The **Rough Guide** to

Thailand's
Beaches & Islands

written and researched by

Paul Gray and Lucy Ridout

D1020944

ROUGH GUIDES

www.roughguides.com

Contents

Underwater Thailand
colour section
following p.304

Ao Phang Nga colour
section following p.432

3

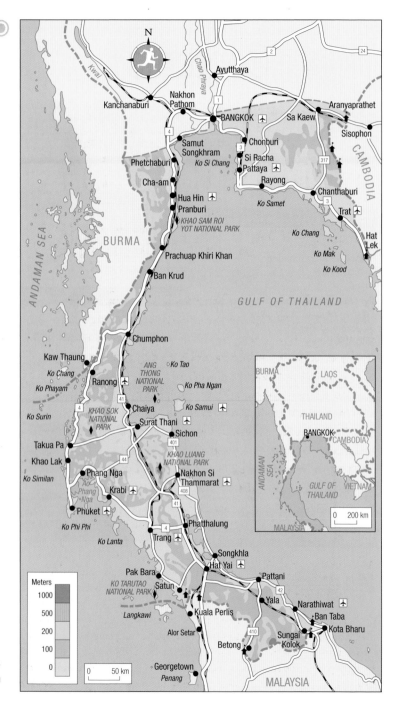

Introduction to

Thailand's
Beaches & Islands

**Despite myriad cultural attractions, sand and sea are
what most Thailand holidays are about, and with over
three thousand kilometres of tropical coastline there are
plenty of stunning white-sand beaches to choose from. In
addition, the peculiar shape of the country – which is often
likened to an elephant's head, with Bangkok as the eye,
the east coast as the chin, and the peninsular Andaman
and Gulf coasts forming the trunk – means you can dive,
swim and sunbathe all year round, for when the monsoon
rains are battering one coast you merely have to cross to
the other to escape them.**

 Geographical differences have given distinctive
character to each of the coasts. The **Andaman
coast** is the most dramatic, edged by sheer
limestone cliffs carved by wind and water
into strange silhouettes, and interleaved with
thick bands of mangrove forest. The **Gulf
coast** begins and ends quietly with relatively
flat, featureless stretches to the south of Bangkok and down towards the
Malaysian border, but peaks at its midpoint, where the peninsular mountains
march into the sea to form the wildly varied landscapes of the Samui
archipelago and the Ang Thong National Marine Park. A fair chunk of the
east coast is dominated by the rigs of offshore oil and gas exploration, but

5

the islands that lie further out have forested spines and gorgeous strands. In short, you'll find great beaches on all three coasts: idyllic confections of clear turquoise waters at invitingly balmy temperatures, sand so soft that it squeaks underfoot, and palm trees laden with coconuts. The Thai royal family started the craze for seaside holidays by making regular trips to Hua Hin in the early 1900s, and the subsequent construction of the Southern Railway Line soon opened up the region to the rest of the population. Inspired by American GIs who'd discovered Thailand's attractions during their R&R breaks from Vietnam, it wasn't long before foreign

▲ Wat Yai Suwannaram, Phetchaburi

holidaymakers followed suit, and these days **tourism** is the main industry in nearly all Thailand's coastal areas. Many of the most beautiful spots have been well and truly discovered, and a number have developed into full-blown high-rise resorts that seem to have more in common with the Costa del Sol than the rest of Southeast Asia. But you need only venture a few kilometres from such anomalies to encounter a more traditional scene of fishing communities, rubber plantations and Buddhist temples. Some forty percent of Thais still earn their living from the land or the sea, and around 85 percent of the population are **Theravada Buddhists**, a faith that colours all aspects

▲ Longtail boats at Hat Rin, Ko Pha Ngan

▲ Young long-tailed macaques, Ang Thong National Marine Park

of daily life – from the tiered temple rooftops that dominate the skyline, to the omnipresent saffron-robed monks and the packed calendar of festivals.

Where to go

Airline schedules decree that many beach holidays begin in **Bangkok**, and despite initial impressions, Thailand's crazy, polluted capital is well worth a couple of days of your time. Within its historic core you'll find the country's most dazzling works of art and architecture, which make a good antidote to the mind-boggling array of traditional markets and contemporary boutiques, hip bars and outstanding restaurants, in the fashionable downtown area.

Fact file

• Known as Siam until 1939, Thailand lies wholly within the tropics, covering 511,770 square kilometres and divided into 76 provinces or *changwat*. The **population** of 63 million is made up of ethnic Thais (75 percent) and Chinese (14 percent), with the rest mainly immigrants from neighbouring countries and hill-tribespeople; the national language is *phasaa thai*. **Buddhism** is the national religion, practised by some 85 percent of Thais, and Islam the largest minority religion. Average life expectancy is 72 years.

• Since 1932 the country has been a constitutional monarchy; **King Bhumibol**, also known as Rama IX (being the ninth ruler of the Chakri dynasty), has been on the throne since 1946. The elected National Assembly (*Rathasapha*) has five hundred MPs in the House of Representatives (*Sapha Phuthaen Ratsadon*), led by a prime minister, and two hundred members of the Senate (*Wuthisapha*).

• Tourism is the country's main **industry**, and its biggest exports are computers and components, vehicles and vehicle parts, textiles and rubber.

Rat or raja?

There's no standard system of **transliterating** Thai script into Roman, so you're sure to find that the Thai words in this book don't always match the versions you'll see elsewhere. Maps and street signs are the biggest sources of confusion, so we've generally gone for the transliteration that's most common on the spot; where it's a toss-up between two equally popular versions, we've used the one that helps best with pronunciation. However, sometimes you'll need to do a bit of lateral thinking, bearing in mind that a classic variant for the town of Satun is Satul, while among street names, Thanon Rajavithi could come out as Thanon Ratwithi – and it's not unheard of to find one spelling posted at one end of a road, with another at the opposite end. See p.487 for an introduction to the Thai language.

Within easy striking distance of Bangkok, the east coast resort of **Pattaya** is the country's most popular – and least interesting – destination, a concrete warren of hotels and strip joints that makes its money from package tourists who are unaware of what they're missing. Yet just a few kilometres beyond sits the diminutive island of **Ko Samet**, whose superb sands are lined with more conducive beach bungalows. East again, just inside the Cambodian border, **Ko Chang** has retained its upland forest despite the relentless march of resort-style facilities along its shores; but for old-style Thai beach charm, you'll need to press on, to tiny, charming **Ko Mak** and wild, unsullied **Ko Kood**.

After an interesting inland diversion at the atmospheric, temple-filled town of **Phetchaburi**, the peninsular Gulf coast kicks off with the historic resort of **Hua Hin**, now disfigured by excessive hotel development; better to keep going to **Pak Nam Pran**'s arty boutique hotels or unspoilt **Prachuap Khiri Kan**, with its handsome promenade and shady sands. The main draw on this side of the peninsula, though, is the Samui archipelago to the south: **Ko Samui** itself is the most developed of the three main islands here, but has largely kept its good looks and offers an appealing variety of beachside accommodation, restaurants and facilities; **Ko Pha Ngan**, with its small resorts and desolate coves, is still firmly backpacker territory, drawing

▲ Gulf coast fishermen

party people – to **Hat Rin** – and solitude seekers in equal parts; and **Ko Tao** is the remotest outcrop of the three, but has established itself as one of the world's leading centres for scuba-diving courses. On the mainland to the south, **Nakhon Si Thammarat** is a great place to recharge your cultural – and culinary – batteries.

Across the peninsula, there's extraordinary drama and beauty all along the Andaman coast. Underwater highlights begin with the polychromatic reefs of the **Ko Surin** and **Ko Similan** island chains, while above water there's the islet-studded bay of **Ao Phang Nga**, the curvy white-sand shores of party-island **Ko Phi Phi** and the primeval cliffs of **Krabi's Railay peninsula**. There's grandeur inland, too, in the lofty tropical rainforests of **Khao Sok National Park**. Sadly, the big resort island of **Phuket** is increasingly denuded of its natural beauty, but five million visitors a year are still drawn to its dozen different beaches, which offer everything from luxurious five-star seclusion to seedy nightlife. **Ko Lanta** is, for the moment at least, a calmer alternative for families, while independent travellers will much prefer the uncommercial islands of **Ko Jum**, **Ko Yao Noi** and **Ko Phayam**.

Spectacular limestone backdrops continue down the Andaman coast into the provinces of the deep south, where the main attractions are teeming sea life and unfrequented sands. The quietest spot of all is the national park of **Ko Tarutao**, though **Ko Lipe** is a rather rowdy, semi-detached neighbour, with the fastest development on this stretch of littoral; half a dozen other varied islands down here offer an appealing balance of remoteness and facilities.

Traditional massage

Combining elements of yoga and acupressure, **traditional Thai massage** originated as an Ayurvedic therapy in India, and was imported to Thailand – along with Buddhism – by missionary monks around two thousand years ago. As well as stretching muscles and loosening joints, it seeks to stimulate pressure points along the body's energy lines, in order to redress energy imbalances and release blockages, stimulate blood circulation and detoxify organs. Thais will visit a masseur for many conditions, including fevers, headaches, backaches and stomach problems. But even if you're perfectly healthy, you'll enjoy emerging from a massage feeling both relaxed and energized – the effect is similar to that of taking a yoga class without doing any of the hard work. For more on traditional massage, see p.56.

When to go

The **climate** of most of Thailand is governed by three seasons: rainy (roughly May–Oct), caused by the southwest monsoon dumping moisture gathered from the Andaman Sea and the Gulf of Thailand; cool (Nov–Feb); and hot (March–May). The **rainy season** is the least predictable of the three, varying in length and intensity from year to year, but usually it gathers force between June and August, coming to a peak in September and October, when unpaved roads are reduced to mud troughs and some islands become inaccessible.

Within this scheme, slight variations are found from region to region. In southern Thailand, temperatures are more consistent throughout the year, with less variation the closer you get to the equator. The rainy season hits the **Andaman coast** harder than anywhere else in the country: heavy rainfall usually starts in May and persists until November. The **Gulf coast** of the southern peninsula lies outside this general pattern – with the sea immediately to the east, this coast and its offshore islands feel the effects of the northeast monsoon, which brings rain between October and January, especially in November, but suffers less than the Andaman coast from the southwest monsoon.

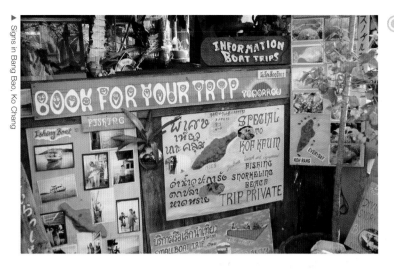

Overall, the **cool season** is generally the **best time** to come to Thailand, and the most popular: as well as having more manageable temperatures and less rain, it offers waterfalls in full spate and the best of the flowers in bloom.

Average daily maximum temperatures (°C) and monthly rainfall (mm)

	Jan	Feb	Mar	Apr	May	Jun	Jul	Aug	Sep	Oct	Nov	Dec
Bangkok												
°C	26	28	29	30	30	29	29	28	28	28	27	26
mm	11	28	31	72	190	152	158	187	320	231	57	9
Pattaya												
°C	26	28	29	30	30	29	29	28	28	28	27	26
mm	12	23	41	79	165	120	166	166	302	229	66	10
Ko Samui												
°C	26	26	28	29	29	28	28	28	28	27	26	25
mm	38	8	12	63	186	113	143	123	209	260	302	98
Phuket												
°C	27	28	28	29	28	28	28	28	27	27	27	27
mm	35	31	39	163	348	213	263	263	419	305	207	52

16

things not to miss

It's not possible to explore every inch of Thailand's coastline in one trip – and we don't suggest you try. What follows is a selective taste of the highlights: outstanding beaches, spectacular dives, exuberant festivals and unforgettable temples – arranged in five colour-coded categories to help you discover the very best things to see, do and experience. All highlights have a page reference to take you straight into the guide, where you can find out more.

01 Full moon party at Hat Rin, Ko Pha Ngan Page **287** • *Apocalypse Now* without the war…

02 **Ko Tao** Page **296** • Take a dive course, or just explore this remote island's contours by boat or on foot.

03 **The Grand Palace, Bangkok** Page **110** • No visitor should miss this huge complex, which encompasses the country's holiest and most beautiful temple, Wat Phra Kaeo, and its most important image, the Emerald Buddha.

04 **Phetchaburi** Page **237** • Many of the temples in this charming, historic town date back three hundred years and are still in use today.

05 **Seafood** Page **40** • Fresh fish, curried with vegetables, steamed whole with ginger and mushrooms or simply barbecued, hot and sour soup with prawns and lemon grass, spicy salads of papaya and crab...the only problem is knowing when to stop.

06 Snorkelling off Ko Surin Page 336 • Camp out on this remote chain of national park islands to make the most of the spectacular turquoise waters and shallow reefs.

07 Songkhran Page 54 • Thai New Year is the excuse for a national water fight – and tourists are definitely fair game.

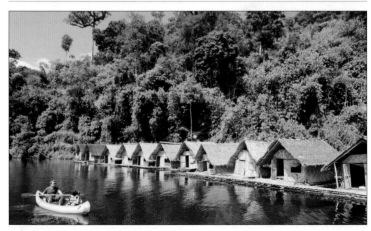

08 Khao Sok National Park Page 337 • Mist-clad outcrops, steamy jungle and the vast Cheow Lan lake.

09 **Chatuchak Weekend Market, Bangkok** Page **140** • Thailand's top shopping experience features over eight thousand stalls selling everything from cooking pots to designer lamps.

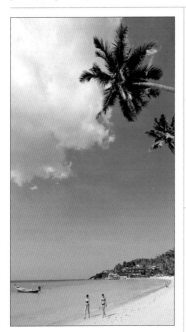

11 **Ko Kood** Page **225** • An untamed beauty, fringed by very pretty beaches.

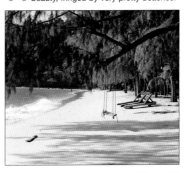

12 **Night markets** Page **41** • After-dark gatherings of dramatically lit pushcart kitchens, which are usually the best-value and most entertaining places to eat.

10 **Ko Pha Ngan** Page **284** • The island is dotted with beautiful beaches, so head out to secluded Bottle Beach or Thong Nai Pan, or gear up for the fun at Hat Rin.

13 Rock-climbing on the Railay peninsula Page

408 • Even novice climbers can scale the cliffs here for unbeatable views of Krabi's stunning coastline.

14 Krung Ching waterfall, Nakhon Si Thammarat

Page **312** • On the northern flank of Khao Luang, the south's highest mountain, Krung Ching is southern Thailand's most spectacular drop, reachable only by a nature trail through dense, steamy jungle.

15 Ko Tarutao National Marine Park Page **455** •

Spectacular islands, with a surprising variety of landscapes, including the shining white crescent of Ko Lipe's Pattaya Beach.

16 Vegetarian festival, Phuket Page **358** • During Taoist

Lent, fasting Chinese devotees test their spiritual resolve with public acts of gruesome self-mortification.

Basics

Basics

Getting there

Thailand currently has international airports in Bangkok, Hat Yai, Krabi, Phuket and Ko Samui. The vast majority of travellers fly into Bangkok's Suvarnabhumi Airport (see p.78).

Airfares to Thailand generally depend on the **season**, with the highest being approximately mid-November to mid-February, when the weather is best (with premium rates charged for flights between mid-Dec and New Year), and in July and August to coincide with school holidays. You will need to book several months in advance to get reasonably priced tickets during these peak periods.

The cheapest way of getting straight to most **regional Thai airports** is usually to buy a flight to Bangkok and then a domestic add-on; see p.33 for details of domestic airlines. However, for flights to **Phuket** you also have the option of flying nonstop from Sydney (with Jetstar) as well as on a through-ticket from any international departure point via Kuala Lumpur (with Malaysia Airlines or Air Asia), Singapore (Singapore/Silk Air), Seoul (Korean Air) or Hong Kong (Cathay Pacific/Dragonair), and from Penang with Firefly. For **Ko Samui** there are flights from Singapore, Hong Kong (both Bangkok Airways), KL (Berjaya Airlines and Firefly) and Penang (Firefly); and for

Six steps to a better kind of travel

At Rough Guides we are passionately committed to travel. We feel strongly that only through travelling do we truly come to understand the world we live in and the people we share it with – plus tourism has brought a great deal of **benefit** to developing economies around the world over the last few decades. But the extraordinary growth in tourism has also damaged some places irreparably, and of course **climate change** is exacerbated by most forms of transport, especially flying. This means that now more than ever it's important to **travel thoughtfully** and **responsibly**, with respect for the cultures you're visiting – not only to derive the most benefit from your trip but also to preserve the best bits of the planet for everyone to enjoy. At Rough Guides we feel there are six main areas in which you can make a difference:

- Consider what you're contributing to the **local economy**, and how much the services you use do the same, whether it's through employing local workers and guides or sourcing locally grown produce and local services.
- Consider the **environment** on holiday as well as at home. Water is scarce in many developing destinations, and the biodiversity of local flora and fauna can be adversely affected by tourism. Try to patronize businesses that take account of this.
- Travel with a purpose, not just to tick off experiences. Consider **spending longer** in a place, and getting to know it and its people.
- Give thought to how often you **fly**. Try to avoid short hops by air and more harmful night flights.
- Consider **alternatives to flying**, travelling instead by bus, train, boat and even by bike or on foot where possible.
- Make your trips "**climate neutral**" via a reputable carbon offset scheme. All Rough Guide flights are offset, and every year we donate money to a variety of charities devoted to combating the effects of climate change.

Krabi you can fly long-haul via KL with Air Asia, or nonstop from Oslo and Munich with Krabi Airline.

Flights from the UK and Ireland

The fastest and most comfortable way of reaching Thailand **from the UK** is to fly nonstop from London to Bangkok with Qantas/British Airways, Thai Airways or Eva Airways, a journey time of about eleven and a half hours. These airlines usually keep their prices competitive, at around £500/730 plus tax in low season/high season. Fares on indirect scheduled flights to Bangkok are always cheaper than nonstop flights and start at £380/550 plus tax, though these journeys can take anything from two to twelve hours longer.

There are no nonstop flights from any **regional airports** in Britain or from any **Irish airports**, and rather than routing via London, you may find it convenient to fly to another hub such as Frankfurt (with Lufthansa), Zurich (with Swiss), Abu Dhabi (with Etihad) or Dubai (with Emirates), and take a connecting flight from there. Return flights from Newcastle upon Tyne with Emirates, for example, with good connections in Dubai, currently start at around £530, including taxes, and from Dublin via Amsterdam with Aer Lingus and China Airlines, at around €800.

Flights from the US and Canada

There are no nonstop flights from North America to Bangkok, as Thai Airways recently abandoned its "ultra-long-haul" services from New York and Los Angeles and now only flies from LA via Osaka (5 weekly). However, plenty of other airlines run daily flights to Bangkok from major East and West Coast cities with only **one stop** en route; it's generally easier to find a reasonable fare on flights via Asia than via Europe, even if you're departing from the East Coast. From New York expect to pay around US$1150/1350 return in low season/high season, including taxes, from LA US$950/1150. Air Canada has the most convenient service to Bangkok from the largest number of Canadian cities; from Vancouver, expect to pay around

Can$1450/1600 in low season/high season; from Toronto, Can$1650/1825. Cheaper rates are often available if you're prepared to make two or three stops and take more time.

Minimum **flying times**, including stop-overs, are twenty hours from New York or Toronto (westbound or eastbound), nineteen hours thirty minutes from LA, eighteen hours from Vancouver.

Flights from Australia and New Zealand

There's no shortage of **scheduled flights** to Bangkok **from Australia**, with direct services from major cities operated by Thai Airways, Qantas/British Airways, Jetstar and Emirates (around 9hr from Sydney and Perth), and plenty of indirect flights via Asian hubs, which take at least eleven and a half hours. You can also fly nonstop to Phuket from Sydney (with Jetstar) and Perth (on Thai). There's often not much difference between the fares on nonstop and indirect flights, which start from around Aus$700/1200 (excluding taxes) in low/high season from Sydney and most major eastern Australian cities. Fares from Perth and Darwin are up to Aus$100/200 cheaper.

From **New Zealand**, Thai Airways runs nonstop twelve-hour flights between Auckland and Bangkok, charging from NZ$1100/1700 (excluding taxes) in low/high season. BA/Qantas and Emirates flights from Auckland make brief stops in Sydney, adding at least a couple of hours to the trip, and other major Asian airlines offer indirect flights via their hubs (from 17hr): fares for indirect flights also start at about NZ$1100/1700. From Christchurch and Wellington you'll pay NZ$150–300 more than from Auckland.

Flights from South Africa

From South Africa, Thai Airways, code-sharing with South African Airways, operate three nonstop flights a week from Johannesburg to Bangkok, taking eleven and a half hours and costing around ZAR10,500 return in low season, ZAR12,000 in high season, including taxes. Otherwise, you'll be making a stop either in the Middle East or in Hong Kong or Southeast Asia, with fares starting at around ZAR7500/10,000 low/high season.

Airlines

Aer Lingus ⓦ www.aerlingus.com
Air Canada ⓦ www.aircanada.com
Air New Zealand ⓦ www.airnewzealand.com
Bangkok Airways ⓦ www.bangkokair.com
Berjaya Air ⓦ www.berjaya-air.com
British Airways ⓦ www.ba.com
Cathay Pacific ⓦ www.cathaypacific.com
Emirates ⓦ www.emirates.com
Etihad Airways ⓦ www.etihadairways.com
EVA Air ⓦ www.evaair.com
Firefly ⓦ www.fireflyz.com.my
Jetstar ⓦ www.jetstar.com
Korean Air ⓦ www.koreanair.com
Krabi Airline ⓦ www.krabi-airline.com
Lufthansa ⓦ www.lufthansa.com
Malaysia Airlines ⓦ www.malaysiaairlines.com
Qantas Airways ⓦ www.qantas.com
Qatar Airways ⓦ www.qatarairways.com
Silk Air ⓦ www.silkair.com
Singapore Airlines ⓦ www.singaporeair.com
South African Airways ⓦ www.flysaa.com
Swiss ⓦ www.swiss.com
Thai Airways ⓦ www.thaiair.com
Tiger Airways ⓦ www.tigerairways.com

Travel agents and tour operators worldwide

Adventure Center US ☏ 1-800/228-8747 or
510/654-1879, ⓦ www.adventurecenter.com.
Hiking and "soft adventure" specialist agent, offering
dozens of packages to Thailand with well-regarded
tour operators from all over the world.
All Points East (formerly Gecko Travel) UK
☏ 023/9225 8859, Thailand ☏ 081 885 9490;
ⓦ www.allpointseast.com. Southeast Asia specialist
operating small-group adventure holidays with
off-the-beaten-track itineraries. Also offers motorbike
tours and family-oriented tours.
Andaman Discoveries Thailand ⓦ www
.andamandiscoveries.com. Village-based homestay
community tourism programmes around Khuraburi
on the north Andaman coast that allow visitors to
experience daily activities such as batik making,
cashew nut farming and roof-thatching.
Asian Trails Thailand ⓦ www.asiantrails.net. Well-
regarded company that does self-drive tours, cycling
and motorcycling adventures, homestay programmes,
river- and sea cruises, plus more typical package tours.
Creative Events Asia Thailand ⓦ www
.creativeeventsasia.com. Wedding specialists for
everything from paperwork to the ceremony and guest
accommodation.
Crooked Trails US ☏ 206/383-9828, ⓦ www
.crookedtrails.com. Not-for-profit community-based

tourism organization offering homestays along the
Andaman coast, usually featuring volunteer work as
well as cultural tours.
Flight Centre US ☏ 1-866/967-5351, Canada
☏ 1-877 967 5302, UK ☏ 0870/499 0040, Australia
☏ 13 31 33, New Zealand ☏ 0800/243 544, South
Africa ☏ 0860 400 727; ⓦ www.flightcentre.com.
Guarantees to offer the lowest international air fares.
Grasshopper Adventures Thailand ☏ 087 929
5208, UK ☏ 020/8123 8144, US ☏ 818/921-7101,
Australia ☏ 03/9016 3172; ⓦ www.grasshopper
adventures.com. Cycling tours around Bangkok and
longer rides to Krabi.
Intrepid Travel US ☏ 1-1 800/970-7299, Canada
☏ 1-866/360-1151, UK ☏ 0203 147 7777, Ireland
☏ 01 524 0071, Australia ☏ 1300/364 512, New
Zealand ☏ 0800/600 610; ⓦ www.intrepidtravel
.com. Well-regarded small-group adventure tour
operator that uses local transport and travellers'-style
accommodation.
Nature Trails Thailand ⓦ www.naturetrails
thailand.com. Specialist bird-watching tours in
Thailand's national parks.
North South Travel UK ☏ 01245/608 291,
ⓦ www.northsouthtravel.co.uk. Competitive travel
agency, offering discounted fares worldwide. Profits
are used to support projects in the developing world,
especially the promotion of sustainable tourism.
Responsible Travel UK ☏ 01273 600030,
ⓦ www.responsibletravel.com. One-stop shop

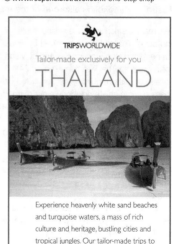

for scores of fair-trade, ethically inclined holidays in Thailand, including trips that focus on wildlife, meditation, family activities and village life.

Spice Roads Thailand ⊛ www.spiceroads.com. Escorted bike tours through Thailand.

STA Travel US ☎ 1-800/781-4040, UK ☎ 0871/2300 040, Australia ☎ 134 782, New Zealand ☎ 0800/474 400, South Africa ☎ 0861/781 781; ⊛ www.statravel .com. Worldwide specialists in independent travel. Good discounts for students and under-26s.

Symbiosis UK ☎ 0845/123 2844, US ☎ 1-866/ 723-7903; ⊛ www.symbiosis-travel.com. Upmarket, off-the-beaten-track tours with an environmentally sensitive, fair-trade focus, including homestays on the Andaman coast and kayaking at Khao Sok and Ko Tarutao.

Telltale Travel UK ☎ 0800/011 2571, ⊛ www .telltaletravel.co.uk. Tailor-made tours with accommodation mainly in upscale homestays in Bangkok and beyond.

Trailfinders UK ☎ 0845/058 5858, Ireland ☎ 01/677 7888, Australia ☎ 1300/780 212; ⊛ www.trailfinders.com. One of the best-informed and most efficient agents for independent travellers.

Travel Cuts US ☎ 1-800/592-CUTS, Canada ☎ 1-866/246-9762; ⊛ www.travelcuts.com. Popular, long-established specialists in budget travel, including student and youth discount offers.

USIT Ireland ☎ 01/602 1906, Northern Ireland ☎ 028/9032 7111, with branches in Athlone, Belfast, Cork, Dublin, Galway, Limerick and Waterford, ⊛ www.usit.ie. Ireland's main outlet for discounted, youth and student fares.

Travel via neighbouring countries

Sharing land borders with Burma, Laos, Cambodia and Malaysia, Thailand works well as part of many overland itineraries, both across Asia and between Europe and Australia. Bangkok is also one of the major regional flight hubs for Southeast Asia.

The main restrictions on overland routes in and out of Thailand are determined by where the permitted land crossings lie and by **visas**. For a guide to Thai visa rules see pp.24–25. Details of visa requirements for travel to Thailand's immediate neighbours are outlined below, but should be double-checked before you travel. All **Asian embassies** are located in Bangkok (see p.167), where many Khao San tour agents also offer to get your visa for you, but beware: some are reportedly **faking the stamps**, which could get you in pretty serious trouble, so it's safer to go to the embassy yourself.

The right paperwork is also crucial if you're planning to **drive your own car or motorbike** into Thailand; see the Golden Triangle Rider website (⊛ www.gt-rider.com) for advice.

Burma

There is no overland access from **Burma** into Thailand and access in the opposite direction is restricted. Western tourists are only allowed to make limited-distance trips into Burma at a few points, including Kaw Thaung (Victoria Point) near Ranong; see p.323. Tourists who intend to enter Burma by air can buy four-week tourist visas at the Burmese embassy in Bangkok for B800; apply to the embassy and you can collect the next day.

Cambodia

At the time of writing, six overland crossings on the **Thai-Cambodia border** are open to non-Thais. See the relevant town accounts for specific details on all the border crossings; for travellers' up-to-the-minute experiences, plus an account of the common **scam** on through-transport from Bangkok to Siem Reap, consult ⊛ www .talesofasia.com/cambodia-overland.htm.

Most travellers use either the crossing at Poipet, which has transport connections to Sisophon, Siem Reap and Phnom Penh and lies just across the border from the Thai town of Aranyaprathet (see p.201), with its transport to Chanthaburi and Bangkok; or they follow the route from Sihanoukville in Cambodia via Koh Kong and Hat Lek to Trat (see p.205), which is near Ko Chang on Thailand's east coast. The Trat route is the fastest option if you're travelling nonstop from Bangkok to Cambodia. There are also two crossings in Chanthaburi province (see p.201), with transport to and from Pailin in Cambodia, and a couple more in the northeast.

Visas for Cambodia are issued to travellers on arrival at Phnom Penh and Siem Reap airports, and at all the above-listed land borders; you need US$20 and two photos for this. If you do need to buy an advance thirty-day visa, you can do so online or from the Cambodian Embassy in Bangkok. This costs about B1000; apply before noon and you can collect your visa the following day after 5pm.

Laos and Vietnam

There are five main points along the **Lao border** where tourists can cross into Thailand: Houayxai (for Chiang Khong); Vientiane (for Nong Khai); Khammouan (aka Tha Khaek, for Nakhon Phanom); Savannakhet (for Mukdahan); and Pakxe (for Chong Mek). All these borders can also be used as exits into Laos, but as they're not coastal regions they are not covered by this book.

Visas are required for all non-Thai visitors to Laos. A thirty-day **visa on arrival** can be bought for US$30–42 (depending on your nationality), plus one photo, at Vientiane, Louang Phabang and Pakxe airports, and all the above-listed land borders. Or you can buy one in advance from the Lao Embassy in Bangkok for B400–1700; this can be collected the following day – or in less than an hour if you pay an extra B200.

If you have the right Lao visa and Vietnamese exit stamp, you can travel **from Vietnam** to Thailand via Savannakhet in a matter of hours; you'll need to use Vietnam's Lao Bao border crossing, west of Dong Ha, where you can catch a bus to Savannakhet and then another bus across the new Mekong bridge to Mukdahan. All travellers into Vietnam need to buy a visa in advance. Thirty-day visas can take up to four working days to process at the embassy in Bangkok and cost B1000.

Malaysia and Singapore

Travelling between Thailand and **Malaysia and Singapore** has in the past been a straightforward and very commonly used overland route, with plentiful connections by bus, minibus, share-taxi and train, most of them routed through the southern Thai city and transport hub of Hat Yai. However, because of the ongoing **violence in Thailand's deep south** (see p.441), all major Western governments are currently advising people not to travel to or through Songkhla, Pattani, Yala and Narathiwat provinces, unless essential (and consequently most insurance companies are not covering travel there). This encompasses Hat Yai and the following border crossings to and from Malaysia: at Padang Besar, on the main rail line connecting Butterworth in Malaysia (and, ultimately, Kuala Lumpur and Singapore) with Hat Yai and Bangkok; at Sungai Kolok, terminus of a railway line from Hat Yai and Bangkok, and at adjacent Ban Taba, both of which are connected by road to nearby Kota Bharu in Malaysia; and at the road crossings at Sadao, south of Hat Yai, and at Betong, south of Yala. (The routes towards Kota Bharu and Betong pass through particularly volatile territory, with martial law declared in Pattani, Yala and Narathiwat provinces; however, martial law is not in effect in Hat Yai itself nor the districts of Songkhla province through which the Bangkok–Butterworth rail line and the Hat Yai–Sadao road pass.)

Nevertheless, the provinces of Trang and Satun on the west coast are not affected, and it's still perfectly possible to travel **overland via Satun**: by ferry between Satun's Thammalang pier and Kuala Perlis or the island of Langkawi, or by air-con minibus between Ban Khuan and Kangar (see p.461); or by boat between Ko Lanta, Ko Lipe and Langkawi (see p.447). For up-to-the-minute advice, consult your government travel advisory (see p.51).

Most Western tourists can spend thirty days in Malaysia and fourteen days in Singapore without having bought a visa beforehand, and there are useful Thai embassies or consulates in Kuala Lumpur, Kota Bharu, Penang and Singapore (see p.25).

Visas

There are three main entry categories for visitors to Thailand; for all of them, under International Air Travel Association rules, your passport should be valid for at least six months. As visa requirements are subject to frequent change, you should always consult before departure a Thai embassy or consulate, a reliable travel agent, or the Thai Ministry of Foreign Affairs' website at ⓦ www.mfa.go.th /web/2637.php. For further, unofficial but usually reliable, details on all visa matters, go to ⓦ www.thaivisa.com and especially their various moderated forums.

Most Western passport holders (that includes citizens of the UK, Ireland, the US, Canada, Australia, New Zealand and South Africa) are allowed to enter the country for short **stays** without having to apply for a visa – officially termed the **tourist visa exemption**. You'll be granted a thirty-day stay at an international airport but, in a recent change, only fifteen days at an overland border; the period of stay will be stamped into your passport by immigration officials upon entry. You're supposed to be able to somehow show proof of means of living while in the country (B10,000 per person, B20,000 per family), and in theory you may be put back on the next plane without it or sent back to get a sixty-day tourist visa from the nearest Thai embassy, but this is unheard of. You are also required to show proof of tickets to leave Thailand again within the allotted time. This is rarely checked by Thai immigration authorities, though there have been a few cases recently, mostly at the Cambodian border. However, if you have a one-way air ticket to Thailand and no evidence of onward travel arrangements, it's best to buy a tourist visa in advance: some airlines will stop you boarding the plane without one, as they would be liable for flying you back to your point of origin if you did happen to be stopped.

If you're fairly certain you may want to stay longer than fifteen/thirty days, then from the outset you should apply for a **sixty-day tourist visa** from a Thai embassy or consulate, accompanying your application – which generally takes several days to process – with your passport and two photos. The sixty-day visa costs, for example, US$35 or £28 in the UK; multiple-entry versions are available, costing US$35 or £28 per entry, which may be handy if you're going to be leaving and re-entering Thailand. Ordinary tourist visas are valid for three months, ie you must enter Thailand within three months of the visa being issued by the Thai embassy or consulate, while multiple-entry versions are valid for six months. Visa application forms can be downloaded from, for example, the Thai Ministry of Foreign Affairs' website.

Thai embassies also consider applications for **ninety-day non-immigrant visas** (£45 or US$65 single entry, for example, on £100 or US$175 multiple-entry) as long as you can offer a reason for your visit, such as study, business or visiting family/friends (there are different categories of non-immigrant visa for which different levels of proof are needed). As it can be a hassle to organize a ninety-day visa, it's generally easier to apply for a thirty-day extension to your sixty-day visa once inside Thai borders.

It's not a good idea to **overstay** your visa limits. Once you're at the airport or the border, you'll have to pay a fine of B500 per day before you can leave Thailand. More importantly, however, if you're in the country with an expired visa and you get involved with police or immigration officials for any reason, however trivial, they are obliged to take you to court, possibly imprison you, and deport you.

Border runs, extensions and re-entry permits

Setting aside the caveats about proof of funds and onward tickets above, it's generally easy to get a new fifteen-day tourist visa exemption by hopping **across the border** into a neighbouring country and back. Such tourist visa exemptions can be **extended** within Thailand for up to a further ten days, sixty-day tourist visas for a further thirty days, at the discretion of immigration officials; extensions cost B1900 and are issued over the counter at immigration offices (*kaan khao muang*; ☎1111 for 24hr information in English, ⊛www.immigration .go.th) in nearly every provincial capital – most offices ask for one or two photos as well, plus two photocopies of the main pages of your passport including your Thai arrival card, arrival stamp and visa. Many Khao San tour agents offer to get your visa extension for you, but beware: some are reportedly faking the stamps, which could get you into serious trouble. Immigration offices in Bangkok and at Suvarnabhumi Airport, as well as at border checkpoints, also issue **re-entry permits** (B1000 single re-entry, B3800 multiple) if you want to leave the country and come back again while maintaining the validity of your existing visa.

Thai embassies and consulates abroad

For a full listing of Thai diplomatic missions abroad, consult the Thai Ministry of Foreign Affairs' website at ⊛www.mfa.go.th/web /10.php.

Australia 111 Empire Circuit, Yarralumla, Canberra ACT 2600 ☎02/6206 0100, ⊛canberra.thai embassy.org; plus consulate at 131 Macquarrie St, Sydney, NSW 2000 ☎02/9241 2542–3, ⊛thaiconsulatesydney.org.

Burma 94 Pyay Rd, Dagon Township, Rangoon ☎01/226721.

Cambodia 196 Preah Norodom Blvd, Sangkat Tonle Bassac, Khan Chamcar Mon, Phnom Penh ☎023/726306–10, ⊛www.thaiembassy.org /phnompenh.

Canada 180 Island Park Drive, Ottawa, ON, K1Y 0A2 ☎613/722-4444, ⊛www.magma.ca /~thaiott; plus consulate at 1040 Burrard St, Vancouver, BC, V6Z 2R9 ☎604/687-1143, ⊛www .thaicongenvancouver.org.

Laos Vientiane, ⊛www.thaiembassy.org/vientiane: embassy at Avenue Kaysone Phomvihane, Saysettha District ☎021/214581–2, consular section at Unit 15 Bourichane Rd, Ban Phone Si Nuan, Muang Si Sattanak ☎021/453916; plus consulate at Khanthabouly District, Savannakhet Province, PO Box 513 ☎041/212373.

Malaysia 206 Jalan Ampang, 50450 Kuala Lumpur ☎03/2148 8222, ⊛www.thaiembassy.org /kualalumpur; plus consulates at 4426 Jalan Pengkalan Chepa, 15400 Kota Bharu ☎09/748 2545; and 1 Jalan Tunku Abdul Rahman, 10350 Penang ☎04/226 9484.

New Zealand 2 Cook St, PO Box 17226, Karori, Wellington ☎04/476 8616–9, ⊛www .thaiembassynz.org.nz.

Singapore 370 Orchard Rd, Singapore 238870 ☎6737 2158, ⊛www.thaiembassy.sg.

South Africa 428 Pretorius/Hill St, Arcadia, Pretoria 0083 ☎012/342 5470, ⊛www .thaiembassy.co.za.

UK and Ireland 29–30 Queens Gate, London SW7 5JB ☎020/7589 2944, ⊛www.thaiembassyuk .org.uk. Visa applications by post are not accepted here, but can be sent to various honorary consulates, including those in Hull (⊛www.thaiconsul-uk.com) and Dublin (⊛www.thaiconsulateireland.com).

US 1024 Wisconsin Ave NW, Suite 401, Washington, DC 20007 ☎202/944-3600, ⊛www.thaiembdc .org; plus consulates at 700 North Rush St, Chicago, IL 60611 ☎312/664-3129, ⊛www.thaichicago .net; 611 North Larchmont Blvd, 2nd Floor, Los Angeles, CA 90004 ☎323/962-9574, ⊛www .thai-la.net; and 351 E 52nd St, New York, NY 10022 ☎212/754-1770, ⊛www .thaiconsulnewyork.com.

Vietnam 63–65 Hoang Dieu St, Hanoi ☎04/823-5092–3; plus consulate at 77 Tran Quoc Thao St, District 3, Ho Chi Minh City ☎08/932-7637–8, ⊛www.thaiembassy.org/hochiminhcity.

Health

Although Thailand's climate, wildlife and cuisine present Western travellers with fewer health worries than in many Asian destinations, it's as well to know in advance what the risks might be, and what preventive or curative measures you should take.

For a start, there's no need to bring huge supplies of nonprescription medicines with you, as Thai **pharmacies** (*raan khai yaa*; typically open daily 8.30am–8pm) are well stocked with local and international branded medicaments, and of course they are generally much less expensive than at home. Nearly all pharmacies are run by trained English-speaking pharmacists, who are usually the best people to talk to if your symptoms aren't acute enough to warrant seeing a doctor. The British pharmacy chain Boots now has branches in many big cities and operates a 24-hour health advice line (℡1800 200444 or 02 233 0575). These are the best place to stock up on some Western products such as **tampons** (which Thai women do not use).

Hospital (*rong phayabaan*) cleanliness and efficiency vary, but generally hygiene and healthcare standards are good and the ratio of medical staff to patients is considerably higher than in most parts of the West. As with head pharmacists, doctors speak English. Several Bangkok hospitals are highly regarded (see p.167), and all provincial capitals have at least one hospital: if you need to get to one, ask at your accommodation for advice on, and possibly transport to, the nearest or most suitable. In the event of a major health crisis, get someone to contact your embassy (see p.167) and insurance company – it may be best to get yourself transported to Bangkok or even home.

There have been outbreaks of **Avian Influenza** (**bird flu**) in domestic poultry and wild birds in Thailand which have led to a small number of human fatalities, believed to have arisen through close contact with infected poultry. There has been no evidence of human-to-human transmission in Thailand, and the risk to humans is believed to be very low. However, as a precaution, you should avoid visiting live animal markets and other places where you may come into close contact with birds, and ensure that poultry and egg dishes are thoroughly cooked.

Inoculations

There are no compulsory **inoculation** requirements for people travelling to Thailand from the West, but you should consult a doctor or other health professional, preferably at least four weeks in advance of your trip, for the latest information on recommended immunizations. Most doctors strongly advise vaccinations or boosters against polio, tetanus, diphtheria, hepatitis A and, in many cases, typhoid, and in some cases they might also recommend protecting yourself against cholera, Japanese B encephalitis, rabies, hepatitis B and tuber-culosis. There is currently no vaccine against malaria; for information on prophylaxis, see opposite. If you forget to have all your inoculations before leaving home, or don't leave yourself sufficient time, you can get them in Bangkok at, for example, the Thai Red Cross Society's Queen Saovabha Institute or Global Doctor; see p.167 for details.

Mosquito-borne diseases

Mosquitoes in Thailand spread not only malaria, but also diseases such as dengue fever, especially during the rainy season. The main message, therefore, is to **avoid being bitten** by mosquitoes. You should smother yourself and your clothes in **mosquito repellent** containing the chemical compound DEET, reapplying regularly (shops, guest houses and department stores all over Thailand stock it, but if you want the highest-strength repellent, or convenient roll-ons or sprays, do your shopping before you leave home). DEET is strong stuff, and if you have sensitive skin, a natural alternative is citronella (available in the UK as Mosi-guard), made from a blend of eucalyptus oils; the Thai version is made with lemon grass.

At night you should sleep either under a **mosquito net** sprayed with DEET or in a bedroom with **mosquito screens** across the windows (or in an enclosed air-con room). Accommodation in tourist spots nearly always provides screens or a net (check both for holes), but if you're planning to go way off the beaten track or want the security of having your own mosquito net just in case, wait until you get to Bangkok to buy one, where department stores sell them for much less than you'd pay in the West. Plug-in insecticide vaporizers, knock-down insect sprays and mosquito coils – also widely available in Thailand – help keep the insects at bay; electronic "buzzers" are useless.

Malaria

Thailand is **malarial**, with the disease being carried by mosquitoes that bite from dusk to dawn, but the risks involved vary across the country.

There is a significant risk of malaria, mainly in rural and forested areas, in a narrow strip along the **borders with Burma** (excluding, for example, resorts and road and rail routes along the Gulf coast), **Laos** and **Cambodia** (including Ko Chang). The only anti-malarial drugs that are currently likely to be effective in these areas are **Doxycycline** and **Malarone**, whose use should be discussed with your travel health adviser, especially as prophylaxis advice can change from year to year. Doxycycline is sold across the counter in Thai branches of Boots but Malarone is not currently available in Thailand.

Elsewhere in Thailand the risk of malaria is considered to be so low that anti-malarial tablets are not advised.

The **signs of malaria** are often similar to flu, but are very variable. The incubation period for malignant malaria, which can be fatal, is usually 7–28 days, but it can take up to a year for symptoms of the benign form to occur. The most important symptom is a raised temperature of at least 38°C beginning a week or more after the first potential

exposure to malaria: if you suspect anything, go to a hospital or clinic immediately.

Dengue fever

Dengue fever, a debilitating and occasionally fatal viral disease that is particularly prevalent during and just after the rainy season, is on the increase throughout tropical Asia, and is endemic to many areas of Thailand, especially in the south. Unlike malaria, dengue fever is spread by mosquitoes that can bite during daylight hours, so you should also use mosquito repellent during the day. Symptoms include fever, headaches, fierce joint and muscle pain ("breakbone fever" is another name for dengue), and possibly a rash, and usually develop between five and eight days after being bitten.

There is no vaccine against dengue fever; the only treatment is lots of rest, liquids and paracetamol (or any other acetaminophen painkiller, not aspirin), though more serious cases may require hospitalization.

Rabies

Rabies is widespread in Thailand, mainly carried by dogs (between four and seven percent of stray dogs in Bangkok are reported to be rabid), but also cats and monkeys. It is transmitted by bites, scratches or even occasionally licks. Dogs are everywhere in Thailand and even if kept as pets they're never very well cared for; hopefully their mangy appearance will discourage the urge to pat them, as you should steer well clear of them. Rabies is invariably fatal if the patient waits until symptoms begin, though modern vaccines and treatments are very effective and deaths are rare. The important thing is, if you are bitten, licked or scratched by an animal, to vigorously clean the wound with soap and disinfect it, preferably with something containing iodine, and to seek medical advice regarding treatment right away.

Other bites and stings

Thailand's seas are home to a few dangerous creatures that you should look out for, notably **jellyfish**, which tend to be washed towards the beach by rough seas during the monsoon season but can appear at any time of year. All manner of stinging and non-stinging jellyfish can be found in Thailand – as a general rule, those with the longest tentacles tend to have the worst stings – but reports of serious incidents are rare; ask around at your resort or at a local dive shop to see if there have been any sightings of poisonous varieties. You also need to be wary of poisonous **sea snakes**, **sea urchins** and a couple of less conspicuous species – **stingrays**, which often lie buried in the sand, and **stonefish**, whose potentially lethal venomous spikes are easily stepped on because the fish look like stones and lie motionless on the sea bed.

If **stung or bitten** you should always seek medical advice as soon as possible, but there are a few ways of alleviating the pain or administering your own first aid in the meantime. If you're stung by a jellyfish, wash the affected area with salt water (not fresh water) and, if possible, with vinegar (failing that, ammonia, citrus fruit juice or even urine may do the trick), and try to remove the fragments of tentacles from the skin with a gloved hand, forceps, thick cloth or credit card. The best way to minimize the risk of stepping on the toxic spines of sea urchins, stingrays and stonefish is to wear thick-soled shoes, though these cannot provide total protection; sea urchin spikes should be removed after softening the skin with ointment, though some people recommend applying urine to help dissolve the spines; for stingray and stonefish stings, alleviate the pain by immersing the wound in hot water while awaiting help.

In the case of a **poisonous snake bite**, don't try sucking out the poison or applying a tourniquet: wrap up and immobilize the bitten limb and try to stay still and calm until medical help arrives; all provincial hospitals in Thailand carry supplies of antivenins. For more on Thai snakes, see p.481.

Some of Thailand's wilder, less developed beaches are plagued by **sandflies**, tiny, barely visible midges whose bites can trigger an allergic response, leaving big red weals and an unbearable itch, and possible infection if scratched too vigorously. Many islanders say that slathering yourself in (widely available) coconut oil is the best deterrent as sandflies apparently don't like the smell.

Applying locally made camphor-based yellow oil (see p.204) quells the itch, but you may need to resort to antihistamines for the inflammation. **Leeches** aren't dangerous but can be a bother when walking in forested areas, especially during and just after the rainy season. The most effective way to get leeches off your skin is to burn them with a lighted cigarette, or douse them in salt; oily suntan lotion or insect repellent sometimes makes them lose their grip and fall off.

Worms and flukes

Worms can be picked up through the soles of your feet, so avoid going barefoot. They can also be ingested by eating undercooked meat, and liver **flukes** by eating raw or undercooked freshwater fish. Worms which cause schistosomiasis (bilharziasis) by attaching themselves to your bladder or intestines can be found in freshwater rivers and lakes. The risk of contracting this disease is low, but you should avoid swimming in most freshwater lakes.

Digestive problems

By far the most common travellers' complaint in Thailand, **digestive troubles** are often caused by contaminated food and water, or sometimes just by an overdose of unfamiliar foodstuffs. For advice on food and water hygiene, see p.40 and p.45.

Stomach trouble usually manifests itself as simple **diarrhoea**, which should clear up without medical treatment within three to seven days and is best combated by drinking lots of fluids. If this doesn't work, you're in danger of getting **dehydrated** and should take some kind of rehydration solution, either a commercial sachet of ORS (oral rehydration solution), sold in all Thai pharmacies, or a do-it-yourself version, which can be made by adding a handful of sugar and a pinch of salt to every litre of boiled or bottled water (soft drinks are not a viable alternative). If you can eat, avoid fatty foods.

Anti-diarrhoeal agents such as Imodium are useful for blocking you up on long bus journeys, but they only attack the symptoms and may prolong infections; an antibiotic such as ciprofloxacin, however, can often reduce a typical attack of traveller's diarrhoea to one day. If the diarrhoea persists for a week or more, or if you have blood or mucus in your stools, or an accompanying fever, go to a doctor or hospital.

HIV and AIDS

AIDS is widespread in Thailand, primarily because of the sex trade (see p.138). **Condoms** (*meechai*) are sold in pharmacies, convenience stores, department stores, hairdressers and even street markets.

Should you need to have treatment involving an **injection** at a hospital, try to check that the needle has been sterilized first; this is not always practicable, however, so you might consider carrying your own syringes. Due to rigorous screening methods, Thailand's medical blood supply is now considered safe from HIV/AIDS infection.

Medical resources for travellers

UK & Ireland

Hospital for Tropical Diseases Travel Clinic London ☎ 0845 155 5000 or 020/7387 4411, ⓦ www.thehtd.org.

MASTA (Medical Advisory Service for Travellers Abroad) UK ☎ 0870 606 2782 or ⓦ www.masta.org for the nearest clinic.
NHS Travel Health Website ⓦ www.fitfortravel .scot.nhs.uk.
Travel Medicine Services Belfast ☎ 028/9031 5220.
Tropical Medical Bureau Dublin ☎ 1850 487674, ⓦ www.tmb.ie.

US & Canada

Canadian Society for International Health ☎ 613/241-5785, ⓦ www.csih.org. Extensive list of travel health centres.
CDC ⓦ www.cdc.gov/travel. Official US government travel health site.
International Society for Travel Medicine ☎ 1-770/736-7060, ⓦ www.istm.org. Has a full list of travel health clinics.

Australia, New Zealand & South Africa

Travellers' Medical and Vaccination Centre ⓦ www.tmvc.com.au, in Australia ☎ 1300/658 844. Travel clinics in Australia, New Zealand and South Africa.

Getting around

Travel in Thailand is both inexpensive and efficient, if not always speedy. Unless you travel by plane, long-distance journeys in Thailand can be arduous, especially if a shoestring budget restricts you to hard seats and no air-conditioning.

Nonetheless, the wide range of transport options makes travelling around Thailand easier than elsewhere in Southeast Asia. **Buses** are fast and frequent and can be quite luxurious; **trains** are slower but safer and offer more chance of sleeping during overnight trips; moreover, if travelling by day you're likely to follow a more scenic route by rail than by road. Inter-town **songthaews**, **share-taxis** and air-con **minibuses** are handy, and **ferries** provide easy access to all major islands. Local transport comes in all sorts of permutations, both public and chartered.

For an idea of the frequency and duration of transport services, check the **travel details** section at the end of each chapter.

Inter-town buses

Buses, overall the most convenient way of getting around the country, come in two main categories: **ordinary** (*rot thammadaa*; usually orange-coloured) and **air-con** (*rot air* or *rot thua*; usually blue). Ordinary and many air-con buses are run by Baw Khaw Saw (BKS), the government-controlled transport company, while privately owned air-con buses, some of which operate from Baw Khaw Saw terminals, also ply the most popular long-distance routes. Be warned that long-distance overnight buses, particularly the private air-con buses, seem to be involved in more than their fair share of accidents; because of this, some travellers prefer to do the overnight journeys by train and then make a shorter bus connection to their destination.

Ordinary buses

Ordinary buses are incredibly inexpensive and generally cover short-range routes between main towns (up to 150km), running frequently during daylight hours. Each bus is staffed by a team of two or three – the driver, the fare collector and the optional "stop" and "go" yeller – who often personalize the vehicle with stereo systems, stickers, jasmine garlands and the requisite Buddha image or amulet. With an entertaining team and eye-catching scenery, journeys can be fun, but there are drawbacks. For a start, the teams work on a commission basis, so they pack as many people in as possible and might hang around for thirty minutes after they're due to leave in the hope of cramming in a few extra. They also stop so often that their average speed of 60km per hour can only be achieved by hurtling along at breakneck speeds between pick-ups, often propelled by amphetamine-induced craziness. To flag down an ordinary bus from the roadside you should wait at the nearest **bus shelter**, or **sala**, usually located at intervals along the main long-distance bus route through town or on the fringes of any decent-sized settlement, for example on the main highway that skirts the edge of town. Where there is only a bus shelter on the "wrong" side of the road, you can be sure that buses travelling in both directions will stop there for any waiting passengers; simply leave your bag on the right side of the road to alert the bus driver and wait in the shade. If you're in the middle of nowhere with no *sala* in sight, any ordinary bus should stop for you if you flag it down.

Air-con buses

Most Thais making journeys of 100km or more choose to travel by **air-con bus**, and on many routes, including most services out of Bangkok, non-air-con options have been replaced by second-class air-con vehicles. On the busiest routes air-con services depart every twenty to thirty minutes, while on less popular journeys there may be only three or four a day. Whatever the frequency, passengers are often allotted specific seats, and on the longest journeys may get blankets, snacks and nonstop DVDs.

On some routes you have a choice of three or even four classes of air-con bus, with the **second-class** service being the cheapest, slowest (with the most frequent stops), and least comfortable (no toilets, for instance), and the **VIP** (or even "super VIP") services having the fewest seats (generally 24–32 instead of 44) and more leg room for reclining.

Air-con services can cost up to twice as much as the ordinary buses (two or three times as much for VIP buses). Not all air-con buses have toilets, so it's always worth using bus station facilities before you board; and make sure you have some warm clothes, as temperatures can get chilly, even with the blanket.

On a lot of long-distance routes **private air-con buses** are indistinguishable from government ones and operate out of the same Baw Khaw Saw bus terminals. The major private companies, such as Nakhon-chai (☎02 936 0009) and Sombat Tour (☎02 570 9030), have roughly similar fares, though naturally with more scope for price variation, and offer comparable facilities and standards of service. The opposite is unfortunately true of a number of the smaller, private, unlicensed companies, several of which have a poor reputation for service and comfort, but gear themselves towards farang customers with bargain fares and convenient timetables. The long-distance tour buses that run **from Thanon Khao San** in Banglamphu to Surat Thani are a case in point; travellers frequently complain about shabby furnishings, ineffective air-conditioning, unhelpful (even aggressive) drivers, lateness and a frightening lack of safety awareness – and there are frequent reports of theft from luggage, too, and even the spraying of "sleeping gas" so that hand luggage can be rifled without interruption. Generally it's best to travel with the government or licensed private bus companies from the main bus terminals (who have a reputation with their regular Thai customers to maintain) or to go by train instead – the extra comfort and peace of mind are well worth the extra baht.

Tickets and timetables

Tickets for all buses can be bought from the departure terminals, but for ordinary buses it's normal to buy them on board. Air-con buses may operate from a separate station or office, and tickets for the more popular routes should be booked a day in advance. As a rough indication of **fares**, a trip from Bangkok to Surat Thani, a distance of 640km, costs B500–800 for VIP, B490 for first-class air-con and B400 for second-class air-con.

Long-distance buses often depart in clusters around the same time (early morning or late at night, for example), leaving a gap of five or more hours during the day with no services at all. Local TAT offices sometimes keep up-to-date bus **timetables** in English, or go to the bus terminal the day before you want to leave and check with staff there. That said, if you turn up at a bus terminal in the morning for a medium-length journey (150–300km), you're almost always guaranteed to be on your way within two hours.

Songthaews, share-taxis and air-conditioned minibuses

In rural areas, the bus network is often supplemented by **songthaews** (literally "two rows"), which are open-ended vans (or occasionally cattle-trucks) onto which the drivers squash as many passengers as possible on two facing benches, leaving latecomers to swing off the running board at the back. As well as their essential role within towns (see p.33), songthaews ply set routes from larger towns out to their surrounding suburbs and villages, and, where there's no call for a regular bus service, between small towns: some have destinations written on in Thai, but few are numbered. In most towns you'll find the songthaew "terminal" near the market; to pick one up between destinations just flag it down. To indicate to the driver that you want to get out, the normal practice is to rap hard with a coin on the metal railings as you approach the spot (or press the bell if there is one).

In the deep south (see p.442) they do things with a little more style 1ww **share-taxis** connect many of the major towns, though they are inexorably being replaced by more comfortable **air-conditioned minibuses**. Many similar private air-con minibuses are now cropping up on popular routes elsewhere in the country; they generally depart frequently and cover the distance faster than the ordinary bus service, but can be uncomfortably cramped when full and are not ideal for travellers with huge rucksacks, who may be required to pay extra. As with full-sized buses (see opposite), be wary of unlicensed private companies that offer minibuses solely for farangs from Bangkok's Thanon Khao San.

In many cases, long-distance songthaews and air-con minibuses will drop you at an exact address (for example a particular guest house) if you warn them far enough in advance. As a rule, the **cost** of inter-town songthaews is comparable to that of air-con buses, with that of air-con minibuses perhaps a shade more.

Trains

Managed by the State Railway of Thailand (SRT), the **rail** network consists of four main lines and a few branch lines. In the area covered by this book is the **Eastern Line, which** has two branches, one running from Bangkok to Aranyaprathet on the Cambodian border, the other connecting Bangkok with Si Racha and Pattaya. Meanwhile, the **Southern Line** extends via Hua Hin, Chumphon and Surat Thani, with

Train information

For 24hr **train information**, phone the State Railway of Thailand (SRT) in Bangkok on ☏02 220 4444, or on its free Hotline ☏1690. The SRT website (⊛www.railway.co.th) carries English-language timetables, a breakdown of ticket prices from Bangkok and a link to the new booking website, ⊛www.thairailway ticket.com.

spurs off to Trang and Nakhon Si Thammarat, to Hat Yai (see the travel warning on p.441), where it branches: one line continues down the west coast of Malaysia, via Butterworth, where you change trains for Kuala Lumpur and Singapore; the other heads down the eastern side of the peninsula to Sungai Kolok on the Thailand–Malaysia border (20km from Pasir Mas on Malaysia's interior railway).

Fares depend on the class of seat, whether or not you want air-conditioning, and on the speed of the train; those quoted here exclude the "speed" supplements, which are discussed below. Hard, wooden or thinly padded third-class seats are a bit cheaper than buses (Bangkok–Surat Thani B297, or B397 with air-con), and are fine for about three hours, after which numbness sets in. For longer journeys you'd be wise to opt for the padded and often reclining seats in second class (Bangkok–Surat B438, or B578 with air-con). On long-distance trains, you also usually have the option of second-class berths (Bangkok–Surat B498–548, or B758–848 with air-con), with day seats that convert into comfortable curtained-off bunks in the evening; lower bunks, which are more expensive than upper, have a few cubic centimetres more of space, a little more shade from the lights in the carriage, and a window. Female passengers can sometimes request a berth in an all-female section of a carriage. Travelling first class (Bangkok–Surat B1279) means a two-person air-con sleeping compartment, complete with washbasin.

There are several different **types of train**: slowest of all is the third-class-only Ordinary service, which is generally (but not always) available only on short and medium-length journeys and has no speed supplement. Next comes the misleadingly named Rapid train (B50–110 supplement), which from Bangkok to Surat Thani, for example, takes twelve or thirteen hours; the Express (B150 supplement), which does the same route in around twelve hours; and the Special Express (B170 supplement), which covers the ground in between nine and eleven hours. Among the last-mentioned, fastest of all are the mostly daytime Special Express Diesel Railcars, which can generally be relied on to run on time. Nearly all long-distance

trains have **dining cars**, and rail staff will also bring meals to your seat.

Booking at least one day in advance is strongly recommended for second- and first-class seats on all lengthy journeys, and sleepers should be booked as far in advance as possible (reservations open sixty days before departure). You can make bookings for any journey in Thailand at the train station in any major town, as well as by phone, though you have to pay for the tickets before 4pm the next day at a train station. It's now also possible to book online, at least three days in advance, at Ⓦwww.thairailwayticket.com, though currently the website is allocated only ten percent of available seats. Otherwise, you can arrange advance bookings over the internet with reputable Thai travel agencies such as Traveller 2000 (Ⓦwww.traveller2000 .com) or Thai Focus (Ⓦwww.thaifocus.com). For details on how to book trains out of Bangkok **in person**, see p.164.

The SRT publishes clear and fairly accurate free **timetables** in English, detailing types of trains and classes available on each route, as well as fares; the best place to get hold of them is over the counter at Bangkok's Hualamphong Station or, if you're lucky, the TAT office in Bangkok. These English-only timetables cover the services that the SRT think will appeal to tourists; other, slow trains covering short- and medium-length routes are also shown on mostly Thai national timetables.

The SRT also sells twenty-day **rail passes** (available only in Thailand), covering unlimited train journeys in second- (or third-) class seats for B1500, or B3000 with all supplements thrown in. However, unless you're on a whistle-stop tour of all four corners of the country, the rail network is not really extensive enough to make them pay.

Ferries

Regular **ferries** connect all major islands with the mainland, and for the vast majority of crossings you simply buy your ticket on board. Safety standards are generally just about adequate but there have been a small number of sinkings in recent years – avoid travelling on boats that are clearly overloaded or in poor condition. In tourist areas competition ensures that prices are kept low, and fares tend to vary with the speed of the crossing, if anything: thus Chumphon–Ko Tao costs between B200 (6hr) and B550 (1hr 30min).

On the east coast and the Andaman coast boats generally operate a reduced service during the monsoon season (May–Oct), when the more remote spots become inaccessible. Ferries in the Samui archipelago are fairly constant year-round. Details on island connections are given in the relevant chapters.

Flights

The domestic arm of **Thai Airways** (☎02 356 1111, ⓦwww.thaiair.com) offers the widest choice of internal flights, flying for example from Bangkok to Hat Yai, Ko Samui, Krabi, Phuket and Surat Thani. However, with deregulation, several smaller airlines have recently broken into the volatile market, including one or two cheap, no-frills companies. **Bangkok Airways** (☎02 265 5555, ⓦwww.bangkokair .com) is Thai Airways' main competitor at home, covering major destinations from Bangkok such as Ko Samui, Phuket and Trat, as well as a Pattaya–Ko Samui–Phuket triangle and Ko Samui–Krabi.

Among the newcomers on the scene, **Air Asia** (☎02 515 9999, ⓦwww.airasia.com) currently flies from Bangkok to Hat Yai, Krabi, Phuket, Ranong and Surat Thani; **Nok Air** (☎1318 or 02 900 9955, ⓦwww.nokair .com), part-owned by Thai Airways, covers Bangkok to Hat Yai, Nakhon Si Thammarat, Phuket and Trang, and, in partnership with SGA Airlines, Bangkok to Hua Hin; and **One-Two-Go** (☎1126 or 02 229 4100–1, ⓦwww.fly12go.com), operated by Orient Thai Airlines, has flights from Bangkok to Hat Yai, Phuket and Trang. These routings change surprisingly frequently and at the very minor airports, schedules are erratic and flights are sometimes cancelled, so always check ahead.

To give an idea of **fares**, on the Bangkok–Surat Thani route Thai Airways charges from B2750 one-way, Air Asia from B1300 (plus B50 per checked-in bag).

If you're planning to use the internal network a lot, you might want to consider buying an **airpass**, although certain taxes and fees are extra and the passes must be bought outside Thailand from one of the airlines' offices or a travel agent. Of the two available, Bangkok Airways' Discovery Airpass is the easier to use: you buy between three and six flight coupons, generally for US$60 each, confirming the first flight before departure, though the others (valid for two months after the first flight) can be left open; a coupon for Bangkok–Ko Samui costs US$75. (Similar coupons are available for international flights by Bangkok Airways and flights with its partners, Siem Reap Airways and Lao Airlines.) Thai Airways' Discover Thailand pass covers three one-way flights within a three-month period for US$199; you fix the routes when you buy the pass, but dates of travel can be changed in Thailand. Up to five additional flights can be added for US$59 each.

Local transport

Most sizeable towns have some kind of **local transport system**, comprising a network of songthaews or even longtail boats. For details of Bangkok's bus network, see p.85.

Songthaews

Within medium-sized and large towns, the main transport role is often played by **songthaews**. The size and shape of vehicle used varies from town to town – and in some places they're known as "tuk-tuks" from the noise they make, not to be confused with the smaller tuk-tuks, described below, that operate as private taxis – but all have the tell-tale two facing benches in the back. In some towns, songthaews follow fixed routes; in others, they act as communal taxis, picking up a number of people who are going in roughly the same direction and taking each of them right to their destination. To hail a songthaew just flag it down, and to indicate that you want to get out, either rap hard with a coin on the metal railings, or ring the bell if there is one. Fares within towns are around B10–20, depending on distance.

Longtail boats

Wherever there's a decent public waterway, there'll be a **longtail boat** ready to ferry you along it. Another great Thai trademark, these elegant, streamlined boats are powered by deafening diesel engines – sometimes custom-built, more often adapted from cars or trucks – which drive a propeller mounted on a long shaft that is swivelled for steering. Longtails carry between eight and twenty passengers: generally you'll have to charter the whole boat, but on popular fixed routes, for example between small, inshore islands and the mainland, it's cheaper to wait until the boatman gets his quorum.

Taxi services

Taxis also come in many guises, and in bigger towns you can often choose between taking a tuk-tuk, a samlor and a motorbike taxi. The one thing common to all modes of chartered transport, bar Bangkok's metered taxis, is that you must establish the **fare** beforehand: although drivers nearly always pitch their first offers too high, they do calculate with traffic and time of day in mind, as well as according to distance – if successive drivers scoff at your price, you know you've got it wrong.

Tuk-tuks

Named after the noise of its excruciatingly unsilenced engine, the three-wheeled, open-sided **tuk-tuk** is the classic Thai vehicle. Painted in primary colours, tuk-tuks blast their way round towns and cities on two-stroke engines, zipping around faster than any car and taking corners on two wheels. They aren't as dangerous as they look though, and can be an exhilarating way to get around, as long as you're not too fussy about exhaust fumes. Fares come in at around B50 for a medium-length journey (over B100 in Bangkok) regardless of the number of passengers – three is the safe maximum, though six is not uncommon. See p.92 for advice on how to avoid being ripped off by Bangkok tuk-tuk drivers.

Samlors

Tuk-tuks are also sometimes known as samlors (literally "three wheels"), but the original **samlors** are tricycle rickshaws propelled by pedal power alone. Slower and a great deal more stately than tuk-tuks, samlors still operate in one or two towns around the country.

A further permutation are the motorized samlors, where the driver relies on a motorbike rather than a bicycle to propel passengers to their destination. They look much the same as cycle samlors, but often sound as noisy as tuk-tuks.

Motorbike taxis

Even faster and more precarious than tuk-tuks, **motorbike taxis** feature both in towns and in out-of-the-way places. In towns – where the drivers are identified by coloured, numbered vests – they have the advantage of being able to dodge traffic jams, but are obviously only really suitable for the single traveller, and motorbike taxis aren't the easiest mode of transport if you're carrying luggage. In remote spots, on the other hand, they're often the only alternative to hitching or walking, and are especially useful for getting between bus stops on main roads, around car-free islands and to national parks or ancient ruins.

Within towns motorbike-taxi fares can start at B10 for very short journeys, but for trips to the outskirts the cost rises steeply – about B200 for a twenty-kilometre round trip.

Vehicle rental

Despite first impressions, a high accident rate and the obvious mayhem that characterizes Bangkok's roads, **driving** yourself around Thailand can be fairly straightforward. Many roads, particularly in the south, are remarkably uncongested. Major routes are clearly signed in English, though this only applies to some minor roads; unfortunately there is no perfect English-language map to compensate (see p.68).

Outside the capital, its immediate environs and the eastern seaboard, local drivers are generally considerate and unaggressive; they very rarely use their horns for example, and will often indicate and even swerve away when it's safe for you to overtake. The most inconsiderate and dangerous road-users in Thailand are bus drivers and lorry drivers, many of whom drive ludicrously fast, hog the road, race round bends on the wrong side of the road and use their horns remorselessly; worse still, many of them are tanked up on amphetamines, which makes them quite literally fearless.

Bus and lorry drivers are at their worst after dark (many of them only drive then), so you are strongly advised **never to drive at night** – a further hazard being the inevitable stream of unlit bicycles and mopeds in and around built-up areas, as well as poorly signed roadworks, which are often not made safe or blocked off from unsuspecting traffic. Orange signs, or sometimes just a couple of tree branches or a pile of stones on the road, warn of hazards ahead.

As for local **rules of the road**, Thais drive on the left, and the speed limit is 60km per hour within built-up areas and 90km per hour outside them. Beyond that, there are few rules that are generally followed – you'll need to keep your concentration up and expect the unexpected from fellow road-users. Watch out especially for vehicles pulling straight out of minor roads, when you might expect them to give way. An oncoming vehicle flashing its lights means it's coming through no matter what; a right indicator signal from the car in front usually means it's not safe for you to overtake, while a left indicator signal usually means that it is safe to do so.

Theoretically, foreigners need an international **driver's licence** to rent any kind of vehicle, but most car-rental companies accept national licences, and the smaller operations have been known not to ask for any kind of proof whatsoever; motorbike renters very rarely bother. A popular current rip-off, notably on Ko Pha Ngan and Ko Tao, is for small agents to charge renters exorbitant amounts for any minor damage to a jeep or motorbike, even paint chips, that they find on return – they'll claim that it's very expensive to get a new part shipped over from the mainland. Check out any vehicle carefully before renting; on the two islands mentioned, we've tried to recommend agents who don't indulge in this practice.

Petrol (*nam man*, which can also mean oil) currently costs around B20 a litre, though it's been as high as B43 in recent years. The big fuel stations are the least costly places to fill up (*hai tem*), and many of these also have toilets and simple restaurants, though some of the more decrepit-looking fuel stations on the main highways only sell diesel. Most small villages have easy-to-spot roadside huts where the fuel is pumped out of a large barrel.

Renting a car

If you decide to **rent a car**, go to a reputable dealer, such as Avis, Budget or SMT National (see below), or a rental company recommended by TAT, and make sure you get insurance from them. There are international car-rental places at many airports, including Bangkok's Suvarnabhumi, which is not a bad place to kick off, as you're on the edge of the city and within fairly easy, signposted reach of the major regional highways.

Car-rental places in provincial capitals and resorts are listed in the relevant accounts in this book. The price of a small car at a reputable company is generally about B1500 per day. In some parts of the country, where there are no dedicated car-rental agencies, you'll still be able to rent a car or air-con minibus with driver, for around B1800 per day.

Jeeps or basic four-wheel drives are a lot more popular with farangs, especially on beach resorts and islands like Pattaya, Phuket and Ko Samui, but they're notoriously **dangerous**; a huge number of tourists manage to roll their jeeps on steep hillsides and sharp bends. Jeep rental usually works out somewhere between B900 and B1200 per day.

International companies will accept your credit-card details as surety, but smaller agents will usually want to hold on to your passport.

Car rental agencies

Avis Ⓦ www.avisthailand.com
Budget Ⓦ www.budget.co.th
Master Ⓦ www.mastercarrental.com
SMT National Ⓦ www.nationalcar.com or www.smtrentacar.com
Thai Rentacar Ⓦ www.thairentacar.com

Renting a motorbike

One of the best ways of exploring the countryside is to **rent a motorbike**. Bikes of around 100c, either fully automatic or with step-through gears, are best if you've never ridden a motorbike before, but aren't really suited for long slogs. If you're going to hit the dirt roads you'll certainly need something more powerful, like a 125–250cc trail bike. These have the edge in gear choice and are the best bikes for steep slopes, though an inexperienced rider may find these machines a handful; the less widely available 125–250cc road bikes are easier to control and much cheaper on fuel.

Rental **prices** for the day usually work out at somewhere around B150–200 for a small bike and B500 for a good trail bike, though you can bargain for a discount on a long rental. Renters will often ask for a deposit and your passport or credit-card details; insurance is not often available, so it's a good idea to make sure your travel insurance covers you for possible mishaps.

Before signing anything, **check the bike** thoroughly – test the brakes, look for oil leaks, check the treads and the odometer, and make sure the chain isn't stretched too tight (a tight chain is more likely to break) – and preferably take it for a test run. As you will have to pay an inflated price for any damage when you get back, make a note on the contract of any defects such as broken mirrors, indicators and so on. Make sure you know what kind of fuel the bike takes as well.

As far as **equipment** goes, a helmet is essential – most rental places provide poorly made ones, but they're better than nothing. Helmets are obligatory on all motorbike journeys, and the law is often rigidly enforced with on-the-spot fines in major tourist resorts. You'll need sunglasses if your helmet doesn't have a visor. Long trousers, a long-sleeved top and decent shoes will provide a second skin if you go over, which most people do at some stage. Pillions should wear long trousers to avoid getting nasty burns from the exhaust. For the sake of stability, leave most of your luggage in baggage storage and pack as small a bag as possible, strapping it tightly to the bike with bungy cords – these are usually provided. Once on the road, oil the chain at least every other day, keep the radiator topped up and fill up with oil every 300km or so.

For expert **advice** on motorbike travel in Thailand, check out David Unkovich's website (Ⓦwww.gt-rider.com).

Cycling

The options for **cycling** in Thailand are numerous, and most Thai roads are in good condition and clearly signposted. The secondary **roads** (distinguished by their three-digit numbers) are paved but carry far less traffic than the main arteries and are the preferred cycling option. Traffic is reasonably well behaved and personal safety is not a major concern as long as you "ride to survive"; dogs, however, can be a nuisance on minor roads so it's probably worth having rabies shots before your trip. There are bike shops in nearly every town and basic equipment and repairs are cheap.

The traffic into and out of Bangkok is dense so it's worth hopping on a bus or train for the first 50–100km to your starting point. The Bangkok Skytrain and intercity air-con buses, taxis and most Thai domestic planes (no bike box required) will **carry your bike** free of charge. The Bangkok subway does not allow bikes. Intercity trains will only transport your bike (for a fare – about the price of a person) if there is a luggage carriage attached, unless you dismantle it and carry it as luggage in the compartment with you. Intercity non-air-con buses and songthaews will carry your bike on the roof for a fare (about the price of a person).

Local one-day cycle tours and **bike-rental outlets** (B30–100 per day) are listed throughout this book. For details of organized **cycle tours** see p.21. For detailed accounts of cycling in Thailand see Biking Southeast Asia with Mr Pumpy at Ⓦwww.mrpumpy.net.

Cycling practicalities

Strong, light, quality **mountain bikes** are the most versatile choice; 26-inch wheels are standard throughout Thailand and are strongly recommended; dual-use (combined road and off-road) tyres are best for touring. As regards panniers and **equipment**, the most important thing is to travel light. Carry a few spare spokes, but don't overdo it with too many tools and spares; parts are cheap in Thailand and most problems can be fixed quickly at any bike shop.

Bringing your bike from home is the best option as you are riding a known quantity.

orting it by plane should be straightforward, but check with the airlines for details. Most Asian airlines do not charge extra.

Buying in Thailand is also a possibility: the range is reasonable and prices tend to be cheaper than in the West or Australia. In Bangkok, the best outlet is Probike at 237/2 Thanon Rajdamri (actually off Soi Sarasin next to Lumphini Park; ☏02 253 3384, ⊛www.probike.co.th); Velo Thailand (see p.86) also sell international-brand aluminium-frame bikes, as well as renting mountain bikes for B300 per day. You can also rent good mountain bikes through the Bangkok cycle-tour operator Spice Roads (☏02 712 5305, ⊛www.spiceroads.com), for B280–400 per day.

Hitching

Public transport being so inexpensive, you should only have to resort to **hitching** in the most remote areas, in which case you'll probably get a lift to the nearest bus or songthaew stop quite quickly. On routes served by buses and trains, hitching is not standard practice, but in other places locals do rely on regular passers-by (such as national park officials), and you can make use of this "service" too. As with hitching anywhere in the world, think twice about hitching solo or at night, especially if you're female. Like bus drivers, truck drivers are notorious users of amphetamines, so you may want to wait for a safer offer.

Accommodation

For the simplest double room prices start at a bargain B150 in the outlying regions, B200 in Bangkok, and B400 in the pricier resorts. Tourist centres invariably offer a tempting range of more upmarket choices but in these areas rates fluctuate according to demand, plummeting during the off-season, peaking over the Christmas fortnight and, in some places, rising at weekends throughout the year.

Guest houses, bungalows and hostels

Most of Thailand's **budget accommodation** (❶–❸) is in **guest houses** and **bungalows.** These are small, traveller-friendly hotels whose services nearly always include an inexpensive restaurant and safe storage for valuables and left luggage, and often also run to internet access (sometimes even in-room wi-fi) and a tour desk. The difference between guest houses and bungalows is mostly in their design, with "bungalows" – which are generally found on the beach and in rural areas – mostly comprising detached or semi-detached rooms in huts, villas, chalets or indeed bungalows, and "guest houses" being either a purpose-built mini hotel or a converted home. En-suite showers and flush toilets are common in both, but at the

cheaper places you might be showering with a bowl dipped into a large water jar, and using squat toilets.

Many guest houses and bungalows offer a spread of options to cater for all budgets: their **cheapest rooms** will often be furnished with nothing more than a double bed, a blanket and a fan (window optional, private bathroom extra) and might cost anything from B150–300 for two people, depending on the location and the competition. A similar room with **en-suite** bathroom, and possibly more stylish furnishings, generally comes in at B200–600, while for a room with **air-con,** and perhaps a TV and fridge as well, you're looking at B350–1500.

In the most popular tourist centres at the busiest times of year, the best-known guest houses are often full night after night. Some

Accommodation prices

Throughout this guide, guest houses, bungalows and hotels have been categorized according to the **price codes** given below. These categories represent the **minimum** you can expect to pay in the **high season** (roughly July, Aug and Nov–Feb) for a **double room**, booked via the hotel website where available; there may, however, be an extra "peak" supplement for the Christmas–New Year period. If travelling on your own, expect to pay between sixty and one hundred percent of the rates quoted for a double room. Where a place also offers **dormitory beds**, the price per bed is given in the text, instead of being indicated by a price code. Top-end hotels will add **seven percent tax** and **ten percent service charge** to your bill; the price codes below are based on net rates after taxes have been added.

① B250 and under ④ B601–900 ⑦ B2001–3000
② B251–400 ⑤ B901–1400 ⑧ B3001–4500
③ B401–600 ⑥ B1401–2000 ⑨ B4501 and over

will take **bookings** and advance payment via their websites, but for those that don't it's usually a question of turning up and waiting for a vacancy. At most guest houses **checkout time** is either 11am or noon.

Generally you should be wary of taking accommodation advice from a **tout** or tuk-tuk driver, as they demand commission from guest-house owners, which, if not passed directly on to you via a higher room price, can have a crippling effect on the smaller guest houses. If a tout claims your intended accommodation is "full" or "no good" or has "burnt down", it's always worth phoning to check yourself. Touts can come into their own, however, on islands such as Ko Lanta where it can be a long and expensive ride to your chosen beach, and frustrating if you then discover your bungalows are full; island touts usually sweet-talk you on the boat and then

transport you for free to view their accommodation, ideally with no obligation to stay.

With only 25 registered **youth hostels** in the country, bookable via Ⓦwww.tyha.org, it's not worth becoming a Hostelling International member just for your trip to Thailand, especially as card-holders get only a small discount and room rates anyway work out the same as or more expensive than guest-house equivalents. In addition, hostels mostly cater for Thai students and so may not be staffed by English-speakers.

Budget hotels

Thai sales reps and other people travelling for business rather than pleasure rarely use guest houses, opting instead for **budget hotels**, which offer rooms for around B150–600. Usually run by Chinese-Thais, these functional three- or four-storey places are found in every sizeable town, often near

Bathroom etiquette

Although modern, Western-style bathrooms are commonplace throughout Thailand, it's as well to be forewarned about local bathroom etiquette.

Sit-down **toilets** are the norm but public amenities, especially at bus and train stations, and in some homes and old-style guest houses and hotels, tend to be squat toilets. Thais traditionally don't use **paper** but wash rather than wipe themselves after going to the toilet. Modern bathrooms are fitted with a special hose for this purpose, while more primitive bathrooms just provide a **bucket of water and a dipper**. Thais always use their left hand for washing – and their right hand for eating (see p.43). As Thai plumbing is notoriously sluggish, where toilet paper is provided, it's normal to throw it in the waste basket and not down the U-bend. If a toilet is not plumbed in, you flush it yourself with water from the bucket. In really basic hotel bathrooms with no **shower** facilities, you also use the bucket and dipper for scoop-and-slosh bathing.

the bus station or central market. Beds are large enough for a couple, so it's quite acceptable for two people to ask and pay for a "single" room (*hawng thiang diaw*, literally a "one-bedded room"). Though the rooms are generally clean, en suite and furnished with either a fan or air-con, there's rarely an on-site restaurant and the atmosphere is generally less convivial than at guest houses. A number of budget hotels also double as brothels, though as a farang you're unlikely to be offered this sideline, and you might not even notice the goings-on.

Advance reservations are accepted over the phone, but this is rarely necessary, as such hotels rarely fill up. The only time you may have difficulty finding a budget hotel room is during Chinese New Year (a moveable three-day period in late Jan or Feb), when many Chinese-run hotels close and others get booked up fast.

Tourist hotels

The rest of the accommodation picture is all about **tourist hotels** which, like anywhere in the world, come in all sizes and qualities and are often best booked via online discount accommodation booking services (see box below). One way or another, it's a good idea to **reserve ahead** in popular tourist areas during peak season.

Rates for **middle-ranking hotels** (❹–❻) fall between B600 and B2000. For this you can expect many of the trimmings of a top-end hotel – air-con, TV and mini-bar in the room, plus an on-site pool, restaurant and perhaps nightclub – but with dated and possibly faded furnishings and little of the style of the famous big names; they're often the kind of places that once stood at the top of the range, but were outclassed when the multinational luxury hotels muscled in.

Online booking agents

Asia Hotels ⓦ www.asia-hotels.com
Hotel Thailand ⓦ www.hotelthailand.com
Passion Asia ⓦ www.passionasia.com
Sawadee ⓦ www.sawadee.com
Thai Focus ⓦ www.thaifocus.com

Many of Thailand's **expensive hotels** (❼–❾) belong to the big international chains: Sheraton, Marriott and Sofitel all have a strong presence in the country and are closely followed by upmarket home-grown groups such as Amari, Dusit and Centara. Between them they maintain premium standards in Bangkok and major resorts at prices of B3000 (£60/US$85) and upward for a double – far less than you'd pay for equivalent accommodation in the West.

Thailand also boasts an increasing number of deliciously stylish **luxury hotels**, many of them designed as intimate, small-scale **boutique** hotels, with chic, minimalist decor, exceptional service and excellent facilities that often include private plunge pools and a spa. A night in one of these places will rarely cost you less than B6000 (£120/US$170), and may set you back more than twice as much, though they're still often outstanding value for the honeymoon-style indulgence that they offer; see accommodation listings for Bangkok, Ko Samui, Khao Lak and Phuket for some suggestions. As in the West, however, the term "boutique" is overused, and a "boutique" guest house or hotel may in practice be little more than "small". Many luxury hotels quote rates in US dollars, though you can always pay in baht.

Homestays

As guest houses have become increasingly hotel-like and commercial in their facilities and approach, many tourists looking for old-style local hospitality are choosing **homestay accommodation** instead. Homestay facilities are nearly always simple and cheap, at around B150 per person per night, with guests staying in a shared spare room and eating with the family. Homestays give an unparalleled insight into typical Thai (usually rural) life and can often be incorporated into a programme that includes experiencing village activities such as rice-farming, squid-fishing, rubber-tapping or silk-weaving. They are also a positive way of supporting small communities, as all your money will feed right back into the village. As well as listed homestays in Pha To (see p.259), Khuraburi (see p.333), Ko Yao Noi (see p.386) and Krabi (see p.396), there are many others bookable through tour operators detailed on p.21 or via www.homestaythai.org, though partici-pants in the latter organization may not speak much English.

National parks and camping

Nearly all the **national parks** have accom-modation facilities, usually comprising a series of simple concrete bungalows that cost at least B600 for two or more beds plus a basic bathroom. Because most of their custom comes from Thai families and student groups, park officials are sometimes loath to discount them for lone travellers, though a few parks do offer dorm-style accommodation at around B100 a bed. In most parks, advance booking is unnecessary except at weekends and national holidays.

If you do want to pre-book, you can do so up to sixty days ahead of your stay at www.dnp.go.th/National_park.asp. As credit-card payment is not yet possible, you need to pay in cash or via bank draft within two days of booking, most conveniently at any branch of Krung Thai bank, or at desig-nated international banks, or at the National Park headquarters in question; see the "Reservation" section of individual national park webpages at the site given above for comprehensive details. The few national parks that accept phone bookings themselves are highlighted in the guide chapters. If you turn up without booking, check in at the park headquarters, which is usually adjacent to the visitor centre.

In a few parks, private operators have set up low-cost guest houses on the outskirts, and these generally make more attractive and economical places to stay.

Camping

You can usually **camp** in a national park for a nominal fee of B60 per two-person tent, and some national parks also rent out fully equipped tents from B150 (bookable through a separate section on the above-listed website). Unless you're planning an extensive tour of national parks, though, there's little point in lugging a tent around Thailand: accommodation everywhere else is very inexpensive, and anyway there are no campsites inside town perimeters, though camping is allowed on nearly all islands and beaches, many of which are national parks in their own right.

Food and drink

Bangkok is the country's main culinary centre, boasting the cream of gourmet Thai restaurants and the best international cuisines. The rest of the country is by no means a gastronomic wasteland, however, and you can eat well and cheaply in even the smallest provincial towns, many of which offer the additional attraction of regional specialities. In fact you could eat more than adequately without ever entering a restaurant, as itinerant food vendors hawking hot and cold snacks materialize in even the most remote spots, as well as on trains and buses – and night markets often serve customers from dusk until dawn.

Hygiene is a consideration when eating anywhere in Thailand, but being too cautious means you'll end up spending a lot of money and missing out on some real local treats. Wean your stomach gently by avoiding excessive amounts of chillies and too much fresh fruit in the first few days.

You can be pretty sure that any noodle stall or curry shop that's permanently packed with customers is a safe bet. Furthermore,

For a detailed **food and drink glossary**, see p.493.

because most Thai dishes can be cooked in under five minutes, you'll rarely have to contend with stuff that's been left to smoulder and stew. Foods that are generally considered high risk include salads, ice cream, shellfish and raw or undercooked meat, fish or eggs. If you're really concerned about health standards you could stick to restaurants and food stalls displaying a "**Clean Food Good Taste**" sign, part of a food sanitation project set up by the Ministry of Public Health, TAT and the Ministry of Interior.

Most restaurants in Thailand are open every day for lunch and dinner; we've noted exceptions throughout the guide. In a few of the country's most expensive restaurants, mostly in Bangkok, a ten percent service charge and possibly even seven percent VAT may be added to your bill.

For those interested in **learning Thai cookery**, short courses designed for visitors are held in Bangkok, Ko Samui, Ko Chang, Ao Nang and Phuket; see the relevant accounts for details.

Where to eat

A lot of tourists eschew the huge range of Thai **places to eat**, despite their obvious attractions, and opt instead for the much "safer" restaurants in guest houses and hotels. Almost all tourist accommodation has a kitchen, and while some are excellent, the vast majority serve up bland imitations of Western fare alongside equally pale versions of common Thai dishes. Having said that, guest houses do serve comfortingly familiar Western breakfasts.

Throughout the country most **inexpensive Thai restaurants** and cafés specialize in one general food type or preparation method, charging around B40–50 a dish – a "noodle shop", for example, will do fried noodles and/ or noodle soups, plus maybe a basic fried rice, but they won't have curries or meat or fish dishes. Similarly, a restaurant displaying whole roast chickens and ducks in its window will offer these sliced, usually with chillies and sauces and served over rice, but

their menu probably won't extend to noodles or fish, while in "curry shops" your options are limited to the vats of curries stewing away in the hot cabinet.

To get a wider array of low-cost food, it's sometimes best to head for the local **night market** (*talaat yen*), a term for the gatherings of open-air night-time kitchens found in every town. Sometimes operating from 6pm to 6am, they are typically to be found on permanent patches close to the fruit and vegetable market or the bus station, and as often as not they're the best and most entertaining places to eat, not to mention the least expensive – after a lip-smacking feast of savoury dishes, a fruit drink and a dessert you'll come away no more than B150 poorer.

A typical night market has maybe thirty-odd "specialist" pushcart kitchens (*rot khen*) jumbled together, each fronted by several sets of tables and stools. Noodle and fried-rice vendors always feature prominently, as do sweets stalls, heaped high with sticky rice cakes wrapped in banana leaves or thick with bags of tiny sweetcorn pancakes hot from the griddle – and no night market is complete without its fruit-drink stall, offering banana shakes and freshly squeezed orange, lemon and tomato juices. In the best setups you'll find a lot more besides: curries, barbecued sweetcorn, satay sticks of pork and chicken, deep-fried insects, fresh pineapple, watermelon and mango and – if the town's by a river or near the sea – heaps of fresh fish. Having decided what you want, you order from the cook (or the cook's dogsbody) and sit down at the nearest table; there is no territorialism about night markets, so it's normal to eat several dishes from separate stalls and rely on the nearest cook to sort out the bill.

Some large markets, particularly in Bangkok, have separate **food court** areas where you buy coupons first and select food and drink to their value at the stalls of your choice. This is also usually the modus operandi in the food courts found in department stores and shopping centres across the country.

For a more relaxing ambience, Bangkok and the larger towns have a range of **upmarket restaurants**, some specializing in **"royal" Thai cuisine**, which is differentiated

Fruits of Thailand

You'll find **fruit** (*phonlamai*) offered everywhere in Thailand – neatly sliced in glass boxes on hawker carts, blended into delicious shakes and served as a dessert in restaurants. The fruits described below can be found in all parts of Thailand, though some are seasonal. The country's more familiar fruits include forty varieties of **banana** (*kluay*), dozens of different **mangoes** (*mamuang*), three types of **pineapple** (*sapparot*), **coconuts** (*maprao*), **oranges** (*som*), **lemons** (*manao*) and **watermelons** (*taeng moh*).

To avoid stomach trouble, **peel all fruit** before eating it, and use common sense if you're tempted to buy it pre-peeled on the street, avoiding anything that looks fly-blown or seems to have been sitting in the sun for hours.

Custard apple (soursop; *noina*; July–Sept). Inside the knobbly, muddy green skin is a creamy, almond-coloured blancmange-like flesh, with a strong flavour of strawberries and pears, and a hint of cinnamon, and many seeds.

Durian (*thurian*; April–June). Thailand's most prized, and expensive, fruit has a greeny-yellow, spiky exterior and grows to the size of a football. Inside, it divides into segments of thick, yellow-white flesh which gives off a disgustingly strong stink that's been compared to a mixture of mature cheese and caramel. Not surprisingly, many airlines and hotels ban the eating of this smelly delicacy on their premises. Most Thais consider it the king of fruits, while most foreigners find it utterly foul in both taste and smell.

Guava (*farang*; year-round). The apple of the tropics has green textured skin and sweet, crisp pink or white flesh, studded with tiny edible seeds. Has five times the vitamin C content of an orange and is sometimes eaten cut into strips and sprinkled with sugar and chilli.

Jackfruit (*khanun*; year-round). This large, pear-shaped fruit can weigh up to 20kg and has a thick, bobbly, greeny-yellow shell protecting sweet yellow flesh. Green, unripe jackfruit is sometimes cooked as a vegetable in curries.

Longan (*lamyai*; July–Oct). A close relative of the lychee, with succulent white flesh covered in thin, brittle skin.

Lychee (*linjii*; April–May). Under rough, reddish-brown skin, the lychee has sweet, richly flavoured white flesh, rose-scented and with plenty of vitamin C.

Mangosteen (*mangkut*; April–Sept). The size of a small apple, with smooth, purple skin and a fleshy inside that divides into succulent white segments that are sweet though slightly acidic.

Papaya (paw-paw; *malakaw*; year-round). Looks like an elongated watermelon, with smooth green skin and yellowy-orange flesh that's a rich source of vitamins A and C. It's a favourite in fruit salads and shakes, and sometimes appears in its green, unripe form in salads, notably som tam.

Pomelo (*som oh*; Oct–Dec). The largest of all citrus fruits, it looks rather like a grapefruit, though it is slightly drier and has less flavour.

Rambutan (*ngaw*; May–Sept). The bright red rambutan's soft, spiny exterior has given it its name – *rambut* means "hair" in Malay. Usually about the size of a golf ball, it has a white, opaque flesh of delicate flavour, similar to a lychee.

Rose apple (*chomphuu*; year-round). Linked in myth with the golden fruit of immortality; small and egg-shaped, with white, rose-scented flesh.

Sapodilla (sapota; *lamut*; Sept–Dec). These small, brown, rough-skinned ovals look a bit like kiwi fruit and conceal a grainy, yellowish pulp that tastes almost honey-sweet.

Tamarind (*makhaam*; Dec–Jan). A Thai favourite and a pricey delicacy – carrying the seeds is said to make you safe from wounding by knives or bullets. Comes in rough, brown pods containing up to ten seeds, each surrounded by a sticky, dry pulp which has a sour, lemony taste.

mainly by the quality of the ingredients and the way the food is presented. Great care is taken over how individual dishes look: they are served in small portions and decorated with carved fruit and vegetables in a way that used to be the prerogative of royal cooks, but has now filtered down to the common folk. The cost of such delights is not prohibitive, either – a meal in one of these places is unlikely to cost more than B500 per person.

Vegetarians and vegans

Very few Thais are **vegetarian** (*mangsawirat*) but, if you can make yourself understood, you can often get a non-meat or fish alternative to what's on the menu; simply ask the cook to exclude meat and fish: *mai sai neua, mai sai plaa*. You may end up eating a lot of unexciting vegetable fried rice and *phat thai* minus the shrimps, but in better restaurants you should be able to get veggie versions of most curries; the mushroom version of chicken and coconut soup is also a good standby: ask for *tom kha hed*. Browsing food stalls also expands your options, with barbecued sweetcorn, nuts, fruit and other non-meaty goodies all common. The two ingredients that you will have to consider compromising on are the fermented **fish sauce** and **shrimp paste** that are fundamental to most Thai dishes; only in the vegan Thai restaurants described below, and in tourist spots serving specially concocted Thai and Western veggie dishes, can you be sure of avoiding them.

If you're **vegan** (*jay,* sometimes spelt "*jeh*") you'll need to stress when you order that you don't want egg, as they get used a lot; cheese and other dairy produce, however, don't feature at all in Thai cuisine. Many towns will have one or more **vegan restaurants** (*raan ahaan jay*), which are usually run by members of a temple or Buddhist sect and operate from unadorned premises off the main streets; because strict Buddhists prefer not to eat late in the day, most of the restaurants open early, at around 6 or 7am, and close by 2pm. Most of these places have a yellow and red sign, though few display an English-language name. Nor is there ever a menu: customers simply choose from the trays of veggie stir-fries and curries,

nearly all of them made with soya products, that are laid out canteen-style. Most places charge around B40 for a couple of helpings served over a plate of brown rice.

How to eat

Thai food is eaten with a **fork** (left hand) and a **spoon** (right hand); there is no need for a knife as food is served in bite-sized chunks, which are forked onto the spoon and fed into the mouth. Cutlery is often delivered to the table wrapped in a perplexingly tiny pink napkin: Thais use this, not for their lap, but to give their fork, spoon and plate an extra wipe-down before they eat. Steamed **rice** (*khao*) is served with most meals, and indeed the most commonly heard phrase for "to eat" is *kin khao* (literally, "eat rice"). **Chopsticks** are provided only for noodle dishes, and northeastern sticky-rice dishes are always eaten with the **fingers of your right hand**. Never eat with the fingers of your left hand, which is used for washing after going to the toilet.

So that complementary taste combinations can be enjoyed, the dishes in a Thai meal are served all at once, even the soup, and shared communally. The more people, the more taste and texture sensations; if there are only two of you, it's normal to order three dishes, plus your own individual plates of steamed rice, while three diners would order four dishes, and so on. Only put a serving of one dish on your rice plate each time, and then only one or two spoonfuls.

Bland food is anathema to Thais, and restaurant tables everywhere come decked out with **condiment sets,** usually featuring fish sauce with chopped chillies; vinegar with chopped chillies; sugar; and dried chillies – and often extra bowls of ground peanuts and a bottle of chilli ketchup as well. If you do bite into a **chilli**, the way to combat the searing heat is to take a mouthful of plain rice and/or beer: swigging water just exacerbates the sensation.

What to eat

Four fundamental tastes are identified in Thai cuisine – spiciness, sourness, saltiness and sweetness – and diners aim to share a variety of dishes that impart a balance of these flavours, along with complementary textures. Lemon grass, basil, coriander, galangal, chilli, garlic, lime juice, coconut milk and fermented fish sauce (used instead of salt) are some of the distinctive components that bring these tastes to life. The repertoire of main dishes described below – along with Chinese-style stir-fries such as sweet-and-sour and chicken with cashew nuts – is pretty much standard throughout Thailand, but when you get out into the provinces, you'll have the chance to sample a few local specialities, too.

Curries

Thai curries (**kaeng**) have as their foundation a variety of curry pastes, elaborate and subtle blends of herbs, spices, garlic, shallots and chilli peppers that are traditionally ground together with pestle and mortar. The use of some of these spices, as well as of coconut cream, was imported from India long ago; curries that don't use coconut cream are naturally less sweet and thinner, with the consistency of soups.

While some curries, such as *kaeng karii* (mild and yellow) and *kaeng matsaman* (literally "Muslim curry", with potatoes, peanuts and usually beef), still show their roots, others have been adapted into quintessentially Thai dishes, notably *kaeng khiaw wan* (sweet and green), *kaeng phet* (red and hot) and *kaeng phanaeng* (thick and savoury, with peanuts). *Kaeng som* generally contains vegetables and fish and takes its distinctive sourness from the addition of tamarind. Traditionally eaten during the cool season, *kaeng liang* uses up gourds or other bland vegetables, but is made aromatic by the heat of peppercorns and shallots and the fragrance of basil leaves.

Soups

Thai soups, an essential component of most shared meals, are eaten simultaneously with other dishes, not as a starter. They are often flavoured with the distinctive tang of lemon grass, kaffir lime leaves and galangal, and garnished with fresh coriander, and can be extremely hot if the cook adds liberal handfuls of chillies to the pot. Two favourites are **tom kha kai**, a creamy coconut chicken soup; and **tom yam kung**, a hot and sour

prawn soup without coconut milk. **Khao tom**, a starchy rice soup that's generally eaten for breakfast, meets the approval of few Westerners, except as a traditional hangover cure.

Salads

One of the lesser-known delights of Thai cuisine is the **yam** or salad, which can often impart all four of the fundamental flavours in an unusual and refreshing harmony. *Yam* can be made in many permutations – with noodles, meat, seafood or vegetables, for example – but at the heart of every variety is a liberal squirt of fresh lime juice and a fiery sprinkling of chopped chillies. As well as *khao yam* described in the box on regional cuisine, salads to look out for include *yam som oh* (pomelo), *yam hua plee* (banana flowers) and *yam plaa duk foo* (crispy fried catfish).

Noodle and rice dishes

Thais eat noodles when Westerners would dig into a sandwich – for lunch, as a late-night snack or just to pass the time. Sold on street stalls everywhere, they come in assorted varieties – including *kway tiaw* (made with rice flour) and *ba mii* (egg noodles), *sen yai* (wide) and *sen lek* (thin) – and get boiled up as soups (*nam*), doused in gravy (*rat na*) or stir-fried (*haeng*, "dry", or *phat*, "fried"). Most famous of noodle dishes is *kway tiaw phat thai* (usually abbreviated to **phat thai**, meaning "Thai fry-up"), a delicious combination of fried noodles, beansprouts, egg, tofu and spring onions, sprinkled with ground peanuts and the juice of half a lime, and often spiked with tiny dried shrimps.

Fried rice (**khao pat**) is the other faithful standby that's guaranteed to feature on menus right across the country. Also popular are cheap, one-dish meals served on a bed of steamed rice, notably *khao kaeng* (with curry), *khao na pet* (with roast duck) and *khao muu daeng* (with red-roasted pork).

Desserts

Desserts (*khanom*) don't really figure on most restaurant menus, but a few places offer bowls of *luk taan cheum*, a jellied concoction of lotus or palm seeds floating in a syrup scented with jasmine or other aromatic

Southern Thai food

Southern Thai cuisine displays a marked Malaysian and Muslim aspect as you near the border and, as you'd expect in a region bounded by sea, the salty flavours associated with seafood are prevalent. Liberal use of **turmeric** is another distinctive feature, which gives many southern dishes a yellow hue, notably *plaa khluk khamin*, grilled fish rubbed with turmeric, garlic and salt. A huge variety of **curries** are dished up in the south, many of them substituting shrimp paste for the fish sauce used elsewhere in Thailand. Three curries that are now found nationally seem to have taken root in Thailand on the peninsula: the rich and usually fairly mild Muslim curry, *kaeng matsaman*; *kaeng phanaeng* (a corruption of Penang, an island off the west coast of Malaysia), a thick, savoury curry also usually made with beef; and the Indian-style chicken curry served over lightly spiced saffron rice, known as *kaeng karii kai*. Other curries are rather more distinctive: *kaeng leuang* ("yellow curry") features fish, turmeric, pineapple, squash, beans and green papaya, while *kaeng tai plaa* is a powerful combination of fish stomach with potatoes, beans, pickled bamboo shoots and turmeric.

Satays feature more down here, as does delicious *hor mok* (sometimes known as *khai plaa mok*), a kind of seafood soufflé made with coconut milk and red curry paste. In Muslim areas, you'll come across *khao mok kai*, the local version of a biryani: chicken and rice cooked with turmeric, cinnamon, cloves and other Indian spices and served with clear chicken soup. Also popular, especially in Phuket, Nakhon Si Thammarat and Trang, is *khanom jiin* (literally, "Chinese pastry"), rice noodles topped with hot, sweet or fishy sauce (the latter Malay-style *naam yaa*, made with ground fish) and served with crispy raw vegetables.

Markets in the south often serve *khao yam* for breakfast or lunch, a deliciously refreshing salad of dried cooked rice, dried shrimp, grated coconut and lemon grass served with a sweet sauce. You'll find many types of **roti** in the south, too – pancake-like bread sold hot from pushcart griddles and, in its plain form, rolled with sickly sweet condensed milk and sugar. Other versions include *roti kluay* (with banana), *roti khai* (with egg), *savoury mataba* (with minced chicken or beef) and, served with curry sauce for breakfast, *roti kaeng*.

---

flowers. Coconut milk is a feature of most other desserts, notably delicious coconut ice cream, *khao niaw mamuang* (sticky rice with mango), and a royal Thai cuisine special of coconut custard (*sangkhayaa*) cooked inside a small pumpkin, whose flesh you can also eat.

Drinks

Thais don't drink water straight from the tap, and nor should you; plastic bottles of drinking **water** (*nam plao*) are sold country-wide, in even the smallest villages, for around B10 and should be used even when brushing your teeth. Cheap restaurants and hotels generally serve free jugs of boiled water, which should be fine to drink, though they are not as foolproof as the bottles.

Night markets, guest houses and restaurants do a good line in freshly squeezed **fruit juices** such as lemon (*nam manao*) and orange (*nam som*), which often come with salt and sugar already added, particularly upcountry. The same places will usually do **fruit shakes** as well, blending bananas (*nam kluay*), papayas (*nam malakaw*), pineapples (*nam sapparot*) and others with liquid sugar or condensed milk (or yoghurt, to make lassi). Fresh **coconut water** (*nam maprao*) is another great thirst-quencher – you buy the whole fruit dehusked, decapitated and chilled – as is **pandanus-leaf juice** (*bai toey*); Thais are also very partial to freshly squeezed **sugar-cane juice** (*nam awy*), which is sickeningly sweet.

Bottled and canned brand-name **soft drinks** are sold all over the place, with a particularly wide range in the ubiquitous 7–Eleven chain stores. Soft-drink bottles are returnable, so some shops and drink stalls have an amazing system of pouring the contents into a small plastic bag (fastened with an elastic band and with a straw inserted) rather than charging you the extra for taking away the bottle. The larger restaurants keep their soft drinks refrigerated, but smaller cafés and shops add **ice** (*nam khaeng*) to glasses and bags. Most ice is produced commercially under hygienic conditions, but it might become less pure in transit so be wary (ice cubes are generally a better bet than shaved ice) – and don't take ice if you have diarrhoea. For those travelling with children, or just partial themselves to **dairy products**, UHT-preserved milk and chilled yoghurt drinks are widely available (especially at 7–Eleven stores), as are a variety of soya drinks.

Weak Chinese **tea** (*nam chaa*) makes a refreshing alternative to water and often gets served in Chinese restaurants and roadside cafés, while posher restaurants keep stronger Chinese and Western-style teas. Instant Nescafé is usually the **coffee** (*kaafae*) offered to farangs, even if freshly ground Thai-grown coffee – notably several kinds of hill-tribe coffee from the mountains of the north – is available. If you would like to try traditional Thai coffee, most commonly found at Chinese-style cafés in the south of the country or at outdoor markets, and prepared through filtering the grounds through a cloth, ask for *kaafae thung* (literally, "bag coffee"), normally served very bitter with sugar as well as sweetened condensed milk alongside a glass of black or Chinese tea to wash it down with. Fresh Western-style coffee (*kaafae sot*) in the form of Italian espresso, cappuccino and other derivatives has recently become popular among Thais, so you'll now come across espresso machines in large towns all over the country (though some of these new coffee bars, frustratingly, don't open for breakfast, as locals tend to get their fix later in the day).

Alcoholic drinks

The two most famous local **beers** (*bia*) are Singha, which has six percent alcohol content (ask for "*bia sing*"), and Chang, which delivers 6.4 percent alcohol at slightly cheaper prices: in shops around B30 for a 330ml bottle, B50 for a 660ml bottle. All manner of foreign beers are now brewed in Thailand, including Heineken and Asahi, and in the most touristy areas you'll find imported bottles from all over the world.

Wine is now found on plenty of upmarket and tourist-oriented restaurant menus, but expect to be disappointed both by the quality and by the price, which is jacked up by heavy taxation. Thai wine is now produced at several vineyards, including at Château de Loei near Phu Reua National Park in the northeast, which produces quite tasty reds, whites including a dessert wine, a rosé and brandy.

At about B80 for a hip-flask-sized 375ml bottle, the local **whisky** is a lot better value, and Thais think nothing of consuming a bottle a night, heavily diluted with ice and soda or Coke. The most palatable and widely available of these is Mekong, which is very pleasant once you've stopped expecting it to taste like Scotch; distilled from rice, Mekong is 35 percent proof, deep gold in colour and tastes slightly sweet. If that's not to your taste, a pricier Thai **rum** is also available, Sang Som, made from sugar cane, and even stronger than the whisky at forty percent proof. Check the menu carefully when ordering a bottle of Mekong from a bar in a tourist area, as they often ask up to five times more than you'd pay in a guest house or shop. A hugely popular way to enjoy whisky or rum at beach resorts is to pick up a bucket, containing a quarter-bottle of spirit, a mixer, Red Bull, ice and several straws, for around B200: that way you get to share with your friends and build a sandcastle afterwards.

You can **buy** beer and whisky in food stores, guest houses and most restaurants; **bars** aren't strictly an indigenous feature as Thais traditionally don't drink out without eating, but you'll find plenty of Western-style drinking holes in Bangkok and larger centres elsewhere in the country, ranging from ultra-hip haunts in the capital to basic, open-to-the-elements "**bar-beers**".

Culture and etiquette

Tourist literature has marketed Thailand as the "Land of Smiles" so successfully that a lot of farangs arrive in the country expecting to be forgiven any outrageous behaviour. This is just not the case: there are some things so universally sacred in Thailand that even a hint of disrespect will cause deep offence. TAT publishes a special leaflet on the subject, entitled Dos and Don'ts in Thailand, reproduced at Ⓦ www.tourismthailand.org.

The monarchy

It is both socially unacceptable and a criminal offence to make critical or defamatory remarks about the **royal family**. Thailand's monarchy might be a constitutional one, but almost every household displays a picture of King Bhumibol and Queen Sirikit in a prominent position, and respectful crowds mass whenever either of them makes a public appearance. The second of their four children, Crown Prince Vajiralongkorn, is the heir to the throne; his younger sister, Princess Royal Maha Chakri Sirindhorn, is often on TV and in the English newspapers as she is involved in many charitable projects. When addressing or speaking about royalty, Thais use a special language full of deference, called *rajasap* (literally "royal language").

Thailand's **lèse majesté laws** are among the most strictly applied in the world, increasingly invoked as the Thai establishment becomes ever more uneasy over the erosion of traditional monarchist sentiments and the rise of critical voices, particularly on the internet (though these are generally quickly censored). Accusations of lèse majesté can be levelled by and against anyone, Thai national or farang, and must be investigated by the police. As a few high-profile cases involving foreigners have demonstrated, they can be raised for seemingly minor infractions, such as defacing a poster or being less than respectful in a work of fiction. Transgressions are met with jail sentences of up to fifteen years.

Aside from keeping any anti-monarchy sentiments to yourself, you should be prepared to stand when the **king's anthem** is played at the beginning of every cinema programme, and to stop in your tracks if the town you're in plays the **national anthem** over its public address system – many small towns do this twice a day at 8am and again at 6pm, as do some train stations and airports. A less obvious point: as the king's head features on all Thai currency, you should never step on a coin or banknote, which is tantamount to kicking the king in the face.

Religion

Almost equally insensitive would be to disregard certain **religious** precepts. **Buddhism** plays a fundamental role in Thai culture, and Buddhist monuments should be treated with respect – which basically means wearing long trousers or knee-length skirts, covering your arms and removing your shoes whenever you visit one.

All **Buddha images** are sacred, however small, tacky or ruined, and should never be used as a backdrop for a portrait photo, clambered over, placed in a position of inferiority or treated in any manner that could be construed as disrespectful. In an attempt to prevent foreigners from committing any kind of transgression the government requires a special licence for all Buddha statues exported from the country (see p.65).

Monks come only just beneath the monarchy in the social hierarchy, and they too are addressed and discussed in a special language. If there's a monk around, he'll always get a seat on the bus, usually right at the back. Theoretically, monks are forbidden to have any close contact with women, which means, as a female, you mustn't sit or stand next to a monk, or even brush against his robes; if it's essential to pass him something, put the object down so that he can then pick it up – never hand it over directly. Nuns, however, get treated like ordinary women.

See p.472 for more on religious practices in Thailand.

The body

The Western liberalism embraced by the Thai sex industry is very unrepresentative of the majority Thai attitude to the body. **Clothing** – or the lack of it – is what bothers Thais most about tourist behaviour. As mentioned above, you need to dress modestly when entering temples, but the same also applies to other important buildings and all public places. Stuffy and sweaty as it sounds, you should keep short shorts and vests for the real tourist resorts, and be especially diligent about covering up and, for women, wearing bras in rural areas. Baring your flesh on beaches is very much a Western practice: when Thais go swimming they often do so fully clothed, and they find topless and nude bathing offensive.

According to ancient Hindu belief, the **head** is the most sacred part of the body and the **feet** are the most unclean. This belief, imported into Thailand, means that it's very rude to touch another person's head or to point your feet either at a human being or at a sacred image – when sitting on a temple floor, for example, you should **tuck your legs beneath you** rather than stretch them out towards the Buddha. These hierarchies also forbid people from wearing **shoes** (which are even more unclean than feet) inside temples and most private homes, and – by extension – Thais take offence when they see someone sitting on the "head", or prow, of a boat. **Putting your feet up** on a table, a chair or a pillow is also considered very uncouth, and Thais will always take their shoes off if they need to stand on a train or bus seat to get to the luggage rack, for example. On a more practical note, the **left hand** is used for washing after going to the toilet (for more on bathroom etiquette see p.38), so Thais never use it to put food in their mouth, pass things or shake hands – as a farang though, you'll be assumed to have different customs, so left-handers shouldn't worry unduly.

Social conventions

Thais never shake hands with each other, instead using the **wai** to greet and say goodbye and to acknowledge respect, gratitude or apology. A prayer-like gesture made with raised hands, the *wai* changes according to the relative status of the two people involved: Thais can instantaneously assess which *wai* to use, but as a farang your safest bet is to go for the "stranger's" *wai*, which requires that your hands be raised close to your chest and your fingertips placed just below your chin. If someone makes a *wai* at you, you should generally *wai* back, but it's safer not to initiate.

Public displays of **physical affection** in Thailand are more common between friends of the same sex than between lovers, whether hetero- or homosexual. Holding hands and hugging is as common among male friends as with females, so if you're caressed by a Thai acquaintance of the same sex, don't assume you're being propositioned.

Finally, there are three specifically Thai **concepts** you're bound to come across, which may help you comprehend a sometimes laissez-faire attitude to delayed buses and other inconveniences. The first, **jai yen**, translates literally as "cool heart" and is something everyone tries to maintain: most Thais hate raised voices, visible irritation and confrontations of any kind, so losing one's cool can have a much more inflammatory effect than in more combative cultures. Related to this is the oft-quoted response to a difficulty, **mai pen rai** – "never mind", "no problem" or "it can't be helped" – the verbal equivalent of an open-handed shoulder shrug, which has its basis in the Buddhist notion of karma (see p.474). And then there's **sanuk**, the wide-reaching philosophy of "fun", which, crass as it sounds, Thais do their best to inject into any situation, even work. Hence the crowds of inebriated Thais who congregate at waterfalls and other beauty spots on public holidays (travelling solo is definitely not *sanuk*), the reluctance to do almost anything without high-volume musical accompaniment, and the national waterfight which takes place every April on streets right across Thailand.

Thai names

Although all Thais have a first **name** and a family name, everyone is addressed by their first name – even when meeting strangers – prefixed by the title "**Khun**" (Mr/Ms); no one is ever addressed as Khun Surname, and even the phone book lists people by their given name. In Thailand you will often be addressed in an Anglicized version of this convention, as "Mr Paul" or "Miss Lucy" for example. Bear in mind though, that when a man is introduced to you as Khun Pirom, his wife will definitely not be Khun Pirom as well (that would be like calling them, for instance, "Mr and Mrs Paul"). Among friends and relatives, **Phii** ("older brother/sister") is often used instead of Khun when addressing older familiars (though as a tourist you're on surer ground with Khun), and **Nong** ("younger brother/sister") is used for younger ones.

Crime, safety and the law

As long as you keep your wits about you, you shouldn't encounter much trouble in Thailand. Theft and pickpocketing are two of the main problems – not surprising considering that a huge percentage of the local population scrape by on under US$5 per day – but the most common cause for concern is the number of con-artists who dupe gullible tourists into parting with their cash. There are various Thai laws that tourists need to be aware of, particularly regarding passports, the age of consent and smoking in public.

Theft

To **prevent theft**, most travellers prefer to carry their valuables with them at all times, but it's often possible to use a locker in a hotel or guest house – the safest are those that require your own padlock, as there are occasional reports of valuables being stolen by hotel staff. **Padlock your luggage** when leaving it in hotel or guest-house rooms, as well as when consigning it to storage or taking it on public transport. Padlocks also come in handy as extra security on your room, particularly on the doors of beachfront bamboo huts.

Theft from some long-distance **overnight buses** is also a problem, with the majority of reported incidents taking place on the temptingly cheap buses run by private companies direct from Bangkok's Thanon Khao San (as opposed to those that depart from the government bus stations) to destinations such as Surat Thani and southern beach resorts. The best solution is to go direct from the bus stations; see p.30 for further advice.

Personal safety

On any bus, private or government, and on any train journey, never keep anything of value in luggage that is stored out of your sight and be wary of accepting food and drink from fellow passengers as it may be drugged. This might sound paranoid, but there have been enough **drug-muggings** for TAT to publish a specific warning about the problem. Drinks can also be spiked in bars and clubs; at Full Moon Parties on Ko Pha Ngan this has led to sexual assaults against farang women, while prostitutes sometimes spike drinks so they can steal from their victim's room.

Violent crime against tourists is not common, but it does occur, and there have been several serious attacks on women travellers in recent years. However, bearing in mind that fourteen million foreigners visit

Reporting a crime or emergency

In emergencies, contact the English-speaking **tourist police**, who maintain a 24-hour toll-free nationwide line (☏1155) and have offices in the main tourist centres; getting in touch with the tourist police first is invariably more efficient than directly contacting the local police, ambulance or fire service. The tourist police's job is to offer advice and tell you what to do next, but they do not file crime reports, which must be done at the nearest police station.

TAT has a special department for mediating between tourists, police and accused persons (particularly shopkeepers and tour agents) called the Tourist Assistance Center, or **TAC**; it's based in the TAT office on Thanon Rajdamnoen Nok, Bangkok (daily 8.30am–4.30pm; ☏02 281 5051).

The British Embassy in Bangkok provides **advice** for British victims of crime in Thailand and also posts practical tips and a list of useful contacts on its website (☏02 305 8333 ext. 2334, 2318, ⓦukinthailand.fco.gov.uk/en/help-for -british-nationals).

Thailand every year, the statistical likelihood of becoming a victim is extremely small. **Obvious precautions** for travellers of either sex include locking accessible windows and doors at night – preferably with your own padlock (doors in many of the simpler guest houses and beach bungalows are designed for this) – and not travelling alone at night in a taxi or tuk-tuk. Nor should you risk jumping into an unlicensed taxi at the airport in Bangkok at any time of day: there have been some very violent robberies in these, so take the well-marked licensed, metered taxis instead, or one of the airport buses.

Unfortunately, it is also necessary for female tourists to think twice about spending time alone with a **monk**, as not all men of the cloth uphold the Buddhist precepts and there have been rapes and murders committed by men wearing the saffron robes of the monkhood. See p.475 for more about the changing Thai attitudes towards the monkhood.

Though unpalatable and distressing, Thailand's high-profile **sex industry** is relatively unthreatening for Western women, with its energy focused exclusively on farang men; it's also quite easily avoided, being contained within certain pockets of the capital and a couple of beach resorts.

As for **harassment** from men, it's hard to generalize, but most Western women find it less of a problem in Thailand than they do back home. Outside the main tourist spots, you're more likely to be of interest as a foreigner rather than a woman and, if travelling alone, as an object of concern rather than of sexual aggression.

Among hazards to watch out for in the natural world, **riptides** claim a number of tourist lives every year, particularly off Phuket, Ko Chang (Trat), Hua Hin, Cha-am and Ko Samui during stormy periods of the monsoon season, so always pay attention to warning signs and red flags, and always ask locally if unsure. **Jellyfish** can be a problem on any coast, especially just after a storm (see p.27). For advice on **road safety** see p.34.

Regional issues

It's advisable to travel with a guide if you're going off the main roads in certain **border areas** or, if you're on a motorbike, to take advice before setting off.

Because of the **violence in the deep south**, all Western governments are currently advising against travel to or through the border provinces of Songkhla, Yala, Pattani and Narathiwat, unless essential – see p.441 for further details. For up-to-the-minute advice on current political troublespots, consult your government's travel advisory.

Scams

Despite the best efforts of guidebook writers, TAT and the Thai tourist police, countless travellers to Thailand get scammed every year. Nearly all **scams** are easily avoided if you're on your guard against anyone who makes an unnatural effort to befriend you.

Governmental travel advisories

Australian Department of Foreign Affairs Ⓦ www.dfat.gov.au, Ⓦ www.smartraveller .gov.au

British Foreign & Commonwealth Office Ⓦ www.fco.gov.uk

Canadian Department of Foreign Affairs Ⓦ www.international.gc.ca

Irish Department of Foreign Affairs Ⓦ www.foreignaffairs.gov.ie

New Zealand Ministry of Foreign Affairs Ⓦ www.mft.govt.nz

US State Department Ⓦ www.travel.state.gov

South African Department of Foreign Affairs Ⓦ www.dfa.gov.za

We have outlined the main scams in the relevant sections of this guide, but con artists are nothing if not creative, so if in doubt walk away at the earliest opportunity. The worst areas for scammers are the busy tourist centres, including many parts of Bangkok and the main beach resorts.

Many **tuk-tuk drivers** earn most of their living through securing **commissions** from tourist-oriented shops; this is especially true in Bangkok, where they will do their damnedest to get you to go to a gem shop (see p.163). The most common tactic is for drivers to pretend that the Grand Palace or other major sight you intended to visit is closed for the day (they usually invent a plausible reason, such as a festival or royal occasion; see p.108), and to then offer to take you on a round-city tour instead, perhaps even for free. The tour will invariably include a visit to a gem shop. The easiest way to avoid all this is to take a **metered taxi**; if you're fixed on taking a tuk-tuk, ignore any tuk-tuk that is parked up or loitering and be firm about where you want to go.

Self-styled **tourist guides**, **touts** and anyone else who might introduce themselves as **students** or **businesspeople** and offer to take you somewhere of interest, or invite you to meet their family, are often the first piece of bait in a well-honed chain of con-artists. If you bite, chances are you'll end up either at a gem shop or in a gambling den, or, at best, at a tour operator or hotel that you had not planned to patronize. This is not to say that you should never accept an invitation from a local person, but be extremely wary of doing so following a street encounter in Bangkok or the resorts. Tourist guides' ID cards are easily faked.

For many of these characters the goal is to get you inside a dodgy **gem shop**, nearly all of which are located in Bangkok. There is a full run-down of advice on how to avoid falling for the notorious low-grade gems scam on p.163, but the bottom line is that if you are not experienced at buying and trading in valuable gems you will definitely be ripped off, possibly even to the tune of several thousand dollars. Check the 2Bangkok website's account of a typical gem scam (Ⓦ www.2bangkok.com/2bangkok/Scams /Sapphire.shtml) before you shell out any cash at all.

A less common but potentially more frightening scam involves a similar cast of warm-up artists leading tourists into a **gambling** game. The scammers invite their victim home on an innocent-sounding pretext, get out a pack of cards, and then set about fleecing the incomer in any number of subtle ways. Often this can be especially scary as the venue is likely to be far from hotels or recognizable landmarks. You're unlikely to get any sympathy from police, as gambling is **illegal** in Thailand.

Age restrictions and other laws

Thai law requires that tourists **carry their original passports** at all times, though sometimes it's more practical to carry a photocopy and keep the original locked in a safety deposit. The **age of consent** is 15, but the law allows anyone under the age of 18, or their parents, to file charges in retrospect even if they consented to sex at the time. It is against the law to have sex with a prostitute who is under 18. It is illegal for **under-18s** to buy cigarettes or to drive and you must be 20 or over to **buy alcohol** or be allowed into a **bar or club** (ID checks are often enforced in Bangkok). It is illegal for anyone to **gamble** in Thailand (though many do).

Smoking in public is widely prohibited. The ban covers all air-conditioned public buildings (including restaurants but usually excluding bars and clubs) and air-conditioned trains, buses and planes and even extends to parks and the street; violators are subject to a B2000 fine. Dropping cigarette butts, **littering** and spitting in public places can also earn you a B2000 fine. There are fines for **overstaying your visa** (see p.24), **working without a permit**, and **not wearing a motor-cycle helmet** and violating other **traffic laws** (see p.35).

Drugs

Drug-smuggling carries a maximum penalty in Thailand of death and **dealing drugs** will get you anything from four years to life in a Thai prison; penalties depend on the drug and the amount involved. Travellers caught with even the smallest amount of drugs at airports and international borders are prose-cuted for trafficking, and no one charged with trafficking offences gets bail. Heroin, amphetamines, LSD and ecstasy are classed as Category 1 drugs and carry the most severe penalties: even **possession** of Category 1 drugs for personal use can result in a **life sentence**. Away from international borders, most foreigners arrested in posses-sion of small amounts of cannabis are released on bail, then fined and deported, but the law is complex and prison sentences are possible.

Despite occasional royal pardons, don't expect special treatment as a farang: you only need to read one of the first-hand accounts by foreign former prisoners (see p.483) or read the blogs at ⓦwww.thai prisonlife.com to get the picture. The **police** actively look for tourists doing drugs, report-edly searching people regularly and randomly on Thanon Khao San, for example. They have the power to order a urine test if they have reasonable grounds for suspicion, and even a positive result for marijuana consumption could lead to a year's impris-onment. Be wary also of **being shopped** by a farang or local dealer keen to earn a financial reward for a successful bust (there are setups at the Ko Pha Ngan full moon parties, for example), or having substances slipped into your luggage (simple enough to perpetrate unless all fastenings are secured with padlocks).

If you are arrested, ask for your embassy to be contacted immediately, which is your right under Thai law (see p.167 for phone numbers), and embassy staff will talk you through procedures; the website of the British Embassy in Thailand also posts useful infor-mation, including a list of English-speaking lawyers, at ⓦukinthailand.fco.gov.uk/en/help -for-british-nationals. The British charity Prisoners Abroad (ⓦwww.prisonersabroad .org.uk) carries a detailed survival guide on its website, which outlines what to expect if arrested in Thailand, from the point of appre-hension through trial and conviction to life in a Thai jail; if contacted, the charity may also be able to offer direct support to a British citizen facing imprisonment in a Thai jail.

The media

To keep you abreast of world affairs, there are several English-language newspapers in Thailand, though a mild form of censorship affects the predominantly state-controlled media, even muting the English-language branches on occasion.

Newspapers and magazines

Of the hundreds of **Thai-language newspapers and magazines** published every week, the sensationalist daily tabloid *Thai Rath* attracts the widest readership, with circulation of around a million, while the moderately progressive *Matichon* is the leading quality daily, with an estimated circulation of 600,000.

Alongside these, two daily **English-language papers** – the *Bangkok Post* (Ⓦwww.bangkokpost.com) and the *Nation* (Ⓦwww.nationmultimedia.com) – are capable of adopting a fairly critical attitude to governmental goings-on and cover major domestic and international stories as well as tourist-related issues. The *Nation* has recently adopted a split personality, covering mostly business news on its main pages while carrying a lively, poppy tabloid, the *Xpress*, inside. The *Post*'s *Spectrum* supplement, which comes inside the Sunday edition, stands out for its investigative journalism. Both the *Post* and *Nation* are sold at most newsstands in the capital as well as in major provincial towns and tourist resorts; the more isolated places receive their few copies at least one day late. Details of local English-language publications are given in the relevant guide accounts.

You can also pick up **foreign publications** such as *Newsweek*, *Time* and the *International Herald Tribune* in Bangkok and the major resorts; from Monday to Saturday, the *IHT* now publishes a special Thai edition, though it's short on Thai news. English-language bookstores such as Bookazine and some expensive hotels carry air-freighted, or sometimes locally printed and stapled, copies of foreign national newspapers for at least B50 a copy; the latter are also sold in tourist-oriented minimarkets in the big resorts.

Television

There are six government-controlled, terrestrial **TV channels** in Thailand: channels 3, 5 (owned and operated by the army), 7 and 9 transmit a blend of news, documentaries, soaps, sports, talk and quiz shows, while the more serious-minded PBS (formerly Thaksin Shinawatra's ITV) and NBT are public-service channels, owned and operated by the government's public relations department. **Cable** networks – available in many mid-range and most upmarket hotel rooms – carry channels from all around the world, including CNN from the US, BBC World from the UK and sometimes ABC from Australia, as well as English-language movie channels, MTV and various sports and documentary channels. Both the *Bangkok Post* and the *Nation* print the daily TV and cable **schedule**.

Radio

Thailand boasts over five hundred **radio stations**, mostly music-oriented, ranging from Virgin Radio's Eazy (105.5 FM), which serves up Western pop, to Fat Radio, which plays Thai indie sounds (104.5 FM). Chulalongkorn University Radio (101.5 FM) plays classical music from 9.30pm to midnight every night. Net 107 on 107 FM is one of several stations that include English-language news. With a **shortwave radio** – or by going **online** – you can pick up the BBC World Service (Ⓦwww.bbc.co.uk/worldservice), Radio Australia (Ⓦwww.radioaustralia.net.au), Voice of America (Ⓦwww.voanews.com), Radio Canada (Ⓦwww.rcinet.ca) and other international stations right across Thailand. Times and wavelengths change regularly, so get hold of a recent schedule just before you travel or consult the websites for frequency and programme guides.

Festivals

Nearly all Thai festivals have a religious aspect. The most theatrical are generally Brahmin (Hindu) in origin, honouring elemental spirits and deities with ancient rites and ceremonial costumed parades. Buddhist celebrations usually revolve round the local temple, and while merit-making is a significant feature, a light-hearted atmosphere prevails, as the wat grounds are swamped with food and trinket vendors and makeshift stages are set up to show *likay* folk theatre, singing stars and beauty contests.

Few of the **dates** for religious festivals are fixed, so check with TAT for specifics (ⓦwww .tourismthailand.org). The names of the most touristy celebrations are given here in English; the more low-key festivals are more usually known by their Thai name (*ngan* means "festival"). Some of the festivals below are designated as national holidays – see p.69.

A festival calendar

January–May

Bangkok and Phuket *Chinese New Year* (three days between mid-Jan and late Feb). The new Chinese year is welcomed in with exuberant parades of dragons and lion dancers, Chinese opera performances and fireworks.
Nationwide Maha Puja (particularly Wat Benjamabophit in Bangkok and Wat Mahathat in Nakhon Si Thammarat; Feb full-moon day). A day of merit-making marks the occasion when 1250 disciples gathered spontaneously to hear the Buddha preach, and culminates with a candlelit procession round the local temple's bot.
Nationwide Kite fights and flying contests (particularly Sanam Luang, Bangkok; late Feb to mid-April).
Nationwide Songkhran (particularly Bangkok's Thanon Khao San; usually April 13–15). The most exuberant of the national festivals welcomes the Thai New Year with massive waterfights, sandcastle building in temple compounds and the inevitable parades and "Miss Songkhran" beauty contests. See p.12.
Nationwide Visakha Puja (particularly Bangkok's Wat Benjamabophit and Nakhon Si Thammarat's Wat Mahathat; May full-moon day). The holiest day of the Buddhist year, commemorating the birth, enlightenment and death of the Buddha all in one go; the most public and photogenic part is the candlelit evening procession around the wat.

Sanam Luang, Bangkok Raek Na (early May). The royal ploughing ceremony to mark the beginning of the rice-planting season; ceremonially clad Brahmin leaders parade sacred oxen and the royal plough, and interpret omens to forecast the year's rice yield. See p.111.

June–December

Hua Hin Jazz Festival (a weekend in late June; ⓦwww.huahinjazzfest.com). Well-known musicians from Thailand and abroad play for free at various special outdoor venues throughout the beach resort.
Bangkok International Film Festival (most recently held over a week in Sept, but has also been staged in Jan and July; ⓦwww.bangkokfilm.org). An annual chance to preview new and unusual Thai films alongside features and documentaries from Southeast Asia and beyond.
Nakhon Si Thammarat Tamboon Deuan Sip (Sept or Oct). Merit-making ceremonies to honour dead relatives, accompanied by a ten-day fair. See p.307.
Phuket and Trang Vegetarian Festival (Ngan Kin Jeh; Oct or Nov). Chinese devotees become vegetarian for a nine-day period and then parade through town performing acts of self-mortification such as pushing skewers through their cheeks. Celebrated in Bangkok's Chinatown by most food vendors and restaurants turning vegetarian for about a fortnight. See p.146 and p.358.
Nationwide Tak Bat Devo and Awk Pansa. Offerings to monks and general merrymaking to celebrate the Buddha's descent to earth from Tavatimsa heaven and the end of the Khao Pansa retreat.
Surat Thani Chak Phra (mid-Oct). The town's chief Buddha images are paraded on floats down the streets and on barges along the river. See p.262.
Nationwide Thawt Kathin (the month between Awk Pansa and Loy Krathong, generally Oct–Nov). During the month following the end of the monks' rainy-season retreat, it's traditional for the laity

to donate new robes to the monkhood and this is celebrated in most towns with parades and a festival. **Nationwide** Loy Krathong (full moon in Nov). Baskets (*krathong*) of flowers and lighted candles are floated on any available body of water (such as ponds, rivers, lakes, canals and seashores) to honour water spirits and celebrate the end of the rainy season. Nearly every town puts on a big show, with bazaars, public entertainments and fireworks.

Wat Saket, Bangkok Ngan Wat Saket (first week of Nov). Probably Thailand's biggest temple fair, held around the Golden Mount, with all the usual festival trappings.

Nationwide New Year's Eve Countdown (Dec 31). Most cities and tourist destinations welcome in the new year with fireworks, often backed up by food festivals, beauty contests and outdoor performances.

Entertainment and sport

Bangkok is the best place to catch authentic performances of classical Thai dance, though more easily digestible tourist-oriented shows are staged in most of the big tourist centres as well as in Bangkok. The country's two main Thai boxing stadia are also in the capital, but you'll come across local matches in the provinces too.

Drama and dance

Drama pretty much equals **dance** in classical Thai theatre, and many of the traditional dance-dramas are based on the *Ramakien*, the Thai version of the Hindu epic the *Ramayana*, an adventure tale of good versus evil which is taught in all the schools.

Of the three main genres of traditional Thai theatres, the most spectacular is **khon**, a stylized drama performed in masks and elaborate costumes by a troupe of highly trained classical dancers accompanied by a chorus and classical *phipat* orchestra.

Serious and refined, **lakhon** *chatri* is derived from *khon* and performed at shrines like Bangkok's Erawan as entertainment for the spirits and a token of gratitude from worshippers. Dancers perform as an ensemble, wearing ornate costumes and accompanied by a *phipat* orchestra.

Likay is much more popular and light-hearted, with lots of comic interludes, bawdy jokes and panto-style over-the-top acting and singing, plus improvisations and topical satire. *Likay* troupes travel around the country doing shows at temple fairs and other events, often for free.

Nang thalung, or shadow plays (see p.310), are performed mainly in the far south, with two-dimensional puppets crafted from buffalo hide playing out scenes from popular dramas against a backlit screen, while the storyline is told through songs, chants and musical interludes.

Thai boxing

Thai boxing (*muay thai*) enjoys a following similar to soccer or baseball in the West: every province has a stadium and whenever the sport is shown on TV you can be sure that large noisy crowds will gather round the sets in streetside restaurants. The best place to see Thai boxing is at one of Bangkok's two main stadia, which between them hold bouts every night of the week (see p.157), but many tourist resorts also stage regular matches.

There's a strong spiritual and **ritualistic** dimension to *muay thai*, adding grace to an otherwise brutal sport. Each boxer enters the ring to the wailing music of a three-piece *phipat* orchestra, wearing the statutory red or blue shorts and, on his head, a sacred rope headband or *mongkhon*. The fighter then bows, first in the direction of his birth-place and then to the north, south, east and west, honouring both his teachers and the spirit of the ring. Next he performs a slow dance, claiming the audience's attention and demonstrating his prowess as a performer.

Any part of the body except the head may be used as an **offensive weapon** in *muay thai*, and all parts except the groin are fair targets. Kicks to the head are the blows which cause most knockouts. As the action hots up, so the orchestra speeds up its tempo and the betting in the audience becomes more frenetic.

A number of *muay thai* gyms and camps offer training **courses** for foreigners, including several in Bangkok (see p.157); Fairtex Muay Thai in Pattaya (⊛www.fairtexbkk.com); the Thai Boxing Garden in Hua Hin (see p.248); the Muay Thai Martial Arts Academy (MTMAA) in Surat Thani (⊛www.muaythai training.com); Jungle Gym on Ko Pha Ngan (see p.292); Monsoon Gym on Ko Tao (see p.302); Suwit Gym on Phuket (⊛www .bestmuaythai.com); and UK–Thai-run Ko Yao Noi Gym on Ko Yao Noi (see p.385).

Spas and traditional massage

With their focus on indulgent self-pampering, spas are usually associated with high-spending tourists, but the treatments on offer at Thailand's five-star hotels are often little different from those used by traditional medical practitioners, who have long held that massage and herbs are the best way to restore physical and mental well-being.

Thai massage (*nuad paen boran*; see also p.10) is based on the principle that many physical and emotional problems are caused by the blocking of vital energy channels within the body. The masseur uses his or her feet, heels, knees and elbows, as well as hands, to exert a gentle pressure on these channels, supplementing this acupressure-style technique by pulling and pushing the limbs into yogic stretches. This distinguishes Thai massage from most other massage styles, which are more concerned with tissue manipulation.

Nearly every hotel and guest house will be able to put you in touch with a **masseur**, and on the more popular beaches, it can be hard to walk a few hundred metres without being offered a massage – something Thai tourists are just as enthusiastic about as foreigners. Thai masseurs do not use oils or lotions and the client is treated on a mat or mattress; you'll often be given a pair of loose-fitting trousers and perhaps a loose top to change into. English-speaking masseurs will often ask if you have any problem areas on your body that you want them to avoid; if your masseur doesn't speak English, the simplest way to signal this is to point at the offending area while saying *mai sabai* ("not well"); if you're in pain during a massage, wincing usually does the trick, perhaps adding *jep* ("it hurts"). A session should ideally last two hours and will cost from around B300.

The **science** behind Thai massage has its roots in Indian Ayurvedic medicine, which classifies each component of the body according to one of the four elements (earth, water, fire and air), and holds that balancing these elements within the body is crucial to good health. Many of the stretches and manipulations fundamental to Thai massage are thought to have derived from yogic practices introduced to Thailand from India by Buddhist missionaries in about the second century BC; Chinese acupuncture and reflexology have also had a strong influence. In the nineteenth century, King

Rama III ordered a series of murals illustrating the principles of Thai massage to be painted around the courtyard of Bangkok's Wat Pho, and they are still in place today, along with statues of ascetics depicted in typical massage poses.

Wat Pho has been the leading school of Thai massage for hundreds of years, and it is possible to take courses there as well as to receive a massage (see p.116). Masseurs who trained at Wat Pho are considered to be the best in the country and masseurs all across Thailand advertise this as a credential, whether or not it is true. Many Thais consider blind masseurs to be especially sensitive practitioners. While Wat Pho is the most famous place to take a **course** in Thai massage, you will find others at southern beach resorts.

All **spas** in Thailand feature traditional Thai massage and herbal therapies in their programmes, but most also offer dozens of other international treatments, including facials, aromatherapy, Swedish massage and various body wraps. Spa centres in upmarket hotels and resorts are usually open to non-guests but generally need to be booked in advance; day spas that are not attached to hotels are found in some of the bigger cities and resorts and some of these may not require reservations.

Thailand's most famous luxury spas include the Oriental Spa, run by the renowned five-star *Oriental Hotel* in Bangkok (see p.168); the Banyan Tree spas at the hotels of the same name in Bangkok (see p.168) and Phuket (see p.362); the Prana Spa at the *Tongsai Bay* on Samui (see p.275); the elegant spa rooms at *Le Vimarn Cottages* on Ko Samet (p.198); and the dedicated wellness and detox retreat *The Spa* on Ko Chang (see p.220).

Meditation centres and retreats

Of the hundreds of meditation temples in Thailand, a few cater specifically for foreigners by holding meditation sessions and retreats in English. Novices as well as practised meditators are generally welcome at these wats, but absolute beginners might like to consider the regular retreats at Wat Suan Mokkh and Wat Khao Tham, which are conducted by supportive and experienced Western teachers and include talks and interviews on Buddhist teachings and practice. The meditation taught is mostly Vipassana, or "insight", which emphasizes the minute observation of internal sensations; the other main technique you'll come across is Samatha, which aims to calm the mind and develop concentration (these two techniques are not entirely separate, since you cannot have insight without some degree of concentration).

Longer **retreats** are for the serious-minded only. All the temples listed below welcome both male and female English-speakers, but strict segregation of the sexes is enforced and many places observe a vow of silence. Reading and writing are also discouraged, and you'll generally not be allowed to leave the retreat complex unless absolutely necessary, so try to bring whatever you'll need in with you. All retreats expect you to wear modest clothing, and some require you to wear white – check ahead whether there is a shop at the retreat complex or whether you are expected to bring this with you.

An average day at any one of these monasteries starts with a **wake-up call** at around 4am and includes several hours of **group meditation** and chanting, as well as time put aside for chores and personal reflection. However long their stay, visitors are usually expected to keep the eight Buddhist precepts, the most restrictive of these being the abstention from food after midday and from alcohol, tobacco, drugs and sex at all times. Most wats ask for a minimal daily **donation** (around B150) to cover the costs of the simple accommodation and food.

Further details about many of the temples listed below – including how to get there – are given in the relevant sections in the guide chapters. Though a little out of date, *A Guide to Buddhist Monasteries and Meditation Centres in Thailand*, published by the World Fellowship of Buddhists, contains plenty of useful general information. An even more useful resource is ⓦwww.dhammathai.org, which provides lots of general background, practical advice and details of meditation temples and centres around Thailand.

Outdoor activities

The vast majority of beach itineraries include a stint snorkelling or diving, and the big resorts of Pattaya, Phuket and Ko Samui offer dozens of other watersports as well. There is also a developing interest in more unusual outdoor activities, such as rock-climbing and kayaking.

Diving and snorkelling

Clear, warm waters (averaging 28°C), prolific marine life and affordable prices make Thailand a very rewarding place for **diving** and **snorkelling**. Most islands and beach resorts have at least one dive centre that organizes trips to outlying islands, teaches novice divers and rents out equipment, and in the bigger resorts there are dozens to choose from.

Thailand's three coasts are subject to different monsoon **seasons**, so you can dive all year round; the seasons run from November to April along the Andaman coast (though there is sometimes good diving here up until late Aug), and all year round on the Gulf and east coasts. See *Underwater Thailand* colour section, for a roundup of the country's premier diving and snorkelling spots and a guide to some of its spectacular marine life.

Whether you're snorkelling or diving, try to minimize your impact on the fragile reef structures by **not touching the reefs** and by asking your boatman not to anchor in the middle of one; **don't buy coral souvenirs**, as tourist demand only encourages local entrepreneurs to dynamite reefs.

Should you scrape your skin on coral, wash the wound thoroughly with boiled water, apply antiseptic and keep protected until healed. Wearing a T-shirt is a good idea when snorkelling to stop your back from getting sunburnt.

Diving

It's usually worth having a look at several **dive centres** before committing yourself to a trip or a course. Always verify the dive instructors' PADI (Professional Association of Diving Instructors) or equivalent accreditation and check to see if the dive shop is a member of PADI's International Resorts and Retailers Association (IRRA) as this guarantees a certain level of professionalism. You can view a list of IRRAs in Thailand at ⓦwww.padi.com.

We've highlighted IRRA dive shops that are accredited Five-Star centres, as these are considered by PADI to offer very high standards, but you should always consult other divers first if possible. Some dive operators do fake their PADI credentials. Avoid booking ahead over the internet without knowing anything else about the dive centre, and be wary of any operation offering extremely cheap courses: maintaining diving equipment is an expensive business in Thailand so any place offering unusually good rates will probably be cutting corners and compromising your safety. Ask to **meet your instructor** or dive leader, find out how many people there'll be in your group, check out the kind of instruction given (some courses are over-reliant on videos) and look over the equipment, checking the quality of the air in the tanks yourself and also ensuring there's an oxygen cylinder on board. Most divers prefer to travel to the dive site in a decent-sized **boat** equipped with a radio and emergency medical equipment rather than in a longtail. If this concerns you, ask the dive company about their boat before you sign up; firms that use longtails generally charge less.

Insurance should be included in the price of courses and introductory dives; for

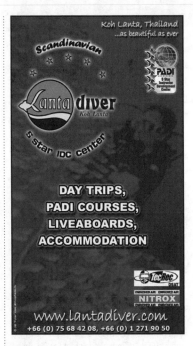
qualified divers, you're better off checking that your general travel insurance covers diving, though some diving shops can organize cover for you. There are **recompression chambers** in Pattaya, on Ko Samui, on Ko Tao and on Phuket and it's a good idea to check whether your dive centre is a member of one of these outfits, as recompression services are extremely expensive for anyone who's not.

For books on diving in Thailand see p.484.

Trips and courses

All dive centres run programmes of one-day **dive trips** (featuring two dives) and **night dives** for B1300–4500 plus equipment, and many of the Andaman coast dive centres also do three- to seven-day **live-aboards** to the exceptional reefs off the remote Similan and Surin islands (from B11,800).

Renting a full set of diving **gear**, including wetsuit, from a dive centre costs about B500 per day; most dive centres also rent **underwater cameras** for about B1000–1500 per day.

All dive centres offer a range of **courses** from beginner to advanced level, with equipment rental usually included in the cost; Ko Tao is now the largest dive-training centre in Southeast Asia, with around fifty dive companies including plenty of PADI Five-Star centres. The most popular courses are the one-day **introductory** or resort dive (a pep talk and escorted shallow dive, open to anyone aged 10 or over), which costs anything from B2000 for a very local dive to B7100 for an all-inclusive day-trip to the Similan Islands; and the four-day **open-water course**, which entitles you to dive without an instructor (from B9,800 including at least two dives a day). Kids' Bubblemaker courses, for children aged 8–10, cost around B2000.

Snorkelling

Boatmen and tour agents on most beaches offer **snorkelling** trips to nearby reefs and many dive operators welcome snorkellers to tag along for discounts of thirty percent or more; not all diving destinations are rewarding for snorkellers though, so check the relevant account in this book first. As far as snorkelling **equipment** goes, the most important thing is that you buy or rent a mask that fits. To check the fit, hold the mask against your face, then breathe in and remove your hands – if it falls off, it'll leak water. If you're buying equipment, you should be able to kit yourself out with a mask, snorkel and fins for about B1000, available from most dive centres. Few places rent fins, but a mask and snorkel set usually costs about B100 a day to rent, and if you're going on a snorkelling day-trip they are often included in the price.

National parks and wildlife observation

Thailand's hundred-plus **national parks**, which are administered by the National Park, Wildlife and Plant Conservation Department (☎02 562 0760, ⊛www.dnp .go.th/National_park.asp), are generally the best places to observe wildlife. **Khao Sok** (see p.337) is southern Thailand's most popular inland park, while bird-watchers consider the coastal flats at **Khao Sam Roi Yot** (see p.251) to be one of the country's primary observation spots. Many of southern Thailand's protected reserves are **marine parks**, including the archipelagos of

Ko Surin (see p.336), Ko Similan (see p.348), Ang Thong (see p.268) and Ko Tarutao (see p.455).

All parks charge an **entrance fee**, which for foreigners is usually B200 (B100 for children), though some charge B100 and a few charge B400. Waymarked hiking **trails** in most parks are generally limited and rarely very challenging and decent park maps are hard to come by, so for serious national park treks you'll need to hire a guide and venture beyond the public routes. Nearly all parks provide **accommodation** and/or campsites (see p.40). Some national parks **close** for several weeks or months every year for conservation, safety or environmental reasons; dates are listed on the National Parks' website.

For an introduction to Thailand's coastal environment and wildlife, see p.478.

Rock-climbing

The limestone karsts that pepper southern Thailand's Andaman coast make ideal playgrounds for **rock-climbers**, and the sport has really taken off here in the past fifteen years. Most climbing is centred round **East Railay** and **Ton Sai** beaches on Laem Phra Nang in Krabi province (see p.408), where there are dozens of routes within easy walking distance of tourist bungalows, restaurants and beaches. **Offshore Deep Water Soloing** – climbing a rock face out at sea, with no ropes, partner or bolts and just the water to break your fall – is also huge round here. Several **climbing schools** at East Railay and Ton Sai provide instruction (from B1000 per half-day), guides and all the necessary equipment (about B2400 per day for two people). Ko Phi Phi (see p.413) also offers a few routes and a couple of climbing schools, as does the quieter and potentially more interesting Ko Yao Noi (see p.383) and Ko Lao Liang (see p.448). There are also less developed climbing areas on Ko Tao (see p.302). For an introduction to climbing on Railay and elsewhere in south Thailand see ⊛www.railay.com.

Kayaking

Sea-kayaking is also centred around Thailand's Andaman coast, where the limestone outcrops, sea caves, *hongs*

(hidden lagoons), mangrove swamps and picturesque shorelines of Ao Phang Nga in particular (see *Ao Phang Nga* colour section) make for rewarding paddling. Kayaking day-trips around Ao Phang Nga can be arranged from any resort in Phuket, at Khao Lak, at all Krabi beaches and islands, and on Ko Yao Noi; multi-day kayaking expeditions are also possible as are self-guided trips from Ko Yao Noi lasting up to a month. Paddle Asia (ⓦwww.paddleasia.com) offer four- to eight-day sea-kayaking trips around the

Trang islands and the Tarutao National Marine Park islands (from US$820 per person) and over on Ko Samui, Blue Stars (see p.269) organize kayaking trips around the picturesque islands of the Ang Thong National Marine Park. Many other beach resorts rent kayaks (from B150 per hr) for casual, independent coastal exploration.

You can go **river-kayaking** on the Lang Suan River near Pha To (see p.259) and on the Sok River in Khao Sok National Park (see p.337).

Gay and lesbian Thailand

Buddhist tolerance and a national abhorrence of confrontation and victimization combine to make Thai society relatively tolerant of homosexuality, if not exactly positive about same-sex relationships. Most Thais are extremely private and discreet about being gay, generally pursuing a "don't ask, don't tell" understanding with their family. The majority of people are horrified by the idea of gay-bashing and generally regard it as unthinkable to spurn a child or relative for being gay.

Hardly any Thai celebrities are out, yet the predilections of several respected social, political and entertainment figures are widely known and accepted. There is no mention of homosexuality at all in Thai law, which means that the **age of consent** for gay sex is fifteen, the same as for heterosexuals. However, this also means that gay rights are not protected under Thai law.

Although excessively physical displays of affection are frowned upon for both hetero-sexuals and homosexuals, Western gay couples should get no hassle about being seen together in public – it's much more acceptable, and common, in fact, for friends of the same sex (gay or not) to walk hand-in-hand, than for heterosexual couples to do so.

Transvestites (known as *katoey* or "ladyboys") and **transsexuals** are also a lot more visible in Thailand than in the west. You'll find cross-dressers doing ordinary jobs, even in small upcountry towns, and there are a number of transvestites and

transsexuals in the public eye too – including national volleyball stars and champion *muay thai* boxers. The government tourist office vigorously promotes the transvestite cabarets in Pattaya, Phuket and Bangkok, all of which are advertised as family enter-tainment. *Katoey* also regularly appear as characters in soap operas, TV comedies and films, where they are depicted as harmless figures of fun. Richard Totman's book *The Third Sex* offers an interesting insight into Thai *katoey*, their experiences in society and public attitudes towards them.

The scene

Thailand's gay scene is mainly focused on **mainstream venues** like karaoke bars, restaurants, massage parlours, gyms, saunas and escort agencies. For the sake of discretion, gay venues are usually inter-mingled with straight ones. Bangkok, Phuket and Pattaya have the biggest concentrations of farang-friendly gay bars and clubs, and they all host flamboyant annual **Gay Pride festivals** as well (check the websites listed below for schedules). For a detailed guide to the gay and lesbian scene throughout the country, see the *Utopia Guide to Thailand* by John Goss, which can be downloaded via ⓦwww.utopia-asia.com.

Thai **lesbians** generally eschew the word lesbian, which in Thailand is associated with male fantasies, instead referring to themselves as either *tom* (for tomboy) or *dee* (for lady). There are hardly any dedicated *tom-dee* venues in Thailand, but we've listed established ones where possible; unless otherwise specified, gay means male throughout this guide.

The farang-oriented gay **sex industry** is a tiny but highly visible part of Thailand's gay scene. With its tawdry floor shows and host services, it bears a dispiriting resemblance to the straight sex trade, and is similarly most active in Bangkok, Pattaya and Patong (on Phuket). Like their female counterparts in the heterosexual fleshpots, many of the boys working in the gay sex bars that dominate these districts are underage; note that anyone caught having sex with a prostitute

below the age of 18 faces imprisonment. A significant number of gay prostitutes are gay by economic necessity rather than by inclination. As with the straight sex scene, we do not list commercial gay sex bars in the guide.

Information and contacts for gay travellers

Anjaree PO Box 322, Rajdamnoen PO, Bangkok 10200 ⓔanjaree@loxinfo.com. General information on the lesbian community in Thailand.
Bangkok Lesbian ⓦwww.bangkoklesbian.com. Organized by foreign lesbians living in Thailand, Bangkok Lesbian hosts regular parties and posts general info and listings of the capital's lesbian-friendly hangouts on its website.
Gay People in Thailand ⓦwww.thaivisa.com /forum/Gay-People-Thailand-f27.html. Popular forum for gay expats.
Long Yang Club ⓦwww.longyangclub.org /thailand. This international organization was founded to promote friendship between men of Western and Eastern origin and runs regular socials.
Utopia ⓦwww.utopia-asia.com and ⓦwww .utopia-asia.com/womthai.htm. Asia's best gay and lesbian website lists clubs, events, accommodation, tour operators and organizations for gays and lesbians and has useful links to other sites in Asia and the rest of the world.

Travelling with children

Despite the relative lack of child-centred attractions in Thailand, there's plenty to appeal to families, both on the beach and inland, and Thais are famously welcoming to young visitors.

Of all the **beach resorts** in the country, two of the most family friendly are the islands of Ko Samui and Ko Lanta. Both have plenty of on-the-beach accommodation for mid- and upper-range budgets, and lots of easygoing open-air shorefront restaurants so that adults can eat in relative peace while kids play within view. Both islands also offer many day-tripping activities, from elephant riding to snorkelling. Phuket is another family favourite, though shorefront accommodation

here is at a premium; there are also scores of less mainstream alternatives. In many beach resorts older kids will be able to go kayaking or learn rock climbing and many dive centres will teach the PADI children's scuba courses on request: the Bubblemaker programme is open to 8-year-olds and the Discover Scuba Diving day is designed for anyone over 10. National **parks** and their waterfalls and caves are good for days out, and there are plenty of opportunities to go rafting and **elephant-riding**. Bangkok has several child-friendly **theme parks** and activity centres (see p.155), as does the beach resort of Pattaya (see p.184).

Should you be in Thailand in January, your kids will be able to join in the free entertainments and activities staged all over the country on **National Children's Day** (Wan Dek), which is held on the second Saturday of January. They also get free entry to zoos that day, and free rides on public buses.

Practicalities

Many of the expensive **hotels** listed in this guide allow one or two under-12s to share their parents' room for free, as long as no extra bedding is required. It's often possible to cram two adults and two children into the double rooms in budget and mid-range hotels (as opposed to guest houses), as beds in these places are usually big enough for two. An increasing number of guest houses now offer three-person rooms, and may even provide special family accommodation. Decent cots are available free in the bigger hotels, and in some smaller ones (though cots in these places can be a bit grotty), and top-and mid-range rooms often come with a small fridge. Many hotels can also provide a **babysitting** service.

Few museums or transport companies offer student reductions, but in some cases children get **discounts**; these vary a lot and we've cited them in the guide only where available and relevant. One of the more bizarre provisos is the State Railway's regulation that a child aged 3 to 12 qualifies for half-fare only if under 150cm tall; some stations have a measuring scale painted onto the ticket-hall wall. Most domestic airlines charge ten percent of the full fare for under-2s, and fifty percent for under-12s.

Although most Thai babies don't wear them, **disposable nappies** (diapers) are sold at convenience stores, pharmacies and supermarkets in big resorts and sizeable towns; for stays on lonely islands, consider bringing some washable ones as back-up. A **changing mat** is another necessity as there are few public toilets in Thailand, let alone ones with baby facilities (though posh hotels are always a useful option). International brands of powdered

milk are available throughout the country, and brand-name baby food is sold in big towns and resorts, though some parents find restaurant-cooked rice and bananas go down just as well. Thai women do not **breastfeed** in public.

For touring, child-carrier backpacks are ideal. Opinions are divided on whether or not it's worth bringing a **buggy** or three-wheeled **stroller**. Where they exist, Thailand's pavements are bumpy at best, and there's an almost total absence of ramps; sand is especially difficult for buggies, though less so for three-wheelers. Buggies and strollers do, however, come in handy for feeding and even bedding small children, as highchairs and cots are only provided in the more upmarket hotels. You can buy buggies fairly cheaply in most towns, but if you bring your own and then wish you hadn't, most hotels and guest houses will keep it for you until you leave. Bring an appropriately sized **mosquito net** or buy one locally in any department store; a mini **sun tent** for the beach is also useful. Taxis and car-rental companies almost never provide baby **car seats**, and even if you bring your own you'll often find there are no seatbelts to strap them in with. Most department stores have dedicated kids' sections selling everything from bottles and dummies. There are even several Mothercare outlets in Bangkok.

Even more than their parents, children need protecting from the sun, unsafe drinking water, heat and unfamiliar **food**. Consider packing a jar of a favourite spread so that you can always rely on toast if all else fails to please. As with adults, you should be careful about unwashed fruit and salads and about dishes that have been left uncovered for a long time. As diarrhoea could be dangerous for a child, rehydration solutions (see p.28) are vital if your child goes down with it. Other significant **hazards** include thundering traffic; huge waves, strong currents and jellyfish; and the **sun** – not least because many beaches offer only limited shade, if at all. Sunhats, sunblock and waterproof suntan lotions are essential, and can be bought in the major resorts. You should also make sure, if possible, that your child is aware of the dangers of **rabies**; keep children away from **animals**, especially dogs and monkeys, and ask your medical advisor about rabies jabs.

Information and advice

Nancy Chandler's Family Travel ⓦwww .nancychandler.net/travelwkids.asp. Plenty of unusual ideas on Thai-style entertainment for kids, plus tips, links and Thailand-themed kids' books.
Thailand 4 Kids ⓦwww.thailand4kids.com. Sells an e-book guide covering the practicalities of family holidays in Thailand.

Travel essentials

Addresses

Thai **addresses** can be immensely confusing, mainly because property is often numbered twice, first to show which real estate lot it stands in, and then to distinguish where it is on that lot. Thus 154/7–10 Thanon Rajdamnoen means the building is on lot 154 and occupies numbers 7–10. There's an additional idiosyncrasy in the way Thai roads are sometimes named: in large cities a minor road running off a major road is often numbered as a soi ("lane" or "alley", though it may be a sizeable thoroughfare), rather than given its own street name. Thanon Sukhumvit, for example – Bangkok's longest – has minor roads numbered Soi 1 to Soi 103, with odd numbers on one side of the road and even on the other; so a Thanon Sukhumvit address could read something like 27/9–11 Sukhumvit Soi 15, which would mean the property occupies numbers 9–11 on lot 27 on minor road number 15 running off Thanon Sukhumvit.

Charities and volunteer projects

Reassured by the plethora of well-stocked shopping plazas, efficient services and apparent abundance in the ricefields, it is easy to forget that life is extremely hard for many people in Thailand. Countless **charities** work with Thailand's many poor and disad-vantaged communities: listed below are a few that would welcome help in some way from visitors. The website of the *Bangkok Post* also carries an extensive list of charitable foundations and projects in Thailand at ⓦwww.bangkokpost.com/outlookwecare. For longer-term placements, see p.67; and for organized holidays that feature volunteer activities see p.21.

Human Development Foundation 100/11 Kae Ha Klong Toey 4, Thanon Damrongrathhaphipat, Klong Toey, Bangkok ☏02 671 5313, ⓦwww .mercycentre.org. Since 1972, this organization has been providing education and support for Bangkok's street kids and slum-dwellers as well as caring for those with HIV/AIDS. It now runs more than thirty kindergartens in the slums. Contact the centre for information about donations and volunteering, or visit it to purchase cards and gifts. *The Slaughterhouse: Stories from Bangkok's Klong Toey* Slum (see p.483) gives an eye-opening insight into this often invisible side of Thai life.

Koh Yao Children's Community Center Ko Yao Noi ⓦwww.koyao-ccc.com. Aims to improve the English-language and lifelong learning skills of islanders on Ko Yao Noi. Visitors welcome. See p.385.

Lifelong Learning Foundation (Thailand) 64–66 Soi 101/1 Thanon Ladprao, Bangkok ☏081 894 6936, ⓦwww.trangsea.com. Promoting nature conservation and the personal development of sea gypsies and other local people in Trang province, this nonprofit organization will accept donations, but also encourages partnerships with sympathetic overseas organizations, and especially welcomes the custom of tourists at its resorts at Ban Chao Mai (see p.447) and on Ko Mook (see p.451) and Ko Libong (see p.447), and on its award-winning tours.

The Students' Education Trust (SET) ⓦwww .thaistudentcharity.org. High-school and further education in Thailand is a luxury that the poorest kids cannot afford so many are sent to live in temples instead. The SET helps such kids pursue their education and escape from the poverty trap. Some of their stories are told in *Little Angels: The Real-Life Stories of Twelve Thai Novice Monks* (see p.483). SET welcomes donations and sponsorship.

Thai Child Development Foundation Pha To Ⓦ www.thaichilddevelopment.org. This small Thai-Dutch-run village project in Chumphon province helps educate, feed and look after needy local children. The foundation welcomes donations of games, toys, clothes, educational materials and money, and takes on volunteers for one to three months, but you can also support it by joining one of the eco-tours organized by its sister outfit Runs 'N Roses (see p.259).

We-Train International House Bangkok Ⓦ www .we-train.co.th. Hotel in northern Bangkok whose profits help provide emergency housing, a clinic, a rape crisis centre, a training centre and other support for women and children, as well as a research institute.

Costs

Thailand can be a very cheap place to travel. At the bottom of the scale, you can manage on a **budget** of about B650 (£13/US$19) per day if you're willing to opt for basic accommodation, eat, drink and travel as the locals do, and stay away from the more expensive resorts like Phuket, Ko Samui and Ko Phi Phi – and you'd have to work hard to stick to this daily allowance in Bangkok. On this budget, you'll be spending around B200 for a dorm or shared room (more for a single room), around B200 on three meals (eating mainly at night markets and simple noodle shops, and eschewing beer), and the rest on travel (sticking to non-air-con buses and third-class trains where possible) and incidentals. With extras like air-conditioning in rooms and on long-distance buses and trains, taking the various forms of taxi rather than buses or shared songthaews for cross-town journeys, and a meal and beer in a more touristy restaurant, a day's outlay would look more like B1000 (£20/US$30). Staying in well-equipped, mid-range hotels and eating in the more exclusive restaurants, you should be able to live very comfortably for around B2000 a day (£40/US$60).

Travellers soon get so used to the low cost of living in Thailand that they start **bargaining** at every available opportunity, much as Thai people do. Although it's expected practice for a lot of commercial transactions, particularly at markets and when hiring tuk-tuks and unmetered taxis (though not in supermarkets or department stores), bargaining is a delicate art that requires humour, tact and patience. If your price is way out of line, the vendor's vehement refusal should be enough to make you increase your offer: never forget that the few pennies or cents you're making such a fuss over will go a lot further in a Thai person's hands than in your own.

It's rare that foreigners can bargain a price down as low as a Thai could, anyway, while **two-tier pricing** has been made official at government-run sights, as a kind of informal tourist tax: at national museums and historical parks, for example, foreigners often pay a B30–40 admission charge while Thais get in for B10; and at national parks, foreigners pay up to B400 entry while Thais generally pay just B20. A number of privately owned tourist attractions follow a similar two-tier system, posting an inflated price in English for foreigners and a lower price in Thai for locals.

Big-spending shoppers who are departing via Suvarnabhumi, Hat Yai, Pattaya or Phuket airports can save some money by claiming a **Value Added Tax refund** (Ⓦ www.rd.go.th/vrt), though it's a bit of a palaver for seven percent (the current rate of VAT). The total amount of your purchases (gems are excluded) from participating shops needs to be at least B5000 per person, of which a minimum of B2000 per shop per day. You'll need to show your passport and fill in an application form (to which original tax invoices need to be attached) at the shop. At the relevant airport, you'll need to show your form and purchases to customs officers before checking in, then make your claim from VAT refund officers – from which fees of at least B100 are deducted.

Customs regulations

The **duty-free** allowance on entry to Thailand is 200 cigarettes (or 250g of tobacco) and a litre of spirits or wine.

To **export antiques** or newly cast **Buddha images** from Thailand, you need to have a licence granted by the Fine Arts Department (the export of antique Buddhas is forbidden).

Licences can be obtained for example through the Office of Archeology and National Museums, 81/1 Thanon Si Ayutthaya (near the National Library), Bangkok (☎02 628 5032), or through the national museum in Phuket (see p.379). Applications take at least three working days in Bangkok, generally more in the provinces, and need to be accompanied by the object itself, some evidence of its rightful possession, two postcard-sized colour photos of it, taken face-on and against a white background, and photocopies of the applicant's passport; furthermore, if the object is a Buddha image, the passport photocopies need to be certified by your embassy in Bangkok. Some antiques shops can organize all this for you.

Departure taxes

International and domestic **departure taxes** are included in the price of all tickets.

Electricity

Mains **electricity** is supplied at 220 volts AC and is available at all but the most remote villages and basic beach huts. Where electricity is supplied by generators and/or solar power, for example on the smaller, less populated islands, it is often rationed to evenings only. If you're packing phone and camera chargers, a hair-dryer, laptop or other appliance, you'll need to take a set of travel-plug adapters with you as several plug types are commonly in use, most usually with two round pins, but also with two flat-blade pins, and sometimes with both options.

Insurance

Most visitors to Thailand will need to take out **specialist travel insurance**, though you should check exactly what's covered. Insurers will generally not cover travel in Songkhla, Yala, Pattani and Narathiwat provinces in the deep south, as Western governments are currently advising against going to these areas unless it's essential – see p.441 for further details. Policies generally also exclude so-called **dangerous sports** unless an extra premium is paid: in Thailand this can mean such things as scuba-diving, whitewater rafting and trekking.

Internet

Internet access is very widespread and very cheap in Thailand. You'll find traveller-oriented **internet cafés** in every touristed town and resort in the country – there are at least twenty in the Banglamphu district of Bangkok, for example – and even remote islands like Ko Mak and Ko Phayam provide internet access via satellite phones. In untouristed neighbourhoods throughout the country you can always check your email at the ubiquitous online games centres, favourite after-school haunts that are easily spotted from the piles of schoolboy pumps outside the door. Competition keeps prices low: upcountry you could expect to pay as little as B20 per hour, while rates in tourist centres average B1 per minute or B2 by satellite. Some mid-sized towns and cities in Thailand also offer a public internet service, called **Catnet**, at the government telephone office (usually located inside or adjacent to the main post office). To use the service, you need to buy a B100 card with a Catnet PIN, which should give you around three hours of internet time at any of these public terminals.

Small but increasing numbers of budget guest houses and cheap hotels, especially in Bangkok, offer **wi-fi** in all or parts of their establishment; most upmarket hotels have it, though rates are sometimes astronomical. Plenty of cafés, bars and other locations across the country provide wi-fi, but some places such as Starbuck's charge around B150 per hour for the privilege. For a list of hotspots nationwide, try ⓦwww .jiwire.com; for free locations, go to ⓦwww .stickmanweekly.com.

Laundry

Guest houses and hotels all over the country run low-cost, same-day **laundry** services. In some places you pay per item, in others you're charged by the kilo (generally from B30–50 per kg); ironing is often included in the price.

Left luggage

Most major train stations have **left luggage** facilities, where bags can be stored for up to twenty days (from B30–80 per item per day); at bus stations you can usually persuade someone official to look after your stuff for a few hours. Many guest houses and hotels also offer an inexpensive and reliable service and there's also left luggage at Bangkok and Phuket international airports (B50–100 per day).

Living in Thailand

The most common source of **employment** in Thailand is **teaching English**, especially in Bangkok. You can search for openings at schools all over Thailand on Ⓦ www.ajarn .com, which also features extensive general advice on teaching and living in Thailand. Another useful resource is the excellent Ⓦ www.thaivisa.com, whose scores of well-used forums focus on specific topics that range from employment in Thailand to legal issues and cultural and practical topics.

If you're a qualified **dive instructor**, you might be able to get seasonal work at one of the major resorts – in Phuket, Khao Lak and Ao Nang and on Ko Chang, Ko Phi Phi, Ko Lanta, Ko Samui and Ko Tao, for example. A tourist visa does not entitle you to work in Thailand, so, legally, you'll need to apply for a **work permit**.

Study, work and volunteer programmes

For voluntary work at smaller grassroots projects, see p.64.
Gibbon Rehabilitation Project Ⓦ www .gibbonproject.org. Phuket project that resocializes abused pet gibbons before releasing them back into the forests. Volunteers welcome. See p.379.
Phuket English teachers Ⓦ www .phukethasbeengoodtous.org. Welcomes short- and longer-term volunteers to teach and assist on its Practical English Language programme at schools on Phuket. The aim of the foundation is to improve kids' standards of English so that they can get the better-paid jobs in Phuket's tourist industry.
Reefcheck Thailand Ⓦ www.thaiecolodge.com /reefcheck.php. The Thai chapter of the international marine conservation NGO welcomes interested paying volunteer divers, trainee divers and snorkellers to help survey local reefs, especially along the north Andaman coast, including the Surin and Similan islands. Based on Ko Ra (see p.334).
Starfish Ventures Ⓦ www.starfishvolunteers .com. Paying volunteer and gap-year placements at environmental and social community projects in Rayong and Phuket.

Volunteer Teaching in Thailand Ⓦ www .volunteerteacherthailand.org. Continuing the good work begun by the thousands of volunteers who came to Khao Lak to help rebuild lives and homes following the 2004 tsunami, this organization teaches English to Khao Lak kids and adults to enhance their future prospects in the local tourist industry. Teaching experience is appreciated but not essential.

Mail

Overseas airmail usually takes around seven days from Bangkok, a little longer from the more isolated areas (it's worth asking at the post office about their express EMS services, which can cut this down to three days and aren't prohibitively expensive). **Post offices**, many of which offer money-wiring facilities (in association with Western Union) and parcel-packing, are generally open Monday to Friday 8.30am to 4.30pm, Saturday 9am to noon; some close Monday to Friday noon to 1pm and may stay open until 6pm, and a few open 9am to noon on Sundays and public holidays. Almost all main post offices across the country operate a **poste restante** service and will hold letters for one to three months. Mail should be addressed: *Name* (family name underlined or capitalized), Poste Restante, GPO, *Town or City*, Thailand. It will be filed by surname, though it's always wise to check under your first initial as well. The smaller post offices pay scant attention to who takes what, but in the busier GPOs you need to show your passport, pay B1 per letter or B2 per parcel received, and sign for them.

Post offices are the best places to buy **stamps**, though hotels and guest houses often sell them too, charging an extra B1 per stamp. An airmail letter of under 10g costs B17 to send to Europe or Australia and B19 to North America; standard-sized postcards cost B12, larger ones and aerogrammes B15, regardless of where they're going. The **surface** rate for parcels to the UK is B950 for the first kg, then B175 per kg; to the US B550 for the first kg, then B140 per kg; and to Australia B650 for the first kg, then B110 per kg; the package should reach its destination in three months. The **airmail** rate for parcels to the UK is B900 for the first kg, then B380 per kg; to the US B950 for the first kg, then B500 per kg; and to Australia

B750 for the first kg, then B350 per kg; the package should reach its destination in one or two weeks.

Maps

For most major destinations, the **maps** in this book should be all you need, though you may want to supplement them with larger-scale maps of Bangkok and the whole country. Bangkok bookshops are the best source of these; where appropriate, detailed local maps and their stockists are recommended throughout the guide. If you want to buy a map before you get there, Rough Guides' 1:1,200,000 map of Thailand is a good option – and, since it's printed on special rip-proof paper, it won't tear. Reasonable alternatives include the 1:1,500,000 maps produced by Nelles and Bartholomew.

For **drivers**, the best atlas (also in CD format) is *Thailand Deluxe Atlas* published by thinknet (Ⓦwww.thinknet.co.th): at a scale of 1:550,000 it's bilingual and regularly updated, but costs B550. It's available at most bookstores in Thailand where English-language material is sold. If you can't get hold of that, you could go for the relevant 1:300,000 maps of each province published by PN Map Centre; some of the detail on these maps is only in Thai, but they should have enough English to be useful.

Money and banks

Thailand's unit of currency is the **baht** (abbreviated to "B"), divided into 100 satang – which are rarely seen these days. Coins come in B1 (silver), B2 (golden), B5 (silver) and B10 (mostly golden, encircled by a silver ring) denominations, notes in B20, B50, B100, B500 and B1000 denominations, inscribed with Western as well as Thai numerals, and generally increasing in size according to value.

At the time of writing, **exchange rates** were around B35 to US$1, B45 to €1 and B50 to £1. A good site for current exchange rates is Ⓦwww.xe.com. Note that Thailand has no black market in foreign currency. Because of severe currency fluctuations in the late 1990s, a few tourist-oriented businesses now quote their prices in **US dollars**, particularly luxury hotels and dive centres.

Banking hours are Monday to Friday from 8.30am to 3.30 or 4.30pm, but exchange kiosks in the main tourist centres are always open till at least 5pm, sometimes 10pm, and upmarket hotels change money 24 hours a day. The Suvarnabhumi Airport exchange counters also operate 24 hours, while exchange kiosks at overseas airports with flights to Thailand usually keep Thai currency.

Sterling and US dollar **traveller's cheques** are accepted by banks, exchange booths and upmarket hotels in every sizeable Thai town, and most places also deal in a variety of other currencies; everyone offers better rates for cheques than for straight cash. Generally, a total of B33 in commission and duty is charged per cheque – though kiosks and hotels in isolated places may charge extra – so you'll save money if you deal in larger cheque denominations.

American Express, Visa and MasterCard **credit and debit cards** are accepted at top hotels as well as in some posh restaurants, department stores, tourist shops and travel agents, but surcharging of up to seven percent is rife, and theft and forgery are major industries – try not to let the card out of your sight, always demand any carbon copies, and never leave cards in baggage storage. With a debit or credit card and personal identification number (PIN), you can also withdraw cash from hundreds of 24-hour **ATMs** around the country. Almost every town now has at least one bank with an ATM that accepts overseas cards (all the banks marked on our maps throughout the guide have ATMs), and there are a growing number of stand-alone ATMs in supermarkets.

Opening hours and public holidays

Most **shops** open long hours, usually Monday to Saturday from about 8am to 8pm, while department stores operate daily from around 10am to 9pm. Private office hours are generally Monday to Friday 8am to 5pm and Saturday 8am to noon, though in tourist areas these hours are longer, with weekends worked like any other day. Government offices work Monday to Friday

8.30am to noon and 1 to 4.30pm, and national museums tend to stick to these hours too, but some close on Mondays and Tuesdays rather than at weekends.

Many tourists only register **national holidays** because trains and buses suddenly get extraordinarily crowded: although banks and government offices shut on these days, most shops and tourist-oriented businesses carry on regardless, and TAT branches continue to dispense information. Some national holidays are celebrated with theatrical festivals, for a calendar of which see p.54. The only time an inconvenient number of shops, restaurants and hotels do close is during **Chinese New Year**, which, though not marked as an official national holiday, brings many businesses to a standstill for several days in late January or February. You'll notice it particularly in the south, where most service industries are Chinese-managed.

Thais use both the Western Gregorian **calendar** and a Buddhist calendar – the Buddha is said to have died (or entered Nirvana) in the year 543 BC, so Thai dates start from that point: thus 2010 AD becomes 2553 BE (Buddhist Era).

National holidays

Jan 1 Western New Year's Day.
Feb (day of full moon) Maha Puja: commemorates the Buddha preaching to a spontaneously assembled crowd of 1250.
April 6 Chakri Day: the founding of the Chakri dynasty.
April (usually 13–15) Songkhran: Thai New Year.
May 1 National Labour Day.
May 5 Coronation Day.
May (early in the month) Royal Ploughing Ceremony: marks start of rice-planting season.
May (day of full moon) Visakha Puja: the holiest of all Buddhist holidays, which celebrates the birth, enlightenment and death of the Buddha.
July (day of full moon) Khao Pansa: the start of the annual three-month Buddhist rains retreat, when new monks are ordained.
Aug 12 Queen's birthday.
Oct 23 Chulalongkorn Day: the anniversary of Rama V's death.
Dec 5 King's birthday: also celebrated as national Fathers' Day.
Dec 10 Constitution Day.
Dec 31 Western New Year's Eve.

Phones

Local **calls within Thailand** are very cheap (as little as B1 for 3min from a coin payphone), but inter-provincial rates cost B3–12 per min; dial ☎1234 before the zero to reduce this to B0.50–2 per min. Deregulation of the Thai telecommunications industry has made **calling internationally** from Thailand a convoluted, though cheaper, business, with the state-owned companies, CAT (contact centre ☎1322, Ⓦwww .cattelecom.com) and TOT (☎1100, Ⓦwww .tot.co.th), competing for business: each now offers a premium-rate service with its own **prefix** (CAT's ☎001 and TOT's ☎007), as well as a cheaper, generally lower-quality, VOIP (voice-over-internet protocol) prefix (CAT's ☎009 and TOT's ☎008). Visitors can access these prefixes variously on mobile phones or via phone cards, while many private international call offices (where your call is timed and you pay at the end) in tourist areas such as Bangkok's Thanon Khao San now use ☎009 or 008 to access the lower VOIP rates – plus a service charge to the customer, of course.

When **dialling** any number in Thailand, you must now always preface it with what used to be the area code, even when dialling from the same area. Where we've given several line numbers – eg ☎02 431 1802–9 – you can substitute the last digit, 2, with any digit between 3 and 9. For **directory enquiries** within Thailand, call ☎1133.

All mobile phone numbers in Thailand have recently been changed from nine to ten digits, by adding the number "8" after the initial zero (you may still come across cards and brochures giving the old nine-digit number). Note also, however, that Thais tend to change mobile-phone providers – and therefore numbers – comparatively frequently, in search of a better deal.

One final local idiosyncrasy: Thai phone books list people by their first name, not their family name.

Phone cards

The most flexible **phone card** available is TOT's **Pin Phone 108** Card, which allows both domestic and international calls. Equipped with a pin number, it can be used from any payphone or fixed landline. Offering the same services, the **TOT Card** has no PIN number but can only be used in special TOT green and yellow payphones, not in the more commonly found stainless steel payphones. With either of these cards, which are available in B50–500 denominations from 7–Eleven and Family Mart supermarkets, for example, calls to the UK and Australia cost B9 (☎007) or B7 (☎008) per minute, US and Canada B9 (☎007) or B5 (☎008), New Zealand B17 (☎007) or B15 (☎008) and South Africa B32 (☎007) or B7 (☎008); calls to Ireland currently cost B24 per minute with either prefix.

CAT's cards are available from most post offices and many supermarkets, but can only be used for international calls. Their Thaicard, available in B100–1000 denominations, can be used in designated purple cardphones – if you can't happen to find one, head for the nearest government telephone centre, which is usually located within or adjacent to a town's main post office. With a Thaicard, you use the ☎001 prefix, at rates roughly comparable with TOT's ☎007 phone-card charges. CAT's **Phone Net** cards, which use the ☎009 prefix and come in B200–500 denominations, can be used, in conjunction with a PIN number, from any payphone or fixed landline or from a mobile with international roaming. Rates are roughly comparable with TOT's ☎008 phone-card charges, though there's currently a long-term special promotion of B2 per minute to landlines in the UK, US and Canada, B2.5 Ireland, Australia and New Zealand and B4 South Africa.

There's also a **private cardphone system** called **Lenso** (@www.lensophonecard.com), which operates mostly in Bangkok and tourist centres. To use Lenso's yellow phones, you either need a special Lenso phone card (available from shops such as 7-Eleven and Family Mart in B200, B300 and B500 denominations), or you can use a credit card. Rates, however, are generally higher than TOT's phonecard rates. If you're really hunting for a telephonic bargain, keep your eyes peeled for new, smaller **private phone cards**, such as Dee (@www.thookdee.com) and

Hello by Hatari (@www.hatari.net), which use call-back and/or PIN number systems, and offer international calls to the most popular destinations for as little as B1 per minute.

Mobile phones

An increasing number of tourists are taking their **mobile phones** (*moe toe*) to Thailand. Visitors from the US may well need to have a dual- or tri-band phone, but GSM 900Hz and 1800Hz, and 3G, the systems most commonly found in other parts of the world, are all available in Thailand. Most foreign networks have links with Thai networks, but it's worth checking with your phone provider before you travel; it's also worth checking how much coverage there is for your network within Thailand. For a list of network types and providers in Thailand, along with coverage maps and roaming partners, go to @www.gsmworld.com/roaming.

If you want to use your mobile a lot in Thailand, it may well be worth getting hold of a rechargeable **Thai SIM card** with a local phone number. An AIS 1-2-Call card (@www.one-2-call.ais.co.th) will give you the widest coverage in Thailand, and top-up cards are available at 7-Eleven stores across the country. Their call rates start at B0.75 per minute within Thailand; international call rates depend on the prefix used (see above), ranging from B7 per minute to the UK, for example, on ☎008 or 009, through B9 on ☎007, to B18 on ☎001. Texts cost B2 domestic, B9 to the UK, for example.

Your own network operator may be able to give you useful advice before you leave home about **exchanging SIM cards**, including any unlocking codes that may be necessary. Thai SIM cards are available at mobile phone outlets all over the country, but the best place to buy a card and have any necessary technical adjustments made, including setting up voicemail, is the Mah Boon Krong Centre in Bangkok (see p.158); an AIS 1-2-Call SIM card, for example, will cost you around B300, including your first B50 worth of calls, though look out for periodic special offers that include substantial credit bonuses.

International dialling codes

Calling from abroad, the international **country code** for Thailand is **66**, after which you leave off the initial zero of the Thai number. For **international directory enquiries** and operator services, call ☎100.

Calling from Thailand, you'll need the relevant country code (see p.69 for information on prefixes):

Australia 61
Canada 1
Ireland 353
New Zealand 64
South Africa 27
UK 44
US 1

Photography

Most towns and all resorts have at least one **camera shop** where you will be able to get your digital pictures downloaded onto a CD for B100–150; the shops all have card readers. In tourist centres many internet cafés also offer CD-burning services, though if you want to email your pictures, bringing your own cable will make life easier.

Time

Thailand is in the same time zone year-round, with no daylight savings period. It's five hours ahead of South Africa, seven hours ahead of GMT, twelve hours ahead of US Eastern Standard Time, three hours behind Australian Eastern Standard Time and five hours behind New Zealand Standard Time.

Tipping

It is usual to **tip** hotel bellboys and porters B20, and to round up taxi fares to the nearest B10. Most guides, drivers, masseurs, waiters and maids also depend on tips, and although some upmarket hotels and restaurants will add an automatic ten percent service charge to your bill, this is not always shared out.

Tourist information

The **Tourism Authority of Thailand**, or **TAT** (☯www.tourismthailand.org), maintains offices in several cities abroad and has 31 branches within Thailand (all open daily 8.30am–4.30pm, though a few close noon–1pm for lunch) plus counters at Suvarnabhumi International Airport. Regional offices should have up-to-date information on local festival dates and transport schedules, but none of them offers accommodation booking, and service can be variable. You can contact the TAT tourist assistance phoneline from anywhere in the country for free on ☎1672 (daily 8am–8pm). In Bangkok, the Bangkok Tourism Division is a better source of information on the capital (see p.84). In some smaller towns that don't qualify for a local TAT office, the information gap is filled by a **municipal tourist assistance office**, though at some of these you may find it hard to locate a fluent English speaker.

TAT offices abroad

Australia and New Zealand Suite 2002, Level 20, 56 Pitt St, Sydney, NSW 2000 ☎02/9247 7549, ☯www.thailand.net.au.
South Africa Contact the UK office.
UK and Ireland 1st Floor, 17–19 Cockspur St, London SW1Y 5BL ☎0870/900 2007, ☯www.tourismthailand.co.uk.
US and Canada 61 Broadway, Suite 2810, New York, NY 10006 ☎212/432-0433, ✉info@tatny.com; 611 North Larchmont Blvd, 1st Floor, Los Angeles, CA 90004 ☎323/461-9814, ✉tatla@tat.or.th.

Travellers with disabilities

Thailand makes few provisions for its disabled citizens and this obviously affects **travellers with disabilities**, but taxis, comfortable hotels and personal tour guides are all more affordable than in the West and most travellers with disabilities find Thais only too happy to offer assistance where they can. Hiring a local tour guide to accompany you on a day's sightseeing is particularly recommended: government tour guides can be arranged through any TAT office.

Most **wheelchair-users** end up driving on the roads because it's too hard to negotiate the uneven pavements, which are high to allow for flooding and invariably lack dropped kerbs. Crossing the road can be a trial, particularly in Bangkok and other big cities, where it's usually a question of climbing steps up to a bridge rather than taking a ramped underpass. Few buses and trains have ramps but in Bangkok some Skytrain stations and all subway stations have lifts.

Several **tour companies** in Thailand specialize in organizing trips featuring adapted facilities, accessible transport and escorts. The Bangkok-based Help and Care Travel Company (℡081 375 0792, Ⓦwww .wheelchairtours.com) designs **accessible holidays** in Thailand for slow walkers and wheelchair users and its website carries a (short) list of wheelchair-accessible hotels in the main tourist centres. Phuket-based Worldwide Dive and Sail (℡076 383819, Ⓦwww.worldwidediveandsail.com) special-izes in **diving and sailing** liveaboard trips for deaf and hard-of-hearing people, and Mermaid's Dive Centre in Pattaya (℡038 232219, Ⓦwww.learn-in-asia.com /handicapped_diving.htm; see p.185) runs Inter-national Association of Handicapped Divers programmes for **disabled divers** and instructors.

Guide

Guide

Bangkok

CHAPTER 1 # Highlights

✳ **Thanon Khao San** Legendary hangout for Southeast Asia backpackers; the place for cheap sleeps, baggy trousers and tall tales. See p.93

✳ **The Grand Palace** The country's least missable sight, incorporating its holiest and most dazzling temple, Wat Phra Kaeo. See p.110

✳ **Wat Pho** Admire the Reclining Buddha and the lavish architecture, and leave time for a relaxing massage. See p.115

✳ **The National Museum** The central repository of the country's artistic riches. See p.118

✳ **The canals of Thonburi** See the Bangkok of yesteryear on a touristy but memorable longtail boat ride. See p.129

✳ **Jim Thompson's House** An elegant Thai design classic. See p.135

✳ **Chatuchak Weekend Market** Eight thousand stalls selling everything from triangular pillows to secondhand Levis. See p.140

✳ **63rd-floor sundowner** Fine cocktails and jaw-dropping views, especially at sunset, at *The Sky Bar* and *Distil*. See p.152

✳ **Thai boxing** Nightly bouts at the national stadia, complete with live musical accompaniment and frenetic betting. See p.157

▲ Ramayana mural, Wat Phra Kaeo, the Grand Palace

Bangkok

T he headlong pace and flawed modernity of Bangkok match few people's visions of the capital of exotic Siam. Spiked with scores of high-rise buildings of concrete and glass, it's a vast flatness that holds a population of at least nine million, and feels even bigger. But under the shadow of the skyscrapers you'll find a heady mix of chaos and refinement, of frenetic markets, snail's-pace traffic jams and hushed golden temples, of dispiriting, zombie-like sex shows and early-morning alms-giving ceremonies. One way or another, the place will probably get under your skin – and if you don't enjoy the challenge of taking on the "Big Mango", you can spend a couple of days on the most impressive temples and museums, have a quick shopping spree and then strike out for the beaches.

Most budget travellers head for the **Banglamphu** district, where if you're not careful you could end up watching DVDs all day long and selling your shoes when you run out of money. The district is far from having a monopoly on Bangkok accommodation, but it does have the advantage of being just a short walk from the major sights in the **Ratanakosin** area: the dazzling ostentation of the **Grand Palace** and **Wat Phra Kaeo**, lively and grandiose **Wat Pho** and the **National Museum**'s hoard of exquisite works of art. Once those cultural essentials have been seen, you can choose from a whole bevy of lesser sights, including **Wat Benjamabophit** (the "Marble Temple"), especially at festival time, and **Jim Thompson's House**, a small, personal museum of Thai design.

City of angels

When Rama I was crowned in 1782, he gave his new capital a grand 43-syllable name to match his ambitious plans for the building of the city. Since then, 21 more syllables have been added. Krungthepmahanakhornbowornrattanakosinmahintarayutthaya-mahadilokpopnopparatratchathaniburiromudomratchaniwetmahasathanamornpiman-avatarnsathitsakkathattiyavisnukarprasit is certified by the Guinness Book of Records as the longest place name in the world, roughly translating as "Great city of angels, the supreme repository of divine jewels, the great land unconquerable, the grand and prominent realm, the royal and delightful capital city full of nine noble gems, the highest royal dwelling and grand palace, the divine shelter and living place of the reincarnated spirits". Fortunately, all Thais refer to the city simply as Krung Thep, "City of Angels", though plenty can recite the full name at the drop of a hat. Bangkok – "Village of the Plum Olive" – was the name of the original village on the Thonburi side; with remarkable persistence, it has remained in use by foreigners since the time of the French garrison.

BANGKOK DISTRICTS

For livelier scenes, explore the dark alleys of **Chinatown**'s bazaars or head for the water: the great **Chao Phraya River**, which breaks up and adds zest to the city's landscape, is the backbone of a network of **canals** that remains fundamentally intact in the west-bank Thonburi district. Inevitably the waterways have earned Bangkok the title of "Venice of the East", a tag that seems all too apt when you're wading through flooded streets in the rainy season. Back on dry land, **shopping** varies from touristic outlets pushing silks, handicrafts and counterfeit watches, through home-grown boutiques selling street-wise fashions and stunning contemporary decor, to thronging local markets where half the fun is watching the crowds. Similarly, the city offers the country's most varied **entertainment**, ranging from traditional dancing and the orchestrated bedlam of Thai boxing, through hip bars and clubs playing the latest imported sounds, to the farang-only sex bars of the notorious Patpong district, a tinseltown Babylon that's the tip of a dangerous iceberg.

Arrival

Unless you arrive in Bangkok by train, be prepared for a long trip into the city centre. Suvarnabhumi Airport is 25km out and the three bus stations are not much closer in, though at least the Eastern Terminal is hard by a Skytrain stop.

By air

Bangkok's main airport is **Suvarnabhumi** (coded "BKK" and pronounced "soo-wanna-poom"; Ⓦ www.bangkokairportonline.com), 25km east of central Bangkok between Highways 7 and 34. At the time of writing, the only scheduled flights using the old **Don Muang Airport** (coded "DMK";

ⓦ www.donmuangairportonline.com), 25km north of the city, were Nok Air and One-Two-Go's domestic services. However, there's been a fair bit of politically motivated toing and froing of domestic airlines between the two airports over the past few years: it may well be that the woefully underused Don Muang will again close to scheduled flights altogether, or it might, conceivably, be allowed to handle a greater range of low-cost flights. If you do wind up at Don Muang, the best way to get into the city centre is by licensed, metered taxi from the desk outside Arrivals (about B300–350).

Suvarnabhumi Airport

At **Suvarnabhumi**, which bears more of a resemblance to a shopping mall than an airport, you'll find plenty of 24-hour exchange booths, ATMs, cafés and restaurants, as well as several bookshops, pharmacies and Internet cafés. In the **arrivals hall** on Floor 2, there's a tourist police booth; two TAT information desks, which are helpful but marooned at the hall's far east and west corners (daily 8am–10pm; ⓣ 02 134 0040); and Thai Hotels Association accommodation desks, with prices generally cheaper than rack rates; while car-rental companies, including Avis and Budget (see p.167), have booths beside the luggage conveyor belts (though you'll have to pick your car up from the Public Transportation Center; see below). There are pricey, 24-hour left-luggage depots, charging B100 per item per day, both in arrivals and in the **departures hall** on Floor 4, which is also home to a post office. On Floor 3, there's a 24-hour clinic run by Samitivej Hospital.

Airport transport

On the other side of the huge airport complex from the terminal building stands the Public Transportation Center, which means taking a free, ten-minute ride on an Express shuttle bus from Gate 5 outside arrivals or Gate 10 outside departures – be sure not to confuse these with the much slower Ordinary shuttle buses, which ferry airport staff around the complex. However, because of the inconvenience involved, taxis and many buses now pick up and drop off at the terminal building, as detailed below. A high-speed **rail link** from Suvarnabhumi (SARL) that's currently reported to be opening in early 2010 will be the quickest means of getting downtown. Nonstop Airport Express trains to the City Air Terminal at Makkasan Station (which connects with the subway system at Phetchaburi Station) are planned to take about fifteen minutes, while the (much cheaper) stopping Airport City Line services to Phaya Thai (an interchange with the Skytrain system) should take around thirty minutes. The TAT offices in the arrivals hall have full details of all airport transport.

The most economical way of getting into the city is by **public air-con bus** (B22–34) or **minibus** (B40–70), with the following routes, mostly 24-hour, likely to be useful to visitors: #552 from the **Public Transportation Center** along Thanon Sukhumvit via Ekamai (for the Eastern Bus Station and Skytrain), turning left along Thanon Ratchadapisek to Khlong Toey via Queen Sirikit Convention Centre (for the subway); and #556 to Democracy Monument, Thanon Rajdamnoen Klang (for Banglamphu guest houses) and the Southern Bus Terminal from Gate 8, Floor 1 of the terminal building.

The dedicated, air-conditioned **airport bus** (daily 5am–midnight; at least every 30min; B150) is fine for lone travellers, but at most times of the day, the convenience of a taxi is going to be cheaper for a group of two or more, or at least not much more expensive. These buses depart from outside Gate 8, Floor 1 of the terminal building, covering four routes: #AE1 terminates at Sala Daeng Skytrain station, via Pratunam, Thanon Rajdamri and a circuit

BANGKOK ①

CENTRAL CHAO PHRAYA EXPRESS-BOAT PIERS

- N15 Thewet (all boats except blue flag)
- N14 Rama VIII Bridge (no flag; Mon–Fri rush hours only)
- N13 Phra Arthit (no flag and orange flag)
- N12 Phra Pinklao Bridge (all boats except blue flag)
- N11 Thonburi Railway Station (no flag; Mon–Fri rush hours only)
- N10 Wang Lang (all boats)
- N9 Chang (no flag and orange flag)
- N8 Thien (no flag and orange flag)
- N7 Ratchini (no flag; Mon–Fri rush hours only)
- N6 Saphan Phut (no flag and orange flag)
- N5 Rachawongse (all boats except blue flag)
- N4 Harbour Department (no flag and orange flag)
- N3 Si Phraya (all boats except blue flag)
- N2 Wat Muang Kae (no flag; Mon–Fri rush hours only)
- N1 Oriental (no flag and orange flag)
- Central Sathorn (all boats)

Samsen Station

Phya Thai Palace

Victory Monument

Suan Pakkad Palace Museum

Makkasan Station City Air Terminal

Baiyoke II Tower

Pratunam Market

Tha Saphan Hua Chang

Jim Thompson's House ★

Bumrungrad

British Embassy

Erawan Shrine

Ratcha-damri

Royal Bangkok Sports Club

Chulalongkorn University

Queen Saovabha Institute

Lumphini Park

Suan Lum Night Bazaar

American Embassy

Lumphini Stadium

Bangkok Christian

BNH

Immigration Department

M. R. Kukrit's Heritage Home

TAT HQ

Ban Kamthieng

Emporium

Queen Sirikit National Convention Centre (QSNCC)

RAMA IX (PHRA RAM 9)

0 _____ 1 km

81

west along Thanon Suriwong and east along Thanon Silom; #AE2 goes to Thanon Khao San in Banglamphu, via Pratunam, Thanon Phetchaburi, Democracy Monument, Sanam Luang, Thanon Phra Arthit, Thanon Phra Sumen and Thanon Chakrabongse; #AE3 runs the length of Sukhumvit and Ploenchit roads, via the Eastern Bus Terminal and Ekamai Skytrain, to the Erawan Shrine, before doubling back via Thanon Phetchaburi to Sukhumvit Soi 3; and #AE4 runs to Hualamphong Station, via Victory Monument, Siam Square, Thanon Phrayathai and Thanon Rama IV.

From the Public Transportation Center, there are also **long-distance buses** to Pattaya (a few Pattaya services each day pick up at Floor 1 of the terminal building), Rayong, Chanthaburi and Trat on the east coast.

Taxis to the centre are comfortable, air-conditioned and reasonably priced, although the driving can be hairy. Walk past the pricey taxis and limousines on offer within the baggage hall and arrivals hall and ignore any tout who may offer a cheap ride in an unlicensed and unmetered vehicle, as newly arrived travellers are seen as easy prey for robbery, and the cabs are untraceable. Licensed and metered public taxis are operated from clearly signposted and well-regulated counters, outside the arrivals hall's Gates 3 and 10. Even including the B50 airport pick-up fee and around B65 tolls for the overhead expressways, a journey to Thanon Silom downtown, for example, should set you back around B300, depending on the traffic.

Airport accommodation

With time to kill and money to spare before your onward journey, you might want to rest and clean up in one of the **day rooms** in the airport's transit area (US$80 per one person, US$87 per two people, for 4hr). Day rooms (B4500 from 8am–6pm, or B3000 for 4hr) are also available at the airport **hotel**, the four-star *Novotel Suvarnabhumi* (☎02 131 1111, ⓦwww.accorhotels.com; ⑨). Offering Thai, Japanese, Chinese and international restaurants, a swimming pool and fitness centre, the *Novotel* is a ten-minute walk from the terminal building – or catch the shuttle bus from outside Gate 4, Floor 2. Just outside the airport complex, to the north near Highway 7, *Queens Garden Resort* (☎02 172 6114, ⓦwww.queensgardenresort.net; ⑤) is a more economical choice, providing hot water, air-con, minibar and satellite TV in all bedrooms and 24-hour pick-ups (B150).

By train

Travelling to Bangkok by **train** from Malaysia and most parts of Thailand, you arrive at **Hualamphong Station**, which is centrally located, at the southern end of the subway line (see map, p.125). The most useful of the city buses serving Hualamphong is the #159 (non-air-con), which runs west to Democracy Monument, Rajdamnoen Klang (for Banglamphu) and the Southern Bus Terminal, and east to MBK, Siam Square, Chatuchak and the Northern Bus Terminal. See box on p.88 for other bus routes via Hualamphong. The Airport Express #AE4 bus service to Suvarnabhumi departs approximately hourly from 7am to 11pm from the east side of the station on Thanon Rong Muang. Station **facilities** include an exchange booth, several ATMs, an internet centre and a makeshift **left-luggage** "office", actually just bags piled up in a corner (daily 4am–11pm; B30–80 per day, depending on size). A more economical, and possibly more secure place to store baggage is the *TT2 Guest House* (see p.99), about fifteen minutes' walk from the station (B15–20 per item per day).

One service the station does not provide is itinerant tourist assistance staff; anyone who comes up to you in or around the station concourse and offers help/information/transport or ticket-booking services is almost certainly a **con-artist**, however many official-looking ID tags are hanging round their neck. This is a well-established scam to fleece new arrivals and should be avoided at all costs (see p.51). For train-related questions, contact the 24-hour "Information" counter close by the departures board (there's more advice on buying onward rail tickets on p.164). The station area is also fertile ground for **dishonest tuk-tuk drivers**, so you'll need to be extra suspicious to avoid them – take a metered taxi or public transport instead.

A handful of trains **from Hua Hin** and other local trains on the Southern line pull in at the small and very quiet **Thonburi Station**, from where it's a short ride in a red public songthaew or an 850-metre walk east to the N11 express-boat pier (Bangkok Noi; Mon–Fri rush hours only), just across the Chao Phraya River from Banglamphu and Ratanakosin; at other times you'll need to use the N10 Tha Wang Lang express boat stop instead, which is 500m south of N11, through the Siriraj hospital compound.

By bus

Buses come to a halt at a number of far-flung spots. All services from the north and northeast terminate at the **Northern and Northeastern Bus Terminal** (**Mo Chit**) on Thanon Kamphaeng Phet 2; some east-coast buses also use Mo Chit, including several daily services from Pattaya, Rayong (for Ko Samet), Chanthaburi and Trat (for Ko Chang and the Cambodian border). The quickest way to get into the city centre from Mo Chit is to hop onto the Skytrain at Mo Chit Station, or the subway at the adjacent Chatuchak Park Station, fifteen minutes' walk from the bus terminal on Thanon Phaholyothin, and then change onto a city bus if necessary. Otherwise, it's a long bus or taxi ride into town: city buses from the Northern Bus Terminal include ordinary #159 to Siam Square, Hualamphong Station, Banglamphu and the Southern Bus Terminal; and ordinary and air-conditioned #3, and air-conditioned #509 and #512 to Banglamphu; for details of these routes see pp.88–89.

Most buses to and from east-coast destinations such as Pattaya, Ban Phe (for Ko Samet) and Trat (for Ko Chang) use the **Eastern Bus Terminal** (**Ekamai**; (☏02 391 2496) between sois 40 and 42 on Thanon Sukhumvit. This bus station is right beside the Ekamai Skytrain stop (see p.90), and is also served by lots of city buses, including air-conditioned #511 to and from Banglamphu and the Southern Bus Terminal (see box, p.88); alternatively, you can use the Khlong Saen Saeb canal boat service which transports passengers to and from the edge of Banglamphu (see p.89) via a pier at Tha Ekamai, at the end of Sukhumvit Soi 63, easiest reached by taxi. There's a left-luggage booth at the bus terminal (daily 6am–6pm; B30 per day) and several places to stay quite nearby (see p.105), as well as a cineplex a few minutes' walk west, between sois 61 and 63.

The huge, airport-like **Southern Bus Terminal**, or **Sathaanii Sai Tai** (☏02 434 7192), handles transport to and from all points south of the capital, including Hua Hin, Chumphon (for Ko Tao), Surat Thani (for Ko Samui and Ko Pha Ngan), Phuket and Krabi, as well as buses for destinations west of Bangkok. The terminal has recently been relocated to the junction of Thanon Borom Ratchonni and Thanon Phutthamonthon Sai 1 in Taling Chan, an inter-minable 11km west of the Chao Phraya River and Banglamphu, so access to and from city accommodation can takes an age, even in a taxi. City buses serving Sathaanii Sai Tai include #124 for Banglamphu, #511 for Banglamphu and Thanon Sukhumvit, and #516 for Thewet and Banglamphu (see box, p.88), but note that when arriving in Bangkok most long-distance bus services make a more convenient **stop before reaching the terminus** (via a time-consuming U-turn), towards the eastern end of Thanon Borom Ratchonni, much nearer Phra Pinklao Bridge and the river; the majority of passengers get off here and it's highly recommended to do the same rather than continue to the terminal. The above-listed city buses all cross the river from this bus drop, as do many additional services, and this is also a faster and cheaper place to grab a taxi into town. The bus terminal itself has lots of facilities, including a food hall, internet access, ATMs and scores of shops. The left-luggage office is beside the *Black Canyon Coffee Shop*, near the information booth on the ticket-sales floor (5am–9pm; B20–60 per day).

Orientation

Bangkok can be a tricky place to get your bearings as it's huge and ridiculously congested, with largely featureless modern buildings and no obvious centre. The boldest line on the map is the **Chao Phraya River**, which divides the city into Bangkok proper on the east bank, and **Thonburi**, part of Greater Bangkok, on the west.

The historical core of Bangkok proper, site of the original royal palace, is **Ratanakosin**, cradled in a bend in the river. Three concentric canals radiate eastwards around Ratanakosin: the southern part of the area between the canals is the old-style trading enclave of **Chinatown** and Indian Pahurat, connected to the old palace by Thanon Charoen Krung (aka New Rd); the northern part is characterized by old temples and the **Democracy Monument**, west of which is the backpackers' ghetto of **Banglamphu**. Beyond the canals to the north, **Dusit** is the site of many government buildings and the nineteenth-century Vimanmek Palace, and is linked to Ratanakosin by the three stately avenues, Thanon Rajdamnoen Nok, Thanon Rajdamnoen Klang and Thanon Rajdamnoen Nai.

"New" Bangkok begins to the east of the canals and beyond the main rail line and Hualamphong Station, and stretches as far as the eye can see to the east and north. The main business district and most of the embassies are south of **Thanon Rama IV**, with the port of Khlong Toey at the southern edge. The diverse area north of Thanon Rama IV includes the sprawling campus of Chulalongkorn University, huge shopping centres around **Siam Square** and a variety of other businesses. A couple of blocks northeast of Siam Square stands the tallest building in Bangkok, the 84-storeyed **Baiyoke II Tower**, whose golden spire makes a good point of reference. To the east lies the swish residential quarter off **Thanon Sukhumvit**.

Information and maps

The official source of information on the capital is the **Bangkok Tourism Division**, part of the Bangkok Metropolitan Administration (BMA), whose main office is next to Phra Pinklao Bridge at 17/1 Thanon Phra Arthit in Banglamphu (daily 9am–7pm; ☎02 225 7612–5, ⒲www.bangkoktourist.com). This is supported by strategically placed satellite booths around the capital (daily 9am–5pm), including in front of the Grand Palace, at the Erawan Shrine, at River City and Mah Boon Krong shopping centres, in front of Robinson Department Store on Thanon Silom, and in front of Banglamphu's Wat Chana Songkhram.

For advice on destinations further afield you need to visit the **Tourism Authority of Thailand** (**TAT**), which maintains a Tourist Service Centre within walking distance of Banglamphu, at 4 Rajdamnoen Nok (daily 8.30am–4.30pm; ☎02 283 1500 ext 1620; freephone tourist assistance 8am–8pm ☎1672, ⓦwww.tourismthailand.org), a twenty-minute stroll from Thanon Khao San, or a short ride in air-conditioned bus #503. TAT also has booths at Suvarnabhumi Airport, but its headquarters (daily 8.30am–4.30pm; ☎02 250 5500) is out at 1600 Thanon Phetchaburi Mai, 350m west of the junction with Sukhumvit Soi 21 and the Phetchaburi subway stop, or 150m east of the junction with Sukhumvit Soi 3 and Tha Nana Nua on the Khlong Saen Saeb canal boat service (see map, p.80). Note, however, that the many other shops and offices across the capital displaying "TAT Tourist Information" signs or similar are **not official Tourism Authority of Thailand centres** and will not be dispensing impartial advice: the Tourism Authority of Thailand never uses the acronym TAT on its office-fronts or in its logo.

To get around Bangkok on the cheap, you'll need to buy a **bus map**. Of the several available, the most useful and reliable is Bangkok Guide's *Bus Routes & Map*. For a far more personal guide to Bangkok's most interesting shops, markets, restaurants and back streets, look for the famously idiosyncratic hand-drawn **maps** *Nancy Chandler's Map of Bangkok* and *Nancy Chandler's Map of Khao San and Old Bangkok* (ⓦwww.nancychandler.net).

City transport

Transport can undoubtedly be a headache in a city where it's not unusual for residents to spend three hours getting to work – and these are people who know where they're going. However, the recent openings of the subway system and the elevated train network called the Bangkok Transit System, or BTS Skytrain, have radically improved movement in downtown areas of the city. Unfortunately for tourists, these systems do not stretch as far as Ratanakosin or Banglamphu, where boats still provide the best means of hopping from one sight to another.

The main form of transport in the city is **buses**, and once you've mastered the labyrinthine complexity of the route maps you'll be able to get to any part of the city, albeit slowly. Catching the various kinds of **taxi** is more expensive, and you'll still get held up by the daytime traffic jams. **Boats** are obviously more limited in their range, but they're regular and as cheap as buses, and you'll save a lot of time by using them whenever possible – a journey between Banglamphu and the GPO, for instance, will take around thirty minutes by water, half what it would usually take on land. The **Skytrain** and **subway** each have a similarly limited range but are also worth using whenever suitable for all or part of your journey; their networks roughly coincide with each other at the east end of Thanon Silom, at the corner of Soi Asoke and Thanon Sukhumvit, and on Thanon Phaholyothin by Chatuchak Park (Mo Chit), while the Skytrain joins up with the Chao Phraya River express boats at the vital hub of Sathorn/Saphan Taksin (Taksin Bridge). **Walking** might often be quicker than travelling by road, but the heat can be unbearable, pavements are poorly maintained and the engine fumes are stifling.

Buses

Bangkok is served by over four hundred bus routes, reputedly the world's largest bus network, on which operate two main types of bus service (though

Tours of the city

The Bangkok Metropolitan Administration tourist office (see p.84) runs year-round **tours** of the city's historic centre in a "tram" (more like an open-sided bus), which covers a forty-minute circuit from the Grand Palace down to Wat Pho, up to Banglamphu, and back to the palace (daily 9am–5pm, every 45min; B30). From mid-December to mid-January, the same office has in previous years offered night-time tours by bicycle or open-topped double-decker bus, and may do so in future years, too. As part of the BMA's greening of the city, it's also possible to pick up bicycles and maps from this office, and seven other locations in and around Ratanakosin, for a self-guided tour along clearly marked cycle lanes (Aug–April Mon–Fri 10am–6pm, Sat & Sun 10am–8pm; free, passport required as deposit); unfortunately, local drivers tend to block or ignore the lanes, which makes the prospect a lot less enticing. Real Asia (℡02 665 6364, 🅦www.realasia.net) does full-day canal and walking tours through Thonburi and leads outings by train to the historic fishing port of Samut Sakhon (both B2000, including lunch and boat trips).

Unlikely as it sounds, there are several companies offering **cycle tours** of the city's outer neighbourhoods and beyond; these are an excellent way to gain a different perspective on Thai life and offer a unique chance to see traditional communities close up. The most popular, longest-running bicycle tours are the ABC Amazing Bangkok Cyclist Tours, which start in the Thanon Sukhumvit area and take you across the river to surprisingly rural khlong- and riverside communities; tours operate every day year-round, cover up to 30km depending on the itinerary, and need to be reserved in advance through Real Asia (see above; B1000–2000 including bicycle). Bangkok Bike Rides (℡02 712 5305, 🅦www.bangkokbikerides.com or www.spiceroads.com; B1000–2500 per person, minimum two people) also operates from the Sukhumvit area and runs a programme of different daily tours within Greater Bangkok, including Ko Kred, as well as to the floating markets and canalside neighbourhoods of Damnoen Saduak. Velo Thailand runs two different bike tours out of its cycle shop at 88 Thanon Samsen Soi 2 on the edge of Banglamphu (℡02 629 1745, 🅦www.velothailand.com). The 1pm tour goes to Thonburi (3–4hr; B1000), while the after-dark tour (6–9pm; B1100) takes in floodlit sights including Wat Pho, Wat Arun and the Pak Khlong Talat flower market.

For details of Thonburi canal tours, see p.129, and for Chao Phraya Express tourist boats, see p.88.

controversial plans, opposed by the transport unions and poorer commuters, to do away with non-air-con services are under discussion). On **ordinary** (non-air-con) buses, which are either red and white, blue and white, or small and green, fares range from B7 to B8.50; most routes operate from about 4am to 10pm, but some maintain a 24-hour service (see box, p.88). **Air-conditioned** buses are generally either blue, orange or white (some are articulated) and charge between B12 and B25 according to distance travelled; most stop in the late evening, but a few of the more popular routes run 24-hour services. As buses can only go as fast as the car in front, which at the moment is averaging 4km per hour, you'll probably be spending a long time on each journey, so you'd be well advised to pay the extra for cool air – and the air-conditioned buses are usually less crowded, too.

Some of the most useful city-bus routes are described in the box on p.88; for a comprehensive roundup of bus routes in the capital, buy a copy of Bangkok Guide's *Bus Routes & Map* (see p.85), or log onto the Bangkok Mass Transit Authority website (🅦www.bmta.co.th), which gives details of all city-bus routes, bar airport buses.

Boats

Bangkok was built as an amphibious city around a network of canals – or **khlongs** – and the first streets were constructed only in the second half of the nineteenth century. Many canals remain on the Thonburi side of the river, but most of those on the Bangkok side have been turned into roads. The Chao Phraya River itself is still a major transport route for residents and non-residents alike, forming more of a link than a barrier between the two halves of the city.

Express boats

The Chao Phraya Express Boat Company operates the vital **express-boat** (*reua duan*; ⓦ www.chaophrayaboat.co.th) services, using large water buses to plough up and down the river, between clearly signed piers (*tha*), which appear on all Bangkok maps. Tha Sathorn, which gives access to the Skytrain network at Saphan Taksin Station, has been designated "Central Pier", with piers to the south of here numbered S1, S2, etc, those to the north N1, N2 and so on – the important stops in the centre of the city are outlined in the box below and marked on our city map (see p.80). In future, express-boat services may be extended downriver to Samut Prakan.

No-flag, local-line boats call at every pier between Wat Rajsingkorn, just upriver of Krung Thep Bridge, in the south, and Nonthaburi, ninety minutes away to the north, but only operate during rush hour (Mon–Fri roughly 6–8.40am & 3–6pm, every 20min). Boats do not necessarily stop at every landing – they only pull in if people want to get on or off, and when they do stop, it's not for long – so when you want to get off, be ready at the back of the

---

Central stops for the Chao Phraya express boats

N15 Thewet (all boats except blue flag) – for Thewet guest houses.

N14 Rama VIII Bridge (no flag) – for Samsen Soi 5.

N13 Phra Arthit (no flag and orange flag) – for Thanon Phra Arthit, Thanon Khao San and Banglamphu guest houses.

N12 Phra Pinklao Bridge (all boats except blue flag) – for Royal Barge Museum and Thonburi shops.

N11 Thonburi Railway Station (or Bangkok Noi; no flag) – for trains to Kanchanaburi.

N10 Wang Lang (aka Siriraj or Prannok; all boats) – for Siriraj Hospital and hospital museums.

N9 Chang (no flag and orange flag) – for the Grand Palace, Sanam Luang and the National Museum.

N8 Thien (no flag and orange flag) – for Wat Pho, and the cross-river ferry to Wat Arun.

N7 Ratchini (aka Rajinee; no flag).

N6 Saphan Phut (Memorial Bridge; no flag and orange flag) – for Pahurat, Pak Khlong Talat and Wat Prayoon.

N5 Rachawongse (aka Rajawong; all boats except blue flag) – for Chinatown.

N4 Harbour (Marine) Department (no flag and orange flag).

N3 Si Phraya (all boats except blue flag) – walk north past the *Sheraton Royal Orchid Hotel* for River City shopping complex, head south for the GPO.

N2 Wat Muang Kae (no flag) – for the GPO.

N1 Oriental (no flag and orange flag) – for Thanon Silom.

Central Sathorn (all boats) – for the Skytrain (Saphan Taksin Station) and Thanon Sathorn.

Useful bus routes

For buses from Suvarnabhumi Airport, see p.79; for more details on Banglamphu bus stops and routes, see p.96.

#3 (ordinary and air-con, 24hr): **Northern Bus Terminal**–Chatuchak Weekend Market–Thanon Phaholyothin–Thanon Samsen–Thanon Phra Arthit (for **Banglamphu guest houses**)–Thanon Sanam Chai (for **Museum of Siam**)–Thanon Triphet–Memorial Bridge (for **Pak Khlong Talat**)–Taksin Monument (for **Wongwian Yai**) –Wat Suwan.

#15 (ordinary): Thanon Ratchadaphisek–Krung Thep Bridge–Thanon Charoen Krung–Thanon Silom–Thanon Rajdamri–**Siam Square**–Thanon Lan Luang–Sanam Luang–Thanon Phra Arthit (for **Banglamphu guest houses**).

#16 (ordinary and air-con): Thanon Srinarong–Thanon Samsen–**Thewet** (for guest houses)–Thanon Phitsanulok–Thanon Phrayathai–**Siam Square**–Thanon Suriwong.

#25 (ordinary and air-con, 24hr): Pak Nam (for **Ancient City** buses)–Thanon Sukhumvit–**Eastern Bus Terminal**–Siam Square–**Hualamphong Station**–Thanon Yaowarat (for **Chinatown**)–Pahurat–**Wat Pho**–Tha Chang (for the **Grand Palace**); some #25 buses (ordinary only) only go as far as Hualamphong Station, while during rush hours some #25 buses take the expressway, missing out Siam Square.

#53 circular (also anti-clockwise; ordinary): Thewet–Thanon Krung Kasem–**Hualamphong Station**–Thanon Yaowarat (for **Chinatown**)–Pahurat–Pak Khlong Talat–Thanon Maharat (for **Wat Pho** and the **Grand Palace**)–Sanam Luang (for **National Museum**)–Thanon Phra Arthit and Thanon Samsen (for **Banglamphu guest houses**)–Thewet.

#56 circular (also clockwise; ordinary, stops at 7pm): Thanon Phra Sumen–Wat Bowoniwes–Thanon Pracha Thipatai–Thanon Ratchasima (for **Vimanmek Palace**)–Thanon Rajwithi–Krung Thon Bridge–Thonburi–Phrapokklao Bridge–Thanon Chakraphet (for **Chinatown**)–Thanon Mahachai–Democracy Monument–Thanon Tanao (for **Khao San guest houses**)–Thanon Phra Sumen.

#124 (ordinary): Sanam Luang–Thanon Rajinee, near Information Centre (for **Banglamphu guest houses**)–Phra Pinklao Bridge–**Southern Bus Terminal**–Mahidol University.

boat in good time for your pier. The only boats to run all day, every day are on the limited-stop **orange-flag** service (Nonthaburi to Wat Rajsingkorn in 1hr; roughly 6am–6.40pm, every 5–20min). Other limited-stop services run during rush hour, flying either a **yellow flag** (Nonthaburi to Tha Sathorn or Rajburana, far downriver beyond Krung Thep Bridge, in about 50min; Mon–Fri roughly 6–8.40am & 4–7pm), a **blue flag** (Nonthaburi to Tha Sathorn Mon–Fri 7–7.45am, Tha Sathorn to Nonthaburi Mon–Fri 5–6.25pm, stopping only at Wang Lang; 35min), or a **green-and-yellow flag** (Pakkred to Tha Sathorn Mon–Fri 6.15–8.05am, Tha Sathorn to Pakkred Mon–Fri 4.05–6.05pm; about 50min).

Tickets can be bought on board, and cost B9–13 on no-flag boats according to distance travelled, B14 flat rate on orange-flag boats, B19–28 on yellow-flag boats, B19–29 on blue-flag boats and B12–31 on green-and-yellow flag boats. Don't discard your ticket until you're off the boat, as the staff at some piers impose a B1 fine on anyone disembarking without one.

The Chao Phraya Express Boat Company also runs **tourist boats**, distinguished by their light-blue flags, between Sathorn (departs every 30min 9.30am–3pm on the hour and half-hour) and Phra Arthit piers (departs every 30min 10am–3.30pm on the hour and half-hour). In between (in both directions), these boats call in at Oriental, Si Phraya, Rachawongse, Saphan Phut, Thien, Maharat (near Wat Mahathat and the Grand Palace) and Wang Lang. On-board guides provide

#159 (ordinary): **Southern Bus Terminal**–Phra Pinklao Bridge–Democracy Monument–**Hualamphong Station**–MBK Shopping Centre–Thanon Ratchaprarop–Victory Monument–Chatuchak Weekend Market–**Northern Bus Terminal**.

#503 (air-con): Sanam Luang–Democracy Monument (for **Banglamphu guest houses**)–Thanon Rajdamnoen Nok (for **TAT** and **boxing stadium**)–Wat Benjamabophit–Thanon Sri Ayutthaya (for **Thewet guest houses**)–Victory Monument–**Chatuchak Weekend Market**–Rangsit. Note, however, that during rush hours, some #503 buses take the expressway, missing out Chatuchak Weekend Market.

#507 (air-con): **Southern Bus Terminal**–Phra Pinklao Bridge (for **Banglamphu guest houses**)–Sanam Luang–Thanon Charoen Krung (New Road)–Thanon Chakraphet–Thanon Yaowarat (for **Chinatown** and **Wat Traimit**)–**Hualamphong Station**–Thanon Rama IV–Bang Na Intersection–Pak Nam (for **Ancient City** buses).

#508 (air-con): Thanon Maharat–**Grand Palace**–Thanon Charoen Krung–Siam Square–Thanon Sukhumvit–**Eastern Bus Terminal**–Pak Nam (for **Ancient City** buses). Note, however, that during rush hours, some #508 buses take the expressway, missing out the Eastern Bus Terminal.

#509 (air-con): **Northern Bus Terminal**–Chatuchak Weekend Market–Victory Monument–Thanon Rajwithi–Thanon Sawankhalok–Thanon Phitsanulok–Thanon Rajdamnoen Nok (for **TAT** and **boxing stadium**)–Democracy Monument–Thanon Rajdamnoen Klang (for **Banglamphu guest houses**)–Phra Pinklao Bridge–Thonburi.

#511 (air-con, 24hr): **Southern Bus Terminal**–Phra Pinklao Bridge (for **Banglamphu guest houses**)–Democracy Monument–Thanon Lan Luang–Thanon Phetchaburi–Thanon Sukhumvit–**Eastern Bus Terminal**–Pak Nam (for **Ancient City** buses). Note, however, that between 4.30am and 8.30pm, some #511 buses take the expressway, missing out the Eastern Bus Terminal.

#512 (air-con): **Northern Bus Terminal**–Chatuchak Weekend Market–Thanon Phetchaburi–Thanon Lan Luang–Democracy Monument (for **Banglamphu guest houses**)–Sanam Luang–Tha Chang (for **Grand Palace**)–Pak Khlong Talat.

running commentaries, and a one-day ticket for unlimited trips, which also allows you to use other express boats within the same route on the same day, costs B150; one-way tickets are also available, costing, for example, B19 from Phra Arthit to Oriental.

Cross-river ferries

Smaller than express boats are the slow **cross-river ferries** (*reua kham fak*), which shuttle back and forth between the same two points. Found at or beside every express-boat stop and plenty of other piers in between, they are especially useful for exploring Thonburi. Fares are generally B3, payable at the entrance to the pier.

Canal boats

Longtail boats (*reua hang yao*) ply the **canals** of Thonburi like commuter buses, stopping at designated shelters (fares are in line with those of express boats), and are available for individual rental here and on the river (see box, p.129). On the Bangkok side, **Khlong Saen Saeb** is well served by passenger boats, which run at least every fifteen minutes during daylight hours from the Phan Fah pier at the Golden Mount (handy for Banglamphu, Ratanakosin and Chinatown), and head way out east to Wat Sribunruang, with useful stops at Thanon Phrayathai, aka Saphan Hua Chang (for Jim Thompson's House and Ratchathevi Skytrain stop); Pratunam (for the Erawan Shrine); Thanon Witthayu (Wireless Rd); and

▲ Canal boat on Khlong Saen Saeb

Soi Nana Nua (Soi 3), Thanon Asok Montri (Soi 21, for TAT headquarters and Phetchaburi subway stop), Soi Thonglo (Soi 55) and Soi Ekamai (Soi 63), all off Thanon Sukhumvit. This is your quickest and most interesting way of getting between the west and east parts of town, if you can stand the stench of the canal. You may have trouble actually locating the piers as few are signed in English and they all look very unassuming and rickety; see the map on p.80 for locations and keep your eyes peeled for a plain wooden jetty – most jetties serve boats running in both directions. Once on the boat, state your destination to the conductor when he collects your fare, which will be between B10 and B24. Due to the construction of some low bridges, all passengers change onto a different boat at Tha Pratunam – just follow the crowd.

The Skytrain

Although its network is limited, the **BTS Skytrain**, or *rot fai faa* (ⓦ www.bts .co.th), provides a much faster alternative to the bus, and is clean, efficient and vigorously air-conditioned. There are only two Skytrain lines, which interconnect at Siam Square (**Central Station**). Both run every few minutes from around 6am to midnight, with **fares** of B15–40 per trip depending on distance travelled. You buy tickets from machines that accept only coins, but you can change notes at staffed counters. You'd really have to be motoring to justify buying a day **pass** at B120, while the twenty-trip, thirty-trip and forty-trip cards, for B440, B600 and B800 respectively (valid for thirty days), are designed for long-distance commuters.

The **Sukhumvit Line** runs from Mo Chit (stop N8) in the northern part of the city to On Nut (Soi 77, Thanon Sukhumvit; E9) in around thirty minutes, though there are plans to extend the line eastward towards Samrong. The **Silom Line** runs from the National Stadium (W1), via Saphan Taksin (Taksin, or Sathorn, Bridge; S6) where it links up with express boats on the Chao Phraya River, to Wongwian Yai (S8) in Thonburi (an eventual continuation to Thanon Phetkasem is planned).

The subway

Bangkok's underground rail system, the **MRT subway** (or metro; in Thai, *rot fai tai din*; ⓦwww.bangkokmetro.co.th), has similar advantages to the Skytrain, though its current single line connects few places of interest for visitors. It runs every few minutes between around 6am and midnight from Hualamphong train station, via Silom (near Sala Daeng Skytrain station), Sukhumvit (near Asoke Skytrain) and Chatuchak Park (near Mo Chit Skytrain), to Bang Sue train station in the north of the city. Plans are afoot to continue the line westwards from Hualamphong along Thanon Charoen Krung, then across to Thonburi, finally completing a loop back to Bang Sue. Pay your **fare** of between B15 and B39 at a staffed counter or machine, where you'll receive a token to put through an entrance gate (the various day passes and stored-value cards available are unlikely to be worthwhile for visitors).

Taxis

Bangkok **taxis** come in three forms, and are so plentiful that you rarely have to wait more than a couple of minutes before spotting an empty one of any description. Neither tuk-tuks nor motorbike taxis have meters, so you should agree on a price before setting off, and expect to do a fair amount of haggling.

For nearly all journeys, the best and most comfortable option is to flag down one of Bangkok's metered, air-conditioned **taxi cabs**; look out for the "TAXI METER" sign on the roof, and a red light in the windscreen in front of the passenger seat, which means the cab is available for hire. Starting at B35, fares are displayed on a clearly visible meter that the driver should reset at the start of each trip (say "*poet meter, dai mai khrap/kha?*" to ask him to switch it on), and increase in stages on a combined distance/time formula; as an example, a medium-range journey from Thanon Ploenchit to Thanon Sathorn will cost around B50 at a quiet time of day. Try to have change with you as cabs tend not to carry a lot of money; tipping of up to ten percent is common, though occasionally a cabbie will round down the fare on the meter. If a driver tries to quote a flat fare rather than using the meter, let him go, and avoid the now-rare unmetered cabs (denoted by a "TAXI" sign on the roof). Getting a metered taxi in the middle of the afternoon when the cars return to base for a change of drivers can sometimes be a problem; if you want to book a metered taxi (B20 surcharge), call Siam Taxi Co-operative on ☏1661 or Taxi Radio on ☏1681.

Somewhat less stable though typically Thai, **tuk-tuks** have very little to recommend them. These noisy, three-wheeled, open-sided buggies, which can carry three medium-sized passengers comfortably, fully expose you to the worst of Bangkok's pollution and weather. Locals might use tuk-tuks for short journeys – though you'll have to bargain hard to get a fare lower than the taxi-cab flagfall of B35 – while for a longer trip from Thanon Convent to Siam Square, for example, drivers will ask for as much as B200. Be aware, also, that tuk-tuk drivers tend to speak less English than taxi drivers – and there have been cases of robberies and attacks on women passengers late at night. During the day it's quite common for tuk-tuk drivers to try and **con** their passengers into visiting a jewellery, tailor's or expensive souvenir shop with them, for which they get a hefty commission; the usual tactic involves falsely informing tourists that the Grand Palace, or whatever their destination might be, is closed (see p.108), and offering instead a ridiculously cheap, even free, city tour.

Motorbike taxis generally congregate at the entrances to long sois – pick the riders out by their numbered, coloured vests – and charge around B10 for short trips down into the side streets. If you're short on time and have nerves of steel, it's also possible to charter them for hairy journeys out on the main roads (a trip from Thanon Convent to Siam Square will cost around B80). Crash helmets are compulsory on all main roads in the capital (traffic police fine non-wearers on the spot), though they're rarely worn on trips down the sois and the local press has reported complaints from people who've caught head-lice this way (they suggest wearing a headscarf under the helmet).

Accommodation

If your time in Bangkok is limited, you should think especially carefully about what you want to do in the city before deciding which part of town to stay in. Traffic jams are so appalling here that easy access to Skytrain, subway or river transport can be crucial. Advance reservations are recommended where possible during high season (Nov–Feb), though some guest houses will only take cash deposits.

For ultra-cheap double rooms under B400, your widest choice lies with the no-frills guest houses on and around **Banglamphu**'s Thanon Khao San, though there are plenty of well-appointed mid-priced options here too, with air-con and swimming pools. Other, far smaller and less interesting travellers' ghettoes that might be worth bearing in mind are the generally dingy **Soi Ngam Duphli**, off the south side of Thanon Rama IV, which nevertheless harbours a couple of decent shoestring options, as well as mid-range and expensive rooms; and **Soi Kasemsan I**, which is very handily placed next to Siam Square and firmly occupies the moderate range, averaging B700 for a double, though with a few rooms for B500. Otherwise, the majority of the city's moderate and expensive rooms are scattered widely across the **downtown areas**, around Siam Square and Thanon Ploenchit, to the south of Thanon Rama IV and along **Thanon Sukhumvit**, and to a lesser extent in **Chinatown**. As well as easy access to transport links and shops, the downtown views from accommodation in these areas are a real plus, especially from the deluxe hotels that are scenically sited along the banks of the Chao Phraya River.

For accommodation **near Suvarnabhumi Airport** see p.82, though the eastern Sukhumvit hotels (see p.106) are also worth considering.

Banglamphu

Nearly all backpackers head straight for **Banglamphu**, Bangkok's long-established travellers' ghetto, location of the cheapest accommodation and some of the best nightlife in the city, and arguably the most enjoyable area to base yourself in the city. It's within easy reach of the Grand Palace and has enough bars, restaurants and shops to keep any visitor happy for a week or more, though some people find this insularity tiresome after just a few hours.

At the heart of Banglamphu is the legendary **Thanon Khao San** (@www.khaosanroad.com), almost a caricature of a travellers' centre, crammed with internet cafés and dodgy travel agents, the sidewalks lined with cheap backpackers' fashions, racks of bootleg PlayStation games, tattooists and hair-braiders. It's a lively, high-energy base: great for shopping and making travel arrangements (though beware the innumerable Khao San scams; see p.50), and a good place to meet other travellers. It's especially fun at night when young Thais from all over the city gather here to browse the clothes stalls, mingle with the crowds of foreigners and squash into the bars and clubs that have made Khao San *the* place to party.

The cheapest sleeps are concentrated in the lanes immediately west of Khao San, around the neighbourhood temple **Wat Chana Songkhram**, and along riverside **Thanon Phra Arthit**, where you'll also find some upscale places offering prime views over the Chao Phraya. About ten minutes' walk north from Thanon Khao San, the guest houses along the **Thanon Samsen sois** enjoy a more authentically Thai environment, while the **Thewet** area, a further fifteen minutes' walk in the same direction or a seven-minute walk from the Thewet express-boat stop, is more local still.

We've listed only the cream of the options in each small enclave of Banglamphu: if your first choice is full there will almost certainly be a vacancy somewhere just along the soi, if not right next door. **Theft** is a problem in Banglamphu, particularly at the cheaper guest houses, so don't leave anything valuable in your room and heed the guest houses' notices about padlocks and safety lockers. Traveller-oriented **facilities** in Banglamphu are second to none and include a clinic, numerous travel agents, and internet, mail, laundry and phone services; for details see pp.166–169.

ACCOMMODATION

Bella Bella House	H
Buddy Lodge	Q
D & D Inn	P
KC Guest House	F
Khao San Palace Hotel	N
Lamphu Treehouse	K
Lek House	M
Live Good	L
Merry V	G
Navalai River Resort	D
New Siam 2	J
Old Bangkok Inn	S
Peachy Guest House	I
Phra Nakorn Norn Len	C
Sawatdee Guest House	A
Siam Oriental	R
Sri Ayutthaya	B
Vimol Guest House	E
Wally House	O

EATING, DRINKING & NIGHTLIFE

Ad Here the 13th	5
Aquatini	D
Bangkok Bar	8
Bar Bali	7
Brick Bar	16
Café Democ	18
The Club	15
Gulliver's Traveler's Tavern	10
Hemlock	7
Hippie de Bar	11
Kai Yang Boran	19
Kaloang	1
Kinlom Chom Saphan	2
Lotash Seed	9
May Kaidee	17
May Kaidee 2	4
Nattaporn	21
Padthai Thipsamai	20
Popaing	6
Prakorb House	13
Roti Mataba	3
Susie Pub	14
Tom Yam Kung	12

▲ Sukhumvit

0   200 m

★ Khlong Saen Saeb stop

LAN LUANG

King Prajadhipok (Rama VII) Museum

Tha Phan Fah

Khlong Saen Saeb

Tha Damrong Rak

Golden Mount & Wat Saket

THANON BORIPHAT

Mahakhan Fort Community

Khlong Ong Ang

THANON MAHACHAI

Ⓢ Queen's Gallery

Loh Prasat

Wat Rajnadda

⑳

RAJDAMNOEN KLANG

THANON PRACHA THIPATAI

Ⓚ

THANON DINSO

Democracy Monument

McDonald's

City Hall

Sao Ching Cha

Wat Suthat

THANON DINSO

THANON BAMRUNG MUANG

RAJDAMNOEN NOK

RAJDAMNOEN KLANG

THANON MAHANNOP

⑱

Rim Khob Fa Books

Bus stop 8

October 14 Memorial

Aporia

Ratchadamnoen P.O.

THANON TANAO

Wat Bowoniwes

THANON PHRA SUMEN

Tori's Books

Ⓛ

⑰

Chang Toin

DAMNOEN KLANG NEUA

SOI DAMNOEN KLANG TAI

THANON TANAO

TROK SIN

Chao Poh Seua

⑲

Temple Supplies

TROK NAWA

SOI SIDSAK

HANG KRABUE

THANON BOWONNIWES

Banglamphubon P.O.

Night Market

Ⓙ ⑨

Viengtai Hotel

⑭

THANON RAM BHUTTRI

⑯

Ⓜ Ⓝ Ⓞ

THANON KHAO SAN

ETC

Ⓞ Ⓟ

K.S. Center

RAJDAMNOEN KLANG

BUNSRI

DAMNOEN KLANG NEUA

THANON TANAO

THANON BURANASIT

THANON PHRAENG PHUTON

PHRAENG PHUTON

THANON KANLAYANA MAITRI

▶ Wat Rajabophit

Ⓑ Bus stop 4

TROK KRAISI

THANON CHAKRABONGSE

Police Station

Ⓘ

Sor Vorapin's Gym

Bus stop 6

⑬⑮ ⑫⑪⑩

True

TROK MAYOM

Bus stop 7

★ Minibuses to Kanchanaburi

Royal Ratanakosin Hotel

THANON ATSADANG

Night Market

THANON BURANASIT

TROK SA-KE

THANON LAK MUANG

Lak Muang

Wat Chana Songkhram

Ⓗ

SOI RAM BHUTTRI

Ⓖ

TROK RONG MAI

THANON PHRA

National Gallery

CHAO FA

PINKLAO

RAJINEE

PHRA PINKLAO

Bangkok Tourism

Bus stop 5

National Theatre

National Museum

THANON PHRA CHAN

Sanam Luang

THANON NA PHRA THAT

THANON RAJDAMNOEN NAI

Wat Mahathat

N

BANGLAMPHU

95

Banglamphu's bus stops and routes

Buses running out of Banglamphu have many different pick-up points in the area: to make things simpler, we've assigned numbers to these **bus stops**, though they are not numbered on the ground. Where there are two bus stops on the same route they share a number. Bus stops are marked on the Banglamphu map on p.94. For a more detailed breakdown of Bangkok's bus routes see p.88.

Bus stop 1: Thanon Krung Kasem, north side
#53 to Hualamphong train station (buses start from here)

Bus stop 2: Thanon Phra Arthit, south side, near *Hemlock*; and Thanon Phra Sumen, south side, near *Banglumpoo Place* hotel
#3 to the Museum of Siam, Pak Khlong Talat
#9 to Wat Pho, Pak Khlong Talat
#53 to the Grand Palace and Chinatown

Bus stop 3: Thanon Phra Arthit, north side, near *New Siam Riverside*; and Thanon Phra Sumen, north side, opposite *Banglumpoo Place* hotel
#3 to Chatuchak Weekend Market and Mo Chit Northern Bus Terminal
#53 to Hualamphong train station (change at Bus Stop 1, but same ticket)
#56 (from Phra Sumen stop only) to Thanon Ratchasima for Vimanmek Palace and Dusit

Bus stop 4: Thanon Chakrabongse, near the 7–Eleven
#15, to Jim Thompson's House, Siam Square, Thanon Silom and Patpong
#30 to the Southern Bus Terminal
#32 to Wat Pho

Banglamphu is served by plenty of **public transport**. Airport express bus #AE2 runs to Banglamphu **from Suvarnabhumi Airport** (see p.79) and has many drop-offs in the area but only one pick-up point, outside the *Mayompuri Restaurant* on Thanon Chakrabongse, about 50m from the west end of Thanon Khao San. Chao Phraya **express boat** stops N13 (Phra Arthit), N14 (Rama VIII Bridge) and N15 (Thewet), detailed in the box on p.87, are nearby. Banglamphu is also served by **public longtail boats** along Khlong Saen Saeb (see p.89), useful for Siam Square and the Skytrain. The other fast way to get on to the BTS system is to take a taxi from Banglamphu to BTS National Stadium. For a list of the most useful **buses** in and out of Banglamphu and where to catch them, see the box above. All Banglamphu accommodation is marked on the map on p.94.

Thanon Khao San and around

🏃 **Buddy Lodge** 265 Thanon Khao San
☎02 629 4477, ⓦwww.buddylodge.com.
The most stylish and expensive hotel on Khao San and right in the thick of the action. The charming, colonial-style rooms are done out in cream, with louvred shutters, balconies, air-con and polished dark-wood floors, though they aren't as pristine as you might expect for the price. There's a beautiful rooftop pool, a spa, in-room wi-fi and several bars and restaurants downstairs in the *Buddy Village* complex. Specify an upper-floor location away from Khao San to ensure a quieter night's sleep. ❼

D & D Inn 68–70 Thanon Khao San ☎02 629 0526, ⓦwww.khaosanby.com. The attractive seventh-floor rooftop pool, with expansive views (and wi-fi), is the clincher at this good-value, mid-sized hotel located in the midst of the throng. Rooms all have air-con and TV and are comfortably furnished and perfectly fine, if not immaculate. The cheapest single rooms don't have windows. ❹

Bus Stop 5: Thanon Rajinee (Rachini), near Bangkok Tourism Information Centre
#124 (non-air-con) to Southern Bus Terminal

Bus stop 6: Thanon Chakrabongse, outside the *Mayompuri Restaurant*
AE2 Airport Express to Suvarnabhumi Airport

Bus stop 7: Thanon Rajdamnoen Klang, north side, outside Lottery Building
#2 to Ekamai Eastern Bus Terminal
#47 to Jim Thompson's House, Thanon Silom and Patpong
#47, #79 to Siam Square
#59, #503 (air-con; non-expressway), #509 to Chatuchak Weekend Market
#47 to Lumphini boxing stadium
#59 to Don Muang Airport
#70, #201, #503, #509 to TAT and Ratchadamnoen boxing stadium
#70 (non-expressway) to Dusit
#157 (air-con) to Mo Chit Northern Bus Terminal
#159 (non-air-con) to Hualamphong train station
#511 to Ekamai Eastern Bus Terminal and Pak Nam (for Ancient City buses)

Bus stop 8: Thanon Rajdamnoen Klang, south side
#44, #512 to Sanam Luang, the Grand Palace and Wat Pho
#60, #512 to Pak Khlong Talat
#79 to Taling Chan weekend floating market
#159 (non-air-con), # 511 and #516 to Southern Bus Terminal

Khao San Palace Hotel 139 Thanon Khao San ☏ 02 282 0578. Clean and well-appointed hotel with a rooftop pool. All rooms have bathrooms and windows and some also have air-con and TV. The best rooms are in the new wing; they're nicely tiled and some have panoramic views, making them good value. Fan ❸ , air-con ❸ – ❹
Lek House 125 Thanon Khao San ☏ 02 281 8441. Classic old-style Khao San guest house, with twenty small, basic rooms, all with shared bathrooms and thin partition walls but thick mattresses. Less shabby than many others in the same price bracket and friendlier than most. Can get noisy at night as it's right next to the popular *Silk Bar*. ❶
Live Good East off Thanon Tanao ☏ 02 282 5092. Cheap and simple rooms in this friendly, back-alley guest house, just off the veggie restaurants soi, 1min from Khao San. Budget options have fans, wall views and shared bathrooms. En-suite fan rooms are larger and have outlooks of sorts. Shared bathroom ❶ , en suite ❷
Siam Oriental 190 Thanon Khao San ☏ 02 629 0312, ⓦ www.siamorientalgroup.com. Small hotel right in the middle of Thanon Khao San, offering slightly scruffy rooms in a cheery shade of mauve,

all with attached bathrooms and most with a window. Some rooms have air-con and a few also have balconies. ❷
Wally House 189/1–2 Thanon Khao San ☏ 02 282 7067. Small guest house behind the family restaurant, with very cheap, very small, bottom-budget fan rooms, some of them en suite. Set back from the road so quieter than many. ❶ – ❷

West: around Wat Chana Songkhram, Phra Arthit and the river

Bella Bella House Soi Ram Bhuttri ☏ 02 629 3090. The pastel-coloured rooms in this guest house are no frills but well priced and a few boast lovely views over Wat Chana Songkhram. The cheapest share bathrooms, and the most expensive have air-con. In-room wi-fi available throughout. Fan ❷ – ❸ , air-con ❸
KC Guest House 64 Trok Kai Chae, off Thanon Phra Sumen ☏ 02 282 0618, ⓦ www.kcguesthouse.com. Friendly, family-run little guest house with exceptionally clean, tiled-floor rooms, with and without private bathrooms and air-con, and a terrace eating area on the soi. Fan ❷ , air-con ❸

Merry V Soi Ram Bhuttri ☎02 282 9267. Large, efficiently run guest house offering some of the cheapest accommodation in Banglamphu. Bottom-end rooms are basic and small, many share bathrooms and it's pot luck whether you get a window or not. Better en suites and air-con versions are also available and there's a useful noticeboard in the downstairs restaurant. Fan ❶, en suite ❸, air-con ❸

Navalai River Resort 45/1 Thanon Phra Arthit ☎02 280 9955, ⓦwww.navalai.com. Style-conscious riverfront hotel, with an elegant rooftop pool, modishly furnished rooms, and river views from the most desirable. There's air-con, private balconies and wi-fi throughout and the excellent riverside *Aquatini* restaurant is at ground level (see p.143). ❼–❽

New Siam 2 50 Trok Rong Mai ☎02 282 2795, ⓦwww.newsiam.net. Very pleasant and wellrun small hotel whose en-suite fan and air-con rooms stand out for their thoughtfully designed extras such as in-room safes, cable TV and drying rails on the balconies. Occupies a quiet but convenient location and has a small streetside pool. Popular with families, and triple rooms are also available. ❹

Peachy Guest House 10 Thanon Phra Arthit ☎02 281 6471. Popular, good-value, very cheap, long-running Bangkok institution set round a small, late-night courtyard bar. Offers lots of clean, simple, wooden-floored rooms, most with shared bathrooms but some with air-con. Fan and shared bathroom ❶, air-con and shared bathroom ❶, air-con and bathroom ❸

North: Samsen sois and Thewet

Lamphu Treehouse 155 Saphan Wanchat, Thanon Phracha Thipatai ☎02 282 0991, ⓦwww.lamphutreehotel.com. Named after the *lamphu* trees (as in Banglamphu, "place with *lamphu* trees") that line the adjacent canal, this attractively turned-out mid-range guest house offers smart, modish air-con rooms, all with balconies and plenty of polished teakwood fittings. There's a pool, and wi-fi in the lobby. It's in a quiet neighbourhood but just a few minutes' walk from Democracy, Khao San and the river. ❺

Old Bangkok Inn 609 Thanon Phra Sumen ☎02 629 1787, ⓦwww.oldbangkokinn.com. This chic little boutique guest house has just ten air-con rooms, each of them individually styled in dark wood, with antique north-Thai partitions, Burmese doors, beds and ironwork lamps, plus elegant contemporary-accented bathrooms. All rooms have a PC with free broadband access, wi-fi and DVD player. Some also have a tiny private garden. A 10min walk from Khao San. ❽–❾

Phra Nakorn Norn Len 46 Thewet Soi 1, Thewet ☎02 628 8188, ⓦwww.phranakorn-nornlen.com. What was once a seedy short-time motel has been transformed into a bohemian haven with genuine eco-conscious and socially engaged sensibilities and a tangible fair-trade philosophy. Every one of the thirty comfortable, though not luxurious, rooms has been hand-painted to a different retro Thai design, and each has a platform bed, cute modern bathroom, balcony, CD player, wi-fi and air-con. The downstairs areas are filled with the owner's twentieth-century collectibles; the rooftop enjoys unrivalled views of Wat Indraviharn's huge standing Buddha and is partly given over to growing organic veg for the restaurant. ❼

Sawatdee Guest House 71 Soi 16, Thanon Sri Ayutthaya, Thewet ☎02 281 0757. Cheap and basic, but friendlier than many in the Thewet area, this long-running old-style guest house offers basic no-frills fan rooms with partition walls, either with or without private bathroom. ❷–❸

Sri Ayutthaya 23/11 Soi 14, Thanon Sri Ayutthaya, Thewet ☎02 282 5942. The most attractive guest house in Thewet, where the good-sized rooms (choose between fan rooms with or without private bathroom and en suites with air-con) are elegantly done out with wood-panelled walls and beautiful polished wood floors. ❸–❹

Vimol Guest House 358 Samsen Soi 4 ☎02 281 4615. Old-style, family-run guest house in a quiet but interesting neighbourhood that has just a smattering of other tourist places. The simple, cramped, hardboard-walled rooms are ultra basic and have shared bathrooms but are possibly the cheapest in Banglamphu. ❶

Ratanakosin

Several small, upmarket hotels have recently opened on the west side of Ratanakosin, which put you in a peerless location, in a quiet, traditional, heavily Chinese neighbourhood of low-rise shophouses, overlooking the river and on the doorsteps of Wat Pho and the Grand Palace. Furthermore, the restaurants and nightlife of Banglamphu are within walking distance if you fancy a bit more of a buzz, while the sights of Thonburi, Chinatown, and Saphan Taksin Skytrain station are just a public boat ride away. All accommodation listed below is marked on the map on p.109.

Arun Residence 36 Soi Pratu Nokyung, Thanon Maharat ☏02 221 9158, ⒲www.arunresidence .com. Stunning views of Wat Arun and charming, wooden-floored rooms that mix traditional and contemporary Thai styles. Occupying an eccentrically converted shophouse (plumbing can sometimes be a problem), the hotel also has a library with internet access, a rooftop bar and a good European and Thai restaurant, *The Deck*, where breakfast (included in the price) is served. ❽

Aurum: The River Place 394/27–29 Soi Pansook, Thanon Maharat ☏02 622 2248, ⒲www.aurum -bangkok.com. Modelled on a French townhouse, with wooden shutters and wrought-iron balconies, this spruce, four-storey hotel is set back slightly from the river but offers views of the water from most bedrooms. Splashed with colourful Thai fabrics and sporting heavily varnished wooden floors, the well-equipped rooms are a little on the small side, apart from those on the top floor. There's a daytime riverside café, *The Coffee Place*, where complimentary breakfast is served. ❽

Chakrabongse Villas 396 Thanon Maharat ☏02 224 6686, ⒲www.thaivillas.com. Riverside luxury accommodation with a difference: in the luxuriant gardens of hundred-year-old Chakrabongse House overlooking Wat Arun, four tranquil villas beautifully furnished in dark wood and silk, with polished teak floors. All have air-con and cable TV, and there's a small, attractive swimming pool and an open-sided riverfront pavilion for relaxing or dining (if ordered in advance). ❾

Chinatown and Hualamphong Station area

Not far from the Ratanakosin sights, and within fifteen minutes' walk of Siam Square, **Chinatown** (**Sampeng**) is among the most frantic and fume-choked parts of Bangkok – and there's quite some competition. If you're in the mood, however, it's got plenty of interest, sees barely any Western overnighters, and is also very handy for **Hualamphong Station**.

Hualamphong is on the **subway** system, and Chinatown is served by a number of useful **bus** routes (see box, p.88). All accommodation listed below is marked on the map on p.125.

Baan Hualamphong 336/20 Soi Chalong Krung ☏02 639 8054, ⒲www.baanhualampong.com. This once strikingly stylish, now slightly faded wooden guest house is still the most welcoming in the soi, not least for its traveller-friendly vibe. There are big, bright, double rooms plus five-person dorms at B220 per bed, but all but one room share bathrooms. Has kitchen facilities, inviting lounging areas and a small roof terrace, provides a left-luggage service and is open 24hr; 5min from Hualamphong. Fan ❸, air-con ❹

Bangkok Center 328 Thanon Rama IV ☏02 238 4848, ⒲www.bangkokcentrehotel.com. The most interesting thing about this otherwise rather mediocre, old-fashioned hotel is its location, a couple of steps from the subway's exit 4 and just across the road from the train station. Rooms are air-con and adequate for the price and there's a pool, restaurant and wi-fi throughout. ❻

FF Guest House 338/10 Trok La-O, off Thanon Rama IV ☏02 233 4168. Tiny, family-run guest house offering ten cheap, cell-like but perfectly acceptable wooden-floored fan rooms with shared bathrooms. No other facilities, nor much English spoken. A 5min walk from the train and subway stations. ❶

Shanghai Mansion 479 Thanon Yaowarat, next to *Scala* sharks fin restaurant ☏02 221 2121, ⒲www.shanghai-inn.com. The most design-conscious accommodation in Chinatown has embraced the modern Chinoiserie look with gusto. Rooms are prettily done out in silks, lacquer-look furniture and lanterns, featuring a lot of sumptuous reds and purples. There's barely any daylight in the hotel (only the noisy street-front suites have windows and views) but standard rooms are cosily isolated from the Chinatown frenzy and all have air-con, TV and free wi-fi. ❼–❽

The Train Inn 428 Thanon Rong Muang ☏02 215 3055, ⒲www.thetraininn.com. Just a couple of minutes' walk from Hualamphong's side exit off platform 3, and open 24hr, this is a decent, traveller-oriented choice for weary rail passengers. Rooms – "first", "second" and "third class" – mostly share bathrooms and can be a bit scruffy, but are all air-con and the majority are a reasonable size. ❸–❹

TT2 Guest House 516 Soi Kaeo Fa (formerly Soi Sawang and known to taxi drivers as such), off Thanon Maha Nakorn ☏02 236 2946,

Ⓔttguesthouse@hotmail.com. A long-running, traveller-friendly budget place, this guest house is clean and well run, has simple singles, doubles and triples, and stores left luggage at B15–20 a day. All rooms share bathrooms. Roughly a 15min walk from either Hualamphong or the N3 Si Phraya express-boat stop; from Hualamphong, cross Thanon Rama IV, then walk left for 250m, cross Thanon Maha Nakorn and walk down it for 275m as far as Soi Kaeo Fa, where you turn left and then first right. The guest house is opposite Wat Kaeo Jam Fa. No check-in between midnight and 5.30am. ❷

Siam Square, Thanon Ploenchit and northern downtown

Siam Square – not really a square, but a low-slung grid of streetwise fashion shops, cinemas and inexpensive restaurants between Thanon Phrayathai and Thanon Henri Dunant – and nearby **Thanon Ploenchit** are as central as Bangkok gets: all the accommodation listed here is within walking distance of a Skytrain station. On hand are the city's best shopping possibilities – notably the phalanx of malls along Thanon Rama I – and a wide choice of Thai and international restaurants and food courts. There's no ultra-cheap accommodation around here, but a few scaled-up guest houses complement the expensive hotels. Concentrated in their own small "ghetto" on **Soi Kasemsan 1**, which runs north off Thanon Rama I, between the Bangkok Metropolitan Art Museum and Jim Thompson's House, these offer typical travellers' facilities and basic hotel comforts – air-conditioning and en-suite hot-water bathrooms – at moderate prices; the Khlong Saen Saeb canal-boat pier, Tha Saphan Hua Chang (easily accessed via Thanon Phrayathai), is especially handy for heading west to the Golden Mount and beyond, to Ratanakosin. All accommodation listed below is marked on the map opposite, unless otherwise stated.

Inexpensive and moderate

A-One Inn 25/13 Soi Kasemsan 1, Thanon Rama I ☎02 215 3029 or 02 216 4770, ⓦwww.aoneinn .com. The original upscale guest house, and still justifiably popular, with a 24hr Internet café, wi-fi and a reliable left-luggage room. Bedrooms all have satellite TV and come in a variety of sizes, including family rooms; discounts for longer stays. ❹

The Bed & Breakfast 36/42 Soi Kasemsan 1, Thanon Rama I ☎02 215 3004, Ⓕ02 215 2493. Bright, clean and family-run, though some of the rooms – carpeted and with en-suite telephones – are a bit cramped. As the name suggests, a simple breakfast – coffee, toast and fruit – is included. ❹

Golden House (VIP Guest House) 1025/5–9 Thanon Ploenchit ☎02 252 9535–7, ⓦwww .goldenhouses.net. Very clean and welcoming, small hotel in a peerless location. The plain but attractive, parquet-floored bedrooms are equipped with air-con, hot water, cable TV, free wi-fi and mini-bar – ask for one of the three larger front rooms with bay windows, which leave just enough space for a couple of armchairs. Breakfast included. Weekly and monthly discounts available. ❻

Jim's Lodge 125/7 Soi Ruam Rudee, Thanon Ploenchit ☎02 255 3100, ⓦwww.jimslodge.com. In a relatively peaceful residential area, with friendly and helpful staff; offers international standards, including satellite TV and mini-bars, on a smaller scale and at bargain prices; no swimming pool, but there is a roof garden with outdoor Jacuzzi. ❻

Reno Hotel 40 Soi Kasemsan 1, Thanon Rama I ☎02 215 0026–7, ⓦwww.renohotel.co.th. Friendly hotel, boasting large, comfortable, en-suite rooms with air-con, hot water, baths and TV (some with fridges), and a small swimming pool. Far more stylish than the bedrooms is the bar-restaurant, refurbished in contemporary Thai style, where breakfast is served (included in the price). Internet access. ❺

Wendy House 36/2 Soi Kasemsan 1, Thanon Rama I ☎02 214 1149–50, ⓦwww.wendyguest house.com. Friendly and well-run guest house, with smart, clean and comfortable rooms, all with fridge, cable TV and wi-fi access. Internet terminals in the ground-floor café, where breakfast (included in the price) is served. Discounted weekly rates. Internet bookings accepted. ❺

White Lodge 36/8 Soi Kasemsan 1, Thanon Rama I ☎02 216 8867 or 02 215 3041, Ⓕ02 216 8228. Cheapest guest house on the soi, with shining white cubicles and a lively, welcoming atmosphere – the best rooms, bright and quiet, are on the upper floors. ❸

EATING, DRINKING & NIGHTLIFE

Aoi	5
Bali	11
Brown Sugar	16
Club Culture	1
Curries & More	12
Food Loft	A
Genji	G
Gianni	15
Home Kitchen	9
Inter	10
Jim Thompson's Café	4
Mah Boon Krong food courts	8
Once upon a Time	3
Pisces	6
Polo Fried Chicken	17
Saxophone	2
Taling Pling	14
Thang Long	13
The Tunnel	5
Vanilla Brasserie	4
Zen	4

ACCOMMODATION

A-One Inn	D
The Bed & Breakfast	B
Courtyard by Marriott	I
Four Seasons	J
Golden House	K
Jim's Lodge	G
Pathumwan Princess Hotel	F
Reno Hotel	A
Swissôtel Nai Lert Park	L
Ten Face	C
Wendy House	E

DOWNTOWN: AROUND SIAM SQUARE & THANON PLOENCHIT

Expensive

Courtyard by Marriott 155/1 Soi Mahadlekluang 1, Thanon Rajdamri ☎02 690 1888, ⓦwww .courtyardbangkok.com. On a quiet, but very handy soi, this hotel offers most of the facilities of a five-star, but at more manageable prices. The modern design is seductive, gleaming white outside, candy colours and plenty of natural light inside, and there's a long, narrow, infinity pool, a fitness centre and reasonably priced massage rooms. ❽

Four Seasons 155 Thanon Rajdamri ☎02 250 1000, ⓦwww.fourseasons.com. The stately home of Bangkok's top hotels, formerly the *Regent*. Afternoon tea is still served in the monumental lobby, which is adorned with magnificent, vibrant eighteenth-century-style murals depicting the Thai cosmology, and flanked by acclaimed Thai, Italian and Japanese restaurants and a steakhouse. Large and luxurious rooms are decorated in warm Thai colours and dark wood, and there's an excellent concierge service. ❾

Pathumwan Princess Hotel 444 Thanon Phrayathai ☎02 216 3700, ⓦwww.pprincess.com. At the southern end of MBK Shopping Centre, affordable luxury (at the lower end of this price code) that's recently been refurbished in a crisp, modern style and is popular with families and businessmen. With Korean and Italian restaurants, a large, saltwater swimming pool with hot and cold Jacuzzis, a health spa and a huge fitness club. ❾

Reflections 224/2–9 (between sois 18 and 20; see map, p.91) Thanon Pradiphat ☎02 270 3344, ⓦwww.reflections-thai.com. Urban guerrilla meets kitsch at this idiosyncratic pop-art hotel, where every room was designed by a different artist. Browse the website to make your choice. The 36 rooms come in two sizes and all have air-con, a balcony or terrace, and in-room wi-fi, though few are luxurious. The location in an unfashionable neighbourhood is not great: it's a 10min walk south then west from BTS Saphan Kwai, but Chatuchak Weekend Market is only 20min away. There's a spa and art shop on site. ❼

Siam City Hotel 477 Thanon Sri Ayutthaya (see map, p.80) ☎02 247 0123, ⓦwww.siamhotels .com. Elegant, welcoming luxury hotel north of downtown (next to Phaya Thai Skytrain and Suan Pakkad). Choose between an "Ayutthaya" room, done out in sharp, modern Thai style, and a larger "Siam" room with a soothing, more traditional flavour. There's a spa, health club, swimming pool and a comprehensive array of restaurants including Chinese, Japanese and Italian. At the lower end of this price code. ❾

Swissôtel Nai Lert Park 2 Thanon Witthayu ☎02 253 0123, ⓦwww.swissotel .com. This welcoming, low-rise hotel is distinguished by its lushly beautiful gardens, overlooked by many of the chic and spacious, balconied bedrooms; set into the grounds are a landscaped swimming pool, tennis courts, squash court and popular spa and health club. Good deli-café, cool bar and Japanese (see p.145), French and Chinese restaurants. ❾

Ten Face 81 Soi 2, Soi Ruam Rudee ☎02 695 4242, ⓦwww.tenfacebangkok.com. The name comes from Totsagan, the ten-faced demon of the *Ramayama* (see p.111), and without being gimmicky, this place ingeniously combines sleek, contemporary design with striking artworks inspired by the national myth. All the rooms are spacious suites with espresso machines, free wi-fi, SIM cards and iPods, some with small kitchens; ask for a room at the back if you're worried about noise from the nearby expressway. There's a fusion restaurant, fitness centre, long, narrow "dipping" pool and shuttle service to Ploen Chit Skytrain, plus a special concierge, who DJs in the ultra-hip *Sita Bar* and dispenses the lowdown on Bangkok parties and happenings. ❾

Downtown: south of Thanon Rama IV

South of Thanon Rama IV, the area sometimes known as **Bangrak** contains a full cross-section of places to stay. Tucked away at its eastern edge and handy for Lumphini subway station, there are one or two decent, cheap guest houses in the small travellers' ghetto of **Soi Ngam Duphli** and nearby Soi Saphan Khu. Bangrak also hosts several good medium-range places, as well as the capital's biggest selection of top hotels, which are among the most opulent in the world. Traversed by the Skytrain, this area is especially good for eating and for gay and straight nightlife, mostly near the east end of **Thanon Silom** (around which several gay-friendly hotels are scattered), and has its fair share of interesting shops. Staying by the river itself in the atmospheric area around **Thanon Charoen Krung**, also known as **New Road**, has the added advantage of easy access to express boats. All accommodation listed opposite is marked on the maps on p.104 and p.80.

Inexpensive

ETC Guest House 5/3 Soi Ngam Duphli ☎02 287 1477–8, ⓦwww.etc.co.th. Above a branch of the recommended travel agent of the same name, and very handy for Thanon Rama IV, though consequently a little noisy. Helpful and very clean, catering mainly to Japanese travellers. Rooms come with fans and are further cooled by air-conditioning in the corridors; hot-water bathrooms are either shared or en suite. Breakfast is included and free internet and wi-fi are available. ❷

New Road Guest House 1216/1 Thanon Charoen Krung, between sois 34 and 36 ☎02 630 6994–8, ⓦwww.jysktravel.com. Thai headquarters of Danish backpacker travel agent and tour operator Jysk, offering a wide choice of accommodation around a courtyard off New Rd, as well as interesting canal (see p.129) and Thailand (see p.169) tours. There are ten-bunk dorms (with air-con planned) and basic bunk-bedded twins sharing bathrooms, as well as free hammocks on the roof. En-suite rooms, some with air-con and cable TV, sport attractive wooden floors, minibars, Thai decorative touches and well-equipped, hot-water bathrooms. Guests hang out in the restaurant, the sociable bar with pool table or the DVD room; internet access and free baggage storage are available, as well as showers for guests with an evening departure. Dorms from B90, fan ❷–❸, air-con ❺

Sala Thai Daily Mansion 15 Soi Saphan Khu ☎02 287 1436. The pick of the area, at the end of a quiet, shaded alley off Soi Saphan Khu, near Soi Sri Bamphen. A clean and efficiently run place, with bright, modern rooms with wall fans, sharing hot- and cold-water bathrooms, and a large, leafy roof garden. Good rates for single rooms. Fan ❸, air-con ❹

Moderate

Baan Saladaeng 69/2 Soi 3, Thanon Saladaeng ☎02 636 3038, ⓦwww .baansaladaeng.com. On a tiny, central alley, this chic designer guest house offers nine individually styled rooms, such as the Pop Art Mania Room and the Moroccan Suite, some with outdoor shower/bath and terrace. Air-con, rain showers, minibars, cable TV, comfy beds and free wi-fi throughout. No children. Continental breakfast included. ❺–❼

Intown Residence 1086/6 Thanon Charoen Krung ☎02 639 0960–2, ⓦwww.tarad.com/intownbkk. Clean, welcoming, rather old-fashioned and very good-value Thai-Chinese hotel with a coffee shop, where most bedrooms are set back from the noisy main road. There's a wide variety of comfortable, old and new rooms, in plain or slightly chintzy

styles, all with air-con, hot-water bathrooms, mini-bars and satellite TVs. Good weekly and monthly discounts available. ❹

Lub.d 4 Thanon Decho ☎02 634 7999, ⓦwww .lubd.com. Buzzing, upmarket hostel with air-con and hot water throughout and an industrial feel to the stylishly lit decor. This crisp modernity extends to the bedrooms, among which the dorms (some women-only) and the cheaper, bunk-bedded private rooms share large bathroom areas, while the top-of-the-range en-suite doubles boast TVs. There's wi-fi throughout, a popular bar and café, a travel agency, washing machines, storage facilities and free internet terminals, but no kitchen. Discounts in the private rooms for single travellers. Dorms B520–750 (towels extra), rooms ❺–❻

Malaysia Hotel 54 Soi Ngam Duphli ☎02 679 7127–36, ⓦwww.malaysiahotelbkk.com. Once a travellers' legend famous for its compendious noticeboard, now better known for its seedy 24hr coffeeshop and massage parlour. The accommodation itself is reasonable value though: the rooms are large and have air-con, mini-bars and hot-water bathrooms; some have cable TV. There's a swimming pool (B50 per day for non-guests) and internet access. Gay-friendly. ❹

Urban House 35/13 Soi Yommarat, Thanon Saladaeng ☎02 636 3244 or 081 492 7778, ⓦwww.urbanh.com. On a quiet but very central sub-soi, this modern, cubist building is more impressive from outside than in, but the six rooms are smart, bright and well equipped, done out in browns and creams. Air-con, hot water, fridges and cable TV in all rooms, small kitchens in half of them. Free internet and wi-fi. No children under 10. Light breakfast included. ❺

Expensive

Bangkok Marriott Resort 257 Thanon Charoennakorn ☎02 476 0022, ⓦwww .marriott.com. A luxury retreat from the frenetic city centre, well to the south on the Thonburi bank, but connected to Taksin Bridge (for the Skytrain and Chao Phraya express boats), 10min away, by hotel ferries every 15min. Arrayed around a highly appealing, landscaped swimming pool, the tranquil, riverside gardens are filled with birdsong, while the stylish and spacious bedrooms come with varnished hardwood floors and balconies. There's a fitness centre, a branch of the classy Mandara Spas, and among a wide choice of eateries, a good Japanese teppanyaki house and a bakery-café. ❾

Luxx 6/11 Thanon Decho ☎02 635 8800, ⓦwww .staywithluxx.com. Welcoming boutique hotel offering a good dose of contemporary style at reasonable prices (with a new, larger branch with a

104

DOWNTOWN: SOUTH OF THANON RAMA IV

ACCOMMODATION
Baan Saladaeng	J
Intown Residence	B
Lub.d	G
Luxx	H
Metropolitan	L
Millennium Hilton	A
New Road Guest House	D
Peninsula Bangkok	F
Rose Hotel	C
Sukhothai	M
Swiss Lodge	I
Tarntawan Place Hotel	E
Urban House	K

EATING, DRINKING & NIGHTLIFE
Aoi	15	Khrua Aroy Aroy	21
Baan Khanitha	26	La Boulange	22
The Balcony	9	Lucifer	12
The Barbican	6	Mei Jiang	F
Celadon	M	Noriega's	9
Chai Karr	17	O'Reilly's	14
Coffee Society	13	Parkbridge	10
Cy'an	L	Ratree Seafood	16
Dick's Café	2	The Sky Bar & Distil	20
Disco Disco	11	Somboon Seafood	5
DJ Station	11	Sphinx	9
Eat Me	24	Taling Pling	23
GOD (Guys on Display)	8	Tapas Bar	9
Harmonique	3 & 19	Tawandang German Brewery	27
Himali Cha-Cha	4	Telephone Pub	9
Home Cuisine	25	Tongue Thai	7
Jim Thompson's Saladaeng Café	11	Zen	18
JJ Park	11		

Legend
- (S) – BTS Skyrain station
- (M) – Subway station
- (N1) – Express-boat pier

pool, *XL*, about to open on Soi Lang Suan). Decorated in white, grey and natural teak, the rooms feature DVD players, free wi-fi and cute wooden baths surmounted by rain showers. Breakfast included. ❼

Metropolitan 27 Thanon Sathorn Tai ☎02 625 3333, ⓦwww.metropolitan.como.bz. The height of chic, minimalist urban living, where the rooms are stylishly decorated in dark wood, creamy Portuguese limestone and lotus-themed contemporary artworks. There's a very seductive pool, a fine spa, a well-equipped fitness centre, an excellent restaurant, *Cy'an* (see p.147), and a fiercely hip bar. ❾

Millennium Hilton 123 Thanon Charoennakorn ☎02 442 2000, ⓦwww.hilton.com. Impressive new hotel with a twelve-storey lobby atrium, decorated throughout in modern Asian style. Its fourth-floor saltwater pool, fringed with white sand, is known as The Beach. There's also a secluded spa and a top-floor bar, *360*, 130m above the river with huge picture windows, while every restaurant also boasts views of the Chao Phraya: Cantonese *Yuan*, with good-value lunchtime dim sum, a steakhouse and an international buffet with its own refrigerated cheese room. On the Thonburi bank, with shuttle boats across to River City shopping centre and Taksin Bridge. ❾

Peninsula Bangkok 333 Thanon Charoennakorn ☎02 861 2888, ⓦwww.peninsula .com. Superb top-class hotel to rival the *Oriental* across the river. Service is flawless, the ultra-luxurious decor stylishly blends traditional Western and Asian design, and every room has a panoramic view of the Chao Phraya. The lovely riverside gardens shelter a three-tiered pool, a beautiful spa run by ESPA, a fitness centre and tennis courts. On the Thonburi bank, with shuttle boats across to a reception area by the *Shangri-La Hotel* off Thanon Charoen Krung and down to Taksin Bridge. ❾

Rose Hotel 118 Thanon Suriwong ☎02 266 8268–72, ⓦwww.rosehotelbkk.com. Set back from the main road but very handy for the city's nightlife, this thirty-year-old hotel has been cleverly refurbished: the compact rooms (all with bathtubs) now boast a simple but stylish, retro look, in keeping with the age of the place. Suites and the ground-floor public rooms, where continental breakfast (included in the price) is served, are more elegant again, and there's a beautiful, new swimming pool at the back. Frequent discounts. ❼

Sukhothai 13/3 Thanon Sathorn Tai ☎02 344 8888, ⓦwww.sukhothai.com. The most elegant of Bangkok's top hotels, its decor inspired by the walled city of Sukhothai: low-rise accommodation, as well as a beautiful garden spa, all coolly furnished in silks, teak and granite. Service is of the highest standard and the architecture makes the most of the views of the surrounding six acres of gardens, lotus ponds and pools dotted with statuary. Health club, 25-metre infinity pool, squash and tennis courts, and excellent restaurants including *Celadon* (see p.147). ❾

Swiss Lodge 3 Thanon Convent ☎02 233 5345, ⓦwww.swisslodge.com. Swish, friendly, good-value, boutique hotel, with high standards of service, just off Thanon Silom and ideally placed for business and nightlife. The tiny terrace swimming pool confirms the national stereotypes of neatness and clever design, while the *Three on Convent* restaurant branches out into North Californian wine-country cuisine. ❽

Tarntawan Place Hotel 119/5–10 Thanon Suriwong ☎02 238 2620, ⓦwww.tarntawan .com. Set back from the main road, a pretty, flower-strewn lobby announces this gracious, well-run, gay-friendly hotel. The decent-sized, well-equipped rooms are pleasant and homely, with free wi-fi. Guests also receive free breakfast and internet access, as well as reduced-price entry to a gym and swimming pool on Soi Thaniya. Discounted fortnightly and monthly rates; in the off-season, excellent-value three-night packages. ❼

Thanon Sukhumvit

Thanon Sukhumvit is Bangkok's longest road – it keeps going east all the way to Cambodia – but for such an important artery it's way too narrow for the volume of traffic that needs to use it, and is further hemmed in by the overhead Skytrain line that runs above it. Packed with high-rise hotels and office blocks, an impressive array of specialist restaurants (from Lebanese to Lao), tailors, bookstores and stall after stall selling cheap souvenirs and T-shirts, it's a lively place that attracts a high proportion of single male tourists to its enclaves of girlie bars on Soi Nana Tai, Soi Cowboy and the Clinton Entertainment Plaza. But for the most part it's not a seedy area, and is home to many expats and middle-class Thais. The majority of overnighters are business travellers but Sukhumvit also has a couple of exceptional mid-priced guest houses.

The most central accommodation is between and along sois 1 to 21; hotels further east are quite convenient for **Suvarnabhumi Airport** but far from the main shopping and eating hubs. Even in central Sukhumvit, many of the sois are refreshingly quiet, even leafy; transport down the longer sois is provided by motorbike-taxi (*mohtoesai*) drivers who wait at the soi's mouth, clad in numbered waistcoats.

Thanon Sukhumvit is well served by the **Skytrain (BTS)**, and there's an interchange with the **subway** at BTS Sukhumvit. It is, however, a long way

ACCOMMODATION		EATING, DRINKING & NIGHTLIFE			
Amari Boulevard Hotel	**A**	Al Ferdoss	**4**	Gaeng Pa Lerd Rod	**12**
The Atlanta	**B**	Aoi	**13**	Gallery 11	**16**
Grand Business Inn	**H**	Baan Khanitha	**5**	Himali Cha-Cha	**10**
Imm Fusion	**E**	Basil	**7**	Le Dalat Indochine	**6**
PS Guesthouse	**C**	Bed Supperclub	**3**	Long Table	**11**
Rex Hotel	**D**	Cabbages and Condoms	**8**	Nest	**2**
Suk 11	**G**	Cheap Charlie's	**17**	Q Bar	**1**
Sukhumvit On-Nut		Dosa King	**18**	Suda Restaurant	**9**
Guesthouse	**F**	Face Bangkok (La Na Thai & Hazara)	**15**	Vientiane Kitchen (Khrua Vientiane)	**14**

from the main Ratanakosin sights, and getting there by **bus** or even **taxi** can take an hour or more, especially during rush hour (7–9am & 3–7pm). Useful buses for getting to Ratanakosin include #508 and #25; full details of bus routes are given on p.88. **Airport bus** #AE3 from Suvarnabhumi stops all the way along Thanon Sukhumvit (see p.79).

A much faster way to cross town is by public **longtail boat** along Khlong Saen Saeb; this canal service begins near Democracy Monument in the west of the city and runs parallel with part of Thanon Sukhumvit (see p.89). All accommodation listed below is marked on the map opposite.

Central Sukhumvit

Amari Boulevard Hotel Soi 5 ☏02 255 2930, ⓦwww.amari.com. Rooms in the deluxe category and above at this long-running but modernized four-star tourist hotel enjoy fine views of the Bangkok skyline and have either wi-fi or broadband. The attractive sixth-floor rooftop swimming pool and garden terrace become the Thai-food restaurant *Season* in the evenings. ❽–❾

The Atlanta At the far southern end of quiet, residential Soi 2 ☏02 252 1650, ⓦwww .theatlantahotel.bizland.com. A Bangkok institution, this classic, five-storey budget hotel was built in 1952 around a famously photogenic Art Deco-style lobby and continues to emphasize an old-fashioned hospitality ("Bangkok's bastion of wholesome tourism"). It offers some of the cheapest accommodation on Sukhumvit: rooms are simple and some are pretty scruffy, though they are all en suite and some have air-con while others have small balconies. There's a swimming pool, wi-fi and internet access and a left-luggage facility. The hotel restaurant serves an extensive Thai menu, including lots of vegetarian dishes, and shows classic movies set in Asia. ❹

Grand Business Inn 2/4–2/11 Soi 11 ☏02 254 7981, ⓦwww.grandbusinessinn.net. Popular, good-value mid-range hotel offering 127 large, comfortable, standard-issue air-con rooms, all with bathtubs, cable TV and broadband access. In a very central location just a few metres from BTS Nana. Advance reservations essential. ❻

🏃 **PS Guesthouse** 26/1 Soi 8 ☏02 255 2309, ⓔpsguesthouse@hotmail.com. This small, calm, friendly guest house offers eight well-equipped rooms, each with air-con, TV, safety box, fridge, free tea and coffee and refreshingly green, plant-screened balconies. Pay a little extra for in-room kitchen facilities. Complimentary wi-fi in the lobby and some rooms. ❻

🏃 **Suk 11** Behind the 7–Eleven store at 1/3 Soi 11 ☏02 253 5927, ⓦwww.suk11 .com. One of the most unusual little hotels in Bangkok, this is also the most backpacker-orientated guest house in the area. The interior of the apparently ordinary apartment-style building has been transformed to resemble a village of traditional wooden houses, accessed by a dimly lit plankway that winds past a variety of guest rooms, terraces and lounging areas. The rooms themselves are simple but comfortable, they're all air-conditioned and some are en suite. B250 beds in five-person air-con dorms are also available. It's well run and thoughtfully appointed, keeps informative noticeboards, provides free breakfast, has wi-fi and washing machines, stores left luggage (B20 per day), and accepts advance reservations via the website. ❹

Eastern Sukhumvit: for Ekamai Bus Station and Suvarnabhumi Airport

Imm Fusion 1594/50 Thanon Sukhumvit, 30m walk west along Thanon Sukhumvit from BTS On Nut, exit 5, beyond Soi 50 ☏02 331 5555, ⓦwww .immhotel.com. Step through the entrance of this attractive and welcoming mid-range hotel and you're in another world, a Moroccan themed one done out in rich earthy colours, wrought ironwork, pretty tiles and plenty of Moorish arches. Rooms are comfortable and equally tasteful, and come with air-con, TV, safety box and wi-fi. There's a gorgeous indoor pool, spa and restaurant and the staff are charming. ❻

Rex Hotel Between sois 32 and 34 (opposite Soi 49), about 300m west from BTS Thong Lo, exit 2 ☏02 259 0106. The best value accommodation close to the Eastern Bus Terminal (one stop on the BTS), this old-fashioned but attractively refurbished hotel is comfortable and run with an old-world graciousness. A rooftop pool and a restaurant complement the spacious air-con rooms, and rates include breakfast. ❺

Sukhumvit On-Nut Guesthouse 125/2 Sukhumvit Soi 89, a 12min walk east from BTS On Nut, exit 3 or, a B20 motorcycle taxi ride from the mouth of adjacent Soi 81 ☏02 742 4525, extn. 2, ⓦwww.bangkok-guesthouse.com. This backpacker-oriented guest house shares premises with a small language school on a quiet

residential soi in a low-rise, unpretentious neighbourhood and makes for a calm introduction to
the city. Many rooms have air-con but all share
bathrooms; options range from four- and

eight-bed fan and air-con dorms (from B169 per
bed) to doubles with private balconies and a
mattress on the floor; facilities include a café and
internet access. ➍

Ratanakosin

The only place to start your exploration of Bangkok is **Ratanakosin**, the royal
island on the east bank of the Chao Phraya, where the city's most important and
extravagant sights are. When Rama I developed Ratanakosin for his new capital
in 1782, after the sacking of Ayutthaya and a temporary stay across the river in
Thonburi, he paid tribute to its precursor by imitating Ayutthaya's layout and
architecture – he even shipped the building materials downstream from the
ruins of the old city. Like Ayutthaya, the new capital was sited for protection
beside a river and turned into an artificial island by the construction of
defensive canals, with a central **Grand Palace** and adjoining royal temple, **Wat
Phra Kaeo**, fronted by an open cremation field, **Sanam Luang**; the Wang Na
(Palace of the Second King), now the **National Museum**, was also built at this
time. **Wat Pho**, which predates the capital's founding, was further embellished
by Rama I's successors, who have consolidated Ratanakosin's pre-eminence by
building several grand European-style palaces (now housing government institutions); Wat Mahathat, the most important centre of Buddhist learning in
southeast Asia; the National Theatre; the National Gallery; and Thammasat and
Silpakorn universities.

Bangkok has expanded eastwards away from the river, leaving the Grand
Palace a good 5km from the city's commercial heart, and the royal family
have long since moved their residence to Dusit, but Ratanakosin remains the
ceremonial centre of the whole kingdom – so much so that it feels as if it
might sink into the boggy ground under the weight of its own mighty
edifices. The heavy, stately feel is lightened by traditional shophouses selling
herbal medicines, pavement amulet sellers and studenty canteens along the
riverside road, **Thanon Maharat**; and by **Sanam Luang**, still used for
cremations and royal ceremonies, but also functioning as a popular open park
and the hub of the modern city's bus system. Despite containing several of
the country's main sights, the area is busy enough in its own right not to have
become a swarming tourist zone, and strikes a neat balance between liveli-
ness and grandeur.

Ratanakosin is within easy walking distance of Banglamphu, but is best
approached from the river, via the **express-boat piers** of Tha Chang (the
former bathing place of the royal elephants, which gives access to the Grand
Palace) or Tha Thien (for Wat Pho). A **word of warning**: when you're
heading for the Grand Palace or Wat Pho, you may well be approached
by someone, possibly pretending to be a student or an official, who will tell
you that the sight is closed when it's not, or some other lies to try to lead
you away from the entrance, because they want to lead you on a shopping
trip for souvenirs, tailored clothes or, if you seem really gullible, gems (see
p.163). The opening hours of the Grand Palace – but not Wat Pho – are
indeed sometimes erratic because of state occasions, but you can check the
details out on its website, ⓦ www.palaces.thai.net – and even if it's closed on
the day you want to visit, that's no reason to throw yourself at the mercy of
these shysters.

RATANAKOSIN

N8 Express-boat pier

THONBURI

Tha Bangkok Noi (N11)

Tha Prachan

Tha Wang Lang (Siriraj) (N10)

Tha Maharat

Chao Phraya River

Tha Chang (N9)

Tha Thien
(N8)

Wat Arun

N (compass)

0   200 m

Banglamphu

BANGKOK

Bangkok Tourism Division (i)

National Gallery

National Theatre

National Museum

Thammasat University

Royal Hotel

Mae Toranee Statue

Wat Mahathat

Sanam Luang

Silpakorn University

Lak Muang

Wat Phra Kaeo

Grand Palace

Inner Palace

Wat Rajapradit

Wat Rajabophit

Wat Pho

Wat Pho Massage School

Museum of Siam

Pahurat & Chinatown

RAJDAMNOEN KLANG

THANON PHRA ARTHIT
THANON CHAO FA
THANON CHAKRABONGSE
PHRAPINKLAO BRIDGE
THANON PHRA CHAN
THANON PHRA LAN
THANON NA PHRA THAT
THANON NA PHRA LAN
THANON RAJDAMNOEN NAI
THANON RACHINI
THANON ATSADANG
THANON LAKMUANG
THANON BAMRUNG MUANG
THANON SANAM CHAI
THANON SARANROM
THANON MAHARAT
THANON THAI WANG
THANON CHAROEN KRUNG (NEW ROAD)
THANON FUANG NAKHON
Khlong Lod
SOI PEN PHAT
SOI CHETUPHON
SOI SATTHAKAN

EATING & DRINKING
Na Pralan Café	1
Po	2
Rub Ar Roon	3

ACCOMMODATION
Arun Residence	A
Aurum: The River Place	B
Chakrabongse Villas	C

N7 Tha Ratchini

Wat Phra Kaeo and the Grand Palace

Hanging together in a precarious harmony of strangely beautiful colours and shapes, **Wat Phra Kaeo** is the apogee of Thai religious art and the holiest Buddhist site in the country, housing the most important image, the **Emerald Buddha**. Built as the private royal temple, Wat Phra Kaeo occupies the northeast corner of the huge **Grand Palace**, whose official opening in 1785 marked the founding of the new capital and the rebirth of the Thai nation after the Burmese invasion. Successive kings have all left their mark here, and the palace complex now covers 25 hectares, though very little apart from the wat is open to tourists.

The only **entrance** to the complex in 2km of crenellated walls is the Gate of Glorious Victory in the middle of the north side, on Thanon Na Phra Lan. This brings you onto a driveway with a tantalizing view of the temple's glittering spires on the left and the dowdy buildings of the Offices of the Royal Household on the right: this is the powerhouse of the kingdom's ceremonial life, providing everything down to chairs and catering, even lending an urn when someone of rank dies. A textile museum under the auspices of the queen is scheduled to open among these buildings, perhaps in 2009, but for now you'll have to content yourself with some crafts shopping at the Queen's Support Foundation (see p.159).

Turn left at the end of the driveway for the ticket office and entrance turnstiles: **admission** to Wat Phra Kaeo and the palace is B300 (daily 8.30am–4pm, last admission 3.30pm, weapons museum, Phra Thinang Amarin Winichai and Dusit Maha Prasat interiors closed Sat & Sun; 2hr personal audioguide B200, with passport or credit card as deposit). This includes a free brochure with

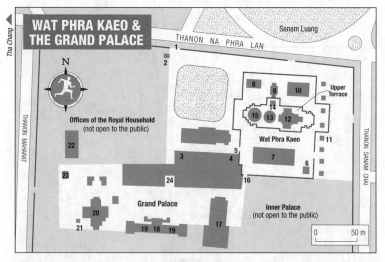

Gate of Glorious Victory	1	Porcelain viharn	9	Phra Thinang Amarin Winichai	17
Queen's Support Foundation Shop	2	Supplementary library	10	Chakri Maha Prasat	18
Ticket office	3	Prangs	11	Weapons museum	19
Royal Decorations & Coins Pavilion	4	Royal Pantheon	12	Dusit Maha Prasat	20
Entrance turnstiles to Wat Phra Kaeo	5	Phra Mondop	13	Mount Krailas model	21
Chapel of the Gandhara Buddha	6	Angkor Wat model	14	Wat Phra Kaeo museum	22
The bot and Emerald Buddha	7	Phra Si Ratana Chedi	15	Café	23
Royal mausoleum	8	Exit from Wat Phra Kaeo	16	Exit from Grand Palace	24

a map (dispensed at the entrance turnstiles) and admission to Dusit Park (within 7 days; see p.132), plus either the missable Ananta Samakhom Throne Hall in Dusit or Sanam Chan Palace in Nakhon Pathom, north of Bangkok. As this is Thailand's most sacred site, you have to **dress in smart clothes**: no vests or see-through clothes; men must wear full-length trousers, women trousers or over-the-knee skirts. Suitable garments can be borrowed from the office to the right just inside the Gate of Glorious Victory (same building as the Queen's Support Foundation shop; free, deposit of B100 per item).

Wat Phra Kaeo

It makes you laugh with delight to think that anything so fantastic could exist on this sombre earth.

W. Somerset Maugham, *The Gentlemen in the Parlour*

Entering the temple is like stepping onto a lavishly detailed stage set, from the immaculate flagstones right up to the gaudy roofs. Reinforcing the sense of unreality, the whole compound is surrounded by arcaded walls, decorated with extraordinary murals of scenes from the *Ramayana*. Although it receives hundreds of foreign sightseers and at least as many Thai pilgrims every day, the temple, which has no monks in residence, maintains an unnervingly sanitized look, as if it were built only yesterday.

The approach to the bot

Inside the entrance turnstiles, you're confronted by six-metre tall **yaksha**, gaudy demons from the *Ramayana*, who watch over the Emerald Buddha from every gate of the temple and ward off evil spirits; the king of the demons, green, ten-faced Totsagan (labelled "Tosakanth"), stands to the left of the entrance by the southwest corner of the golden Phra Si Ratana Chedi. Less threatening is the toothless old codger, cast in bronze and sitting on a plinth immediately inside the turnstiles by the back wall of the bot, who represents a Hindu **hermit** credited with inventing yoga and herbal medicine. In front of him is a large grinding stone where previously herbal practitioners could come to grind their ingredients – with enhanced powers, of course. Skirting around the bot, you'll reach its **main entrance** on the eastern side, in front of which stands a cluster of grey **statues**, which have a strong Chinese feel: next to Kuan Im, the Chinese *bodhisattva* of mercy shown holding a bottle of *amritsa* (sacred elixir), are a sturdy pillar topped by a lotus flower, which Bangkok's Chinese community presented to Rama IV during his 27 years as a monk, and two handsome cows which commemorate Rama I's birth in the Year of the Cow. Worshippers make their offerings to the Emerald Buddha at two small, stand-in Buddhas here, where they can look at the main image through the open doors of the bot without messing up its pristine interior with gold leaf, candle wax and joss-stick ash.

Nearby, in the southeastern corner of the temple precinct, look out for the exquisite scenes of rice sheaves, fish and turtles painted in gold on blue glass on the doors and windows of the **Chapel of the Gandhara Buddha** (labelled "Hor Phra Kanthara Rat"). The decorations allude to the fertility of the ricefields, as this building was crucial to the old royal rainmaking ritual and is still used during the Royal Ploughing Ceremony (see p.54). Adorning the roof are thousands of nagas (serpents), symbolizing water; inside the locked chapel, among the paraphernalia used in the ritual, is kept the Gandhara Buddha, a bronze image in the gesture of calling down the rain with its right hand, while cupping the left to catch it. In times of drought the king would order a week-long rainmaking ceremony to be conducted, during which he was bathed regularly and kept away from the opposite sex while Buddhist monks and Hindu Brahmins chanted continuously.

The bot and the Emerald Buddha

The **bot**, the largest building of the temple, is one of the few original structures left at Wat Phra Kaeo, though it has been augmented so often it looks like the work of a wildly inspired child. Eight *sema* stones mark the boundary of the consecrated area around the bot, each sheltering in a psychedelic fairy castle, joined by a low wall decorated with Chinese porcelain tiles, which depict delicate landscapes. The walls of the bot itself, sparkling with gilt and coloured glass, are supported by 112 golden garudas (birdmen) holding nagas, representing the god Indra saving the world by slaying the serpent-cloud that had swallowed up all the water. The symbolism again reflects the king's traditional role as a rain maker.

Of the bot's three doorways, the largest, in the middle, is reserved for the king himself. Inside, a nine-metre-high pedestal supports the tiny **Emerald Buddha**, a figure whose mystique draws pilgrims from all over Thailand – as well as politicians accused of corruption, who traditionally come here to publicly swear their innocence. Here especially you must act with respect, sitting with your feet pointing away from the Buddha. The spiritual power of the sixty-centimetre jadeite image derives from its legendary past. Reputed to have been created by the gods in India, it was discovered when lightning cracked open an ancient chedi in Chiang Rai in the early fifteenth century. The image was then moved around the north, dispensing miracles wherever it went, before being taken to Laos for two hundred years. As it was believed to bring great fortune to its possessor, the future Rama I snatched it back when he captured Vientiane in 1779, installing it at the heart of his new capital as a talisman for king and country.

Seated in the *Dhyana Mudra* (meditation), the Emerald Buddha has three **costumes**, one for each season: the crown and ornaments of an Ayutthayan king for the hot season; a gilt monastic robe for the rainy season, when the monks retreat into the temples; this is augmented with a full-length gold shawl in the cool season. To this day it's the job of the king himself to ceremonially change the Buddha's costumes – though in recent years, due to the present king's age, the Crown Prince has conducted proceedings. (The Buddha was granted a new set of these three costumes in 1997: the old set is now in the Wat Phra Kaeo Museum (see p.115), while the two costumes of the new set that are not in use are on display among the blinding glitter of crowns and jewels in the Royal Decorations and Coins Pavilion, which lies between the ticket office and the entrance to Wat Phra Kaeo.)

Among the paraphernalia in front of the pedestal sits the tiny, silver Phra Chai Lang Chang (Victory Buddha), which Rama I always carried into battle on the back of his elephant for luck and which still plays an important past in coronation ceremonies. Recently covered in gold, it occupies a prestigious spot dead centre, but is modestly obscured by a fan and by the umbrella of a larger gold Buddha in front. The tallest pair of a dozen standing Buddha images, all made of bronze but encased in gold and raising both hands to dispel fear, are at the front: Rama III dedicated the one on the Emerald Buddha's left to Rama I, the one on his right to Rama II, and Rama IV enshrined relics of the Buddha in their crowns.

The upper terrace

The eastern end of the **upper terrace** is taken up with the **Prasat Phra Thep Bidorn**, known as the **Royal Pantheon**, a splendid hash of styles. The pantheon has its roots in the Khmer concept of *devaraja*, or the divinity of kings: inside are bronze and gold statues, precisely life-size, of all the kings since Bangkok became the Thai capital. Constructed by Rama IV, the building is open only on special occasions, such as Chakri Day (April 6), when the dynasty is commemorated, and Coronation Day (May 5).

From here you get the best view of the **royal mausoleum**, the **porcelain viharn** and the **supplementary library** to the north (all of which are closed to tourists, though you can sometimes glimpse Thai Buddhists worshipping in the library), and, running along the east side of the temple, a row of eight bullet-like **prangs**, each of which has a different nasty ceramic colour. Described as "monstrous vegetables" by Somerset Maugham, they represent, from north to south, the Buddha, Buddhist scripture, the monkhood, the nunhood, the Buddhas who attained enlightenment but did not preach, previous emperors, the Buddha in his previous lives and the future Buddha.

In the middle of the terrace, dressed in deep-green glass mosaics, the **Phra Mondop** was built by Rama I to house the *Tripitaka*, or Buddhist scripture, which the king had revised at Wat Mahathat in 1788, the previous version having been lost in the sack of Ayutthaya. It's famous for the mother-of-pearl cabinet and solid-silver mats inside, but is never open. Four tiny **memorials** at each corner of the mondop show the symbols of each of the nine Chakri kings, from the ancient crown representing Rama I to the present king's discus, while the bronze statues surrounding the memorials portray each king's lucky white elephants, labelled by name and pedigree. A contribution of Rama IV, on the north side of the mondop, is a **scale model of Angkor Wat**, the prodigious Cambodian temple, which during his reign (1851–68) was under Thai rule (apparently, the king had wanted to shift a whole Khmer temple to Bangkok but, fortunately, was dissuaded by his officials). At the western end of the terrace, you can't miss the golden dazzle of the **Phra Si Ratana Chedi**, which Rama IV erected, in imitation of the famous bell-shaped chedis at Ayutthaya's Wat Phra Si Sanphet, to enshrine a piece of the Buddha's breastbone.

The murals

Extending for about a kilometre in the arcades that run inside the wat walls, the **murals of the Ramayana** depict every blow of this ancient story of the triumph of good over evil, using the vibrant buildings of the temple itself as backdrops, and setting them off against the subdued colours of richly detailed landscapes. Because of the damaging humidity, none of the original work of Rama I's time survives: maintenance is a never-ending process, so you'll always find an artist working on one of the scenes. The story is told in 178 panels, labelled and numbered in Thai only, starting in the middle of the northern side opposite the porcelain viharn: in the first episode, a hermit, while out ploughing, finds the baby Sita, the heroine, floating in a gold urn on a lotus leaf and brings her to the city. Panel 109 near the gate leading to the palace buildings shows the climax of the story, when Rama, the hero, kills the ten-headed demon Totsagan (Ravana), and the ladies of the enemy city weep at the demon's death. Panel 110 depicts his elaborate funeral procession, and in 113 you can see the funeral fair, with acrobats, sword-jugglers and tightrope-walkers. In between, Sita – Rama's wife – has to walk on fire to prove that she has been faithful during her fourteen years of imprisonment by Totsagan. If you haven't the stamina for the long walk round, you could sneak a look at the end of the story, to the left of the first panel, where Rama holds a victory parade and distributes thank-you gifts.

The palace buildings

The exit in the southwest corner of Wat Phra Kaeo brings you to the palace proper, a vast area of buildings and gardens, of which only the northern edge is on show to the public. Though the king now lives in the Chitrlada Palace in Dusit, the Grand Palace is still used for state receptions and official ceremonies, during which there is no public access to any part of the palace.

Phra Maha Monthien

Coming out of the temple compound, you'll first of all see to your right a beautiful Chinese gate covered in innumerable tiny porcelain tiles. Extending in a straight line behind the gate is the **Phra Maha Monthien**, which was the grand residential complex of earlier kings.

Only the **Phra Thinang Amarin Winichai**, the main audience hall at the front of the complex, is open to the public. The supreme court in the era of the absolute monarchy, it nowadays serves as the venue for ceremonies such as the king's birthday speech. Dominating the hall are two gleaming, intricately carved thrones that date from the reign of Rama I: a white umbrella with the full nine tiers owing to a king shelters the front seat, while the unusual *busbok* behind is topped with a spired roof and floats on a boat-shaped base. The rear buildings are still used for the most important part of the elaborate coronation ceremony, and each new king is supposed to spend a night there to show solidarity with his forefathers.

Chakri Maha Prasat and the Inner Palace

Next door you can admire the facade of the "farang with a Thai hat", as the **Chakri Maha Prasat** is nicknamed. Rama V, whose portrait you can see over its entrance, employed an English architect to design a purely Neoclassical residence, but other members of the royal family prevailed on the king to add the three Thai spires. This used to be the site of the elephant stables: the large red tethering posts are still there and the bronze elephants were installed as a reminder. The building displays the emblem of the Chakri dynasty on its gable, which has a trident (*ri*) coming out of a *chak*, a discus with a sharpened rim. The only part of the Chakri Maha Prasat open to the public is the ground-floor **weapons museum**, which houses a forgettable display of hooks, pikes and guns.

The **Inner Palace**, which used to be the king's harem (closed to the public), lies behind the gate on the left-hand side of the Chakri Maha Prasat. The harem was a town in itself, with shops, law courts and an all-female police force for the huge population: as well as the current queens, the minor wives and their children (including prepubescent boys) and servants, this was home to the daughters and consorts of former kings, and the daughters of the aristocracy who attended the harem's finishing school. Today, the Inner Palace houses a school of cooking, fruit-carving and other domestic sciences for well-bred young Thais.

Dusit Maha Prasat

On the western side of the courtyard, the delicately proportioned **Dusit Maha Prasat**, an audience hall built by Rama I, epitomizes traditional Thai architecture. Outside, the soaring tiers of its red, gold and green roof culminate in a gilded *mongkut*, a spire shaped like the king's crown, which symbolizes the 33 Buddhist levels of perfection. Each tier of the roof bears a typical *chofa*, a slender, stylized bird's-head finial, and several *hang hong* (swans' tails), which represent three-headed nagas. Inside, you can still see the original throne, the **Phra Ratcha Banlang Pradap Muk**, a masterpiece of mother-of-pearl inlaid work.

When a senior member of the royal family dies, the hall is used for the lying-in-state: the body, embalmed and seated in a huge sealed urn, is placed in the west transept, waiting up to two years for an auspicious day to be cremated.

The Wat Phra Kaeo Museum

In the nineteenth-century Royal Mint in front of the Dusit Maha Prasat – next to a small, basic **café** and an incongruous hair salon – the **Wat Phra Kaeo Museum** houses a mildly interesting collection of artefacts donated to the Emerald Buddha, along with architectural elements rescued from the Grand Palace grounds during restoration in the 1980s. Highlights include the bones of various kings' white elephants, and upstairs, the Emerald Buddha's original costumes and two useful scale models of the Grand Palace, one as it is now, the other as it was when first built. Also on the first floor stands the grey stone slab of the Manangsila Seat, where Ramkhamhaeng, the great thirteenth-century king of Sukhothai, is said to have sat and taught his subjects. It was discovered in 1833 by Rama IV during his monkhood and brought to Bangkok, where Rama VI used it as the throne for his coronation.

Wat Pho (Wat Phra Chetuphon)

Where Wat Phra Kaeo may seem too perfect and shrink-wrapped for some, **Wat Pho** (daily 8am–6pm; B50; Ⓦ www.watpho.com), to the south of the Grand Palace, is lively and shambolic, a complex arrangement of lavish structures which jostle with classrooms, basketball courts and a turtle pond. Busloads of tourists shuffle in and out of the **north entrance**, stopping only to gawp at the colossal Reclining Buddha, but you can avoid the worst of the crowds by using the **main entrance** on Soi Chetuphon to explore the huge compound.

▲ The Reclining Buddha, Wat Pho

115

Visitors' entrances	1	Traditional Medicine Pavilions	5	Rama IV Chedi	9	European Pavilion	13
Entrances to Bot	2	Rama II Chedi	6	Chapel of the Reclining Buddha	10	Café	14
Bot	3	Phra Si Sanphet Chedi	7	Chinese Pavilion	11	Monks' Quarters	15
Massage Pavilions	4	Library	8			Grand Palace	16

Wat Pho is the oldest temple in Bangkok and older than the city itself, having been founded in the seventeenth century under the name Wat Photaram. Foreigners have stuck to the contraction of this old name, even though Rama I, after enlarging the temple, changed the name in 1801 to **Wat Phra Chetuphon**, which is how it is generally known to Thais. The temple had another major overhaul in 1832, when Rama III built the chapel of the Reclining Buddha, and turned the temple into a public centre of learning by decorating the walls and pillars with inscriptions and diagrams on subjects such as history, literature, animal husbandry and astrology. Dubbed Thailand's first university, the wat is still an important centre for traditional medicine, notably **Thai massage**, which is used against all kinds of illnesses, from backaches to viruses. Excellent massages are available in the air-conditioned buildings on the east side of the main compound; allow two hours for the full works (B360 per hr; foot reflexology massage B360 per 45min). There are often long queues here, however, so you might be better off heading over to the massage centre's new premises just outside the temple, at 392/25–28 Soi Pen Phat 1, Thanon Maharat (T02 622 3533 or 02 622 3551, W www.watpomassage.com). At the latter, you can also enrol on a thirty-hour **massage training course** in English, over five days (B8500), and foot-massage courses for B6500.

The eastern courtyard

The main entrance on Soi Chetuphon is one of a series of sixteen monumental gates around the main compound, each guarded by stone **giants**, many of them comic Westerners in wide-brimmed hats – ships which exported rice to China would bring these statues back as ballast.

The entrance brings you into the eastern half of the main complex, where a courtyard of structures radiates from the bot in a disorientating symmetry. To get to the bot, the principal congregation and ordination hall, turn right and cut through the two surrounding cloisters, which are lined with hundreds of Buddha images. The elegant **bot** has beautiful teak doors decorated with mother-of-pearl, showing stories from the *Ramayana* in minute detail. Look out also for the stone bas-reliefs around the base of the bot, which narrate the story of the capture and rescue of Sita from the *Ramayana* in 152 action-packed panels. The plush interior has a well-proportioned altar on which ten statues of disciples frame a graceful, Ayutthayan Buddha image containing the remains of Rama I, the founder of Bangkok (Rama IV placed them there so that the public could worship him at the same time as the Buddha).

Back outside the entrance to the double cloister, keep your eyes open for a miniature mountain covered in statues of naked men in tall hats who appear to be gesturing rudely: they are *rishis* (hermits), demonstrating various positions of healing massage. Skirting the southwestern corner of the cloisters, you'll come to two pavilions between the eastern and western courtyards, which display plaques inscribed with the precepts of traditional medicine, as well as anatomical pictures showing the different pressure points and the illnesses that can be cured by massaging them.

The western courtyard

Among the 99 chedis strewn about the grounds, the four **great chedis** in the western courtyard stand out as much for their covering of garish tiles as for their size. The central chedi is the oldest, erected by Rama I to hold the remains of the most sacred Buddha image of Ayutthaya, the Phra Si Sanphet. Later, Rama III built the chedi to the north for the ashes of Rama II and the chedi to the south to hold his own remains; Rama IV built the fourth, with bright blue tiles, though its purpose is uncertain.

In the northwest corner of the courtyard stands the chapel of the **Reclining Buddha**, a 45-metre-long gilded statue of plaster-covered brick which depicts the Buddha entering Nirvana, a common motif in Buddhist iconography. The chapel is only slightly bigger than the statue – you can't get far enough away to take in anything but a surreal close-up view of the beaming five-metre smile. As for the feet, the vast black soles are beautifully inlaid with delicate mother-of-pearl showing the 108 *lakshanas*, or auspicious signs, which distinguish the true Buddha. Along one side of the statue are 108 bowls: putting a coin in each will bring you good luck and a long life.

Museum of Siam (National Discovery Museum)

The hi-tech and mostly bilingual **Museum of Siam** is an excellent, new attraction that occupies the century-old, European-style, former Ministry of Commerce (Tues–Sun 10am–6pm; free; Ⓦ www.ndmi.or.th). Approached from either Thanon Maharat or Thanon Sanam Chai to the south of Wat Pho (and handy also for Ratchini express-boat pier during weekday rush hours), it looks at what it is to be Thai, with lots of humorous short films and imaginative touches such as shadow-puppet cartoons and war video games. Generally, it's great fun for adults and kids, and there's a nice little indoor-outdoor **café-restaurant** in the grounds run by the Black Canyon chain.

It all kicks off with the prehistory of Southeast Asia, or Suvarnabhumi (Land of Gold) as the Thais call it, and the arrival of Buddhism via missionaries sent by the great Indian emperor, Ashoka (Asoke). Much space is devoted to Ayutthaya, where we learn that during that kingdom's four-hundred-year history, there were no less than twenty outbreaks of war with the Burmese states, before the final annihilation in 1767. Beyond this, look out for a fascinating map of Thonburi, King Taksin's new capital between 1768 and 1782, as drawn by a Burmese spy. In the Bangkok period, there's coverage of the Chinese in Thailand and of early twentieth-century racialism, but next to nothing on the country's Muslims. Towards the end, under the banner of Westernization, visitors can wind up cartoon peep shows and dress up in "colonial" pith helmets.

Wat Mahathat

On Sanam Luang's western side, with its main entrance on Thanon Maharat, eighteenth-century **Wat Mahathat** provides a welcome respite from the surrounding tourist hype, and a chance to engage with the eager monks studying at **Mahachulalongkorn Buddhist University** here. As the nation's centre for the Mahanikai monastic sect (where Rama IV spent 24 years as a monk before becoming king in 1851), and housing one of the two Buddhist universities in Bangkok, the wat buzzes with purpose. It's this activity, and the chance of interaction and participation, rather than any special architectural features, which make a visit so rewarding. The many university-attending monks at the wat are friendly and keen to practise their English, and are more than likely to approach you: diverting topics might range from the poetry of Dylan Thomas to English football results.

Situated in Section Five of the wat is its **Vipassana Meditation Centre**, where sitting and walking meditation practice is available in English (daily 7–10am, 1–4pm & 6–8pm; ☎02 222 6011 or 02 222 4981). Participants generally stay in the simple surroundings of the meditation building itself (donation requested), and must wear white clothes (available to rent at the centre) and observe the eight main Buddhist precepts (see p.57). Talks in English on meditation and Buddhism are held here every evening (8–9pm), as well as at the International Buddhist Meditation Centre (Room 106; ☎02 623 6326 or 089 220 1754, ⓦwww.sirimangalo.org) in the Mahachulalongkorn University building on the second and fourth Saturdays of every month (3–5pm).

The National Museum

At the northwest corner of Sanam Luang, the **National Museum** (Wed–Sun 9am–4pm, some rooms may close at lunchtime; B200 including leaflet with map; ⓦwww.thailandmuseum.com) houses a colossal hoard of Thailand's chief artistic riches, ranging from sculptural treasures in the north and south wings, through bizarre decorative objects in the older buildings, to outlandish funeral chariots and the exquisite Buddhaisawan Chapel, as well as sometimes staging worthwhile temporary exhibitions. It's worth making time for the free **guided tours in English** on Wednesday and Thursday at 9.30am by the National Museum Volunteers (who also organize interesting lectures and excursions; ⓦwww.museumvolunteersbkk.net): they're generally entertaining and their explication of the choicest exhibits provides a good introduction to Thai religion and culture. By the ticket office are a bookshop and a pleasant, air-conditioned **café**, serving drinks, sandwiches and cakes, while the **restaurant** inside the museum grounds, by the funeral chariots building, dishes up decent, inexpensive Thai food.

The first building you'll come to near the ticket office houses an informative overview of the history of Thailand, including a small archeological gem: a black stone **inscription**, credited to King Ramkhamhaeng of Sukhothai, which became the first capital of the Thai nation (c.1278–99) under his rule. Discovered in 1833 by the future Rama IV, it's the oldest extant inscription using the Thai alphabet. This, combined with the description it records of prosperity and piety in Sukhothai's Golden Age, has made the stone a symbol of Thai nationhood.

The main collection: southern building

At the back of the compound, two large modern buildings, flanking an old converted palace, house the museum's **main collection**, kicking off on the ground floor of the **southern building**. Look out here for some historic sculptures from the rest of Asia, including one of the earliest representations of the Buddha, from Gandhara in northwest India. Alexander the Great left a garrison at Gandhara, which explains why the image is in the style of Classical Greek sculpture: for example, the *ushnisha*, the supernatural bump on the top of the head, which symbolizes the Buddha's intellectual and spiritual power, is rationalized into a bun of thick, wavy hair.

Upstairs, the **prehistory** room displays axe heads and spear points from Ban Chiang in the northeast of Thailand, one of the earliest Bronze Age cultures ever discovered. Alongside are many roughly contemporaneous metal artefacts from Kanchanaburi province, as well as some excellent examples of the developments of Ban Chiang's famous pottery. In the adjacent **Dvaravati** room (S7; sixth to eleventh centuries), the pick of the stone and terracotta Buddhas is a small head in smooth, pink clay, whose downcast eyes and faintly smiling full lips typify the serene look of this era. At the far end of the first floor, you can't miss a voluptuous Javanese statue of elephant-headed Ganesh, Hindu god of wisdom and the arts, which, being the symbol of the Fine Arts Department, is always freshly garlanded. As Ganesh is known as the clearer of obstacles, Hindus always worship him before other gods, so by tradition he has grown fat through getting first choice of the offerings – witness his trunk jammed into a bowl of food in this sculpture.

Room S9 next door contains the most famous piece of **Srivijaya** art (seventh to thirteenth centuries), a bronze Bodhisattva Avalokitesvara found at Chaiya (according to Mahayana Buddhism, a *bodhisattva* is a saint who has postponed his passage into Nirvana to help ordinary believers gain enlightenment). With its pouting face and sinuous torso, this image has become the ubiquitous emblem of southern Thailand. The rough chronological order of the collection continues back downstairs with an exhibition of **Khmer** and **Lopburi** sculpture (seventh to fourteenth centuries), most notably some dynamic bronze statuettes and stone lintels. Look out for an elaborate lintel that depicts Vishnu reclining on a dragon in the sea of eternity, dreaming up a new universe after the old one has been annihilated in the Hindu cycle of creation and destruction. Out of his navel comes a lotus, and out of this emerges four-headed Brahma, who will put the dream into practice.

The main collection: northern building

The second half of the survey, in the northern building, begins upstairs with the **Sukhothai** collection (thirteenth to fifteenth centuries), which features some typically elegant and sinuous Buddha images, as well as chunky bronzes of Hindu gods and a wide range of ceramics. The **Lanna** rooms (roughly thirteenth to sixteenth centuries) include a miniature set of golden regalia, among them tiny umbrellas and a cute pair of filigree flip-flops, which would have been enshrined in a chedi. An ungainly but serene Buddha head, carved from grainy, pink sandstone, represents the **Ayutthaya** style of sculpture (fourteenth to eighteenth centuries): the faintest incision of a moustache above the lips betrays the Khmer influences that came to Ayutthaya after its conquest of Angkor. A sumptuous scripture cabinet, showing a cityscape of old Ayutthaya, is a more unusual piece, one of a surviving handful of such carved and painted items of furniture.

Downstairs in the section on **Bangkok** or **Ratanakosin** art (eighteenth century onwards), a stiffly realistic standing bronze brings you full circle. In his zeal for Western naturalism, Rama V had the statue made in the Gandhara style of the earliest Buddha image displayed in the first room of the museum.

The funeral chariots

To the east of the northern building, beyond the café on the left, stands a large garage where the fantastically elaborate **funeral chariots** of the royal family are stored. Pre-eminent among these is the Vejayant Rajarot, built by Rama I in 1785 for carrying the urn at his own funeral. The thirteen-metre-high structure symbolizes heaven on Mount Meru, while the dragons and divinities around the sides – piled in five golden tiers to suggest the flames of the cremation – represent the mythological inhabitants of the mountain's forests. Each weighing around forty tonnes and requiring the pulling power of three hundred men, the teak chariots last had an outing in 2008, for the funeral of the present king's much-revered elder sister, Princess Galyani.

Wang Na (Palace of the Second King)

The sprawling central building of the compound was originally part of the **Wang Na**, a huge palace stretching across Sanam Luang to Khlong Lod, which housed the "second king", appointed by the reigning monarch as his heir and deputy. When Rama V did away with the office in 1887, he turned the palace into a museum, which now contains a fascinating array of Thai *objets d'art*. As you enter (room 5), the display of sumptuous rare gold pieces behind heavy iron bars includes a well-preserved armlet taken from the ruined prang of fifteenth-century Wat Ratburana in Ayutthaya. In adjacent room 6, an intricately carved ivory seat turns out, with gruesome irony, to be a *howdah*, for use on an elephant's back. Among the masks worn by *khon* actors next door (room 7), look out especially for a fierce Hanuman, the white monkey-warrior in the *Ramayana* epic, gleaming with mother-of-pearl.

The huge and varied ceramic collection in room 8 includes some sophisticated pieces from Sukhothai, while the room behind (9) holds a riot of mother-of-pearl items, whose flaming rainbow of colours comes from the shell of the turbo snail from the Gulf of Thailand. It's also worth seeking out the display of richly decorated musical instruments in room 15.

The Buddhaisawan chapel

The second holiest image in Thailand, after the Emerald Buddha, is housed in the **Buddhaisawan chapel**, the vast hall in front of the eastern entrance to the Wang Na. Inside, the fine proportions of the hall, with its ornate coffered ceiling and lacquered window shutters, are enhanced by painted rows of divinities and converted demons, all turned to face the chubby, glowing **Phra Sihing Buddha**, which according to legend was magically created in Sri Lanka and sent to Sukhothai in the thirteenth century. Like the Emerald Buddha, the image was believed to bring good luck to its owner and was frequently snatched from one northern town to another, until Rama I brought it down from Chiang Mai in 1795 and installed it here in the second king's private chapel. Two other images (in Nakhon Si Thammarat and Chiang Mai) now claim to be the authentic Phra Sihing Buddha, but all three are in fact derived from a lost original – this one is in a fifteenth-century Sukhothai style. It's still much loved by ordinary people and at Thai New Year is carried out onto Sanam Luang, where worshippers sprinkle it with water as a merit-making gesture.

The careful detail and rich colours of the surrounding two-hundred-year-old **murals** are surprisingly well preserved; the bottom row between the windows narrates the life of the Buddha, beginning in the far right-hand corner with his parents' wedding.

Tamnak Daeng

On the south side of the Buddhaisawan chapel, the sumptuous **Tamnak Daeng** (Red House) stands out, a large, airy Ayutthaya-style house made of rare golden teak, surmounted by a multi-tiered roof decorated with carved foliage and swan's-tail finials. Originally part of the private quarters of Princess Sri Sudarak, elder sister of Rama I, it was moved from the Grand Palace to the old palace in Thonburi for Queen Sri Suriyen, wife of Rama II; when her son became second king to Rama IV, he dismantled the edifice again and shipped it here to the Wang Na compound. Inside, it's furnished in the style of the early Bangkok period, with some of the beautiful objects that once belonged to Sri Suriyen, a huge, ornately carved box bed, and the uncommon luxury of an indoor toilet and bathroom.

Banglamphu and the Democracy Monument area

Immediately north of Ratanakosin, **Banglamphu**'s most notorious attraction is **Thanon Khao San**, a tiny sliver of a road whose multiple guest houses and buzzing, budget-minded nightlife have made it an unmissable way station for travellers through Southeast Asia. There is cultural interest here too, in a medley of idiosyncratic **temples** within a few blocks of nearby landmark Democracy Monument, and in the typical Bangkok neighbourhoods that connect them, many of which still feel charmingly old-fashioned. The megalithic yellowy wings of the **Democracy Monument** itself (*Anu Sawari Pracha Tippatai*), at the centre of a thunderous roundabout, are anything but charming, but are highly symbolic: they represent the ideals that fuelled the 1932 changeover to a constitutional monarchy and have served as a rallying point for pro-democracy demonstrations ever since. If coming from downtown Bangkok, the fastest way to get to this area is by longtail canal boat along Khlong Saen Saeb (see p.89), whose Phan Fah terminus is five minutes' walk from Democracy Monument. For details on bus and express-boat services to Banglamphu, see p.96.

Around Khao San: Phra Arthit and the riverside walkway

Even if you're staying elsewhere, the **Khao San** area offers great shopping, eating and nightlife and is also a cultural curiosity in its own right, a unique and continually evolving expression of global youth culture fuelled by Thai entrepreneurship. Students from nearby Thammasat University inject an arty Thai vibe into the mix, particularly along **Thanon Phra Arthit**, which borders the Chao Phraya River. There's an attractive **riverside walkway** here too, which begins at the Bangkok Tourism Division's information centre beside Phra Pinklao Bridge and takes you past a couple of beautifully restored century-old mansions, currently occupied by Unicef and the UN's FAO; they show their most elegant faces to the river since in their heyday most visitors would have arrived by boat. The walkway terminates at the whitewashed, renovated octagonal tower of **Phra Sumen Fortress** (Phra Sumeru), one of fourteen built by Rama I in 1783 to protect the royal island of Ratanakosin. Nowadays there's nothing to see inside the fort, but the area around it has been remodelled as grassy riverside **Santichaiprakarn Park** and retains some of the district's last remaining mangrove-like lamphu trees (*duabanga grandiflora*), after which Banglamphu, "the place with lamphu trees", was named.

Wat Rajnadda and the amulet market

Five minutes' walk east of Democracy Monument, at the point where Rajdamnoen Klang meets Thanon Mahachai, stands the assortment of religious buildings known collectively as **Wat Rajnadda** (daily 9am–5pm; free). Its most striking feature is the multi-tiered, castle-like **Loh Prasat**, or "Iron Monastery", whose 37 forbidding metal spires represent the 37 virtues necessary for attaining enlightenment. Modelled on a Sri Lankan monastery, its tiers are pierced by passageways running north–south and east–west – fifteen in each direction at ground level – with small meditation cells at each point of intersection.

In the southeast (Thanon Mahachai) corner of the temple compound, Bangkok's biggest **amulet market**, the **Wat Rajnadda Buddha Center**,

---

Amulets

To invite good fortune, ward off malevolent spirits and gain protection from physical harm, Thais wear or carry at least one **amulet** at all times. The most popular **images** are copies of sacred statues from famous wats, while others show revered monks, kings (Rama V is a favourite) or healers. On the reverse side a *yantra* is often inscribed, a combination of letters and figures also designed to deflect evil, sometimes of a very specific nature: protecting your durian orchards from gales, for example, or your tuk-tuk from oncoming traffic. Individually hand-crafted or mass-produced, amulets can be made from bronze, clay, plaster or gold, and some even have sacred ingredients added, such as special herbs, or the ashes of burnt holy texts. But what really determines an amulet's efficacy is its history: where and by whom it was made, who or what it represents and who consecrated it. Stories of miracle cures and lucky escapes also prompt a rush on whatever amulet the survivor was wearing. Monks are often involved in the making of the images and are always called upon to consecrate them – the more charismatic the monk, the more powerful the amulet. Religious authorities take a relaxed view of the amulet industry, despite its anomalous and commercial functions, and proceeds contribute to wat funds and good causes.

The **belief in amulets** is thought to have originated in India, where tiny images were sold to pilgrims who visited the four holy sites associated with the Buddha's life. But not all amulets are Buddhist-related; there's a whole range of other enchanted objects to wear for protection, including tigers' teeth, rose quartz, tamarind seeds, coloured threads and miniature phalluses. Worn around the waist rather than the neck, the phallus amulets provide protection for the genitals as well as being associated with fertility, and are of Hindu origin.

For some people, amulets are not only a vital form of spiritual protection, but valuable **collectors' items** as well. Amulet-collecting mania is something akin to stamp collecting and there are at least half a dozen Thai magazines for collectors, which give histories of certain types, tips on distinguishing between genuine items and fakes, and personal accounts of particularly powerful amulet experiences. The most rewarding places to watch the collectors and browse the wares yourself are at Wat Rajnadda Buddha Center, probably the best place in Bangkok (see above); along "Amulet Alley" on Trok Mahathat, between Wat Mahathat (see p.118) and the river, where streetside vendors will have cheaper examples; and at Chatuchak Weekend Market (see p.140). Prices start as low as B50 and rise into the thousands.

comprises at least a hundred stalls selling tiny Buddha images of all designs (see box opposite). Alongside these miniature charms are statues of Hindu deities, dolls and carved wooden phalluses, also bought to placate or ward off disgruntled spirits, as well as love potions and CDs of sacred music.

Across the road from Wat Rajnadda, the **Phra Mahakhan Fortress community** occupies the land between the whitewashed crenellations of the renovated eighteenth-century city walls and Khlong Ong Ang. It's a historic neighbourhood and welcomes visitors with informative signboards describing some of its traditions, including massage therapy, fish bladder soup and *likay* popular theatre. Immediately south of the crenellations is a block of shops specializing in Thai and Chinese antiques.

Wat Saket and the Golden Mount

Beautifully illuminated at night, when it seems to float unsupported above the neighbourhood, the gleaming gold chedi east of Wat Rajnadda actually sits atop a structure known as the Golden Mount, within the compound of the late eighteenth-century **Wat Saket**. Being outside the capital's city walls, the wat initially served as a crematorium and then a dumping ground for sixty thousand plague victims left to the vultures because they couldn't afford funeral pyres. There's no sign of this grim episode at modern-day Wat Saket of course, which is these days a smart, buzzing hive of religious activity at the base of the golden hilltop chedi.

The **Golden Mount**, or **Phu Khao Tong** (daily 7.30am–5.30pm; B10), dates back to the early nineteenth century, when Rama III commissioned a huge chedi to be constructed here on ground that proved too soft to support it. The whole thing collapsed into a hill of rubble, but as Buddhist law states that a religious building can never be destroyed, however tumbledown, fifty years later Rama V simply crowned it with the more sensibly sized chedi we see today, in which he placed some relics, believed by some to be the Buddha's teeth. These days the old rubbly base is picturesquely planted with shrubs and shady trees and dotted with gravestones and memorials. Winding stairways take you up to the chedi terrace and a fine view over Banglamphu and Ratanakosin landmarks, including the golden spires of the Grand Palace, the finely proportioned prangs of Wat Arun across the river beyond and, further upriver, the striking superstructure of the Rama VIII Bridge.

Wat Saket hosts an enormous annual **temple fair** in the first week of November, when the mount is illuminated with lanterns and the compound seethes with funfair rides and travelling theatre shows. Easiest **access** to the Golden Mount is along Thanon Boriphat (the specialist street for custom-carved wooden doors), five minutes' walk south from the khlong bridge and Phan Fah canal boat stop at the eastern end of Rajdamnoen Klang.

Sao Ching Cha, Wat Suthat and Thanon Bamrung Muang

About 700m south along Thanon Dinso from Democracy Monument, you can't miss the towering, red-painted teak posts of **Sao Ching Cha**, otherwise known as the **Giant Swing**, just in front of Wat Suthat. This strange contraption was once the focal point of a Brahmin ceremony to honour the Hindu god Shiva's annual visit to earth, in which teams of young men competed to swing up to a height of 25m and grab a suspended bag of gold with their teeth. The act of swinging probably symbolized the rising and setting of the sun, though legend also has it that Shiva and his consort Uma were banned from swinging in heaven because doing so caused cataclysmic floods on earth – prompting Shiva to demand that the practice be continued on earth to ensure moderate rains and bountiful harvests. Accidents were so common with the terrestrial version that it was outlawed in the 1930s.

Were the swing still in operation, you'd get a fine view over adjacent **Wat Suthat** (daily 9am–5pm; B20) and its towering central viharn, Bangkok's tallest. This is one of Thailand's six most important temples, built in the early nineteenth century to house the eight-metre-high statue of the meditating **Phra Sri Sakyamuni Buddha**, which was brought all the way down from Sukhothai by river. It now sits on a glittering mosaic dais surrounded with surreal murals that depict the last 24 lives of the Buddha rather than the more usual ten. The encircling galleries contain 156 serenely posed Buddha images, making a nice contrast to the **Chinese statues** dotted around the temple courtyards, most of which were brought over from China during Rama I's reign, as ballast in rice boats; there are some fun character studies among them, including gormless Western sailors and pompous Chinese scholars.

West from Sao Ching Cha and Wat Suthat, **Thanon Bamrung Muang** is famous as the best place in Thailand to buy **Buddhist paraphernalia**, or *sanghapan*, and is well worth a browse even for tourists. The road is lined with shops selling everything a good Buddhist might need, from household offertory tables to temple umbrellas and cellophane-wrapped Buddha images up to two metres high. They also sell special alms packs for donating to monks, which typically come in saffron-coloured plastic buckets (used by monks for washing their robes, or themselves), and include such necessities as soap, toothpaste, soap powder, toilet roll, candles and incense.

Chinatown

When the newly crowned Rama I decided to move his capital across to the east bank of the river in 1782, the Chinese community living on the proposed site of his palace was obliged to relocate downriver, to the **Sampeng** area. Two centuries on, **Chinatown** has grown into the country's largest Chinese district, a sprawl of narrow alleyways, temples and shophouses packed between Charoen Krung (New Road) and the river, separated from Ratanakosin by the Indian area of **Pahurat** – famous for its cloth and dressmakers' trimmings – and bordered to the east by **Hualamphong** train station.

The **Chinese influence** on Thai culture and commerce has been significant ever since the first Chinese merchants gained a toehold in Ayutthaya in the fourteenth century. Following centuries of immigration and intermarriage, there is now some Chinese blood in almost every Thai citizen, including the king, and Chinese-Thai business interests play an enormous role in the Thai economy. This is played out at its most frantic in Chinatown, whose real estate is said to be amongst the most valuable in the country; there are over a hundred gold and jewellery shops along Thanon Yaowarat alone.

For the tourist, Chinatown is chiefly interesting for its **markets**, shophouses, open-fronted warehouses and remnants of colonial-style architecture, though it also harbours a few noteworthy **temples**. A meander through its most interesting neighbourhoods could easily soak up a whole day, allowing for frequent breaks from the thundering traffic and choking fumes. For the most authentic Chinatown experience it's best to come during the week, as some shops and stalls shut at weekends; on weekdays they begin closing around

HUALAMPHONG, CHINATOWN & PAHURAT

Ⓜ – Subway Station

N

0   200 m

ACCOMMODATION
Baan Hualamphong	D
Bangkok Center	C
FF Guest House	E
Shanghai Mansion	A
The Train Inn	B
TT2 Guest House	F

EATING
Chong Kee	5
Hua Seng Hong	2
Shangri-La	1
T&K Seafood	4
White Orchid Hotel	3

5pm, after which time the neighbourhood's other big draw – its **food** – takes centre stage.

Easiest access is either by **subway** to Hualamphong Station, or by Chao Phraya **express boat** to Tha Rachawongse (Rajawong; N5) at the southern end of Thanon Rajawong. This part of the city is also well served by **buses**, with Hualamphong a useful and easily recognized place to disembark (see boxes, p.88 & p.96). Be warned that buses and taxis may take an unexpectedly circuitous route due to the many and complex **one-way systems** in Chinatown.

Orientation in Chinatown can be tricky: the alleys (often known as trok rather than the more usual soi) are extremely narrow, their turn-offs and other road signs often obscured by mounds of merchandise and thronging crowds, and the longer ones can change their names several times. For a detailed tour of the alleys and markets, use *Nancy Chandler's Map of Bangkok*; alternatively, ask for help at the BMA **tourist information** booth (Mon–Sat 9am–5pm) just northwest of the Chinese Arch on Thanon Yaowarat, beside Soi 5.

Wat Traimit and the Golden Buddha

The obvious place to start a Chinatown tour is on its eastern perimeter, just west of Hualamphong train and subway stations (exit 1), with **Wat Traimit** (daily 9am–5pm) and its famous Golden Buddha, on Thanon Mittaphap Thai-China. You can see the temple mondop's golden spire from quite a distance, a fitting beacon for its gleaming treasure, the world's largest solid-gold Buddha. It's an apt attraction for a community so closely linked with the gold trade, even if the image has nothing to do with China's spiritual heritage. Over 3m tall and weighing five tonnes, the **Golden Buddha** gleams as if coated in liquid metal, seated amidst candles and surrounded with offerings of lotus buds and incense. It's a fine example of the curvaceous grace of Sukhothai art, slim-waisted and beautifully proportioned.

Cast in the thirteenth century, the image was brought to Bangkok by Rama III, completely encased in stucco – a common ruse to conceal valuable statues from would-be thieves. The disguise was so good that no one guessed what was underneath until 1955 when the image was accidentally knocked in the process of being moved to Wat Traimit, and the stucco cracked to reveal a patch of gold. The discovery launched a country-wide craze for tapping away at plaster Buddhas in search of hidden precious metals, but Wat Traimit's is still the most valuable – it's valued, by weight alone, at over US$10 million.

Sampeng Lane, Soi Issaranuphap and Wat Mangkon Kamalawat

From Wat Traimit, walk northwest from the big China Gate roundabout along Thanon Yaowarat, and make a left turn onto Thanon Songsawat, to reach **Sampeng Lane** (also signposted as Soi Wanit 1), one of Chinatown's most enjoyable shopping alleys. Stretching southeast–northwest for about 1km, it's a great place to browse, unfurling itself like a serpentine department store selling everything from Chinese silk pyjama pants to computer games at bargain-basement rates. Similar goods are more or less gathered in sections, so at the eastern end you'll find mostly cheap jewellery and hair accessories, for example, before passing through stalls specializing in ceramics, Chinese lanterns, then shoes, clothes (west of Thanon Rajawong) and, as you near Pahurat, fabrics, haberdashery and irresistibly girlie accessories.

For a rather more sensual experience, take a right about halfway down Sampeng Lane, into **Soi Issaranuphap** (also signed along its course as Yaowarat Soi 11 then Soi 6, and later Charoen Krung sois 16 and 21). Packed with people from dawn till dusk, this long, dark alleyway, which also traverses Charoen Krung, is where you come in search of ginseng roots (essential for good health), quivering fish heads, cubes of cockroach-killer chalk and a gastronome's choice of dried mushrooms and brine-pickled vegetables. Alleys branch off to florid Chinese temples and tiny squares before Soi Issaranuphap finally ends at the Thanon Plaplachai intersection amid a flurry of shops specializing in paper **funeral art**. Believing that the deceased should be well provided for in their afterlife, Chinese people buy miniature paper replicas of necessities to be burned with the body: especially popular are houses, cars, suits of clothing and, of course, money.

If Soi Issaranuphap epitomizes age-old Chinatown commerce, then **Wat Mangkon Kamalawat** (also known as **Wat Leng Nee Yee** or, in English, "Dragon Flower Temple") stands as a fine example of the community's spiritual practices. Best approached via its dramatic multi-tiered gateway 10m up Thanon Charoen Krung from the Soi Issaranuphap junction, Wat Mangkon receives a constant stream of devotees, who come to leave offerings at the altars inside this important Mahayana Buddhist temple. As with the Theravada Buddhism espoused by the Thais, Mahayana Buddhism fuses with other ancient religious beliefs, notably Confucianism and Taoism, and the statues and shrines within Wat Mangkon cover the spectrum. As you pass through the secondary gateway, under the glazed ceramic gables topped with undulating Chinese dragons, you're greeted by a set of four outsize statues of bearded and rather forbidding sages, each symbolically clasping either a parasol, a pagoda, a snake's head or a mandolin. Beyond them, a series of Buddha images swathed in saffron netting occupies the next chamber, a lovely open-sided room of gold paintwork, red-lacquered wood, lattice lanterns and pictorial wall panels inlaid with mother-of-pearl. Elsewhere in the compound are booths selling devotional paraphernalia, a Chinese medicine stall and a fortune-teller.

Pak Khlong Talat and Memorial Bridge Night Bazaar

A browse through the 24-hour flower and vegetable market, **Pak Khlong Talat**, is a fitting way to round off a day in Chinatown, though it's also a great place to come before dawn, when market gardeners from Thonburi and beyond boat and truck their freshly picked produce across the Chao Phraya ready for sale to shopkeepers, restaurateurs and hoteliers. The market has been operating from covered halls between the southern ends of Khlong Lod, Thanon Banmo, Thanon Chakraphet and the river bank since the nineteenth century and is the biggest wholesale market in the capital. The flower stalls, selling twenty different varieties of cut orchids and countless other tropical blooms, spill onto the streets along the riverfront as well and, though prices are lowest in the early morning, you can still get some good bargains in the afternoon.

The riverside end of nearby Thanon Triphet and the area around the base of **Memorial Bridge** (Saphan Phut) hosts a huge **night bazaar** (Tues–Sun 8pm–midnight) that's dominated by cheap and idiosyncratic fashions – and by throngs of teenage fashion victims.

The Chao Phraya **express boat** service stops just a few metres from both markets at Tha Saphan Phut (N6).

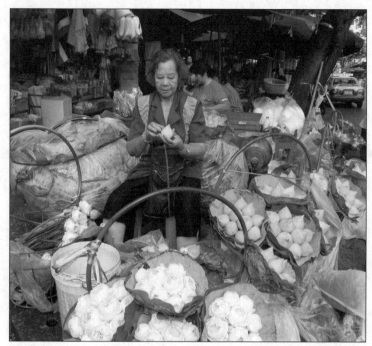

▲ Lotus bud stall, Pak Khlong Talat

Thonburi

For fifteen years between the fall of Ayutthaya in 1767 and the founding of Bangkok in 1782, the west-bank town of **Thonburi**, across the Chao Phraya from modern-day Bangkok, stood in as the Thai capital, under the rule of General Phraya Taksin. Its time in the spotlight was too brief for the building of the fine monuments and temples that graced earlier capitals at Sukhothai and Ayutthaya, but some of its centuries-old **canals**, which once transported everyone and everything, have endured; it is these and the ways of life that depend on them that constitute Thonburi's main attractions. In some quarters, life on this side of the river still revolves around these khlongs: vendors of food and household goods paddle their boats along the canals that crisscross the residential areas, and canalside factories use them to ferry their wares to the Chao Phraya River artery. Venture onto the backroads just three or four kilometres west of the river and you find yourself surrounded by market gardens and rural homes, with no hint of the throbbing metropolis across on the other bank. The most popular way to explore these old neighbourhoods is by **boat**, but joining a bicycle tour of the older neighbourhoods is also very rewarding (see p.86). Most boat trips also encompass Thonburi's imposing riverside Temple of the Dawn, **Wat Arun**, and often the **Royal Barge Museum** as well, though both are easily visited by yourself.

Getting to Thonburi is simply a matter of crossing the river. Either use Phra Pinklao or Memorial/Phra Pokklao **bridge**, take a **cross–river ferry**, or hop on the **express ferry**, which makes several stops on the Thonburi bank.

Royal Barge Museum

Since the Ayutthaya era, kings of Thailand have been conveyed along their country's waterways in royal barges. For centuries these slender, exquisitely elegant, black-and-gold wooden vessels were used on all important royal outings, and even up until 1967 the current king would process down the Chao Phraya to Wat Arun in a flotilla of royal barges at least once a year, on the occasion of

Exploring Thonburi by boat

The most popular way to explore the sights of Thonburi is by **boat**, taking in Wat Arun and the Royal Barge Museum, then continuing along Thonburi's network of small canals. The easiest option is to take a **fixed-price trip** from one of the piers on the Bangkok side of the Chao Phraya, most conveniently from Tha Phra Arthit in Banglamphu, Tha Chang near Wat Pho or the River City pier off Thanon Charoen Krung; see below for a select list of operators. You can also charter your own longtail from these piers and others such as Tha Sathorn, and from many five-star riverside hotels, but bear the listed prices in mind when negotiating and be specific about your itinerary.

Many of the fixed-price tours include visits to one of Thonburi's two main **floating markets**, both of which are heavily touristed and rather contrived. **Wat Sai** floating market happens daily from Monday to Friday but is very commercialized, and half of it is land-based anyway, while **Taling Chan** floating market is also fairly manufactured but more fun, though it only operates on Saturdays and Sundays (approx 9am–3pm). Taling Chan market is held on Khlong Chak Phra, in front of Taling Chan District Office, a couple of kilometres west of Thonburi train station, and can also be reached by taking bus #79 from Banglamphu. Arguably more photogenic, and certainly a lot more genuine, are the individual **floating vendors** who continue to paddle from house-to-house in Thonburi, touting anything from hot food to plastic buckets. You've a good chance of seeing some of them in action on almost any longtail boat tour on any day of the week, particularly in the morning.

Mitchaopaya Travel Service Tha Chang ☎02 623 6169. Offers trips of varying durations: in 1hr (B1000 per boat), you'll go out along Khlong Bangkok Noi and back via Khlong Mon, passing Wat Arun and the Royal Barge Museum without stopping; in 90min (B1300), you'd have time to stop at either or you could do a longer route, coming back along Khlong Bangkok Yai; while in 2hr (B1500) you'll have time to go right down the back canals on the Thonburi side and visit an orchid farm. On Sat & Sun, the 90min and 2hr trips take in Taling Chan floating market.

New Road Guest House see p.103. Recommended four-hour longtail trips with a knowledgeable, English-speaking guide that take you deep into Thonburi, passing orchards and taking in an orchid farm, with a drop-off at Wat Pho or the Grand Palace possible on the way back. B700 per person.

Real Asia ☎02 665 6364, Ⓦwww.realasia.net. Runs guided full-day walking and boat tours of the Thonburi canals for B2000 per person.

River City pier longtails ☎02 237 0077 ext. 180. Private longtail trips for B800 per 1hr per boat for two people.

Tha Phra Arthit longtails Pier in front of *The Old Phra Arthit Gastronobar*, 200m south of the N13 Tha Phra Arthit express boat pier, Banglamphu. An enjoyable 90min loop via Khlong Bangkok Noi, Khlong Chak Phra and Khlong Bangkok Yai that takes in a variety of different khlong-side residences, temples and itinerant floating vendors, but won't include any stops. B850 per 1hr per boat for two people; B1300 per 90min per boat for two to six; B1600 per 2hr per boat for up to six people.

Wan Fah River City Shopping Centre pier ☎02 639 0704, Ⓦwww.wanfahcruise.com. A 2hr cruise of the west-bank canals by a combination of longtail and converted rice barge. Daily 2.30pm; B700 per person.

Kathin, the annual donation of robes by the laity to the temple at the end of the rainy season. But the hundred-year-old boats are becoming quite frail, so such an event is now rare: the last full-scale royal procession was floated for Kathin in 2007, to mark the king's 80th birthday. A **royal barge procession** along the Chao Phraya is a magnificent event, all the more spectacular because it happens so infrequently. Fifty or more barges fill the width of the river and stretch for almost 1km, drifting slowly to the measured beat of a drum and the hypnotic strains of ancient boating hymns, chanted by over two thousand oarsmen dressed in luscious brocades.

The eight beautifully crafted vessels at the heart of the ceremony are housed in the **Royal Barge Museum** on the north bank of Khlong Bangkok Noi (daily 9am–5pm; B30; ⓦ www.thailandmuseum.com). Up to 50m long and intricately lacquered and gilded all over, they taper at the prow into imposing mythical figures after a design first used by the kings of Ayutthaya. Rama I had the boats copied and, when those fell into disrepair, Rama VI commissioned the exact reconstructions still in use today. The most important is *Sri Suphanahongse*, which bears the king and queen and is graced by a glittering five-metre-high prow representing the golden swan Hamsa, mount of the Hindu god Brahma. In front of it floats *Anantanagaraj*, fronted by a magnificent seven-headed naga and bearing a Buddha image. The newest addition to the fleet is *Narai Song Suban*, which was commissioned by the current king for his golden jubilee in 1996; it is a copy of the mid-nineteenth-century original and is crowned with a black Vishnu (Narai) astride a garuda figurehead. A display of miniaturized royal barges at the back of the museum recreates the exact formation of a traditional procession.

The museum is a feature of most canal tours but is easily visited on your own. Just take the Chao Phraya **express boat** to Tha Phra Pinklao (N12) or, if coming from Banglamphu, take the cheaper, more frequent cross-river ferry (B4) from under Pinklao bridge, beside the tourist information office, to Tha Phra Pinklao across the river, then walk up the road a hundred metres and take the first left down Soi Wat Dusitaram. If coming by **bus** from the Bangkok side (#507, #509 and #511 all cross the river here), get off at the first stop on the Thonburi side, which is right beside the mouth of Soi Wat Dusitaram. Signs from Soi Wat Dusitaram lead you through a jumble of walkways and stilt-houses to the museum, about ten minutes' walk away.

Wat Arun

Almost directly across the river from Wat Pho rises the enormous, five-spired prang of **Wat Arun** (daily 8am–5pm; B20; ⓦ www.watarun.org), the Temple of Dawn, probably Bangkok's most memorable landmark and familiar as the silhouette used in the TAT logo. It looks particularly impressive from the river as you head downstream from the Grand Palace towards the *Oriental Hotel*, but is ornate enough to be well worth stopping off for a closer look. All boat tours include half an hour here, but Wat Arun is also easily visited by yourself, although tour operators will try to persuade you otherwise: just take a B4 cross-river **ferry** from the pier adjacent to the Chao Phraya express-boat pier at Tha Thien.

A wat has occupied this site since the Ayutthaya period, but only in 1768 did it become known as the Temple of Dawn – when General Phraya Taksin reputedly reached his new capital at the break of day. The temple served as his royal chapel and housed the recaptured Emerald Buddha for several years until the image was moved to Wat Phra Kaeo in 1785. Despite losing its special status after the relocation, Wat Arun continued to be revered and its corncob

▲ Wat Arun

prang was reconstructed and enlarged to its present height of 81m by Rama II and Rama III.

The prang that you see today is classic Ayutthayan style, built as a representation of Mount Meru, the home of the gods in Khmer cosmology. By climbing the two tiers of the square base that supports the **central prang**, you not only enjoy a good view of the river and beyond, but also get a chance to examine the tower's distinctive decorations. Both this main prang and the four minor ones that encircle it are studded all over with bits of broken porcelain, ceramic shards and tiny bowls that have been fashioned into an amazing array of polychromatic flowers. The statues of mythical *yaksha* demons and half-bird, half-human *kinnari* that support the different levels are similarly decorated. The crockery probably came from China, possibly from commercial shipments that were damaged at sea, and the overall effect is highly decorative and far more subtle than the dazzling glass mosaics that clad most wat buildings. On the first terrace, the mondops at each cardinal point contain statues of the Buddha at birth (north), in meditation (east), preaching his first sermon (south) and entering Nirvana (west). The second platform surrounds the base of the prang proper, whose closed entranceways are guarded by four statues of the Hindu god Indra on his three-headed elephant Erawan. In the niches of the smaller prangs stand statues of Phra Pai, the god of the wind, on horseback.

Dusit

Connected to Ratanakosin via the boulevards of Rajdamnoen Klang and Rajdamnoen Nok, the spacious, leafy area known as **Dusit** has been a royal district since the reign of Rama V, King Chulalongkorn (1860–1910). The first Thai monarch to visit Europe, Rama V returned with radical plans for the modernization of his capital, the fruits of which are most visible in Dusit, notably at **Vimanmek Palace** and **Wat Benjamabophit**, the so-called "Marble Temple". Even now, **Rama V** still commands a loyal following and the statue of him, helmeted and on horseback, which stands at the Thanon U-Thong Nai-Thanon Sri Ayutthaya crossroads, is presented with offerings every week and is also the focus of celebrations on Chulalongkorn Day (Oct 23). On December 2 Dusit is also the venue for the spectacular annual **Trooping the Colour**, when hundreds of magnificently uniformed Royal Guards demonstrate their allegiance to the king by parading around Suan Amporn, across the road from the Rama V statue. Across from Chitrlada Palace, **Dusit Zoo** makes a pleasant enough place to take the kids.

Today, the Dusit area retains its European feel, and much of the country's decision-making goes on behind the high fences and impressive facades along its tree-lined avenues: the building that houses the **National Parliament** is here, as is Government House (used mainly for state functions), and the king's official residence, Chitrlada Palace, occupies the eastern edge of the area. Normally a calm, stately district, in 2008 Dusit became the focus of the **mass anti-government protest** by the royalist PAD movement, whose thousands-strong mass of yellow-shirted supporters occupied Government House and part of Rajdamnoen Nok for an extraordinary three months, creating a heavily defended temporary village in this most refined of neighbourhoods.

From Banglamphu, you can get to Dusit by taking the #70 (non-expressway) **bus** from Rajdamnoen Klang and getting off outside the zoo and Elephant Museum on Thanon U-Thong Nai, or the #56 from Thanon Phra Sumen and alighting at the Thanon Ratchasima entrance to Vimanmek Palace (see box, p.96); alternatively, take the **express boat** to Tha Thewet and then walk. From downtown Bangkok, easiest access is by bus from the Skytrain and subway stops at Victory Monument; there are many services from here, including #28 and #108.

Dusit Park

Breezy, elegant **Vimanmek Palace** (daily 9.30am–4pm; compulsory free guided tours every 30min, last tour 3.15pm; B250, or free with a Grand Palace ticket, which remains valid for one week; Ⓦwww.palaces.thai.net) was built by Rama V as a summer retreat on Ko Si Chang, from where it was transported bit by bit in 1901. The ticket price also covers entry to a dozen other specialist collections in the **Dusit Park** palace grounds, including the Support Museum and Elephant Museum. All visitors are treated to free performances of traditional Thai dance daily at 10.30am and 2pm. Note that the same **dress rules** apply here as to the Grand Palace (see p.111). The main **entrance** to the extensive Vimanmek Palace compound is on Thanon Rajwithi, but there are also ticket gates on Thanon Ratchasima, and opposite Dusit Zoo on Thanon U-Thong Nai.

Vimanmek Palace

Built almost entirely of golden teak without a single nail, the coffee-coloured, L-shaped Vimanmek Palace is encircled by delicate latticework verandas that look out onto well-kept lawns, flower gardens and lotus ponds. Not surprisingly, this "Celestial Residence" soon became Rama V's favourite palace, and he and his enormous retinue of officials, concubines and children stayed here for lengthy periods between 1902 and 1906. All of Vimanmek's 81 rooms were out of bounds to male visitors, except for the king's own apartments in the octagonal tower, which were entered by a separate staircase.

On display inside is Rama V's collection of **artefacts** from all over the world, including *bencharong* ceramics, European furniture and bejewelled Thai betel-nut sets. Considered progressive in his day, Rama V introduced many newfangled ideas to Thailand: the country's first indoor bathroom is here, as is the earliest typewriter with Thai characters, and some of the first portrait paintings – portraiture had until then been seen as a way of stealing part of the sitter's soul.

The Support Museum

Elsewhere in the Vimanmek grounds a dozen handsome, pastel-painted royal residences have been converted into tiny, specialist interest museums, including collections of antique textiles, photographs taken by the King, royal ceremonial paraphernalia and antique clocks. The most interesting of these is the **Support Museum Abhisek Dusit Throne Hall**, which is housed in another very pretty building, formerly used for meetings and banquets, immediately behind (to the east of) Vimanmek. The Support Museum showcases the exquisite handicrafts produced under Queen Sirikit's charity project, Support, which works to revitalize traditional Thai arts and crafts. Outstanding exhibits include a collection of handbags, baskets and pots woven from the *lipao* fern that grows wild in southern Thailand; jewellery and figurines inlaid with the iridescent wings of beetles; gold and silver nielloware; and lengths of intricately woven silk from the northeast.

Chang Ton Royal Elephant National Museum

Just behind (to the east of) the Support Museum, inside the Thanon U-Thong Nai entrance to the Vimanmek compound, stand two whitewashed buildings that once served as the stables for the king's white elephants. Now that the sacred pachyderms have been relocated, the stables have been turned into the **Royal Elephant National Museum** (Ⓦ www.thailandmuseum.com). Inside you'll find some interesting pieces of elephant paraphernalia, including sacred ropes, mahouts' amulets and magic formulae, as well as photos of the ceremony in which a white elephant is granted royal status.

In Thailand the most revered of all elephants are the so-called **white elephants** – actually tawny brown albinos – which are considered so sacred that they all, whether wild or captive, belong to the king by law. The present king, Rama IX, has eleven, the largest royal collection in use. Before an elephant can be granted official "white elephant" status, it has to pass a stringent assessment of its physical and behavioural characteristics. Key qualities include a paleness of seven crucial areas – eyes, nails, palate, hair, outer edges of the ears, tail and testicles – and an all-round genteel demeanour, manifested, for instance, in the way in which it cleans its food before eating, or in a tendency to sleep in a kneeling position. The expression "white elephant" probably derives from the legend that the kings used to present their enemies with one of these exotic creatures. The animal required expensive attention but, being royal, could not be put to work in order to pay for its upkeep. The recipient thus went bust trying to keep it.

Dusit Zoo (Khao Din)

Across Thanon U-Thong from the Elephant Museum is the side entrance into **Dusit Zoo**, also known as **Khao Din** (daily 8am–9pm; B100, children B50), which was once part of the Chitrlada Palace gardens, but is now a public park; the main entrance is on Thanon Rajwithi, and there's a third gate on Thanon

Rama V, within walking distance of Wat Benjamabophit. All the usual suspects are here in the zoo, including big cats, elephants, orang-utans, chimpanzees and a reptile house, but the enclosures are pretty basic. However, it's a reasonable place for kids to let off steam, with plenty of shade, a full complement of English-language signs, a lake with pedalos and lots of foodstalls.

Wat Benjamabophit

Wat Benjamabophit (aka Wat Bencha; daily 7am–5pm; B20) is an interesting fusion of classical Thai and nineteenth-century European design, with its Carrara marble walls – hence the tourist tag "**The Marble Temple**" – complemented by the bot's unusual stained-glass windows, Victorian in style but depicting figures from Thai mythology. Inside, a fine replica of the highly revered Phra Buddha Chinnarat image of Phitsanulok presides over the small room containing Rama V's ashes. The courtyard behind the bot houses a gallery of Buddha images from all over Asia, set up by Rama V as an overview of different representations of the Buddha.

Wat Benjamabophit is one of the best temples in Bangkok to see religious **festivals** and rituals. Whereas monks elsewhere tend to go out on the streets every morning in search of alms, at the Marble Temple the ritual is reversed, and meritmakers come to them. Between about 6 and 7.30am, the monks line up on Thanon Nakhon Pathom, their bowls ready to receive donations of curry and rice, lotus buds, incense, even toilet paper and Coca-Cola; the demure row of saffron-robed monks is a sight that's well worth getting up early for. The evening candlelight processions around the bot during the Buddhist festivals of Maha Puja (in Feb) and Visakha Puja (in May) are among the most entrancing in the country.

Wat Benjamabophit is just a two-hundred-metre walk south of the zoo's Thanon Rama V entrance, or about 600m from Vimanmek's U-Thong Nai gate. Coming by bus #70 from Banglamphu, get off at the crossroads in front of the Rama V statue and walk east along Thanon Sri Ayutthaya.

Downtown Bangkok

Extending east from the main rail line and south to Thanon Sathorn, **downtown Bangkok** is central to the colossal expanse of Bangkok as a whole, but rather peripheral in a sightseer's perception of the city. This modern high-rise area is where you'll find the main financial district, around Thanon Silom, and the chief shopping centres, around Siam Square and Thanon Ploenchit, in addition to the smart hotels, restaurants and bars, the embassies and airline offices. Scattered widely across the downtown area are three attractive museums housed in traditional teak buildings: **Jim Thompson's House**, the **Ban Kamthieng** and the **Suan Pakkad Palace Museum**. Downtown's other tourist highlights include **Siam Ocean World**, a hi-tech aquarium that both kids and adults can enjoy, and the noisy and glittering **Erawan Shrine**.

All of the sights reviewed here are within walking range of a **Skytrain** station, while Ban Kamthieng is also served by the **subway**. If you're heading downtown from Banglamphu, allow at least an hour to get to any of the places mentioned here by **bus**. Depending on the time of day, it may be quicker to take an **express boat** downriver, and then change onto the **Skytrain**. It might also be worth considering the regular **boats** on Khlong Saen Saeb (see p.89).

Jim Thompson's House

Just off Siam Square at the north end of Soi Kasemsan 2, Thanon Rama I, **Jim Thompson's House** (daily from 9am, viewing on frequent 30–40min guided tours in several languages, last tour 5pm; B100, students & under-25s B50; ☎02 216 7368, ⓦwww.jimthompsonhouse.org) is a kind of Ideal Home in elegant Thai style, and a peaceful refuge from downtown chaos. The house was the residence of the legendary American adventurer, entrepreneur, art collector and all-round character whose mysterious disappearance in the jungles of Malaysia in 1967 has made him even more of a legend among Thailand's farang community. National Stadium is the closest **Skytrain** station, but the house is walkable from Central Station (Siam), and a canalside path presents a shortcut from the Khlong Saen Saeb **pier** at Saphan Hua Chang.

Apart from putting together this beautiful home, Thompson's most concrete contribution was to turn traditional silk-weaving from a dying art into the highly successful international industry it is today. The complex now includes a **shop** (closes 6pm), part of the Jim Thompson Thai Silk Company chain (see p.160). Above the shop, the **Jim Thompson Center for the Arts** is a fascinating gallery that hosts both traditional and modern temporary exhibitions on textiles and the arts, such as royal maps of Siam in the nineteenth century or an interactive show that celebrated the hundredth anniversary of Thompson's birth and the vibrant evolution of Bangkok over the same period. There's also an excellent **bar-restaurant** (last food orders 4.45pm), which serves a similar menu to *Jim Thompson's Saladaeng Café* (see p.147). Ignore any con men at the entrance to the soi looking for mugs to escort on rip-off shopping trips, who'll tell you that the house is closed when it isn't.

The grand, rambling **house** is in fact a combination of six teak houses, some from as far afield as Ayutthaya and most more than two hundred years old. Like all traditional houses, they were built in wall sections hung together without nails on a frame of wooden pillars, which made it easy to dismantle them, pile them onto a barge and float them to their new location. Although he had trained as an architect, Thompson had more difficulty in putting them back together again; in the end, he had to go back to Ayutthaya to hunt down a group of carpenters who still practised the old house-building methods. Thompson added a few unconventional touches of his own, incorporating the elaborately carved front wall of a Chinese pawnshop between the drawing room and the bedroom, and reversing the other walls in the drawing room so that their carvings faced into the room.

The impeccably tasteful **interior** has been left as it was during Jim Thompson's life, even down to the place settings on the dining table – Thompson entertained guests most nights and to that end designed the house like a stage set. Complementing the fine artefacts from throughout Southeast Asia is a stunning array of Thai arts and crafts, including one of the best collections of traditional Thai paintings in the world. Thompson picked up plenty of bargains from the Thieves' Quarter (Nakhon Kasem) in Chinatown, before collecting Thai art became fashionable and expensive. Other pieces were liberated from decay and destruction in upcountry temples, while many of the Buddha images were turned over by ploughs, especially around Ayutthaya. Some of the exhibits are very rare, such as a headless but elegant seventh-century Dvaravati Buddha and a seventeenth-century Ayutthayan teak Buddha, but Thompson also bought pieces of little value and fakes simply for their looks – a shopping strategy that's all the more sensible in the jungle of today's Thai antiques trade.

After the guided tour, you're free to look again, at your leisure, at the former rice barn and gardener's and maid's houses in the small, jungly **garden**, which display some gorgeous traditional Thai paintings and drawings, as well as small-scale statues and Chinese ceramics.

Siam Ocean World

Spreading over two spacious basement floors at the east end of the Siam Paragon shopping centre on Thanon Rama I, **Siam Ocean World** is a highly impressive, Australian-built aquarium (daily 9am–10pm, last admission 9pm; B750, children 80–120cm tall B600, under 80cm free; ☎02 687 2000, Ⓦwww.siamoceanworld .com). Despite the relatively high admission price, it gets packed at weekends and during holidays, and can be busy with school groups on weekday afternoons – there are often long queues for the twenty-minute glass-bottomed boat rides (normally B150, though free at the time of writing, on special promotion), which give a behind-the-scenes look at the aquarium's workings. Among other outstanding features of this US$30-million development are an eight-metre-deep glass-walled tank, which displays the multi-coloured variety of a coral reef drop-off to great effect, touch tanks for handling starfish, and a long, under-ocean tunnel where you can watch sharks and rays swimming over your head. In this global piscatorial display of around four hundred species, locals such as the Mekong giant catfish and the Siamese tigerfish are not forgotten, while regularly spaced touch-screen terminals provide information in English about the creatures on view. Popular daily highlights include shark feeds (currently 1pm & 4pm), and it's even possible to walk with the sharks (wearing a diving helmet; B2000 for 15min) or dive with them for thirty minutes, costing from B5300 for an experienced diver to B6600 for a first-timer (including admission price; Ⓦwww.sharkdive.org). You can also watch – through 3D glasses – underwater and other nature films in "4D X-venture", where the chairs move and there are occasional sprays of water (normally B250, though free at the time of writing, on special promotion).

The Erawan Shrine

For a glimpse of the variety and ubiquity of Thai religion, drop in on the **Erawan Shrine** (*Saan Phra Prom* in Thai), at the corner of Thanon Ploenchit and Thanon Rajdamri underneath Chit Lom Skytrain station. Remarkable as much for its setting as anything else, this shrine to Brahma, the ancient Hindu creation god, and Erawan, his elephant, squeezes in on one of the busiest and noisiest intersections in modern Bangkok. And it's not the only one: half a dozen other Hindu shrines are dotted around Ratchaphrasong intersection, most notably **Trimurti**, who combines the three main gods, Brahma, Vishnu and Shiva, on the opposite corner outside Central World Plaza. Modern Bangkokians see Trimurti as a sort of Cupid figure, and those looking for love bring red offerings.

Towering over the Erawan Shrine, the *Grand Hyatt Erawan Hotel* is the reason for its existence and its name. When a string of calamities held up the building of the original hotel in the 1950s, spirit doctors were called in, who instructed the owners to build a new home for the offended local spirits: the hotel was then finished without further mishap. Ill fortune struck the shrine itself, however, in early 2006, when a young, mentally disturbed, Muslim man smashed the Brahma statue to pieces with a hammer – and was then brutally beaten to death by an angry mob. An exact replica of the statue was quickly installed, incorporating the remains of the old statue to preserve the spirit of the deity.

Be prepared for sensory overload here: the main structure shines with lurid glass of all colours and the overcrowded precinct around it is almost buried under scented garlands and incense candles. You might also catch a group of traditional dancers performing here to the strains of a small classical orchestra – worshippers hire them to give thanks for a stroke of good fortune. To increase their future chances of such good fortune, visitors buy a bird or two from the flocks incarcerated in cages here; the bird-seller transfers the requested number of captives to a tiny hand-held cage, from which the customer duly liberates the animals, thereby accruing merit. People set on less abstract rewards will invest in a lottery ticket from one of the physically disabled sellers: they're thought to be the luckiest you can buy.

Suan Pakkad Palace Museum

The **Suan Pakkad Palace Museum** (daily 9am–4pm; B100; ⓦwww .suanpakkad.com), five minutes' walk from Phaya Thai Skytrain station, at 352–4 Thanon Sri Ayutthaya, stands on what was once a cabbage patch but is now one of the finest gardens in Bangkok. Most of this private collection of beautiful Thai objects from all periods is displayed in four groups of traditional wooden houses, which were transported to Bangkok from various parts of the country. You can either take a guided tour in English (free) or explore the loosely arranged collection yourself (a leaflet and bamboo fan are handed out at the ticket office, and some of the exhibits are labelled). The attached **Marsi Gallery**, in the modern Chumbhot-Pantip Center of Arts on the east side of the garden, displays some interesting temporary exhibitions of contemporary art (ⓣ02 246 1775–6, ext. 229 for details).

The highlight of Suan Pakkad is the renovated **Lacquer Pavilion**, across the reedy pond at the back of the grounds. Set on stilts, the pavilion is actually an amalgam of two eighteenth- or late seventeenth-century temple buildings, a *ho trai* (library) and a *ho khien* (writing room), one inside the other, which were found between Ayutthaya and Bang Pa-In. The interior walls are beautifully decorated with gilt on black lacquer: the upper panels depict the life of the Buddha while the lower ones show scenes from the *Ramayana*. Look out especially for the grisly details in the tableau on the back wall, showing the earth goddess drowning the evil forces of Mara. Underneath are depicted some European dandies on horseback, probably merchants, whose presence suggests that the work was executed before the fall of Ayutthaya in 1767. The carefully observed details of daily life and nature are skilful and lively, especially considering the restraints which the lacquering technique places on the artist, who has no opportunity for corrections or touching up.

Divided between House no. 8 and the Ban Chiang Gallery in the Chumbhot-Pantip Center of Arts is a very good collection of elegant, whorled pottery and bronze jewellery, which the former owner of Suan Pakkad Palace, Princess Chumbhot, excavated from tombs at Ban Chiang, the major Bronze Age settlement in the northeast. Scattered around the rest of the museum are some attractive Thai and Khmer religious sculptures among an eclectic jumble of artefacts, including fine ceramics and some intriguing kiln-wasters, failed pots which have melted together in the kiln to form weird, almost rubbery pieces of sculpture; an extensive collection of colourful papier-mâché *khon* masks; beautiful betel-nut sets; monks' elegant ceremonial fans; and some rich teak carvings, including a two-hundred-year-old temple door showing episodes from *Sang Thong*, a folk tale about a childless king and queen who discover a handsome son in a conch shell.

Patpong

Concentrated into a small area between the eastern ends of Thanon Silom and Thanon Suriwong, the neon-lit go-go bars of the **Patpong** district loom like rides in a tawdry sexual Disneyland. In front of each bar, girls cajole passers-by with a lifeless sensuality while insistent touts proffer printed menus and photographs detailing the degradations on show. Inside, bikini-clad women gyrate to Western music and play hostess to the (almost exclusively male) spectators; upstairs, live shows feature women who, to use Spalding Gray's phrase in *Swimming to Cambodia*, "do everything with their vaginas except have babies".

Patpong was no more than a sea of mud when the capital was founded on the marshy river bank to the west, but by the 1960s it had grown into a flash district of dance halls for rich Thais, owned by a Chinese millionaire godfather, educated at the London School of Economics and by the OSS (forerunner of the CIA), who gave his name to the area. In 1969, an American entrepreneur turned an existing teahouse into a luxurious nightclub to satisfy the tastes of soldiers on R&R trips from Vietnam, and so Patpong's transformation into a

Thailand's sex industry

Bangkok owes its reputation as the carnal capital of the world to a **sex industry** adept at peddling fantasies of cheap thrills on tap. More than a thousand sex-related businesses operate in the city, but the gaudy neon fleshpots of Patpong and Sukhumvit's Soi Nana and Soi Cowboy give a misleading impression of an activity that is deeply rooted in Thai culture: the overwhelming majority of Thailand's prostitutes of both sexes (estimated at anywhere between 200,000 and 700,000) work with Thai men, not farangs.

Prostitution and polygamy have long been intrinsic to the Thai way of life. Until Rama VI broke with the custom in 1910, Thai kings had always kept concubines, only a few of whom would be elevated to royal mothers. The practice was aped by the nobility and, from the early nineteenth century, by newly rich merchants keen to have lots of sons. Though the monarch is now monogamous, many men of all classes still keep **mistresses**, known as *mia noi* (minor wives); the common view is that an official wife (*mia luang*) should be treated like the temple's main Buddha image – respected and elevated upon the altar – whereas the minor wife is like an amulet, to be taken along wherever you go. For less wealthy men, prostitution is a far cheaper option: at least two-fifths of sexually active Thai men are thought to visit brothels twice a month.

The **farang sex industry** is a relatively new development, having started during the Vietnam War, when the American military set up seven bases around Thailand. The GIs' appetite for "entertainment" attracted women from surrounding rural areas to cash in on the boom, and Bangkok joined the fray in 1967. By the mid-1970s, the GIs had left, but tourists replaced them, lured by advertising that diverted most of the traffic to Bangkok and Pattaya. Sex tourism has since grown to become an established part of the Thai economy and has spread to Phuket, Hat Yai, Ko Samui and Chiang Mai.

The majority of the women who work in the country's go-go bars and "bar-beers" (outdoor hostess bars) come from the poorest rural areas of north and northeast Thailand. **Economic refugees**, they're easily drawn into an industry in which they can make in a single night what it takes a month to earn in the rice fields. In some villages, money sent home by prostitutes in Bangkok far exceeds financial aid given by the government. Many women from rural communities opt for a couple of lucrative years in the sex bars to help pay off family debts and improve the living conditions of parents stuck in the poverty trap.

Many bar-girls, and male prostitutes too, are looking for longer term **relationships** with their farang customers, bringing a temporary respite from bar work and perhaps even a ticket out. A surprising number of one-night transactions do develop into some sort of holiday romance, with the young woman accompanying her farang "boyfriend" (often twice her age) around the country and maintaining contact after he's returned home. It's a common joke that some bar-girls field half a dozen mobile phones so they can juggle all their various "sponsors". An entire sub-genre of novels

Western sex reservation began. At first, the area was rough and violent, but over the years it has wised up to the desires of the affluent farang, and now markets itself as a packaged concept of Oriental decadence. The centre of the skin trade lies along the interconnected sois of **Patpong 1 and 2**, where lines of go-go bars share their patch with respectable restaurants, a 24-hour supermarket and an overabundance of pharmacies. By night, it's a thumping theme park, whose blazing neon promises tend towards self-parody, with names like *Thigh Bar* and *Chicken Divine*. Budget travellers, purposeful besuited businessmen and noisy lager louts throng the streets, and even the most demure tourists – of both sexes – turn out to do some shopping at the night market down the middle of Patpong 1, where hawkers sell fake watches, bags and designer T-shirts. By day, a relaxed hangover descends on the place. Bar-girls hang out at foodstalls and cafés in respectable dress, often recognizable by faces that are pinched and

and confessional memoirs (among them the classic *Hello, My Big Big Honey!: Letters to Bangkok Bar Girls and Their Revealing Interviews*) testifies to the role money plays in all this, and highlights the delusions common to both parties, not to mention the cross-cultural incomprehension.

Despite its ubiquity, prostitution has been **illegal** in Thailand since 1960, but sex-industry bosses easily circumvent the law by registering their establishments as clubs, karaoke bars or massage parlours, and making payoffs to the police. Sex workers, on the other hand, often endure exploitation and violence from pimps and customers rather than face fines and long rehabilitation sentences. Hardly surprising that many prefer to go freelance, working the clubs and bars in non-red-light zones such as Thanon Khao San. Life is made even more difficult because abortion is illegal in Thailand. The **anti-prostitution law** does attempt to treat sex workers as victims rather than criminals, penalizing parents who sell their children and punishing venue managers and customers with a jail sentence or heavy fine, but this is reportedly haphazardly enforced, owing to the number of influential police and politicians allegedly involved in the sex industry. A high-profile voice in the struggle to improve the **rights of sex workers** is the Empower Foundation (🌐 www.empowerfoundation .org), which not only organizes campaigns and runs education centres for bar workers but also manage its own bar in Chiang Mai.

Inevitably, **child prostitution** is a significant issue in Thailand, but NGOs such as EPCAT (🌐 www.epcat.net) say numbers have declined over the last decade, due to zero-tolerance and awareness campaigns. The government has also strengthened legislation against hiring a prostitute under the age of 18, and anyone caught having sex with an under-15 is now charged with rape. The disadvantaged are still targeted by traffickers, however, who "buy" children from desperately poor hill-tribe and other minority families and keep them as bonded slaves until the debt has been repaid. Street kids and other orphans, including those displaced by the 2004 tsunami and by the ongoing conflict in the deep south, are especially vulnerable to pimps and predators.

The spectre of **AIDS** also puts the problems of the sex industry into sharp focus. UN AIDS statistics from 2004 reported that about one in twenty female sex workers in Bangkok was infected with HIV/AIDS and more than one in a hundred of the general adult Thai population. However, the rate of new HIV infections is in decline, down to 19,000 in 2003, thanks to aggressive AIDS awareness campaigns, particularly those of the Population and Community Development Association (PDA; 🌐 www.pda.or.th /eng), a Bangkok-based NGO, which also runs the famous **Cabbages and Condom** restaurants on Bangkok's Thanon Sukhumvit. It continues to campaign and educate the public, spurred on by fears that young Thais are too complacent about the virus, and by recent reports of a worrying rise in new infections.

strained from the continuous use of antibiotics and heroin in an attempt to ward off venereal disease and boredom. Farang men slump at the bars on Patpong 2, drinking and watching videos, unable to find anything else to do in the whole of Bangkok.

The small dead-end alley to the east of Patpong 2, **Silom 4** (ie Soi 4, Thanon Silom), hosts some of Bangkok's hippest nightlife, its bars, clubs and pavements heaving at weekends with the capital's bright young things. There are many gay venues on Silom 4, but the focus of the scene has shifted to **Silom 2**, while in between, **Soi Thaniya**'s hostess bars and restaurants cater to Japanese tourists.

Ban Kamthieng (Kamthieng House)

Another reconstructed traditional Thai residence, **Ban Kamthieng** (Tues–Sat 9am–5pm; B100; ⓦwww.siam-society.org) was moved in the 1960s from Chiang Mai to 131 Thanon Asok Montri (Soi 21), off Thanon Sukhumvit, and set up as an ethnological museum by the Siam Society. The delightful complex of polished teak buildings makes a pleasing oasis beneath the towering glass skyscrapers that dominate the rest of Sukhumvit, and is easily reached from the Asok Skytrain and Sukhumvit subway stops. It differs from Suan Pakkad and Jim Thompson's House in being the home of a rural family, and the objects on display give a fair insight into country life for the well-heeled in northern Thailand.

The house was built on the banks of the Ping River in the mid-nineteenth century, and the ground-level display of farming tools and fish traps evokes the upcountry practice of fishing in flooded rice paddies to supplement the supply from the rivers. Upstairs, the main display focuses on the ritual life of a typical Lanna household, explaining the role of the spirits, the practice of making offerings, and the belief in talismans, magic shirts and male tattoos. The rectangular lintel above the door is a *hum yon*, carved in floral patterns that represent testicles and designed to ward off evil spirits. Walk along the open veranda to the authentically equipped kitchen to see a video lesson in making spicy frog soup, and to the granary to find an interesting exhibition on the ritual practices associated with rice-farming. Elsewhere in the Siam Society compound you'll find an esoteric bookshop and an antiques outlet.

Chatuchak and the outskirts

The amorphous clutter of Greater Bangkok doesn't harbour many attractions, but both **Chatuchak Weekend Market** and the cultural theme park of **Muang Boran** are worth making the effort for.

Chatuchak Weekend Market (JJ)

With over eight thousand open-air stalls to peruse, and wares as diverse as Lao silk, Siamese kittens and designer lamps, the enormous **Chatuchak Weekend Market**, or **JJ** as it's usually abbreviated, from "Jatu Jak" (Sat & Sun 7am–6pm), is Bangkok's most enjoyable – and exhausting – shopping experience. It occupies a huge patch of ground between the Northern Bus Terminal and Mo Chit Skytrain (N8)/Chatuchak Park subway stations, and is best reached by Skytrain or subway if you're coming from downtown areas; Kamphaeng Phet subway station is the most convenient as it exits right into the most interesting, southwestern, corner of the market. Coming from Banglamphu, you can either get a bus to the nearest Skytrain stop at National Stadium or Ratchathewi, or take the #59, #503 (non-expressway version) or #509 bus all the way from Rajdamnoen Klang (about 1hr); see p.96 for details.

Though its primary customers are Bangkok residents in search of idiosyncratic fashions and homewares, Chatuchak also has plenty of collector- and tourist-oriented **stalls**. Aside from trendy one-off clothes and accessories, best buys include antique lacquerware, unusual sarongs, traditional cotton clothing and crafts from the north, jeans, silver jewellery, and ceramics, particularly the five-coloured *bencharong*. The market is divided into 26 numbered **sections**, plus a dozen unnumbered ones, each of them more or less dedicated to a particular genre, for example household items, young fashions, plants, secondhand books, or crafts. If you have several hours to spare, it's fun just to browse at whim, but if you're looking for souvenirs, handicrafts or traditional textiles you should start with sections 22, 24, 25 and 26, which are all in a cluster at the southwest (Kamphaeng Phet subway) end of the market; sections A, B and C, behind the market's head office and information centre, are also full of interesting artefacts. *Nancy Chandler's Map of Bangkok* has a fabulously detailed and informatively annotated **map** of all the sections in the market; it's best bought before you arrive but is available at Teak House Art in Section 2, near Kamphaeng Phet subway's exit 2. Maps are also posted at various points around the market and for specific help you can also ask at the market office near Gate 1 off Thanon Kamphaeng Phet 2.

The market also contains a controversial **wildlife** section that has long doubled as a clearing-house for protected and endangered species such as gibbons, palm cockatoos and Indian pied hornbills, many of them smuggled in from Laos and Cambodia and sold to private animal collectors and foreign zoos. The illegal trade goes on beneath the counter, despite occasional crackdowns, but you're bound to come across fighting cocks around the back, miniature flying squirrels being fed milk through pipettes, and iridescent red and blue Siamese fighting fish, kept in individual jars and shielded from each other's aggressive stares by sheets of cardboard.

There's no shortage of **foodstalls** inside the market compound, particularly at the southern end, where you'll find plenty of places serving inexpensive *phat thai* and Isaan snacks. Close by these stalls is a classy little juice bar called *Viva* where you can rest your feet while listening to the manager's jazz tapes. The biggest restaurant here is *Toh Plue*, whose main branch is on the edge of the block containing the market office and makes a good rendezvous point (there's a second branch beside Kamphaeng Phet subway station's exit 1). For veggie food, head for *Chamlong's* (also known as *Asoke*), an ultra-cheap food-court-style restaurant just outside the market on Thanon Kamphaeng Phet (across Thanon Kamphaeng Phet 2; 5min walk from Kamphaeng Phet subway's exit 1; Sat & Sun 8am–noon). You can **change money** (Sat & Sun 8am–6pm) in the market building at the south end of the market, and there are several ATMs here too. A few very small electric **trams** circulate around the market's main inner ringroad, transporting weary shoppers for free, though they always seem to be full.

Muang Boran Ancient City

A day-trip out to the **Muang Boran Ancient City** open-air museum (daily 8am–5pm; B300, children B200; Ⓦwww.ancientcity.com), 33km southeast of Bangkok, is a great way to enjoy the best of Thailand's architectural heritage in relative peace and without much effort. Occupying a huge park shaped like Thailand itself, the museum comprises more than 116 traditional Thai buildings scattered around pleasantly landscaped grounds and is best toured by rented **bicycle** (B50; B150 per tandem; B200 per three-seater), though you can also make use of the circulating **tram** (B150 round trip, children B75), and doing it on foot is just about possible. Many of the buildings are copies of the country's most famous monuments, and are located in the appropriate "region" of the park, with everything from Bangkok's Grand Palace (central region) to the spectacularly sited hilltop Khmer Khao Phra Viharn sanctuary (northeast) represented here. There are also some original structures, including a rare scripture library rescued from Samut Songkhram (south), as well as some painstaking reconstructions from contemporary documents of long-vanished gems, of which the Ayutthaya-period Sanphet Prasat palace (central) is a particularly fine example. A team of restorers and skilled craftspeople maintains the buildings and helps keep some of the traditional techniques alive; if you come here during the week you can watch them at work.

To get to Muang Boran from Bangkok, take air-conditioned **bus** #511 to **Samut Prakan** on the edge of built-up Greater Bangkok, then change onto songthaew #36, which passes the entrance to Muang Boran. Although bus #511 runs from Banglamphu via Thanon Rama I and Thanon Sukhumvit (see p.88), the journey is likely to be much faster if you cross downtown Bangkok by Skytrain (and boat and/or subway if necessary) and pick up the #511 at the Ekamai Skytrain stop.

A couple of kilometres east of Samut Prakan, the **Crocodile Farm** (daily 7am–6pm; B300, children B200) figures on tour-group itineraries, but is a depressing place. The thirty thousand reptiles kept here are made to "perform" for their trainers in hourly shows and are subsequently turned into handbags, shoes, briefcases and wallets, a selection of which are sold on site. Songthaews run from Samut Prakan.

Eating

As you'd expect, nowhere in Thailand can compete with Bangkok's diversity when it comes to food: it boasts an astonishing fifty thousand places to eat, almost one for every hundred citizens. Although prices are generally higher here than in the provinces, it's still easy to dine well on a budget. For **Thai** food, the best gourmet restaurants in the country operate from the downtown districts around Thanon Sukhumvit and Thanon Silom, proffering wonderful royal, traditional and regional cuisines that definitely merit a visit. Over in Banglamphu, Thanon Phra Arthit is known for its idiosyncratic little restaurant-bars angled at young Thai diners. At the lower end of the price scale, one-dish meals from around the country are rustled up at the **food courts** of shopping centres and department stores, as well as at **night markets** and **street stalls**, which are so numerous in Bangkok that we can only flag the most promising areas – but wherever you're staying, you'll hardly have to walk a block in any direction before encountering something appealing.

For the non-Thai cuisines, Chinatown naturally rates as the most authentic district for pure **Chinese** food, while there's a sprinkling of Indian and (mostly southern Thai) **Muslim** restaurants around Silom's Maha Uma Devi Temple and nearby Thanon Charoen Krung. Sukhumvit's Soi 3 is a hub for **Middle Eastern** cafés, complete with hookah pipes at the outdoor tables; and good, comparatively cheap **Japanese** restaurants are concentrated on Soi Thaniya, at the east end of Thanon Silom. The place to head for inexpensive,

Western, **travellers' food** – from herbal teas and hamburgers to muesli – as well as a hearty range of veggie options, is Thanon Khao San; standards vary, but there are some definite gems among the blander establishments. Meanwhile, downtown Bangkok has a good quota of **coffee shops**, including several branches of local company *Black Canyon* and the ubiquitous *Starbucks*.

In the more expensive restaurants listed below you may have to pay a ten percent **service charge** and seven percent VAT. Most restaurants in Bangkok are open every day for lunch and dinner; we've noted exceptions in the listings below.

Banglamphu and the Democracy Monument area

Copycat entrepreneurship means that Khao San is stacked full of **backpacker restaurants** serving near-identical Western and (mostly) watered-down Thai food; there's even a lane, one block east, parallel to Thanon Tanao (behind *Burger King*), that's dominated by **vegetarian** cafés, following a trend started by *May Kaidee*. Hot-food stalls selling very cheap **night-market** snacks operate until the early hours. Things are more varied down on Thanon Phra Arthit, with its arty little **café-restaurants** favoured by Thammasat University students, while the riverside places, on Phra Arthit and further north off Thanon Samsen and in Thewet, tend to be best for **seafood** with a view. For the real old-fashioned Thai taste, though, browse southern Thanon Tanao and its network of sois south of Democracy and west of Sao Ching Cha (the Giant Swing), where traditional shophouses have been selling **specialist sweets and savouries** for generations; none have signs or numbers in English, however. See the map on p.94 for locations of the places listed below.

Around Khao San

Lotash Seed Thanon Ram Bhuttri. A tiny pocket of Buddhist calm in an increasingly frantic street, this cosy restaurant has understated lotus imagery and a menu full of delicious Thai classics and one-offs, plus cocktails and wines. The roll-your-own *miang* stuffed tea-leaf starters are a delicious opener and there are great curries, plus *yam taleh* (seafood salad) and a long vegetarian menu. Mains B80–150.

May Kaidee East off Thanon Tanao ⓦwww .maykaidee.com. Simple, neighbourhood Thai vegetarian restaurant, with two outlets on opposite sides of the soi, that still serves some of the best veggie food in Banglamphu despite having spawned a row of competitors on the same alley. Try the tasty green curry with coconut, the Vietnamese-style veggie spring rolls or the sticky black-rice pudding. May Kaidee herself also runs vegetarian cookery classes (see p.167). Most dishes B60–70.

Popaing Soi Ram Bhuttri. Popular place for cheap seafood: mussels and cockles cost just B50 per plate, squid B70, or you can get a large helping of seafood noodles for B100. Eat in the low-rent restaurant area or on the street beneath the temple wall.

Prakorb House Thanon Khao San. Archetypal travellers' haven, with only a few tables, and an emphasis on wholesome ingredients. Herbal teas, mango shakes, delicious pumpkin curry, and lots more besides (B50–90).

Tom Yam Kung Thanon Khao San. Occasionally mouth-blastingly authentic Thai food served in the courtyard of a beautiful early twentieth-century villa that's hidden behind Khao San's modern clutter. The menu (B115–300) includes spicy fried catfish, coconut-palm curry with tofu and shrimps in sugar cane. Well-priced cocktails, draught beer and a small wine list.

Phra Arthit area

Aquatini *Navalai River Resort*, 45/1 Thanon Phra Arthit, next to Tha Phra Arthit express-boat pier. Occupying a nice wooden deck in a perfect breezy riverfront spot beside the express boat pier (even better after sunset when the boats stop running), this hotel restaurant does exceptionally good mid-priced Thai food. Seafood's a speciality: the deep-fried ruby fish served with cashew nuts and bell peppers is very good, and their tangy coconut milk *tom kha kai* soup is especially delicious. Most seafood mains B200–300.

Hemlock 56 Thanon Phra Arthit ☎02 282 7507. Small, stylish, recommended air-con restaurant that's very popular with students and young Thai couples. Offers a long and interesting menu of unusual Thai dishes (mostly about B80), including banana-flower salad, coconut and mushroom curry, grand lotus rice and various *larb* and fish dishes. The traditional *miang* starters (shiny green wild tea leaves filled with chopped vegetables, fish and meat) are also very tasty, and there's a good vegetarian selection. Mon–Sat 5pm–midnight; worth reserving a table on Fri and Sat nights.

Roti Mataba 136 Thanon Phra Arthit. Famous outlet for the ever-popular fried Indian breads, or *rotis*, served here in lots of sweet and savoury varieties, including with vegetable and meat curries, and with bananas and condensed milk (from B10). Mon–Sat 8.30am–10pm.

Thanon Samsen and Thewet

Kaloang Beside the river at the far western end of Thanon Sri Ayutthaya. Flamboyant service and excellent seafood attracts an almost exclusively Thai clientele to this open-air riverside restaurant. Dishes well worth sampling include the fried rolled shrimps served with a sweet dip, the roast squid cooked in a piquant sauce and the steamed butter fish (mains B150–300).

Kinlom Chom Saphan Riverside end of Thanon Samsen Soi 3. This sprawling, waterside seafood restaurant boasts close-up views of the lyre-like Rama VIII Bridge and is always busy with a youngish Thai crowd. The predominantly seafood menu (B130–300) features everything from crab to grouper cooked in multiple ways, including with curry, garlic or sweet basil sauces, but never with MSG. As well as the usual complement of *tom yam* and *tom kha* soups, there are *yam* salads and meat options including stir-fried ostrich with herbs.

May Kaidee 2 33 Thanon Samsen, between the khlong and Soi 1 ⓦwww.maykaidee.com. Air-con branch of Banglamphu's best-loved Thai veggie restaurant and cooking school; see p.143.

South: Thanon Tanao and around

Kai Yang Boran 474–476 Thanon Tanao, immediately to the south of the Chao Poh Seua Chinese shrine (no English sign). Locally famous grilled chicken and *som tam* restaurant (with air-con). Daily 9am–8pm.

Nattaporn 94 Soi Phraeng Phuton, west off southern Thanon Tanao. This family has been specializing in its famous home-made fresh coconut ice-cream for over sixty years, topping it with classic Thai condiments like sweetcorn, red beans and taro balls. They also do chocolate, coffee and ice-tea flavours. To find it, take the first left off Soi Phraeng Phuton and follow it round until you reach Nattaporn, on the corner of the next sub-soi. Mon–Sat 9am–4pm.

Padthai Thipsamai 313 Thanon Mahachai (no English sign), near Wat Rajnadda ⓦwww.thipsamai.com. The most famous *phat thai* in Bangkok, flash-fried by the same husband-and-wife team since 1966. The "extra" option is huge, comes with especially juicy prawns, and is wrapped in a translucent, paper-thin omelette. Best washed down with fresh coconut juice. Daily except alternate Wed, from 5.30pm.

Ratanakosin

The places reviewed below are especially handy for sightseers, but there are also plenty of street stalls around Tha Chang and a load of simple, studenty restaurants off the north end of Thanon Maharat near Thammasat University, as well as a decent restaurant at *Arun Residence* and a daytime café at *Aurum* (see p.99). See the map on p.109 for locations of the places listed below.

Na Pralan Café Thanon Na Phra Lan. This small, cheap café is ideally placed for refreshment after your tour of the Grand Palace. Popular with students, it occupies a quaint old air-con shophouse with battered, artsy decor. The menu, well thought out with some unusual twists, offers mostly Thai salads and one-dish meals with rice, and a range of ice creams, coffees, teas and beers. Mon–Sat 10.30am–10pm, Sun 10.30am–6pm.

Rub Ar Roon Opposite Wat Pho at 310–2 Thanon Maharat. Among many open-fronted, century-old shophouses on this stretch, this cosy, congenial café used to be a dispensary and still has its original teak cabinets. The Thai food is varied and very reasonably priced, and there are sandwiches, espressos, Thai herbal teas and fruit shakes. Daily 8am–6pm.

Chinatown and Pahurat

Much of the fun of Chinatown dining is in the browsing of the night-time hot-food stalls that open up all along Thanon Yaowarat, around the mouth of Soi Issaranuphap (Yaowarat Soi 11) and along Soi Phadungdao; wherever there's a crowd you'll be sure of good feed. Pan Siam's *Good Eats: Chinatown* map, available from major bookshops, is also a great resource for the weirder local specialities. See the map on p.125 for locations of the places listed below.

Chong Kee 84 Soi Sukon 1, near Wat Traimit. Delicious and moreishly cheap pork satay and sweet toast. Tues–Sun 9.30am–7pm, Mon 9.30am–2pm.

Hua Seng Hong 371 Thanon Yaowarat. Braised goose feet is one of the specialities here, but more familiar alternatives include wonton noodle soup and stir-fried crab noodles. Dishes from B160.

Shangri-La 306 Thanon Yaowarat (corner of Thanon Rajawong). Cavernous banquet-hall serving Cantonese classics (B100–1000), including lots of seafood, and lunchtime dim sum. Very popular, especially for family gatherings.

T&K (Toi & Kid's Seafood) 49 Soi Phadungdao, just off Thanon Yaowarat. Known for their barbecued seafood, with everything from prawns (B150 a serving) to oysters (B30 each) on offer. Eat at streetside tables or inside with air-con. Daily 4.30pm–2am.

White Orchid Hotel 409–421 Thanon Yaowarat. Recommended for its dim sum, with bamboo baskets of prawn dumplings, spicy spare ribs, stuffed bean curd and the like, served in three different portion sizes at fairly high prices. Dim sum 11am–2pm & 5–10pm. All-you-can-eat lunchtime buffets also worth stopping by for.

Downtown: Around Siam Square and Thanon Ploenchit

In this area, there are also branches of *Taling Pling* (see p.148), on Floor 3, Central World Plaza (☎02 613 1360–1); *Jim Thompson's Café* (see p.147), on the ground floor of Central World Plaza (☎02 255 9813–4) and at Jim Thompson's House; and *Aoi* (see p.147), in the Siam Paragon shopping centre on Thanon Rama I (☎02 129 4348–50). See the map on p.101 for locations of the places listed below.

Bali 15/3 Soi Ruam Rudee ☎02 250 0711. Top-notch, reasonably priced Indonesian food in a cosy nook, including plenty of options for veggies and authentic desserts. Blow out on the seven-course *rijstaffel* for B400 or restrain yourself with the excellent four-course version for B260. Closed Sun.

Curries & More 63/3 Soi Ruam Rudee ☎02 253 5408–9. And a whole lot more…this offshoot of *Baan Khanitha* (see p.149) offers something for everyone, including European-style fish, steaks and pasta, as well as curries from around the country (from B240). Try the delicious *chu chi khung nang*, deep-fried freshwater prawns with mild, Indian-style curry, or the prawn and pomelo salad. The modern, white-painted interior is hung with contemporary paintings, but the garden, surrounded by waterfalls and with water flowing over the transparent roof, is the place to be.

Food Loft Floor 7, Central Chidlom, Thanon Ploenchit. Bangkok's best department store lays on a suitably upscale food court of all hues – Thai, Vietnamese, Malay, Chinese, Japanese, Indian,

Italian (by *Gianni* – see below). Choose your own ingredients and watch them cooked in front of you, eat in the stylish, minimalist seating areas and then ponder whether you have room for a Thai or Western dessert. There's another, recently opened branch of *Food Loft* on Floor 7 of Zen department store in Central World Plaza.

Genji *Swissôtel Nai Lert Park*, 2 Thanon Witthayu ☎02 253 0123. Excellent, genteel Japanese restaurant, serving authentic food in a contemporary setting overlooking the hotel's beautiful gardens, with a sushi bar, teppanyaki grill tables and private dining rooms.

Gianni 34/1 Soi Tonson, Thanon Ploenchit ☎02 252 1619, ⓦwww.giannibkk.com. One of Bangkok's best independent Italian restaurants, offering a sophisticated blend of traditional and modern in both its decor and food. Offerings include a belt- (and bank-) busting tasting menu for B1290 and innovative pastas. Gianni also runs a couple of classy *Bar Italia* café-restaurants, on the ground floor of Gaysorn Plaza and on Floor 6 of Central World Plaza.

Yellow-flag heaven for veggies

Every autumn, for nine days during the ninth lunar month (between late Sept & Nov), Thailand's Chinese community goes on a **meat-free** diet to mark the onset of the Vegetarian Festival (Ngan Kin Jeh), a sort of Taoist version of Lent. Though the Chinese citizens of Bangkok don't go in for skewering themselves like their compatriots in Trang and Phuket (see p.358), they do celebrate the Vegetarian Festival with gusto: some people choose to wear only white for the duration, all the temples throng with activity, and nearly every restaurant and foodstall in Chinatown turns vegetarian for the period, flying small yellow flags to show that they are upholding the tradition and participating in what's essentially a nightly veggie food jamboree. For vegetarian tourists this is a great time to be in town – just look for the yellow flag and you can be sure all dishes will be one hundred percent vegan. Soya substitutes are a popular feature on the vegetarian Chinese menu, so don't be surprised to find pink prawn-shaped objects floating in your noodle soup or unappetizingly realistic slices of fake duck. Many hotel restaurants also get in on the act during the Vegetarian Festival, running special veggie promotions for a week or two.

Home Kitchen (Khrua Nai Baan) 94 Soi Lang Suan ☎02 253 1888. Like an upcountry restaurant in the heart of the city, this congenial, unpretentious spot offers a choice between air-con and outdoor tables behind a huge open kitchen. On the inexpensive picture menu, you're bound to find something delicious, among dozens of soups – how about the *kaeng liang*, with shrimp, pumpkin and mixed vegetables, for B150? – six kinds of *laap* and a huge array of seafood. Success has spawned a smarter new branch, but with the same menu and just two doors away. Daily 8am–midnight.

Inter 432/1–2 Soi 9, Siam Square. Honest, efficient Thai restaurant that's popular with students and shoppers, serving good one-dish meals from B50, as well as curries, soups, salads and seafood, in a no-frills, fluorescent-lit canteen atmosphere.

Mah Boon Krong Shopping Centre Corner of Rama I and Phrayathai roads. Two good food courts, operating on a coupon system, at the north end of MBK: the long-running area on Floor 6 is a great introduction to Thai food, with English names and pictures of a huge variety of tasty, cheap one-dish meals from all over the country displayed at the various stalls, as well as fresh juices and a wide range of desserts; the slightly upmarket version on Floor 5 is an international affair, spanning specialities from India, Italy, Vietnam, China and Japan, as well as good homegrown cuisine at *Nara Thai*. Both daily 10am–10pm.

Once upon a Time 32 Soi 17, Thanon Phetchaburi ☎02 252 8629. The antique, rustic feel of this restaurant verges on the kitsch, but it's a genteel, quiet place, spread across several old wooden houses in a lush compound. And the Thai food, which includes traditional appetisers and desserts and lots of salads, is very good – try the omelette with sweet basil leaves and the pomelo salad. It's halfway down the soi directly opposite Panthip Plaza, on the right.

Pisces 36/6 Soi Kasemsan 1, Thanon Rama I. Drawing plenty of custom from the local guest houses, a friendly, family-run restaurant, neat and colourful, serving a wide variety of breakfasts and cheap, tasty Thai food, with lots of vegetarian options. Daily 8am–1pm & 5–10pm.

Polo Fried Chicken (Kai Thawt Jay Kee Soi Polo) Soi Polo, Thanon Witthayu ☎02 655 8489. On the access road to the snobby polo club, Bangkok's most famous purveyor of the ultimate Thai peasant dish, fried chicken. All manner of northeastern dishes, including fish, sausages and loads of salads, fill out the menu, but it would be a bit perverse to come to this basic, air-con restaurant and not have the classic combo of finger-licking chicken (B80 for a half), *som tam* and sticky rice. Daily 7am–10pm.

Thang Long 82/5 Soi Lang Suan ☎02 251 3504. Excellent Vietnamese food, such as lemon grass fish (B215) in this stylish, minimalist and popular restaurant, all stone floors, ornamental plants and whitewashed walls.

Vanilla Brasserie Ground floor, Siam Paragon shopping centre ☎02 610 9383. Sophisticated restaurant, patisserie, crêperie, glacier and chocolatier that's a shrine to Western gourmet delights: delicious parma ham and mascarpone crêpes, salads and other main courses, spot-on desserts, and excellent teas and coffees. Their small *Vanilla Industry* café on Siam Square Soi 11 should have reopened by the time you read this. Daily 10am–11pm.

Zen Floor 6 (north end), Central World Plaza ☎02 255 6462; Floor 3, MBK shopping centre ☎02 620 9007–8; and Floor 4, Siam Centre ☎02 658 1183–4. Good-value Japanese restaurant with wacky and colourful modern wooden design and a sushi bar. Among a huge range of dishes, the complete meal sets (with pictures to help you choose) are filling and particularly good. Meanwhile, the recently opened, slightly upmarket Cucina Zen, towards the south end of Floor 3, Central World Plaza (☎02 613 1580–1), promises contemporary Japanese cuisine.

Downtown: south of Thanon Rama IV

Two popular groupings of street stalls off Thanon Silom are worth noting: the top end of Thanon Convent and, away to the west opposite the Maha Uma Devi Temple, Soi 20. In this area, there are also branches of *Baan Khanitha* (see p.149) at 69 Thanon Sathorn Tai, at the corner of Soi Suan Phlu (☎02 675 4200–1), and *Zen* (see above), at 1/1 Thanon Convent (☎02 266 7150–1). See the maps on p.104 and p.80 for locations of the places listed below.

Aoi 132/10–11 Soi 6, Thanon Silom ☎02 235 2321–2. The best place in town for a Japanese blowout, justifiably popular with the expat community. Excellent authentic food and elegant decor. Good-value lunch sets (from B250) available and a superb sushi bar. *Aoi* also operates two *Ramentei* noodle restaurants in this area, at 11/1 Thanon Suriwong (☎02 235 4326) and 23/8–9 Soi Thaniya (☎02 234 8082).

Celadon *Sukhothai Hotel*, 13/3 Thanon Sathorn Tai ☎02 344 8888. Consistently rated as one of the best hotel restaurants in Bangkok and a favourite with locals, serving outstanding traditional and contemporary Thai food – try the banana-flower salad and the red curry with chicken rolls and salted egg – in an elegant setting surrounded by lotus ponds.

Chai Karr 312/3 Thanon Silom, opposite *Holiday Inn* ☎02 233 2549. Folksy, traditional-style wooden decor is the welcoming setting for a wide variety of well-prepared, modestly priced Thai and Chinese dishes, followed by home-made coconut ice cream. Closed Sun.

Cy'an *Metropolitan Hotel*, 27 Thanon Sathorn Tai ☎02 625 3388. Expensive but highly inventive cooking, fusing Asian and Mediterranean (especially North African) elements to produce strong, clean flavours, with great attention to detail. Charming service to go with it, in a stylish room with the best tables on a terrace overlooking the pool.

Eat Me 1/6 Soi Phiphat 2, Thanon Convent ☎02 238 0931. Highly fashionable art gallery and restaurant in a striking, white, modernist building, with changing exhibitions on the walls and a temptingly relaxing balcony. The pricey, far-reaching menu is more international – with dishes such as tenderloin steak fillet with Dijon sauce – than fusion, though the lemon grass crème brûlée is not to be missed. Daily 3pm–1am.

Harmonique 22 Soi 34, Thanon Charoen Krung, on the lane between Wat Muang Kae express-boat pier and the GPO ☎02 237 8175. A relaxing, welcoming, moderately priced restaurant that's well worth a trip: tables are scattered throughout several converted shophouses, decorated with antiques and bric-a-brac, and a quiet, leafy courtyard, and the Thai food is varied and excellent – among the seafood specialities, try the crab (B160) or red shrimp (B85) curries. Closed Sun.

Himali Cha-Cha 1229/11 Soi 47/1, Thanon Charoen Krung, south of GPO ☎02 235 1569. Fine, moderately priced North Indian restaurant, founded by a character who was chef to numerous Indian ambassadors, and now run by his son. Homely atmosphere, attentive service and a good vegetarian selection. There's also a branch down a short alley off the north end of Thanon Convent, opposite *Molly Malone's*.

Home Cuisine Islamic Restaurant 186 Soi 36, Thanon Charoen Krung ☎02 234 7911. The short, cheap menu of Indian and southern Thai dishes here has proved popular enough to warrant a spruce refurbishment in green and white, with comfy booths, pot plants and a few outdoor tables overlooking the colonial-style French embassy. The *khao mok kai* (B60), a typical hybrid version of a chicken biryani, served with aubergine curry, is delicious. Closed Sun lunch.

Jim Thompson's Saladaeng Café 120/1 Soi 1, Thanon Saladaeng ☎02 266 9167. A civilized, reasonably priced haven with tables in the elegantly informal air-con interior or out in the leafy garden. Thai food stretches to some unusual dishes such as southern *khao yam*, a refreshing salad of dried cooked rice, dried shrimps and grated coconut with a sweet sauce. There's pasta, salads and other Western dishes, plus a few stabs at fusion including linguini *tom yam kung*. The array of desserts is mouthwatering, rounded off by good coffee and a wide choice of teas. Daily 11am–11pm.

Khrua Aroy Aroy 3/1 Thanon Pan. Aptly named "Delicious, Delicious Kitchen", this simple shophouse restaurant stands out for its choice of inexpensive, tasty, well-prepared dishes from all around the kingdom, notably *khao soi*, *kaeng matsaman* and *khanom jiin*. Lunch only.

La Boulange 2–2/1 Thanon Convent ☎02 631 0354. A fine choice for breakfast with great croissants and all sorts of tempting patisserie made on the premises. For savoury lunches and dinners, choose from a variety of quiches, plates of charcuterie, sandwiches, salads and simple brasserie dishes such as lamb Provençal.

Le Café Siam 4 Soi Sri Akson, Thanon Chua Ploeng ☎02 671 0030, ⊛www .lecafesiam.com. An early twentieth-century Sino-Thai mansion in a tranquil garden that's difficult to find off the eastern end of Soi Sri Bamphen, but well worth the effort (the restaurant suggests a taxi company ☎02 611 6499; or you can download a map from their website). The French and Thai food, with main courses starting at B250, is superb, served in a relaxing ambience that subtly blends Chinese and French styles, with an especially seductive bar area upstairs. Eve only.

Le Lys 104 Soi Phra Pinit (Soi 7, Thanon Narathiwat Ratchanakharin) ☎02 287 1898–9. In a large, characterful compound – with an air-con room, outdoor tables under a pergola, a bar and a petanque court, the French-Thai owners rustle up excellent, authentic Thai food, supplemented by daily bistro specials such as *assiette de rillettes*.

Mali Soi Jusmag, just off Soi Ngam Duphli ☎02 679 8693. Cosy, informal, low-lit restaurant, mostly air-con with a few cramped tables out front. The Thai menu specializes in salads and north-eastern food, with plenty of veggie options, while pricier Western options run as far as burgers (B180), potato salad, all-day breakfasts, delicious banana pancakes and a few Mexican dishes.

Mei Jiang *Peninsula Hotel*, 333 Thanon Charoennakorn, Klongsan ☎02 861 2888. Probably Bangkok's best Chinese restaurant, with beautiful views of the hotel's riverside gardens

night and day, and very attentive and graceful staff. Cantonese specialities include delicious teas, lobster rolls, smoked duck with tea and excellent lunchtime dim sum such as crystal prawn dumplings – a bargain, starting at B80 a dish.

Ratree Seafood Soi 1, Thanon Silom, opposite Soi Thaniya. Famous and popular streetside stall in the heart of the urban maelstrom, with half-a-dozen tables on the Silom pavement and down the soi behind. The *rot khen* (pushcart kitchen), laden with glistening seafood and even a small water tank for giant shrimp, rolls up about 6pm and barbecues away until around midnight.

Sarah Jane's 55/21 Thanon Narathiwat Ratchana-kharin, between sois 4 & 6 ☎02 676 3338–9. Long-standing restaurant, popular with Bangkok's Isaan population, serving excellent, simple north-eastern dishes, including a huge array of *nam tok* (B85), *laap* and *som tam*, as well as Italian food.

Somboon Seafood Thanon Suriwong, corner of Thanon Narathiwat Ratchanakharin ☎02 234 4499. Highly favoured, bustling seafood restaurant, known for its crab curry (B250) and soy-steamed sea bass, with simple, functional, modern decor and an array of marine life lined up in tanks outside awaiting its gastronomic fate. Daily 4–11.30pm.

Taling Pling 60 Thanon Pan ☎02 234 4872. One of the best Thai restaurants in the city outside of the big hotels, specializing in classic dishes from the four corners of the kingdom. The house deep-fried fish salad (B120) is delicious and refreshing, while the toothsome, deeply flavoured green beef curry with roti (B155) is recommended by the leading Thai restaurant guides. The atmosphere's convivial and relaxing, too.

Tongue Thai 18–20 Soi 38, Thanon Charoen Krung ☎02 630 9918–9. In front of the Oriental Place shopping mall. Very high standards of food and cleanliness, with charming, unpretentious service, in a hundred-year-old shophouse elegantly decorated with Thai and Chinese antiques and contemporary art. Veggies are very well catered for with delicious dishes such as tofu in black bean sauce and deep-fried banana-flower and corn cakes, while carnivores should try the fantastic beef curry (*panaeng neua*; B170).

Thanon Sukhumvit

In this area, there are also branches of the sushi restaurant *Aoi* (see p.147), Floor 4, Emporium shopping centre (☎02 664 8590), and the north-Indian *Himali Cha-Cha* (see p.147), on Soi 31 (☎02 259 6677). For dessert heaven take a stroll around the fifth-floor food stalls in the Emporium, which overflows with luscious gateaux, gelati, mango surprises and other blissful sweets. For those restaurants east of sois 39 and 26 that are not shown on the map, we've given directions from the nearest Skytrain station. See the map on p.106 for locations of the places listed below.

Al Ferdoss Soi 3/1. Long-running Lebanese and Turkish restaurant in the heart of Sukhumvit's Middle Eastern soi, where you can smoke hookah pipes on the streetside terrace and choose from a menu (B80–200) that encompasses shish, hummus, tabouleh and the rest.

Baan Khanitha 36/1 Soi 23 ☎02 258 4128. The big attraction at this long-running favourite haunt of Sukhumvit expats is the setting in a traditional Thai house. The food is upmarket Thai and fairly pricey, and includes lots of fiery salads (*yam*), and a good range of *tom yam* soups, green curries and seafood curries. Most mains cost B190–490.

Basil *Sheraton Grande Hotel*, between sois 12 and 14 ☎02 649 8888. Mouthwateringly fine traditional Thai food with a modern twist is the order of the day at this trendy, relatively informal though high-priced restaurant in the deluxe five-star *Sheraton*. Recommendations include the grilled river prawns with chilli, the *matsaman* curry (both served with red and green rice) and the surprisingly delicious durian cheesecake. Vegetarian menu on request.

Cabbages and Condoms 6–8 Soi 12 ⊛www.pda .or.th/restaurant. The Population and Community Development Association of Thailand (PDA; see p.139) runs this restauarnt – "our food is guaranteed not to cause pregnancy" – so diners are treated to authentic Thai food in the Condom Room, and relaxed scoffing of barbecued seafood in the rainforest beer-garden. Try the spicy catfish salad (B130) or the prawns steamed in a whole coconut (B250). All proceeds go to the PDA, and there's an adjacent shop selling double-entendre T-shirts, cards, key rings and of course, condoms.

Dosa King Soi 11/1 ⊛www.dosaking.net. Usually busy with expat Indian diners, this vegetarian Indian restaurant serves good food from both north and south, including twenty different dosa (southern pancake) dishes, tandooris and the like. It's an alcohol-free zone so you'll have to make do with sweet lassi instead. Most dishes B100–180.

Face Bangkok: La Na Thai and Hazara 29 Soi 38, about 150m walk from BTS Thong Lo Exit 4 ☎02 713 6048, ⊛www.facebars.com. Two restaurants, a bar, a bakery and a spa occupy this attractive compound of traditional, steeply gabled wooden Thai houses. Each restaurant is tastefully styled with appropriate artefacts and fabrics, and the adjacent *Face Bar* makes a chic 'n' funky place for a pre- or post-dinner drink. The very upmarket *Lan Na Thai* restaurant (daily 11.30am–2.30pm &

6.30–11.30pm) serves quality Thai food such as Chiang Mai-style pork curry and deep-fried grouper with tamarind sauce (mains from B400), while the *Hazara* (daily 6.30–11.30pm) specializes in Afghani and north-Indian tandoor cuisine, including murgh Peshawar chicken and the signature cardamom-marinated lamb (B400 and up).

Gaeng Pa Lerd Rod Soi 33/1, no English sign but it's just before the *Bull's Head*. Hugely popular outdoor restaurant whose tables are clustered under trees in a streetside yard and get packed with office workers at lunchtime. Thai curries (from B50) are the speciality here, with dishes ranging from conventional versions, like catfish and beef curries, to more adventurous offerings like fried cobra with chilli, and curried frog.

Gallery 11 Soi 11. Sharing the traffic-free sub-soi with the idiosyncratic *Suk 11* guest house, this restaurant also re-creates an atmosphere of old-fashioned village Thailand, with its wooden building, plentiful foliage, lamplight and staff dressed in late nineteenth-century fashions. The food is good, authentic, mid-priced Thai (mostly B100–200), with plenty of spicy *yam* salads, delicious chicken *larb*, tasty *phanaeng* curry plus Thai desserts, cocktails and imported wines by the glass. It all adds up to a special occasion ambience, but without the pretension or high prices of its better known competitors.

Le Dalat Indochine 14 Soi 23 ☎02 661 7967. There's Indochinese romance aplenty at this delightful early twentieth-century villa decked out in homely style with plenty of photos, pot plants and eclectic curiosities. The extensive, Vietnamese menu (B250–1200) features favourites such as *goi ca* salad of aromatic herbs and shredded pork, *chao tom* shrimp sticks and *ga sa gung*, chicken curry with caramelized ginger.

Suda Restaurant Soi 14. Unpretentious shophouse restaurant whose formica tables and plastic chairs spill out onto the soi and are mainly patronized by budget-conscious expats and their Thai friends. The friendly proprietor serves a good, long menu of Thai favourites (mostly B50–80), including deep-fried chicken in banana leaves, battered shrimps, fried tuna with cashews and chilli, and sticky rice with mango. Mon–Sat 11am–midnight, Sun 4pm–midnight.

Vientiane Kitchen (Khrua Vientiane) 8 Soi 36, about 50m south off Thanon Sukhumvit. Just a 3min walk west then south from BTS Thong Lo (Exit 2) and you're transported into a little piece of Isaan, where the menu's stocked full of northeastern delicacies, a live band sets the mood with heart-felt folk songs, and there are even occasional performances by a troupe of upcountry dancers. The Lao- and Isaan-accented menu (B120–300) includes vegetable curry with ants' eggs, spicy-fried frog, jackfruit curry, and farm chicken with cashews, plus there's a decent range of veggie options such as meat-free *larb* and sweet and sour dishes. With its airy, barn-like interior and mixed clientele of Thais and expats, it's a very enjoyable dining experience.

Nightlife and entertainment

For many of Bangkok's male visitors, nightfall is the signal to hit the city's sex bars, most notoriously in the area off the east end of Thanon Silom known as Patpong (see p.137). Fortunately, Bangkok's **nightlife** has thoroughly grown up and left these neon sumps behind in the past ten years, offering everything from microbreweries and vertiginous, roof-top cocktail bars to fiercely chic clubs and dance bars, hosting top-class DJs: within spitting distance of the beer bellies flopped onto Patpong's bars, for example, lies Soi 4, Thanon Silom, one of the city's most happening after-dark haunts. Along with Silom 4, the high-concept clubs and bars of Sukhumvit and the lively, teeming venues of Banglamphu pull in the style-conscious cream of Thai youth and are tempting an increasing number of travellers to stuff their party gear into their rucksacks. Though Silom 4 started out as a purely **gay** area, it now offers a range of styles in gay, mixed and straight pubs, DJ bars and clubs, while the city's other main gay area is the more exclusive Silom 2 (towards Thanon Rama IV).

Most bars and clubs **open** nightly until 1am, while clubs on Silom 4 and Silom 2 can stay open until 2am. In the past few years, there have been regular "social order" clampdowns by the police, strictly enforcing these closing times, conducting occasional urine tests for drugs on bar customers, and setting up widespread ID checks to curb under-age drinking (you have to be 20 or over to drink in bars and clubs). However, at the time of writing, probably partly due to the political turmoil, things were much more chilled, with clubs staying open into the wee hours on busy nights and little sign of ID checks. It's hard to predict how the situation might develop, but you'll soon get an idea of how the wind is blowing when you arrive in Bangkok – and there's little harm in taking your passport out with you, just in case.

On the cultural front, the most accessible of the capital's performing arts are **Thai dancing**, particularly when served up in bite-size portions in tourist shows, and the graceful and humorous performances at the **Traditional Thai Puppet Theatre**. **Thai boxing** is also well worth watching: the raucous live experience at either of Bangkok's two main national stadia far outshines the TV coverage.

Bars and clubs

The travellers' enclave of **Banglamphu** takes on a new personality after dark, when its hub, Thanon Khao San, becomes a "walking street", closed to all traffic but open to almost any kind of makeshift stall, selling everything from fried bananas and buckets of "very strong" cocktails to share, to bargain fashions and one-off art works. Young Thais crowd the area to browse and snack before piling in to Banglamphu's more stylish bars and indie live-music clubs, most of which are free to enter (though some ask you to show ID first).

Downtown, there's a small knot of bars that are popular with both foreigners and Thais on Soi Sarasin (along the north side of Lumphini Park), as well as a larger concentration around the east end of Thanon Silom. Sarasin's western end (between *Brown Sugar* and Thanon Rajdamri) supports a gaggle of good-time, gay and straight, DJ bars such as the *Seventies Bar* that heave at weekends. On Silom 4, while most of the gay venues have been around for some years now, other bars and clubs have opened and closed with bewildering speed. All the same, on a short, slow bar-crawl around this wide, traffic-free alley lined with pavement tables, it would be hard not to find somewhere to enjoy yourself. If, among all the choice of nightlife around Silom, you do end up in one of Patpong's sex shows, watch out for hyper-inflated bar bills and other cons – plenty of customers get ripped off in some way, and stories of menacing bouncers are legion. A night out on **Thanon Sukhumvit** could also be subsumed by the girlie bars and hostess-run bar-beers (open-sided drinking halls with huge circular bars) on sois Nana and Cowboy, but there's plenty of style on Sukhumvit too, especially in the rooftop bars and enjoyably trendy clubs.

During the cool season (Nov–Feb), an evening out at one of the seasonal **beer gardens** is a pleasant way of soaking up the urban atmosphere (and the traffic fumes). You'll find them in hotel forecourts or sprawled in front of dozens of shopping centres all over the city, most notably Central World Plaza.

Getting back to your lodgings should be no problem in the small hours: many bus routes run a (reduced) service throughout the night, and tuk-tuks and taxis are always at hand – though it's probably best for unaccompanied women to avoid using tuk-tuks late at night.

Banglamphu and Ratanakosin

Except where indicated, all bars listed below are marked on the map on p.94.

Ad Here the 13th 13 Thanon Samsen. Relaxed, sociable little neighbourhood live-music joint where half-a-dozen tables of Thai and expat musos congregate to listen to nightly sets from the in-house blues 'n' jazz quartet (from 10pm onwards). Well-priced beer and plenty of cocktails. Daily 6pm–midnight.

Bangkok Bar Next to *Sawasdee Inn* at 149 Soi Ram Bhuttri ⓦ www.bkkbar.com. Small, dark, tastefully furnished air-con bar-restaurant whose DJs and live indie-rock bands – including occasional big-name appearances – are popular with young Thais and can be a fun introduction to the neighbourhood live-music scene. Daily 6pm–1am.

Bar Bali 58 Thanon Phra Arthit. Typical Phra Arthit bar-restaurant, with just a handful of tables, a small menu of drinking foods and a decent selection of well-priced cocktails. Live music from student singer-songwriters (usually one rather soulful man and his guitar) most nights. Daily 6pm–1am.

Brick Bar *Buddy Village* complex, 265 Thanon Khao San ⓦ www.brickbarkhaosan.com. Massive red-brick vault of a live-music bar whose regular roster of reggae, ska and blues bands, and occasional one-off appearances, are hugely popular with Thai twenty-somethings and teens. Big, sociable tables are set right under the stage and there's food too. The biggest nights are Fridays and

Saturdays when there's a B150 entry charge, which includes one free drink. Daily 7pm–1am.

Café Democ 78 Thanon Rajdamnoen Klang ⓦ www.cafe-democ.com. Fashionable, dark and dinky bar that overlooks Democracy Monument and is spread over one-and-a-half cosy floors, with extra seating on the semi-circular mezzanine. Lots of cocktails, nightly sessions from up-and-coming Thai DJs, and regular trance, techno, house and progressive nights. Tues–Sun 4pm–2am.

The Club 123 Thanon Khao San ⓦ www .theclubkhaosan.com. High ceilings, a central DJ station spinning mostly house music and an intimate dance floor encircled by tables draw a sophisticated young Thai and international crowd. Free entry except for special events when one free drink is included in the B300–500 ticket. Daily 8pm–1am.

Gulliver's Traveler's Tavern Thanon Khao San ⓦ www.gulliverbangkok.com. Infamous, long-established tourist-oriented air-con pub with pool tables, sports TV, reasonably priced beer (happy hours often till 10pm) and a reputation for being something of a pick-up joint. Has a branch on Thanon Sukhumvit. Daily 11am–1am.

Hippie de Bar 46 Thanon Khao San. Invitingly mellow courtyard bar set away from the main fray near *Tom Yam Kung* restaurant. Attracts an indie, mostly Thai crowd, to drink cocktails (B120)

and 3.5-litre towers of draft Heineken (B500) at its wrought-iron tables and artily mismatched furniture. Cool sounds too. Daily 6pm–2am.

Po 230 Tha Thien, Thanon Maharat (see map, p.109). When the Chao Phraya express boats start to wind down around 6pm, this bar takes over the rustic wooden pier and the balcony above with their great sunset views across the river to Wat Arun. It's popular with local students and office workers, hence the loud Thai pop music; avoid the food in favour of beer and Thai whisky.

Susie Pub On the soi between Thanon Khao San and Thanon Ram Bhuttri. Big, dark, phenomenally popular pub that's often standing-room-only on weekend nights. Has a pool table, cheapish beer and DJs playing mainstream pop and generally gets a mixed crowd of farang and Thais. Daily 11am–1am; ID sometimes required.

Siam Square, Thanon Ploenchit and northern downtown

See the map on p.101 for locations of the venues listed below.

Brown Sugar 231/19–20 Soi Sarasin ⓉⓉ02 250 1826. Tightly packed, pricey and atmospheric bar, with a certain crumpled chic, acknowledged as the capital's top jazz venue, with a popular Sunday night jam session.

Club Culture 346/29 Thanon Sri Ayutthaya, opposite *Siam City Hotel* Ⓦ www.club-culture -bkk.com. Huge, attractive former ballroom that's handy for Phaya Thai Skytrain station and trendy amongst Thais and expats. A roster of international and local DJs play house, electronica, trance, drum'n'bass, depending on the night. Tues–Sun 9pm–2am. B400 including two drinks.

Saxophone 3/8 Victory Monument (southeast corner), Thanon Phrayathai ⓉⓉ02 246 5472, Ⓦ www.saxophonepub.com. Lively, easy-going, spacious venue with decent Thai and Western food and a diverse roster of bands – mostly jazz (Mon–Thurs) and blues (Fri–Sun), plus acoustic guitar, funk, rock and reggae – that attracts a good mix of Thais and foreigners.

The Tunnel Soi Lang Suan, behind *Ma Be Ba* restaurant. The after-hours club of the moment, though it suffers from sporadic police clampdowns, hence the dimly lit entrance. The decor is grotto-like with a riot of mosaics, while the music policy is strictly electro and house. Open 10pm till 3–5am or later, depending on the constabulary, busy after 1am. Sun–Thurs free, Fri & Sat B500 including two drinks.

Southern downtown: south of Thanon Rama IV

See the map on p.104 for locations of the venues listed below.

The Barbican 9/4–5 Soi Thaniya, east end of Thanon Silom ⓉⓉ02 233 4141–2. Stylishly modern fortress-like decor to match the name: dark woods, metal and undressed stone. With Guinness on tap and a long menu of imported beers, it could almost be a smart City of London pub – until you look out of the windows onto the soi's incongruous Japanese hostess bars. Good food, DJ sessions Tues & Fri and happy hours Mon–Fri 4–7pm.

Lucifer 76/1–3 Patpong 1. Popular dance club playing trance, techno and house in the dark heart of Patpong, largely untouched by the sleaze around it. Done out with mosaics and stalactites like a satanic grotto, with balconies to look down on the dance-floor action. Free entry on quiet nights, B150 including one drink when busy. Radio City, the interconnected bar downstairs, is only slightly less raucous, with jumping live bands, including famous Elvis and Tom Jones impersonators, and tables out on the sweaty pavement.

Noriega's Soi 4, Thanon Silom. Unpretentious, good-time bar at the end of the alley, with nightly live bands (blues, rock or acoustic, including open mike on Thurs) or DJs. Regular salsa nights; happy hour all night Mon & Tues, till 9pm Wed–Sun.

O'Reilly's Corner of Silom and Thaniya roads. Welcoming Irish bar that's especially good for watching TV sport. Guinness and Kilkenny bitter on draught, multifarious drinks offers including 4–7pm happy hours, popular food and varied live music Tues–Sat eve.

Parkbridge Patpong 2 Ⓦ www.theparkbridge.com. An extraordinary setting in a glass-walled bridge two floors above the sleazy soi, and decor that melds imperial kitsch and urban art styles – think graffiti and silver antlers – mark out this French-run bar-disco. Throw in a 6–9pm happy hour and an imaginative menu of DJs (after 9pm) stretching from Japanese (Wed) to bring-your-own (Sun), and you might find yourself still there at closing time (currently 3am-ish weekdays, 5am weekends).

🏃 **The Sky Bar & Distil** Floor 63, State Tower, 1055 Thanon Silom, cnr of Thanon Charoen Krung ⓉⓉ02 624 9555. Thrill-seekers and view

▲ *The Sky Bar*

addicts shouldn't miss forking out for an al fresco drink here, 275m above the city's pavements – come around 6pm to enjoy the stunning panoramas in both the light and the dark. It's standing only at *The Sky Bar*, a circular restaurant-bar on the edge of the building with almost 360° views, but for the sunset itself, you're better off on the outside terrace of *Distil* on the other side of the building (where bookings are accepted), which has a wider choice of drinks, charming service and huge couches to recline on.

Tapas Bar Soi 4, Thanon Silom. Vaguely Spanish-oriented, pricey bar (but no tapas) with Moorish-style decor, whose outside tables are probably the best spot for checking out the comings and goings on the soi; inside, music ranges from house and hip-hop to Latin jazz and funk. Fri & Sat admission B100, Sun free, Mon–Thurs B200 including 1 drink.

Tawandang German Brewery 462/61 Thanon Rama III ☏02 678 1114–6. A taxi-ride south of Thanon Sathorn down Thanon Narathiwat Ratchanakharin – and best to book a table in advance – this vast all-rounder is well worth the effort. Under a huge dome, up to 1600 revellers enjoy good food and great micro-brewed beer every night. Sundays sees cover bands, but the main attraction from Monday to Saturday is the mercurial live music and cabaret, featuring Fong Naam, led by Bruce Gaston, who blend Thai classical and popular with Western styles of music.

Thanon Sukhumvit

Many clubs in Sukhumvit require you to show ID when you enter, to prove that you are 20 or over. See the map on p.106 for locations of the venues listed below.

Bed Supperclub 26 Soi 11 ☏02 651 3537, ⓦwww.bedsupperclub.com. Worth visiting for the futuristic visuals alone, this seductively curvaceous spacepod bar is still the top nightspot in this happening soi. Inside, the all-white interior is dimly lit and surprisingly cosy, with deep couches inviting drinkers to recline around the edges of the upstairs gallery, getting a good view of the downstairs bar and DJ. The vibe is always welcoming and a lot less pretentious than you might expect; some nights are themed, including a weekly gay night. The cover charge (B700 after 9pm on Wed, Fri & Sat, B600 other nights) is redeemable against two drinks. The restaurant section is starker, lit with glacial ultra-violet, and serving a Pacific Rim fusion menu 7.30–9pm (reservations essential). Bar daily 8pm–2am; ID required.

Cheap Charlie's Soi 11. Idiosyncratic, long-running, low-tech, open-air pavement bar that's famous for its cheap beer, customers' hall-of-fame gallery and lack of tables and chairs. A few lucky punters get to occupy the bar-stools but otherwise it's sidewalk standing room only. Mon–Sat 5.30pm–12.30am.

Long Table 25th Floor, Column Tower, 48 Soi 16. This achingly fashionable 25th-floor restaurant is named for its thirty-metre-long communal centrepiece table, which seats seventy and serves contemporary Thai cuisine. But the real attraction is the sleek, Shanghai-style open-sided balcony bar whose "long-tail" cocktails give you ample time to lounge glamorously on the leather sofas and soak up the wraparound panoramas across downtown skyscrapers. Daily midday–1am.

Nest 9th Floor, *Le Fenix* hotel, Soi 11. Whether you unfurl on a daybed, curl up in a basket-chair or recline under a hooded chaise longue at this aptly named rooftop eyrie you'll get an airy view of the condo-spiked skyline (there are covers for wet days) and a decent choice of cocktails (mostly B300) plus a few light meals. Not as slick or spectacular as the more famous downtown sky bars but very pleasant. Nightly 5pm–1am.

Q Bar 34 Soi 11 ⓦ www.qbarbangkok.com. Very dark, very trendy, New York-style bar occupying two floors and a terrace. Famous for its wide choice of chilled vodkas, and for its music, Q Bar appeals to a mixed crowd of fashionable people, particularly on Friday and Saturday nights when the DJs fill the dance floor. Arrive before 11pm if you want a seat, and don't turn up in shorts, singlets or sandals if you're male. Sun–Thurs B500 including two free drinks, Fri & Sat B700. Daily 8pm–1am; ID required.

Gay Bangkok

The bars, clubs and café-restaurants listed here, mostly at the east end of Thanon Silom, are the most notable of Bangkok's gay nightlife venues; *Bed Supperclub* (see p.153) also hosts a regular gay night. For more general background on gay life in Thailand, contacts and sources of information, most of them concentrated in Bangkok, see p.61. Don't forget **Bangkok Pride** (ⓦ www.bangkokpride.org) in November, when the capital's GLBT community struts its stuff in a week of parades, cabarets, fancy-dress shows and sports contests.

The Balcony Soi 4, Thanon Silom. Unpretentious, fun place with plenty of outdoor seats for people-watching, welcoming staff, reasonably priced drinks, karaoke and decent Thai and Western food.

Coffee Society 12/3 Thanon Silom, between sois 2 and 2/1. Gay-friendly, 24hr coffee shop and restaurant with cosy booths and free wi-fi.

Dick's Café Duangthawee Plaza, 894/7–8 Soi Pratuchai, Thanon Suriwong ☎02 637 0078, ⓦ www.dickscafe.com. Stylish day-and-night café-bar-restaurant (daily 10.30am–2am), hung with exhibitions by gay artists, on a traffic-free soi of go-go bars opposite the prominent Wall St Tower, ideal for drinking, eating decent Thai and Western food or just chilling out.

Disco Disco Soi 2, Thanon Silom. Small, pared-down bar-disco with a minimalist, retro feel, playing good dance music to a fun young crowd.

DJ Station Soi 2, Thanon Silom. Highly fashionable but unpretentious three-storey club, packed at weekends, attracting a mix of Thais and farangs; cabaret show nightly at 11.30pm. B100 including one drink (B200 including two drinks Fri & Sat).

GOD (Guys on Display) 60/18–21 Soi 2/1, Thanon Silom, in a small soi between Soi Thaniya and Soi 2. Large, busy club, somewhat more Thai-oriented and with later hours (till 3–6am) than *DJ Station*; occasional cabaret shows. B140 including one drink before 1am, B280 including two drinks. *Richard's* next door is a smart bar-restaurant that's open till 2am.

JJ Park 8/3 Soi 2, Thanon Silom. Classy, Thai-oriented bar, for relaxed socializing rather than raving, with nightly singers and cabaret acts, and a chill-out annexe, *Club Café*, next door.

Sphinx 98–104 Soi 4, Thanon Silom ☎02 234 7249. Plush decor with a vaguely Egyptian theme, terrace seating and very good Thai and Western food attract a sophisticated crowd to this ground-floor bar and restaurant; karaoke upstairs at *Pharoah's*.

Telephone Pub 114/11–13 Soi 4, Thanon Silom. Bangkok's first Western-style gay bar when it opened in 1987, this cruisey, dimly lit eating and drinking venue has a terrace on the alley, telephones on the tables inside for making new friends and karaoke upstairs.

Bangkok for kids

The following theme parks and amusement centres are all designed for kids, the main drawbacks being that many are located a long way from the city centre. Other attractions kids should enjoy include the Museum of Siam (see p.117), Siam Ocean World aquarium (see p.136), Dusit Zoo (see p.133), cycling around Muang Boran Ancient City (see p.141), and the Traditional Thai Puppet Theatre (see p.157). For general tips on kids' Thailand, see p.62.

Bangkok Butterfly Garden and Insectarium In Suan Rotfai (Railway Park), just north of Chatuchak Weekend Market (Tues–Sun 8.30am–4.30pm; free; ☎02 272 4359). Over 500 butterflies flutter within an enormous landscaped dome. There's also a study centre, plus family-oriented cycle routes and bikes for rent in the adjacent park, which also has a kids' playpark. BTS Mo Chit or Chatuchak Park subway.

Children's Discovery Museum Opposite Chatuchak Weekend Market on Thanon Kamphaeng Phet 4 (Tues–Fri 9am–5pm, Sat & Sun 10am–6pm; B150, kids B120; ☎02 615 7333). Interactive and hands-on zones covering science, the environment, human and animal life. BTS Mo Chit or Chatuchak Park subway.

Dream World Ten minutes' drive north of Don Muang Airport at kilometre-stone 7 Thanon Rangsit-Ongharak (Mon–Fri 10am–5pm, Sat & Sun 10am–7pm; B120, children B95; ☎02 533 1152, ⊛www.dreamworld-th.com). Theme park with different areas such as Snow Land, Dream Garden and Adventure Land. Water rides, a hanging coaster and other amusements. Non-air-con buses #39 and #59 from Rajdamnoen Klang in Banglamphu to Rangsit, then songthaew or tuk-tuk to Dream World; or bus, Skytrain or subway to Mo Chit/Chatuchak Park, then air-con bus #523.

Safari World On the northeastern outskirts at 99 Thanon Ramindra, Minburi (daily 9am–4.30pm; joint ticket to both parks B700, children B450; ☎02 518 1000, ⊛www .safariworld.com). Drive-through safari park, with monkeys, lions, giraffes and zebras, and separate marine park with dolphins and sea lions. Both stage animal shows (phone for times). If you don't have your own car, you can be driven through the park in a Safari World coach. Take air-con bus #60 from Rajdamnoen Klang in Banglamphu or air-con #26 from Victory Monument, then a songthaew to Safari World.

Siam Park On the far eastern edge of town at 101 Thanon Sukhapiban 2 (daily 10am–6pm; B400, children B300; ☎02 919 7200, ⊛www.siamparkcity.com). Waterslides, whirlpools and artificial surf, plus rollercoasters, a small zoo and a botanical garden. Air-con bus #60 from Rajdamnoen Klang in Banglamphu or air-con #501/#1 from Hualamphong Station.

Culture shows and performing arts

Because of the language barrier, most Thai theatre is inaccessible to foreigners and so, with a few exceptions, the best way to experience the traditional **performing arts** is at shows designed for tourists, most notably at **Siam Niramit** and the **Traditional Thai Puppet Theatre**. Many tourist restaurants offer low-tech versions of the Siam Niramit experience, in the form of nightly **culture shows** – usually a hotchpotch of Thai dancing and classical music, with a martial-arts demonstration thrown in; it's always worth calling ahead to reserve, especially if you want a vegetarian version of the set menu. You can, however, witness Thai dancing being performed for its original ritual purpose, usually several times a day, at the the Erawan Shrine (see p.136) and the Lak Muang Shrine outside the northeast corner of the Grand Palace. For background on Thai classical dance and traditional theatre, see p.55.

More glitzy and occasionally ribald entertainment is the order of the day at the capital's two **ladyboy cabaret shows**, where a bevy of luscious transvestites dons

▲ Puppeteers with puppet, the Traditional Thai Puppet Theatre

glamorous outfits and performs over-the-top song and dance routines: Mambo Cabaret plays at the theatre in Washington Square, between Sukhumvit sois 22 and 24 (☏ 02 259 5715; nightly 8pm; Nov–Feb also at 10pm; B800); and New Calypso Cabaret performs inside the *Asia Hotel*, on the west side of Ratchathevi Skytrain station at 296 Thanon Phrayathai (☏ 02 216 8937, ⓦ www.calypsocabaret.com; nightly 8.15 & 9.45pm; B1000 or half-price if booked online 5 days ahead).

National Theatre Sanam Luang, Ratanakosin ☏ 02 224 1342 or 02 222 1012. Closed for a lengthy renovation at the time of writing, but has in the past staged roughly weekly shows of music, *lakhon* (classical dance-drama) and *likay* (folk drama), monthly medley shows, plus outdoor shows of classical music and dancing at the National Museum on dry-season weekends – try the nearby Bangkok Tourism Division for the latest information (see p.84).

Patravadi Theatre 69/1 Soi Wat Rakhang, Thonburi ☏ 02 412 7287, ⓦ www.patravaditheatre .com; free shuttle boat transport from Tha Maharaj in front of Wat Mahathat. Highly regarded, experimental, contemporary theatre company rooted in the traditional arts, who stage a dinner-theatre experience at their riverside restaurant *Studio 9* (Fri & Sat 7.30pm; a la carte menu). They also run classes in classical dance and other disciplines, some of which are accessible to non-Thai speakers.

Sala Chalermkrung 66 Thanon Charoen Krung, on the intersection with Thanon Triphet in Pahurat,

next to Old Siam Plaza ☏ 02 224 4499, ⓦ www .salachalermkrung.com. Mainstream traditional and contemporary theatre, plus regular *khon* performances with English subtitles (Fri & Sat 7.30pm; from B1000).

Siam Niramit Cultural Extravaganza Ratchada Theatre, 19 Thanon Tiam Ruammit, 5min walk from Thailand Cultural Centre subway, following signs for the South Korean embassy (see map, p.91) ☏ 02 649 9222, ⓦ www.siamniramit.com. Unashamedly tourist-oriented but the easiest place to get a glimpse of the variety and spectacle intrinsic to traditional Thai theatre. The eighty-minute show presents a history of regional Thailand's culture and beliefs in a hi-tech spectacular of fantastic costumes and huge chorus numbers, enlivened by acrobatics and flashy special effects. Daily 8pm; B1500; tickets can be bought on the spot or through most travel agents. The complex also includes crafts outlets and a buffet restaurant (dinner B500).

Silom Village Thanon Silom ☏ 02 234 4581, ⓦ www.silomvillage.co.th. This complex of tourist shops stages a nightly 50min show at its Ruen Thep theatre (8.30pm; B600) to accompany a set menu of Thai food (available from 7pm), as well as rather desultory free 15min shows at 7.45pm and 8.45pm at its outdoor restaurant.

Thailand Cultural Centre Thanon Ratchadapisek ☎02 247 0028, ext 4280, ⓦ www.thaicultural center.com; BTS Thailand Cultural Centre. Mainstream classical concerts, traditional and contemporary theatre, and visiting international dance and theatre shows.

Traditional Thai Puppet Theatre Suan Lum Night Bazaar, Thanon Rama IV ☎02 252 9683–4, ⓦ www.thaipuppet.com; Lumphini subway. Entertaining, tourist-oriented performances that are well worth it for both adults and children, using *hun lakhon lek* (jointed stick-puppets), an art form that was developed in the early twentieth century and had all but died out before the late owner of the theatre, Sakorn Yangkeowsod (aka Joe Louis), came to its rescue in the 1980s. Each sixty-centimetre-tall puppet is manipulated by three puppeteers, who are accomplished Thai classical dancers in their own right, complementing their charges' elegant and precise gestures with graceful movements in a harmonious ensemble. Hour-long shows (B900, kids B300) are put on daily at the theatre at 8pm, preceded by a video documentary in English at 7.30pm. The puppets perform *khon*, *lakhon* and *likay* stories, accompanied by synopses in English and live traditional music of a high standard.

Thai boxing

The violence of the average **Thai boxing** match may be offputting to some, but spending a couple of hours at one of Bangkok's two main stadia can be immensely entertaining, not least for the enthusiasm of the spectators and the ritualistic aspects of the fights. Bouts, advertised in the English-language newspapers, are held in the capital every night of the week at the **Rajdamnoen Stadium**, next to the TAT office on Rajdamnoen Nok (☎02 281 4205; Mon, Wed, Sun 6pm, Thurs 5pm), and at **Lumphini Stadium** on Thanon Rama IV (☎02 252 8765 or 02 251 4303, ⓦ www.muaythailumpini.com; Tues & Fri 6.30pm, Sat 4.30pm & 8.30pm; Lumphini subway). Tickets cost B1000–2000, though at Rajdamnoen the view from the B1000 seats is partially obscured. Sessions usually feature ten bouts, each consisting of five three-minute rounds with two-minute rests in between each round, so if you're not a big fan it may be worth turning up an hour late, as the better fights tend to happen later in the billing. It's more fun if you buy one of the less expensive standing tickets, from where you can witness the frantic gesticulations of the betting aficiona-does at close range. For more on Thai boxing, see p.55.

To engage in a little *muay Thai* yourself, visit Sor Vorapin's Gym at 13 Trok Kasap off Thanon Chakrabongse in Banglamphu, which holds *muay Thai* **classes** twice daily (B500 per session; ☎02 282 3551, ⓦ www.thaiboxings.com), or Chacrit Muay Thai School, next to Washington Square Theatre on Sukhumvit, between sois 22 and 24 (Mon–Sat 9am–8pm; drop-in sessions B500; ☎02 260 5826, ⓦ www.chacritmuaythaischool.com). For more serious training there are a couple of well-regarded places for foreigners to train on the outskirts of the city: Jitti's Gym (ⓦ www.jittigym.com) and the Muay Thai Institute (ⓦ www.muaythai-institute.net).

Shopping

Bangkok has a good reputation for shopping, particularly for silk, gems, contemporary interior design and fashions, where the range and quality are streets ahead of other Thai cities, and handicrafts are good buys too. As always, watch out for **fakes**: cut glass masquerading as precious stones (see p.163), old, damaged goods being passed off as antiques, counterfeit designer

clothes and accessories, pirated CDs and DVDs, even mocked-up international driver's licences (though Thai travel agents and other organizations
aren't that easily fooled). Bangkok also has the best English-language
bookshops in the country. Department stores and tourist-oriented shops in
the city keep late **hours**, opening daily at 10 or 11am and closing at about
9pm; many small, upmarket boutiques, for example along Thanon Charoen
Krung and Thanon Silom, close on Sundays. Monday is meant to be
no-street-vendor day throughout Bangkok, a chance for the pavements to
get cleaned and for pedestrians to finally see where they're going, but plenty
of stalls manage to flout the rule.

Downtown Bangkok is full of smart, multi-storeyed **shopping plazas** like
Siam Paragon, Siam Centre and Emporium, which is where you'll find the
majority of the city's fashion stores, as well as designer lifestyle goods and
bookshops. The plazas tend to be pleasantly air-conditioned and thronging with
trendy young Thais, but don't hold much interest for tourists unless you happen
to be looking for a new outfit. You're more likely to find useful items in one of
the city's numerous **department stores**: seven-storey Central Chidlom on
Thanon Ploenchit, which boasts handy services like watch-, garment- and
shoe-repair booths as well as a huge product selection (including large sizes), is
probably the city's best, but the Siam Paragon department store (which also
offers garment and shoe repairs), in the shopping centre of the same name on
Thanon Rama I, is also good. They all have children's departments selling
bottles, slings and clothes, or there are Mothercare concessions inside the
Emporium (between Sukhumvit sois 22 and 24) and Siam Paragon shopping
centres, and in Central Chidlom. The British chain of **pharmacies** Boots the
Chemist has lots of branches across the city, including on Thanon Khao San, in
Siam Paragon, on Patpong, in the Times Square complex between Sukhumvit
sois 12 and 14, and in Emporium.

The best place to buy anything to do with **mobile phones** (see p.70) is the
scores of small booths on Floor 4 of Mah Boon Krong (MBK) Shopping
Centre at the Rama I/Phrayathai intersection. For **computer** hardware and
genuine and pirated software, as well as digital cameras, Panthip Plaza, at 604/3
Thanon Phetchaburi (BTS Ratchathevi or canal stop Tha Pratunam) is the
best place: staff are often very knowledgable and helpful, Mac-heads are catered
for, including authorized resellers, and there are dozens of repair and secondhand booths, especially towards the back of the shopping centre and on the
upper floors.

Markets

For travellers, spectating, not shopping, is apt to be the main draw of Bangkok's
neighbourhood **markets** – notably the bazaars of Chinatown and the blooms
and scents of Pak Khlong Talat, the flower and vegetable market just west of
Memorial Bridge. The massive Chatuchak Weekend Market is an exception,
being both a tourist attraction and a marvellous shopping experience (see
p.140). With the chief exception of Chatuchak, most markets operate daily from
dawn till early afternoon; early morning is often the best time to go to beat the
heat and crowds.

Night-time shoppers will want to make a beeline for **Suan Lum Night
Bazaar**, opposite Lumphini Park at the corner of Thanon Rama IV and
Thanon Witthayu (Lumphini subway), a huge development of hundreds of
booths, which is at its best between 6 and 10pm. Down the narrow alleys of
tiny shops, you'll find colourful street fashions, jewellery and lots of soaps,
candles and beauty products, as well as some interesting contemporary decor:

lighting, paintings, ceramics and woodcarving. At the centre stands the Traditional Thai Puppet Theatre (see p.157), with a popular Thai terrace-restaurant in front, and the attractive women's clothes and furnishings, notably rugs, of the Doi Tung by Mae Fah Luang shop (see below), with a hip Doi Tung coffee house attached. Other options for eating and drinking are uninspiring – your best bet is probably the open-air food court and beer garden, with a stage for nightly live music, by Thanon Witthayu. The lease on the night bazaar ran out in 2007, but amidst very protracted legal wrangling and plenty of colourful rumour, it looks set to remain open for a good few years yet – though it might be worth checking with your hotel before setting out.

Handicrafts, contemporary design and textiles

Samples of nearly all regionally produced **handicrafts** end up in Bangkok, so the selection is phenomenal, and many of the shopping plazas have at least one classy handicraft outlet. Handicraft sellers in Banglamphu tend to tout a limited range compared to the shops downtown, but several places on and around Thanon Khao San sell reasonably priced triangular "axe" pillows (*mawn khwaan*) in traditional fabrics, which make fantastic souvenirs but are heavy to post home; some places sell unstuffed versions which are simple to mail home, but a pain to fill when you return. The cheapest outlet for traditional northern and northeastern textiles – including sarongs, axe pillows and farmers' shirts – is **Chatuchak Weekend Market** (see p.140), where you'll also able to nose out some interesting handicrafts.

Bangkok is also rapidly establishing a reputation for its **contemporary interior design**, fusing minimalist Western ideals with traditional Thai and other Asian craft elements. The best places to sample this, as detailed in the reviews below, are on Floor 4 of the Siam Discovery Centre and Floor 4 of the Siam Paragon shopping centre, both on Thanon Rama I, and Floor 3 of the Gaysorn Plaza on Thanon Ploenchit.

Noted for its thickness and sheen, **Thai silk** became internationally recognized only about fifty years ago after the efforts of American Jim Thompson (see p.135). Much of it comes from the northeast, but you'll find a good range of outlets in the capital. Prices are around B600 per metre for two-ply silk (suitable for thin shirts and skirts), or B800 for four-ply (for suits).

Banglamphu and Ratanakosin

Lofty Bamboo *Buddy Hotel* complex, 265 Thanon Khao San ⓦ loftybamboo.com. Fair-trade outlet for Thai crafts, accessories and jewellery, including silver made by Karen people from north and west Thailand, Lahu hill-tribe bags and recycled textile products from tsunami-affected communities in Phang Nga.

Queen's Support Foundation Grand Palace (on the right just inside the Gate of Glorious Victory). Not-for-profit shop that's especially good for beautiful, top-quality *yan lipao*, traditional basketware made from delicately woven fern stems.

Taekee Taekon 118 Thanon Phra Arthit. Tasteful assortment of traditional textiles and scarves, plus a selection of Thai art cards,

black-and-white photocards and Nancy Chandler greetings cards.

Downtown: around Siam Square and Thanon Ploenchit

Ayodhya Floor 4, Siam Paragon, and Floor 3, Gaysorn Plaza (also Floor 4, Emporium, Thanon Sukhumvit). Gorgeous cushion covers, pouffes covered in dried water-hyacinth stalks, bowls, trays and mats.

D & O Shop Floor 3, Gaysorn Plaza ⓦ www .dandoshop.com. Ten enterprising local designers have formed the Design and Objects Association to showcase their diverse contemporary, often poppy wares here: vases, lamps, tableware, jewellery, bags, stationery, even sandals.

Doi Tung by Mae Fah Luang Floor 4, Siam Discovery Centre, and Suan Lum Night Bazaar, Thanon Rama IV Ⓦ www.doitung.org. Part of the late Princess Mother's development project based at Doi Tung, selling very striking and attractive cotton and linen in warm colours, made up into clothes, cushion covers, rugs and so on, as well as rustic ceramics.

EGG Floor 4, Siam Discovery Centre Ⓦ www.eggthai.com. The main draw here are cushion covers, table settings and boxes which tread a fine line between traditional and modern, featuring floral- and coral-inspired motifs in sumptuous colours.

Exotique Thai Floor 4, Siam Paragon. A collection of small outlets from around the city and the country – including silk-makers and clothes designers down from Chiang Mai – that makes a good, upmarket one-stop shop, much more interesting than Narai Phand (see below). There's everything from jewellery, through celadons, to beauty products, with a focus on home decor and contemporary adaptations of traditional crafts.

Gilles Caffier Floor 4, Siam Discovery Centre Ⓦ www.gillescaffier.com. From a French designer based in Nakhon Pathom, who has spent time in Japan but takes his influences from around the world, clippy leather cushions, signature brown "spaghetti" bowls, and some lovely, subtly coloured modern vases.

Lamont Contemporary Floor 3, Gaysorn Plaza Ⓦ www.lamont-design.com. Beautiful lacquerware bowls, vases and boxes, as well as bronze, glass, crystal and ceramic objects, all in imaginative contemporary styles. Lamont also have a pan-Asian antique shop opposite, and sell both contemporary and antique lines at their branch in the *Sukhothai* hotel (see p.105).

Lofty Bamboo Floor 2, MBK, Siam Square. Branch of Banglamphu's fair-trade Thai crafts outlet.

Narai Phand Ground floor, President Tower Arcade, just east of Gaysorn Plaza, Thanon Ploenchit Ⓦ www.naraiphand.com. This souvenir centre was set up to ensure the preservation of traditional crafts and to maintain standards of quality, as a joint venture with the Ministry of Industry in the 1930s, and has a duly institutional feel, though it makes a reasonable one-stop shop for last-minute presents. It offers a huge assortment of reasonably priced goods from all over the country, including silk and cotton, *khon* masks, *bencharong*, nielloware and celadon, woodcarving, silver, basketware and beauty products.

Niwat (Aranyik) Floor 3, Gaysorn Plaza. A good place to buy that chunky, elegant Thai-style cutlery you may have been eating your dinner with in

Bangkok's posher restaurants, with both traditional and contemporary hand made designs; plus lovely, handmade stainless-steel bowls.

Thann Native Floor 3, Gaysorn Plaza Ⓦ www.thann.info. Striking contemporary rugs, cushion covers and furniture, plus famous spa and beauty products (with a high-concept modern spa next door).

Triphum Floor 3, Gaysorn Plaza, and Floor 4, Siam Paragon. Affordable, hand-painted reproductions of temple mural paintings, Buddhist manuscripts from Burma, repro Buddha statues in many styles, lacquerware, framed amulets and even Buddha's footprints.

Downtown: south of Thanon Rama IV

Jim Thompson's Thai Silk Company Main shop at 9 Thanon Suriwong, corner of Thanon Rama IV (including a branch of their very good café; see p.147), plus branches at the Jim Thompson House Museum and at many department stores, malls and hotels around the city; Ⓦ www.jimthompson.com. A good place to start looking for traditional Thai fabric, or at least to get an idea of what's out there. Stocks silk and cotton by the yard and ready-made items from dresses to cushion covers, which are well designed and of good quality, but pricey. They also have a home furnishings section and a good tailoring service. A couple of hundred metres along Thanon Suriwong from the main branch, at no. 149/4–6, a Jim Thompson Factory Sales Outlet sells remnant home-furnishing fabrics and home accessories at knock-down prices (if you're really keen on a bargain, they have a much larger factory outlet way out east of the centre on Soi 93, Thanon Sukhumvit).

The Legend Floor 3, Thaniya Plaza, corner of Soi Thaniya and Thanon Silom. Stocks a small selection of well-made Thai handicrafts, from wood and wickerware to pretty fabrics and celadon and other ceramics, at reasonable prices. Tamnan Mingmuang, its subsidiary opposite, concentrates on basketry from all over the country: among the unusual items on offer are trays and boxes for tobacco and betel nut made from *yan lipao* (intricately woven fern vines), and bambooware sticky rice containers, baskets and lampshades.

Thanon Sukhumvit

Krisna's Just west of Soi 11. Five-floor emporium of mostly mass-produced but good quality artefacts from Thailand and beyond, especially figurines and Buddha statues in wood, lacquer and silver plus some jewellery and trinkets. Mon–Sat 10am–9pm, Sun 4–7pm.

The Shop @ TCDC Thailand Creative and Design Centre, Floor 6, Emporium, Thanon Sukhumvit, between sois 22 and 24. The retail outlet at Bangkok's design centre sells innovative products dreamt up by local creatives, mostly fairly funky stocking-fillers, bags and household items, with just a whiff of kitsch. Closed Mon.

Thai Celadon Soi 16 (Thanon Ratchadapisek). Classic celadon stoneware made without commercial dyes or clays and glazed with the archetypal blues and greens that were invented by the Chinese to emulate the colour of precious jade. Mainly dinner sets, vases and lamps, plus some figurines.

Tailored clothes

Inexpensive **tailoring shops** crowd Silom, Sukhumvit and Khao San roads, but the best single area to head for is the short stretch of Thanon Charoen Krung between the GPO and Thanon Silom (near the Chao Phraya express boat stops at Tha Oriental and Tha Wat Muang Kae, or ten minutes' walk from Saphan Taksin Skytrain station), where all of the recommended tailors below are. It's generally advisable to avoid tailors in tourist areas such as Thanon Khao San, shopping malls and Thanon Sukhumvit's Soi Nana and Soi 11, although if you're lucky it's still possible to come up trumps here: one that stands apart is Banglamphu's well-regarded Chang Torn, located at 95 Thanon Tanao (℡02 282 9390). For cheap and reasonable shirt and dress material other than silk go for a browse around Pahurat market on the western fringes of Chinatown, though the suit materials are mostly poor, and best avoided.

Prices vary widely depending on material and the tailor's skill. As a very rough guide, for labour alone expect to pay B5000–6000 for a two-piece suit, though some tailors will charge rather more. For middling material, expect to pay about the same again, or anything up to four times as much for top-class cloth. Special deals offering two suits, two shirts, two ties and a kimono for US$99 should be left well alone.

A Song Tailor 8 Trok Chartered Bank, off Thanon Charoen Krung, near the *Oriental Hotel* ℡02 630 9708. Friendly, helpful and a good first port of call if you're on a budget.

Ah Song Tailor 1203 Thanon Charoen Krung, opposite Soi 36 ℡02 233 7574. Younger brother of the above, a meticulous tailor who takes pride in his work. Men's and women's suits.

Golden Wool 1340–1342 Thanon Charoen Krung ℡02 233 0149; and World Group 1302–1304

Thanon Charoen Krung ℡02 234 1527, and 38 Oriental Avenue ℡02 238 3344–8. Part of the same company, they can turn around decent work in three or four days, though prices are slightly on the high side.

Marzotto Tailor 3 Soi 42/1 (Soi Shangri-la Hotel), Thanon Charoen Krung ℡02 233 2880. Friendly business which makes everything from trousers to wedding outfits, and can make a suit in two days, with just one fitting, if necessary.

Fashions

Thanon Khao San is lined with stalls selling low-priced **fashions**: the tie-dyed vests, baggy cotton fisherman's trousers and embroidered blouses are all aimed at backpackers, but they're supplemented by cheap contemporary fashions that appeal to urban Thai trendies as well. The stalls of Banglamphu Market, around the edges of the abandoned New World department store, have the biggest range of inexpensive Thai fashions in this area. Downtown, the most famous area for low-cost, low-quality casual clothes is the warren-like Pratunam Market and the surrounding malls at the corner of Phetchaburi and Ratchaprarop roads, but for the best and latest trends from Thai designers, you should check out the shops in Siam Square and across the road in the more upmarket Siam Centre. Prices vary considerably: street gear in Siam Square is undoubtedly inexpensive (and look out for outlet stores such as Jaspal's in Amarin Plaza, Thanon Ploenchit), while genuine Western brand names are generally competitive but not breathtakingly cheaper than at home; larger sizes can be hard to find. **Shoes** and **leather goods** are good buys in Bangkok, being generally hand made from high-quality leather and quite a bargain: check out branches of the stylish, Italian-influenced Viera by Ragazze (Ⓦ www.ragazze.co.th) in the Silom Complex (Floor 2), Thanon Silom, in Central World Plaza or in the attached Isetan department store.

Central World Plaza Ratchaprasong Intersection, corner of Rama I and Rajdamri. This recently refurbished shopping centre is so huge that it defies easy classification, but you'll find plenty of Thai and international fashions on its lower floors and in the attached Zen department store at its southern end.

Emporium Thanon Sukhumvit, between sois 22 and 24. Enormous and rather glamorous shopping plaza, with a good range of fashion outlets, from exclusive designer wear to trendy high-street gear. Genuine brand name outlets include Versace, Prada, Gucci, Chanel, Louis Vuitton – and Mango.

Gaysorn Plaza Thanon Ploenchit. The most chic of the city's shopping plazas: in amongst Burberry, Emporio Armani and Louis Vuitton, a few Thai names have made it onto the second floor, notably Fly Now, which mounts dramatic displays of women's party and formal gear, alongside more casual wear, and

Myth, a gathering of six cutting-edge local designers for men and women in one store.

Mah Boon Krong (MBK) At the Rama I/ Phrayathai intersection. Labyrinthine shopping centre which houses hundreds of small, mostly fairly inexpensive outlets, including plenty of high-street fashion shops.

Siam Centre Thanon Rama I. Particularly good for hip local labels, many of whom have made the step up from the booths of Siam Square across the road – look out for Baking Soda, Fly Now, Greyhound, Headquarter, Jaspal, Kloset, Senada and Theatre – as well as international names like Nike and Quiksilver.

Siam Square Worth poking around the alleys here, especially near what's styled as the area's "Center-point" between sois 3 and 4. All manner of inexpensive boutiques, some little more than booths, sell colourful street gear to the capital's fashionable students and teenagers.

Books

English-language **bookstores** in Bangkok are always well stocked with everything to do with Thailand, and most carry fiction classics and popular paperbacks as well. The capital's **secondhand** bookstores are not cheap, but you can usually part-exchange your unwanted titles.

Aporia 131 Thanon Tanao, Banglamphu. This is one of Banglamphu's main outlets for new books and keeps a good stock of titles on Thai and Southeast Asian culture, a decent selection of travelogues, plus some English-language fiction. Also sells secondhand books.

Asia Books Branches on Thanon Sukhumvit between sois 15 and 19, in Landmark Plaza between sois 4 and 6, in Times Square between sois 12 and 14, and in Emporium between sois 22 and 24; in Peninsula Plaza and in the Central World Plaza, both on Thanon Rajdamri; in Siam Discovery Centre and Siam Paragon, both on Thanon Rama I; and in Thaniya Plaza on Soi Thaniya off Thanon Silom. English-language bookstore (and publishing house) that's especially recommended for its books on Asia – everything from guidebooks to cookery books, novels to art (the Sukhumvit 15–19 branch has the very best Asian selection). Also stocks bestselling novels and coffee-table books.

Bookazine Silom Complex, Thanon Silom; Soi 4, Siam Square; Gaysorn Plaza, Thanon Ploenchit;

and at the mouth of Sukhumvit Soi 5. Alongside a decent selection of English-language books about Asia and novels, these shops stock a wide range of foreign newspapers and magazines.

Books Kinokuniya 3rd Floor, Emporium Shopping Centre, between sois 22 and 24 on Thanon Sukhumvit, with branches at Floor 6, Isetan, in the Central World Plaza, and Floor 3, Siam Paragon, Thanon Rama I. Huge, efficient English-language bookstore with a wide selection of books ranging from bestsellers to travel literature and from classics to sci-fi; not so hot on books about Asia though.

Dasa Book Cafe between sois 26 and 28, Thanon Sukhumvit Ⓦ www.dasabookcafe.com. Appealingly calm secondhand bookshop that's intelligently and alphabetically, categorized, with sections on everything from Asia to chick-lit, health to gay and lesbian interest. Browse its stock online, or enjoy coffee and cakes in situ.

Shaman Books Thanon Khao San (3 branches), Banglamphu. Well-stocked secondhand bookshop where all books are logged on the computer. Lots of books on Asia (travel, fiction, politics and history) as well as a decent range of novels and general interest books.

Ton's Bookseller 327/5 Thanon Ram Bhuttri, Banglamphu. Exceptionally well stocked with titles about Thailand and Southeast Asia, particularly political commentary and Buddhist studies.

Jewellery and gems

Bangkok boasts the country's best **gem and jewellery** shops, and some of the finest lapidaries in the world, making this *the* place to buy cut and uncut stones such as rubies, blue sapphires and diamonds. However, countless gem-buying tourists get badly **ripped off**, so be extremely wary. Never buy anything through a tout or from any shop recommended by a "government official"/"student"/"businessperson"/tuk-tuk driver who just happens to engage you in conversation on the street, and note that there are no government jewellery shops despite any information you may be given to the contrary. Always check that the shop is a member of the **Thai Gem and Jewelry Traders Association** by calling the association or visiting their website (☏02 630 1390–7, ⓦwww.thaigemjewelry.or.th). To be doubly sure, you may want to seek out shops that also belong to the TGJTA's **Jewel Fest Club** (ⓦwww.jewelfest.com), which guarantees quality and will offer refunds; see their website for a directory of members. For independent professional advice or precious stones certification, contact the Asian Institute of Gemological Sciences, located on the sixth floor of the Jewelry Trade Center Building, 919/1 Thanon Silom (☏02 267 4325, ⓦwww .aigsthailand.com), which also runs reputable **courses**, such as a five-day (15hr) introduction to gemstones (US$250).

A common **scam** is to charge a lot more than what the gem is worth based on its carat weight. Get it tested on the spot, ask for a written guarantee and receipt. Don't even consider **buying gems in bulk** to sell at a supposedly vast profit elsewhere: many a gullible traveller has invested thousands of dollars on a handful of worthless multi-coloured stones, believing the vendor's reassurance that the goods will fetch at least a hundred percent more when resold at home. Gem scams are so common in Bangkok that TAT has published a brochure about it and there are several websites on the subject, including the very informative ⓦwww.2bangkok.com/2bangkok/Scams /Sapphire.shtml, which describes the typical scam in detail and advises on what to do if you get caught out; it's also updated with details of the latest scammers. Most victims get no recompense at all, but you have more chance of doing so if you contact the website's recommended authorities while still in Thailand.

The most exclusive of the reputable **gem outlets** are on Thanon Silom, notably in the Jewelry Trade Center (Silom Galleria); you can get an idea of prices at the online catalogue ⓦwww.thaigem.com. Other recommended outlets include the nearby, American-owned Lambert, Silom Shanghai Building, Soi 17, Thanon Silom (☏02 236 4343, ⓦwww.lambertgems.com); the very upscale Kim's in Oriental Place in front of the *Oriental*; and Johnny's Gems at 199 Thanon Fuang Nakhon, near Wat Rajabophit (☏02 224 4065). Thongtavee, Floor 2, River City, and in the Jewelry Trade Center, outlets of a famous Burmese **jade** factory in Mae Sai in northern Thailand, sells beautiful jade jewellery, as well as carved Buddha statues, chopsticks and the like. The hub of Bangkok's **gold** trade is Chinatown, specifically Thanon Yaowarat, which boasts over a hundred outlets. For cheap **silver** earrings, bracelets and necklaces, you can't beat the traveller-orientated jewellery shops along Trok Mayom in Banglamphu.

Moving on from Bangkok

Bangkok is the terminus of all major highways and rail lines, and **public transport** between the capital and the beaches is inexpensive and plentiful. Bangkok is also the best place to make arrangements for onward travel from Thailand, and all the major **Asian embassies** are here (see p.167), so getting the appropriate **visas** should be straightforward.

Travel within Thailand

As well as reliable one-way transfers, many of the Bangkok travel agents listed on p.169 offer day and overnight excursion to popular destinations. For details of **specialist Thai tour operators** offering more distinctive cultural, cycling and trekking packages, see p.21. For information on Thailand's **domestic flight network**, see p.33.

By train

Nearly all trains depart from **Hualamphong Station**, whose 24-hour "Information" booth keeps English-language **timetables**, or you can try phoning the Train Information Hotline on ☎1690; the State Railway of Thailand website (Ⓦwww.railway.co.th) also carries timetables and a fare chart. For a guide to destinations and journey times from Bangkok, see "Travel details" on p.169. For details on city transport to and from Hualamphong, left-luggage facilities at the station, and a warning about **con-artists** operating at the station, see p.82. **Tickets** for overnight trains and other busy routes should be booked at least a day in advance (further ahead for travel on national holidays), and are best bought from Hualamphong, either at the clearly signed State Railway **advance booking office** at the back of the station concourse (daily 8.30am–4pm) or, outside those hours, from the main ticket counters. Train tickets can also be bought through almost any travel agent and through some hotels and guest houses for a booking fee of about B50. Hualamphong's advance booking office also sells **joint rail and boat** and **rail and bus tickets** to Ko Samui, Ko Pha Ngan, Ko Tao, Krabi and Ko Phi Phi. Sample prices include B768 for the train to Surat Thani (second-class air-con sleeper), plus either B250 for bus and boat connections to Ko Samui or B250 for bus connections to Krabi.

A few other services leave from sleepy **Thonburi Station** (sometimes still referred to by its former name, **Bangkok Noi Station**), across the river from Banglamphu in Thonburi. These include a handful of commuter services (not listed on English-language timetables) **to Hua Hin**, Prachuap Khiri Khan and Lang Suan. Thonburi Station is about 850m west of the Railway Station N11 express-boat pier (in use Mon–Fri rush hours only; at other times get off at N10 and walk an extra 500m to N11, through the Siriraj Hospital compound); frequent red songthaews run passengers between the N10 pier and the train station (5 min), or you can walk it in about fifteen minutes by heading up the only road that runs away from the pier, passing a temple, walking alongside (under) the flyover, and turning right at the far edge of the market when you see the station sign.

By bus

Bangkok's **three main bus terminals** are distributed around the outskirts of town and are described in full on p.83. Leave plenty of time to reach them, especially if setting off from Banglamphu, from where you should allow at least an hour and a half (outside rush hour) to get to the Eastern Bus Terminal, and a good hour to get to the Northern or Southern terminals. Seats on the most popular long-distance air-con bus services (such as to Krabi, Phuket and Surat Thani) should be **reserved** ahead of time, ideally at the relevant bus station as hotels and guest houses may book you on to one of the dodgy budget tourist buses described on p.30.

Getting to Suvarnabhumi and Don Muang airports

At the time of writing, all **international flights** depart from **Suvarnabhumi Airport** (coded **BKK**), about 25km east of Bangkok, as do the vast majority of **domestic flights**; however, the future role of the old **Don Muang Airport** (coded **DMK**), about 25km north of the city, remains uncertain (see p.78), and may be used for some international routes, so double-check to be absolutely sure. Currently only domestic services with Nok Air and One-Two-Go are using Don Muang.

Getting to either airport by bus, minibus or taxi can be severely hampered by traffic jams, so leave plenty of **time**. Also note that Suvarnabhumi is enormous but ill-served by travelators, so allow loads of time to get to your gate; there are also a bewildering number of (expensive) shops to engross you en route. Domestic and international **departure taxes** are included in the ticket price. In addition to the transport options described below, both airports are served by slow, crowded **city buses** (see p.88).

For more informataion on **facilities** at both airports see p.78.

Getting to Suvarnabhumi

When the **Suvarnabhumi Airport Rail Link** finally opens for business (currently slated for early 2010), this will be the fastest way of getting to **Suvarnabhumi Airport** from downtown areas. Non-stop Airport Express trains from the City Air Terminal at Makkasan Station (which connects with the subway system at Phetchaburi station) should take about fifteen minutes to the airport, while stopping Airport City Line services from Phaya Thai (an interchange with the BTS Skytrain system) will take around thirty minutes and cost a lot less; a luggage check-in facility is also planned at Makkasan; see p.79.

The Suvarnabhumi **Airport Express bus services** #AE1–AE4 that serve Silom, Banglamphu, Sukhumvit and Hualamphong, as described in detail on p.79, are less useful on the outward journey, mainly because the traffic often makes it impossible for them to stick to their schedules. The most reliable is service #AE2 **from Banglamphu**, which has a printed timetable and dedicated information and ticket sales booth at its pick-up point in front of the *Mayompuri Restaurant* at the west end of Thanon Chakrabongse (at least hourly 7am–11.15pm; B150; 1hr or 90min during rush hour 4–6pm; ☎02 622 3000, ⓦwww.airportexpressthai.com). For the same price most travellers opt instead for one of the private **minibus services** to Suvarnabhumi (at least every 2hr; B150; 90min) organized through guest houses and travel agents in Banglamphu and everywhere else around the city.

A **metered taxi** to Suvarnabhumi can cost anything from B160 to B350 (plus up to B75 in expressway tolls), depending on where you are and how bad the traffic is; on this route, drivers will nearly always try to leave their meters off and agree an inflated price with you – say *"poet meter, dai mai khrap/kha?"* to get them to switch the meter on. If you leave the downtown areas before 7am or after 9pm you can get to the airport in half an hour, but at other times you should set off about an hour and a half before you have to check in.

Getting to Don Muang

There are currently no scheduled airport bus or minibus services to **Don Muang**, so the fastest, most reliable option is a **metered taxi** (B150–350 plus B75 in expressway tolls).

By tourist bus

Many Bangkok tour operators sell tickets for unlicensed **budget tourist buses** to popular long-distance destinations such as Surat Thani (for Ko Samui) and Krabi (for Ko Phi Phi), and to places closer at hand such as Ko Samet and Ko Chang. Prices can vary considerably but often work out just as cheap as air-con buses from the public bus terminals and, crucially, are more convenient as they mostly leave from the Khao San area in Banglamphu. The big drawbacks, however, are the **lack of comfort** and **poor safety**, which particularly applies to the long-distance **overnight services** (see p.30). It is standard practice for budget tour operators, especially those on Thanon Khao San, to assure you that overnight transport will be in a large, luxury VIP bus despite knowing it's actually a clapped-out old banger. **Security** on overnight tourist buses is a serious problem, and because they're run by unlicensed private companies there is no insurance against loss or theft of baggage: don't keep anything of value in luggage that's stored out of sight, even if it's padlocked, as luggage gets slashed and rifled in the roomy baggage compartment. In addition, passengers often find themselves dumped on the outskirts of their destination city, at the mercy of unscrupulous touts. If you are planning a journey to Surat Thani, consider taking the train instead – the extra comfort and peace of mind are well worth the extra baht – or at the least, opt for a government bus or licensed private bus from the relevant terminal. Services to Ko Samet and Ko Chang are usually by air-con minibus; these are usually cramped and can go scarily fast but luggage is generally secure. Bear in mind that Khao San tour operators open up and go bust all the time; see p.169 for recommended travel agents and never hand over any money until you see the ticket.

Leaving Thailand

If buying onward **international air tickets**, be warned that there are many dodgy, transient travel agents in Bangkok, particularly on and around Thanon Khao San, which is known for its shady operators who display fake TAT licences, issue false tickets and flee with travellers' money overnight. The best advice is to use one of the tried and tested **agents** listed on p.169. Never hand over any money until you've called the airline to check your reservation personally (for phone numbers see below) and have been given the ticket; double-check that it's a return ticket if that's what you paid for. For advice on getting to Suvarnabhumi and Don Muang airports, see the box on p.165.

For information on travelling overland **to Cambodia** see boxes on p.201 and p.205; for advice on routes south **to Malaysia** see p.23.

Listings

Airlines Aeroflot ☎02 251 0617–8; Air Asia ☎02 515 9999; Air Canada ☎02 670 0400; Air France ☎02 635 1191; Air India ☎02 653 2288; Air New Zealand ☎02 235 8280–3; Bangkok Airways ☎1771 or ☎02 265 5555; British Airways ☎02 627 1701; Cathay Pacific ☎02 263 0606; China Airlines ☎02 250 9888; Druk Air ☎02 237 9201–3; Emirates ☎02 664 1040; Etihad ☎02 253 0099; Eva Air ☎02 269 6288; Finnair ☎02 634 0238–9; Garuda ☎02 679 7371–2; Gulf Air ☎02 254 7931–4; Japan Airlines ☎02 649 9500; KLM ☎02 635 2400; Korean Air ☎02 635 0465–9; Lao Airlines ☎02 236 9822; Lufthansa ☎02 264 2400; Malaysia Airlines ☎02 263 0565–71; Nok Air ☎1318 or 02 900 9955; One-Two-Go ☎1126; Pakistan International (PIA) ☎02 234 2961–5; PB Air ☎02 261 0222; Philippine Airlines ☎02 633 5713; Qantas Airways ☎02 627 1701; Royal Brunei ☎02 637 5151; SGA ☎02 664 6099; Singapore Airlines

⊤02 353 6000; Sri Lankan Airlines ⊤02 236 8450; Swiss ⊤02 204 7744; Thai Airways ⊤02 356 1111; United Airlines ⊤02 353 3939; Vietnam Airlines ⊤02 655 4137–40.

Airport enquiries Suvarnabhumi: flight information ⊤02 132 0000, airport information counter ⊤02 132 9324–9; Don Muang: domestic departures ⊤02 535 1192, domestic arrivals ⊤02 535 1253; ⊛www.donmuangairportonline.com.

Car rental Avis ⊤02 251 1131–2, ⊛www .avisthailand.com: 2/12 Thanon Witthayu (Wireless Road), Suvarnabhumi and Don Muang airports. Budget ⊤02 203 0250, ⊛www.budget.co.th: 19/23 Building A, Royal City Avenue, Thanon Phetchaburi Mai and Suvarnabhumi Airport. National (SMT Rent-A-Car) ⊤02 722 8487, ⊛www.nationalcarrental.co.th: 727 Thanon Srinakharin and Suvarnabhumi Airport.

Cookery classes Nearly all the five-star hotels will arrange Thai cookery classes for guests if requested; the most famous are held at the *Oriental Hotel* (on Thanon Charoen Krung (⊤02 659 9000, ⊛www.mandarinoriental.com; B4500; Mon–Sat), while the *Bangkok Marriott* (see p.103) offers morning classes aboard a converted rice barge, the *Manohra* (⊤02 476 0022, ext 1416, ⊛www.manohracruises.com; B2600; Mon–Fri), including a market tour to buy ingredients. In a grand, century-old building at 233 Thanon Sathorn Tai (⊤02 673 9353–4, ⊛www.blueelephant.com), the *Blue Elephant* offers courses that range from B2800 for a half-day to a five-day private course for professional chefs for B68,000. Also recommended in the southern downtown area is Baipai, 150/12 Soi Naksuwan, Thanon Nonsee, off Thanon Rama III (⊤02 294 9029, ⊛www.baipai.com; B1600, including transfers from central hotels; closed Mon), who run thorough, morning classes in a quiet, suburban house. Banglamphu's famous vegetarian cook, May Kaidee, shares her culinary expertise at the 33 Thanon Samsen branch of her restaurant chain (⊤089 137 3173, ⊛www .maykaidee.com; see p.143) for B1200 per day. Set in an orchard in a rural part of Nonthaburi, *Thai House* (⊤02 903 9611 or 997 5161, ⊛www .thaihouse.co.th) runs one- (B3500) to three-day (B16,650) cooking courses, all including transfers from downtown, the latter including vegetable- and fruit-carving and home-stay accommodation in traditional wooden houses.

Couriers DHL Worldwide (⊤02 345 5000 ⊛www .dhl.co.th) has several Bangkok depots.

Embassies and consulates See ⊛www.mfa.go .th/web/2694.php for a full list, with links. Australia, 37 Thanon Sathorn Tai ⊤02 344 6300, ⊛www .austembassy.or.th; Burma (Myanmar), 132 Thanon

Sathorn Nua ⊤02 234 4789; Cambodia, 518/4 Thanon Pracha Uthit (Soi Ramkhamhaeng 39) ⊤02 957 5851–2; Canada, 15th floor, Abdulrahim Place, 990 Thanon Rama IV ⊤02 636 0540, ⊛www.international.gc.ca/bangkok; China, 57 Thanon Rajadapisek ⊤02 245 7033 or 02 245 7036; India, 46, Sukhumvit Soi 23 ⊤02 258 0300–5, ⊛indianembassy.gov.in/bangkok; Indonesia, 600–602 Thanon Phetchaburi ⊤02 252 3135–9, ⊛www.kbri-bangkok.com; Ireland (honorary consul), 28th Floor, Q House Lumpini Building, 1 Thanon Sathorn Tai ⊤02 677 7500, ⊛www.irelandinthailand.com; Laos, 502/1–3 Soi Sahakarnpramoon, Thanon Pracha Uthit ⊤02 539 6667–8, ext 106, ⊛www.bkklaoembassy.com; Malaysia, 35 Thanon Sathorn Tai ⊤02 629 6800; New Zealand, 14th Floor, M Thai Tower, All Seasons Place, 87 Thanon Witthayu ⊤02 254 2530; Singapore, 129 Thanon Sathorn Tai ⊤02 286 2111; South Africa, Floor 12A, M Thai Tower, All Seasons Place, 87 Thanon Witthayu ⊤02 659 2900, ⊛www.saembbangkok.com; UK, 14 Thanon Witthayu ⊤02 305 8333; US, 120 Thanon Witthayu ⊤02 205 4000; Vietnam, 83/1 Thanon Witthayu ⊤02 650 8979.

Emergencies For English-speaking help in any emergency, call either the tourist police on their free 24hr phoneline ⊤1155 or the Tourist Assistance Centre on ⊤02 281 5051. The tourist police headquarters is on the eastern edge of town at 2107 Bangkok Tower, Thanon Phetchaburi Mai (east of Phetchaburi subway station and the Wat Mai Chong Lom stop on the Saen Saeb canal-boat service; ⊤02 308 0333), or drop in at the more convenient Chana Songkhram Police Station at the west end of Thanon Khao San in Banglamphu (⊤02 282 2323). In the evenings, you'll also find tourist police in Suan Lum Night Bazaar and at the Silom end of Patpong 1.

Exchange The Suvarnabhumi Airport exchange desks and those in the upmarket hotels are open 24hr, while many other exchange booths stay open till 8pm or later, especially along Khao San, Sukhumvit and Silom roads and in the major shopping malls. You can also withdraw cash from hundreds of ATMs around the city and at the airports.

Hospitals, clinics and dentists Most expats rate the private Bumrungrad International Hospital, 33 Sukhumvit Soi 3 ⊤02 667 1000, emergency ⊤02 667 2999, ⊛www.bumrungrad.com, with its famously five-star accommodation, as the best and most comfortable in the city, followed by the BNH (Bangkok Nursing Home) Hospital, 9 Thanon Convent ⊤02 686 2700, emergency ⊤02 632 1000, ⊛www.bnhhospital.com; Bangkok Hospital

Medical Centre, 2 Soi Soonvijai 7, Thanon Phetchaburi Mai, ⏂02 310 3000, emergency ⏂17192, ⓦwww.bangkokhospital.com; and the Samitivej Sukhumvit Hospital, 133 Sukhumvit Soi 49 ⏂02 711 8000, ⓦwww.samitivej.co.th. Other recommended private hospitals include Bangkok Mission Hospital, 430 Thanon Phitsanulok, cnr Thanon Lan Luang, just east of Banglamphu ⏂02 282 1100, ⓦwww.tagnet.org/mission-net, and Bangkok Christian Hospital, 124 Thanon Silom ⏂02 233 6981–9, ⓦwww.bkkchristianhosp.th .com. You can get vaccinations and malaria advice, as well as rabies advice and treatment, at the Thai Red Cross Society's Queen Saovabha Memorial Institute (QSMI) and Snake Farm on the corner of Thanon Rama IV and Thanon Henri Dunant (Mon–Fri 8.30am–noon & 1–4pm, Sat 8.30am– noon; ⏂02 252 0161–4, ⓦwww.redcross.or.th). Among general clinics, there's one in Banglamphu on Soi Rambuttri run by the Bangkok Hospital (⏂02 629 5260; daily 8am–7pm; B300 per consultation), and Global Doctor, Ground Floor, *Holiday Inn Hotel*, 981 Thanon Silom (cnr Thanon Surasak) ⏂02 236 8442–4, ⓦwww.globaldoctor clinic.com, is recommended. For dental problems, try the Bumrungrad Hospital's dental department on ⏂02 667 2300, or the following dental clinics (not 24hr): Dental Hospital 88/88 Sukhumvit Soi 49 ⏂02 260 5000–15, ⓦwww.dentalhospital bangkok.com; Siam Family Dental Clinic 292/6 Siam Square Soi 4 ⏂02/255 6664–5, ⓦwww .siamfamilydental.com.

Immigration office About 600m down Soi Suan Phlu, off Thanon Sathorn Tai (Mon–Fri 8.30am– 4.30pm; ⏂1178, 1111 or 02 287 3101–10, ⓦwww .immigration.go.th); see p.25 for information on visa extensions. Be very wary of any Khao San tour agents who offer to organize a visa extension for you: some are reportedly faking the relevant stamps and this has caused problems at immigration.

Internet access An increasing number of hotels, guest houses and a few restaurants and bars offer wi-fi, occasionally for free, more usually for a minimal fee; True provide free wi-fi to the whole Siam Square area. For a list of other hotspots, try ⓦwww.jiwire.com; for free locations, go to ⓦwww .stickmanweekly.com. Banglamphu is packed with places offering internet access, in particular along Thanon Khao San, where competition keeps prices very low. To surf in style, head for *True*, housed in a beautiful early twentieth-century villa at the back of *Tom Yam Kung* restaurant, where you also can sip coffee, recline on retro sofas and browse lifestyle mags. The Ratchadamnoen Post Office on Banglam-phu's Soi Damnoen Klang Neua (Mon–Fri 8.30am– 4.30pm) also has very cheap public Catnet internet

booths. On Thanon Sukhumvit the Time Internet Centre on the second floor of Times Square, between sois 12 and 14 (daily 9am–midnight) is reliable. The TOT office on the north side of Thanon Ploenchit near Central Chidlom offers cheap surfing in quite a civilized atmosphere, with refreshments available, and there's a branch of *True* (see above) on Soi 3, Siam Square, that's only a little more expensive. Elsewhere in the downtown area, during the day, there are several, rather noisy, places on Floor 7 of the MBK Shopping Centre (Zone D, towards the *Pathumwan Princess Hotel*), while *Chart Gallery Café* on the ground floor of River City shopping centre offers a bit more style and tranquil-lity, as well as food and drink while you're online. There's a Catnet centre in the public telephone office on Thanon Charoen Krung (see opposite).

Laundry Nearly all guest houses and hotels offer same-day laundry services (about B35 per kg), or there are several self-service laundries on and around Thanon Khao San, including Wearever on Thanon Samsen, between sois 1 and 3, which has sofas, coffee and free wi-fi.

Left luggage At Suvarnabhumi Airport (B100 per day); Don Muang Airport (B75 per day); Ekamai Eastern Bus Terminal (B30 per day); Southern Bus Terminal (B20–60 per day); Hualamphong train station (B30–80 per day); and most hotels and guest houses.

Massage and spas Traditional Thai massage sessions and courses are held at Wat Pho (see p.116), while luxurious and indulgent spa and massage treatments are available at many posh hotels across the city, including most famously at the *Banyan Tree Hotel* on Thanon Sathorn Tai (⏂02 679 1054, ⓦwww.banyantreespa.com) and the *Oriental* on Thanon Charoen Krung (⏂02 659 9000, ⓦwww.mandarinoriental.com), and more affordably at *Buddy Lodge* on Thanon Khao San in Banglamphu (⏂02 629 4477). One of Banglamphu's most popular massage centres is the uninvitingly clinical looking but highly rated Pian's on Soi Susie Pub (daily 7.30am–12.30am, ⏂02 629 0924), where a Thai massage costs B180 per hr and you can also study Thai, Swedish, herbal and foot massage (about B5000 for a 30hr course, or B250 for a 1hr introduction). In the Silom area, Ruen Nuad, 42 Thanon Convent (⏂02 632 2662–3; daily 10am–9pm), offers excellent Thai massages (B350 for 1hr, B600 for 2hr), as well as aromatherapy and herbal massages, in an air-conditioned, characterful wooden house, down an alley opposite the BNH Hopsital and behind *Naj* restaurant. At the other end of Thanon Silom, in Sun Square, a small shopping arcade on the south side of the road between Soi 21 and 23, Nicolie (daily 10.30am–10pm; ☎02 233 6957, ⓦwww .nicolie-th.com) provides superb Thai (B1600 per 90min) and other massages, as well as facials and scrubs, in a soothing environment decorated with Asian *objets d'art*. Recommended alternatives on Sukhumvit include the delightful Divana Massage and Spa at 7, Soi 25 (☎02 661 6784, ⓦwww .divanaspa.com; from B1150); Pimmalai, in an old wooden house 50m east of BTS On Nut, exit 1, between sois 81 and 83 (☎02 742 6452, ⓦwww.pimmalai.com; 3–4hr packages B700–3400); and the Thai massage at no-frills Bann Phuan on Soi 11 (B300 per hr). For more on spa treatments see Basics p.56.

Post offices The GPO is at 1160 Thanon Charoen Krung (postcode 10501), near Wat Muang Kae express-boat pier and walkabon from Si Phraya pier. Poste restante, which is kept for two months, can be collected here. This and most other services at the GPO are open Mon–Fri 8am–8pm, Sat & Sun 8am–1pm; the parcel-packing service, however, operates Mon–Fri 8am–5pm, Sat 9am–noon. If you're staying on or near Thanon Khao San in Banglamphu, it's more convenient to use the local postal, packing and poste restante services at either Ratchadamnoen Post Office, Soi Damnoen Klang Neua, Bangkok 10200 (Mon–Fri 8am–5pm, Sat 9am–1pm); or Banglamphubon PO, Soi Sibsam Hang, Bangkok 10203 (daily 8am–5pm). On Thanon Sukhumvit use Nana PO, between sois 4 and 6, Thanon Sukhumvit, Bangkok 10112 (Mon–Fri 8.30am–8pm, Sat, Sun & hols 9am–5pm).

Telephones International cardphones are dotted all over the city, so there's now little call for the public telephone offices in or adjacent to post offices, though their booths do at least guarantee some peace and quiet. The largest and most convenient is the CAT office in the compound of the GPO on Thanon Charoen Krung (Mon–Fri 8am–8pm, Sat & Sun 8am–4pm) which, as well as cardphones, offers a fax and internet service, a free collect-call service and even video-conferencing (see above for location details). The Ratchadamnoen post office in Banglamphu (see above) also has international telephone offices attached, but these close at 5pm. Many entrepreneurs, particularly on Thanon Khao San, advertise very cheap international calls through the internet.

Travel agents Diethelm Travel has branches all over Indochina and is especially good for travel within Thailand and to Cambodia, China, Laos and Vietnam: 12th Floor, Kian Gwan Building II, 140/1 Thanon Witthayu ☎02 660 7000, ⓦwww .diethelmtravel.com; Asian Trails sells flights, does interesting Thailand tours (see p.21) and runs scheduled and private transfers to many coastal destinations from Bangkok hotels and the airport: 9th Floor, SG Tower, 161/1 Soi Mahadlek Luang 3, Thanon Rajdamri ☎02 626 2000, ⓦwww .asiantrails.net; Jysk at *New Road Guest House*, 1216/1 Thanon Charoen Krung, between sois 34 and 36 ☎02 630 6994–8, ⓦwww.jysktravel.com, is a reliable agent for train, bus and air tickets, as well as their own unusual tours, including live-aboard sea safaris around Ko Kood. Educational Travel Centre (ETC) sells air tickets and Thailand tours and has offices inside the *Royal Hotel*, 2 Thanon Rajdamnoen Klang, Banglamphu ☎02 224 0043, ⓦwww.etc.co.th, at 180 Thanon Khao San, Banglamphu ☎02 629 1885, and at 5/3 Soi Ngam Duphli ☎02 286 9424; Olavi Travel sells air tickets and budget transport within Thailand and is opposite *Gulliver's Traveler's Tavern* at 53 Thanon Chakrabongse, Banglamphu ☎02 629 4711–3, ⓦwww.olavi.com. On Sukhumvit, the helpful Thai Overlander at #407, between sois 21 and 23, ☎02 258 4778-80, ⓦwww.thaioverlander.com (Mon–Fri 8.30am–5.30pm, Sat 8.30am–4pm) sells train and air tickets and day-trips. Royal Exclusive, 9 The Place, 18/2 Thanon Chan ☎02 676 4182–7, ⓦwww.royalexclusive.com, is good for travel to Burma, Cambodia, Laos and Vietnam, and also sells air and train tickets; and the Bangkok branch of the worldwide STA Travel is a reliable outlet for cheap international flights: 14th Floor, Wall Street Tower, 33 Thanon Suriwong ☎02 236 0262, ⓦwww .statravel.co.th. For Bangkok tour operators special-izing in trips within Thailand see p.21.

Travel details

Trains

Bangkok Hualamphong Station to: Aranyaprathet (2 daily; 5–6hr); Butterworth (Malaysia; 1 daily; 21hr); Cha-am (5 daily; 3hr 10min–3hr 50min); Chumphon (12 daily; 7hr–9hr 30min); Don Muang airport (27 daily; 50min); Hua Hin (12 daily; 4–5hr); Nakhon Si Thammarat (2 daily; 15–16hr); Pattaya (1 daily; 3hr 45min); Phetchaburi (11 daily; 2hr 45min–3hr 45min); Prachuap Khiri Khan (11 daily; 5–7hr); Pranburi (3 daily; 5hr 30min); Si Racha (1 daily; 3hr 15min);

Surat Thani (10 daily; 9–12hr); Trang (2 daily; 15–16hr).

Thonburi (Bangkok Noi) Station to: Hua Hin (4 daily; 4hr–4hr 30min).

Buses

Eastern Bus Terminal to: Ban Phe (for Ko Samet; 12 daily; 3hr–3hr 30min); Chanthaburi (every 30min; 4–5hr); Laem Ngop (for Ko Chang; 2 daily; 5hr 15min); Pattaya (every 30min; 2hr 30min–3hr 30min); Rayong (every 40min; 2hr 30min–3hr); Si Racha (every 30min; 2–3hr); Trat (6 daily; 5–6hr).

Northern Bus Terminal to: Aranyaprathet (hourly; 4hr 30min); Pattaya (every 30min; 2–3hr); Rayong (every 30min; 2hr 30min–3hr 30min); Si Racha (every 30min; 2hr); Trat (5 daily; 4hr 30min).

Southern Bus Terminal to: Cha-am (every 40min; 2hr 45min–3hr 15min); Chumphon (roughly hourly; 7–9hr); Hat Yai (13 daily; 12hr); Hua Hin (every 40min; 3–4hr); Ko Pha Ngan (2 daily; 14hr); Ko Samui (8 daily; 13hr); Krabi (8 daily; 12–14hr); Nakhon Si Thammarat (19 daily; 12hr); Phang Nga (6 daily; 12hr); Phetchaburi (every 40min; 2hr 15min); Phuket (15 daily; 12hr); Prachuap Khiri Khan (every 30min; 4–5hr); Pranburi (every 40min; 3hr 30min); Ranong (6 daily; 8hr); Satun (5 daily; 16hr); Surat Thani (10 daily; 10–12hr); Takua Pa (10 daily; 12–13hr); Trang 11 daily; 12–14hr).

Flights

Bangkok to: Hua Hin (2 daily; 50min); Ko Samui (20 daily; 1hr–1hr 30min); Krabi (5 daily; 1hr 20min); Nakhon Si Thammarat (3 daily; 1hr 5min); Phuket (21 daily; 1hr 20min); Ranong (3 weekly; 1hr 5min); Surat Thani (4 daily; 1hr 15min); Trang (2 daily; 1hr 30min); Trat (3 daily; 1hr 5min).

2

The east coast

CHAPTER 2 # Highlights

✳ **Ko Si Chang** Tiny, barely tourated island with craggy coastlines, glorious views, and an appealingly laid-back ambience. See p.175

✳ **Ko Samet** Pretty (and popular) little island fringed with dazzlingly white beaches. See p.190

✳ **Trat** Welcoming guest houses and an atmospheric old quarter make for a worthwhile stopover. See p.202

✳ **Ko Chang** Head for Lonely Beach if you're in the mood to party, or to Hat Khlong Phrao for a more tranquil scene. See p.207

✳ **Ko Mak** Lovely, lazy, palm-filled little island with peaceful white-sand beaches. See p.221

✳ **Ko Kood** The real beauty of the east – untamed and as yet largely undeveloped. See p.225

▲ Hat Sai Kaew, Ko Samet

2

The east coast

ocated within just a few hours' drive from the capital, the **east coast** resorts and islands attract a mixed crowd of weekending Bangkokians, pleasure-seeking expats and sybaritic tourists. Transport connections are good and, for overlanders, there are several Cambodian border crossings within easy reach. Beautiful beaches are not the whole picture, however, as the westernmost stretch of the east coast is also crucial to Thailand's industrial economy, its natural gas fields and deep-sea ports having spawned massive development along the first 200km of coastline, an area often dubbed the **Eastern Seaboard**. The initial landscape of refineries and depots shouldn't deter you though, as offshore it's an entirely different story, with island sands as glorious as many of those at the more celebrated southern retreats and enough peaceful havens to make it worth packing your hammock.

The first worthwhile stop comes 100km east of Bangkok at the town of **Si Racha**, which is the point of access for tiny **Ko Si Chang**, whose dramatically rugged coastlines and low-key atmosphere make it a restful retreat. In complete contrast, nearby **Pattaya** is Thailand's number-one package-tour destination, its customers predominantly middle-aged Western and Chinese males enticed by the resort's sex-market reputation and undeterred by its lacklustre beach. Things soon look up, though, as the coast veers sharply eastwards towards Ban Phe, revealing the island of **Ko Samet**, the prettiest of all the beach resorts within comfortable bus-ride range of Bangkok.

East of Ban Phe, the landscape becomes lusher and hillier around **Chanthaburi**, the dynamo of Thailand's gem trade and one of only two eastern provincial capitals worth visiting. The other is **Trat**, 68km further along the highway, and an important hub both for transport into **Cambodia** via Hat Lek – one of this region's two main border points, the other being Aranyaprathet – and for the forty islands of the Ko Chang archipelago. The star of this island group is large, forested **Ko Chang** itself, whose long, fine beaches have made it into Thailand's latest resort destination. A host of smaller, less-developed islands fill the sea between Ko Chang and the Cambodian coast, most notably the temptingly diverse trio of **Ko Wai**, **Ko Mak** and **Ko Kood**.

Highway 3 extends almost the entire length of the east coast, beginning in Bangkok as Thanon Sukhumvit, and known as such when it cuts through towns, and hundreds of **buses** ply the route, connecting all major mainland destinations. It's also possible to travel between the east coast and the northeast and north without doubling back through the capital: the most direct routes into **Isaan** start from Pattaya, Rayong and Chanthaburi. Bangkok's Suvarnabhumi Airport is less than 50km from Si Racha, and there are two domestic **airports** along the east coast itself: at U-Tapao naval base, southeast of Pattaya, and just west of Trat.

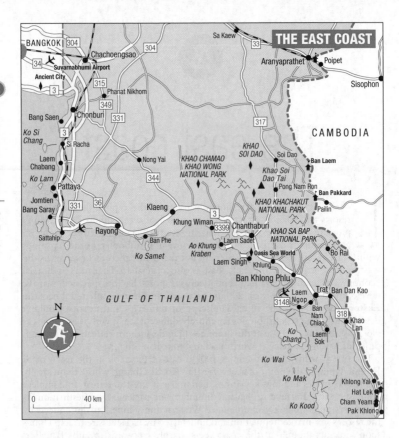

Though a rail line connects Bangkok with Si Racha and Pattaya, it is served by just one slow **train** a day in each direction; a branch line makes two journeys a day to Aranyaprathet near the Cambodian border.

Si Racha

The eastbound journey out of Bangkok is not at all scenic, dominated initially by traffic-choked suburban sprawl and then by the industrial landscape of the petrochemical and shipping industries that power Thailand's Eastern Seaboard. The first major population centre is the provincial capital of **Chonburi**, whose only notable attraction is its annual October bout of buffalo-racing. Twenty kilometres on and you reach the fast-growing town of **SI RACHA**, a prosperous residential and administrative hub for the Eastern Seaboard's industries and home to a sizeable population of expat families. The town is best known though as the source of *nam phrik Si Racha*, the chilli-laced ketchup found on every kitchen table in Thailand, and as the departure point for the island of **Ko Si Chang** (see opposite). Si Racha's only sight is the Sino–Thai "island temple" of **Wat Ko Loy**, a gaudy hexagon presided over by a statue of the Chinese Goddess of Mercy, Kuan Im, and located on an islet at the end of a 1500-metre-long causeway, adjacent to the pier for boats to Ko Si Chang.

Buses to Si Racha leave frequently from both Bangkok's Eastern (Ekamai) and Northern (Mo Chit) bus terminals, and from Pattaya, Rayong and Trat further east. They all drop passengers near the huge Robinsons/Pacific Park shopping centre on Thanon Sukhumvit in Si Racha's town centre. It's about 2.5km from here to the end of the Ko Si Chang pier, known as Tha Wat Ko Loy, which is west off the Thanon Chermchompon/Thanon Surasak junction. A motorbike taxi or tuk-tuk will drive you there for B30–40 or, if walking, take any road west towards the sea as far as Thanon Chermchompon (also spelt Jermjompol), then head north up Chermchompon until you reach the junction for the Ko Si Chang pier and Wat Ko Loy. White songthaews from Naklua, the northern suburb of Pattaya, run about twice an hour to Si Racha, dropping passengers near the clocktower, about 1km south down Thanon Chermchompon from the pier junction. The one slow **train** a day from Bangkok departs the capital at 6.55am, takes over three hours, and arrives at the train station on the far eastern edge of town, a tuk-tuk ride from the pier.

The most atmospheric of the cheap places **to stay** are the very simple, cabin-like, en-suite fan rooms of *Sri Wattana* (☎038 311037; ❶), built on a jetty jutting out over the waterfront, with a pleasant sea-view terrace; the hotel is on Soi Sri Wattana, directly across Thanon Chermchompon from Thanon Si Racha Nakhon 3, about 500m south of the pier junction. For flashier, air-con digs, head for the eleven-storey *City Hotel* (☎038 322700, ⓦwww.citysriracha .com; ❼), 300m south of Pacific Place at 6/126 Thanon Sukhumvit, which has wi-fi and a pool. For **eating**, Thanon Si Racha Nakhon 3 is a good place to browse, lined with restaurants and night-time foodstalls, or there's an official night market by the day market and clocktower further south down Thanon Chermchompon.

Ko Si Chang

The unhurried pace and absence of consumer pressures make tiny, rocky **KO SI CHANG** an engaging place to wind down for a few days. Unlike most other east-coast destinations, it offers no real beach life – though the water can be beautifully clear and there are opportunities to dive and snorkel – and there's little to do here but explore the craggy coastline by kayak or ramble up and down its steep contours on foot or by motorbike. The island is famous as the location of one of Rama V's summer palaces, parts of which have been prettily restored, and for its rare white squirrels, who live in the wooded patches inland.

Arrival and information

Ferries to Ko Si Chang leave from Tha Wat Ko Loy in Si Racha (see opposite), departing approximately hourly from 7am to 8pm (45min; B40), and wending their way past the congestion of international cargo boats and Thai supply barges that anchor in the protected channel between the mainland and Ko Si Chang. On **arrival**, all boats dock first at Tha Lang (also signed as Tateawavong Bridge), with many then continuing to Tha Bon a short distance up the east coast. Samlor drivers meet the boats and charge B40 to most accommodation, or B80 to Hat Tham Pang; as they are paid commission by some hotels and restaurants, be wary of any opinionated remarks. The first boat back to the mainland leaves Tha Lang at 6am and the last at 6pm; the same boats depart Tha Bon about fifteen minutes earlier.

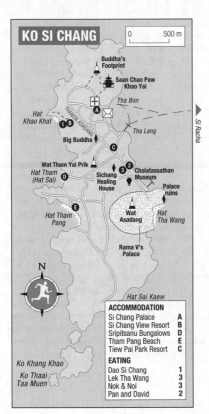

KO SI CHANG

0   500 m

Buddha's
Footprint

Saan Chao Paw
Khao Yai

Tha Bon

Hat
Khao Khat

Big Buddha

Tha Lang

Wat Tham Yai Prik

Hat Tham
(Hat Sai)

Sichang
Healing
House

Cholatassathan
Museum

Palace
ruins

Hat Tham
Pang

Wat
Asadang

Hat
Tha Wang

Rama V's
Palace

N

Hat Sai Kaew

Ko Khang Khao

Ko Thaai
Taa Muen

ACCOMMODATION
Si Chang Palace   A
Si Chang View Resort   B
Sripitsanu Bungalows   D
Tham Pang Beach   E
Tiew Pai Park Resort   C

EATING
Dao Si Chang   1
Lek Tha Wang   3
Nok & Noi   3
Pan and David   2

Si Racha

Both piers connect with Thanon Asadang, a small ring road on which you'll find the market, shops and many of the island's houses. Much of the rest of the island is accessible only by paths and tracks. In town it's easy enough to walk from place to place, but to really enjoy what Ko Si Chang has to offer you'll need to either rent a **motorbike** from the pier (B250), or charter a samlor for the day. The island's trademark **samlors** are driven by distinctive, elongated 1200cc motorbikes and virtually monopolize the roads, as there are barely any private cars on Ko Si Chang; a tour of the island will only set you back around B250.

There are **exchange facilities** and an ATM at the bank between the two piers; the hospital is also near Tha Bon. For a fee of B50, non-guests can use the **swimming pool** at *Si Chang Palace* hotel. The charming Sichang Healing House (daily except Wed 9am–5pm; ☎038 216467) offers Ayurvedic **massage** (from B400) and herbal treatments at its cute little garden retreat west off the road to the old palace. It also sells watercolour views of Ko Si Chang. For detailed **information** on Ko Si Chang, consult the website ⓦwww .ko-sichang.com, compiled by David at *Pan and David Restaurant*.

Ko Si Chang celebrates three particularly interesting **festivals**. **Songkhran** is marked here from April 17–19 with sandcastle-building, greasy-pole-climbing and an exorcist ritual for any islanders who have suffered unpleasant deaths over the previous year. At **Visakha Puja**, the full-moon day in May when Buddha's birth, death and enlightenment are honoured, islanders process to the old palace with hand-crafted Chinese lanterns. And on September 20, Ko Si Chang honours its royal patron **King Chulalongkorn's birthday** with a *son et lumière* in the palace grounds and a beauty contest staged entirely in costumes from the Chulalongkorn era.

Accommodation

Because water on the island has to be bought from a private desalination company at six times the price it costs on the mainland, **accommodation** on Ko Si Chang is expensive and disappointingly poor value. West-coast accommodation enjoys the best views, while Thanon Asadang and east-coast options are more convenient for restaurants and shops. Booking ahead is advisable for weekends and public holidays. For the very finest sea views, nothing can beat **camping**: the cliffs at Hat Khao Khat are a particularly popular site, though quite exposed. You can rent tents for B100 from Uncle Juk on Hat Tham Pang (☎081 822 5540), but phone ahead to reserve one for weekends.

Si Chang Palace Across from Tha Bon on Thanon Asadang ☎038 216276, ⓦwww.sichangpalace .com. The most upmarket place on the island has good air-con rooms, the best of them enjoying fine eastward sea views. There's a pool here too. ❺
Si Chang View Resort Hat Khao Khat ☎038 216210, ⓔjiyakiat@yahoo.com. Run by a friendly, English-speaking family, the thirteen well-maintained fan and air-con rooms occupy a couple of two-storey buildings in a nice garden set back from a prime cliffside spot (not quite visible from the rooms sadly) above Hat Khao Khat. There's wi-fi and fresh coffee in the restaurant. Fan ❹, air-con ❺
Sripitsanu Bungalows Hat Tham ☎038 216336. Remote and stunningly located place whose dozen large, plain and rather haphazardly maintained fan and air-con rooms and bungalows sit almost right at the edge of the cliff – some are actually built into the rockface. It's a gorgeous spot, with unsurpassed views and the possibility of swimming at low tide, though there's not much English spoken. Some bungalows have their own cooking facilities.

From *Tiew Pai*, cross Thanon Asadang and walk a few metres to the left, then follow signs up the first right, a narrow road heading uphill; it's a 10min walk from here. Fan ❸, air-con ❹
Tham Pang Beach Hat Tham Pang ☎038 216179. The busiest west-coast accommodation, whose twenty fairly rudimentary concrete bungalows – all with bathroom, fans, verandas and partial sea views – are stacked in tiers up the cliffside behind Ko Si Chang's only real beach. There's a restaurant plus beach equipment for rent. Reservations essential for weekends. ❸
Tiew Pai Park Resort Thanon Asadang ☎038 216084, ⓦwww.tiewpai.com. Very central and cheaper than the competition, this is most backpackers' first choice. Bungalows and rooms are crammed around a scruffy garden across the road from the restaurant and many are pretty basic; the best value are the en-suite fan bungalows (with TV and fridge) and there are also some cheap single rooms with shared bathrooms. Fan ❷–❸, air-con ❹

Around the island

The main sights on the island are **Rama V's old palace** on the southeast coast and the popular Chinese pilgrimage temple **Saan Chao Paw Khao Yai** on the northeastern tip, with west-coast **Hat Tham Pang** the main beach. **Fishing** boats with a skipper can be chartered from the two Ko Si Chang piers for B1500 per day, or *Tiew Pai Park Resort* does half-day fishing trips for B2000 per ten-person boat.

Rama V's Palace and around

The most famous sight on the island is the partially ruined Rama V's Palace, which occupies a large chunk of gently sloping land midway down the east coast, behind pebbly **Hat Tha Wang**. It's an enjoyable place to explore and can be reached on foot from *Tiew Pai Park Resort* in about half an hour. Shortly before reaching the palace grounds, you'll pass the small and less than riveting **Cholatassathan Museum** (Tues–Sun 9am–5pm; entry by donation), established by the resident Aquatic Resources Research Institute to provide an introduction to the coral and marine life around Ko Si Chang.

Built in the 1890s as a sort of health resort for sickly royals, **Rama V's Palace**, or **Phra Judhadhut Ratchathan** (daily 9am–5pm; free), formed the heart of an extensive complex comprising homes for royal advisers, chalets for convalescents, quarters for royal concubines and administrative buildings. By the turn of the twentieth century, however, Rama V (King Chulalongkorn) had lost interest in his island project and so in 1901 his golden teak palace was moved piece by piece to Bangkok, and reconstructed there as Vimanmek Palace; its foundations are still visible just south of the palace's Saphan Asadang pier. Following recent renovations, the elegant design of the palace grounds is apparent once more. They fan out around an elaborate labyrinth of fifty interlinked ponds and a

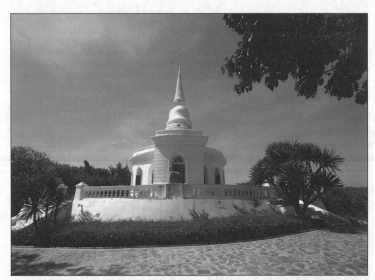

▲ Wat Asadang, Ko Si Chang

maze of stone steps and balustrades that still cling to the shallow hillside. Close to the shore, four of the original Western-style **villas** have been reconstructed to house displays, of varying interest, on Chulalongkorn's relationship with Ko Si Chang; one of them also doubles as a coffee shop. Inland, signs direct you up the hillside to the palace's unusual whitewashed shrine, **Wat Asadang**, whose circular walls are punctuated with Gothic stained-glass windows and surmounted by a chedi.

Hat Tham Pang and around

The main beach on the west coast, and the most popular one on the island, is small, crowded **Hat Tham Pang**, a B80 samlor ride from either pier. Its sandy front is packed with deckchairs and beach umbrellas and you can rent snorkels, kayaks, inner tubes and fishing rods here too. The best **snorkelling** spots are further south, around the tiny islands off Ko Si Chang's southern tip, particularly off the north coast of **Ko Khang Khao**, forty minutes by kayak from Hat Tham Pang.

North of Hat Tham Pang, and also accessible via a fork off Thanon Asadang opposite *Tiew Pai* (a 10min walk), you'll find the **Wat Tham Yai Prik** temple and meditation centre, which is open to interested visitors and holds frequent retreats. Unusually, nuns as well as monks here wear brown (rather than white) and everyone participates in the upkeep of the monastery: you can see some of the fruits of their labour in the extensive roadside orchard. Just west of the wat, the dramatically situated *Sripitsanu Bungalows* offers glorious views over the pretty, rocky cove known as **Hat Tham** or **Hat Sai**, which is only really swimmable at low tide.

North to Saan Chao Paw Khao Yai

Back down on the ring road, if you continue in a northwesterly direction, you'll pass beneath the gaze of a huge yellow Buddha before reaching the rocky northwest headland of **Khao Khat**, a few hundred metres further on. The uninterrupted panorama of open sea makes this a classic sunset spot, and there's a path along the cliffside.

From here the road heads east to reach the showy, multi-tiered Chinese temple, **Saan Chao Paw Khao Yai** (Shrine of the Father Spirit of the Great Hill), stationed at the top of a steep flight of steps and commanding a good view of the harbour and the mainland coast. Established here long before Rama V arrived on the island, the shrine was dedicated by Chinese seamen who saw a strange light coming out of one of the **caves** behind the modern-day temple. The caves, now full of religious statues and related paraphernalia, are visited by boatloads of Chinese pilgrims, particularly over Chinese New Year. Continue on up the cliffside to reach the small pagoda built for Rama V and enshrining a **Buddha's Footprint**. Two very long, very steep flights of stairs give access to the footprint: the easternmost one starts at the main water-front entrance to the Chinese temple and takes you past a cluster of monks' meditation cells, while the westerly one rises further west along the ring road and offers the finest lookouts.

Eating

One of the most enjoyable **places to eat** on the island is *Pan and David Restaurant* (Mon, Tues, Thurs & Fri 11am–9.30pm, Sat 8.30am–10pm, Sun 8.30am–8.30pm), 200m before the entrance to the old palace grounds, which is run by a sociable and well-informed American expat and his Thai wife. The long and delicious menu (B50–395) includes authentically fiery *som tam*, home-made fettuccine, fillet steak, Thai curries, brownies and home-made fresh strawberry ice cream, as well as good-value Italian wine. *Nok and Noi,* across the road from *Pan and David*, and the locally famous *Lek Tha Wang*, slightly further down the road towards the palace, are both well known for their seafood. *Dao Si Chang*, on the clifftop in front of *Si Chang View Resort*, also specializes in seafood and is a great spot for a sunset dinner.

Pattaya

With its streets full of high-rise hotels and hustlers on every corner, **PATTAYA** is the epitome of exploitative tourism gone mad, but most of Pattaya's two million annual visitors don't mind that the place looks like the Costa del Sol because what they are here for is sex. The city swarms with male and female **prostitutes**, spiced up by a sizeable population of transvestites (*katoey*), and plane-loads of Western men flock here to enjoy their services in the rash of hostess bar-beers, go-go clubs and massage parlours for which "Patpong-on-Sea" is notorious. The signs trumpeting "Viagra for Sale" say it all. Pattaya also has the largest **gay scene** in Thailand, with several exclusively gay hotels and an entire zone devoted to gay sex bars.

Pattaya's evolution into sin city began with the Vietnam War, when it got fat on selling sex to American servicemen. When the soldiers and sailors left in the mid-1970s, Western tourists were lured in to fill their places, and ex-servicemen soon returned to run the sort of joints they had once blown their dollars in. These days, at least half the bars and restaurants in Pattaya are Western-run. More recently, there has been an influx of criminal gangs from Germany, Russia and Japan, who reportedly find Pattaya a convenient centre for running their rackets in passport and credit-card fraud, as well as child pornography and prostitution; expat murders are a regular news item in the *Pattaya Mail*.

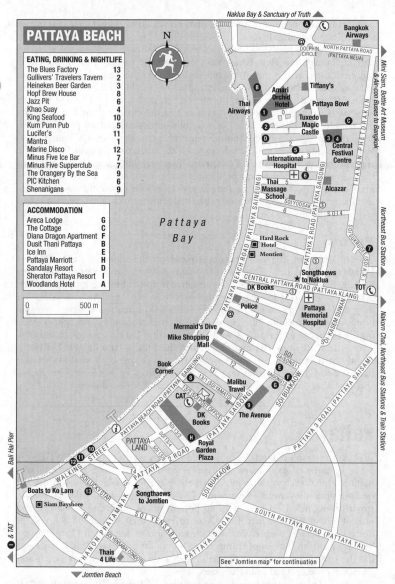

Naklua Bay & Sanctuary of Truth

PATTAYA BEACH

N

EATING, DRINKING & NIGHTLIFE

The Blues Factory	13
Gullivers' Travelers Tavern	2
Heineken Beer Garden	3
Hopf Brew House	8
Jazz Pit	6
Khao Suay	4
King Seafood	10
Kum Punn Pub	5
Lucifer's	11
Mantra	1
Marine Disco	12
Minus Five Ice Bar	7
Minus Five Supperclub	7
The Orangery By the Sea	9
PIC Kitchen	6
Shenanigans	9

ACCOMMODATION

Areca Lodge	G
The Cottage	C
Diana Dragon Apartment	F
Dusit Thani Pattaya	B
Ice Inn	E
Pattaya Marriott	H
Sandalay Resort	D
Sheraton Pattaya Resort	I
Woodlands Hotel	A

0   500 m

Bangkok
Airways

DOLPHIN
CIRCLE
NORTH PATTAYA ROAD
(PATTAYA NEUA)

Mini Siam, Bottle Art Museum
& Air-con Buses to Bangkok

Tiffany's

Amari
Orchid
Hotel

Pattaya Bowl

Thai
Airways

Tuxedo
Magic
Castle

Thai
Airways

Central
Festival
Centre

International
Hospital

Alcazar

Thai
Massage
School

SOI YODSAK

SOI 014

Northeast Bus Station

*Pattaya
Bay*

Hard Rock
Hotel

Montien

Songthaews
to Naklua

Nakorn Chai, Northeast Bus Stations & Train Station

TOT

CENTRAL PATTAYA ROAD
(PATTAYA KLANG)

DK Books

Police

Pattaya
Memorial
Hospital

Mermaid's Dive

SOI
SAISONG1

Mike Shopping
Mall

Book
Corner

Malibu
Travel

CAT

The Avenue

DK
Books

Royal
Garden
Plaza

PATTAYA-
LAND

Bali Hai Pier

Boats to Ko Larn

Siam Bayshore

Songthaews
to Jomtien

SOI YENSABAI

SOUTH PATTAYA ROAD (PATTAYA TAI)

Thais
4 Life

THANON PRATAMNAK

SOI YENSABAI CONDOTEL

i & TAT

See "Jomtien map" for continuation

Jomtien Beach

Meanwhile, local tourism authorities are trying hard to improve **Pattaya's image**, and with surprising success have begun enticing families and older couples with a catalogue of more wholesome entertainments such as theme parks, golf courses, shopping plazas and year-round diving. Russian holiday-makers seem particularly keen and Cyrillic script is now much in evidence around the resort. A recent flush of more sophisticated boutique hotels and restaurants is also starting to bring in a younger Thai crowd, which has brightened the picture a little. But in truth the beach here is far from pristine – way outshone by Ko Samet just along the coast – so after-hours "entertainment" is still the primary inducement.

Arrival and information

Dozens of air-con **buses** run from **Bangkok**'s Eastern and Northern bus terminals to Pattaya, and there's a slightly less frequent service from the Southern Bus Terminal. In addition there are up to seven buses a day from **Suvarnabhumi Airport** to Pattaya (some operate direct from Arrivals, others from the public transport terminal), and at least four in the opposite direction (☎038 231142). All Bangkok and most airport buses arrive at and depart from the bus station on North Pattaya Road (☎038 429877). Metered taxis from Suvarnabhumi cost around B1300 (90min); returning to the airport from Pattaya costs from B800 per car or B450 per person in a shared minibus arranged through any hotel.

Coming **by bus from Si Racha**, **Rayong** or **Trat** you'll probably get dropped on Thanon Sukhumvit, the resort's eastern limit, from where songthaews will ferry you into town. If heading on to these towns, you need to pick up your bus from one of the drops on Thanon Sukhumvit, but if you're going **to Ko Samet** or **Ko Chang** it's much easier and not much more expensive to use the tourist minibus services run by Samet Island Tour on Soi Yamato (☎038 427277, ⓦwww.malibu-samet.com) and Koh Chang Travel on Soi Post Office (☎038 710145, ⓦwww.kohchangtravel.com), both of which operate door-to-door services to the Ban Phe pier (for Ko Samet; B230), and the Ko Chang piers (B500); tickets can also be booked through most tour agents. Some airport and most **local buses** use the Baw Kaw Saw government bus station on Thanon Chaiyapruk in Jomtien.

It's also possible to get to Pattaya direct **from Isaan and the north**: Nakorn Chai buses to and from Chiang Mai, Chiang Rai, Khorat and Ubon use a terminus on Thanon Sukhumvit, across from the Central Pattaya Road intersection (☎038 424871); other bus services to the northeast use the Northeastern Bus Station on Central Pattaya Road, just east of the Pattaya 3 Road intersection.

Pattaya is on a branch line of the eastern rail line, and there's one slow **train** a day in each direction between the resort and Bangkok. Pattaya's station (☎038 429285) is on Thanon Sukhumvit, about 500m north of the Central Pattaya Road intersection. Pattaya's **U-Tapao airport** (☎038 245595) is located at the naval base near Sattahip, about 25km south of the resort, and runs Bangkok Airways flights to and from Ko Samui and Phuket.

There's a municipal **tourist service centre** (daily 8.30am–4.30pm) on the beach at the mouth of Walking Street; the **TAT** office is inconveniently located at 609 Thanon Pratamnak between South Pattaya and Jomtien (daily 8.30am– 4.30pm; ☎038 428750, ⓔtatchon@tat.or.th). Alternatively, call the 24-hour Pattaya City Call Centre **information service** on ☎1337. The weekly *Pattaya Mail* (ⓦwww.pattayamail.com) is one of several **local newspapers** that fills readers in on the often lurid goings-on.

Orientation

At the heart of this ever-expanding playground is the four-kilometre-long **Pattaya Beach**, the noisiest, most unsightly zone of the resort, crowded with yachts and tour boats and fringed by a sliver of sand and a paved beachfront walkway. The densest glut of hotels, restaurants, bars, fast-food joints, souvenir shops and tour operators is halfway down Pattaya Beach Road (also signed as Pattaya Saineung), in **Central Pattaya** (Pattaya Klang), between

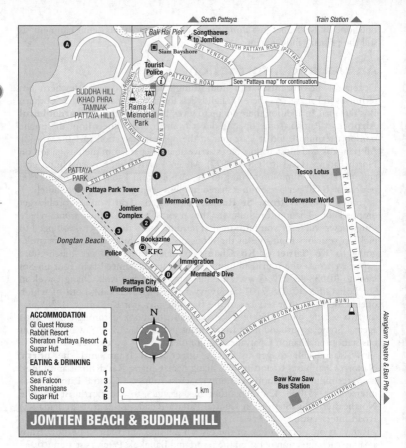

Bali Hai Pier
★ Songthaews to Jomtien
SOUTH PATTAYA ROAD (PATTAYA TAI)
SOI YENSABAI
Siam Bayshore
Tourist Police
PATTAYA 3 ROAD
See "Pattaya map" for continuation
TAT
BUDDHA HILL (KHAO PHRA TAMNAK PATTAYA HILL)
Rama IX Memorial Park
THANON TABPHAYA
THANON PRATAMNAK (PATTAYA HILL)
PATTAYA PARK
SOI PATTAYA PARK
THEP PRASIT
Tesco Lotus
THANON SUKHUMVIT
Pattaya Park Tower
Mermaid Dive Centre
Underwater World
Jomtien Complex
Dongtan Beach
Bookazine
KFC
Police
Immigration
Mermaid's Dive
JOMTIEN BEACH ROAD (THANON HAT JOMTIEN)
Pattaya City Windsurfing Club
THANON WAT BOONKANJANA (WAT BUN)
Alangkarn Theatre & Ban Phe
N
Baw Kaw Saw Bus Station
THANON CHAIYAPRUK

ACCOMMODATION
GI Guest House — D
Rabbit Resort — C
Sheraton Pattaya Resort — A
Sugar Hut — B

EATING & DRINKING
Bruno's — 1
Sea Falcon — 3
Shenanigans — 2
Sugar Hut — B

0 — 1 km

JOMTIEN BEACH & BUDDHA HILL

sois 6 and 13, but after dark the action moves to the neon zone south of Soi 13/2. Here, in **South Pattaya**, and specifically along ultra-sleazy **Walking Street**, sex is peddled in hundreds of go-go bars, discos, massage parlours and open-sided bar-beers. The gay district is also here, in the lanes known as **Pattayaland** sois 1, 2 and 3 (or **Boyz Town**), but actually signed as sois 13/3, 13/4 and 13/5. The quietest and least sleazy end of town to stay in is **North Pattaya**, between Central Pattaya Road and North Pattaya Road (Thanon Hat Pattaya Neua).

South around the headland from South Pattaya, **Jomtien Beach** (sometimes spelt Chom Tian) is also fronted by enormous high-rises, many of them condominiums. Though the atmosphere here is not as frantic as in Pattaya, Jomtien also flounders under an excess of bar-beers and shops flogging tacky souvenirs and, like its neighbour, is forever under construction. The nicest stretch of sand is **Dongtan Beach**, beyond the northern end of Jomtien Beach Road: shady, and car-free between 10am and 5pm, it is Pattaya's main gay beach, though used by all. The bulge of land behind Dongtan Beach, separating Jomtien from South Pattaya, is Khao Phra Tamnak, variously translated as **Pattaya Hill** or **Buddha Hill**, site of several posh hotels and the Pattaya Park waterpark and funfair.

Transport

Public **songthaews** – known locally as baht buses – circulate continuously around the resort from dawn until at least 11pm. In **Pattaya** most follow a standard anticlockwise route up Pattaya 2 Road as far as North Pattaya Road and back down Pattaya Beach Road, for a fixed fee of B10 per person; avoid jumping in a parked songthaew, however, as you'll be charged for chartering the whole vehicle. Songthaews **to Jomtien** start from the junction of Pattaya 2 Road and South Pattaya Road and cost B10 to *KFC* or up to B30 to Thanon Wat Boonkanjana. Songthaews **to Naklua**, beyond north Pattaya, head north from the junction of Pattaya 2 Road and Central Pattaya Road and cost B10 to Naklua Soi 12.

Motorbike rental is available everywhere from B200 per day, but beware of faulty vehicles, and of scams – sometimes rented bikes get stolen by touts keen to keep the customer's deposit, so you may want to use your own lock. Avis **car rental** (ⓦwww.avisthailand.com) have offices inside the *Dusit Resort* (☎038 361627) and the *Hard Rock Hotel* (☎038 428755) in North Pattaya; Budget (☎038 710717, ⓦwww.budget.co.th) has an office in Tipp Plaza on Beach Road, between sois 10 and 11; and many of the motorbike touts also rent out jeeps for about B1200 per day.

Accommodation

There's no travellers' scene in Pattaya and **hotels** offering doubles under B450 outside low season are almost impossible to find; the cheapest alternatives are often rooms above the bars on sois 6, 13/2, 13/3 and 13/4.

Areca Lodge 198/21 Soi Saisong 13 (aka Soi Diana Inn), Central Pattaya ☎038 410123, ⓦwww.arecalodge.com. Unusually stylish place for Pattaya, with pleasantly furnished air-con rooms in two wings built around two swimming pools, all of them with balconies. Wi-fi in public areas. ❻

The Cottage Off Pattaya 2 Rd, North Pattaya ☎038 425650, ⓦwww.thecottagepattaya.com. Good-value, simply furnished semi-detached brick bungalows, all with air-con, pleasantly set among tall trees within a mature tropical garden away from the main road but opposite the Central Festival shopping centre. Facilities include two small swimming pools and wi-fi in most rooms. ❺

Diana Dragon Apartment 198/16 Soi Saisong 13 (aka Soi Diana Inn), Central Pattaya ☎038 423928, ⓦwww.dianapattaya.co.th. This long-running Pattaya institution has the cheapest doubles in town, and they're good value considering the competition: huge and quite light, with either fan or air-con, plus use of the pool at *Diana Inn*, 100m away. Fan ❸, air-con ❹

Dusit Thani Pattaya 240/2 Pattaya Beach Rd, North Pattaya ☎038 425611, ⓦwww.dusit.com. In the less sleazy part of town, this upper-bracket Thai chain hotel is one of only a few Beach Rd hotels to be actually on the beach (the others are the southern end). Sea-view rooms are worth paying extra for as the impressive panoramas take in the whole bay. ❾

GI Guest House 75/14 Soi 5 (Soi Post Office), off Beach Rd, Jomtien ☎038 232968, ⓔgitravel @gmail.com. Bright, cheery air-con rooms with TV in a small block across the road from the GI Tour office. Sea views cost a bit extra. ❹

Ice Inn Corner of Saisong 12 and Pattaya 2 Rd, Central Pattaya ☎038 720671, ⓦwww.iceinn pattaya.com. Cheap fan-cooled singles and reasonably priced doubles in this small thirty-room hotel behind a handicrafts shop a few metres from the busier bar-beer sois. Rooms are simple but are all en suite; all doubles have air-con. ❸–❹

Pattaya Marriott 218 Pattaya Beach Rd, Central Pattaya ☎038 412120, ⓦwww.marriotthotels .com/pyxmc. Located in the heart of the resort (attached to the Royal Garden Plaza shopping centre), and across the road from the beach, this international chain hotel is both very central and refreshingly calm, not least because it's designed around a huge swimming pool and tropical garden full of palms. Not surprisingly it's the first choice for anyone in Pattaya on business. Rooms are capacious and comfortable and have either pool- or sea view. Facilities include a spa, floodlit tennis courts, mountain-bike rental and a kids' club. ❹

Rabbit Resort Dongtan beachfront, Jomtien ☎038 303303, ⓦwww.rabbitresort.com. Beautiful place that's the most appealing option in Jomtien, and located on the nicest stretch of beach, the predominantly but not exclusively gay Dongtan Beach. Most accommodation is in teakwood cottages that are elegantly furnished with Thai fabrics and antiques and have garden-style bathrooms; there are also some "forest rooms" in a two-storey block. All are set around a tropical garden just metres off the beach. ⑨

Sandalay Resort Between sois 1 and 2, Pattaya Beach Rd, North Pattaya ☎038 422660, ⓦwww .sandalayresort.com. This hundred-room hotel with swimming pool is in the quieter northern part of town just across the road from the beach. It has contemporary-styled, well-designed, though quite small, standard air-con rooms plus impressively large deluxe versions. Both options are available with sea view and tiny balcony at extra cost, but all have free wi-fi. Good discounts often available. ⑦

Sheraton Pattaya Resort 437 Thanon Pratamnak (Cliff Rd), South Pattaya ☎038 259888, ⓦwww .starwoodhotels.com. Pattaya's best hotel is smaller and more intimate than most in its class and offers five-star rooms in its two hotel wings as well as in private pavilions. The beautiful series of freeform swimming pools is set within lush gardens – compensating for the minuscule private beach – though it's built on a hill so be prepared

for lots of steps. You'll need transport to get to the shops and restaurants of downtown Pattaya. ⑨

Sugar Hut 391/18 Thanon Tabphaya, midway between South Pattaya and Jomtien ☎038 251686, ⓦwww.sugar-hut.com. The most characterful accommodation in Pattaya comprises a charming collection of 33 Ayutthaya-style traditional wooden bungalows set in a fabulously profuse garden with three swimming pools. The bungalows are in tropical-chic style, with low beds, open-roofed shower rooms, mosquito nets and private verandas; the more expensive ones have a sitting room as well. You'll need your own transport as it's nowhere near the restaurants, shops or sea. ⑧

Woodlands Hotel and Resort 164 Thanon Pattaya-Naklua, North Pattaya ☎038 421707, ⓦwww.woodland-resort.com. A quiet, unpretentious and welcoming family-friendly garden resort 100m north of the Dolphin Circle, 400m from a scruffy but quiet thread of beach. The quite elegant, wooden-floored air-con rooms are in two storeys set round the pools and garden; the most expensive in each category have direct access to the pool from ground-floor balconies. Broadband throughout. ⑦–⑧

The resort

Many tourists in Pattaya spend the days recovering from the night before, but there's an increasing number of other resort-style attractions, including theme parks, watersports facilities, dive centres and golf courses.

Theme parks and indoor attractions

One of Pattaya's most enjoyable indoor attractions is **Ripley's Believe It Or Not** (daily 11am–11pm; B380, kids B280), on the third floor of the Royal Garden Plaza on Pattaya Beach Road. It's part of a worldwide chain of museums-of-the-bizarre inspired by the collections of American cartoonist and adventurer Robert Leroy Ripley. The Pattaya branch is good fun, featuring plenty of amusing and outlandish curios from Thailand and beyond – everything from shrunken heads and models of the world's tallest, smallest and fattest men to an exhibition on sharks.

 Mini Siam (daily 8am–10pm; B300, kids B150) is just what it sounds like: the cream of Thailand's finest monuments reconstructed to 1:25 scale, plus miniature replicas of international icons such as the Sydney Opera House and the Statue of Liberty. It's just north of the North Pattaya Road/Thanon Sukhumvit intersection but you can arrange free transport if you call ☎038 727333. Advertised as the only one of its kind in the world, the nearby **Bottle Art Museum** (daily 9am–6.30pm; B200/100), just south of the North Pattaya Road/Thanon Sukhumvit intersection, also deals in miniatures, in this case extraordinarily tiny versions encased in bottles; among the three hundred delicately hand-crafted pieces, painstakingly assembled inside the bottles by their Dutch creator, are Dutch windmills, Thai temples, a Saudi mosque and a British coach and horses.

 The hugely ambitious **Sanctuary of Truth**, or **Wang Boran** (daily 8am–5pm; B500, kids B250; ☎038 225407, ⓦwww.sanctuaryoftruth.com; daily dolphin shows at 11.30am & 3pm), is also a kind of replica, but on a 1:1 scale. Conceived by the man behind the Muang Boran Ancient City complex near Bangkok, it's a majestic 105-metre-high temple-palace built entirely of wood and designed to evoke the great ancient Khmer sanctuaries of Angkor. Though begun in 1981, it is still a work-in-progress, its external walls covered in a growing gallery of beautiful, symbolic woodcarvings inspired by Cambodian, Chinese, Thai and Indian mythologies. The Sanctuary occupies a dramatic seaside spot, behind imposing crenellated walls off the west end of Naklua Soi 12, close to the *Garden Sea View* hotel; from Central Pattaya, take a Naklua-bound songthaew as far as Soi 12, then a motorbike taxi.

If you've been disappointed with local reef life, the small and expensive but rather beautiful aquarium at **Underwater World** (daily 9am–6pm; B450, kids B250 or free if under 90cm tall; Ⓦwww.underwaterworldpattaya.com) might make up for it with its trio of long fibreglass tunnels that transport you through shallow rocks pools to the ocean floor; there are touch pools and masses of reef fish and you can also arrange to dive with the resident sharks and rays. It's on Thanon Sukhumvit, just south of the Thep Prasit junction, near Tesco Lotus.

Diving, snorkelling, watersports and golf

Though Pattaya's reefs are far less spectacular than those along the Andaman Coast, it can be dived year-round, and underwater visibility is consistent. Most **dive trips** focus on the group of "outer islands" about 25km from shore, which include Ko Rin, Ko Man Wichai and Ko Klung Badaan, where you have a reasonable chance of seeing barracuda, moray eels and blue-spotted stingrays. There are also three rewarding wreck dives in the Samae San/Sattahip area. Be careful when choosing a **dive operator** as there are plenty of charlatans around. One of the most reputable is the PADI Five-Star National Geographic Dive Centre Mermaid's Dive Centre, which has branches next to *Siam Bayview* hotel between sois 10 and 11 on Beach Road in Central Pattaya, and on Soi White House in Jomtien; its head office is on Thanon Tabphaya in Jomtien (Ⓣ038 303333, Ⓦwww.mermaiddive.com). It charges B2990 for two dives,

▲ Walking Street, Pattaya

with accompanying snorkellers paying B1000, and B14,000 for the four-day Openwater course.

All tour agents sell **snorkelling** trips to nearby islands, the majority of them going to the reefs and beaches of **Ko Larn**. You can also make your own way to Ko Larn by public boat from the Bali Hai pier at the far southern end of Walking Street (approximately hourly 7am–6.30pm; 45min; B20). Beachfront stalls in Pattaya and Jomtien offer **water-skiing**, **jet-skiing** and **parasailing**, but for **windsurfing** you need to go to the Pattaya City Windsurfing Club opposite Soi 6 in Jomtien (B400 per hr). The more family-oriented **Pattaya Park Water Park** (daily 11am–10pm; ☎038 251201, ⓦwww.pattayapark .com), whose gigantic 240-metre-high tower on Buddha Hill, at the far northern end of Jomtien, is visible from all over the resort, features water slides, a Viking ship, a 170-metre tower jump, and other funfair-style rides, as well as panoramic revolving restaurants, 52 floors up. Jomtien songthaews will drop you about 750m from the entrance.

On dry land, there are over fifteen international-standard **golf courses** within easy reach of Pattaya (ⓦwww.thaigolfer.com), some of them designed by famous golfers; visitors' green fees start at around B1000.

Eating

In among the innumerable low-grade Western cafés that dominate Pattaya's **restaurant** scene are a few much classier joints serving good, sophisticated cuisine – at top-end prices. For the cheapest, most authentic Thai food, just head for the nearest of Pattaya's myriad building sites and you'll find street stalls catering to the construction-site workers.

Bruno's 306/63 Chateau Dale Plaza, Thanon Tabphaya, Jomtien ⓦwww.brunos-pattaya.com. A local institution that's a favourite with expats celebrating special occasions. The food is upscale, expensive, European – Provençal-style rack of lamb, sirloin steak, dark-chocolate mousse – and there's a cellar of some 150 wines. Main dishes from B200. Daily noon–2.30pm & 6pm–late.

Khao Suay Ground Floor, Central Festival Centre, Pattaya 2 Rd, North Pattaya. A long menu of good modern Thai food (most mains about B110) draws Thai families to this tiny café inside the shopping centre. The varied options include prawns with long beans and chillis, fish and tamarind soup, and Isaan sausage salad.

King Seafood Opposite Soi 15, Walking St, South Pattaya. Considered to be the best of South Pattaya's three famously enormous seafront seafood restaurants, at the heart of super-seedy Walking Street. Tiger prawns, giant lobsters and the rest for B150–300. Daily 11am–1am.

🏃 **Mantra** Amari Orchid hotel, Beach Rd, North Pattaya ⓦwww.mantra-pattaya.com. Setting the standard unexpectedly high for Pattaya, this large, beautifully designed bar-restaurant creates an ambience somewhere between a contemporary Shanghai hotel and a maharaja's palace with its silken drapes, lacquered shuttering, cosy romantic booths and burnished amber glow throughout. Downstairs there's an open-plan view of the five different, equally eclectic kitchens specializing in Japanese, Chinese, Thai, Indian and Mediterranean food. A meal might begin with avocado sushi, supplemented with bite-sized Peking duck, continue with seafood linguine, and end with lemon grass and pandanus crème brulée. The walk-in wine cellar keeps over 150 imported wines. Mains B270–600. Daily 5–11pm, Sunday brunch 11am–3pm.

Minus Five Supperclub Amari Nova Suites, Soi Sukrudee, North Pattaya ☎038 489488, ⓦwww .minus5pattaya.com. A copycat version of Bangkok's ultra-trendy Bed Supperclub, Minus Five brings a welcome dash of style to Pattaya's dining scene. Here, you loll on comfy loungers in an all-white diner as you're served a three-course dinner of modern Pacific-fusion cuisine (goats cheese and pomegranate salad, steamed monkfish with bacon and cider) for B950; there's a live band until 10pm and house music until closing. The super-cool Icebar is in the same building. Nightly from 6pm, last orders at midnight.

The Orangery By the Sea The Avenue plaza, Pattaya 2 Rd, Central Pattaya. Like its Bangkok sister in the Siam Paragon mall, this invitingly summery conservatory of a restaurant serves several different cuisines – Thai, Chinese, Russian,

French – prepared in discrete kitchens, so a typical meal might feature shrimp spring rolls, *matsaman* curry and *crêpe suzette*. A major draw is that after 6pm you get to sit on swing seats on the plant-filled roof terrace: a great spot for sipping delicious berry smoothies and forgetting where you are. Mains B160–400.

PIC Kitchen Soi 5, North Pattaya. One of Pattaya's top traditional Thai restaurants, set in a stylish series of teak buildings with the option of Thai-style cushion seating. Elegantly presented curries, lots of different seafood platters (served grilled or fried, laced with chilli and/or coconut, or accompanied by asparagus and mushroom), spicy salads and some vegetarian dishes. Mains from B150. Daily 11am–2pm & 6–11pm.

Sea Falcon Dongtan beachfront, Jomtien. Popular, mid-priced almost-on-the beach restaurant known for its lobster and steak. There's even a three-course lobster blowout (featuring bisque and thermidor) for B600.

Sugar Hut 391/18 Thanon Tabphaya, Jomtien. Attached to the charming hotel of the same name (see p.184), this restaurant gives you the chance to soak up the ambience and enjoy the tropical gardens without shelling out for a bungalow (though the food's not cheap either). Meals are served in an open-sided *sala* and the menu is mainly classy Thai; recommendations include fried catfish in coconut milk and chilli, and chicken baked with pineapple. Set menus from B500–750.

Drinking, nightlife and entertainment

Entertainment is Pattaya's *raison d'être* and the **nightlife** is what most tourists come for, as do expats from Laem Chabang port, oilfield workers from the Arabian Gulf and shore-leave marines on R&R. Of the thousand plus bars in the resort, the vast majority are staffed by women and men whose aim is to get bought for the night. Sex makes more money than booze in Pattaya – depending on who you believe, there are between six thousand and twenty thousand Thais working in Pattaya's **sex industry**; most depressing of all is that this workforce includes children as young as 10, despite fairly frequent high-profile paedophile arrests. It is, however, just about possible to have a night out without getting entangled in sleaze, either at one of the growing number of hostess-free **bars** listed below, a few of which are surprisingly style-conscious, or at one of the **family-oriented** cabarets and cultural extravaganzas.

However you choose to spend your evening, be warned that Pattaya is notorious for its transvestite **pickpockets** who target drunk men walking home in the early hours: while one "distracts" the victim from the front, the other extracts the wallet from behind.

Bars

The vast majority of Pattaya's bars are open-air "**bar-beers**", which group themselves in neon clusters all over North, Central and South Pattaya so that there's barely a 500-metre stretch of road without its rowdy enclave. The setup is the same in all of them: from mid-afternoon the punters – usually lone males – sit on stools around a brashly lit circular bar, behind which the hostesses keep the drinks, bawdy chat and well-worn jokes flowing. Beer is generally inexpensive, the atmosphere low-key and good-humoured, and, though most of the hostesses are aiming to score for the night, couples as well as single women drinkers are almost always made welcome.

Drinks are a lot more expensive in the bouncer-guarded **go-go bars** on Walking Street in South Pattaya, where near-naked hostesses serve the beer and live sex shows keep the boozers hooked through the night. The scene follows much the same pattern as in Patpong, Nana and Soi Cowboy in Bangkok, with the women dancing on a small stage in the hope they might be bought for the night – or the week. Go-go dancers, shower shows and striptease are also the mainstays of the **gay scene**, centred on Pattayaland Soi 3 (Soi 13/5), South Pattaya.

Despite the proliferation of lonely men and business-minded working girls, there are more and more **bars** aimed at couples, families and singles who just want a fun, even sophisticated, night out, the best of which are listed here.

The Blues Factory Soi Lucky Star, Walking Street, South Pattaya Ⓦ www.thebluesfactorypattaya.com. Considered to be the best live-music venue in Pattaya, with nightly sets (except Mon) from the famously charismatic rock guitarist Lam Morrison and his band, and (except on Wed) from the house blues band as well. Happy hour 8.30–10pm.

Gulliver's Traveler's Tavern Pattaya Beach Rd, north of Soi 1, North Pattaya. Like its branches on Bangkok's Khao San and Sukhumvit roads, this is a big-screen sports pub with pool tables, wi-fi and a streetside beer-garden.

Heineken Beer Garden Central Festival Centre, Pattaya 2 Road, North Pattaya. Outdoor tables and live music nightly (from about 8pm) from Thai singers and bands, doing mostly Thai pop and country.

Hopf Brew House Pattaya Beach Rd, between sois 13/1 (Yamato) and 13/2 (Post Office), Central Pattaya. Cavernous and very popular air-con beer hall that brews its own Pilsener and wheat beer, serves generous wood-fired pizzas and stages live music nightly. Attracts a youngish crowd, including vacationing couples.

Jazz Pit Soi 5, North Pattaya. Nightly live jazz (from 8pm) from the in-house trio in the cosy lounge-bar adjacent to the *PIC Kitchen* restaurant, and occasional high-profile celeb jamming sessions.

Kum Punn Pub Soi 2, North Pattaya. Typically Thai take on a country-and-western bar (lots of wood and the occasional buffalo head) that's known for its live bands who play nightly sets of authentic Thai folk music as well as soft rock.

Minus Five Ice Bar *Amari Nova Suites*, Soi Sukrudee, North Pattaya ☎ 038 489488, Ⓦ www .minus5pattaya.com. Your chance to literally chill-out at this cube of a bar sculpted entirely from ice, right down to the draught beer kegs on the ice-cold counter. For B500 (or B300 before 8pm) you get lent a winter coat and mittens and are given twenty minutes to down as many vodka shots as you can. Then it's back out into the warmth of the trendy Bangkok-style bar adjacent, or to the *Supperclub* restaurant next door (see p.186). Phone for free transport for groups of four or more. 6pm–2am.

Shenanigans The Avenue plaza, Pattaya 2 Rd, Central Pattaya; and Jomtien Complex Condotel, Thanon Tabphaya, Jomtien. Both branches of this long-established Irish pub keep Guinness, Kilkenny Bitter and John Smith, serve UK-style pub food, and show big-screen sports. Leather sofas, pool tables plus free internet and wi-fi are additional draws, not to mention the 4.30–7pm happy hour.

Cabarets

Tour groups – and families – constitute the main audience at Pattaya's **transvestite cabarets**. Glamorous and highly professional, these shows are performed three times a night at Alcazar, opposite Soi 4 on Pattaya 2 Road in North Pattaya (daily 6pm, 8pm & 9.30pm); and at Tiffany's, north of Soi 1 on Pattaya 2 Road in North Pattaya (daily 6pm, 7.30pm & 9pm). Each theatre has a troupe of sixty or more transvestites who run through twenty musical-style numbers in fishnets and crinolines, ball gowns and leathers, against ever more lavish stage sets. All glitz and no sleaze, the shows cost from B500 per person. The even more ambitious **cultural extravaganza** staged by Alangkarn in southern Jomtien (Thurs–Tues from 6pm; B1000) features a highly theatrical medley of Thai classical dance, martial arts, acrobatics and pyrotechnics, while Tuxedo Magic Castle, north of Central Festival on Pattaya 2 Road, North Pattaya, is a family-friendly show of classic **magic tricks and illusions** (shows nightly from 6.30pm; B450, kids B225). Any tour agent will organize tickets and transport to all the above shows.

Listings

Airlines Fairtex Arcade, 179/85–212, North Pattaya Rd ☎ 038 412382; Thai Airways, inside the *Dusit Resort*, North Pattaya ☎ 038 420995.

Bookshops Very good English-language selections at DK Books on Soi 13/2 and at the Beach Rd/ Central Pattaya Rd junction; and at Bookazine, in

The Avenue, Central Festival and Royal Garden shopping plazas. One of Pattaya's best secondhand bookshops is Thais4Life (Mon–Sat noon–6pm; ⓦ www.thais4life.com) at 504 Soi Yensabai Condotel, off Soi 17 (Soi VC), South Pattaya; run as a charity, it sells all its books for B80 and donates profits to medical and other needy projects including Baan Jing Jai orphanage.

Cinemas Several English-language screenings a day at the multiplexes: Major Cineplex, The Avenue plaza, Pattaya 2 Rd, Central Pattaya; Central Cineplex, Central Festival Centre, Pattaya 2 Rd, North Pattaya; and Royal Garden Plaza, South Pattaya.

Emergencies For all emergencies, call the tourist police on the free, 24hr phone line ☎ 1155 or contact them at their office beside TAT on Buddha Hill, between South Pattaya and Jomtien. Pattaya's main police station is more central, on Beach Rd, between sois 8 and 9, in Central Pattaya (☎ 038 425937).

Hospitals and dentists The best-equipped hospital is the private Bangkok-Pattaya Hospital ☎ 1719 or 038 259999, ⓦ www.bangkokpattaya hospital.com on Thanon Sukhumvit, about 400m north of the intersection with North Pattaya Rd. It also has dental services, as does the private

Pattaya International Hospital on Soi 4 ☎ 038 428374, ⓦ www.pih-inter.com.

Immigration office Soi 5, off Jomtien Beach Road, Jomtien (Mon–Fri 8.30am–4.30pm; ☎ 038 252750). Many travel agents offer cheap visa-renewal day-trips to Cambodia, including Five Star Visa Runs on Soi 13, South Pattaya ☎ 038 416088.

Massage In among the full-body soaps and "full-service" massage joints you'll find the innocent Thai Massage Development School (Soi Yodsak, Central Pattaya; daily 10am–10pm; ☎ 038 414115), where you can have a proper traditional massage (B300 per 60min) and also learn Thai massage (60hr over two weeks; B5000).

Shopping The main shopping plazas – the Avenue, Pattaya 2 Rd, South Pattaya; Central Festival Centre, Pattaya 2 Rd, North Pattaya; and Royal Garden Plaza in South Pattaya – are all good for designer boutiques, international brands and smart gift and handicraft outlets.

Yoga and fitness The huge, sleek California Wow fitness centre at The Avenue, Pattaya 2 Rd, Central Pattaya (daily 6am–11pm; ☎ 038 399999, ⓦ www.californiawowx.com), issues B800 day passes covering full use of all the gym equipment plus access to the many daily yoga and fitness classes.

Rayong

Few farang travellers choose to stop for longer than they have to in the busy and rapidly expanding provincial capital of **RAYONG**, 65km southeast of Pattaya, whose main concern is the Eastern Seaboard's petrochemical and shipping industries. But it's a useful place for **bus connections**, particularly if you're travelling between the east coast and the northeast or north (see p.232 for destinations), or if you're trying to get to Ko Samet; Ban Phe, the ferry pier for Ko Samet, is about 17km east and served by frequent songthaews from Rayong bus station (every 30min; 20min).

If you get stuck in town overnight, try the basic but serviceable fan and air-con **rooms** at *Burapa Palace*, 100m east of the bus station at 69 Thanon Sukhumvit (☎ 038 622946; ❸), or the huge, upscale business-oriented *Star Hotel* (☎ 038 614901, ⓦ www.starhotel.th.com; ❺) just behind and to the west of the bus station, near the lively market, on Soi 4 of the Rayong Trade Centre complex.

The region's best **hospital**, the private Bangkok-Rayong Hospital (☎ 038 921999, ⓦ www.rayonghospital.com), is on Soi Saengchan Neramit, on the southwest edge of town. The **TAT office** (☎ 038 655420, ✉ tatryong@tat .or.th) for the Rayong region and Ko Samet is inconveniently located 7km east of Rayong town centre at 153/4 Thanon Sukhumvit (Highway 3), on the way to Ban Phe; any Ban Phe-bound bus or songthaew will drop you at its door.

Ko Samet

Blessed with the softest, squeakiest sand within weekending distance of Bangkok, the tiny island of **KO SAMET**, which measures just 6km from top to toe, is a favourite escape for Thais, expats and tourists. Its fourteen small but dazzlingly white beaches are breathtakingly beautiful, lapped by pale blue water and in places still shaded by coconut palms and the occasional cajeput (*samet*) tree that gave the island its name. But they are also crowded, developed to full capacity with over fifty sprawling, albeit low-rise bungalow developments, a disfiguring number of which pay scant attention to landscaping and rubbish disposal. It's a sobering state of affairs considering that much of the island's coastline has been protected as part of the Khao Laem Ya – Mu Ko Samet **national park** since 1981; all visitors to Ko Samet are required to pay the standard national park fee on arrival (B200, 3- to 14-year-olds B100), and most hoteliers also pay rent to park authorities, but there's little evidence that this income has been used to improve the island's infrastructure.

Samet's best **beaches** are along the **east coast**, where you'll find nearly all the bungalow resorts, though there's one rather exclusive beach on the otherwise largely inaccessible west coast, and the north-coast shoreline retains a pleasingly village ambience. Most islanders and many resort staff live in the **northeast**, near the island's main pier, in the ramshackle, badly drained village of **Na Dan**, which has small shops and cheap foodstalls as well as Samet's only school, health centre and wat. A few narrow tracks, mostly signed at crucial junctions, cross the island's forested central ridge to link the east and west coasts with the trans-island dirt-road, but much of the **interior** is dense jungle, home to hornbills, gibbons and spectacular butterflies. The evergreen vegetation belies the fact that there are no rivers on this unusually dry island, which gets only scant rainfall in an average year. Lack of rain is another plus point for tourists, though it means water is a precious and expensive commodity as it has to be trucked in from the mainland.

The trend across the island is upmarket and in high season you'll be hard pressed to secure an en-suite bungalow for under B700, though a few simple no-frills B300 huts do remain. The most backpacker-oriented beaches are east-coast **Ao Hin Kok**, **Ao Phai** and **Ao Tub Tim**, with Ao Hin Kok and Ao Phai both quite lively in the evenings; the travellers' vibe at nearby **Ao Nuan** is more alternative, with **Ao Thian** and north-coast **Ao Noi Na** also worth investigating. **Hat Sai Kaew** and **Ao Wong Duan** are the biggest centres on the east coast, dominated by upper scale accommodation aimed at families, package tourists and Bangkok trendies. Samet's super-deluxe accommodation is on west-coast **Ao Phrao** and southern beauty **Ao Kiu**.

All beaches get packed on **weekends** and national holidays, when booking ahead is advisable, though, unusually for Thailand, walk-in guests are often offered the best rates. Many bungalow managers raise their prices by sixty percent during peak periods and sometimes for weekenders as well: the rates quoted here are typical weekday high-season rates.

Getting to Ko Samet

The mainland departure-point for Ko Samet is the small coastal town of **BAN PHE**, 17km east of Rayong, 80km southeast of Pattaya, and about 200km from Bangkok. It's served by hourly buses **from Bangkok**'s Eastern (Ekamai) Bus Terminal, by songthaews from the nearby provincial capital of **Rayong** (which has bus connections to many towns; see p.189), and by fast but cramped tourist minibuses from Bangkok's **Thanon Khao San** (about 4hr; B250) and **Pattaya**

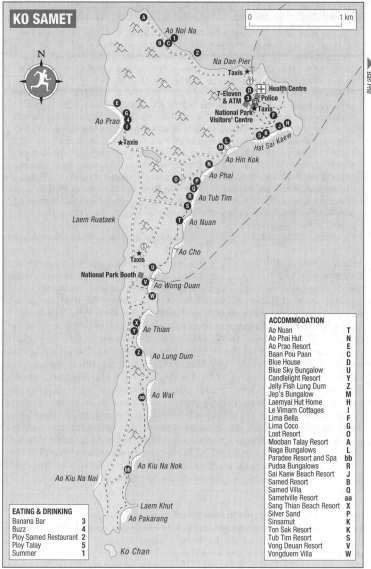

▲ Ban Phe

KO SAMET

N

0   1 km

Ao Noi Na

Na Dan Pier
★ Taxis

7-Eleven
& ATM ✚ Health Centre
Police
★ Taxis
National Park
Visitors' Centre

Ao Prao

★ Taxis

Hat Sai Kaew

Ao Hin Kok

Ao Phai

Ao Tub Tim

Laem Ruataek

Ao Nuan

Taxis
★

Ao Cho

National Park Booth ■

Ao Wong Duan

Ao Thian

Ao Lung Dum

Ao Wai

Ao Kiu Na Nok

Ao Kiu Na Nai

Laem Khut

Ao Pakarang

Ko Chan

ACCOMMODATION	
Ao Nuan	T
Ao Phai Hut	N
Ao Prao Resort	E
Baan Pou Paan	C
Blue House	D
Blue Sky Bungalow	U
Candlelight Resort	Y
Jelly Fish Lung Dum	Z
Jep's Bungalow	M
Laemyai Hut Home	H
Le Vimarn Cottages	I
Lima Bella	F
Lima Coco	G
Lost Resort	O
Mooban Talay Resort	A
Naga Bungalows	L
Paradee Resort and Spa	bb
Pudsa Bungalows	R
Sai Kaew Beach Resort	J
Samed Resort	B
Samed Villa	Q
Sametville Resort	aa
Sang Thian Beach Resort	X
Silver Sand	P
Sinsamut	K
Ton Sak Resort	S
Tub Tim Resort	V
Vong Deuan Resort	V
Vongduern Villa	W

EATING & DRINKING	
Banana Bar	3
Buzz	4
Ploy Samed Restaurant	2
Ploy Talay	5
Summer	1

(about 90min; B230). A meter-taxi ride from **Suvarnabhumi Airport** should cost around B2000. Coming by bus from **Chanthaburi** or **Trat**, you'll most likely be dropped on Highway 3, from where a songthaew or motorbike taxi will take you the remaining 5km to the Ban Phe piers.

The area around Ban Phe's main Taruaphe pier-head has many **tour desks** selling onward bus tickets and private transfers, plus minimarkets, internet centres and the well-stocked Blue Sky secondhand bookshop. Places **to stay**

Moving on from Ko Samet

The first **boat** leaves Ko Samet's Na Dan pier at 6.30am, and in theory there's then an hourly service across to Ban Phe until 6pm, but if you have a plane to catch you should allow for boat no-shows and delays. There are also at least three daily departures from Ao Wong Duan (8.30am, 11.30am & 3.30pm), and in high season you'll find at least one Ban Phe boat a day from Ao Cho and Ao Prao.

There are several options for transport from Ban Phe **to Bangkok**. Cherdchai's large, air-con **buses** leave from the bus station 400m east of *Christie's* and go direct to Bangkok's Ekamai **Eastern Bus Terminal** (hourly 4am–7pm; 3hr 30min); tourist minibuses to **Pattaya** and **Khao San** (both B250) leave from the tour agencies in the two sois behind *Christie's* but are best booked on Samet; and private minivans run direct to Bangkok's **Victory Monument** from opposite the *Diamond Hotel* (hourly 6.30am–7.30pm; 3hr; B250). For **Ko Chang**, you can also book tourist minibuses direct to the port at Laem Ngop, through agencies on Ko Samet or in Ban Phe (B250). The same agencies sell bus tickets to **Phnom Penh** and **Siem Reap** (B2000), but read the warnings on p.201 first. For all other destinations, including **Chanthaburi** and **Trat**, flag down a songthaew from the roadside in front of any of the piers and change at **Rayong** bus station.

include *Christie's* (☎038 651976; Je_christie@hotmail.com; ❸), opposite the Taruaphe pier, which has four good air-con rooms above its restaurant. Across the soi, *Tan Tan Too* (☎087 485 6913; ❷–❸) offers a couple of equally good rooms with either fan or air-con, while 100m west along the road, the decent enough *Diamond Hotel* (☎038 651757; fan ❷, air-con ❸) is open 24 hour.

Most **boats to Ko Samet** run from Ban Phe's main Taruaphe pier (opposite one of the 7-Eleven shops) **to Na Dan** on Ko Samet's north coast; they depart approximately hourly from 8am to 5pm during high season (Nov–Feb) and on national holidays, and every two hours at other times, take thirty minutes and cost B50. Na Dan is convenient for Hat Sai Kaew, Ao Hin Kok, Ao Phai, Ao Tub Tim and Ao Nuan. Less frequent boat services also run from the Taruaphe pier **to Ao Wong Duan**, halfway down Samet's east coast (at least 2 daily; 40min; B70), and from the Chokkrisda pier, about 100m west of Taruaphe, to Ao Wong Duan. There are also direct services operated by individual resorts and several 24-hour **speedboat** services such as that run by Shair Buay, that will take you to any beach (☎089 8316270, ⓦwww.shairbuaysamed.com; B1500–2200 for a boat carrying up to 10 people); Shair Buay is located by Ban Phe's third main pier, the Nuan Tip pier, which is opposite the Cherdchai bus station, 400m east of *Christie's*.

Island transport, information and activities

Samet's principal road is a rough and deeply rutted dirt track that runs north–south and gives access to all the main beaches. Fleets of green songthaew **share-taxis** shuttle passengers up and down it, waiting for fares at the Na Dan pier, near the Hat Sai Kaew National Park office, behind Ao Wong Duan, and at Ao Prao; they will also pick up from accommodation if you get staff to phone them. Transfer rates are fixed and are generally charged per trip not per person, with most routes (eg Na Dan to Ao Prao or Hat Sai Kaew to Wong Duan) costing B200–B250. You need to be pretty confident to negotiate the mud and potholes on a **motorbike**, available for rent at Na Dan pier and on almost every beach (B400 per day), which is why it's become fashionable to rent a lumbering four-wheeled ATV instead, either from the Na Dan pier-head or via hotels elsewhere (from B1500 per 24hr).

Shops and stalls in Na Dan and on all the main beaches sell basic travellers' necessities. There are **ATMs** at the Na Dan pier-head, beside the Hat Sai Kaew national park office and on Ao Wong Duan; the bigger bungalows also change money. There are **internet centres** around the National Park office on the Na Dan road, a couple of which have wi-fi, and on almost every beach, and the island's **post office** is at *Naga Bungalows* on Ao Hin Kok. CP Travel on Hat Sai Kaew (☎038 644136), in the beach-access arcade near the National Park office, sells domestic and international **air tickets** as well as bus and minibus tickets for onward travel (see box opposite). It also sells a few new books. Ko Samet's **health centre** and **police station** (☎038 644111) are on the Na Dan–Hat Sai Kaew road, but for anything serious you should go to the Bangkok-Rayong hospital in Rayong (see p.189). Many bungalows have **safety deposits** and it's worth making use of them: theft is an issue on Samet and there are occasional instances of drinks being spiked by freelance bar-girls and punters waking next day without their valuables.

Samet has no decent coral reefs of its own, so you'll have to take a boat trip to the islands of Ko Kudi, Ko Thalu and Ko Mun, off the northeast coast, to get good **snorkelling** (from B500 from most beaches) or **diving**; Ploy Scuba on Hat Sai Kaew charges B2700 for two dives and B15,000 for the four-day PADI Openwater course (☎038 644 212, ⓦwww.ployscuba.com). From the main beaches you can also organize **boat trips** around Samet itself (from B350), rent kayaks and jet skis and arrange banana boat rides and parasailing.

Hat Sai Kaew and Na Dan

From **NA DAN** pier, a ten-minute walk south along the road brings you to **HAT SAI KAEW**, or Diamond Beach, named for its long and extraordinarily beautiful stretch of luxuriant sand, so soft and clean it squeaks underfoot – a result, apparently, of its unusually high silicon content. Unsurprisingly, it's the busiest beach on Samet, its shorefront packed with bungalows, restaurants, beachwear stalls, deckchairs and parasols, though the northern end is slightly more peaceful.

Accommodation

Much of the **accommodation** here is crammed uncomfortably close together and prices are high. Cheap rooms are sometimes available above the shops and restaurants on the Na Dan road.

Blue House On the Na Dan road ☎086 332 5903. Budget, mostly windowless singles and simple en-suite fan and air-con options in two different locations on the Na Dan road. Fan ❷, air-con ❸
Laemyai Hut Home ☎038 644282. The fan bungalows here are the best of the cheapest options on this beach, not least because they're dotted round a shaded sandy garden in one of the prettiest spots, under the Laem Yai headland at the quieter northern end. Fan bungalows are simple, with platform beds; air-con versions are also available. Fan ❹, air-con ❺
Lima Bella ☎02 938 1811, ⓦwww.limabella .com. This hip but invitingly homely little garden haven occupies a quiet heliconia-filled plot with its own pretty swimming pool, about 3min walk from the beach. Its 26 architecturally striking, design-conscious air-con rooms have daybeds, DVD

players and free wi-fi; some have separate mezzanine bedrooms or living areas and many have bathtubs. The ambience is more intimate and private than most hotels on Samet and it's popular with families. It's expensive, but discounts are often available on request. ❽
Sai Kaew Beach Resort ☎038 644197, ⓦwww.samedresorts.com. This popular and highly efficient resort has over 150 rooms, most of them in distinctive and thoughtfully if quite simply designed blue-and-white air-con bungalows; many have their own tiny lawn, and the priciest have uninterrupted sea views. The "deluxe cottages" occupy their own grassy haven with swimming pool, in front of a separate and pretty but minute little patch of sandy shoreline; they have garden bathrooms and private decks. ❽–❾

Sinsamut ☏038 644134, ⓦwww.sinsamut -kohsamed.com. Initial appearances aren't encouraging here, with various types of rooms stuffed into cheek-by-jowl little blocks behind the restaurant midway down the beach, but most rooms are pleasant inside, with bright, contemporary decor, and some have outdoor space. The quirky fan-cooled "*katom*" bungalows, set around a grassy little roof garden, enjoy the best outlook. Fan ❹, air-con ❺

Ton Sak Resort ☏038 644314, ⓦwww.tonsak .com. The timbered cabins here are packed very close together, but the surrounding borders of shrubs add a little privacy, and few are more than 100m from the water. Interiors are comfortable if a little old-fashioned, and have air-con and modern bathrooms. ❼–❽

Eating and drinking

At sundown the deckchairs give way to the low tables, mats and cushions that the **restaurants** spread out along the sand. By far the most popular is *Ploy Talay*, which, like many other places on Hat Sai Kaew, serves barbecued seafood dinners, buffet style, plus à la carte choices, but livens up proceedings with nightly entertainment from its Filipino cover band and its troupe of athletic fire-jugglers, who spark up around 8.30pm. Away from the sea, the growing number of congenial little bars and restaurants on the Na Dan road tend to serve cheaper and more interesting menus; in particular, the tiny *Banana Bar*, not far from the police station, serves tastily authentic yellow, green and *matsaman* curries, as well as *tom yum* and spicy salads.

Ao Hin Kok

Separated from Hat Sai Kaew by a low promontory on which sits a mermaid statue (a reference to the early nineteenth-century poem, *Phra Abhai Mani*, by famous local poet Sunthorn Phu), **AO HIN KOK** is much smaller than its neighbour, and has more of a travellers' vibe. Just three sets of bungalows overlook the petite white-sand beach from the slope on the far side of the dirt road, and you can walk here from Na Dan in about fifteen minutes.

The long-running, consciously traveller-focussed, English-run *Naga Bungalows* (☏038 644168, ⓔsuewildnaga@gmail.com; ❷–❸) has some of the cheapest **accommodation** on Ko Samet, with prices consistent year round

▲ Fire-jugglers on Ko Samet

and at weekends. It offers simple bamboo and wood huts stacked in tiers up the slope, with decks, mosquito nets and shared bathrooms, as well as pricier concrete bungalows with their own adjacent bathroom. Its restaurant does lots of vegetarian dishes, and sells home-made bread, cakes and pizzas. Next door but one, *Jep's Bungalow* (T038 644112, W www.jepbungalow.com; fan ❷–❸, air ❺–❼) has a spread of options in unremarkable wooden chalets and concrete bungalows, the latter with air-con and TV and ranged up the shady, terraced, sandy-soiled garden. It has internet access and a tour desk and a 🏃 **restaurant**, which serves up a great menu of authentic Thai dishes (including popular *som tam* sets), seafood, Indian curries, Japanese food, brownies and the rest at its tables on the beach, set under trees strung with fairylights and given extra atmosphere by mellow music. A nearby cappuccino stall does various fresh and liqueur coffees.

Ao Phai

Narrow but sparkling little **AO PHAI**, around the next headland, is Samet's party beach, with the shoreside *Silver Sand* bar and disco known for its late-night dance music and fire-juggling shows fuelled by cocktails and buckets of vodka Red Bull (Saturday is unofficial gay night). Not everyone has to join in though, as the bungalows on the fringes of the bay are far enough away for a good night's sleep. There's a minimarket on the beach, a dive shop, tour service and exchange facilities, and you can walk to Na Dan pier in twenty minutes.

Ao Phai Hut (T038 644075; fan ❹, air-con ❺) sits on the rocky divide between Ao Phai and Hin Kok and offers a wide range of rather variable split-bamboo and concrete **huts**, the more basic ones set in a scruffy area among the trees, the pricier options, some of them with air-con, occupying a scenic spot overlooking the rocky end of the shore. At the centre of the beach, party-hub *Silver Sand* (T038 644301, W www.silversandresort.samet.i8.com; fan ❹, air-con ❺–❻) has a spread of well-turned-out rooms, including whitewashed, air-con chalets ranged around a pretty garden; they all come with safety boxes, verandas and good modern bathrooms, and some have polished wooden floors. The huge villa-style bungalows at well-managed *Samed Villa* (T038 644094, W www.samedvilla.com; ❻–❼) are packed into a fairly small area along the rocks at the southern end of the bay (good views from the front row) and up the slope behind the restaurant. Interiors are luxurious and well furnished and especially good for families; they all have air-con and TV and free tea and coffee. Immediately behind *Sea Breeze*, on the road to Wong Duan, the two-storey block that is *Lost Resort* (T038 644041, W www.thelostresort.net; fan ❸, air-con ❺) sits peacefully in a grove of tall trees, just a couple of minutes' walk from the beach but with no sea view. The twelve rooms here can be fan or air-con and are of a good standard and well priced.

Ao Tub Tim

Also known as Ao Pudsa, **AO TUB TIM** is another cute white-sand bay sandwiched between rocky points, partly shaded with palms and backed by a wooded slope. It has just two bungalow operations and feels secluded, if a bit crowded, but is only a short stroll from Ao Phai and the other beaches further north, and a half-hour hike from Na Dan pier.

The most popular **place to stay** is the sprawling, well-run 🏃 *Tub Tim Resort* (T038 644025, W www.tubtimresort.com; fan ❹–❺, air-con ❻–❼), with over sixty handsome chalet-style wooden bungalows of various sizes and designs, all with classy modern furnishings and outdoor space. Their restaurant is very good indeed, especially for Thai favourites like *haw mok* (fish curry steamed in banana leaf). At adjacent *Pudsa Bungalows* (☎038 644030; fan ❹, air-con ❻) you get large, sturdy huts, including some especially well located fan ones that sit on the northern rocks alongside the footpath (next to *Samet Villa*'s much pricier ones on neighbouring Ao Phai) and enjoy direct sea views.

Ao Nuan

Clamber up over the next headland (which gives you a fine panorama over Hat Sai Kaew) to reach Samet's smallest and most laid-back beach, the secluded **AO NUAN**. This is effectively the private domain of *Ao Nuan* bungalows (no phone; shared bathroom ❹, en suite ❻), whose octagonal veggie restaurant and simple, idiosyncratic huts hark back to a mellower, old-school island vibe, entirely removed from the commercialism of the other beaches (though room rates are definitely modern-day). The nine sturdy timber huts are each built to a slightly different design and dotted across the slope that drops down to the bay, with a few hanging right over the beach. The furnishing is spartan – the cheapest have just a platform bed and a mosquito net, and all but three share bathrooms – but they all have fans and 24-hour electricity and one has air-con. Because it's some way off the main track, the beach gets hardly any through-traffic and so feels quiet and private. Although not brilliant for swimming, the rocky shore reveals a good patch of sand when the tide withdraws; the more consistent beach at Ao Tub Tim is only five minutes' walk to the north and Ao Cho, which has some coral, is a five-minute walk south along the footpath.

Ao Wong Duan

The horseshoe bay of **AO WONG DUAN**, a ten-minute walk round the next-but-one point from Ao Nuan, is Samet's second most popular beach after Hat Sai Kaew. Though it's not as pretty and suffers even more from hordes of day-trippers, it does offer some attractive upscale accommodation; most guests are either package tourists, Pattaya overnighters, or weekending Bangkokians so shoestring travellers aren't well catered for. Although the beach is fairly long and broad, the central shorefront is almost lost under a knot of tiny bars (many with irresistibly comfy armchairs) and tourist shops, and the main stretch of beach all but disappears at high tide. Facilities include minimarkets, ATMs, money exchange and internet access. At least two direct **boats** a day should run from Ban Phe to Wong Duan (see p.192), and vice versa.

Blue Sky Bungalow (☎089 936 0842; fan ❹, air-con ❺) is the last remaining bastion of budget **accommodation** on Wong Duan, with just a handful of basic wooden fan bungalows plus some air-con concrete ones set up on the hill at the north, rocky, end of the bay, above the *Blue Sky Restaurant*. Ideally located in the middle of the beach, *Vong Deuan Resort* (☎038 651777, ⓦwww .vongdeuan.com; ❼–❽) comprises attractive air-con bungalows in various designs set around a pretty tropical garden, including nice cottages with dark-wood exteriors, contemporary styled interiors and garden bathrooms. Service is efficient, attentive and hotel-like, which makes it a favourite with older guests. The younger, hipper crowd mostly goes for *Vongduern Villa* (☎038 644260, ⓦwww.vongduernvilla.com; ❺–❽), which has character, even if it's not quite pristine. Occupying a big chunk of the bay's southern end, it features various types and standards of room, all of them design-conscious and air-con, and ranging from whitewashed timber huts built on stilts and with picture windows, decks and modern furnishings to more minimalist versions kitted out with dark-wood floors and Japanese-style platform beds. There's also an attractive restaurant deck jutting out over the water.

Ao Thian (Candlelight Beach) and Ao Lung Dum

A favourite with Thai students, who relish the natural beauty of its slightly wild setting, **AO THIAN** ("Candlelight Beach") and contiguous Ao Lung Dum display almost none of the commerce of Wong Duan, a couple of minutes' walk over the hill, though the scenic shorefront is fronted by an unbroken line of bungalows and the eponymous "candlelight" lighting is long gone. The narrow, white-sand coastline is dotted with wave-smoothed rocks and partitioned by larger outcrops that create several distinct bays; as it curves outwards to the south you get a great view of the island's east coast. To get here either take a **boat** from Ban Phe to Ao Wong Duan and then walk, or pay B250 for a place on the scheduled direct speedboats (up to 6 daily from Taruaphe pier).

Towards Ao Thian's northern end, *Sang Thian Beach Resort* (T038 644255, Wwww.sangthain.com; ⑥) has very tasteful air-con timber chalets built up the cliffside on a series of decks and steps – decor is navy-and-white chic, and views, mostly encompassing the sea, are pretty; it also has much less interesting compact brick **bungalows** up the northern slope. Further down the shore, the ten very nice wooden bungalows belonging to *Candlelight Resort* (T089 247 9597; fan ④, air-con ⑤) are strung out in a long line, with each one facing the water, making them good value considering the competition.

At its southern end, Ao Thian becomes **AO LUNG DUM**, and the various little bungalow outfits fringing the shore here are pretty similar: *Jelly Fish Lung Dum* (T038 644331; fan ④, air-con ⑤) is just about the cheapest, and all sixteen of its bungalows are right on the rocky shore, practically overhanging the water.

Ao Wai and Ao Kiu

A fifteen-minute walk along the coast path from Lung Dum brings you to **AO WAI**, a very pretty white-sand bay, partially shaded and a good size considering it supports just one (large) **bungalow** operation, *Sametville Resort* (T038 651681, Wwww.sametvilleresort.com; fan ⑤, air-con ⑥–⑧), which also spills across on to neighbouring little Ao Hin Kaleng. Bungalows in all categories vary in quality, but you've plenty to choose from, unless you come at a weekend when it tends to fill up with Thai groups. There's usually a morning **boat** here from Ban Phe (Mon–Sat 10am, Sun 9am; B90) plus possible extra ones on weekends, but call the resort to confirm.

Over an hour's walk south of Ao Thian, via a track that begins behind *Vong Deuan Resort* on Ao Wong Duan and can be joined at the southern end of Ao Thian, the gorgeous little twin bays of **AO KIU** – Ao Kiu Na Nok on the east coast and Ao Kiu Na Nai on the west – are separated by just a few hundred metres of land. Both beaches are the domain of Samet's most exclusive hotel, the very luxurious, five-star, butler-service villa resort *Paradee Resort and Spa* (T038 644283, Wwww.paradeeresort.com; ⑨ published rates from B17,800).

Ao Prao (Paradise Bay)

Across on the upper west coast, the rugged, rocky coastline only softens into beach once, at **AO PRAO**, also known as Paradise Bay, on the northwestern stretch, some 4km north of Ao Kiu Na Nai. This is Samet's top-notch beach, dominated by two expensively elegant resorts, plus one slightly more affordable option, and nothing else to lower the tone. If you're only visiting for the day, the most direct route from the east-coast beaches is via the inland track from behind *Sea Breeze* on Ao Phai, which takes about twenty minutes on foot, though the track from the back of *Tub Tim* on Ao Tub Tim will also get you there. If staying on Ao Prao, your hotel will arrange boat transfers.

Ao Prao Resort (℡038 644101, Ⓦwww.samedresorts.com; ❾) boasts some of the most luxurious **accommodation** on the island, in comfortable wooden chalets set in a mature tropical garden that slopes down to the beach. All chalets have air-con, TVs and balconies looking out to sea. There's a dive centre, boat tours and kayak rental, and a picturesquely sited restaurant extending over the water. The even more indulgent *Le Vimarn Cottages* (℡038 644104, Ⓦwww.samedresorts.com; ❾, prices start from B10,500) is owned by the same company and comprises charming, gorgeously furnished cottages, a delightful spa and a swimming pool. Its very refined *Buzz* restaurant serves highly regarded, highly priced Thai food (mains cost up to B600) in its chic modern dining room and upstairs terrace. *Lima Coco* (℡089 105 7080, Ⓦwww.limacoco.com; ❼–❾) is younger, trendier and cheaper, with a Bangkok contemporary chic look and lots of white walls, brightly coloured cushions, day beds and decks. Rooms are built up the side of the hill, with the priciest enjoying front-row sea views.

Ao Noi Na

West of Na Dan, the island's north coast – known simply as **AO NOI NA** even though it's not strictly a single bay – has a refreshingly normal village feel compared to the rest of Samet. There are an increasing number of places to stay along the narrow coastal road here, offering serene views across the water to the mainland hills behind Ban Phe, and just one white-sand beach of note at the far western end. Though this beach has been hogged by the luxurious *Mooban Talay Resort*, it's not private and you can walk there from Na Dan pier in about 25 minutes. En route you'll pass several good **restaurants**, including a floating seafood restaurant, ⚓ *Ploy Samed Restaurant,* where diners have to ring a bell on the shore to alert the boatman to come over and pick you up; rock lobster is a speciality, and you eat on a deck at low tables with your feet dangling above the water.

Less than fifteen minutes' walk from Na Dan, Scottish-run *Baan Pou Paan* (℡081 172 4486, Ⓔlizziecj@hotmail.com; ❹–❺) is a chilled-out boutique **guest house** offering three beautiful en-suite fan and air-con bungalows built on stilts in the sea, with large decks and unparalleled views, plus another three air-con rooms in the building at the water's edge; they're all furnished with cushions, lamps and lots of plants, and prices stay the same year-round and at weekends. There's a stunningly sited eating area at the end of a jetty, for diners at the hotel's *Summer* restaurant, whose speciality is modern Mediterranean (evenings only; mains B120–380). Guests can either swim off the jetty or from the tiny beaches to either side, and there's table tennis and free wi-fi. Next-door-but-one, the dozen bungalows at British-managed *Samed Resort* (℡038 644334, Ⓦwww.samed-resort.com; shared bathrooms ❷, fan ❸, air-con ❺) occupy a wide sandy grove just across the road from a tiny, almost private beach; though the beach is a bit scruffy it has shade, with hammocks, and good swimming. Bungalows range from old-style bamboo huts with shared bathroom to en-suite fan and air-con bungalows; interiors in all are modern and cheery. You can also rent tents here (B300 for two including bedding). The shoreside restaurant, and its lively bar, has a pool table, table tennis and free wi-fi. Ten minutes' walk further west, you reach the poshest place on Ao Noi Na – and one of the classiest on the island: *Mooban Talay Resort* (℡038 644251, Ⓦwww.moobantalay.com; ❾), a secluded haven at the end of the road, set under the trees on a gorgeous, quiet, white-sand beach. Accommodation is in large, attractive bungalows, all with platform beds, garden bathrooms and outdoor seating: the priciest, seafront ones have enormous decks, and there's a beachside pool.

Chanthaburi and around

For over five hundred years, the seams of rock rich in sapphires and rubies that streak the hills of eastern Thailand have drawn prospectors and traders of all nationalities to the provincial capital of **CHANTHABURI**, 80km east of Ban Phe. Many of these hopefuls established permanent homes in the town, particularly the Shans from Burma, the Chinese and the Cambodians. Though the veins of precious stones have now been all but exhausted, Chanthaburi's reputation as a gem centre has continued to thrive and this is still one of the most famous places in Thailand to trade in gems (most of them now imported from Sri Lanka and elsewhere), not least because Chanthaburi is as respected a cutting centre as Bangkok, and Thai lapidaries are considered among the most skilled – and affordable – in the world.

Chanthaburi is an exceptionally fertile province, renown for its abundance of orchards, particularly durian, rambutan and mangosteen, which are celebrated

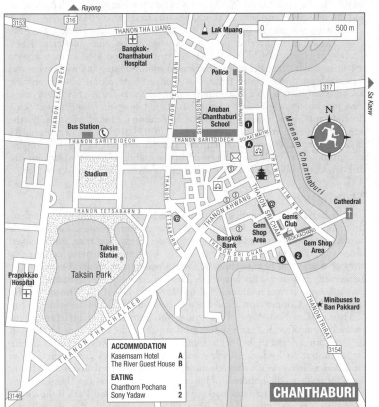

ACCOMMODATION	
Kasemsarn Hotel	A
The River Guest House	B
EATING	
Chanthorn Pochana	1
Sony Yadaw	2

CHANTHABURI

Trat ▼

with an annual **fruit festival**, held in May or June. Its barely developed coastline is also very pretty, popular with Thai visitors for its empty beaches and shady casuarina trees that are just perfect for long seafood lunches. Though most foreign tourists passing through this province are either racing to cross the **Cambodian border** or have their sights set firmly on Ko Chang, a deviation via **the Chanthaburi coast** offers a much calmer, and very Thai, alternative.

Arrival, information and accommodation

Even if you're not planning a visit to Chanthaburi, you may find yourself stranded here for a couple of hours between **buses**, as this is a major transit point for east-coast services (including most Rayong–Trat buses) and a handy terminus for buses to and from the northeast. Eight daily buses make the scenic six-hour Chanthaburi–Sa Kaew–Khorat journey in both directions, with Sa Kaew being a useful interchange for buses to **Aranyaprathet and the Cambodian border** (see box opposite). Buses to and from all these places, as well as Bangkok's Eastern (Ekamai) and Northern (Mo Chit) stations (a few of which go via Suvarnabhumi Airport), use the Chanthaburi **bus station** (☎039 311299) on Thanon Saritdidech, about 750m northwest of the town centre and market. Chartered songthaew taxis from here to the Ko Chang piers at Laem Ngop charge B500.

The best **hospital** in town is the private Bangkok-Chanthaburi Hospital at 25/14 Thanon Tha Luang (☎039 319888, ⒲www.bangkokchanthaburi.com) and the **police** are further east along the same road (☎039 311111).

The two nicest **places to stay** are near the river. Traveller-oriented *The River Guest House* sits on the river bank on the edge of the gems quarter at 3/5–8 Thanon Sri Chan (☎039 328211; ❶–❷); it serves good food at its waterside restaurant and has internet access. Its cheapest rooms are tiny and windowless and share bathrooms; the better fan and air-con en-suite rooms have river-view balconies but narrow beds. Five minutes' walk north up Thanon Sri Chan, or less than ten minutes' walk east of the bus station (past the thought-provoking Buddhist aphorisms adorning the wall of the Anuban Chanthaburi School), is the unexpectedly contemporary *Kasemsarn Hotel* (☎039 312340, ⒠kasemsarnhotel1 @yahoo.com; ❹–❺), at 98/1 Thanon Benchama-Rachutit. Its comfortable air-con rooms are built round a central atrium and done out in whitewash and dark wood; they all have free wi-fi and there's a smart coffee shop downstairs.

The Town

Chanthaburi's most interesting neighbourhoods are close to the **river**, particularly along Thanon Rim Nam, with its mix of pastel-painted, colonial-style housefronts and traditional wooden shophouses, many displaying finely carved latticework. This district is home to a large Catholic Vietnamese community, most of whom fled here in waves following religious persecution between the eighteenth century and the late 1970s. The earliest refugees constructed what is now, following several revamps, Thailand's largest cathedral, the **Church of the Immaculate Conception**, located across the footbridge from the southern end of Thanon Rim Nam. West of the bridge, the **gem dealers' quarter** begins, centred around Trok Kachang and Thanon Sri Chan (the latter signed in English as "Gem Street") and packed with dozens of gem shops. Most lie empty during the week, but on Fridays, Saturdays and Sunday mornings they come alive as local dealers arrive to sift through mounds of tiny coloured stones and classify them for resale to the hundreds of buyers who drive down from Bangkok.

West of the gem quarter and market, the landscaped **Taksin Park** is the town's recreation area and memorial to King Taksin of Thonburi, the general who

Overland into Cambodia via Aranyaprathet–Poipet and Chanthaburi province

The most commonly used **overland crossing into Cambodia** is at **Poipet**, which lies just across the border from the Thai town of **Aranyaprathet**. The border here is open daily from 7am to 8pm and officials will issue thirty-day Cambodian **visas on arrival** (see p.22; ⓦwww.thaivisa.com for its visa-run forum; and ⓦwww.talesofasia.com /cambodia-overland.htm for a very detailed description of the crossing and for advice on onward transport into Cambodia). Once you're through, it's about three hours in a share-taxi or tourist bus to reach Siem Reap, 150km away. If you need a **hotel** in Aranyaprathet, try either the comfortable fan and air-con rooms at *Inter Hotel* at 108/7 Thanon Chatasingh (☎037 231291, ⓦwww.ourweb.info/interhotel; fan ❷, air-con ❸), or the cheaper en-suite rooms at *Aran Garden II*, 110 Thanon Rat Uthit (fan ❶, air-con ❷).

To reach Aranyaprathet from east-coast towns, the easiest route is to take a bus **from Chanthaburi** to the town of **Sa Kaew**, 130km to the northeast, and then change to one of the frequent buses for the 55-kilometre ride east to Aranyaprathet. **From Bangkok**, you can travel to Aranyaprathet by **train** (2 daily; 6hr), though you'll need to catch the 5.55am to ensure reaching the border before 5pm; the other leaves at 1.05pm. Return trains depart Aranyaprathet at 6.35am and 1.35pm. Tuk-tuks will take you the 4km from the train station to the border post. Alternatively, take a **bus** from Bangkok's Northern (Mo Chit) Bus Terminal to Aranyaprathet (at least hourly; 4hr 30min), then a tuk-tuk from the bus station to the border post. The last Aranyaprathet– Bangkok bus leaves at 7pm. It's also possible to buy a **through ticket to Siem Reap** from Trat and Ko Chang, or from Thanon Khao San in Bangkok (B200–600), but this option is dogged by **scams** (including a visa "service charge", described in detail at ⓦwww.talesofasia.com/cambodia-overland-bkksr-package.htm and on the forum at ⓦwww.thaivisa.com), can take up to ten hours longer than doing it independently, often travels via the less convenient Pailin or O'Smach border crossings instead, and nearly always uses clapped-out buses or even pick-ups on the Cambodian side, despite the promised "luxury bus".

There are also two less-used crossings in **Chanthaburi province**, giving access to the Cambodian town of **Pailin**, just east of the border. Daung Lem Border Crossing at **Ban Laem** is 88km northeast of Chanthaburi and the Phsa Prom border crossing is at **Ban Pakkard** (aka Chong Phakkat), 72km northeast of Chanthaburi. There's a minibus service in the morning from Chanthaburi (just east across the bridge from *The River Guest House*) to Ban Pakkard (1hr; B150), or you can take a songthaew from Chanthaburi to **Pong Nam Ron**, 42km north of Chanthaburi on Highway 317 (90min), then charter another to either border pass. The borders are open daily from 7am to 8pm and issue **visas on arrival**; if entering Thailand via this route you'll probably be obliged to show proof of onward travel from Thailand.

reunited Thailand between 1767 and 1782 after the sacking of Ayutthaya by the Burmese. Chanthaburi was the last Burmese bastion on the east coast – when Taksin took the town he effectively regained control of the whole country. The park's heroic bronze statue of Taksin is featured on the back of the B20 note.

Eating

A few metres up the road from the *Kasemsarn Hotel* on Thanon Benchama-Rachutit, *Chanthorn Phochana* **restaurant** at 102/5–8 Thanon Benchama-Rachutit serves a delicious range of spicy *yam* salads, Thai curries and stir-fries. Another place that's worth investigating is the tiny vegetarian Indian restaurant *Sony Yadaw*, opposite *The River Guest House*. **Foodstalls** in the market and along the riverside sois sell Vietnamese spring rolls (*cha gio*) with sweet sauce, and locally made Chanthaburi rice noodles (*sen Chan*); *sen Chan* are popularly used in *phat thai* throughout Thailand, but in Chanthaburi they're also crucial to the local noodle soup, *muu liang*, whose dark broth is flavoured with pungent herbs.

Coastal Chanthaburi

An ideal base from which to appreciate the understated charm of **coastal Chanthaburi** is the New Zealand–Thai owned *Faasai Resort* (☎039 417404, Ⓦwww.faasai.com; ❺–❻), a fifteen-room environmentally conscious **resort** in **KHUNG WIMAN**, just off Route 3399, about 30km southwest of Chanthaburi, or 80km east of Ban Phe. Its comfortable, family-friendly, air-con bungalows sit in a tropical garden with views to the Cardamon mountains on the Cambodian border, and there's a swimming pool, wi-fi and Wat Pho-trained massage therapists on site. Very unusually, the resort also has its own private little **wetland conservation area**, where you can sit bird-watching, swim in the natural spring pool or kayak along the rivulet. The quiet, shady, bronze-sand beach of Hat Khung Wiman is ten minutes' walk away and *Faasai* rents bicycles, motorbikes and cars and organizes interesting local tours. On Khung Wiman beach itself you can also stay in one of the eight rather chic Moroccan-inspired rooms at *Al Medina Beach House* (☎085 838 1200, Ⓦwww.almedinabeach.com; ❽–❾).

A couple of kilometres southeast of Hat Khung Wiman and you're at the lip of **AO KHUNG KRABEN**, a deep, lagoonlike scoop of a bay that's occasionally visited by dugongs and is edged by dense mangrove forest. A wide swathe of this mangrove swamp is protected under a royal conservation project and crossed by a kilometre-long boardwalk; you can also rent kayaks here (Oct–May Tues–Sun 8.30am–4pm) to follow a signed riverine trail. Access is via **LAEM SADET** on the southern curve of the bay. Across the road from the mangrove project, down on Laem Sadet's beach road, the impressively stocked **KKB Aquarium** (daily 8.30am–4.30pm; free) is another royal initiative and displays a multicoloured variety of reef fish, some seahorses and a few larger marine creatures, with informative English signage. A bridge across the next estuary at Ban Pak Nam Khaem Nu, and another one further east, means that it's now possible to continue on to **LAEM SING**, 25km southeast, via scenic coastal backroads 4002 and 6001. Hat Laem Sing is another long and lovely gold-sand beach, popular on Sundays for seafood lunches, but it's most famous for the chance to swim with Irawaddy and pink humpback **dolphins** at nearby **Oasis Sea World** (daily 9am–6pm; shows every 2hr; B180; swims B400; last swims from 3.45pm; Ⓦswimwithdolphins.information.in.th), 25km south of Chanthaburi. The dolphinarium is offered as a day-trip from Pattaya and Ko Chang, but don't expect a particularly heart-warming experience: you'll be encouraged to take "your" dolphin through a set routine of tricks and to then grab hold of its tail as it pulls you round the pool for a couple of minutes.

Trat and around

The small and pleasantly unhurried provincial capital of **TRAT**, 68km east of Chanthaburi, is the perfect place to stock up on essentials, extend your visa, or simply take a break before striking out again. Most travellers who find themselves here are heading either for Ko Chang, via the nearby port at **Laem Ngop**, for the outer islands, or for Cambodia, via the border at **Hat Lek**, 91km southeast of town. But Trat itself has its own distinctive, if understated, old-Thailand charm and there are lots of welcoming guest houses to tempt you into staying longer.

Though there are no real sights in town, the historic neighbourhood down by Khlong Trat, where you'll find most of the guest houses and traveller-oriented restaurants, is full of old wooden shophouses and narrow, atmospheric sois. The covered market in the heart of town is another fun place to wander. Out-of-town attractions that make enjoyable focuses for a leisurely cycle ride (ask at *Cool Corner* restaurant for detailed directions and other recommended routes) include the ornate seventeenth-century **Wat Buppharam**, 2km west of Trat Department Store, and the nearby lake. Slightly further afield, in the **mangrove forest** near Dan Khao, 5.5km southeast of town, a boardwalk with informative English signs takes you through the swamp; after dark it's a good place to see twinkling fireflies too. The boardwalk access is currently unsigned in English, but head for Dan Kao and after about 5.4km you'll pass dolphin statues on your left; the track to the mangroves is about 100m further on, on the right (if you get to the estuary and road's end you've gone about 500m too far).

Arrival and information

Trat is served by **buses** from Bangkok's Eastern (Ekamai) Bus Terminal (about every 2hr; 5–6hr), and Northern (Mo Chit) Bus Terminal (5 daily; 4hr 30min),

Yellow oil

Trat is famous across Thailand for the **yellow herbal oil** mixture, *yaa luang*, invented by one of its residents, Mae Ang Ki, and used by Thais to treat many ailments: sniff it for travel sickness and blocked sinuses, or rub it on to relieve mosquito and sandfly bites, ease stomach cramps, or sterilize wounds. Ingredients include camphor and aloe vera. It's well worth investing in a lip-gloss-sized bottle of the stuff before heading off to the sandfly-plagued islands; you can buy it for about B100 at Trat market and at nearby Tratosphere bookshop. There are now several imitations, but Mae Ang Ki's original product has a tree logo to signify that it's made by royal appointment.

the latter going via Suvarnabhumi Airport (4hr 10min). It also has useful bus connections with Ban Phe (for Ko Samet), Chanthaburi, Pattaya and Si Racha. All buses terminate at the bus station, 1.5km northeast of central Trat on Highway 318, from where songthaews shuttle passengers into the town centre (B20, or B60 if chartered) or on to the **departure points for the islands** (see p.206).

Tiny Trat **airport** (☎039 525767) is served by Bangkok Airways flights to and from Bangkok. The airport is about 16km from the Ko Chang piers at Laem Ngop and there's an airport shuttle direct to Ko Chang hotels for B350 per person, including ferry ticket. Trat town is a thirty-minute, B500 taxi ride from the airport. The Bangkok Airways office (☎039 525299) is on the northern edge of Trat, just beyond the Highway 317 turn-off to Khlong Yai, across from the Bangkok-Trat Hospital, but you can also buy tickets at the travel agent in the town centre (see p.206).

The Trat and Ko Chang **TAT office** (daily 8.30am–4.30pm; ☎039 597259, ✉tattrat@tat.or.th) is out in Laem Ngop, but any guest house will help you out with **information** on transport to the islands or into Cambodia. Alternatively, drop by the Tratosphere bookshop at 23 Soi Kluarimklong (☎039 523200) for tips on Trat and the islands from the knowledgeable French owner, or visit *Cool Corner* restaurant for a browse through the travellers' comment books.

Accommodation

Most **guest houses** in Trat are small and friendly and are well used to fielding travellers' queries about the islands and Cambodia. All those listed here are within ten minutes' walk of the covered market.

Ban Jaidee 67 Thanon Chaimongkon ☎039 520678, ✉maneesita@hotmail.com. Very calm, inviting and rather stylish guest house with a pleasant seating area downstairs and just seven simple bedrooms upstairs. The nicest rooms are in the original building and have polished wood floors, though those in the modern extension are further from the traffic noise. All rooms share bathrooms. ❶

Basar Garden 87 Thanon Thoncharoen ☎039 523247. Just three big en-suite rooms in a lovely atmospheric old wooden house at the greener end of town. Curtains and drapes made from faded batik sarongs add to the faintly bohemian ambience and all rooms have fans and mosquito nets. ❷

Residang House 87/1–2 Thanon Thoncharoen ☎039 530103, ⓦwww.trat-guesthouse.com.

Comfortably appointed, good-value three-storey German–Thai-managed guest house. Rooms are large, light and clean and all have windows, thick mattresses and bathrooms; some also have wi-fi and air-con and there are family rooms too. Internet access downstairs. Fan ❷, air-con ❸

S.A. Hotel Just off Thanon Sukhumvit ☎039 511141. Though hardly deluxe, the best hotel in town is off the main road and has large air-con rooms, all with bathrooms and French windows. ❸

Sawaddee 90 Thanon Lak Muang ☎039 530063, ✉sawaddee_Trat@yahoo.com. Friendly place above an internet café where the thin walls are faced with woven bamboo matting but the furnishings are pretty and there's a window in each room. All rooms share bathrooms. Cheap singles. ❶

Overland into Cambodia via Hat Lek–Koh Kong

Many travellers use the **Hat Lek–Koh Kong border crossing** (daily 7am–8pm) for overland travel into Cambodia: **visas on arrival** are issued here (see p.23) and Koh Kong has reasonable transport connections to Sihanoukville and, via Sre Ambel, Phnom Penh. For a comprehensive guide to the crossing and to the various transport options – and scams – on both sides of the border, see ⓦ www.talesofasia.com /cambodia-overland.htm and the ⓦ www.thaivisa.com forum. Trat travel agents (see p.206) also do all-inclusive transport via Hat Lek to Siem Reap, Phnom Penh and Sihanoukville for B750/1000, but see the warnings on p.201.

The only way to get to **Hat Lek** is by minibus from Trat, 91km northwest. **Minibuses** leave Trat bus station approximately every 45 minutes between 6am and 5pm (1hr–1hr 30min; B120), though you can also arrange to be picked up from the Suparat Tour office (Tanakavee Transport; daily 6am–11.30pm; ☏ 039 511481) in central Trat. In the reverse direction, the timetable is almost the same.

Hat Lek (on the Thai side) and Koh Kong (in Cambodia) are on opposite sides of the Dong Tong River estuary, but a bridge connects the two banks. Once through immigration, taxis ferry you into **Koh Kong** town for onward transport to Sihanoukville and Phnom Penh or for guest houses should you arrive too late for connections (mid-afternoon onwards). **Vans and share-taxis** to Phnom Penh take seven to eleven hours, depending on the state of the road; the trip to Sihanoukville takes around the same time but you need to change in Sre Ambel. The alternative is to take the daily **speedboat** service to Sihanoukville (departs Koh Kong pier at 8am; 4hr), or to Sre Ambel (daily at 7am; 3hr) for road connections to Phnom Penh. However, though much faster, this can be a nerve-racking, even dangerous experience, especially in rough weather, as the boats used were built for river travel not open seas.

Eating

Two of the best and cheapest **places to eat** in Trat are at the covered day market on Thanon Sukhumvit, and the night market (5–9pm), between Soi Vichidanya and Soi Kasemsan, east of Thanon Sukhumvit.

Cool Corner 49-51 Thanon Thoncharoen. Run single-handedly by a local writer/artist, this place has lots of personality, both in its cute hand-painted decor, and in its traveller-oriented menu of real coffee, Indian chai, veggie specials, quality breakfasts and great Thai curries (from B50). A good place to while away an extra hour or three, listening to the mellow music and perusing the travellers' comment books.

Kluarimklong Soi Kluarimklong. More Bangkok than Trat in its style and menu, this unexpectedly classy little place has both an indoor and a courtyard dining area and serves delicious, upmarket Thai food (dishes B50–80), including

steamed *haw mok thalay* fish curry with coconut and lots of spicy *yam* salads and *tom yum* soups.

Raan Ahaan Mangsawirat No English sign, but follow the soi near *Ban Jaidee*, off Thanon Chaimongkon. Typical no-frills, very cheap Thai vegetarian place, where you choose two portions of veggie curry, stir-fry or stew from the trays laid out in the display cabinet, and pay about B30 including rice. Shuts about 2pm.

Rabieng Mai Beside the lake, south of Wat Bos, on the southwest corner of town. Mid-priced Thai seafood place – with famously good catfish curries – whose lake views make it a good focus for a hike or cycle trip out to Wat Buppharam. Mains B60–180.

Listings

Bookshops The French-Thai run Tratosphere, at 23 Soi Kluarimklong, is a cut above most secondhand bookshops and a very good source of local information; you can also buy

curios from all over Thailand here, and hammocks.

Cooking course At Tratosphere bookshop (B800 per three dishes).

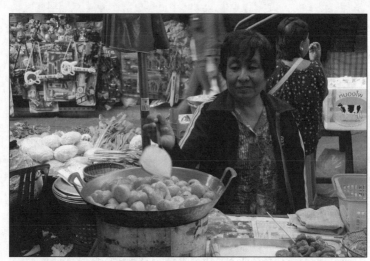
▲ Trat's night market

Emergencies For all emergencies, call the tourist police on the free, 24hr phone line ☎1155, or contact the local police station off Thanon Vivatthana ☎039 511239.

Hospital The best hospital is the private Bangkok–Trat Hospital ☎039 522555, ⓦwww .bangkoktrathospital.com, part of the Bangkok Hospital group, which also offers dental care services; it's on the Sukhumvit Highway, 1km north of Trat Department Store.

Immigration office Located in Laem Ngop, 100m west of the TAT office (Mon–Fri 8.30am–4.30pm; ☎039 597261).

Massage Available all over town and from Wat Pho-trained Pu at Tratosphere bookshop, who also teaches massage (30hr; B4500).

Travel agencies International and domestic flights from Koh Chang TT Travel on Thanon Sukhumvit ☎039 531420 (closed Sun); they also book accommodation on the islands (B200–5000), arrange taxis to Trat airport and transport to Cambodia, provide local information and rent motorbikes.

Moving on to the islands: Laem Ngop and nearby ports

All ferries to Ko Chang and Ko Wai and some services to Ko Mak leave from one of four different piers west along the coast from the small port town of **LAEM NGOP**, 17km southwest of Trat, which is served by songthaew share-taxis from Trat's bus station and, less frequently, from Thanon Sukhumvit in the town centre; they cost B50 (20–40min) per person or B150 if chartered (for the latter price you get collected from your guest house) and should drop you at the correct pier. Details of the different boat services are given in the relevant island accounts. Long-distance transport direct to Laem Ngop is either by **tourist minibus** from Bangkok's Thanon **Khao San**, **Pattaya** or **Ko Samet**, or by public bus from **Bangkok**'s Eastern (Ekamai) Bus Terminal (2 daily at 7.45am & 9.45am; 5hr 15min; return buses depart Laem Ngop at 12.30pm, 2pm & 4pm). All other **public transport**, including most buses from Bangkok's Eastern Bus Terminal and all buses from Bangkok's Mo Chit Northern Bus Terminal, Suvarnabhumi Airport, Pattaya, Rayong and the Cambodian border, terminates in **Trat**. If you're going to the remote **Long Beach** on Ko Chang you can take a direct songthaew to Salak Pet (B150, including car ferry) from the temple compound behind *KFC* and Trat Department Store.

Some boats to Ko Mak and nearly all boats to Ko Kood depart from **LAEM SOK**, 30km south of Trat; boat tickets bought in Trat should include free transfers to Laem Sok, but there's also a Laem Sok songthaew service that leaves from the town centre and takes thirty minutes (see map, p.203). A few boats to the outer islands depart from **BAN DAN KAO**, on the river estuary 6km northeast of Trat town; Dan Kao songthaews leave from the town centre and take ten minutes.

Ko Chang

Edged with a chain of long, mostly white-sand beaches and dominated by a broad central spine of jungle-clad hills, **KO CHANG** is developing fast but still feels green. It's Thailand's second largest island, after Phuket, but unlike its bigger sister has no villages or tourist facilities within its steeply contoured and densely forested interior, just a few rivers, waterfalls and hiking trails that come under the auspices of the Mu Ko Chang National Park. Some of its marine environment is also protected, as the national park extends to over forty other islands in the Ko Chang archipelago. Ko Chang's own coast, however, has seen major development over the past decade, and the island is now well established as a mainstream destination, crowded with package tourists and all the usual resort facilities, and suffering the inevitable inflated prices and inappropriate architecture. That said, it's still possible to find accommodation to suit most budgets and though the beaches may be busy they're undeniably handsome, with plenty of inviting places to swim, stroll, or snooze under a palm tree.

At 30km north to south, Ko Chang has plenty of coast to explore. The western **beaches** are the prettiest and the most congested, with **White Sand Beach** (**Hat Sai Khao**) drawing the biggest crowds to its mainly upmarket and increasingly overpriced mid-range accommodation; smaller **Hat Kai Bae** is also busy. Most backpackers opt for so-called **Lonely Beach** (officially **Hat Tha Nam**), with its roadside village of travellers' accommodation and famous beachfront party scene; those in search of quiet choose the more laid-back **Hat Khlong Phrao**, a long and lovely sweep of sand that caters to most pockets, or the jetty village of **Bang Bao**, which has bay views but no direct beach access. Every beach has **currency exchange** and most have **ATMs**, along with minimarkets, tour agents, dive shops (see p.219), internet access, clothes stalls and souvenir shops. White Sand Beach and Hat Kai Bae have the densest concentrations of facilities. During **peak season**, accommodation on every beach tends to fill up very quickly, so it's worth booking ahead. The island gets a lot quieter (and cheaper) from June to October, when heavy downpours and fierce storms can make life miserable, though sunny days are common too; be especially careful of riptides on all the beaches during the monsoon season.

Getting to Ko Chang

Access to Ko Chang **from the mainland** is by boat from the **Laem Ngop coast**, 17km southwest of Trat; details of transport to Laem Ngop are given opposite. During high season there are also boats to Ko Chang **from Ko Wai**, **Ko Mak** and **Ko Kood**; for details of these services, which all terminate at Bang Bao on Ko Chang's southwest coast, see relevant island accounts.

The main **Laem Ngop–Ko Chang boat services** are operated by two different car ferry companies from two different piers, but unless you're in your own vehicle you'll likely just get taken to the next departing service.

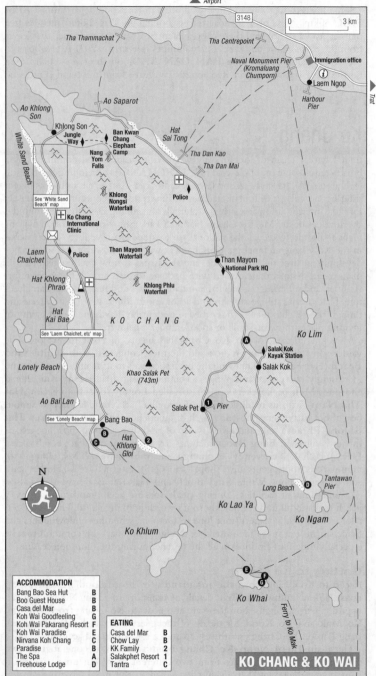

Airport

3148

0   3 km

Tha Thammachat

Tha Centrepoint

Naval Monument Pier
(Kromaluang
Chumporn)

Immigration office

Laem Ngop

Trat

Harbour
Pier

Ao Khlong
Son

Khlong Son

Jungle
Way

Ban Kwan
Chang
Elephant
Camp

Hat
Sai Tong

Ao Saparot

Nang
Yom
Falls

Tha Dan Kao

Tha Dan Mai

White Sand Beach

Khlong
Nongsi Waterfall

Police

See 'White Sand
Beach' map

Ko Chang
International
Clinic

Than Mayom
Waterfall

Laem
Chaichet

Police

Khlong Phlu
Waterfall

Than Mayom
National Park HQ

Hat Khlong
Phrao

Hat
Kai Bae

K O   C H A N G

See 'Laem Chaichet, etc' map

Ko Lim

A

Salak Kok
Kayak Station

Salak Kok

Lonely Beach

Khao Salak Pet
(743m)

Ao Bai Lan

See 'Lonely Beach' map

Bang Bao

Salak Pet   1   Pier

B

2

C

Hat
Khlong
Gloi

N

Long Beach

D

Tantawan
Pier

Ko Lao Ya

Ko Ngam

Ko Khlum

E

F

G

Ko Whai

Ferry to Ko Mak

ACCOMMODATION
Bang Bao Sea Hut	B
Boo Guest House	B
Casa del Mar	B
Koh Wai Goodfeeling	G
Koh Wai Pakarang Resort	F
Koh Wai Paradise	E
Nirvana Koh Chang	C
Paradise	B
The Spa	A
Treehouse Lodge	D

EATING
Casa del Mar	B
Chow Lay	B
KK Family	2
Salakphet Resort	1
Tantra	C

KO CHANG & KO WAI

Ko Mak, Ko Kham & Ko Kood

Moving on from Ko Chang

Every tour agency on Ko Chang offers transport direct from Ko Chang **to Bangkok** (big bus/minibus to Khao San Road B350/550, 5hr; minibus to Sukhumvit Road hotels B900, 5hr); **Suvarnabhumi Airport** (minibus B900, whole taxi B3900; 5hr); Ban Phe (for Ko Samet, B250); Pattaya (B500); and Cambodia (minibus to Siem Reap B750, 12hr; see warnings on p.201); and Bangkok Airways runs a shuttle bus service to Trat Airport (contact the office in central Hat Sai Khao on ℡039 551654; B350 per person). Prices include the ferry crossing from Ko Chang but may not include transport from your Ko Chang accommodation to the ferry pier. Share-taxis transport passengers to the ferry piers from all Ko Chang's western beaches (simply wait on the side of the road and flag one down), or you can charter your own; drivers should take you to whichever ferry is next to depart.

From November to May, car ferries to the mainland leave Ko Chang at least every 45 minutes between about 7am and 6pm, departing from Ao Saparot or Tha Dan Kao on the northeast coast and arriving at either Tha Thammachat (25min) or Tha Centrepoint (45min) near Laem Ngop. During the rest of the year boats may only run every two hours.

From September to June, Bang Bao Boat (℡087 054 4300, ⓦwww.bangbaoboat .com) runs one or two daily boats from Ko Chang direct to the **outer islands** (one slow boat and sometimes one speedboat as well); timetables vary according to how busy things are, so check locally first, and see relevant island accounts for more details. Tickets are sold at every tour agency on Ko Chang, and transfers to the Bang Bao pier are sometimes included: **Ko Wai** (1hr/15min; B300/400), **Ko Mak** (2hr/1hr; B400/550), and **Ko Kood** (5hr including transfer/2hr; B700/900). Other speedboat services come and go but any tour agency will have current details.

Ferries run between 6.30am and 7pm, at least once an hour from November to May and at least once every two hours during the rest of the year. Fares are competitive and change frequently: expect to pay about B100 single or B160 return, and not much more if you have a vehicle, though deals on the latter can vary considerably. Centrepoint Ferry (℡039 538196) runs from Tha Centrepoint, 3km west of Laem Ngop, to Tha Dan Kao (45min); and Ferry Ko Chang (℡039 518588) runs from Tha Thammachat, 9km west of Laem Ngop, to Ao Saparot (25min).

On Ko Chang, **songthaew share-taxis** meet boats at Tha Dan Kao and Ao Saparot and transport passengers to west-coast beaches (B50 to White Sand Beach, 25min; B100 to Lonely Beach, 1hr; B150 to Bang Bao, 1hr 15min). If you're heading **to Salak Pet** or **Long Beach** on Ko Chang's southeast coast, you can make use of the bargain B150 songthaew service that departs central Trat, behind the *KFC*, and takes you all the way to Salak Pet, car-ferry passage included.

Island transport and information

A wide road runs nearly all the way round the island, served by **songthaew share-taxis** which tend to charge according to how many passengers they have as well as the distance travelled (usually B50–150 per person). You can rent **motorbikes and cars** on every beach, but the road is notoriously dangerous, with steep hills, sharp, unexpected hairpins and many reckless drivers, so think twice if you're an inexperienced motorcyclist – accidents happen every day and fatalities are all too frequent. Goodquality **mountain bikes** are available through Ko Chang Gym in the VJ Plaza complex in Laem Chaichet (℡081 003 8468; B400 per 6hr).

Island activities

Tour agents on every beach will sell you tickets for the **activities** described below and prices should include return transport from your accommodation. If you're still looking for something unusual to do you might consider taking a **microlight flight** over Ko Chang (15min; B1700 per person) from the Koh Chang Flying Club; its airfield is just past the turnoff to Khlong Phlu falls in Khlong Phrao. For information on snorkelling and diving in the Ko Chang archipelago, see p.219.

Ko Chang or "Elephant Island" is named for its hilly profile rather than its indigenous pachyderms, but there are several **elephant camps** on the island that have brought in their own lumbering forest dwellers so that tourists can ride and help bathe them. The one with the best reputation is **Ban Kwan Chang Elephant Trek** (℡089 815 9566), based in a forested area in the north of the island, east of Khlong Son village, near Nang Yom Waterfall. It was set up by the man behind the Asian Elephant Foundation and is staffed by ten Suay mahouts and their elephants from Ban Ta Klang village in northeast Thailand, which has for centuries been a traditional centre for working elephants. Visitors can either do a forty-minute elephant ride through adjacent plantations (B500) or extend the ride to an hour and bathe the elephants as well (B900). Nearby Thai–British-run **Jungle Way** leads guided **treks** through the forest here as well as more strenuous hikes on the northern Chang Noi peninsular (℡089 223 4795, Ⓦwww.jungleway.com; from B600). If you're in the area, you could make the easy 300m walk to tiny **Nang Yom falls**, 500m beyond Ban Kwang Elephant Camp, but Khlong Phlu falls in Khlong Phrao are more satisfying (see p.213).

For a more demanding physical challenge, make an afternoon of it at **Treetop Adventure Park**, just south of the *Dusit Princess* hotel on Ao Bai Lan, south of Lonely Beach (daily 9am–5pm; B950 including transport; ℡084 310 7600, Ⓦwww .treetopadventurepark.com), an enjoyable and professionally managed jungle activity centre where you get to swing through the trees on a series of trapezes, flying foxes, aerial skateboards, rope ladders and webs. Everyone gets a full safety harness and gloves and starts off with a training session before tackling the two adventure courses (or the special kids' one), which take around two hours in all, though there's no limit to repeat attempts.

Also at Ao Bai Lan, and the perfect place to tease out any sore muscles, is **Bailan Herbal Sauna** (daily 4–8pm; ℡086 252 4744). This charming, creatively designed US-Thai-run herbal steam sauna is an alternative little haven of adobe buildings with glass-bottle windows, secluded within a patch of roadside forest. Entry into the sociable communal sauna costs B200, with home-made DIY herbal treatments (kaffir lime for hair, white-mud for face and turmeric for skin) mostly just a bargain B50. Lao and herbal massage are also available (B350–700), along with fresh juices and spirulina. For more conventional **spa and detox treatments**, *The Spa* near Salak Kok on the east cost (see p.220) offers the biggest range and is an appealingly tranquil place to while away a few hours. On Hat Khlong Phrao, Baan Zen (℡086 530 9345, Ⓦwww.baanzen.com) runs **yoga classes** and short courses (from B900 per lesson) as well as **reiki** courses. The amiable chef who runs the recommended *KaTi* restaurant in nearby Khlong Phrao teaches well-regarded **cooking classes** at her restaurant (KaTi Culinary Cooking School; 6hr; B1200 for three to nine dishes; ℡081 903 0408, Ⓔkati-culinary@hotmail.com.

The widely distributed detailed free maps and quarterly Ko Chang guides published by Whitesands Publications (Ⓦwww.whitesandsthailand.com) are a handy source of **information** and advertisements, and the website provides an accommodation-booking service, but for more intelligent insights and opinionated advice, check out Ⓦwww.iamkohchang.com, compiled by a Ko Chang resident.

The island's **post office** is 2km south of the southern end of White Sand Beach, across from the access road to Hat Sai Mook. The private 24 hour **Ko Chang International Clinic** (☎039 551555, ⓦ www.bangkoktrathospital.com), part of the Bangkok Hospital Group, is located between southern White Sand Beach and Hat Kai Mook, 1km south of *Ploma Resort*; it deals with minor injuries and has a dental service, and will transfer seriously ill patients to its parent Bangkok-Trat Hospital in Trat. There's also a small clinic in Khlong Phrao. The island's main **police station** is at Dan Mai on the northeast coast (☎039 5586191), and there are police boxes on White Sand Beach and at Hat Khlong Phrao's Ko Chang Plaza.

Though mosquitoes don't seem to be much in evidence, Ko Chang is one of the few areas of Thailand that's still considered to be **malarial**, so you may want to start taking your prophylactics before you get here (see p.27). Staff at the Ko Chang International Clinic, however, say that the risk to tourists is minimal and that cases are confined to those who work and stay overnight in the island's jungle interior. **Sandflies** can be more of a problem on the southern beaches (see p.28). Watch out for **jellyfish**, which plague the west coast in April and May, and for **snakes**, including surprisingly common cobras, sunbathing on the overgrown paths into the interior. The other hazard is **theft** from rooms and bungalows: use your own padlock on bags (and doors where possible) or, better still, make use of hotel safety boxes.

White Sand Beach (Hat Sai Khao)

Framed by a broad band of fine white sand at low tide, a fringe of casuarinas and palm trees and a backdrop of forested hills, **Hat Sai Khao**, more commonly referred to as **White Sand Beach**, is, at 2.5km long, the island's longest beach and its most commercial, with scores of mid-range and upmarket hotel and bungalow operations squashed in along the shore, plus dozens of shops, travel agents, bars and restaurants lining the inland side of the

WHITE SAND BEACH (HAT SAI KHAO)

N

Ao Saparot & Tha Dan Kao

Police box
7- Eleven
@ Earthlink
Pharmacy

EATING & DRINKING
Bamboo Resort	6
Hungry Elephant	8
Invito	9
Norng Bua Food Centre	7
Oodie's Place	4
Pen's	1
Sabay Bar	5
Texas Steakhouse	3
Tonsai	2

ACCOMMODATION
Arunee Resort	E
Cookies Hotel	G & H
Fisherman Hill Resort	I
KC Grande Resort	D
Maylamean Bungalows	B
Star Beach	C
White Sand Beach Resort	A
Yakah	F

White Sand Plaza
Bangkok Airways
Koh Chang Adventure Travel
SOI KERT MANEE
Ploy Scuba Diving
@ Bookshop
Scuba Evolution
V- Mart
Grand View Plaza
Ploma Cliff Resort

0   500 m

⑧ ⑨ Ko Chang International Clinic ▼ & post office

2

THE EAST COAST | Ko Chang

211

road. The vibe is much more laid-back and traveller-oriented at the far quieter northern end of the beach, however, beyond *KC Grande*, and this is where you'll find the most budget-priced accommodation, some of it pleasingly characterful and nearly all of it enjoying its own sea view. An extra bonus is that the road is well out of earshot up here, and there's hardly any passing pedestrian traffic. There are some low-key beach **bars** up there too, and more along the shorefront in the central beach area – all of them quite different in feel from the rash of brash, Pattaya-style bar-beers inland from *Plaloma Cliff Resort* in southern Hat Sai Khao. Wherever you stay on Hat Sai Khao, be careful when swimming as the **currents** are very strong and there's no lifeguard service.

A good **tour agent** on Hat Sai Khao – for flights, day-trips, onward transport, car and bike rental – is the helpful Koh Chang Adventure Travel, 100m north of Soi Kert Manee, opposite *Bamboo Resort* (⊕081 887 9515).

Accommodation

Arunee Resort ⊕039 551075, ⓔaruneeresorttour @hotmail.com. Built in a partitioned wooden row-house just across the road from the beach, the sixteen very simple terraced rooms here all have a small veranda, mattress, fan and en-suite bathroom and are a good price for central Hat Sai Khao. The friendly owner has a tour desk and internet shop out front. ❷

Cookies Hotel ⊕081 861 4227, ⓦwww .cookieskohchang.com. If you want hotel-style facilities at affordable prices this is good option, right in the middle of the beach. Rooms are in two locations, with the far less interesting site being across the road, with only shops and traffic to look at through the picture windows. Better to pay the extra and go for the two-storey sea-view "superior" building, set round the shorefront swimming pool. Rooms are large and comfortable and all have air-con, polished wooden floors and a veranda. ❼

Fisherman Hill Resort Soi Kert Manee ⊕081 429 3827. Local, family-run place ranged in a garden of mature fruit trees up the hillside about 200m east off the road. It offers some of the cheapest rooms in central Hat Sai Khao, in very simple huts with fan and deck and shared bathroom, plus others with bathrooms and some less good-value ones with air-con across the soi (though discounts can often be negotiated). Fan ❷, air-con ❺

KC Grande Resort ⊕039 551199, ⓦwww.kckoh chang.com. The largest and priciest hotel on the beach is able to charge top dollar because it spreads over a huge area of the northern shorefront. Accommodation ranges from rows of air-con bungalows set in landscaped gardens fronting the beach to deluxe sea-view rooms in the three-storey hotel block. Facilities are good and include two pools. ❽–❾

Maylamean Bungalows ⊕086 144 5865. In the cluster of funky, north-beach cliffside shanty bungalows, this one stands out both for its lilac paintwork and its en-suite wooden huts, while also built on stilts steeply up the cliffside, are larger and a bit more private than many of its neighbours. ❹

Star Beach ⊕087 558 4085. Ten basic, cheerily painted plywood huts squat limpet-like on the rock-face here, just above the sand on the quiet, funky northern stretch of White Sand Beach. Rooms are very simple but are all en suite and enjoy high-level sea views and breezes. ❷

White Sand Beach Resort ⊕081 863 7737, ⓦwww.whitesandbeachresort.net. Spread across a long, attractive stretch of uncommercialized beach at the far north end of the beach, *White Sand* offers a big range of nicely spaced huts, many of them lapping up uninterrupted sea views. Interiors are fairly simple, but have air-con, wooden floors, TVs, and a faintly contemporary style. For a proper peaceful beach vibe and a little bit of affordable comfort, within 10min walk of resort facilities, this is a good option considering the competition. If arriving by songthaew, get off at the 7-Eleven beside *KC Grande* and phone for transport. ❺–❻

Yakah ⊕039 551 1086. Just eleven teak-log bungalows in a tiny, crowded enclave right on the beach, all pretty nice inside and with air-con, TV, fridge and at least partial sea view; avoid the one next to the drainage khlong if you can. ❻

Eating and drinking

Bamboo Resort A popular restaurant, that sets its tables out on the sand, partly because of its nightly high-season fireshows at 8.30pm. As for food, there's a fresh seafood barbecue every night, a good Thai menu and a variable Italian one (pizzas from B200). plus cheapish house wine by the glass too.

Hungry Elephant Opposite the sign for *Saffron* hotel, 2km south of southern White Sand Beach. The French and Thai food at this unassuming roadside place has a good reputation with local expats. The Thai chef trained at the Alliance Française in Bangkok and does toothsome steaks – au poivre, chateaubriand and crème cognac – mostly for about B260. Good espressos too.

Invito On the hill, about 800m south of *Plaloma Resort*. Expensive but highly rated, authentic Italian food (from B300) including wood-fired pizzas, pastas and imported wines. Daily 5–11pm.

Norng Bua Food Centre Very cheap night-market-style Thai food, including noodle soups, fried noodles and satays.

Oodie's Place One of Ko Chang's most famous live-music venues, with live blues, rock, reggae and r'n'b played most nights, plus daily movies, and a Euro-Asian menu with a French accent; most main dishes cost B60–200.

Pen's Tiny beachfront restaurant in the northern bungalow cluster that serves exceptionally good home-style Thai food at fairly cheap prices.

Sabay Bar One of Ko Chang's longest-running institutions, where you can choose to sit in the chic air-con bar and watch the nightly live sets from the in-house cover band (from 9pm), or lounge on mats and cushions on the sand and listen in via the outdoor speakers. You pay for the pleasure, however, as drinks are pricey. Also stages fire-juggling shows on the beach and full-moon parties.

Texas Steakhouse Rooftop restaurant that serves delicious ribs (from B300), plus imported steaks (from B220) and a few Thai dishes.

Tonsai The atmosphere at this mostly vegetarian restaurant is pleasingly mellow: seating is on Thai-style cushions scattered around a circular platform wedged between half a dozen trees, and the menu (B50–180) includes Thai curries, pastas, Vietnamese sausage and around fifty cocktails.

Laem Chaichet and Hat Khlong Phrao

Four kilometres south of Hat Sai Khao, the scenic, rocky cape at **LAEM CHAICHET** curves round into sweeping, casuarina-fringed **HAT KHLONG PHRAO**, one of Ko Chang's nicest beaches, not least because it has yet to see the clutter and claustrophobic development of both its neighbours. For the moment at least, most of the restaurants, bars and shops are way off the beach, along the roadside, with the shorefront left mainly to a decent spread of accommodation. Laem Chaichet protects an inlet and tiny harbour and offers beautiful views south across the bay and inland to the densely forested mountains. To the south, Hat Khlong Phrao begins with a nice kilometre-long run of beach that's interrupted by a wide khlong, whose estuary is the site of some characterful stilt homes and seafood restaurants. At low tide you can just about wade across it; more reliably, during daylight hours, you can rent your own kayak from almost anywhere along the beach, or make use of the boatman who ferries guests at *Aana Resort* to the private patch of sand behind *Panviman Resort*. (After dark, you can use your kayak to paddle upriver to see the fireflies twinkling in the khlongside *lamphu* trees.) Beyond the estuary, the long southern beach is partly shaded by casuarinas and backed in places by a huge coconut grove that screens the shore from the road; it's quite a hike to the roadside shops and restaurants from here though, at least a kilometre along a rutted track.

Upstream from Hat Khlong Phrao, the khlong that divides the beach in two tumbles into Ko Chang's most famous cascade, **Khlong Phlu Falls** (Nam Tok Khlong Phlu), a couple of kilometres east off the main road. Signs lead you inland to a car park and some hot-food stalls, where you pay your national park entry fee (B200, kids B100) and walk the final 500m to the twenty-metre-high waterfall (best in the rainy season) that plunges into an invitingly clear pool defined by a ring of smooth rocks.

Both Chaichet and Khlong Phrao have roadside tourist villages with **ATMs**, minimarkets, tour agents, dive centres, internet access, shops and restaurants. The **police** have a post at Chaichet, and in Khlong Phrao there's a **clinic**, a fuel

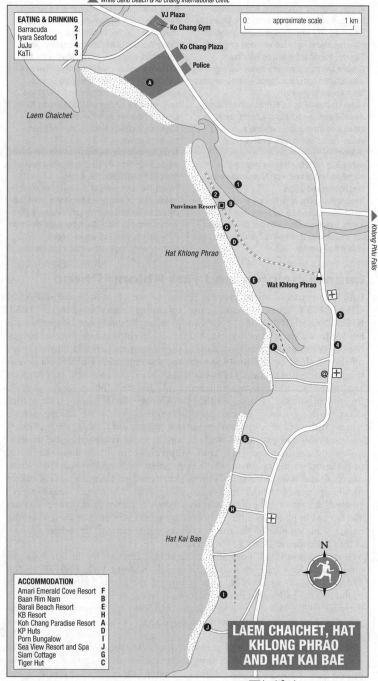

▲ White Sand Beach & Ko Chang International Clinic

EATING & DRINKING

Barracuda	2
Iyara Seafood	1
JuJu	4
KaTi	3

VJ Plaza
Ko Chang Gym
Ko Chang Plaza
Police

0   approximate scale   1 km

Laem Chaichet

Ⓐ

Ⓑ ❶
❷
Panviman Resort ◼ Ⓑ

Ⓒ

Ⓓ

Hat Khlong Phrao

Ⓔ Wat Khlong Phrao

▶ Khlong Phlu Falls

❸

Ⓕ ❹

@ ✠

Ⓖ

Ⓗ ✠

Hat Kai Bae

N

@ ✠

Ⓘ

Ⓙ

**LAEM CHAICHET, HAT
KHLONG PHRAO
AND HAT KAI BAE**

ACCOMMODATION

Amari Emerald Cove Resort	F
Baan Rim Nam	B
Barali Beach Resort	E
KB Resort	H
Koh Chang Paradise Resort	A
KP Huts	D
Porn Bungalow	I
Sea View Resort and Spa	J
Siam Cottage	G
Tiger Hut	C

▼ Lonely Beach

station and a community temple, Wat Khlong Phrao. And from the southern end of Khlong Phrao it's only a few hundred metres south to the start of the Kai Bae tourist village amenities.

Accommodation

Amari Emerald Cove Resort ☎ 039 552000, Ⓦ www.amari.com. Top-of-the-scale chain hotel that occupies a lovely tranquil spot on the southern beach, complete with its own palm-shaded sandy terrace and huge seafront swimming pool. Rooms are in low-rise three-storey blocks set around the pool, tropical garden and lagoons, and are typical deluxe style, with wooden floors and balconies. ❾

Baan Rim Nam ☎ 087 005 8575, Ⓦ www .iamkohchang.com. Peaceful, scenic and unusual, this converted fishing family's house is built on stilts over the wide, attractive khlong at the end of a walkway through the mangroves. Run by the British author of the best Ko Chang website, it has just three comfortable air-con rooms with good bathrooms and free wi-fi, plus a big deck for soaking up views of the khlongside village, but no restaurant. You can borrow kayaks and it's a couple of minutes' walk to the beach and *Barracuda* restaurant, or 20min to the main Khlong Phrao facilities. ❺

Barali Beach Resort ☎ 039 557238, Ⓦ www .baralikohchang.com. One of the more elegant spots on the southern beach, with forty tastefully designed, Balinese-style rooms, furnished with four-poster beds, sunken baths and lots of polished wood, and set around a beachfront tropical garden with an infinity-edge swimming pool. ❾

Koh Chang Paradise Resort ☎ 039 551100, Ⓦ www.kohchangparadise.com. The biggest and most popular place to stay on the Chaichet end of the beach occupies a huge area between the road and the shore so offers easy access to the beach as well as shops and restaurants. Its generously designed concrete bungalows have French windows and comfortable, hotel-style, air-con interiors. Some have private plunge pools and there's also a central swimming pool. ❽–❾

KP Huts ☎ 084 099 5100. Though the fifty timber huts here are very simple for the price, they are attractively scattered through the broad shoreside coconut grove (about 1.5km from roadside amenities) with plenty of sea views. Even some of the cheapest options (with shared bathrooms) are right on the shore, and a few are raised high on stilts for an extra-seductive panorama; en-suite huts are huge, and some are designed for families. Shared bathroom ❸, en suite ❹–❺

Tiger Hut ☎ 084 109 9660. One of the few budget-minded, old-school travellers' beach bungalows left on Ko Chang, occupying a sandy beachfront garden just south of the khlong and about 2km down a track from the main road. The woven-bamboo huts have simple but fresh interiors and there's a restaurant deck and bar with pool table plus motorbike rental. Shared bathroom ❷, en suite ❸

Eating and drinking

Restaurants on Hat Khlong Phrao worth making a special effort for include the beachfront-shack *Barracuda*, between *Tiger Hut* and *Panviman Resort*, which serves especially good, mid-priced seafood; and, for its khlongside setting, the posh *Iyara* seafood restaurant, built on stilts over the estuary behind *Tiger Hut*. On the roadside, *KaTi* restaurant and cookery school (see p.210) serves great Thai food, including infinite permutations of red, green, yellow and southern curries, plus delicious home-made ice-creams and inventive mint, lychee and lemon smoothies. Across from the *Amari* turnoff, *JuJu* beer garden is run by a French musician and known for its **world music** band, its jam sessions and its good-quality visiting musicians.

Hat Kai Bae

Narrow, pretty little **HAT KAI BAE** (see map opposite) presents a classic picture of white sand, pale blue water and overhanging palms, but in places the shorefront is very slender indeed – and filled with bungalows – and the beach can disappear entirely at high tide. The beach is bisected by a khlong and rocky point, with most of the accommodation to the south. Seaward views from the southernmost end take in the tiny island of Ko Man Nai, whose sandy shores are easily reached by kayak, half an hour offshore from *Sea View Resort*. Kai Bae's roadside tourist village is busy and stretches a couple of kilometres. It's got plenty of shops, bars and restaurants, as well as ATMs, currency exchange, dive shops (see p.219), a secondhand bookshop and internet access.

The most famous of the dwindling number of budget **accommodation** options on the beach is *Porn Bungalow* (☎089 099 8757, Ⓦwww.pornsbungalows -kohchang.com; ❷–❺), which has scores of fan bungalows in various styles, set under palm trees along a big expanse of the shorefront. The cheapest are in old-style bamboo and concrete huts; the most luxurious are spacious wooden cabins with wraparound decks. *Porn's* over-water restaurant deck does seafood barbecues nightly in high season and has a pool table and bar. Also affordably priced considering the competition, but at the northern end of Hat Kai Bae, is *Siam Cottage* (☎089 153 6664; ❸), whose 36 wooden bungalows face each other across a narrow lot that runs down to the sea. There's a restaurant and internet access here and bungalows have modern, cheerily painted interiors with a hint of style, plus fans and private decks. The best of Kai Bae's mid-priced options is the attractive shorefront *KB Resort* (☎039 557125, Ⓦwww .kbresort.com; fan ❺, air-con ❼) with 49 good-quality bungalows set around a tropical garden with swimming pool. The air-con bungalows have huge windows, many of which enjoy direct sea views; fan versions stand further back. The swankiest beachfront hotel is *Sea View Resort and Spa* (☎081 830 7529, Ⓦwww .seaviewkohchang.com; ❼–❾), set around a lawn and tropical flower garden towards the southern end of Hat Kai Bae. It has a swimming pool and a pretty spa and its air-con "spa" (hotel) rooms and cottages are large, light and airy.

LONELY BEACH & AO BAI LAN

▲ Hat Kai Bae

Siam Beach

Lonely Beach

Minimart

Ao Bai Lan

Dusit Princess Resort

Treetop Adventure Park

Bang Bao ▼

ACCOMMODATION
Bhumiyama Beach Resort	B
Nature Beach	A
Paradise Cottage	F
Siam Hut	C
The Sunflower	D
Sunset Hut	E

EATING
Coffee House	2
Saïan	3
Sign Ngam	1

❶ Ploy Scuba Diving
❷ Scuba Evolution
Motorbike Repair
BB Divers
Bailan Herbal Sauna

N

0   150 m

Lonely Beach (Hat Tha Nam) and Ao Bai Lan

Hat Tha Nam – dubbed **LONELY BEACH** before it became Ko Chang's top place to party – is small and lively, with a shorefront that's occupied by just four sets of increasingly expensive accommodation and a hinterland village, ten minutes' walk away, that's the most traveller-oriented on the island.

It's here, overlooking the rocks immediately south of the beach, and along the sandy sois that run inland to the main road, that backpackers feel most at home, in little bungalows and guest houses squashed any old how beneath the remaining trees, with every other shop-shack offering tattoos or internet access. Despite the creeping concrete, creatively designed little wood and bamboo bar-restaurants abound, some of them offering chilled, low-key escapes from the loud dance music, all-night parties and B250 buckets of vodka Red Bull that the beachfront places are notorious for, others cranking it up just as hard and fast. The most intense partying mostly happens down on the beach, usually at *Nature Beach*, which kicks off most high-season nights with seafood barbecues, live music and fire-juggling shows.

Day and (especially) night, you should be extremely careful when swimming off Lonely Beach, especially around *Siam Beach* at the northern end, as the steep shelf and dangerous current result in a sobering number of double-figure **drownings** every year, particularly during the monsoon season; do your swimming further south and don't go out at all when the waves are high. Also be careful with your belongings – many a drunken night sees cameras, phones and wallets pilfered unnoticed. Among the roadside shops you'll find an **ATM** and a dive shop (see p.219), plus tour agents and motorbike rental and repair.

A fifteen-minute walk along the road and over the hill from the southern end of Lonely Beach village will bring you to **AO BAI LAN**, which hasn't got much of a beach to speak of, but is the site of two of Ko Chang's most interesting attractions, the **Treetop Adventure Park** and the **Bailan Herbal Sauna** (see p.210 for both).

Accommodation

Bhumiyama Beach Resort Central beach area ☏ 081 860 4623, ⓦ www.bhumiyama.com. The poshest place on the beach has just 45 attractively furnished rooms, in deluxe two-storey bungalows and hotel wings set around grassy seafront lawns and a good-sized swimming pool. Interiors are quite chic – bungalows have four-poster beds and polished wooden floors – and all have bathtubs; only the premier rooms have sea views. ❽–❾

Nature Beach Central beach area ☏ 081 803 8933. Responsible for Lonely Beach's party reputation, this place is hugely popular and, at the time of writing, was planning to upgrade all 65 of its tasteful but simple fan and air-con bungalows. Prices have always been on the high side because it occupies a prime location in the middle of the beach and is at the heart of the action (so if you prefer a quiet night's sleep it's best to head elsewhere). There's a tour desk, internet access and massage, plus a big restaurant and bar with live music, DJs and the rest. ❸–❺

🏃 **Paradise Cottage** On the rocky shore, a 10min walk south along the rocks from the sandy beach ☏ 081 773 9337, ⓔ loengbkk @hotmail.com. Backpacker chic is the style here, where accommodation is no frills but there's an air of Bangkok sophistication about the design, especially the communal wooden decks whose

hammocks and easy chairs are perfect for lounging, horizon-gazing and sipping cocktails; there's wi-fi here too. Though the 32 en-suite wood and thatch huts are fairly simple they are also in good condition and look stylish; they all have fans and mozzie nets. The slightly more expensive ones have sea views, and the rest are enveloped by banana trees in the tropical, heliconia-filled-garden. There's no sand here, but you can swim off the rocks at high tide. ❸

Siam Hut Central beach area ☏ 086 609 7772, ⓦ www.siamhutkohchang.com. The cheapest place to stay right on the beach has rows and rows of primitive, split-bamboo huts – eighty in total – all of them en suite and with little else but plank floors, mattresses and mozzie nets. It's first come, first served for the prime seafront spots. Fan ❷–❸, air-con ❹

The Sunflower Inland, on Soi Sunset ☏ 084 017 9960, ⓦ www.the-sunflower.com. Run by a genial German and his Thai family, the two-dozen bungalows here are set under palm and banana trees 200m from the roadside village and equidistant from the rocky coast at *Sunset*, a 5min walk south of the sandy beach. Choose between old bamboo huts with shared bathrooms, sturdy wooden fan bungalows with open-roofed bathrooms, and concrete bungalows; all have good thick mattresses and are kept very clean. The restaurant is good and has wi-fi. Shared bathroom ❷, en suite ❸, air-con ❹

Sunset Hut 5min walk south beyond *Siam Hut*, on the rocks ☎ 081 818 7042. The good-quality concrete en-suite bungalows here have proper beds and big windows and some also have perfect, private, over-sea decks. There are also some cheaper en-suite huts at the back plus a few big air-con bungalows. The seafront deck-restaurant and bar attracts a lively crowd and holds occasional parties. Though you can only swim here at high tide, it's a short walk to the sandy beach and just 400m inland to roadside shops and restaurants. Fan ❷—❸, air-con ❹—❺

Diving and snorkelling in the Ko Chang archipelago

Because there's just one tide a day in the inner Gulf, the **reefs** of the Ko Chang archipelago are much less colourful and varied than Andaman coast dive sites, and they can get very crowded, but they're rewarding enough to make a day-trip worthwhile. The main **dive and snorkel sites** are west of Ko Mak, in the national marine park around **Ko Rang** and its satellite islets. These range from beginners' reefs with lots of hard corals and anemones at depths of 4–6m, frequented by plenty of reef fish – including a resident ten-thousand-strong shoal of yellow fusiliers – and the occasional moray eel, to the more challenging 25-metre dive at the Pinnacles. There are also some technical wreck dives of Japanese boats from World War II and even some centuries-old Chinese trading ships. The coral around Ko Yuak, off Ko Chang's Hat Kai Bae, is mostly dead, though some operators still sell trips there.

Dive shops on Ko Chang
The biggest concentration of dive shops is on Ko Chang, though there are also some on Ko Wai, Ko Mak and Ko Kood (see relevant accounts for details). Some **Ko Chang dive shops** have their main office in Bang Bao, where most boats depart, as well as a branch office or agent elsewhere on the island; those listed below are the main reputable operators. All dive shops will organize pick-ups from any beach. See p.59 for a general introduction to diving in Thailand and for advice on what to look for in a dive centre.

Waves permitting, Ko Chang dive shops run trips year round, though during the **monsoon season**, from June to September, visibility can be poor. **Prices** for local dive trips, with two tanks, average B2200–2900, or B1000 for accompanying snorkellers. Dive courses cost about B14,500 for the four-day Openwater, and B4500 for the one-day Discover Scuba introduction.

BB Divers Lonely Beach and Bang Bao ☎ 086 155 6212, ⓦ www.bbdivers.com. Belgian-run, PADI Five-Star IDC centre which uses fishing boats (with sun decks) rather than speedboats.

Ploy Scuba Diving Hat Sai Khao, Hat Kai Bae, Lonely Beach and Bang Bao ☎ 086 155 1331, ⓦ www.ployscuba.com. Big Thai run-operation.

Scuba Dreams Hat Kai Bae ☎ 089 472 8782, ⓦ www.scuba-dreams.com.

Scuba Evolution Hat Sai Khao, Hat Kai Bae, Lonely Beach ☎ 087 926 4973, ⓦ www.scuba-evolution.com. British-run dive company that specializes in technical and wreck diving.

Snorkelling
From about November to May, several companies run dedicated **snorkelling trips** to reefs and islands around Ko Chang, Ko Wai and Ko Rang. Tickets are sold by tour agents on every beach and prices range from B600 to B1250, depending on the size of the boat (some take as many as a hundred people in high season) and the number of islands visited. In general the more islands "featured" (sailed past), the less time there is for snorkelling, though nearly all the actual snorkelling happens around **Ko Rang**.

Eating

Along the roadside you'll find some good, cheap, local Thai **restaurants**, including the Isaan specialist *Sign Ngam*, beside the khlong bridge at the north end of the village, which does several types of *som tam*, catfish curry and snakehead fish soup (B25–60). Invitingly idiosyncratic *Coffee House* (8am–3pm), on Soi Sunset, serves strong coffee and breakfasts, and *Saïan*, on parallel Soi Warapura, is run by a young French chef who serves charcuterie plates, bakes his own baguettes and croissants and does filet mignon and mushroom and pork tagliatelle. The restaurant at *The Sunflower* (open high season only) dishes up very generous set breakfasts for B150 and authentically spicy Thai curries.

Bang Bao and Hat Khlong Gloi

Almost at the end of the west-coast road, the southern harbour village of **BANG BAO**, much of it built on stilts off a central jetty, is the departure point for boat trips and transfers to the outer islands and is also an increasingly popular place to stay. Though it has no beach of its own, you're within a short motorbike ride of both undeveloped Hat Khlong Gloi, 2km to the east, and Lonely Beach, 5km up the coast. Accommodation is mostly in jetty homes and bungalows, often with exceptional bay views, and some pleasingly chilled bar-restaurants share the outlook. Bang Bao is, however, almost entirely given over to tourist facilities, and vanloads of day-trippers clog the jetty village as they linger over the trinket shops, clothes stalls and dive shops (see opposite). Seafood lunches are another attraction, most famously at the long-running *Chow Lay* restaurant.

The cushions, hammocks and swing-seats at the cool and funky Ibiza-vibe *Casa del Mar* **lounge-bar** and guest house (☎083 174 5695, ⓦwww .casadelmarkohchang.com; ❺–❻), halfway along the jetty's east side, are an ideal place to escape the day-tripping crowds. Aside from stunning panoramas of the bay, there's good music and free wi-fi plus Thai and Western food, cocktails (happy hour 6–8pm) and Saturday evening parties; **accommodation** is in one of seven tasteful fan or air-con rooms. Other places to stay on the main jetty

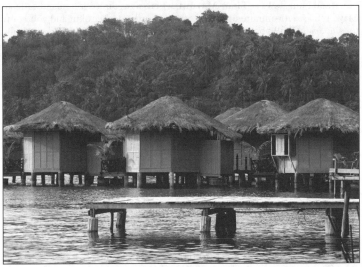

▲ Jetty bungalows, Bang Bao

include the no-frills jetty huts with shared bathrooms at *Paradise* (℡089 934 8044; ❶); the jetty rooms at *Boo Guest House* (℡089 831 1874; ❸), which are very clean but have no particular view; and the very attractive *Bang Bao Sea Hut* (℡081 285 0570; ❼), whose fourteen tastefully modern, octagonal over-sea villas – with air-con and polished wood floors – overlook the harbour and are connected to the main jetty by a series of walkways.

Secluded on a narrow neck of land across the bay to the west of the village, boutique little *Nirvana Koh Chang* (℡039 558061, ⓦwww.nirvanakohchang .com; ❾) is a relaxed and lushly landscaped retreat with private forest walks, a cliffside boardwalk, two pools and access to two swimmable coasts but no real beach. Accommodation is in fifteen rather chic, Balinese-accented villas, some with direct sea views. Even if you're not staying you could come and eat at the dramatically sited waterside *Tantra* restaurant, creatively furnished with woodcarvings from the Indonesian archipelago and serving a menu of contemporary Thai dishes and seafood; set lunches are B300 or you could book the dinner package (B1000), which includes sunset drinks, food and transport.

The nearest swimmable beach to Bang Bao and *Nirvana* is long, sandy **Hat Khlong Gloi**, 2km east of the village and not far short of the end of the tarmac. It's backed by a lagoon and a long stretch of beach-scrub and for the time being at least has nothing much more than a couple of small beach cafés, a few deckchairs, and the construction site for a ten-room resort; it can still get quite busy though. *KK Family* café (℡081 715 3940) rents tents on the beach (B250 including bedding) or you can pitch your own for B100.

The east coast

Beaches along the mangrove-fringed **east coast** are less inviting than those in the west, but this side of Ko Chang is much less developed and makes for a fun day-trip; it's about 35km from Khlong Son in the north to Salak Pet in the south.

South of the piers at Ao Saparot and Tha Dan Kao, the east-coast road runs through long swathes of rubber and palm plantations, with jungle-clad hills to the west and bronze-coloured beaches to the east, passing the national park office and bungalows at **Than Mayom**, where signs direct you inland to Than Mayom falls, a 45-minute uphill hike away. South another 6km and you come to *The Spa* (℡039 553091, ⓦwww.thespakohchang.com; ❼–❾), a beautifully designed upscale but reasonably priced wellness and detox retreat specializing in colema treatments (coffee enemas); it also has branches on Ko Samui and in Chiang Mai. It's set in a lovely mature tropical garden that runs down to the mangrove-ringed bay of western **Ao Salak Kok** and welcomes day visitors for massage, herbal saunas and facials (from B500) as well as guests who don't want to detox. The restaurant has a good reputation and the menu includes raw-food dishes, goats' yoghurt and halal meals. Fork left at the junction just south of *The Spa* to reach the southern edge of the bay and its small fishing settlement, **SALAK KOK**, site of the award-winning Salak Kok Kayak Station, a community tourism venture that runs **kayak tours** along a marked route through the mangroves (B100 per hr for kayak rental or B200 with guide) and does mangrove seafood-dinner cruises (℡081 919 3995; B1200) on a wooden catamaran too.

From Salak Kok, continue down to the tip of the southeastern headland to reach **Hat Sai Yao**, or **LONG BEACH**, the prettiest white-sand beach on this coast, which is good for swimming and has some coral close to shore. The famous *Treehouse* bungalows from Lonely Beach have relocated here under new management as *Treehouse Lodge* (℡081 847 8215, ⓦwww.tree-house.org; ❷; closed in low season); accommodation is in simple, idiosyncratic, thatched bamboo huts and it all feels pretty remote. A daily songthaew travels here from Lonely Beach (10am; B100) but if coming from Trat, either take the 3pm Ko Wai boat from Laem Ngop, which will drop you near *Treehouse Lodge*, or use the Trat-Salak Pet songthaew service; staff from *Treehouse Lodge* should meet both the boat and the songthaew.

Most day-trippers turn right not left just after *The Spa* and head instead for the little fishing port of **SALAK PET** on the south coast. Still a fairly quiet spot, Salak Pet is best known for its excellent **seafood restaurant**, *Salakphet Resort*, whose bayside dining deck offers fine views and food that's so good people travel here all the way from Trat just for lunch; crabs are a speciality – particularly stir-fried with black pepper, or with curry powder – but it's all fresh so the possibilities are infinite.

Ko Wai

Lovely, palm-edged little **KO WAI** (or Ko Whai), 10km south of Ko Chang, is only 3km long and 1.5km wide – perfect for circumnavigating in a kayak – and is encircled by sparkling turquoise water and several reefs. It has just a few **places to stay** (Oct–May only). Of these, the ultra laid-back *Koh Wai Paradise* (T081 762 2548; ❷) has the prettiest beach, on the northern headland, and offers forty very basic, no-frills-at-all bamboo huts in varying sizes (electricity 6–11pm only); unfortunately it serves lunch to the hordes of day-trippers from Ko Chang so it's not always peaceful. Further south, on a secluded brown-sand beach, *Koh Wai Goodfeeling* (T081 850 3410; ❷) has its reception off the main pier and just seven simple en-suite bungalows spread across the rocky coast. To the east, a twenty-minute walk from *Paradise*, the more comfortable though less atmospheric *Koh Wai Pakarang Resort* (T084 113 8946, Wwww.kohwaipakarang.com; fan ❹–❺, air-con ❼) has 39 en-suite wood and concrete beachside bungalows, a restaurant pavilion built off the pier, plus internet access and nightly movies.

Boats from the mainland to Ko Wai depart from Laem Ngop's Tha Kromaluang Pier, 3km west of Laem Ngop and 20km southwest of Trat, once a day at 3pm (approximately Nov–May; 2hr 30min; B250). From approximately June to September, Bang Bao Boat (T087 054 4300, Wwww.bangbaoboat.com) runs one slow service and usually one speedboat as well to Ko Wai **from Ko Chang** (1–2 daily; 20min, B400; 45min, B300) and **Ko Mak** (1–2 daily; 20min, B400; 45min, B300). Several companies on Ko Chang also offer day-trips to Ko Wai.

Ko Mak

Small, slow-paced, peaceful **KO MAK** (sometimes spelt "Maak") makes an idyllically low-key alternative to Ko Chang, 20km to the northwest. Home to little more than four hundred people, many of them descended from the islands' five main clans, Ko Mak measures just sixteen square kilometres and is dominated by coconut and rubber plantations. A couple of narrow concrete roads traverse the island; elsewhere a network of red-earth tracks cuts through the trees. The island is shaped like a star, with fine white-sand beaches along the northwest coast at **Ao Suan Yai** and the southwest coast at **Ao Kao**, where most of the island's (predominantly mid-range and upper-bracket) tourist accommodation is

Laem Ngop & Ko Chang

Laem Ngop

Ko Kood, Laem Ngop & Laem Sok

EATING & DRINKING

Baan Sabaay	**2**
Beach Café	**G**
Food Garden	**1**
Noodle Stop	**4**
Tal@y Bar	**3**
TK Hut	**F**

ACCOMMODATION

Ao Kao Resort	**J**
Baan Koh Mak	**G**
Bamboo Hideaway Resort	**C**
Goodtime	**D**
Island Hut	**I**
Koh Mak Residence	**E**
Koh Mak Resort	**B**
Monkey Island	**H**
Suchanaree Resort	**A**
TK Hut	**F**

KO MAK

concentrated; the principal village of **Ban Ao Nid** is on the southeast coast and there's another village at **Ban Laem Son** on the east coast. The main beaches are just about within walking distance of each other, and other parts of the island are also fairly easy to explore on foot, or by mountain bike, motorbike or kayak – the best way to discover the empty undeveloped beaches hidden along the north and eastern coasts. The **reefs** of Ko Rang are also less than an hour's boat ride away so snorkelling and diving trips are quite popular.

During the **rainy season**, from early June through September, choppy seas mean that boat services to Ko Mak are much reduced. Most Ko Mak accommodation stays open – and offers tempting discounts – but the smaller places often don't bother to staff their restaurants. Islanders say that it can be very pleasant during this "green season", though you may be unlucky and hit a relentlessly wet few days.

Getting to Ko Mak

As the island gets more popular, **boat services** from the mainland and the other islands are increasing: check W www.kohmak.com for current routes and schedules. Boats arrive at one of Ko Mak's three **piers** – at *Koh Mak Resort* on Ao Suan Yai, at the *Makathanee Resort* on Ao Kao or at Ao Nid – and are always met by a modest welcoming committee of accommodation staff offering free transport. When it comes to moving on, all hotels keep current boat schedules and can sell you a ticket; if going to Ko Chang be sure to pre-book a taxi from the arrival pier to your hotel at the same time as not all Ko Mak boats dock at the main piers.

In principle, there's at least one year-round slow boat **from the Trat mainland**, which departs from Laem Ngop Pier, in Laem Ngop, some 20km southwest of Trat (3hr; B300). From approximately October to May, up to five daily speedboat services also operate from this pier to Ko Mak (B450; 45min). In addition, there are currently three daily October to May services to Ko Mak from Laem Sok, 30km south of Trat (B300–450 including free transfer from central Trat; 40min–1hr 10min). If you stay over in Trat you can consult Trat guest houses and tour agents for the best option, and buy tickets from them; if arriving direct from Bangkok, Ko Samet or elsewhere, and bypassing Trat, you'll likely be whisked straight to Laem Ngop by waiting taxi drivers (see p.206). A taxi service all the way **from Bangkok** to Ko Mak is also available (B1100 including boat transfer; Ⓦ www.kohmak.com).

Except during the rainy season, there are also a number of boat services from nearby islands. Between September and June there's one daily Bang Bao slow boat and usually a speedboat as well (ⓣ087 054 4300, Ⓦwww.bangbaoboat .com) **from Ko Chang** (slow boat 2hr, B400; speedboat 50min, B550) to Ko Mak, via **Ko Wai** (1hr, B300; 20min, B400). **From Ko Kood** you have the option of one daily ferry (45min; B250) and at least a couple of speedboats (35min–1hr; B350).

Island practicalities

The best one-stop shop for **information** about Ko Mak and transport to Trat and the other islands is the comprehensive website Ⓦ www.kohmak.com and its creator, who runs *Ball Café* at the Ao Nid pier-head (Nov–May daily 7am–6pm; ⓣ086 972 4918), where you can also access the internet (and wi-fi), rent mountain bikes and quaff cappuccinos; it's a twenty-minute walk from *Island Hut* on Ao Kao or about thirty minutes from *Koh Mak Resort*. There are additional information centres and tour agents on Ao Suan Yai and Ao Kao.

The island has no public transport and virtually no traffic of any sort, so most visitors rent a **mountain bike** (B150 per day) or **motorbike** (B350 per day), either from one of the hotels, from the shop next to the *White Elephant Restaurant* on the Ao Nid road, about 300m south of the T-junction, or from the Koh Mak Information Centre in front of *Makathanee Resort* on Ao Kao. The island does have some long and potentially interesting signed **mountain-bike routes** – discreet concrete posts enigmatically carved with route numbers A1-C7 – but the explanatory map for navigating them is currently out of print: either ask about them at *Ball Café* or simply go exploring. Apparently it's possible to walk, wade and swim around the entire perimeter of the island in ten hours.

There is as yet no major commercial development on the island and **no bank or ATM**, just a few local shops in Ban Ao Nid and along its access road, and another behind *Baan Ko Mak* on the Ao Kao road. Bungalows on both beaches will **change money** and *Koh Mak Resort* on Ao Suan Yai does Visa card cash advances. For **internet access** on Ao Kao go to *Ao Kao Resort*, *Makathanee Resort* or *Baan Sabaay* restaurant (which has wi-fi too), and on Ao Suan Yai go to *Koh Mak Resort*, which is also a **postal agent**. There's a small **clinic** off the Ao Nid road, though for anything serious a speedboat will whisk you back to the mainland.

The mediocre reefs of Ko Rang (see p.219), part of the Ko Chang National Marine Park, are less than an hour's boat ride west of Ko Mak and are the island's main **diving and snorkelling** destination; they're also the main focus of Ko Chang dive and snorkel boats, so you won't be alone. Snorkelling and inland excursions to Ko Kood are also available. Island dive shops, which operate from October through May only, include the British-run Koh Mak Divers (ⓣ083 297 7724, Ⓦwww.kohmak-divers.com), on the Ao Kao road just east of *Island Hut*, and German-run Paradise Divers at *Koh Mak Resort* on Ao Suan Yai (Ⓦwww.thailandtauchen.com). Out of season, contact British freelance dive instructor Stuart (☎089 062 5071) at his house near *Baan Chai Lay* resort towards the western end of Ao Kao. Prices average B2300 for two fun dives, and B650 for snorkellers. Most hotels can also book snorkelling trips to the nearby Ko Rayang islands.

Ao Kao

Ko Mak's longest and nicest beach is **AO KAO** on the southwest coast, a pretty arc of sand that's overhung with stooping palm trees and backed in places by mangroves. The beach is divided towards its southern end by a low rocky outcrop that's straddled by *Ao Kao Resort*, with *Sunset Resort* occupying the southern headland beyond, while the long western beach is shared by a dozen other sets of bungalows. The roadside inland from the main accommodation area is where you'll find most of the restaurants and bars: if you're walking from the southern end, by far the easiest access is via the beach, tides permitting.

Koh Mak Information Centre (Oct–May daily 7.30am–7pm; ☎081 870 6287, ⓦwww.makathanee.com) at the upmarket *Makathanee Resort*, west of *Baan Koh Mak*, is a one-stop shop for boat and plane tickets, tour and transfer **information** (including Cambodia visa runs), day-trips, and bicycle and motorbike rental.

Accommodation

Ao Kao Resort ☎039 501001, ⓦwww.kohmak .com. This long-running and efficiently managed set of upscale bungalows occupies an attractive garden fronting the prettiest part of the beach. Its thirty large, comfortable en-suite timber bungalows come with fan or air-con and some have direct sea views. There's massage and internet access and kayaks and motorbikes for rent. Fan ⑤, air-con ⑧
Baan Koh Mak ☎089 895 7592, ⓦwww .baan-koh-mak.com. The eighteen cute rose-and-lime-painted bungalows here are modern and comfortable, with air-con, comfortable beds and good bathrooms, and each is enclosed within its own white picket fence. There's a very good restaurant here, plus motorbike and kayak rental and boat trips. ⑤
Goodtime ☎039 501000, ⓦwww.goodtime-resort .com, and **Koh Mak Residence** ⓦwww .kohmakresidence.com. Villa developments by these two companies are rented to visiting tourists by the day or week. The serviced houses are luxurious Thai and tastefully styled: most are one-and two-bed homes with a living area, deck and kitchen, plus DVD player, wi-fi and use of a pool. They're located on higher ground inland from Ao Kao's *Makathanee Resort*, around 20min walk from the beach. ⑧–⑨
Island Hut ☎087 139 5537. This family-run little place has the best value and most idyllically sited accommodation on the beach, though not always the friendliest welcome. The two-dozen en-suite rough-hewn timber huts are more artfully designed than they might appear: most have cheery stripey doors and idiosyncratic driftwood artwork; all have fans, hanging space and their own deckchairs on decks or on private sandy porches. Price depends on proximity to the narrow but pretty shore: the most expensive are at the water's edge. ①–③
Monkey Island ☎087 692 1001, ⓦwww .monkeyislandkohmak.com. There's a big range of quality, contemporary styled bungalows here, all in timber and thatch. Top-end "Gorilla" seafront villas are huge, with air-con and the possibility of connecting villas; the large fan and air-con "Chimpanzee" bungalows are also good, while some of the small "Baboon" options share bathrooms. There's a kids' swimming pool, plus wi-fi and internet access. Fan ③–⑤, air-con ⑥
TK Hut ☎087 134 8435, ⓦkohmak.com. One of Ko Mak's first resorts, whose old-fashioned but well-priced wood, stone and concrete bungalows are set around a shady garden of casuarinas and little hedges. Also has a seafront bar and restaurant, internet access, plus kayak and motorbike rental. Rates include buffet breakfast. Fan ④, air-con ⑤–⑥

Eating and drinking

Baan Sabaay Between *Baan Ko Mak* and *Makathanee*, inland side of the road. A congenial and lively place for a few Beer Changs and a chat with island expats. Also serves food and has internet terminals and wi-fi.

Beach Café At *Baan Ko Mak*. The kitchen here serves exceptionally delicious Thai food, including good *tom kha* soups and great *phanaeng* curries. Mains from B60.

Food Garden Opposite *Monkey Island*. A cross between a beer garden and a night market, this very popular, cheap and enjoyable outdoor restaurant comprises several concessions serving *phat thai*, yellow curry, recommended *haw mok* (steamed fish and coconut curry), chicken satay, grilled seafood, *som tam* and beer. Dishes start at B30 and there's a big screen for major sports fixtures.

Noodle Stop Between *Island Hut* and Koh Mak Divers. A good cheap place for noodle soups (B30) and the rest.

Tal@y Bar On the beach in front of *Ko Mak Cottages*. Deckchairs and lamps on the sand and great margaritas (B120) plus a long list of other cocktails. Happy hour 9–10pm.

TK Hut The thrice-weekly all-you-can-eat seafood barbecues here get lots of returnees; from 6.30pm.

Ao Suan Yai and around

Long, curvy **AO SUAN YAI** is not as pretty a beach as Ao Kao, but the sand is fine and the outlook is beautiful, with Ko Chang's hilly profile filling the horizon and Ko Kham and other islets in between. You'll need a bicycle or motorbike to access the variety of restaurants on the Ao Kao road as there's just a couple of **accommodation** options here. The biggest is the extensive *Koh Mak Resort* (℡039 501013, ⓦwww.kohmakresort.com; ⓺–⓽), which offers various air-con bungalows, all enjoying lovely panoramas, the most interesting of which are the very modern, design-conscious, sea-view and beachfront suites – all polished concrete, stacked slate walls, huge picture windows and private little walled gardens. There's a swimming pool and similarly chic pool bar here too, plus currency exchange, Visa cash advance, internet access and a tour desk, plus postal services, a taxi service, motorbike and kayak rental, a dive shop and a pier. Neighbouring *Suchanaree Resort* (℡081 983 2629, ⓔSuchanaree_Tour @hotmail.com; ⓷) couldn't be more different. Comprising just half-a-dozen shoreside bungalows, it's an intimate, friendly little place and deservedly popular. The cute, good-quality, shaggy-thatched wooden bungalows all have fan, mozzie nets and bathrooms.

A couple of kilometres southeast of Ao Suan Yai, accessed via tracks through the rubber plantations, *Bamboo Hideaway Resort* (℡039 501085, ⓦwww .bamboohideaway.com; ⓻) is an idiosyncratic haven, built almost entirely from lengths of polished bamboo. Its eight comfortable air-con rooms all have four-poster beds and hammocks and are connected by a raised bamboo walkway. Although the south coast is just a couple of minutes' walk downhill, Ao Suan Yai has the nearest decent beach. There's a good-sized swimming pool on site, along with the *Naked Fish* restaurant, which specializes in upscale authentic Thai and northeastern food (non-guests can phone for free transport) and is presided over by a genial New Zealand host.

Ko Kood

The fourth-largest island in Thailand, forested **KO KOOD** (also spelt Ko Kut and Ko Kud) is still a wild and largely uncommercialized island. Though it's known for its sparkling white sand and exceptionally clear turquoise water, particularly along the west coast, Ko Kood is as much a nature-lover's destination as a beach-bum's. Swathes of its shoreline are fringed by scrub and

◀ Trat, Ko Chang & Ko Mak

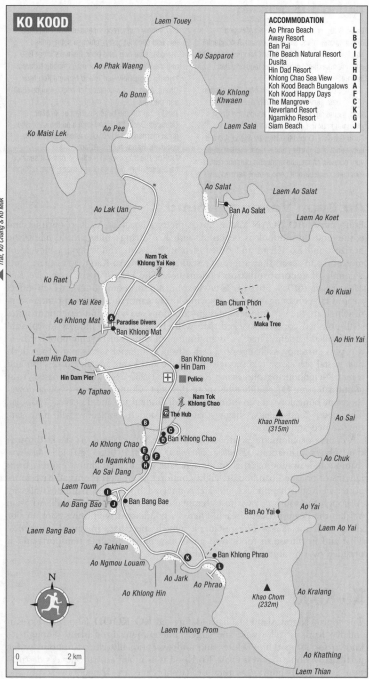

KO KOOD

ACCOMMODATION	
Ao Phrao Beach	L
Away Resort	B
Ban Pai	C
The Beach Natural Resort	I
Dusita	E
Hin Dad Resort	H
Khlong Chao Sea View	D
Koh Kood Beach Bungalows	A
Koh Kood Happy Days	F
The Mangrove	C
Neverland Resort	K
Ngamkho Resort	G
Siam Beach	J

Laem Touey

Ao Sapparot

Ao Phak Waeng

Ao Bonn

Ao Khlong
Khwaen

Ao Pee

Laem Sala

Ko Maisi Lek

Ao Salat

Laem Ao Salat

Ao Lak Uan

Ban Ao Salat

Laem Ao Koet

Nam Tok
Khlong Yai Kee

Ko Raet

Ao Yai Kee

Ao Kluai

Ban Chum Phon

Ao Khlong Mat

A Paradise Divers

Maka Tree

Ban Khlong Mat

Ao Hin Yai

Laem Hin Dam

Ban Khlong
Hin Dam

Hin Dam Pier

✚ ■ Police

Ao Taphao

Nam Tok
Khlong Chao

@ The Hub

Khao Phaenthi
(315m)

Ao Sai

B

C

Ao Khlong Chao

D Ban Khlong Chao

E

Ao Ngamkho

G

Ao Chuk

Ao Sai Dang

H F

Laem Toum

I

Ao Bang Bao

J ● Ban Bang Bae

Ban Ao Yai ●

Ao Yai

Laem Bang Bao

Laem Ao Yai

Ao Takhian

Ao Ngmou Louam

K

● Ban Khlong Phrao

Ao Jark

L

Ao Phrao

Khao Chom
(232m)

Ao Kralang

Ao Khlong Hin

N

Laem Khlong Prom

Ao Khathing

0   2 km

Laem Thian

mangrove rather than broad sandy beaches and those parts of the island not still covered in virgin tropical rainforest are filled with palm groves and rubber plantations. Though the island is 25km long and 12km wide, it supports barely more than 20km of concrete road, with many areas penetrated only by the odd sandy track and, in places, by navigable khlongs, if at all. The highest point on the island, at just 315m, is Khao Phaenthi, towards the southeast. All of this makes Ko Kood a surprisingly pleasant place to explore on foot (or kayak), especially as the cool season brings refreshing breezes most days. The interior is also graced with several waterfalls, the most famous of which is Nam Tok Khlong Chao, inland from Ao Khlong Chao and the focus of occasional day-trips from Ko Chang and Ko Mak.

Because of its lack of roads, Ko Kood has to date been the almost exclusive province of package-tourists, but things are becoming much easier for independent travellers now, with a choice of scheduled boat services from the mainland, as well as from Ko Chang and Ko Mak (and even plans for a possible run to Ban Hat Lek, on the Cambodian border, from Ban Ao Salat on the northeast coast), and the emergence of some budget-minded guest houses. The island is still pretty much a **one-season destination**, however, as rough seas mean that nearly all the boat services only operate from November through May. An increasing number of places are staying open year-round, however, and offer tempting discounts to those willing to chance the rains and the off-season quiet.

Most of Kok Kood's fifteen hundred residents make their living from fishing and growing coconut palms and rubber trees. Many have Khmer blood in them as the island population mushroomed at the turn of the twentieth century when Thais and Cambodians resident in nearby Cambodian territory fled French control. The main settlements are **Ban Khlong Hin Dam**, just inland from the main Hin Dam pier; **Ban Khlong Mat**, a natural harbour-inlet a few kilometres further north up the coast; the stilted fishing village of **Ban Ao Salat** across on the northeast coast; and the fishing community of **Ban Ao Yai** on the southeast coast. On the southwest coast, several of the main beaches also have small villages. Of these, the obvious choice for budget travellers are **Ao Khlong Chao** and **Ao Ngamkho**, which both have a choice of accommodation and eating options and are within walking distance of each other; **Ao Bang Bao** also has cheapish bungalows and is the longer and arguably better beach but has no village and is more isolated. Seclusion is the thing on all the other west-coast beaches, most of which are the province of just one or two upmarket resorts: **Ao Jark** is the most heart-stoppingly gorgeous, and very private, while **Ao Khlong Mat** offers notably good value.

Getting to Ko Kood

In all but the worst weather, Ninmoungkorn (☎086 126 7860) runs a year-round **boat service** to Ko Kood from the **Trat** mainland, departing from Laem Sok, about 30km south of Trat (see p.206), and terminating at Ao Salat on the island's northeast coast during the rainy season but serving west-coast piers at Hin Dam and Bang Bao from November to May (1–2 daily; 2–3hr; B400 including transfer from Trat to the Laem Sok pier). There are also several different companies offering high-season **speedboat** services between the Trat mainland and Ko Kood's western piers and beaches; these are faster and more expensive (up to 4 daily; 1hr 10min–1hr 50min; B600) but can be wet and uncomfortable in all but the flattest seas. Schedules and mainland departure points vary (usual departure points are Laem Sok; Dan Kao, 6km northeast of central Trat; and Laem Ngop Pier, 20km southwest of Trat) and are best checked

with Trat guest houses, the TAT office in Laem Ngop, or tour agents in Trat or
Laem Ngop. Some of the high-season speedboats go via **Ko Mak** (Nov–May,
2–3 daily; 35min–1hr; B350), and Bang Bao Boat runs a connecting service
from Ko Chang and Ko Wai via Ko Mak to Ko Kood (Sept–June, 1 daily
slow boat with speedboat connection, 5hr, B700; 1 daily speedboat, 2hr, B900;
Ⓦwww.bangbaoboat.com). Local tour operators on the islands are the best
source of current timetables. As arrival points for speedboats vary, it's always
worth calling ahead to your accommodation for a pick-up: there are only a few
share-taxis on the island and they don't meet all arrivals. Return schedules from
Ko Kood operate at the same frequency as the outbound services; all Ko Kood
hotels keep current timetables and sell tickets.

Island practicalities

Getting around Ko Kood is mainly a question of walking or renting your own
transport, though you should be able to charter a songthaew for the day for
around B1000. You can rent **kayaks** on every beach, and **motorbikes** through
Koh Kood Happy Days guest house on Ao Ngamkho and The Hub activity
centre on Ao Khlong Chao (from B300 per day), but be warned that the west-
coast road is very narrow, concrete only in parts, and dirt, stone and occasionally
badly rutted in others. The number of hills may also deter you from doing it by
mountain bike, which are available at The Hub (B200 per day) and through
some resorts. Exploring the island **on foot** is both feasible and fun, and south
of Ao Khlong Chao much of the route is shady. From Ao Khlong Chao to Ao
Bang Bao takes about forty minutes; from Ao Bang Bao to Ao Jark is about an
hour's walk, then another twenty minutes to Ao Phrao.

There's **no bank** on Ko Kood, but you can **change money** at *Happy Days*
in Ao Ngamkho and at the biggest resorts. There's a postal agent in the shop
next to *Happy Days* and **internet** access both at *Happy Days* and The Hub on
Ao Khlong Chao. The **police** are in Ban Khlong Hin Dam (Ⓣ039 521745), as
is the **hospital** (Ⓣ039 521852); the shop across from the hospital has a small
pharmacy section and sells antihistamine tablets for sandfly bites (see p.28),
which can be legion on Ko Kood. There is some **malaria** on the island so be
especially assiduous with repellent and nets if you are not taking prophylactics;
there's a malaria-testing station in Ban Khlong Hin Dam.

There are two **dive operators** on Ko Kood: The Hub, part of *Away Resort* in
Ao Khlong Chao (Ⓣ081 835 4517, Ⓦwww.awaykohkood.com), and Paradise
Divers (Ⓣ087 144 5945, Ⓦwww.thailandtauchen.com), whose headquarters are
at *Ko Kood Beach Resort* at Ao Khlong Mat, with another desk at *Happy Days*.
Two dives cost B3000, with snorkellers paying B900; you might prefer to opt
for a local Ko Kood dive as the usual sites around Ko Rang (see p.219) are
always packed with dive boats from Ko Chang and Ko Mak.

The Hub organizes guided kayak **trips** to Khlong Chao Falls and around the
coast, as well as round-island boat tips, snorkelling trips and hikes.

Ao Khlong Chao and Khlong Chao Falls

About 5km south of the main Hin Dam pier, **AO KHLONG CHAO**
(pronounced "Jao") is a fun place to stay because as well as a small sandy beach
– no great beauty but a perfectly pleasant "village" beach – you've got the pretty
two-kilometre-long mangrove-lined Khlong Chao that runs down from the
famous Khlong Chao Falls. Close by the road-bridge that spans the khlong, just
300m from the palm-fringed beach, is a cluster of little guest houses, some of
them built partially on stilts over the river, which offer the cheapest accommodation on the island, as well as a couple of package-tour resorts, complete

with intrusive, late-night karaoke restaurants which unfortunately mar the atmosphere considerably at weekends.

Away Resort's roadside **activity centre** The Hub (Nov–May 8am–8pm) has internet access and wi-fi, runs PADI dive trips and courses, organizes snorkelling and other day trips and rents motorbikes, bicycles and kayaks.

The three-tiered **Nam Tok Khlong Chao** is a pretty if not exceptional waterfall that tumbles down into a large, refreshing pool that's perfect for a dip; it's quietest in the mornings, before the package groups arrive. It takes around twenty minutes to kayak upriver from the Khlong Chao bridge to the jetty near the falls, followed by a ten-minute walk – though you can also walk the whole thing in half an hour, or even take a car or motorbike to within 500m: just follow the signs from the bridge over the khlong in Khlong Chao. The track continues beyond the falls through jungle for another few kilometres before terminating at a rubber plantation, making for a pleasant and very quiet four-hour walk there and back, though watch out for snakes, especially cobras.

Accommodation

Away Resort ☎081 835 4517, ⓦwww .awayresorts.com. The most upmarket place to stay in Khlong Chao occupies a garden that drops down to a rocky chunk of the shore; though there's no beach here you can swim off the jetty, laze in the garden, or take a free kayak across to Ao Khlong Chao beach proper, just a couple of minutes' paddle away. The seaside and sea-view bungalows are large and quite stylish, with air-con, wooden floors and inviting verandas; their cheapest accommodation is in fixed safari-style tents (with fans and hot water) which aren't worth the money. ⑥–⑨
Ban Pai ☎089 931 5683. Has the cheapest rooms in Khlong Chao (with shared bathrooms), in an extended stilt house centred round a lovely breezy communal khlong-side deck. The pricier rooms and bungalows are not such good value but the

home-cooked food is exceptional, especially for fish dishes. ❷–❺
Khlong Chao Sea View ☎087 908 3593. Away from the khlong – and the karaoke-singing weekenders on the north bank – this friendly place is set in a garden beside the road 200m beyond the bridge, from where you can indeed see the sea, 200m away, through the thinly planted palm grove. Its half-dozen bamboo bungalows each have a bathroom and a little veranda and there's good food at the popular garden restaurant too, especially the *phanaeng* curries. Fan ❸, air-con ❺
🏃 **The Mangrove** ☎081 290 7455. The best of the khlong-side options, with very nice sturdy wooden bungalows spaced around a grassy lawn, all with river views. Interiors are modern and well furnished with TV and hot water. Fan ❹, air-con ❺

Ao Ngamkho

Having climbed over the point at the south end of Ao Khlong Chao, the road dips down again to the tiny village at **AO NGAMKHO** and its beach, actually a series of pretty, miniature bays either side of a khlong and between rocky points, with quite rewarding snorkelling and plenty of fish at its southern end.

The backpacker-oriented *Koh Kood Happy Days* (☎087 144 5945, ⓦwww .kohkood-happydays.com; ❸–❹) is beside the road here, 200m from the northern section of the beach, and offers ten en-suite fan and air-con **rooms** in a little guest-house block, all with wooden floors, pretty furnishings and a shared veranda. There's also motorbike rental and internet access, plus a sociable bar and restaurant and a general store next door. Directly on the shore, just south of the khlong, small, friendly *Dusita* (☎081 420 4861, ⓦwww.dusitaresorts.com; ❺–❻) offers plainly outfitted fan and air-con wooden cabins that all enjoy beautiful sea views and some shade among the sparse coconut grove hung with hammocks; it's open November to May only. Also right on the beach, traveller-oriented 🏃 *Ngamkho Resort* (☎081 825 7076, ⓦwww.kohkood-ngamkho.com; ❹) has just nine well-designed and attractively furnished en-suite bamboo bungalows, all with fans, decks and hammocks, plus a restaurant in the secluded little shore-front garden. The twenty sturdy fan and air-con chalets of *Hin Dad Resort* (☎081 762 9519, @hindadresort@hotmail.com; ❻–❼; closed July–Sept) sit atop the little rocky point at the southern end of the bay, with panoramic sea views and easy access to the beach.

Ao Bang Bao

From Ao Ngamkho, follow signs for *The Beach* to reach **AO BANG BAO**, about twenty minutes' walk further south (fifteen minutes west off the main road). This is one of Ko Kood's prettiest beaches, fronted by a longish sweep of bleach-white sand and deliciously clear turquoise water, plus the inevitable fringe of coconut palms, and embraced by a pair of protective promontories. Though *The Beach Natural Resort* (☎086 009940, ⓦwww.thebeachkohkood .com; fan ❺, air-con ❼) doesn't actually sit on the nicest part of the beach, but behind a rocky area towards the northern end, its 34 thatched Balinese-style **bungalows** are tastefully furnished and have garden bathrooms; they're grouped quite closely together so most only offer sea glimpses. Neighbouring *Siam Beach* (☎081 899 6200, ⓦwww.siambeachkohkood.net; fan ❹, air-con ❺–❻) occupies almost all of the best part of the beach, sprawling across an extensive area, and is popular with budget travellers, though it's more isolated than similarly priced options on Ao Ngamkho and Ao Khlong Chao. It offers big, rustic, no-frills timber huts on the seafront with the option of either fan or air-con, and nearly all enjoy uninterrupted bay views. Some of the newer, pricier air-con rooms are in a less idyllic spot close to a khlong and back from the shore a bit. The restaurant cooks up regular seafood barbecues and there's internet access, motorbike and kayak rental.

Ao Jark, Ao Phrao and Ao Yai

Back on the main southbound road at the Ao Bang Bao turnoff, a 35-minute walk through coconut and rubber plantations brings you to **Ao Khlong Hin**, a wild little bay that's dominated by a small coconut-processing centre and is not really great for swimming. Ten minutes further along the road, which hugs the coast so close it gets washed by the waves at high tide, remote and breathtakingly lovely little **AO JARK** sits at the mouth of a wide, serene khlong and feels secluded and private. The only accommodation here, set among the palms between the limpid blue sea and the calm green khlong, is at *Neverland Resort* (☎081 762 6254, ⓦwww.neverlandresort.com; ❻–❼), which offers fourteen comfortable air-con bungalows and fully equipped two-person tents (B450). Prices go up a little at weekends, and from June to October you need to call ahead to make sure it's open.

Continue twenty minutes further along the pretty coastal road to reach the most southerly bay, **AO PHRAO** (about 2km from Ao Jark), a long, stunning beach of white sand backed by densely planted palms and the slopes of Khao Chom. You can stay here at *Ao Phrao Beach* (☎081 429 7145, ⓦwww.kokut .com; ❽; closed June–Sept), in mainly but not exclusively package-oriented clusters of thatched and concrete air-con bungalows; facilities include internet, wi-fi and kayak rental. Behind Ao Phrao, the tiny fishing village of **Ban Khlong Phrao** occupies the mangrove-lined banks of Khlong Phrao (which extends another kilometre inland). There's a clinic here as well as a few small shops and hot-food stalls.

A five-kilometre track that's very steep and rough in places connects Ban Khlong Phrao with **Ao Yai**, the southeast coast's main if rather lacklustre fishing village, built entirely on stilts and jetties around the shoreline of a natural harbour. Its main visitors are the crews of anchored fishing boats from Thailand and Cambodia, who come here for drink, supplies, karaoke and the rest.

North, inland and east

The bays of **northern Ko Kood**, beyond Ao Khlong Chao, are even more thinly populated than the southwest coast, with just a few resorts up here open to tourists who don't come on pre-booked packages. Inland is the island's administrative centre, **Ban Khlong Hin Dam**, 3.5km north of Ao Khlong Chao, site of a few shops, the hospital, police station, school and principal island temple. Ko Kood's main pier is a couple of kilometres to the west, at **Laem Hin Dam**.

The best value of the northwest resorts is Danish-run *Koh Kood Beach Bungalows* (☎081 908 8966, ⓦwww.jysktravel.com; ❼–❽), set above the small, effectively private little bay at **AO KHLONG MAT**, beside the deep natural harbour in the adjacent stilt village, about 2km north of Ban Khlong Hin Dam. The widely spaced, high-roofed Balinese-style bungalows here all have air-con, TV and garden-style bathrooms and each enjoys a sea view from its generous deck. There's a swimming pool, motorbike, bicycle and kayak rental, internet access and a dive shop on site. The company also runs interesting sounding four-day **sea-safaris**: guests sleep in special billets on the deck of a fishing boat and visit various local islands including Ko Mak.

About 5km northwest of Ban Khlong Hin Dam, the small but appealing three-tiered waterfall **Nam Tok Khlong Yai Kee** is basically a miniature version of the famous Nam Tok Khlong Chao and rushes down into a good-sized pool that's ideal for swimming. It's accessible via a five-minute path that's very steep in places, but there are ropes at the crucial points.

East off the road to the north coast, in the mature rainforest near Ban Chum Phon, is a locally famous **five-hundred-year old maka tree** (*Bridelia insulana*), known to islanders as the *dtohn maai yai*, that's an impressive 35m or more in height and drips with lianas and epiphytes. A kilometre-long path that runs through rubber trees and rainforest will get you there, but you'll need to go with a local to stay on the right track.

The road currently serves just one spot on the northeast coast and that's the tiny stilt-village and fishing community of **Ban Ao Salat**, 9km northeast of Ban Khlong Hin Dam. Several of the wooden houses strung out along the jetty-promenade serve food so this is a great place for a fresh-seafood lunch, especially crab. The rainy season boat service usually terminates here.

Travel details

Trains

Aranyaprathet to: Bangkok (2 daily; 5hr 25min–6hr).
Pattaya to: Bangkok (1 daily; 4hr); Si Racha (1 daily; 30min).
Si Racha to: Bangkok (1 daily; 3hr 30min); Pattaya (1 daily; 30min).

Buses

Aranyaprathet to: Bangkok (10 daily; 4hr 30min).
Ban Phe to: Bangkok (14 daily; 3hr); Chanthaburi (6 daily; 1hr 30min); Rayong (every 30min; 30min); Trat (6 daily; 3hr).
Chanthaburi to: Bangkok (Eastern Bus Terminal; 18 daily; 4–5hr); Bangkok (Northern Bus Terminal; 5 daily; 3–4hr); Bangkok (Suvarnabhumi Airport; 4 daily; 3hr); Rayong (8 daily; 2hr); Sa Kaew

(for Aranyaprathet; 8 daily; 3hr); Trat (every 1hr 30min; 1hr 30min).

Laem Ngop to: Bangkok (Eastern Bus Terminal; 2 daily; 5hr 15min).

Pattaya to: Bangkok (Eastern/Northern bus Terminals; every 30min; 2hr 30min)); Bangkok (Southern Bus Terminal; 12 daily; 3hr 30min); Bangkok (Suvarnabhumi Airport; 4 daily; 2hr); Chanthaburi (6 daily; 3hr); Rayong (every 30min; 1hr 30min); Trat (6 daily; 4hr 30min).

Rayong to: Bangkok (Eastern Bus Terminal; every 40min; 2hr 30min–3hr); Bangkok (Northern Bus Terminal; 5 daily; 3hr); Ban Phe (for Ko Samet; every 30min; 30 min); Chanthaburi (every 30min; 2hr).

Si Racha to: Bangkok (Eastern/Northern bus terminals; every 30min; 2hr); Chanthaburi (6 daily; 3hr 30min); Pattaya (every 20min; 30min); Rayong (every 30min; 2hr); Trat (6 daily; 5hr).

Trat to: Bangkok (Eastern Bus Terminal; 6 daily; 5–6hr); Bangkok (Northern Bus Terminal; 5 daily; 4hr 30min); Bangkok (Suvarnabhumi Airport; 5 daily; 4hr 10min); Chanthaburi (11 daily; 1hr 30min); Hat Lek (for the Cambodian border; every 45min; 1hr–1hr 30min); Pattaya (6 daily; 4hr 30min); Rayong (6 daily; 3hr 30min); Si Racha (6 daily; 5hr).

Boats

Ban Phe to: Ko Samet (at least 6 daily; 30min).
Ko Chang to: Ko Kood (Nov–May 1–2 daily; 2hr–5hr); Ko Mak (Sept–June 1–2 daily; 50min–2hr); Ko Wai (Sept–June 1–2 daily; 15min–1hr 15min); Trat province (at least every 2hr; 25min–45min).
Ko Kood to: Ko Chang (Nov–May daily; 2hr); Ko Mak (Nov–May 2–3 daily; 35min–1hr); Trat province (1–5 daily; 1hr 10min–4hr).
Ko Mak to: Ko Chang (Sept–June 1–2 daily; 50min–2hr); Ko Kood (Nov–May 2–3 daily; 35min–1hr); Trat province (1–9 daily; 40min–3hr).
Si Racha to: Ko Si Chang (hourly; 40min).
Trat province to: Ko Chang (at least every 2hr; 25–45min); Ko Kood (1–6 daily; 1hr 10min–4hr); Ko Mak (1–9 daily; 40min–3hr); Ko Wai (Nov–April 1 daily; 2hr 30min).

Flights

Pattaya (U-Tapao) to: Ko Samui (2 daily; 1hr); Phuket (1 daily; 1hr 35min).
Trat to: Bangkok (3 daily; 50min).

3

Southern Thailand: the Gulf coast

CHAPTER 3 # Highlights

* **Phetchaburi** Charming historic town, boasting several fine old working temples. See p.237

* **Leisurely seafood lunches** At the squid-pier restaurants in Hua Hin or under the trees at Ban Krud. See p.248 & p.256

* **Pak Nam Pran** Chic boutique hotels on a long, sandy beach. See p.249

* **Ang Thong National Marine Park** A dramatic boat-trip from Samui or Pha Ngan. See p.268

* **Full moon at Hat Rin** Party on, and on... See p.287

* **Ao Thong Nai Pan on Ko Pha Ngan** Beautiful, secluded bay with good accommodation. See p.293

* **A boat-trip round Ko Tao** Satisfying exploration and great snorkelling. See p.300

* **Nakhon Si Thammarat** Historic holy sites, shadow puppets and excellent cuisine. See p.306

* **Krung Ching waterfall** Walk past giant ferns and screeching monkeys to reach this spectacular drop. See p.312

▲ Khao Wang, Phetchaburi

3

Southern Thailand: the Gulf coast

S
outhern Thailand's gently undulating **Gulf coast** is famed above all for the Samui archipelago, three small idyllic islands lying off the most prominent hump of the coastline. This is the country's most popular seaside venue for independent travellers, and a lazy stay in a Samui beachfront bungalow is so seductive a prospect that most people overlook the attractions of the mainland, where the sheltered sandy beaches and warm clear water rival the top sunspots in most countries. Added to that you'll find scenery dominated by forested mountains that rise abruptly behind the coastal strip, especially impressive in **Khao Sam Roi Yot National Park**, and a sprinkling of historic sights – notably the crumbling temples of ancient **Phetchaburi**. Though not a patch on the islands further south, the stretch of coast around **Cha-am** and **Hua Hin** is popular with weekending Thais escaping the capital and is crammed with condos, high-rise hotels and bars, not to mention a large population of foreign tourists. Far quieter and preferable are the sophisticated little beach resort of **Pak Nam Pran**, just a short distance further south, the welcoming town of **Prachuap Khiri Khan**, fronted by a lovely bay and flanked by an equally appealing beach, and laid-back, lightly developed **Ban Krud**.

Of the islands, **Ko Samui** is by far the most naturally beautiful, with its long white-sand beaches and arching fringes of palm trees. The island's beauty has not gone unnoticed by tourist developers of course, and its varied spread of accommodation these days draws as many package tourists and second-homers as backpackers. In recent years the next island out, **Ko Pha Ngan**, has drawn increasing numbers of backpackers away from its neighbour: its bungalows are generally simpler and cost less than Ko Samui's, and it offers a few stunning beaches with a more laid-back atmosphere. The island's southeastern headland, **Hat Rin**, has no less than three white-sand beaches to choose from, but now provides all the amenities the demanding traveller could want, not to mention its notorious full moon parties. The furthest inhabited island of the archipelago, **Ko Tao**, has taken off as a **scuba-diving** centre, but despite a growing nightlife and restaurant scene, still has the feel of a small, rugged and isolated outcrop.

Tucked away beneath the islands, **Nakhon Si Thammarat**, the cultural capital of the south, is well worth a short detour from the main routes through the centre of the peninsula – it's a sophisticated city of grand old temples,

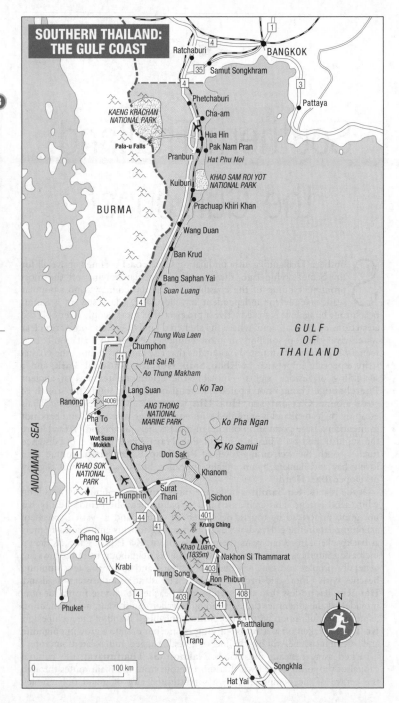

SOUTHERN THAILAND:
THE GULF COAST

Ratchaburi

BANGKOK

Samut Songkhram

Phetchaburi

KAENG KRACHAN
NATIONAL PARK

Pattaya

Pala-u Falls

Cha-am

Hua Hin

Pak Nam Pran

Pranburi

Hat Phu Noi

Kuiburi

KHAO SAM ROI YOT
NATIONAL PARK

BURMA

Prachuap Khiri Khan

Wang Duan

Ban Krud

Bang Saphan Yai

Suan Luang

GULF
OF
THAILAND

Thung Wua Laen

Chumphon

Hat Sai Ri

Ao Thung Makham

Ko Tao

Lang Suan

Ranong

ANG THONG
NATIONAL
MARINE PARK

Ko Pha Ngan

Pha To

Ko Samui

Wat Suan
Mokkh

Chaiya

Don Sak

Khanom

KHAO SOK
NATIONAL
PARK

ANDAMAN SEA

Phunphin

Surat
Thani

Sichon

Krung Ching

Phang Nga

Khao Luang
(1835m)

Nakhon Si Thammarat

Krabi

Thung Song

Ron Phibun

Phuket

Phatthalung

Trang

N

Songkhla

0   100 km

Hat Yai

delicious cuisine and distinctive handicrafts. With its small but significant Muslim population, and machine-gun dialect, Nakhon begins the transition into Thailand's deep south.

The **railway** from Bangkok connects all the mainland towns, including a branch line to Nakhon; nearly all services depart from Hualamphong Station, but a few slow trains (not shown on the English-language timetable) use Thonburi Station. You can also head south from Kanchanaburi by train, changing at Ban Pong (not listed on English-language timetables) or Nakhon Pathom. **Bus** services, along highways 4 (also known as the Phetkasem Highway, or usually Thanon Phetkasem when passing through towns) and 41, are generally faster and more frequent than the trains. From Bangkok, Thai Airways and Air Asia **fly** to Surat Thani, Nok Air to Nakhon Si Thammarat, while Bangkok Airways operates a variety of popular routes to Ko Samui's airport, which is now also served by Thai Airways from the capital. Daily boats run to the islands from two jumping-off points: **Surat Thani**, 650km from Bangkok, has a better choice of routes, but the faster alternatives from **Chumphon**, 200km nearer the capital, take you straight to the tranquillity of Ko Tao.

The Gulf coast has a slightly different **climate** from the Andaman coast and much of the rest of Thailand, being hit heavily by the northeast monsoon's rains, especially in November, when it's best to avoid this part of the country altogether. Most times during the rest of the year should see pleasant, if change-able, weather, with some effects of the southwest monsoon felt on the islands between May and October. Late December to April is the driest period, and is therefore the region's high season, which also includes July and August.

Phetchaburi

Straddling the Phet River about 120km south of Bangkok, the provincial capital of **PHETCHABURI** (sometimes "Phetburi") has been settled ever since the eleventh century, when the Khmers ruled the region, but only really got going six hundred years later, when it flourished as a trading post between the Andaman Sea ports and Burma and Ayutthaya. Despite periodic incursions from the Burmese, the town gained a reputation as a cultural centre – as the ornamentation of its older temples testifies – and after the new capital was established in Bangkok it became a favourite country retreat of Rama IV, who had a hilltop palace built here in the 1850s. Modern Phetchaburi's main claim to fame is as one of Thailand's finest sweet-making centres, the essential ingredient for its assortment of *khanom* being the sugar extracted from the sweet-sapped palms that cover the province. This being very much a cottage industry, today's downtown Phetchaburi has lost relatively little of the ambience that so attracted Rama IV: the central riverside area is hemmed in by historic wats in varying states of disrepair, along with plenty of traditional wooden shophouses.

Despite the attractions of its old quarter, Phetchaburi gets few overnight visitors as most people see it on a day-trip from Bangkok, Hua Hin or Cha-am. It's also possible to combine a day in Phetchaburi with an early-morning expedition from Bangkok to the floating markets of Damnoen Saduak, 40km north; budget tour operators in Bangkok's Thanon Khao San area offer this option as a day-trip package for about B600 per person. The town sees more overnighters during the **Phra Nakhon Khiri Fair**, spread over at least five days in February; it features parades in historic costumes, cooking demonstrations and traditional entertainments such as *likay* and *lakhon*.

Arrival, information and transport

Arriving by **bus**, you may be dropped in one of four places. Through-buses on Highway 4 will set you down at the corner of Thanon Banda-It on the western edge of town. Non-air-con buses to and from Cha-am and Hua Hin use the small terminal in the town centre, less than ten minutes' walk from Chomrut Bridge. The **terminal** for Phetchaburi–Bangkok **air-con buses** is also about ten minutes' walk from Chomrut Bridge, just off Thanon Rajwithi. If you're coming here from Kanchanaburi, you can avoid Bangkok by heading for Ratchaburi, where you can catch an air-con bus that'll put you off at a terminal on the west side of Khao Wang. Phetchaburi **train station** is on the northern outskirts of town.

There's no TAT office in town, but *Rabieng Rimnum Guest House* is a good source of local **information**. **Internet access** is available, for example, at an unnamed shop on Thanon Phongsuriya, five minutes' walk east of Chomrut Bridge. To see the major temples in a day and have sufficient energy left for climbing Khao Wang, you might want to hire a **samlor** for a couple of hours, at about B100 per hour. Alternatively make use of the public **songthaews** that circulate round the town, or **rent** a **bicycle** or **motorbike** from *Rabieng Rimnum Guest House.*

Accommodation

Most travellers **stay** at the *Rabieng Rimnum (Rim Nam) Guest House*, centrally located at 1 Thanon Chisa-in, on the southwest corner of Chomrut Bridge (☎032 425707 or 089 919 7446, ✉rabieng@hotmail.com, ⊛www .rabiengrimnum.com; ❶). Occupying a century-old house next to the Phet River and, less appealingly, a noisy main road, the guest house offers nine simple rooms with shared bathrooms, lots of local information and the best restaurant

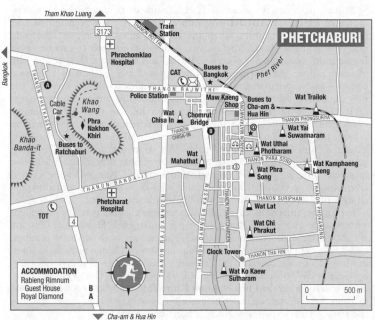

in town; it also organizes day-trips and overnight visits to Kaeng Krachan National Park for bird-watching and hiking. If *Rabieng Rimnum* is full, ask the owners about the sporadically open *Ban Thai Guest House* about 1km south just off Thanon Damnoen Kasem. West of Khao Wang, on the outskirts of town, is Phetchaburi's most upmarket option, the *Royal Diamond* (T032 411061, W www.royaldiamondhotel.com; ●), which has comfortable air-con rooms with hot water, TVs and fridges and is located on Soi Sam Chao Phet, just off the Phetkasem Highway.

The Town

The pinnacles and rooftops of the town's thirty-odd **wats** are visible in every direction, but only a few are worth stopping off to investigate; the following description takes in the top three, which can be seen on a leisurely two-hour circular walk beginning from Chomrut Bridge. Phetchaburi's other significant sight, the palace-museum at Phra Nakhon Khiri, is on a hill about 1km west of the bridge.

Wat Yai Suwannaram

Of all Phetchaburi's temples, the most attractive is the still-functioning seventeenth-century **Wat Yai Suwannaram** on Thanon Phongsuriya, about 700m east of Chomrut Bridge. The temple's fine old teak **sala** has elaborately carved doors, bearing a gash reputedly inflicted by the Burmese in 1760 as they plundered their way towards Ayutthaya. Across from the *sala* and hidden behind high, whitewashed walls stands the windowless Ayutthaya-style bot. The bot compound overlooks a pond, in the middle of which stands a small but well-preserved scripture library, or **ho trai**: such structures were built on stilts over water to prevent ants and other insects destroying the precious documents. Enter the walled compound from the south and make a clockwise tour of the cloisters filled with Buddha statutes before entering the bot itself via the eastern doorway (if the door is locked, one of the monks will get the key for you). The **bot** is supported by intricately patterned red and gold pillars and contains a remarkable, if rather faded, set of murals, depicting Indra, Brahma and other lower-ranking divinities ranged in five rows of ascending importance. Once you've admired the interior, walk to the back of the bot, passing behind the central cluster of Buddha images, to find another Buddha image seated against the back wall: climb the steps in front of this image to get a close-up of the left foot, which for some reason was cast with six toes.

Wat Kamphaeng Laeng

Fifteen minutes' walk east and then south of Wat Yai, the five tumbledown prangs of **Wat Kamphaeng Laeng** on Thanon Phra Song mark out Phetchaburi as the probable southernmost outpost of the Khmer empire. Built to enshrine Hindu deities and set out in a cruciform arrangement facing east, the laterite corncob-style prangs were later adapted for Buddhist use, as can be seen from the two that now house Buddha images. There has been some attempt to restore a few of the carvings and false balustraded windows, but these days worshippers congregate in the modern whitewashed wat behind these shrines, leaving the atmospheric and appealingly quaint collection of decaying prangs and casuarina topiary to chickens, stray dogs and the occasional tourist.

Wat Mahathat

Heading west along Thanon Phra Song from Wat Kamphaeng Laeng, across the river you can see the prangs of Phetchaburi's most fully restored and important temple, **Wat Mahathat**, long before you reach them. Boasting the "Mahathat" title only since 1954 – when the requisite Buddha relics were donated by the king – it was probably founded in the fourteenth century, but suffered badly at the hands of the Burmese. The five landmark prangs at its heart are adorned with stucco figures of mythical creatures, though these are nothing compared with those on the roofs of the main viharn and the bot. Instead of tapering off into the usual serpentine *chofa*, the gables are studded with miniature *thep* and *deva* figures (angels and gods), which add an almost mischievous vitality to the place. In a similar vein, a couple of gold-embossed crocodiles snarl above the entrance to the bot, and a caricature carving of a bespectacled man rubs shoulders with mythical giants in a relief around the base of the gold Buddha, housed in a separate mondop nearby.

Khao Wang

Dominating Phetchaburi's western outskirts stands Rama IV's palace, a stew of mid-nineteenth-century Thai and European styles scattered over the crest of the hill known as **Khao Wang** ("Palace Hill"). During his day, the royal entourage would struggle its way up the steep brick path to the summit, but now there's a **cable car** (daily 8.30am–4.30pm; B70 return, including admission to Phra Nakhon Khiri), which starts from the western flank of the hill off Highway 4; there's also a path up the eastern flank, starting near Thanon Rajwithi. If you do walk up the hill, be warned that hundreds of quite aggressive monkeys hang out at its base and on the path to the top.

Up top, the wooded hill is littered with wats, prangs, chedis, whitewashed gazebos and lots more, in an ill-assorted combination of architectural idioms – the prang-topped viharn, washed all over in burnt sienna, is particularly ungainly. Whenever the king came on an excursion here, he stayed in the airy summer house, **Phra Nakhon Khiri** (daily 9am–4pm; B40; ⓦ www.thailandmuseum .com), with its Mediterranean-style shutters and verandas. Now a museum, it houses a moderately interesting collection of ceramics, furniture and other artefacts given to the royal family by foreign friends. Besides being cool and breezy, Khao Wang also proved to be a good star-gazing spot, so Rama IV, a keen astronomer (see also p.255), had an open-sided, glass-domed observatory built close to his sleeping quarters.

Eating

Phetchaburi's best **restaurant** is the *Rabieng Rimnum* (daily 8.30am–1am), an airy, wooden house with riverside tables attached to the guest house of the same name. It offers a long and interesting menu of inexpensive Thai dishes, from banana-blossom salad to tasty sugar-palm fruit curry with prawns, and is deservedly popular with local diners.

Almost half the shops in the town centre stock Phetchaburi's famous **sweet snacks** (*khanom*), as do many of the souvenir stalls crowding the base of Khao Wang and vendors at the day market on Thanon Matayawong. The most well known local speciality is *maw kaeng* (best sampled from a shop on the west side of Thanon Matayawong just north of Phongsuriya), a baked sweet egg custard made with mung beans and coconut and sometimes flavoured with lotus seeds, durian or taro. Other Phetchaburi classics to look out for include *khanom taan*, small, steamed, saffron-coloured cakes made with local palm sugar, coconut and rice flour, and wrapped in banana-leaf cases; and *thong yot*, orange balls of palm sugar and baked egg-yolk. The town is also known for **khao jae**: originally a Mon dish, it consists of rice in chilled, flower-scented water served with delicate, fried side dishes, such as shredded Chinese radish and balls of shrimp

③

paste, dried fish and palm sugar. It's available at the day market until sold out, usually around 3pm.

Cha-am and around

Forever in the shadow of its more famous neighbour, Hua Hin, 25km to the south, the resort of **CHA-AM** is nevertheless very popular with Thais on short breaks, and it sports a few package-holiday high-rises and Western-style restaurants for Europeans, too. Mostly, though, it's weekending families and partying student groups from Bangkok who eat and drink at the rows of umbrella-shaded tables and deckchairs on the sand, or brave the sea on banana boats or rubber tyres. The long, straight beach here is pleasantly shaded, though rather gritty and very narrow at high tide, and the water is perfectly swimmable, if not pristine. During the week the pace of life in Cha-am is slow, and it's easy to find a solitary spot under the thick canopy of casuarinas, particularly at the northerly end of the beach, but that's rarely possible at weekends, when prices shoot up and traffic thickens considerably.

Arrival and information

Through-**buses** and local services to and from Hua Hin and Phetchaburi stop on Thanon Phetkasem (Highway 4), close to the junction with Thanon Narathip, the main access road to the beach, 1km to the east. Bangkok–Cha-am air-con buses use the depot at the little plaza off the beachfront Thanon Ruamchit, just south of Thanon Narathip. If you're heading for Bangkok, you could also phone for the Hua Hin–Victory Monument air-con minibus to pick you up (see p.244). The **train station**, a few blocks west of the main Phetkasem–Narathip junction, is not included on the State Railways' English-language timetables but a handful of services a day, from either Hualamphong or Thonburi stations in Bangkok, stop there.

Cha-am has a functional pocket of development around the Phetkasem bus stop, but Thanon Ruamchit's three-kilometre seaside promenade is where you'll find most of the hotels, restaurants and a few other tourist-oriented businesses; Thanon Ruamchit's sois are numbered according to whether they're north or south of Thanon Narathip. There are **internet** terminals inside the CAT **phone office**, which is 200m west along Thanon Narathip from the seafront, and at several shops along Thanon Ruamchit – notably the photo shop sandwiched between the 7-Eleven at the Thanon Narathip junction and Siam Commercial Bank. A number of shops along the beachfront rent **motorbikes** as well as **bicycles**, tandems and even three-person bikes. The local **TAT** office (daily 8.30am–4.30pm; ☎032 471005, ⓔtatphet @tat.or.th), which theoretically provides information about Phetchaburi and Prachuap Khiri Khan provinces (including Hua Hin), is on Highway 4, about 1km south of the centre.

Accommodation

There are no obvious backpacker-oriented guest houses in Cha-am; instead you'll find mainly small, mid-range hotels, concentrated on Thanon Ruamchit and the adjoining sois, and upmarket, out-of-town resorts. Many Cha-am hotels give a fifteen- to thirty-percent discount from Sunday to Thursday.

Alila Cha-am 6km north of central Cha-am ☎032 709555, ⓦwww.alilahotels.com. Sleek, eco-friendly hideaway, featuring a triumphal, white-marble staircase up to the lobby and a huge reflective pool as its centrepiece. The accommodation blocks have a striking cubic design but are very comfortable for all that, while creative, beautifully presented food is served at the breezy restaurant, *Clouds Loft*. There are two swimming pools (plus seven villas with private pools), a spa and an events centre offering cooking classes, kite flying and bicycles. ❾

Dusit Resort Hua Hin 14km south of Cha-am and 9km north of Hua Hin at 1349 Thanon Phetkasem ☎032 520009, ⓦhuahin.dusit.com. One of the most luxurious spots on this stretch of coast, with 300 large, elegant rooms set around a tropical garden and lotus-filled lagoon. Facilities include four restaurants, a huge pool and children's pool, a spa, fitness centre, watersports, horseriding, tennis and squash courts and an Avis car rental desk. ❾

Golden Beach Cha-am Hotel Just south of Soi Cha-am North 8 at 208/14 Thanon Ruamchit ☎032 433833, ⓦwww.goldenbeachchaam.com. Good-value 20-storey hotel with a full-height atrium, a swimming pool, gym and internet access, set back from the promenade. The nicely appointed rooms have air-con, hot water, minibars and TVs, as well as balconies, most with sea-views. Breakfast included. ❻

Kaenchan Beach Hotel North of Soi Cha-am North 7 at 241/4 Thanon Ruamchit ☎032 470777–9. Stylish mid-sized hotel, with a papaya-coloured facade, a sixth-floor swimming pool and appealing, sleekly furnished rooms, all with air-con, TV, fridge and hot water, some with sea view. Also has some cheaper terraced bungalows in the garden behind. ❹–❺

Nirandorn 3 Just south of the Narathip junction on Thanon Ruamchit ☎032 470300, ℻032 470303. Clean, well-maintained hotel rooms and a few tightly packed, motel-style bungalows, mostly decorated in crisp, modern whites and browns, with air-con, TVs, fridges and hot water; all rooms in the hotel block are sea-facing, sporting balconies and deckchairs. ❹

Eating and drinking

The choice of **restaurants** in Cha-am is not a patch on the range you get in Hua Hin, but for a change from hotel food you might want to drop by *Poom*, north of Soi Cha-am North 6 at 274/1 Thanon Ruamchit, which serves a good selection of Thai-style seafood dishes (mostly B100–250) on its sea-view terrace – try the shrimps with garlic. Further north beyond Soi 7, *O-Zone* is a welcoming and popular bar-restaurant; attractions here include mellow live music early evening, followed by bands playing Thai and Western pop until midnight, and a menu that encompasses a few Western dishes such as spaghetti with meat sauce, one-plate Thai dishes and more complex offerings such as crispy fried catfish salad. On Thanon Chao Lay (which parallels Thanon Ruamchit), south of Narathip and the Bangkok bus depot, look out for the ornate garden of *Crawford's Irish Bar* (or call ☎032 471774 for a free pick-up); here you can eat Irish stew, steak and kidney pie and Thai food, play pool or watch big-screen sports, and in high season listen to a live band playing Sixties and Seventies covers and Irish ballads.

Phra Ratchaniwet Marukhathaiyawan

Ten kilometres south of Cha-am, on the way to Hua Hin, stands the lustrous seaside palace of Rama VI, **Phra Ratchaniwet Marukhathaiyawan** (aka Mrigadayavan Palace; daily except Wed 8.30am–4.30pm; B30), a rarely visited place, despite the easy access; the half-hourly Cha-am–Hua Hin buses stop within a couple of kilometres' walk of the palace at the sign for Rama VI Camp – just follow the road through the army compound.

Designed by the king himself in a Victorianized Thai style, but completed by an Italian architect in 1923, the complex of sixteen golden teak pavilions stands on over a thousand concrete columns to keep out ants. It's often referred to as "the palace of love and hope" as Rama VI first visited with his pregnant consort, who later miscarried, but it was abandoned to the corrosive sea air after the king's death in 1925. Restoration work began in the 1970s, and today most of the structure looks as it once did, a stylish composition of verandas and lattice-work painted in pastel shades of beige and blue, with an emphasis on cool simplicity. The spacious open hall in the north wing, hung with chandeliers and encircled by a first-floor balcony, was once used as a theatre, and the upstairs rooms, now furnished only with a few black-and-white portraits from the royal family photo album, were given over to royal attendants. The king stayed in the centre room, with the best sea view and access to the promenade, while the south wing contained the queen's apartments.

Hua Hin

Thailand's oldest beach resort, **HUA HIN** used to be little more than an overgrown fishing village with one exceptionally grand hotel, but the arrival of mass tourism, high-rise hotels and farang-managed hostess bars has made a serious dent in its once idiosyncratic charm. With the far superior beaches of Ko Samui, Krabi and Ko Samet so close at hand, there's little to draw the dedicated sunseeker here. The town's most distinctive attractions are its squid-pier restaurants and guest houses on Thanon Naretdamri, characterful spots to stay or enjoy fine seafood (though in recent years plans have been mooted to knock them down and build a shopping plaza), while at the other end of the scale the former *Railway Hotel* provides all the atmosphere you can afford. In addition, the town makes a convenient base for day-trips to Khao Sam Roi Yot National Park to the south and Pala-u Falls in Kaeng Krachan National Park to the west. If none of that appeals, you might consider stopping by for Hua Hin's well-respected **jazz festival** in June (ⓦ www.huahinjazzfest.com).

▲ Hua Hin train station

The **royal family** were Hua Hin's main visitors at the start of the twentieth century, but the place became more widely popular in the 1920s, when the opening of the Bangkok–Malaysia rail line made short excursions to the beach much more viable. The Victorian-style *Railway Hotel* was opened in 1922, originally as a necessary overnight stop on the three-day journey to Malaysia. At the same time Rama VI commissioned the nine-hole Royal Hua Hin Golf Course (now 18 holes; ☎032 512475) to the west of the station, and in 1926 Rama VII had his own summer palace, Klai Klangwon (Far from Worries), erected at the northern end of the beach. It was here, ironically, that Rama VII was staying in 1932 when the coup was launched in Bangkok against the system of absolute monarchy. The current king lives here most of the time now, apparently preferring the sea breezes to the traffic fumes of the capital, which means that the navy is on constant guard duty in the resort and the police are also on their best behaviour; consequently both Thais and expats consider Hua Hin an especially safe place to live and do business – hence the number of farang-oriented real estate agencies in the area.

Arrival and information

All services to the south from Bangkok stop at photogenic Hua Hin **train station**, which has changed little since it was built in the 1920s. It's a ten-minute walk east to the seafront from here, or hop on a motorbike taxi, samlor, tuk-tuk or songthaew. Tiny Hua Hin **airport** (☎032 522300–1) is 6km north of town, beside the Phetkasem Highway, and is currently served only by little SGA Cessna planes (ⓦwww.sga.co.th or www.nokair.com; 2 daily; 50min; B2300) to and from Bangkok's Suvarnabhumi Airport. Green songthaews run to Thanon Sa Song in town from the airport every twenty minutes.

Most government and many private **buses** use the main Baw Khaw Saw terminal, which is well to the south of the centre, between Thanon Phetkasem sois 96 and 98. These include second-class air-con services to and from Bangkok's Southern Bus Terminal, but much faster, first-class air-con buses to the same place, stopping only at Phetchaburi, leave from beside the *Sri Phetkasem* hotel on Thanon Sa Song; nearby, you'll find non-air-con buses to Pranburi (for a faster, air-con service, head for the Baw Khaw Saw). Non-air-con Cha-am and Phetchaburi buses from the Baw Khaw Saw also pick up at a spot just north of the junction of Thanon Phetkasem and Thanon Chomsin, while private **air-con minibuses** to and from Bangkok's Victory Monument are down a soi just behind (departing when full, usually around every 30min; 2hr 30min; B200; ☎086 992 7422). **Lomprayah** (☎032 553739, ⓦwww .lomprayah.com; book at their office on Soi Kanjanomai or through most travel agents) runs a twice-daily bus and catamaran service, beginning in Bangkok and picking up at Hua Hin's clocktower (daily at 8.30am and midnight) to Ko Tao (B850), Ko Pha Ngan (B1200) and Ko Samui (B1400) via Chumphon; you could catch one of their buses in the reverse direction to Banglamphu at 4.45pm or 9.45pm (B400).

There's a **tourist information** office (Mon–Fri 8.30am–8pm, Sat & Sun 9am–5pm; ☎032 511047, ext 100) in the local government buildings on the corner of Thanon Damnern Kasem and Thanon Phetkasem, with a satellite office just up Phetkasem at the clocktower (same times). TAT (ⓦwww .tourismthailand.org) also plan to open an information office in Hua Hin. Among Hua Hin's many English-language **publications** and maps, the *Hua Hin Pocket Guide*, a free, monthly booklet, is worth looking out for, while ⓦwww.huahinafterdark.com is a useful **website**.

Map labels:
- HUA HIN
- A & Cha-am
- 1, Thai Silk & Cultural Village
- SOI 53
- Fishing Pier
- THANON PHETKASEM
- THANON NAEBKEHAT
- SOI 68
- Pala-u Falls
- Polyclinic A
- Fish Market
- THANON CHOMSIN (SOI 55)
- SOI 70
- N
- THANON POONSUK
- Hua Hin Adventure Tour
- Night Market
- B
- SOI 72
- THANON DECHANUCHIT (SOI 51)
- THANON NARETDAMRI
- Boots
- i
- Night Market & Plaza
- Clocktower
- Pharmacy
- Pagoda
- THANON SA SONG
- C
- D
- THANON SRASONG
- THANON AMNUAYSIN (SOI 74)
- Wat Ampharam
- G
- Avis
- Thai Boxing Garden
- SOI BINTABAN
- THANON KAMNOADVITEE
- SOI159
- Lomprayah
- SOI KANJANOMAI
- 5
- H
- Satukarn Square
- Police Station
- Bookazine
- 7-Eleven
- THANON NARETDAMRI
- Tourist Police
- Train Station
- SOI 76
- DAMNERN KASEM (SOI 61)
- i
- Western Tours
- 6
- THANON PHETKASEM
- I
- TRANSPORT
- Airport songthaews B
- Non-air-con buses to Cha-am and Phetchaburi & air-con minibuses to Bangkok A D
- Private air-con buses to Bangkok D
- Songthaews to Khao Takiab & non-air-con buses to Pranburi C
- Khomapastr
- Sunseeker Tours
- J
- San Paulo Hospital
- 0   75 m
- Khao Sam Roi Yot National Park, main bus terminal, Soi 67, K & L
- Royal Golf Course

ACCOMMODATION				EATING & DRINKING	
All Nations	D	Jinning Beach Guest House	L	Chao Lay	3
Anantara Resort & Spa	A	Karoon Hut	C	Hagi	6
Baan Somboon	J	Pattana Guest Home	B	Monsoon	2
Bird	F	Sofitel Centara Grand	H & I	Som Moo Joom	4
Fu-Lay Guest House & Hotel	E	Veranda Lodge	K	Takeang Bar	5
Hilton Hua Hin	G			Youyen	1

Accommodation

A night or two at the former *Railway Hotel* (now the *Sofitel*) is reason in itself to visit Hua Hin, but there are plenty of other **places to stay**. The most unusual guest houses are those built on the squid piers, with rooms strung out along wooden jetties so you can hear, feel – and smell, especially at low tide – the sea beneath you, even if you can't afford a room with an actual sea view. Room rates at many places can drop significantly from Mondays to Thursdays, so don't be afraid to ask for a discount.

About fifteen minutes' walk south down the beach from the *Sofitel*, or 2km by road down Thanon Phetkasem, there's a little knot of accommodation on **Soi 67**. Here, facing each other across the short, narrow soi about 200m back from the beach, are a dozen little guest houses, mainly Scandinavian-Thai run, which share a swimming pool; none comprise more than twenty rooms and most charge about B900. They're very popular with older European couples, many of whom return for several months every winter, so booking is essential. **Resorts** beyond the northern fringes of Hua Hin, on the stretch of coast between Hua Hin and Cha-am, are described on p.242.

Inexpensive and moderate

All Nations 10 Thanon Dechanuchit ☏ 032 512747, ⓦ www.geocities.com/allnationsguest house/. A range of comfortable rooms in varying sizes with balconies, a few with distant sea views, some with air-con; bathrooms with hot water are shared between two rooms. Also has a roof terrace. Good value for Hua Hin and a useful source of local information. Long-term discounts in low season. Fan ❸, air-con ❹

Baan Somboon 13/4 Thanon Damnern Kasem ☏ 032 511538 or 032 553638, ⓦ www .baansomboon.com. Down a quiet but very central soi, this guest house divides between a lovely, old-fashioned house with polished teak floors, decorated with a melange of Thai antiques, woodcarvings and Western "old master" prints, and a small annexe. Spruce, homely rooms come with small, hot-water bathrooms, fridges, TVs and either fan or air-con, and there's a small garden crammed with plants, songbirds and a fish tank. Continental breakfast included. ❺

Bird 31/2 Thanon Naretdamri ☏ 032 511630, ⓔ birdguesthousehuahin@hotmail.com. A friendly little jetty guest house, painted light green and decorated with pot plants and shells. There's a wide variety of rooms, some recently refurbished, so choose carefully: all have TVs and cold-water bathrooms, some have a fridge and/or air-con, while the best fan room occupies the prime end-of-pier position. There's a nice, broad, breezy sea-view terrace at the end. Reserve ahead as it's very popular. Fan ❷–❸, air-con ❹

Fu-Lay Guest House and Hotel 110/1 Thanon Naretdamri, guest house ☏ 032 513145, hotel ☏ 032 513670, ⓦ fulay-huahin.com. *Fu-Lay* is in two halves, with guest house rooms strung along a jetty and hotel accommodation in a low-rise block across the street. The jetty guest house is the most stylish of its kind in Hua Hin, offering attractively appointed air-con rooms with nice hot-water bathrooms and TV, plus some cheap en-suite fan rooms (some with hot water) and a breezy seating area set right over the water. Air-con rooms in the hotel are similar, with some on the upper floors offering sea views from their shared verandas. Fan ❷–❸, air-con ❹–❺

Jinning Beach Guest House East end of Soi 67, off Thanon Phetkasem ☏ 032 532597, ⓦ www .jinningbeachguesthouse.com. Typical Soi 67 guest house under welcoming Danish-Thai management, with seventeen mostly good-sized air-con rooms, some with verandas, and all with TV and fridge. ❺

Karoon Hut 80 Thanon Naretdamri ☏ 032 530242, ⓕ 032 530737. Friendly jetty guest house, with decent fan- and air-con rooms, shared hot showers available and a nice big open-air seating area at the end of the pier. Fan ❸, air-con ❹

Pattana Guest Home 52 Thanon Naretdamri ☏ 032 513393, ⓔ huahinpattana@hotmail.com. Cosy, comfortable rooms with character, in an appealingly traditional, teak former fisherman's house, with a flower-strewn courtyard, quietly located at the end of a small soi. Some rooms have private, cold-water bathrooms, some have balconies. ❷–❸

Expensive

Anantara 5km north of Hua Hin at 43/1 Thanon Phetkasem ☏ 032 520250, ⓦ www.anantara.com. Set in effusive, beautifully designed tropical gardens that run right down to the shore, this is a lovely resort-style idyll, just out of town. Accommodation is in a series of Thai-style pavilions, whose stylishly appointed rooms use plenty of wood. The hotel offers Thai cooking and yoga classes, and has three restaurants, two free-form pools, a charming spa, a fitness centre, two tennis courts and its own stretch of beach, with watersports available. ❾

Hilton Hua Hin 33 Thanon Naretdamri ☏ 032 538999, ⓦ www.huahin.hilton.com. Set bang in the centre of Hua Hin's beachfront, the *Hilton's* high-rise profile disfigures the local skyline, but the facilities are extensive and the views excellent. There's a large, inviting lagoon-like swimming pool right on the seafront, a spa, a kids' club, a panoramic rooftop Chinese restaurant and an impressive indoor-outdoor water garden in the lobby. All three hundred rooms are large and comfortable and have sea-view balconies. ❾

Sofitel Centara Grand 1 Thanon Damnern Kasem ☏ 032 512021–38, ⓦ www.sofitel .com. The original Thai "destination hotel", the main building is a classic of colonial-style architecture, boasting high ceilings, polished wood panelling, period furniture, wide sea-view balconies and a huge, landscaped garden full of topiary animals. Across the road, lush gardens shelter gorgeous, all-white clapboard villas, most with their own marble pools with resistance machines, some with large outdoor jacuzzis. With a total of four swimming pools, a spa, tennis courts, a kids' club, canoeing and a giant chessboard, you need never leave the grounds. You can even tuck into a high tea buffet at *The Museum*, the original lobby, which now displays hotel memorabilia. ❾

Veranda Lodge Beachfront end of Soi 67, off Thanon Phetkasem ☏ 032 533678, ⓦ www .verandalodge.com. Chic 18-room boutique hotel set a little apart from the Soi 67 guest houses in its own beachfront garden. Deluxe rooms have a contemporary look (lime green, pink or china-blue walls) and petite balconies; suites have separate living rooms, small kitchen areas and sea-view balconies. All rooms have air-con and cable TV, and there's a small pool fed by a waterfall and a seafront terrace restaurant. ❽

The resort

The prettiest part of Hua Hin's five-kilometre-long **beach** is the patch in front of and to the south of the *Sofitel*, where the sand is at its softest and whitest. North of here the shore is crowded with tables and chairs belonging to a string of small restaurant shacks, beyond which the beach ends at a Chinese temple atop a flight of steps running down to Thanon Naretdamri. The coast to the north of the pagoda is dominated by the jetties and terraces of the squid-pier guest houses and seafood restaurants, the hub of the original fishing village, which dates back to the early nineteenth century.

South of the *Sofitel*, holiday homes and high-rise condos overshadow nearly the whole run of beach down to the promontory known as Khao Takiab (Chopstick Hill), 6km further south, but during the week it's fairly quiet along here, with just a few widely spaced food stalls along the broad, squeakily soft beach. Kiteboarding Asia (☎081 591 4592–3, ⓦwww.kiteboardingasia.com) offers **kiteboarding** courses and rental from a spot off the end of Soi 75/1, about 2.5km south of the *Sofitel* (B4000 for a 1-day course, B11,000 for 3 days; best conditions from March–May). **Khao Takiab** itself is a wooded outcrop surmounted by a temple and home to a troupe of monkeys; the road to the top is guarded by a tall, golden, standing Buddha and affords good coastal views. Green songthaews run to Khao Takiab every twenty minutes from Thanon Sa Song.

Excursions from Hua Hin

Hua Hin is well placed for **excursions** (see p.249 for tour operators) to Khao Sam Roi Yot National Park, Phetchaburi and Damnoen Saduak floating markets, as well as to the old summer palace of Phra Ratchaniwet Marukhathaiyawan just to the north (see p.242). Another popular day-trip from Hua Hin is 63km west to the fifteen-tiered **Pala-u Waterfall**, situated close to the Burmese border and within **Kaeng Krachan National Park** (B200; ⓦwww.dnp.go.th). Though the falls themselves are hardly exceptional, the route there takes you through lush, hilly landscape and past innumerable pineapple plantations. There's no public transport to the falls, but every tour operator features them in its programme (about B1300 per person). To get there under your own steam, follow the signs from the west end of Thanon Chomsin along Highway 3218. Once inside the park you'll see hundreds of butterflies and may also catch sight of monitor lizards and six species of hornbills. A slippery and occasionally steep path follows the river through the fairly dense jungle up to the falls, passing the (numbered) tiers en route to the remote fifteenth level, though most people opt to stop at the third level, which has the first pool of any decent depth (full of fish but not that clear) and is a half-hour walk from the car park.

Also worth singling out is the trip south to the **Pran River** run by eco-friendly Mermaid Cruises (☎032 632223 or 084 800 7400, ⓦwww.huahincruises.com; B1950 per person, minimum 2 people). The company uses quiet electric-powered longtails – solar-powered boats are planned – that allow you to get close to the wildlife, including three-metre monitor lizards, egrets, ospreys, wild peacocks and six species of kingfisher. The tour includes a stroll on a walkway through the mangrove swamps of the Pranburi Forest Park, lunch and transfers, and kayaking can be worked into the day if you're feeling energetic. Mermaid also run full-day **sea cruises** on a big boat down to Khao Sam Roi Yot, with the opportunity to see dolphins and to fish for squid (same price).

Eating, drinking and entertainment

Hua Hin is renowned for its **seafood**, and some of the best places to enjoy the local catch are the seafront and squid-pier restaurants along Thanon Naretdamri. Fish also features heavily at the large and lively **night market**, which sets up at sunset along Soi 72 (the western end of Thanon Dechanuchit). The biggest concentration of **bars** is in the network of sois between the *Hilton Hotel* and Wat Hua Hin, particularly along Soi Bintaban, Soi Kanjanomai and Thanon Poonsuk; many of these places are so-called "bar-beers", with lots of seating round the bar and hostesses dispensing beer and flirtation through the night.

The **Sasi Garden Theatre**, near the *Hyatt Regency*, about 4km south of the *Sofitel*, stages a performance of classical Thai **dance**, plus traditional fighting and contemporary ballet, with dinner nightly at 7pm (vegetarians catered for); book through any travel agent (B750 including set dinner and transfer; ☎032 512488 or 081 880 4004, ⓦ www.sasirestaurant.com). Tuesdays and Saturdays are fight nights at the **Thai Boxing Garden** off Thanon Poonsuk (☎032 515269), with programmes starting at 9pm and featuring five different fights (B350–500); it's owned by local *muay Thai* champion Khun Chop, who also runs Thai boxing classes every day at 5pm (B300 per hr).

Chao Lay 15 Thanon Naretdamri. Hua Hin's most famous jetty restaurant is deservedly popular, serving up high-quality seafood, including rock lobster, blue crab, scallops, cottonfish, mixed seafood hot plates and specialities such as mackerel curry soufflé (*haw mok*). Most main dishes cost B150–200. Daily 10am–10pm.

Hagi *Sofitel*, corner of Damnern Kasem and Naretdamri roads ☎032 512021–38. Tasty, authentic sushi, including delicious, hand-rolled *temaki* with crispy salmon skin and cucumber, tempura and *teppanyaki* grills at this elegant and welcoming Japanese restaurant. Pick your spot in the Zen-style garden, adorned with black slate, bamboo plants and a rocky pond, or in the air-con section with its sushi counter. Not too pricey, especially if you go for local, rather than imported seafood. Daily 3–11pm.

Monsoon 62 Thanon Naretdamri ☎032 531062. Atmospheric teakwood house, with brass fans, mellow lighting and a garden patio, that serves Thai and Vietnamese food, including Vietnamese *pho* (noodle soup), fresh spring rolls and *luc lac* (warm beef and watercress salad; B250), as well as duck curry and seafood. Also serves afternoon tea, tapas and a vegetarian menu. Daily from 3pm.

Som Moo Joom (Jek Pia) 51/6 Thanon Dechanuchit (corner of Thanon Naebkehat); no English sign. Exceptionally good seafood at very cheap prices has made this bare-bones evening restaurant (6–9pm) extremely popular with Thai holidaymakers. The trademark dish, *moo joom*, is a clear soup with vegetables and pork (or shrimp/squid), but the menu also covers the range of standard seafood dishes. At lunchtime, several popular stalls take over the space, offering seafood, satay and noodle soup with seafood.

Takeang Bar Soi Bintaban. Rustic bar, furnished every inch in wood, down to the wagon wheel lights, that makes a welcome change from the surrounding hostess bars. Live bands play country, rock and pop covers 9pm–2am nightly.

Youyen (Hua Hin Balcony) Thanon Naebkehat, near Soi 51 ☎032 531191–2. The works: lovely terrace seating by the sea, as well as air-con or open-air seating in a big, old house; keen service; and an excellent variety of authentic Thai food – try the delicious stir-fried shrimp with green sauce, green peppercorns, crispy garlic and sweet basil (B280).

Shopping

Hua Hin is famous for *pha khomapastr* (or *pha kiaw*), brightly coloured, hand-printed **cotton** with lovely, swirling *kannok* patterns, usually with strong elements of gold. At Khomapastr, 218 Thanon Phetkasem, just north of the hospital, you can buy it by the piece or yard, or made up into skirts or shirts, for example; it's particularly nice for triangular (or axe) cushion covers and bags. **Silk** and other handicrafts are available at the Thai Silk and Cultural Village (daily 9am–6pm; ☎032 531155–6, ⓦ www.mikeandcotailor.com) at 18 Thanon Naebkehat, about ten minutes' walk north from the town-centre clocktower, or phone for a free pick-up. Every visitor to the "village" (actually a series of open-air workshop pavilions and an air-conditioned shop) is given a free and well-explained guided tour of the entire silk production process, after which you are encouraged to pop in to the attached tailors' shop and get yourself suited up.

Listings

Banks and exchange There are currency-exchange counters all over the resort, especially on Thanon Damnern Kasem and Thanon Naretdamri; most of the main bank branches with ATMs are on Thanon Phetkasem.

Books Bookazine, on the corner of Damnern Kasem and Naretdamri roads. Secondhand bought and sold at BB Books, Satukarn Square, Thanon Damnern Kasem.

Car and motorbike rental Avis (☎032 531238, ⓦwww.avisthailand.com) is based at the *Thanavit Hotel*, on a soi near the corner of Amnuaysin and Phetkasem roads; several Hua Hin tour agencies also act as agents for Budget (☎02 203 0250, ⓦwww.budget.co.th). Among the transport touts who rent out mopeds for around B150 and more per day on Thanon Damnern Kasem, try Khun Dennapa (☎081 942 5615, or Khun Nui on ☎081 306 9179, ⓦwww.den-carrental.com), who also offers cars with or without driver – find them on the pavement in front of the *Sirin Hotel*, near 7-Eleven.

Emergencies For all emergencies, call the tourist police on the free, 24hr phoneline (☎1155), or contact them at their office opposite the *Sofitel* at the beachfront end of Thanon Damnern Kasem (☎032 515995).

Hospital San Paulo, 222 Thanon Phetkasem (☎032 532576–80), south of the tourist office.

Mountain biking Sea Hill Mountain Biking, based on Soi 126, Thanon Phetkasem ☎081 173 4469, ⓦwww.huahin.tourdeasia.org, offers a variety of guided day rides for B1600 and up, including transfers and lunch, as well as rental for B400 per day.

Pharmacy Several in the resort, including the helpful and well-stocked Medihouse (daily 9.30am–11pm) opposite the *Hilton* on Thanon Naretdamri.

Tour operators Western Tours, 11 Thanon Damnern Kasem (☎032 533303–4, ⓦwww .westerntourshuahin.com), sells air tickets and certain bus tickets, and has a weekly roster of day-trips to Khao Sam Roi Yot National Park (B1600 per person, kayaking on Khao Daeng canal B500 extra), Pala-u Falls (B1600), Phetchaburi (B1300) and Damnoen Saduak Floating Market (B1800). Hua Hin Adventure Tour, 69/8 Thanon Phetkasem (☎032 530313, ⓦwww.huahinadventuretour.com), does trips to the same places, plus Prachuap Khiri Khan (from B1700), a boat trip in Kaeng Krachan National Park (from B2200) and snorkelling (B2200). Sunseeker Tours, 166 Thanon Naretdamri (☎032 533666, ⓦwww.sunseekertours.com), offers cruises to local beaches on its motor yacht for around B1500 per person (minimum 4 people), as well as a sunset cruise around Khao Takiab and snorkelling trips.

Pak Nam Pran

The stretch of coast between Hua Hin and Chumphon barely registers on most foreign tourists' radar, but many better-off Bangkokians have favourite beaches in this area, the nicest of which is sophisticated **PAK NAM PRAN**. Just 30km or so south of Hua Hin, Pak Nam Pran used to cater only for families who owned beach villas here, but in the past few years the shorefront homes have been joined by a growing number of enticing, if pricey, boutique hotels, and signs are there's more development to come. For now, facilities consist of just a few minimarkets, car-rental outlets and independent restaurants, plus the possibility of organizing day-trips to nearby Khao Sam Roi Yot National Park through hotel staff. As along much of the Gulf coast, the beach itself is not exceptional (it has hardly any shade and is suffering from erosion in parts), but it is long, with fine sand, and nearly always empty, and you're quite likely to see dolphins playing within sight of the shore. The **beach** (also known as Hat Naresuan) stretches south from Pak Nam Pran town at the mouth of the Pran River – which is known for its colourful fishing boats, specializing in squid – for around 5km to Khao Kalok headland and the tiny Thao Kosa Forest Park.

Practicalities

Easiest **access** is via the town of **PRANBURI**, which straddles Highway 4 and the Southern Rail Line some 23km south of Hua Hin and is served by air-con buses from Bangkok's Southern Bus Terminal as well as local buses from Hua Hin (see p.244), which drop passengers close by the town centre's main intersection. There's no public transport from Pranburi to Pak Nam Pran beach, 10km away, but hotels can arrange transfers and any Pranburi songthaew driver will taxi you there. If making your own way, the easiest route is to turn east off Highway 4 at Pranburi's town-centre traffic lights and then take minor road 3168 down to the sea, picking up the relevant sign for your hotel.

Accommodation

Pak Nam Pran's charming **accommodation** is its biggest draw: for once, "boutique" is the appropriate term, as many of the hotels here offer a dozen or fewer rooms, and the style tends to be more arty than five-star, though you will certainly be comfortable. Some hotels aren't suitable for kids owing to their multiple levels and unfenced flights of steps. Breakfast is generally included in the price of the room. During weekends in high season (Nov–May) you'll need to book ahead; conversely, many places offer weekday discounts.

The following are spread over a two-kilometre stretch of the beachfront road, starting about 4km south of Pak Nam Pran town.

Aleenta Central Pak Nam Pran beach ☎032 618333, ⓦ www.aleenta.com. This stunningly designed hotel, divided between the Main Wing and the newer Frangipani Wing, 500m down the beach, is the resort's sleekest outfit, offering gorgeous circular, thatch-roofed bungalows and very tasteful villa-style rooms, most with uninterrupted sea views, decks and personal plunge pools. The feel is modernist chic, with elegantly understated local furnishings and huge glass windows, and iPods and wi-fi capability rather than TVs in every room. There's a small rooftop pool, a spa and restaurant; yoga and Thai cooking classes are available. ❾

Baan Panali Southern Pak Nam Pran beach, 200m south of *Huaplee* ☎086 051 2333 or 081 844 2484, ⓦ www.baan-panali.com. Not as striking as some of the beach's other offerings, but much cheaper and stylish enough: a cream-painted, adobe-style block with large, colourful, tiled rooms and a cute little swimming pool on its beachfront terrace. All but one room face the sea with a terrace or balcony, and all have air-con, hot showers, TVs and fridges; free bicycles. ❼

Huaplee Lazy Beach Central Pak Nam Pran beach ☎032 630554–5, ⓦ www .huapleelazybeach.com. This exceptionally cute collection of eight idiosyncratic white-cube beachfront rooms around a pretty lawn is the work of the architect-interior designer owners. It's a characterful place of whimsical, marine-themed interiors done out with white-painted wood floors, blue-and-white colour schemes and funky shell and driftwood decor. The rooms are airy and bright but all have air-con, as well as fridges and TVs (no hot water); some have fantastic sea-view terraces. ❽

Jamsawang Resort Northern Pak Nam Pran beach ☎032 570050, ⓦ www.jamsawang.com. One of the cheapest places to stay in the area, run by a friendly family. Dotted around a neatly trimmed garden across the road from the beach, all bungalows have air-con, hot water, fridge and TV; a few ("Thai-style") are comfortable if not especially sophisticated pale-blue concrete affairs, but most are pricier, more stylishly furnished, yellow-painted "Bali-style" bungalows, with garden bathrooms. ❻–❼

Pran Havana Central Pak Nam Pran beach ☎032 570077, ⓦ www.pranhavana.net. More white-cube architecture right next to *Huaplee* at this slightly bigger but equally charming beachfront accommodation, where the warren of individually furnished rooms is accessed by a series of whitewashed steps, wooden walkways and sea-view terraces. Interiors are idiosyncratic seaside-chic, personalized with hand-crafted furnishings and artworks. The price depends on the view; discounts offered for stays of two nights or more (except around Christmas and bank holidays) and on weekdays. ❽–❾

Eating

The simple shorefront **restaurant** *Krua Sawatdikan Khao Kalok* (unsigned in English), by the headland at the far southern end of Pak Nam Pran beach, about 1km from *Baan Panali*, has an extensive menu of very good seafood dishes; mosquitoes are a problem here though, so take repellent. On the edge of Pak Nam Pran town, about 2km north of the *Evason*, seafront *Krua Jaew* (also unsigned in English) offers an enormous, mid-priced menu of 120 mostly fish and seafood dishes, including very good crab curry, seafood curry soufflé (*haw mok thalay*) and pork with garlic.

Khao Sam Roi Yot National Park

With a name that translates as "The Mountain with Three Hundred Peaks", **KHAO SAM ROI YOT NATIONAL PARK** (B200; ☎032 619078, Ⓦ www.dnp.go.th), with its northern entrance 28km south of Pak Nam Pran beach or 63km from Hua Hin, encompasses a small but varied, mosquito-ridden, coastal zone of just 98 square kilometres. The dramatic limestone crags after which it is named are the dominant feature, looming 600m above the Gulf waters and the forested interior, but perhaps more significant are the mud flats and freshwater marsh which attract and provide a breeding ground for thousands of migratory birds. **Bird-watching** at Thung Khao Sam Roi Yot swamp is a major draw, but the famously photogenic Phraya Nakhon Khiri cave is the focus of most day-trips, while a few decent trails and a couple of secluded beaches provide added interest.

Orientation in the park is fairly straightforward. One main inland road runs roughly north–south through it from the R3168 (the road from Pranburi's main junction to Pak Nam Pran), passing in order the turn-off for **Hat Phu Noi**, a quiet, golden-sand beach that offers several resort alternatives to the park's accommodation; the northern park checkpoint; the turn-offs for Ban Bang Pu (the jumping-off point for Tham Phraya Nakhon), Ban Khung Tanot (for Tham Sai) and Hat Sam Phraya (all to the east); then going over Khao Daeng canal; before looping westwards around the main massif, past park headquarters and the southern checkpoint (14km from the northern checkpoint), to Highway 4 at kilometre-stone 286.5. A park brochure with a **map** is available at headquarters.

The park

Khao Sam Roi Yot's most visited attraction is the **Tham Phraya Nakhon** cave system, hidden high up on a cliffside above **Hat Laem Sala**, an unremarkable sandy bay that's inaccessible to vehicles. The usual way to get to Hat Laem Sala is by a five-minute boat ride from the knot of food stalls behind Wat Bang Pu on the edge of **Ban Bang Pu** fishing village (6km from the northern checkpoint); prices are fixed at B300 per boat for the round trip. It's also possible to walk over the headland from behind Wat Bang Pu to Hat Laem Sala, along a signed, but at times steep, 500-metre trail. From Hat Laem Sala, another taxing though shaded trail runs up the hillside to Tham Phraya Nakhon in around thirty minutes.

The huge twin **caves** are filled with stalactites and stalagmites and wreathed in lianas and gnarly trees, but their most dramatic features are the partially collapsed roofs, which allow the sunlight to stream in and illuminate the interiors, in particular beaming down on the famous royal pavilion, Phra Thi Nang Khua Kharunhad, which was built in the second cave in 1890 in honour of Rama V. A three-hour trek south from Tham Phraya Nakhon brings you to

Tham Sai, a thoroughly dark and dank limestone cave, complete with stalactites, stalagmites and petrified waterfalls; lamps are available here for B40. The trek offers some fine coastal views, but a shorter alternative is the twenty-minute trail from **Ban Khung Tanot** village (accessible by road, 8km on from the Ban Bang Pu turn-off).

The next turning off the main road will take you down to **Hat Sam Phraya**, a quiet, kilometre-long beach, while a little further on the road crosses mangrove-fringed **Khao Daeng canal**. From beside Wat Khao Daeng, on the west side of the main road here, you can charter a boat (B400 for up to six people) for a one-hour cruise that's best in the early morning or the late afternoon. Kayaks are available at the same spot for B300 per person (☏089 903 1619), or for B400 from Horizon, across the main road on the beach (☏089 504 3694). A couple of kilometres on, you can scramble up **Khao Daeng** itself, a 157-metre-high outcrop that offers good summit views over the coast, via a thirty-minute trail that begins near the park headquarters. The park's two official **nature trails** also start from close by HQ – the 30-minute "Horseshoe Trail" takes in the forest habitats of monkeys, squirrels and songbirds, while the 45-minute "Mangrove Trail" leads through the swampy domiciles of monitor lizards and egrets, with the chance of encountering long-tailed (crab-eating) macaques.

The park hosts up to three hundred species of **birds** and between September and November the mud flats are thick with migratory flocks from Siberia, China and northern Europe. To the west of Khao Sam Roi Yot lies Thailand's largest freshwater marsh, **Thung Khao Sam Roi Yot**, near the village of Rong Jai (Rong Che). It's accessed not from the main park road, but by turning east off Highway 4, 200m north of kilometre-stone 276, and continuing for 9km (the wetlands are outside the park boundary and not subject to the park entry fee). This is an excellent place for observing waders and songbirds, and is one of only two places in the country where the **purple heron** breeds; punts are available here for one-hour bird-watching excursions (B200 per person).

Practicalities

Like most of Thailand's national parks, Khao Sam Roi Yot is hard to explore without your own **transport**, and its sights are spread too far apart to walk between. The only public transport is an hourly **songthaew** service in the morning from Pranburi to Ban Bang Phu. Otherwise, you could charter a songthaew or motorbike taxi (around B200–300) from Pranburi, or hook up with Khun Lamai Thongsuk (☏089 533 8664), park information officer and local fixer, who offers a **taxi** service, for example, to headquarters from Pranburi (B700) or from the closer bus drop to the south at Kuiburi (B500); you could then rent a **bicycle** from him at HQ. The easiest options are to join a one-day **tour** from Hua Hin or Pak Nam Pran, or to rent your own transport from Hua Hin. As well as at HQ, there are national park **visitor centres** at Hat Laem Sala and Hat Sam Phraya.

Park accommodation is at headquarters, at Hat Sam Phraya, a beach between Khao Daeng canal and Ban Khung Tanot, and at Hat Laem Sala; all three sites have **restaurants**. At Hat Laem Sala it's a choice between camping, at B150–225 per tent, or staying in one of the national park bungalows (B1600–2200 for 6–9 people); at Sam Phraya it's camping only and at the headquarters it's bungalows only (B1200–1400 for 5–7 people). Bungalows must be booked ahead through the National Parks office in Bangkok (see p.40). It's also possible to stay at *Kasemsuk Bungalows* in Ban Khung Tanot near Tham Sai, which have fridges, TVs and cold-water en-suite bathrooms and belong to Khun Lamai (see above; fan ❸, air-con for up to 8 people ❼).

Hat Phu Noi

Given the limitations of the park accommodation, many people prefer to stay a few kilometres to the north at the long, pleasingly shaded beach of **HAT PHU NOI**, where dolphins are a daily sight from October to March – you may even spot the very rare, pink Indo-Pacific humpback dolphin. Hat Phu Noi is signed off the main road into the park, 4km before the northern checkpoint, and is at the end of a two-kilometre side road. Your best bet for a moderately priced **hotel** here is the long-running, eco-conscious and family-friendly *Dolphin Bay* (☏032 559333 or 032 559360, ⓦwww.dolphinbayresort.com; ❻), towards the northern end of the beach. The resort offers about fifty comfortable air-con rooms and bungalows with fridges, hot water and TVs, large children's and adults' pools set in an attractive, palm-fringed lawn, plus a big restaurant with a bar, kids' playground and internet access and wi-fi. Pick-ups from Pranburi (B250–350) can be arranged and there's no shortage of things to do once you're here: songthaews into the park (about B250), boat trips for dolphin-watching, snorkelling or night-time squid-fishing, plus kayak, motorbike and bicycle rental. At the bottom end of Hat Phu Noi but the top of the price range is *Brassiere Beach* (☏032 630554–5, ⓦwww.brassierebeach.com; ❾), under the same architect-designer owners as *Huaplee* at Pak Nam Pran (see p.250). It gets its name from the two conical Nom Sao ("Breast") islands offshore and the mainland spirit house where fishermen leave bras for good luck, and contains rooms with playful monikers like "La Perla". That may sound a bit naff to some, but the hotel itself is the height of quirky chic, airy and light-filled, with elegant tiled floors and a mostly white-and-blue colour scheme. All the spacious rooms have air-con and hot water, some have their own small jacuzzi and pool or an outdoor bathroom, and kayaks and bicycles are available.

South to Chumphon

Most foreign tourists zip through the region immediately south of Khao Sam Roi Yot en route to the more obvious delights of the Ko Samui archipelago, but the unexpectedly charming seaside town of **Prachuap Khiri Khan** and the small beach resort at **Ban Krud** are worth investigating if you're happy to substitute good seafood and laid-back Thai hospitality for full-on resort facilities. Twenty-two kilometres south of Prachuap, Highway 4 passes through Wang Duan, where a sign announces the fact that this is the narrowest part of Thailand: just 10.96km of Thai land separates the Gulf of Thailand from the Burmese border at this point.

Prachuap Khiri Khan and around

Despite lacking any must-see attractions, the tiny, unfrequented provincial capital of **PRACHUAP KHIRI KHAN**, 67km south of Pranburi, makes a pleasant place to break any journey up or down the coast. Its greatest asset is its setting, a huge, palm-fringed, half-moon bay, dotted with colourful fishing boats and tipped by a rocky outcrop at the north end and by a small group of jungly islands to the south – the waterfront promenade in the town centre is great for a seafood lunch with a view. There's a lovely **beach** in the next bay to the south, Ao Manao, and generally Prachuap is a fine spot to settle into small-town Thai life.

The town is contained in a small grid of streets that runs just 250m east to west, between the sea and the train station – with Highway 4 beyond the railway tracks

– and around 1km north to south, from the Khao Chong Krajok hill at the northern end to the Wing 5 air-force base in the south. **Orientation** couldn't be simpler: the major road across from the station to the pier is Thanon Kongkiat, and there are four main north–south roads: Thanon Phitak Chat near the station, Thanon Salacheep, Thanon Susuek and the seafront road, Thanon Chai Thalay.

Arrival and information

Nearly all services on the Southern Line from Bangkok stop at the **train station** at the western end of Thanon Kongkiat. The **non-air-con bus stop** for Chumphon (on departure, roughly hourly in the morning) is nearby on Thanon Kongkiat, while that for Pranburi and Hua Hin is one block east of the station and one block north, on east–west Thanon Thetsaban Bamrung; at the same spot stop second-class **air-con buses** from Bangkok (every 30min), via Pranburi, Hua Hin and Phetchaburi. First-class bus services **from Bangkok** (hourly), via Pranburi and Phetchaburi but bypassing Hua Hin, are based just south of Thanon Kongkiat, on Thanon Phitak Chat. On departure, for the fastest service to Chumphon and Surat Thani you need to wait on Highway 4 at the Highway Police office, about 1km north of the access road into town, for the air-con buses that whizz down from Bangkok; several south-bound services pick up passengers here between 8.30am and 11.30am (and many more around midnight).

There's a small, clued-up **tourist information** office (daily 8.30am–4.30pm, occasionally closing noon–1pm for lunch; ☏032 611491), where town maps are available, at the far northern end of town in a compound of provincial offices; it's on the ground floor of a modern, white building facing the beachfront road. The **post office** is directly behind the *Hadthong Hotel* on Thanon Susuek (Mon–Fri 8.30am–4.30pm, Sat & Sun 9am–noon), and there's an **internet** place one block west and around the corner to the left on Thanon Salacheep. There are ATMs and **currency exchange** on Thanon Salacheep and Thanon Phitak Chat, notably on the latter at Krung Thai Bank, which opens daily. **Motorbikes** can be rented from *Sun Beach Guesthouse*, **bicycles** from the *Hadthong Hotel*, **kayaks** from Kayak Adventures, on the seafront next to *Hadthong*.

Accommodation

Prachuap doesn't get enough visitors to support a wide choice of accommodation, but it does have one outstanding option, the *Sun Beach Guest House*.

Akan Ti Pak Sawatdikan Ao Manao ☏032 661088–90. If you don't mind cosying up to the Thai military, this spruce, wi-fi-enabled air-force hotel on the Wing 5 base puts you right on the beach. All rooms have sea-view balconies, air-con, hot water, TV and fridge. Ten-percent discount on weekdays. No English sign. ⑤

Hadthong Hotel 21 Thanon Susuek, but also with an entrance just south of the pier on the beachfront road ☏032 601050–6, ⒲www.hadthong.com. Well-run spot with comfortable rooms, many sporting balconies and great sea views, most with fridges, and air-con, hot water and TVs all round – plus a 15m swimming pool and snooker club. The cheapest options are in the basement. ③–④

Prachuapsuk Hotel 69 Thanon Susuek ☏032 611019. One of the cheapest places in town, popular with travelling salesmen, this friendly enough place has simple, slightly battered but large en-suite rooms with parquet floors. It's 50m south of the post office or about 300m southeast of the train station. Fan ①, air-con ②

🏃 **Sun Beach Guesthouse** 160 Thanon Chai Thalay, 500m or so down the promenade from the pier ☏032 604770, ⒲www.sunbeach -guesthouse.com. Run by a welcoming and helpful Thai-German couple, this palatial guest house is done out like a Mediterranean villa, with Corinthian columns and smart tiling everywhere. The bright, comfortable, sky-blue rooms come with air-con, hot water, fridges, TVs and balconies, with prices varying according to the quality of the sea view. There's a seductive pool and whirlpool, and free internet access. ④–⑤

The Town

Monkey-infested **Khao Chong Krajok** is Prachuap's main sight: if you climb the 417 steps from Thanon Salacheep to the golden-spired chedi at the summit you get a great perspective on the scalloped coast below and west to the mountainous Burmese border, just 12km away. At the far southern end of town, the long sandy beach at **Ao Manao** is the best place in the area for swimming and sunbathing. The bay is inside the air-force base, so you usually need to sign in at the checkpoint 2km north of the beach itself. To get there, just head south down Thanon Salacheep (or down the promenade and turn right) until you get to the base sign and checkpoint; a tuk-tuk to the beach should cost around B60. On weekdays you're likely to have the sand almost to yourself, but it's a very popular spot with Thai families on weekends when the stalls at the beachfront food centre do a roaring trade in the locally famous *som tam puu* (spicy papaya salad with fresh crab), which you can eat at the deckchairs and tables under the trees on the beach. You can walk to the north end of the bay to the base of an outcrop known as Khao Lommuak, where a memorial commemorates the battle that took place here between Thai and Japanese forces in World War II.

King Mongkut Memorial Park

About 12km south of town, on the beach at Wa Ko (Waghor), the main feature of the **King Mongkut Memorial Park of Science and Technology** (also signed as Phra Chomklao Science Park; daily 9am–5pm) is the extensive and well-stocked **Waghor Aquarium** (B20; ☏032 661726). Highlights include an underwater tunnel, touch pools and fish-feeding at 11am and 2pm (subject to change, so worth phoning in advance to check), and there are display boards and labels for most of the fish in English. It's nothing like as slick as Siam Ocean World in Bangkok, but then again it's less than a tenth of the price. About 500m south along the beach road, the park also contains an astronomy museum that's decidedly low-tech but with enough labels in English to maintain interest. To reach the park, the easiest way is to turn east off Highway 4 at kilometre-stone 335, or you can get there through Ao Manao air-force base, bearing left along the coast all the way.

The park marks the spot where **Rama IV**, known as the father of Thai science, came to observe a solar eclipse on August 18, 1868. Having predicted the eclipse's exact course, King Mongkut decided to publicize science among his subjects by mounting a large expedition, aiming specifically to quash their centuries-old fear that the sun was periodically swallowed by the dragon Rahoo. To this end, he invited scientists all the way from France and the British governor of Singapore, and himself turned up with fifty elephants and all his court, including the astrologers – who, as the leader of the French expedition noted, "could hardly be blamed if they did not display much enthusiasm for the whole project". Unfortunately, both the king and his 15-year-old son contracted malaria at Waghor; Mongkut passed away in Bangkok on October 1, but Chulalongkorn survived to become Thailand's most venerated king, Rama V.

Eating and drinking

Prachuap's famously good seafood is most cheaply sampled at the town's lively and varied main **night market**, which sets up shop in the empty lot around the junction of Thanon Kongkiat and Thanon Phitak Chat. *Plern Smud*, south of the pier on Thanon Chai Thalay, alongside the *Hadthong Hotel*, is probably the town's best **restaurant**, serving delicious pan-fried oysters on its seafood-dominated menu (English-sign at the Thanon Suseuk entrance only, not on the beachfront road). Try not to let the awful muzak put you off at *Ma-prow*, an otherwise mellow, rustic, airy restaurant a little further down the front – it serves tasty crispy fish with green mango salad, as well as a few Western dishes such as fish'n'chips. The sounds improve markedly at *Rome Bar* (*MC Club*) just to the south, an excellent spot for a waterside **drink**, hung with motorcycle memorabilia and home to some of the friendliest bikers you're ever likely to meet.

Ban Krud

Graced with a tranquil, five-kilometre sweep of white sand, pale-blue sea and swaying casuarinas, **BAN KRUD**, 70km south of Prachuap, supports a dozen or so fairly upmarket bungalow outfits and seafood restaurants along the central stretch of its beachfront road. At the beach's northern end are a colourful fishing village, which hosts a Thursday afternoon market, and a panoramic headland beyond, **Khao Thongchai**, that's dominated by the fourteen-metre-high Phra Phut Kitti Sirichai Buddha image and its sparkling modern temple, Wat Phra Mahathat Phraphat. Crowned with nine golden chedis, the temple displays an impressive fusion of traditional and contemporary features, including a series of charming modern stained-glass windows depicting Buddhist stories; reach it via a 1500-metre-long road that spirals up from the beachfront. Other than a visit to the temple and possibly a snorkelling trip to Ko Thalu (B400 per person), the main pastime in Ban Krud is sitting under the trees and enjoying a long seafood lunch or dinner.

Practicalities

Most southbound **buses** drop passengers on Highway 4, from where motorbike taxis (with sidecars) cover the 8km down to the beach; just two Bangkok–Bang Saphan air-con buses a day stop at Ban Krud itself. Near Ban Krud **train** station, about 1km from the beach, are a couple of **ATMs** but no bank as yet. About 1km north of the central beachfront T-junction is friendly *Sala Thai* (℡032 695181, Ⓦ www.salathaibeachresort.com; ❸–❺, including breakfast; discounts for long stays), whose cutesy wooden **bungalows** with air-con, hot water and TV are spread around a pretty garden just across the road from the beach; it also has a restaurant and a popular burger bar. North of the headland and the ramshackle youth hostel, 4km from *Sala Thai* on Hat Tangsai, ✳ *Bayview* is a very welcoming and relaxed spot with a swimming pool, a kids' pool and a lovely area for deckchairs under the beachside casuarinas (℡032 695566–7, Ⓦ www.bayview beachresort.com; ❻ breakfast included). All the well-spaced bungalows boast air-con and hot water, and there's an excellent restaurant, internet access and wi-fi, free bicycles, and kayaks and motorbikes to rent. A surprisingly urban feel pervades *Lumra Resort*, 2km further on (℡032 602714, Ⓦ www.reflections-thai .com; ❻ breakfast included), which often hosts holistic healing courses (Ⓦ www .naturalhealing.co.th). Sister resort to Bangkok's *Reflections Hotel* (see p.102), the concrete rooms, running back in two rows from the beach, have a similarly colourful, modern style. All feature air-con and hot water, but the pick of the bunch are the two beachside affairs, one of which sports an outside wooden bath. Internet access and free pick-ups from the train or bus are available.

Chumphon and around

South Thailand officially starts at **CHUMPHON**, where the main highway splits into west- and east-coast branches, and inevitably the provincial capital saddles itself with the title "gateway to the south". Most tourists take this tag literally and use the town as nothing more than a transport interchange between the Bangkok train and **boats to Ko Tao**, so the town is well equipped to serve these passers-through, offering clued-up travel agents, efficient transport links and plenty of internet cafés. In truth, there's little call for exploring the fairly average beaches, islands and reefs around town when the varied and attractive strands of Ko Tao are just a short hop away, while the Chumphon National Museum is little short of pitiful. The most rewarding direction for day-trippers is inland, through Chumphon province's famously abundant fruit orchards to **Pha To** for some **rafting** on the Lang Suan River.

Arrival and information

Chumphon **train station** is on the northwest edge of town, less than ten minutes' walk from most guest houses and hotels. The government **bus station** is 11km south of town on Highway 4, connected to the centre by songthaews (B50 per person), though if they have enough customers, long-distance services will sometimes drop in town. There are also several private **air-con bus and minibus** services that depart from other parts of town (see map for locations), including minibuses to Ranong (in theory hourly, but will leave early if full); Rungkit buses to Phuket, via Ranong and Khao Lak (4 daily; ☎077 812324), and Chokeanan Tour buses to Bangkok (3 daily; ☎077 511757).

The best **fixer** in town, offering a personal, unbiased service, is Suda at her eponymous guest house, who, as well as tickets to Ko Tao, can arrange bus and train tickets, including hourly air-con minibuses to Surat Thani; twice-daily visa runs via Ranong to Burma (from B650, excluding B500 visa); **motorbike** (B200 per day) and **car rental** (B1000–1300 per day); and jungle treks and rafting on the Lang Suan river (see p.259). Among the bigger multi-purpose **travel agents**, avoid if you can busy Farang Bar, which resembles a human meat-processing factory, in favour of Fame, which offers the same transport services as Suda, as well as a guest house and restaurant, snorkelling trips, airline tickets and twice-daily air-con minibuses to Krabi and Ko Lanta that coincide with boats from Ko Tao.

The provincial **tourist information** centre, at the junction of Thanon Kromluang and Thanon Sala Daeng (Mon–Fri 8.30am–4.30pm; ☏077 504833), can do little more than hand out brochures, while the TAT office covering Chumphon and Ranong (☏077 556191, ⓦwww.tourismthailand.org) is currently 16km south on Highway 4, though planning a move closer to the centre.

Accommodation

Chumphon's **guest houses** are well used to accommodating Ko Tao-bound travellers, so most are happy to store luggage until the night boat leaves and offer shower services to non-guests.

Fame 188/20–21 Thanon Sala Daeng ☏077 571077, ⓦwww.chumphon-kohtao.com. Above the restaurant and tour agency of the same name, this place has good-sized and very clean rooms with mattresses on the floor, fans and hot water in either shared or en-suite bathrooms; internet access. **❶**
Chumphon Guest House (Kae House) Soi 1, Thanon Kromluang ☏077 502900. Sociable place with 24hr check-in, hosted by the effervescent Kae, on a quiet, residential soi with a pleasant outdoor bar-restaurant. Motorcycle rental, boat tickets, internet and informal cooking classes and day-trips around Chumphon. Accommodation ranges from small rooms out front with mattresses on the floor to en-suites with beds in the main wooden house. **❶–❷**

Novotel 15km southeast near Pak Nam ☏077 529529, ⓦwww.novotel-chumphon.com. This new, low-rise luxury hotel on Paradornpab beach, done out in an unobtrusive Thai contemporary style, features spacious rooms with balconies and lots of dark wood, two restaurants (Mediterranean and Thai/international), two swimming pools, a spa, fitness centre, golf course and kids' club. Substantial discounts online. **❽**
Paradorn Inn 180/12 Thanon Sala Daeng ☏077 511598 or 077 511500, ⓦwww.chumphon-paradorn.com. The best value of the town's mid-range hotels, though not particularly welcoming, a shining, white block where all rooms have air-con, hot water and TV. There's a restaurant too. **❷**

Boats to Ko Tao and beyond

There are several different **boat services from Chumphon to Ko Tao**, tickets for all of which are sold by travel agents and guest houses in town. Of these, the Songserm Express is the most likely to be cancelled if the weather is very bad.

The fastest services – about ninety minutes – are **Lomprayah Catamaran** (daily 7am & 1pm; B550; ☏077 558212–3, ⓦwww.lomprayah.com), which has an office on Thanon Tapao and departs from Ao Thung Makham Noi, 27km south of Chumphon; and **Seatran** (daily 7am, plus 1pm in high season; B550; ☏077 521052, ⓦwww.seatranferry.com), which departs from Pak Nam port, 14km southeast of Chumphon. **Songserm Express** (7am; 2hr 30min; B450; ☏077 506205, ⓦwww.songserm-expressboat.com) has an office on Thanon Tapao (tickets can also be bought from a State Railways booth at the station) and departs from Tha Yang, 7km east of town. These three companies' boats continue to Ko Pha Ngan (B750 with Lomprayah and Seatran, B620 Songserm) and Ko Samui (B850 Lomprayah and Seatran, B770 Songserm). All of the above prices include transport to the pier from town, with pick-ups available even from guest houses and from the station, including off the overnight train from Bangkok that arrives around 4am.

There are also two late-night services from Tha Yang, both of which do pick-ups from town guest houses at around 10pm (B50 per person). Of these, the slightly pricier **Ko Jaroen car ferry** (daily 11pm; 6hr; B300; ☏077 580030) is more comfortable and has blankets and pillows for passengers; cheapest of all is the smaller **midnight boat** (daily midnight; 6hr; B200; ☏077 553052).

Suda Guest House Thanon Sala Daeng Soi 3 (aka Soi Bangkok Bank), 30m off Thanon Tha Tapao ☎077 504366 or 085 571 2229. Chumphon's most genuine and welcoming home-stay, offering seven clean and well-maintained fan or air-con rooms, most with shared hot-water bathrooms, one en-suite, in the owner's own modern house. Plenty of information available, B20 showers for passers-through and much more (see p.257). Phone for free transport from train or bus station. Fan ❶–❸, air-con ❷–❸

Eating and drinking

The cheapest place to eat is the **night market**, which sets up along both sides of Thanon Kromluang and is an enjoyable place to munch your way through a selection of fried noodles, barbecued chicken and sticky, coconut-laced sweets. *CSL* on Thanon Sala Daeng is a friendly, informative **internet café** (which also offers drinks, sandwiches and egg breakfasts).

Ahaan Jeh Right next to *Fame* on Thanon Sala Daeng. Tiny place offering a ready-cooked buffet of Thai-Chinese vegetarian food at B20 per serving. Daily 7am to about 5pm, though most dishes will be finished long before then.

Boom (The Bakery Café) Thanon Tha Tapao. Good espressos, tasty brownies and other Western and Thai cakes. Mon–Sat 7.30am–8pm.

Fame 188/20-21 Thanon Sala Daeng. Travellers' restaurant specializing in Italian food, including pizzas available whole or by the slice, as well as plenty of other home-baked goods, Indian dhal, loads of sandwiches, and huge American and veggie breakfasts (B100–120). Daily 4.30am–midnight.

Green Kitchen Behind *Jansom Chumphon Hotel,* between Thanon Suksumer and Thanon Sala Daeng. Good, authentic Vietnamese cuisine such as grilled beef in betel leaves and fresh spring rolls, plus Thai food and some European dishes.

Kozo Sushi Off Thanon Suksumer opposite *Green Kitchen* ☎077 512239. Great Japanese restaurant offering a huge range of dishes on a picture menu – big portions, reasonable prices. Closed Mon.

Papa 2000 Across from the train station on Thanon Kromluang. One of the liveliest places to eat dinner is this huge restaurant, open air with an air-con room, which has an extensive menu of fresh seafood and salads, plenty of Western and Chinese standards – and live music every evening, as well as an attached nightclub.

Inland to Pha To

Chumphon's reputation as a major **fruit-growing** region is well established, and a great way to appreciate this is to head inland for some **rafting** on the pretty if not spectacular Lang Suan River near **PHA TO**. Beginning 71km down Highway 41 from the provincial capital, Highway 4006 winds its exceptionally scenic way westwards for 26km to Pha To, passing through endless plantations of papayas, mangosteens, durians, bananas, rambutans, pomelos and coconuts, plus the occasional *robusta* coffee field as well (over fifty percent of Thailand's *robusta* coffee crop is grown in Chumphon).

Travel agencies and guest houses in town offer either whitewater rafting in an inflatable or a more gentle float on a PVC punt from around B1000 per person, depending on the size of the group, including transport and lunch. Whitewater rafting is also offered by the Thai-Dutch eco-tourism outfit Runs 'N Roses (☎086 172 1090, ⊛www.runsnroses.com), based near Pak Song village in Pha To municipality (see the website on how to get there). In addition, they have **accommodation** in their lodge or bungalows (❺ for two people including all meals) and many more **trips and activities**, including trekking, mountain-bike rental, horse riding, yoga, Thai cooking, cultural and language workshops and plenty for kids to do. Profits support the **Thai Child Development Foundation**, which welcomes donations and volunteers – see p.65 for more details.

Chaiya and around

About 140km south of Chumphon, **CHAIYA** was the capital of southern Thailand under the Srivijayan empire, which fanned out from Sumatra between the eighth and thirteenth centuries. Today there's little to mark the passing of the Srivijayan civilization, but this small, sleepy town has gained new fame as the site of **Wat Suan Mokkh**, a progressively minded temple whose meditation retreats account for the bulk of Chaiya's foreign visitors (most Thais only stop to buy the famous local salted eggs). Unless you're interested in one of the retreats, the town is best visited on a day-trip, either as a break in the journey south, or as an excursion from Surat Thani.

Chaiya is 3km east of Highway 41, the main road down this section of the Gulf coast: **buses** running between Chumphon and Surat Thani will drop you off on the highway, from where you can catch a motorbike taxi or walk into town; from Surat Thani's Talat Kaset II bus station, hourly air-con minibuses and more frequent but slower songthaews take around an hour to reach Chaiya. The town also lies on the main Southern Rail Line, served by nine, mostly overnight **trains** from Bangkok (8–11hr).

The Town

The main sight in Chaiya is **Wat Phra Boromathat** on the western side of town, where the ninth-century chedi – one of very few surviving examples of Srivijayan architecture – is said to contain relics of the Buddha himself. Hidden away behind the viharn in a pretty, red-tiled cloister, the chedi looks like an oversized wedding cake surrounded by an ornamental moat. Its unusual square tiers are spiked with smaller chedis and decorated with gilt, in a style similar to the temples of central Java.

The **National Museum** (Wed–Sun 8am–4pm; B30; ⓦwww.thailandmuseum .com), on the eastern side of the temple, is a bit of a disappointment. Although the Srivijaya period produced some of Thailand's finest sculpture, much of it discovered at Chaiya, the best pieces have been carted off to the National Museum in Bangkok. Replicas have been left in their stead, which are shown alongside fragments of some original statues, two intricately worked 2000-year-old bronze drums, found at Chaiya and Ko Samui, and various examples of Thai handicrafts. The best remaining pieces are a calm and elegant sixth- to seventh-century stone image of the Buddha meditating from Wat Phra Boromathat, and an equally serene head of a Buddha image, Ayutthayan-style in pink sandstone, from **Wat Kaeo**, an imposing ninth- or tenth-century brick chedi on the south side of town. Heading towards the centre from Wat Phra Boromathat, you can reach this chedi by taking the first paved road on the right, which brings you first to the restored base of the chedi at Wat Long, and then after 1km to Wat Kaeo, enclosed by a thick ring of trees. Here you can poke around the murky antechambers of the chedi, three of which house images of the Buddha subduing Mara.

Wat Suan Mokkh

The forest temple of **Wat Suan Mokkh** (Garden of Liberation), 6km south of Chaiya on Highway 41, was founded by the abbot of Wat Phra Boromathat, **Buddhadasa Bhikkhu**, southern Thailand's most revered monk until his death in 1993 at the age of 87. His radical, back-to-basics philosophy, encompassing Christian, Zen and Taoist influences, lives on and continues to draw Thais from all over the country to the temple, as well as hundreds of foreigners. It's not necessary to sign up for one of the wat's retreats to enjoy the temple, however

– all buses from Surat Thani to Chaiya and Chumphon pass the wat, so it's easy to drop by for a quiet stroll through the wooded grounds.

The layout of the wat is centred on the Golden Hill: scrambling up between trees and monks' huts, past the cremation site of Buddhadasa Bhikkhu, you'll reach a hushed clearing on top of the hill, which is the temple's holiest meeting-place, a simple open-air platform decorated with images of Buddha and the Wheel of Law. At the base of the hill, the outer walls of the Spiritual Theatre are lined with bas-reliefs, replicas of originals in India, which depict scenes from the life of the Buddha. Inside, every centimetre is covered with colourful didactic painting, executed by resident monks and visitors in a jumble of realistic and surrealistic styles.

Meditation retreats

Meditation retreats are led by Western and Thai teachers over the first ten days of every month at the International Dharma Heritage, a purpose-built compound 1km from the main temple at Wat Suan Mokkh. Large numbers of foreign travellers, both novices and experienced meditators, turn up for the retreats, which are intended as a challenging exercise in mental development – it's not an opportunity to relax and live at low cost for a few days. Conditions imitate the rigorous lifestyle of a *bhikkhu* (monk) as far as possible, each day beginning before dawn with meditation according to the Anapanasati method, which aims to achieve mindfulness by focusing on the breathing process. Although talks are given on Dharma (the doctrines of the Buddha – as interpreted by Buddhadasa Bhikkhu) and meditation technique, most of each day is spent practising Anapanasati in solitude. To aid concentration, participants maintain a rule of silence, broken only by daily chanting sessions, although supervisors are available for individual interviews if there are any questions or problems. Men and women are segregated into separate dormitory blocks and, like monks, are expected to help out with chores.

Each course has space for about one hundred people – turn up at the information desk in Wat Suan Mokkh as early as possible on the last day of the month to enrol. The fee is B1500 per person, which includes two vegetarian meals a day and accommodation in simple cells. Bring a flashlight (or buy one outside the temple gates) and any other supplies you'll need for the ten days – participants are encouraged not to leave the premises during the retreat. For further information, go to Ⓦwww.suanmokkh.org or telephone ☏077 531552 or 077 431597.

Surat Thani

Uninspiring **SURAT THANI** ("City of the Good People"), 60km south of Chaiya, is generally worth visiting only as the jumping-off point for the Samui archipelago. Strung along the south bank of the Tapi River, with a busy port for rubber and coconuts near the river mouth, the town is experiencing rapid economic growth and paralysing traffic jams. It might be worth a stay, however, when the Chak Phra Festival (see box, p.262) is on, or as a base for seeing the nearby historic town of Chaiya.

Arrival and information

Buses arrive at three different locations, two of which are on Thanon Taladmai in the centre of town: Talat Kaset I on the north side of the road (Phunphin,

The Chak Phra Festival

At the start of the eleventh lunar month (usually in October) the people of Surat Thani celebrate the end of Buddhist Lent with the **Chak Phra Festival** (Pulling the Buddha), which symbolizes the Buddha's return to earth after a monsoon season spent preaching to his mother in heaven. On the Tapi River, tugboats pull the town's principal Buddha image on a raft decorated with huge nagas, while on land sleigh-like floats bearing Buddha images and colourful flags and parasols are hauled across the countryside and through the streets. As the monks have been confined to their monasteries for three months, the end of Lent is also the time to give them generous offerings in the *kathin* ceremony, of which Surat Thani has its own version, called Thot Pha Pa, when the offerings are hung on tree branches planted in front of the houses before dawn. Longboat races, between teams from all over the south, are also held during the festival.

Chumphon, non-air-con Nakhon Si Thammarat and Ranong services, and other local buses) and opposite at Talat Kaset II (many long-distance buses, including those from Krabi, Phang Nga, Phuket, Hat Yai, and Ranong and Nakhon Si Thammarat air-con services). The Baw Khaw Saw terminal, 2km southwest of the centre on the road towards Phunphin, handles mostly services from Bangkok. If you're coming from points south by **air-conditioned minibus** or **share-taxi**, you should be deposited at the door of your destination.

Arriving by **train** means arriving at **Phunphin**, 13km to the west, from where buses run into Surat Thani, via the Baw Khaw Saw bus terminal, every ten minutes or so between around 5.30am and 7.30pm, while share-taxis (based in Surat at Talat Kaset II) charge B140 to charter the whole car into town. It's also possible to buy through-tickets to Ko Samui and Ko Pha Ngan from the train station for the same price as they would be from Surat Thani town, including a connecting bus to the relevant pier. There's a basic **hotel**, *Queen* (℡077 311125; ❶), in Phunphin if you get really stuck.

Arriving by **air**, you can take a B100 Phantip minibus for the 27km journey south from the airport (℡077 441230–1) into Surat Thani, or a combination ticket to Ko Samui (B350) or Ko Pha Ngan (B550). Budget (℡077 441166) have an outlet at the airport for **car rental**.

TAT's helpful office is at the western end of town at 5 Thanon Taladmai (daily 8.30am–noon & 1–4.30pm; ℡077 288817–9 or 077 282352, ✉tatsurat@tat .or.th), while the **tourist police** (℡1155 or 077 405575) are based out on the southern bypass near the junction with Thanon Srivichai, the westward continuation of Thanon Taladmai. Small **share-songthaews** buzz around town, charging around B15–20 per person. There's **internet access**, as well as good coffee, snacks and breakfast, at *Tukta Capuccino* on Thanon Taladmai in front of Talat Kaset II. Surat's best **travel agency** is the helpful and reliable Phantip, in front of Talat Kaset I at 293/6–8 Thanon Taladmai (℡077 272230 or 077 272906), where among many other things you can book train and plane tickets. Thai Airways have an office at 3/27–28 Thanon Karoonrat, off Thanon Chonkasem (℡077 272610).

Accommodation

Most budget **accommodation** in Surat Thani is noisy, grotty and overpriced – you may consider yourself better off on a night boat to one of the islands. If you do get stuck here, head for the *Ban Don Hotel*, above a restaurant at 268/2 Thanon Namuang (℡077 272167; fan ❷, air-con ❸), where most of the very clean rooms with en-suite cold-water bathrooms and fans or air-con and TV are set back from the noise of the main road. In the moderate range, *100 Islands* (*Roi Koh*; ☎077 201150–8, ⓦwww.roikoh.com; ❹ including breakfast) offers attractive, comfortable rooms with air-con and hot water, a small spa and a decent-sized pool set in a lush garden with a waterfall. However, it's right out on the southern bypass near the tourist police and opposite Tesco Lotus. On the western side of the centre by the TAT office, *Wangtai Hotel*, 1 Thanon Taladmai (☎077 283020–39, ⓦwww.wangtaisurat.com; ❺), is Surat Thani's best upmarket option, and surprisingly good value, with over two hundred large, smart rooms around a swimming pool and several good restaurants.

Eating

For large portions of tasty, inexpensive Thai and Chinese **food**, head for the restaurant on the ground floor of the *Ban Don Hotel*. The **night market** between Thanon Si Chaiya and Thanon Ban Don displays an eye-catching range of dishes; a smaller offshoot by Ban Don pier offers less choice but is handy if you're taking a night boat. Also near the night-boat piers on Thanon Ban Don, *Milano* has an authentic oven turning out very tasty and reasonably priced pizza, and serves panini, home-made pasta and a few Italian fish and meat main courses; you can augment these with *som tam* from the popular stall that parks outside in the afternoons. During the day, an unnamed vegetarian restaurant, one block east of Talat Kaset II bus station on Thanon Tha Thong, offers a wide selection of cheap and delicious tray food or fried noodles, (look for the yellow flags outside and a sign saying "vegetarian food"; closes 4pm).

Moving on

For **moving on** to the rest of the mainland, air-con minibuses (to Chumphon, Ranong, Ratchabrapa Dam, Khao Sok, Phang Nga, Phuket, Krabi, Trang and

Boat operators in Surat

Details of **boats to Ko Samui**, **Ko Pha Ngan** and **Ko Tao** are given in the account of each island – see p.266, p.85 and p.297. Phunphin and the bus stations are teeming with touts, with transport waiting to escort you to their employer's boat service to the islands – they're generally reliable, but make sure you don't get talked onto the wrong boat. If you manage to avoid getting hustled, you can buy tickets from Phantip (see p.262) or direct from the **boat operators**: Seatran, in the petrol station on Thanon Taladmai opposite Wat Thammabucha (⊕077 275060–2, ⓦwww.seatranferry.com), has vehicle ferries to Samui (with connecting buses), from Don Sak, 68km east of Surat; Samui Tour, 326/12 Thanon Taladmai (⊕077 282352), handles buses to Ko Samui via the Raja vehicle ferries (ⓦwww.rajaferry.com) from Don Sak; Phangan Tour, also on Thanon Taladmai (⊕077 205799), handles buses to Don Sak for the Raja vehicle ferries to Ko Pha Ngan; tickets for Songserm Express Boats (ⓦwww.songserm -expressboat.com) to Samui, Pha Ngan and Tao (and from there to Chumphon) from Don Sak (or sometimes from the pier at Pak Nam Tapi, just east of Surat town) can be bought at ADV on Thanon Rung Ruang (⊕077 205418–9). The night boats to Ko Samui, Ko Pha Ngan and Ko Tao line up during the day at Ban Don Pier in the centre of Surat; as they're barely glorified cargo boats, it's worth going along there as early as you can, as the first to buy tickets get the more comfortable upstairs mattresses.

Nakhon Si Thammarat) and a dwindling number of share-taxis congregate around Talat Kaset II. Be aware, however, that there have been many reports of overcharging and **scams** by unregistered agents selling tickets for minibus and bus services out of Surat, especially involving any kind of combination ticket, including those heading for Khao Sok National Park (see p.337), Phuket, Krabi and Malaysia. To avoid this, either go direct to the relevant air-con minibus office rather than let yourself be hustled by a tout at Talat Kaset II bus station (local offices are generally on the west side of the station, long-distance ones on the east side, and they all have to be authorized by the provincial office); or walk the short distance to the reliable Phantip Travel (see p.262); or buy a bus ticket direct from the station. If you're heading for Krabi, as well as air-con minibuses, there are roughly hourly non-air-con buses from Talat Kaset II and faster hourly air-con buses through Phantip. For Bangkok, choose between second-class, first-class and VIP buses from the Baw Khaw Saw, and a cheaper VIP service from Sophon Tour, near the corner of Talat Luang and Ban Don roads (⊕077 420275). Buses heading out of Surat to Phang Nga, Phuket and Hat Yai also make a stop at Phunphin train station, which might save you a journey into town and out again. If you're flying out of Surat, you can catch the **airport minibus** from town at the Phantip office (B100; see p.262).

Ko Samui

A million visitors a year, ranging from globetrotting backpackers to suitcase-toting fortnighters, come to southern Thailand just for the beautiful beaches of **KO SAMUI**, 80km from Surat. At 15km across and down, Samui is generally large enough to cope with this diversity – except during the rush at Christmas and New Year – and the paradisal sands and clear blue seas have to a surprising extent kept their good looks, enhanced by a thick fringe of palm trees that gives a harvest of more than two million coconuts each month. However, development behind the beaches – which has brought the islanders far greater prosperity than the crop could ever provide – speeds along in a messy, haphazard fashion with little concern for the environment. At least there's a local bye-law limiting new construction to the height of a coconut palm (usually about three storeys), though this has not deterred either the luxury hotel groups or the real-estate developers who have recently been throwing up estates of second homes for Thais and foreigners.

The island's most appealing beach, **Chaweng**, has seen the heaviest, most crowded development and is now the most expensive place to stay, though it does offer by far the best range of amenities and nightlife, ranging from tawdry bar-beers to hip nightclubs. Its slightly smaller neighbour, **Lamai**, lags a little behind in terms of looks and top-end development, but retains large pockets of backpacker bungalow resorts. The other favourite for backpackers is **Maenam**, which though less attractive again, is markedly quiet, with plenty of room to breathe between the beach and the round-island road. Adjacent **Bophut** is similar in appearance, but generally more sophisticated, with a cluster of boutique resorts, fine restaurants and a distinct Mediterranean feel in its congenial beachfront village. **Choeng Mon**, set apart in Samui's northeast corner, offers something different again: the small, part-sandy, part-rocky bay is tranquil and pretty, the seafront between the handful of upmarket hotels is comparatively undeveloped, and Chaweng's nightlife is within easy striking distance.

No particular **season** is best for coming to Ko Samui (see also p.237). The northeast monsoon blows heaviest in November, but can bring rain at any time between October and January, and sometimes causes high waves and strong currents, especially on the east coast. January is often breezy, March and April are very hot, and between May and October the southwest monsoon blows onto Samui's west coast and causes some rain. At the lower end of Samui's **accommodation** scale, there are very few bungalows left for under B400, while at the most upmarket places you can pay well over B4000 for the highest international standards. The prices listed are based on high-season rates, but out of season (roughly April–June, Oct & Nov) dramatic reductions are possible.

Getting to the island

The most obvious way of getting to Ko Samui is on a **boat** from the **Surat Thani** area; for contact details of **transport companies** in Surat, see p.264. Services may fluctuate according to demand, but the longest-established ferry is the night boat that leaves **Ban Don** pier in Surat Thani itself for **Na Thon** – the main port on Samui – at 11pm every night (6hr); tickets (B200) are sold at the pier on the day of departure.

All the following operators charge B240 to get to Samui, including a connecting bus from Surat or Phunphin train station; total journey time from Surat is around three hours. From **Don Sak**, 68km east of Surat, hourly Seatran vehicle ferries (on Ko Samui ☏077 426000–2) and one Songserm Express Boat a day, at 8am (though sometimes this departs from Pak Nam Tapi pier, on the east side of Surat town; on Ko Samui ☏077 426092), run to Na Thon. Raja vehicle ferries run hourly between Don Sak and **Lipa Noi**, 8km south of Na Thon (on Samui ☏077 415230–3); every two hours to coincide with alternate boats, Samui Tour (on Samui ☏077 421092) runs buses from Surat or Phunphin via the ferry to Na Thon.

From Bangkok, you can buy a through ticket with the State Railway – B498, for example, in a second-class fan bunk, upper tier, to Phunphin station, plus B240 for your bus and boat from there. Overnight bus and boat packages from the government-run Southern Terminal cost around B650 on a basic air-con bus to B1000 on a VIP bus, and are far preferable to the cheap deals offered by dodgy travel agents on Thanon Khao San, as the vehicles used on these latter services are often substandard and many thefts have been reported. The ferry companies, Seatran and Lomprayah (see p.44), offer packages from Bangkok on their VIP buses and fast boats from **Chumphon** (see p.258) for around B1000; the latter also has a "buffet" ticket, allowing you to stop off at Ko Tao and Ko Phangan on the way for B1250.

At the top of the range, you can get to Ko Samui direct **by air** from Suvarna-bhumi Airport with Thai Airways (3 daily; in Bangkok ☏02 356 1111, ⓦwww .thaiair.com), or with Bangkok Airways (about 20 daily; in Bangkok ☏02 265 5555, at Samui airport ☏077 428555, ⓦwww.bangkokair.com), which also operates flights from Chiang Mai, Hong Kong, Krabi, Pattaya, Phuket and Singapore (Dubai, Shanghai, Bali and Kuala Lumpur routes are planned). Berjaya Airlines (ⓦwww.berjaya-air.com) currently operates a twice-weekly service from Kuala Lumpur, while Firefly (ⓦwww.fireflyz.com.my) runs four times a week from KL, more sporadically from Penang.

Air-con minibuses meet incoming flights (and connect with departures) at the **airport** in the northeastern tip of the island, charging B120 to Chaweng for example. As well as bar and restaurant facilities, the recently rebuilt terminals have currency-exchange facilities and ATMs, a Bookazine bookshop, a post office with international telephones and several car rental outlets including Avis (☎084 700 8161, ⓦ www.avisthailand.com).

For information about boats from Ko Samui to **Ko Pha Ngan** see p.285, and to **Ko Tao** see p.297; all offer the same service in the return direction.

Information and island transport

TAT runs a small but helpful office (daily 8.30am–noon & 1–4.30pm; ☎077 420504 or 077 420720–2, ⓔ tatsamui@tat.or.th), tucked away on an unnamed side road in Na Thon (north of the pier and inland from the post office). Another useful source of **information** is ⓦ samui.sawadee.com, a website set up by a German based at Lamai, which handles, among other things, direct bookings at a range of local hotels.

Songthaews, which congregate at the car park near the southerly pier in Na Thon, cover a variety of set routes during the daytime, either heading off clockwise or anti-clockwise on Route 4169, to serve all the beaches; destinations are marked in English and fares range from B40 to Maenam to B60 to Chaweng or Lamai. In the evening, they tend to operate more like taxis and you'll have to negotiate a fare to get them to take you exactly where you want to go. Ko Samui now also sports dozens of **air-con taxis**. By law, they're required to use their meters (flag fall B50, on top of which they're allowed to add a B90 service charge), but at the moment you'd be wasting your breath trying to persuade any driver to do so (though this may change); you might be lucky enough to settle on a flat fare of B300 from Maenam to Chaweng, for example, after some hard bargaining. You'll also see some **motorbike taxis** buzzing about the island, which charge from B30 for a local drop, up to B250 from Na Thon to Chaweng. You can **rent a motorbike** from around B150 in Na Thon and on the main beaches. Dozens are killed on Samui's roads each year, so proceed with great caution, and wear a helmet – apart from any other consideration, you can be landed with an on-the-spot B500 fine by police for not wearing one. In addition, thieves have been snatching bags from the front

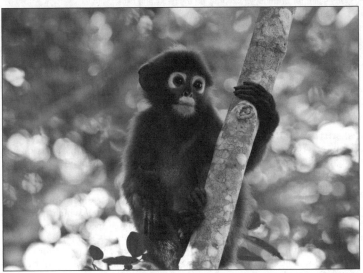

▲ Young long-tailed macaque on Ko Wua Talab, Ang Thong National Marine Park

Even if you don't get your buns off the beach for the rest of your stay, it's worth taking at least a day out to visit the beautiful **Ang Thong National Marine Park**, a lush, dense group of 42 small islands strewn like dragon's teeth over the deep-blue Gulf of Thailand, 31km west of Samui. Once a haven for pirate junks, then a Royal Thai Navy training base, the islands and their coral reefs, white-sand beaches and virgin rainforest are now preserved under the aegis of the National Parks Department. Erosion of the soft limestone has dug caves and chiselled out fantastic shapes that are variously said to resemble seals, a rhinoceros, a Buddha image and even the temple complex at Angkor.

The surrounding waters are home to dolphins, wary of humans because local fishermen catch them for their meat, and *pla thu* (short-bodied mackerel), part of the national staple diet, which gather in huge numbers between February and April to spawn around the islands. On land, long-tailed macaques, leopard cats, common wild pig, sea otters, squirrels, monitor lizards and pythons are found, as well as dusky langurs, which, because they have no natural enemies here, are unusually friendly and easy to spot. Around forty bird species have had confirmed sightings, including the white-rumped shama, noted for its singing, the brahminy kite, black baza, little heron, Eurasian woodcock, several species of pigeon, kingfisher and wagtail, as well as common and hill mynah; island caves shelter swiftlets, whose homes are stolen for bird's nest soup (see box, p.418). The largest land mass in the group is **Ko Wua Talab** (Sleeping Cow Island) where the park headquarters shelter in a hollow behind the small beach. From there it's a steep 430-metre climb (about 1hr return; bring walking sandals or shoes) to the island's peak to gawp at the panorama, which is especially fine at sunrise and sunset: in the distance, Ko Samui, Ko Pha Ngan and the mainland; nearer at hand, the jagged edges of the surrounding archipelago; and below the peak, a secret cove on the western side and an almost sheer drop to the clear blue sea to the east. Another climb from the beach, only 200m but even harder going (allow 40min return), leads to Tham Buabok, a cave set high in the cliff-face. Some of the stalactites and stalagmites are said to resemble lotuses, hence the cave's appellation, "Waving Lotus". If you're visiting in September, look out for the white, violet-dotted petals of **lady's slipper orchids**, which grow on the rocks and cliffs.

The park's name Ang Thong, "Golden Bowl", comes from a landlocked saltwater lake, 250m in diameter, on **Ko Mae Ko** to the north of Ko Wua Talab, which was the inspiration for the setting of bestselling novel and film, *The Beach*. A well-made path (allow 30min return) leads from the beach through natural rock tunnels to the rim of the cliff wall that encircles the lake, affording another stunning view of the archipelago

baskets of moving motorbikes on Samui, so keep yours on your person – or think about upgrading to a **four-wheel drive**, for around B800 a day.

Island activities

For most visitors, the days are spent indulging in a few watersports or just lying on the beach waiting for the next drinks' seller, hair-braider or masseur to come along; some make it to one of Samui's many **spas**, whether independent or attached to one of the posh hotels, for further pampering. For something more active, you should not miss the almost supernatural beauty of the **Ang Thong National Marine Park** (see above), which comprises many of the eighty islands in the Samui archipelago. (Speedboat day-trips to Ko Tao are also available, but they cost a lot of money – around B2000 – for a matter of hours on the island.) A day-trip by rented car or motorbike on the fifty-kilometre round-island road, perhaps making time for a visit to the **Butterfly Garden** and a meal at *Ban Hua Thanon Seafood*, both on the south and the shallow, blue-green water far below, which is connected to the sea by a natural underground tunnel.

Practicalities

There are no scheduled **boats to Ang Thong**, only organized day-trips, which can be easily booked through your accommodation or a travel agent. The main operator is Highway, near *Coffee Island* on Thanon Chonwithi (℡077 421290, Ⓦwww .highseatour.com), whose big boats leave Na Thon every day at 8.30am, returning at around 5pm. In between, there's a two-hour stop to explore Ko Wua Talab (just enough time to visit the viewpoint, the cave and have a quick swim, so don't dally), lunch, some cruising through the archipelago, a visit to the viewpoint over the lake on Ko Mae Ko and a snorkelling stop. Tickets cost B1300 per person (or B1800 with kayaking), including pick-up from your accommodation and the B200 national park fee. Several companies in Maenam, Bangrak and Bophut on Samui do speedboat day-trips to Ang Thong (around B1500–1800), and the luxury yacht *Seatran Discovery* does the trip three times a week for B2700, including hotel pick-up, national park fee and kayaking (℡077 426000–2, Ⓦwww.seatrandiscovery.com). Similar trips run from Ko Pha Ngan (see p.286) and less frequently from Ko Tao; *Seaflower* on Ko Pha Ngan does three-day "treks" (see p.295).

If you want to make the most of the park's beautiful scenery of strange rock formations and hidden caves, take a dedicated **kayaking** trip with Blue Stars, based at Gallery Lafayette near the *Green Mango* nightclub on Chaweng (℡077 413231, Ⓦwww.bluestars.info). For a one-day trip, taking in the lake at Ko Mae Ko and kayaking and snorkelling among the islands in the northern part of the park, they charge B2200, including pick-up from your accommodation and boat over to the park, buffet lunch, snorkelling gear and national-park entrance fee; ask about overnight trips, which were suspended at the time of writing.

It's also possible to **stay** at the headquarters on **Ko Wua Talab**, where the National Parks Department maintains simple two- to eight-berth bungalows (B500–1400) and a restaurant. To book accommodation contact the Ang Thong National Marine Park Headquarters (℡077 280222 or 077 286025, Ⓦwww.dnp.go.th), or the Parks Department in Bangkok (see p.40). Camping is also possible in specified areas, and two-person tents can be rented for around B200 a night. If you do want to stay, you can go over on a boat-trip ticket – it's valid for a return on a later day. For getting around the archipelago from Ko Wua Talab, it's possible to charter a motorboat from the fishermen who live in the park; the best snorkelling is off Ko Thai Plao.

coast, will throw up plenty more fine beaches. Otherwise you could hook up with a **round-island tour**, whether on land with Mr Ung's Magical Safari Tours (bookable through travel agents or your accommodation or contact ℡077 230114 or 081 895 5657; from B1200), which will take you up the rough tracks of the mountainous interior to some spectacular viewpoints; or by boat with Samui Evasion, who sail from Bangrak, via lunch and snorkelling on Ko Taen, and the bird's-nest islands of Ko Si Ko Ha, to Nathon (Mon, Wed & Sat; B1700 per person; ℡077 230159, Ⓦwww.samuievasion.com).

Ko Samui has around a dozen **scuba-diving** companies, offering trips for qualified divers and a wide variety of courses throughout the year, and there's a **recompression chamber** at Bangrak (℡077 427427, Ⓦwww.sssnetwork .com). Most trips for experienced divers, however, head for the waters around Ko Tao (see p.298), which contain the best sites in the region; a day's outing costs around B3500, but of course if you can make your own way to Ko Tao, you'll save money and have more time in the water. Established and reliable

PADI Five-Star dive centres, each with several branches around the island, include Samui International Diving School (Ⓦwww.planet-scuba.net), which has its head office at the *Malibu Resort* towards the north end of Central Chaweng (Ⓣ077 422386); and Easy Divers (Ⓦwww.easydivers-thailand.com), which has its head office opposite *Sandsea Resort*, towards the north end of Lamai (Ⓣ077 231190).

Other worthwhile **activities**, such as treetop cable rides on Maenam, go-karting on Bophut, Thai cookery courses on Chaweng and Lamai, meditation courses near Lamai, and boat trips to Ko Taen and Ko Madsum off the south coast, are detailed in the relevant accounts below.

Na Thon

The island capital, **NA THON**, at the top of the long western coast, is a frenetic half-built town which most travellers use only as a service station before hitting the sand: although most of the main beaches now have post offices, currency-exchange facilities, ATMs, supermarkets, travel agents and clinics, the biggest and best concentration of amenities is here. The town's layout is simple: the three piers come to land at the promenade, Thanon Chonvithi, which is paralleled first by narrow Thanon Ang Thong, then by Thanon Taweeratpakdee, aka Route 4169, the round-island road; the main cross-street is Thanon Na Amphoe, by the central pier.

Accommodation and eating

If you really need a **place to stay** in Na Thon, your best bet is the *Nathon Residence* (Ⓣ077 236081, Ⓣ&Ⓕ077 236058; ❸), on Thanon Taweeratpakdee next to Siam City Bank and near the market, a well-run place with a café downstairs and large, plain but spotless tiled rooms with air-con, cable TV and en-suite bathrooms, some with hot water and fridge, upstairs.

Several stalls and small cafés purvey inexpensive Thai **food** around the market on Thanon Taweeratpakdee and on Thanon Chonvithi (including a lively night market by the piers), and there are plenty of Western-orientated places around the piers. Justifiably popular, especially for breakfast, is cheerful and inexpensive *RT (Roung Thong) Bakery*, with one branch on Thanon Taweeratpakdee, another opposite the southerly pier and a landmark sister operation, a little to the north on the corner of Thanon Na Amphoe, *Coffee Island*: all serve sandwiches, pancakes and pizzas, as well as Thai food and a wide variety of coffees.

Listings

Bookshop Nathon Book Store, Thanon Na Amphoe (Ⓣ077 420332; may close Sun in the future), is a good, helpful secondhand place, with some new titles and a café.

Buses The Baw Khaw Saw government bus station, about 1km south of town off Route 4169, handles a variety of through buses to Bangkok. Phantip travel agent (see below) runs through buses to Krabi, Phang Nga, Phuket and Hat Yai from Na Thon.

Hospital The state hospital (Ⓣ077 421230–2) is 3km south of town off Route 4169.

Immigration office 2km south of town down Route 4169 (Mon–Fri 8.30am–4.30pm; Ⓣ077 421069).

Massage The Garden Home Health Center, 2km north along Route 4169 in Ban Bang Makham, dispenses good traditional Thai massages during the day (B350 per hr; booking advisable on Ⓣ077 421311).

Post office and internet Towards the northern end of the promenade, just north of the central pier (Mon–Fri 8.30am–4.30pm, Sat & Sun 9am–noon), with poste restante and packing services. International telephones and Catnet internet access upstairs (Mon–Fri 8.30am–4pm).

Tourist police 1km south of the town centre on Route 4169 Ⓣ1155, 077 421281 or 077 421360.

Travel agent The reliable Phantip is on Thanon Taweeratpakdee (north of Thanon Na Amphoe; Ⓣ077 421221–2).

Laem Yai and Maenam

LAEM YAI, the steep, tree-covered headland at the island's northwest tip, shelters one exceptional top-end resort, while in contrast, **MAENAM**, 13km from Na Thon in the middle of the north coast, is Samui's most popular beach for budget travellers. Its exposed four-kilometre bay is not the island's prettiest, being more of a broad dent in the coastline, and the sloping, white-sand beach is relatively narrow and slightly coarse by Samui's high standards. But Maenam features many of the cheapest bungalows on the island, unspoilt views of fishing boats and Ko Pha Ngan, and good swimming. Despite the recent opening of some upmarket developments on the shoreline and a golf course in the hills behind, this is still the quietest and most laid-back of the major beaches, with little in the way of nightlife. Though now heavily built up with multi-storey concrete shophouses, the main road is set back far from the sea, connected to the beachside bungalows by an intricate maze of minor roads through the trees. At the midpoint of the bay, **Ban Maenam** is centred on a low-key road down to the fishing pier, which is flanked by several cafés, internet shops, travel agents and small boutiques.

You might be tempted off the beach for a couple of hours of fun with Canopy Adventures (℡077 414150–1 or 087 046 7307, ⊛www.canopyadventuresthailand .com; B1750, including transfers), who offer **cable rides** between treehouses and past waterfalls in the hills 4km above Maenam. At the far west end of the beach, beyond Wat Na Phra Larn, KSK (℡086 267 1169, ⊛www.kohsamuikiteboarding .com) runs **kiteboarding** courses, starting from B4200 for half a day. Other **watersports** such as wakeboarding and kayaking are available at *Moonhut* (see below). For **car rental** on Maenam, contact the helpful Petch Travel (℡077 425276 or 081 797 0699; from around B900 per day), who offer free delivery.

Accommodation

As well as several luxury resorts, Maenam has around thirty inexpensive and moderately priced bungalow complexes, most offering a spread of accommodation; the cheapest of these are at the far eastern end of the bay.

Four Seasons Resort Laem Yai ℡077 243000, ⊛www.fourseasons.com. Ultra-luxury spot, with its own small beach, enjoying lovely views of Ko Pha Ngan and the setting sun. Each of the large, beautiful villas, designed for indoor-outdoor living in a subtle, modern but natural style, using brown and marine colours, has its own infinity-edge swimming pool; the resort lays on a wide range of other activities, from spa treatments to sailing and Thai boxing classes. ❾

Harry's At the far western end, near Wat Na Phra Larn ℡077 425447, ⊛www.harrys-samui.com. Popular, well-run place, set back about 100m from the beach amidst a secluded and shady tropical garden. The public areas feature strong elements of traditional Thai architecture, though not the bungalows, which are nevertheless clean and spacious, with air-con and hot water. Internet access and a decent-sized swimming pool and jacuzzi. ❺

Lolita On the east side of *Santiburi Resort* ℡077 425134, ℮lolitakohsamui@yahoo.com. Quiet, friendly and efficiently run resort in a colourful, grassy garden on a long stretch of beach. Large,

wooden, fan-cooled bungalows, some with hot water, and much smarter air-con rooms cluster around a kitsch, circular bar-restaurant adorned with pink Corinthian columns. Fan ❹, air-con ❻

Maenam Resort 500m west of the village, just beyond *Santiburi Resort* ℡077 247287, ⊛www .maenamresort.com. A welcoming, tranquil resort (no TVs) in tidy, shady grounds, with an especially long stretch of beach. The rooms and large bungalows, with verandas, hot water and fans or air-con, offer good-value comfort. Internet access. Fan ❺, air-con ❻

Maenam Villa At the far eastern end of the bay, next to *SR* ℡077 425501, ℮maenamvilla @hotmail.com. Friendly spot on a spacious triangular plot with kayaks available. Choose between clean, bright, older bungalows with verandas and large, concrete, open-plan villas with air-con, hot water and small terraces. ❸

Moonhut On the east side of the village ℡077 425247, ⊛www.moonhutsamui.com. Welcoming English-run place on a large, sandy, shady plot, with a lively restaurant and beach bar and colourful, substantial and very clean bungalows; all have verandas, mosquito screens, wall fans and en-suite bathrooms, some have hot water and air-con. Fan ③, air-con ⑤

Santiburi Resort 500m west of the village ☏077 425031–8, ☻www.santiburi.com. Luxury hotel in beautifully landscaped grounds spread around a huge freshwater swimming pool and stream. Accommodation is mostly in Thai-style villas, inspired by Rama IV's summer palace at Phetchaburi, each with a large bathroom and separate sitting area, furnished in luxurious traditional design; each has a private outdoor plunge pool. Facilities include watersports on the private stretch of beach, tennis courts, squash court and golf course, a spa, car rental, and an excellent "royal" cuisine restaurant, the *Sala Thai*. ⑨

Shangrilah West of *Maenam Resort*, served by the same access road ☏077 425189, ☻www.geocities.com/pk_shangrilah. Sprawling onto the nicest, widest stretch of sand along Maenam, a flower-strewn compound of smart, well-maintained though tightly packed, en-suite bungalows with verandas, ceiling fans and decent furniture; some boast air-con and hot water, and there are some rather ugly luxury villas with fridges and cable TV. The restaurant serves good Thai food. Fan ④, air-con ⑤–⑦

SR At the far eastern end of the bay ☏077 427524–30, ☻sr_bungalow@hotmail.com. A quiet, welcoming, good-value place, set in a narrow flower garden, with a very good restaurant. Accommodation is in large, smart, concrete bungalows with bathrooms (some with hot water), verandas and chairs. At the moment only those in pole position on the beachfront have air-con, though the owners may install it throughout. Fan ③, air-con ④

Eating

Most visitors to Maenam **eat** in their hotel or resort restaurant, though a couple of other places stand out. At the west end of the bay, signposted on a lane that runs east from Wat Na Phra Larn, *Sunshine Gourmet* does a bit of everything, from cappuccino and home-made yoghurt for all-day breakfast, through own-baked pies, sandwiches and cakes, to international, especially German, main courses, seafood and other Thai dishes. *Angela's Bakery*, opposite the police station on the main through-road to the east of the pier, is a popular, daytime-only expat hangout, offering great breakfasts and a wide choice of sandwiches, salads, soups and Western main courses, as well as cakes, pies and home-made chocolates.

Bophut

The next bay east is **BOPHUT**, which has a similar look to Maenam but shows a marked difference in atmosphere and facilities, with a noticeable French influence. The quiet, two-kilometre beach attracts a mix of young and old travellers, as well as families, and **Ban Bophut**, now tagged "**Fisherman's Village**", at the east end of the bay, is well geared to meet their needs, with a sprinkling of

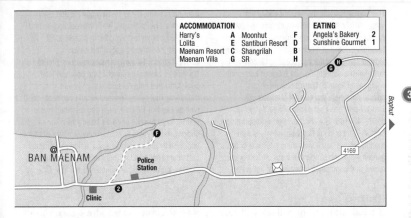

ACCOMMODATION					EATING	
Harry's	A	Moonhut	F		Angela's Bakery	2
Lolita	E	Santiburi Resort	D		Sunshine Gourmet	1
Maenam Resort	C	Shangrilah	B			
Maenam Villa	G	SR	H			

BAN MAENAM

Police Station

Clinic

boutique hotels, and a bank, ATMs, scuba-diving outlets, travel agents, internet cafés, supermarkets and a small bookstore, Book World, at the start of Route 4171, for magazines and bestsellers. While through traffic sticks to Route 4169 to Chaweng and Route 4171 towards the airport, development of the village has been reasonably sensitive, preserving many of its old wooden shophouses on the two narrow, largely car-free streets that meet at a T-junction by the pier. At night, in sharp contrast to Chaweng's frenetic beach road, it's a fine place for a promenade, with a concentration of good upmarket restaurants and low-key farang-run bars. The nicest part of the beach itself is at the west end of the bay, towards *Zazen* resort, but again the sand is slightly coarse by Samui's standards.

Samui Go-kart, a **go-karting** track (daily 9am–8/9pm; ☎077 425097; from B500 for 10min) on the main road 1km west of the village, offers everyone the chance to let off steam without becoming another accident statistic on the roads of Samui. **Watersports** are also catered for, with kayaks, sailing and windsurfing available near the centre of the beach at The Dive Academy, next to *Anantara*. On the main road near the centre of the beach, Peace Tropical Spa (☎077 430199, ⓦwww.peacetropicalspa.com) offers half a dozen types of **massage**, as well as body and facial treatments, at prices noticeably lower than the luxury hotel spas.

Accommodation

There's very little inexpensive accommodation left among Bophut's twenty or so resorts. Most establishments are well spaced out along the length of the beach, though a handful of small, comfortable hotels cluster together in Ban Bophut.

Anantara West of the village on the main road ☎077 428300–9, ⓦwww.anantara.com. Luxury hotel with attentive service in the style of an opulent oriental palace. Blocks of balconied rooms are arrayed round lush gardens, ponds, an attractive swimming pool and a central bar and restaurant, offering contemporary Italian cuisine with Asian influences. There's also a very attractive spa and a huge range of activities, from yoga and traditional crafts classes to tennis and watersports. ❾

Cactus Towards the west end of the beach ☎077 245565, ⓔcactusbung@hotmail.com. Welcoming place where ochre cottages with attractive bed

platforms, small verandas and well-equipped bathrooms stand in two leafy rows running down to the stylish beachside bar-restaurant; the cheapest make do with fans and cold water, while the various air-con bungalows have hot water and TV. Pool table, internet access. Fan ❹, air-con ❺

Juzz'a Pizza 2 East of the village T-junction ☎077 245662–3, ⓦwww.juzzapizza.com. Above a good restaurant (see p.274), four small but smart rooms, well equipped with comfy beds, air-con, hot showers, fridges and cable TV. Two rooms look onto the road, while the other two have beachside terraces with great views. ❻

273

The Lodge Towards the western end of the village ☎077 425337, ⓦwww.lodgesamui.com. Apartment-style block with immaculately clean and tastefully decorated modern rooms, all with balconies looking over the water, and boasting air-con, ceiling fan, mini-bar, satellite TV, plus spacious bathrooms with tubs to soak in. There's a seafront bar downstairs where you can get breakfast. ➐

The Waterfront East of the village T-junction ☎077 427165, ⓦwww.thewaterfrontbophut.com. English-run boutique hotel, sociable and family-friendly, with a small swimming pool in a grassy garden. All of the simply but tastefully decorated rooms and bungalows have air-con, hot water,

mini-bars, safes, cable TV, DVD players and views of the sea. Free pick-ups, wi-fi, internet access and babysitting; breakfast included in the price. ➐

Zazen At the far west end of the beach ☎077 425085, ⓦwww.samuizazen.com. Stylish bungalows clustered round a cute pool and kids' pool, furnished with Asian objets d'art and traditional Thai tables, wardrobes and cabinets, as well as satellite TV, DVD, wi-fi and mini-bar; many sport a tropical-style open-air bathroom with rain shower, rockery and fountain. Other facilities at this eco-friendly resort include a spa, a fine restaurant that hosts Thai dancing Thurs and Sun, cooking classes, table-tennis, pétanque and the like. ➒

Eating

A stroll through the village will turn up a wide choice of good restaurants for dinner, though it's best to book in advance at a couple of the smaller places recommended.

Happy Elephant West of the village T-junction. Good choice of mostly Thai food, including a few unusual dishes and reasonably priced seafood, and friendly service. There's an attractive beachside terrace and a contemporary-style annexe, On the Beach, next door.

Juzz'a Pizza 2 200m south of the village T-junction towards R4169 ☎077 245662–3. Friendly, small, elegant restaurant with a beachside terrace, serving excellent, authentic pizzas, with vegetarian and seafood options and a wide choice of extra toppings, as well as pastas and Thai and Western main courses. Closed Mon.

Samui French Bakery East of the village T-junction. The real deal: delicious, inexpensive croissants, breads, quiches, pizzas and patisserie. Also offers simple, reasonably priced main courses such as chicken breast with ham and cheese, sandwiches and salads. Daily 8am–8pm.

The Shack Grill West of the village T-junction ☎077 246041 or 087 264994. Small, pricey spot, run by an ebullient New Yorker, and focused on the large, open grill at the front of the restaurant: here all manner of local seafood and imported meats, such as Australian beef and New Zealand lamb, are cooked to your liking. Delicious apple pie and decent house wine.

Bangrak

Beyond the sharp headland with its sweep of coral reefs lies **BANGRAK**, sometimes called **Big Buddha Beach** after the colossus that gazes sternly down on the sun worshippers from its island in the bay. The beach is no great shakes, especially during the northeast monsoon, when the sea retreats and leaves a slippery mud flat, but Bangrak still manages to attract the watersports crowd, and every Sunday locals and expats descend for the family-friendly **Secret Garden Party**, with barbecues, drink and live music from around 4 to 10pm.

The **Big Buddha** (*Phra Yai*) is certainly big and works hard at being a tourist attraction, but is no beauty. A short causeway at the eastern end of the bay leads across to a messy clump of souvenir shops and foodstalls in front of the temple, catering to day-tripping Thais as well as foreigners. Here you can at least get a decent cup of coffee or tea, or a sandwich at *Big Buddha Café*. Ceremonial dragon-steps then bring you up to the covered terrace around the Big Buddha, from where there's a fine view of the sweeping north coast. Look out for the B10 rice-dispensing machine, which allows you symbolically to give alms to the monks at any time of the day.

Bangrak's **bungalows** are squeezed together in a narrow, noisy strip between busy Route 4171 and the shore, underneath the airport flight path. Best of a generally disappointing bunch is *Shambala* (☎077 425330, ⓦwww.samui -shambala.com; ❹), an English-run place that's well spread out in a lush garden, with chill-out areas and books to borrow; the large, smart bungalows all have verandas, en-suite bathrooms and fans, and most have hot water; massages and good Thai and Western food are also on offer as well as, diving, snorkelling, kayaking and other activities through in-house dive shop One Hundred Degrees East (☎077 245936–7, ⓦwww.100degreeseast.com).

Choeng Mon

After Bangrak comes the high-kicking boot of Samui's **northeastern cape**, with its small, rocky coves overlooking Ko Pha Ngan and connected by sandy lanes. Songthaews run along Route 4171 to the largest and most beautiful bay, **Choeng Mon**, whose white sandy beach is lined with casuarina trees that provide shade for the bungalows and upmarket resorts. Choeng Mon is now popular enough to support small supermarkets, travel agents and a bank, but on the whole it remains relatively uncommercialized and laid-back.

Accommodation

Boat House Hotel Central Choeng Mon ☎077 425041–52, ⓦwww.imperialhotels.com. Run by the reliable Imperial group, *Boat House* is named after the two-storey rice barges that have been converted into suites in the grounds. It also offers good-value luxury rooms with balconies in more prosaic modern buildings, often filled by package tours. As well as a beachside boat-shaped pool, there's a spa and fitness room. ❾

Island View Tucked in on the east side of the *Boat House Hotel* ☎077 245031, ☎077 425583. Smart, good-value chalets with air-con, hot water, TV and fridge, in a lively compound that crams in a super-market, a dive shop offering kayaks and snorkelling, a small bookshop and a beachfront bar. ❺

Kirati Resort (PP) 200m east of *Island View* ☎077 245360, ✉kirati_family@hotmail.com. Spacious wooden chalets with a few nice decorative touches, fridges and large hot-water bathrooms, in a large, jungley garden. Fan ❹, air-con ❺

Ô Soleil West of the *Boat House Hotel* ☎077 425232, ✉buisseretjean@yahoo.fr. A lovely, orderly, Belgian-run place in a pretty, tranquil garden dotted with ponds. The good-value, well-built, clean bungalows all have TVs and some have hot water, fridges and air-con. Fan ❸, air-con ❹

The Tongsai Bay Cottages and Hotel North side of Choeng Mon ☎077 245480, ⓦwww.tongsaibay.co.th. The island's finest hotel, an easy-going, environmentally aware establish-ment with the unhurried air of a country club, and with excellent service. The luxurious rooms, red-tiled cottages and palatial villas (some with their own pool) command beautiful views over the spacious, picturesque grounds, the private beach (with plenty of non-motorized watersports), a fresh-water and a vast saltwater swimming pool and the whole bay. They all also sport second bathtubs on their secluded open-air terraces, so you don't miss out on the scenery while splashing about. There's an array of very fine restaurants and a delightful health spa, as well as a tennis court, gym and an Avis car-rental desk. ❾

Chaweng

For looks alone, none of the other beaches can match **CHAWENG**, with its broad, gently sloping strip of white sand sandwiched between the limpid blue sea and a line of palm trees. Such beauty has not escaped attention of course, which means, on the plus side, that Chaweng can provide just about anything the active beach bum demands, from thumping nightlife to ubiquitous and diverse watersports. The negative angle is that the new developments are ever more cramped and expensive, while building work behind the palm trees and repairs to the over-commercialized main beach road are always in progress.

The six-kilometre bay is framed between the small island of Ko Matlang at the north end and the 300-metre-high headland above Coral Cove in the south. From

Ko Matlang, where the waters provide some decent snorkelling, an often exposed coral reef slices southwest across to the mainland, marking out a shallow lagoon and **North Chaweng**. This S-shaped part of the beach is comparatively peaceful, though it has some ugly pockets of development; at low tide it becomes a wide, inviting playground, and from October to January the reef shelters it from the worst of the northeast winds. South of the reef, the idyllic shoreline of **Central Chaweng** stretches for 2km in a dead-straight line, the ugly, traffic-clogged and seemingly endless strip of amenities on the parallel main drag largely concealed behind the treeline and the resorts. Around a low promontory is **Chaweng Noi**, a little curving beach in a rocky bay, which is comparatively quiet in its northern part, away from the road. Well inland of Central Chaweng, the round-island road, Route 4169, passes through the original village of **Ban Chaweng**.

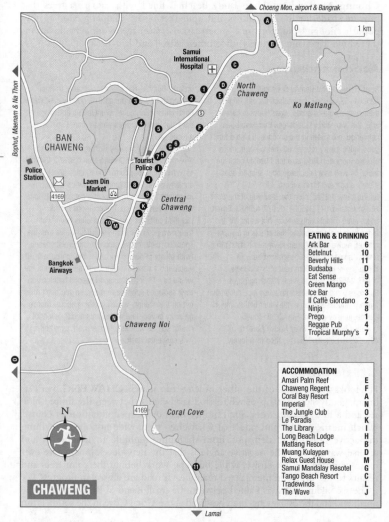

EATING & DRINKING

Ark Bar	6
Betelnut	10
Beverly Hills	11
Budsaba	D
Eat Sense	9
Green Mango	5
Ice Bar	3
Il Caffè Giordano	2
Ninja	8
Prego	1
Reggae Pub	4
Tropical Murphy's	7

ACCOMMODATION

Amari Palm Reef	E
Chaweng Regent	F
Coral Bay Resort	A
Imperial	N
The Jungle Club	O
Le Paradis	K
The Library	I
Long Beach Lodge	H
Matlang Resort	B
Muang Kulaypan	D
Relax Guest House	M
Samui Mandalay Resotel	G
Tango Beach Resort	C
Tradewinds	L
The Wave	J

CHAWENG

South of Chaweng, the road climbs past **Coral Cove**, a tiny, isolated beach of coarse sand hemmed in by high rocks, with some good coral for snorkelling. It's well worth making the trip to the *Beverly Hills Café*, towards the tip of the headland dividing Chaweng from Lamai, for a jaw-dropping view over Chaweng and Choeng Mon to the peaks of Ko Pha Ngan (and for some good, moderately priced food, notably seafood).

Accommodation

Over fifty **bungalow resorts** and **hotels** at Chaweng are squeezed into thin strips running back from the beachfront at right angles. The cheapest digs here are generally little more than functional, while more and more expensive places are sprouting up all the time, offering sumptuous accommodation at top-whack prices.

Inexpensive and moderate

The Jungle Club 2km up a steep, partly paved road from Chaweng Noi ☎081 894 2327, ⓦwww.jungleclubsamui.com. Breezy, French-Thai antidote to Chaweng's commercial clutter: a huge, grassy, shady plot with a small but attractive pool on the edge of the slope to catch the towering views of Ko Pha Ngan and beyond. A chic, open-sided bar-restaurant has been built into the rocks, while some of the smart, varied, en-suite bungalows come with hot water. Free pick-ups twice a day; long-stay discounts. ❹–❼

Long Beach Lodge Towards the north end of Central Chaweng ☎077 422162, ⒻIn077 422372. An unusually spacious and shady, sandy compound. All the orderly, clean bungalows and rooms are a decent size and have hot water, fridge, TV and air-con. Service is friendly, and breakfast is included in the price. ❺–❼

Matlang Resort At the far north end of North Chaweng ☎077 230468–9. Tranquil, friendly place facing a broad stretch of beach with nice views of Ko Matlang. The en-suite wooden bungalows, all with verandas and mosquito screens, some with air-con and hot water, are a little bit battered, but are spread around a very pleasant, shady flower garden. Fan ❸, air-con ❺

Relax Guest House Soi Colibri, Central Chaweng, next to *Betelnut* restaurant ☎077 413836. Functional crashpad, but clean and well maintained by a pleasant family, and good value for the facilities: air-con, hot water and TV. ❸

Samui Mandalay Resotel Central Chaweng, next to *Ark Bar* ☎077 422340, ⒻIn077 422280. Friendly spot offering a wide variety of colourful, rather eccentrically designed bungalows in a narrow strip and rooms in the main building. Clean and well equipped, with air-con, hot water, TV and fridge. ❹–❺

The Wave Central Chaweng ☎077 230803, ⓦwww.thewavesamui.com. One of the cheapest

guest houses on Chaweng, this helpful, English-run place is not on the beach, but above a very popular bar-restaurant on the main road. The pick of the rooms, most of which have fans and share cold-water bathrooms, is the top-floor duplex with air-con, hot water and a rooftop terrace. All kinds of advice and tours available, as well as internet access and a huge library. Fan ❸–❹, air-con ❻

Expensive

Amari Palm Reef North Chaweng ☎077 422015–8, ⓦwww.amari.com. Congenial, eco-friendly luxury hotel that's unpretentious and good value. Spacious accommodation, stretching back across the road from the beach, includes family-friendly duplexes, and there are two elegant restaurants, including *Prego* (see p.278), a full-service spa, two swimming pools and a kids' pool. Various discounts and packages available on their website. ❾

Chaweng Regent At the bottom end of North Chaweng ☎077 230391–400, ⓦwww .chawengregent.com. Reliable, well-run, luxury place offering elegant bungalows and low-rise rooms with private terraces and all mod cons, around lotus ponds, two pools, a fitness centre, sauna and spa. ❾

Coral Bay Resort At the far north end of North Chaweng ☎077 234555, ⓦwww .coralbay.net. A charming, eco-friendly vision of how Chaweng might have developed – if only there'd been more space. In quiet, delightful, ten-acre gardens with over 500 species of plants, the huge, thatched villas have been thoughtfully and tastefully designed with local woods, bamboo and coconut; all have extensive verandas, waterfall showers and DVD players (movies available from the library). There's an attractive pool, a spa and a recommended beachside bar-restaurant; kayaks and snorkels available. ❾

Imperial Chaweng Noi ☎077 422020–36, ⓦwww.imperialhotels.com. The longest-established luxury hotel on Samui is a grand but lively establishment with a Mediterranean feel, set in sloping, landscaped gardens; features include two pools (one sea water, one fresh with a jacuzzi), a spa, tennis court, all kinds of watersports and classes such as Thai cookery. ❾

Le Paradis Central Chaweng ☎077 239041–3, ⓦwww.leparadisresort.com. Set in lush, spacious gardens, twelve luxurious traditional Ayutthaya-style houses on stilts, with living areas underneath and verandas, as well as fourteen stylish contemporary villas with open-air bathrooms. Attractive beachside swimming pool, gym and health spa. ❾

The Library Central Chaweng ☎077 422767–8, ⓦwww.thelibrary.name. High-concept design hotel, based around a library of books, DVDs and CDs with computer terminals. The idea is continued in the rooms, which all sport iMacs and have a sleek, cubic theme; they're divided into suites (downstairs) and studios with balconies (upstairs). There's a blood-red swimming pool, a spa, a fitness centre and a beachfront terrace restaurant, *The Page*. Rack rates from B16,500. ❾

Muang Kulaypan North Chaweng ☎077 230036, ⓦwww.kulaypan.com. Original, stylish boutique hotel arrayed around a large, immaculate garden with a black-tiled swimming pool and an excellent beachside restaurant (see below). Rooms – each with their own private balcony or garden – combine contemporary design with traditional Thai-style comforts. ❾

Tango Beach Resort North Chaweng ☎077 422470, ⓦwww.tangobeachsamui.com. This helpful and welcoming place has a modern Thai style that sets it apart from most of Samui's farang-oriented hotels: a variety of cutesy, colourful, well-equipped rooms are separated by a small, shady pool and a wooden boardwalk that runs down to *Lazy Wave* bar-restaurant. Breakfast included. ❼

Tradewinds Central Chaweng ☎077 414294, ⓦwww.tradewinds-samui.com. A cheerful, well-run place of characterful bungalows and rooms (all with air-con, hot water, mini-bar, cable TV and balcony) with plenty of room to breathe in colourful tropical gardens. The resort specializes in sailing, with its own catamarans (instruction available), as well as offering kayaks and croquet. Breakfast included. ❽

Eating

Chaweng offers all manner of foreign **cuisines**, from French to Russian, much of it of dubious quality. Amongst all this, it's quite hard to find good, reasonably priced Thai food – as well as the places recommended below, it's worth exploring the cheap and cheerful night-time foodstalls at **Laem Din market**, which are popular with local workers, on the middle road between Central Chaweng and Highway 4169. The fame of *Betelnut* has attracted several other well-regarded restaurants to **Soi Colibri**, including Italian, Japanese and Chinese. *The Jungle Club* (see p.277; book the day before) offers **barbecues** for B750, including transfers, a cocktail and a swim.

Betelnut Soi Colibri, a small lane at the south end of Central Chaweng opposite the landmark *Centara Grand Resort* ☎077 413370. By far Samui's best restaurant, serving pricey but exceptional Californian-Thai fusion food. Few tables, so reservations highly recommended.

Budsaba Restaurant At the *Muang Kulaypan Hotel* ☎077 230850. This charming, upmarket beachfront restaurant fully justifies the journey up to North Chaweng: you get to recline in your own seaside *sala* or open-sided hut on stilts while tucking into unusual and excellent Thai dishes such as banana-flower and shrimp salad. Live traditional music and dance Tues, Thurs, Sat & Sun eve.

Eat Sense Central Chaweng, next to *Charlie's Huts* ☎077 414242. Spacious, relaxing, mostly open-air restaurant on the beachfront, serving expensive but delicious Thai food – try the deep-fried prawns with cashew nuts and tamarind sauce.

Il Caffè Giordano North Chaweng, at the start of the Ban Chaweng road. Trim café-bar run by a congenial Florentine. Good coffees of course, plus tiramisu, pizza by the slice, sandwiches and simple pastas; free internet for customers. Daily 8.30am–7pm, sometimes till 10.30pm in high season.

Ninja Near *Charlie's Huts* in Central Chaweng. Popular, well-run, very basic and cheap restaurant, serving simple Thai favourites such as *tom yam*, *som tam* and *phat thai*, as well as crêpes, breakfasts and other Western food. Open 24hr.

Prego *Amari Palm Reef*, North Chaweng ☎077 422015–8. Excellent, chic, open-sided restaurant that would stand on its own two feet in Milan, the head chef's home town. The varied menu of contemporary Italian dishes includes good *antipasti*, pizzas and top-notch risottos, and there's a very good selection of wines. Booking advised in high season.

Drinking and nightlife

Avoiding the raucous hostess bars and English theme pubs on the main through road, the best place to **drink** is on the beach: at night dozens of resorts and dedicated bars lay out candlelit tables with axe cushions for reclining on the sand, especially towards the north end of Central Chaweng and on North Chaweng – if you want somewhere specific to aim for, try *Lazy Wave* at *Tango Beach Resort* or *Jack Bar*, a little further down, for reggae. Meanwhile inland, overlooking the lake from its north shore, *Q Bar* was closed for refurbishment at the time of writing, but has garnered quite a reputation for its cutting-edge music from local and international DJs and its sleek decor.

Ark Bar North end of Central Chaweng. Hosts a very popular beach party, with house and funk DJs and a free barbecue, Wed from 3pm until well into the night.

Green Mango North end of Central Chaweng. Long-standing dance venue, in a huge shed that combines an industrial look with that of a tropical greenhouse. Now with its own alley, Soi Green Mango, lined with other vibrant bars and clubs, including *Sweet Soul Café*, which always seems to be rammed with dancing farangs and Thais.

Ice Bar North side of the lake ⓦ www .icebarsamui.com. Been out in the midday sun with mad dogs and Englishmen? Maybe what you need is a spell at -5°C in this sculpted ice bar – and a vodka. B375, furs included.

Reggae Pub Inland from Central Chaweng across the lake. Chaweng's oldest nightclub, a venerable Samui institution with a memorabilia shop to prove it. It does time now as an unpretentious, good-time, party venue, with plenty of drinking games, pool tables, big-screen sports and live bands most nights in high season.

Tropical Murphy's Opposite *McDonald's* in Central Chaweng. One theme pub that is worth singling out: with draught Guinness and Kilkenny, big-screen sports, quiz nights, live music and decent food, *Murphy's* has turned itself into a popular landmark and meeting place.

Listings

Airline Bangkok Airways, south end of Ban Chaweng on Route 4169 ☏ 077 422512.

Bookshop Bookazine, selling English-language books, newspapers and magazines, has several branches, most conveniently next to *Tropical Murphy's* in Central Chaweng. Saai, North Chaweng at the T-junction of the beach road and the Ban Chaweng road, is good for secondhand, and some new, books.

Cookery courses The highly recommended Samui Institute of Thai Culinary Arts (SITCA; closed Sun; ☏ 077 413172, ⓦ www.sitca.net), on Soi Colibri opposite *Betelnut* restaurant, runs 2hr 30min classes in the morning and afternoon (B1950), and you get to eat what you've cooked with a friend afterwards. They also have a culinary shop selling Thai cooking accessories, ingredients and cookbooks.

Hospital The private Samui International Hospital in North Chaweng (☏ 077 230781–2, ⓦ www.sih .co.th) provides 24hr emergency services, house calls, a dental clinic and travel inoculations.

Internet Dozens of outlets, including at travel agent Travel Solutions (see below).

Pharmacy Boots has a convenient branch in the middle of Central Chaweng, just up the road from *Tropical Murphy's* pub.

Spas Among stand-alone spas, which are generally cheaper than the luxury hotel versions, Living Senses, above *McDonald's* in the Living Square shopping plaza in Central Chaweng (☏ 077 230917, ⓦ www.livingsensesspa.com), has a good reputation for its massages, reflexology, body wraps and scrubs; on a waterfall- and flower-splashed hillside with a plunge pool at the far north end of Chaweng, Eranda offers a wider range of treatments and a little more style, at higher prices (☏ 077 422666, ⓦ www.erandaspa.co.th).

Tourist police Behind *McDonald's* overlooking the lake in Central Chaweng ☏ 1155 or 077 414198.

Travel agent English-run Travel Solutions, just off the main road opposite *Tropical Murphy's* (☏ 077 239007–8, ⓦ www.travelsolutionsthailand.com), is a reliable and knowledgeable agent, for train and bus tickets among many other things.

Watersports Samui Ocean Sports, on the beach by the *Chaweng Regent* at the bottom end of North Chaweng, and south of *Long Beach Lodge* on Central Chaweng (☏ 081 940 1999, ⓦ www .sailing-in-samui.com), rents windsurfers and kayaks, as well as offering sailing lessons, trips and charters.

Lamai

LAMAI is like a second city to Chaweng's capital, not quite as developed and much less frenetic, while lacking the latter's range of chic hotels, restaurants and nightclubs. Development is concentrated into a farang toytown of open-air hostess bars and Western restaurants that has grown up behind the centre of the beach, interspersed with supermarkets, clinics, banks, ATMs, dive shops and travel agents. Running roughly north to south for 4km, the white, palm-fringed beach itself is still a picture, and generally quieter than Chaweng, with far less in the way of watersports – it's quite easy to get away from it all by staying at the peaceful extremities of the bay, where the backpackers' resorts are preferable to Chaweng's functional guest houses. At the northern end, the spur of land that hooks eastward into the sea is perhaps the prettiest spot, though it's beginning to attract some upmarket development: it has more rocks than sand, but the shallow sea behind the coral reef is protected from the high seas of November, December and January.

The original village of **Ban Lamai**, set well back on Route 4169, remains surprisingly aloof, and its wat contains a small museum of ceramics, agricultural tools and other everyday objects. Most visitors get more of a buzz from **Hin Yay** (Grandmother Rock) and **Hin Ta** (Grandfather Rock), small rock formations on the bay's southern promontory, which never fail to raise a giggle with their resemblance to the male and female sexual organs.

Lamai boasts two of Samui's longer-standing and better **spas**. The oldest, *The Spa Resort* (T077 230855, W www.thesparesorts.net; ⑤–⑨; minimum three-night stay), covers everything from Thai massage (B300 per hr) and herbal saunas (B300 per hr) for guests and non-guests, to in-house fasting programmes (US$300 per week). Also on offer are a wide range of other massages, body and facial wraps, and yoga, meditation, massage and raw-food culinary classes. *The Spa* now has two main locations, the original one at the far north end of the beach, the other, more upmarket branch 3km away in the hills above Lamai (connected by shuttle buses), each with a swimming pool and a wide variety of accommodation; there's also a small complex of beachside villas with private saltwater pools, 600m north of the original branch. With less of an emphasis on clean living, and more on pampering, *Tamarind Springs* (T077 230571 or 077 424436, W www.tamarindsprings.com) is set in a beautiful, secluded coconut grove just north of *Spa Resort* off the main road. Here a session in their unique herbal steam room, set between two boulders by a waterfall-fed plunge pool, and a two-hour Thai massage, for example, costs B2600. Facials and other massages, such as head, foot and back, are also available, and there's a café and juice bar, as well as luxury villas on the site to rent (minimum three nights; ⑨).

Accommodation

Lamai's **accommodation** is generally less cramped and slightly better value than Chaweng's, though it presents far fewer choices at the top end of the market. The far southern end of the bay towards the Grandparent Rocks has the tightest concentration of budget bungalows.

Bay View Resort On the bay's northern headland T077 418429, W www.bayviewsamui .com. Neat, stylish bungalows with verandas, minibars and hot-water bathrooms in an extensive, flower-bedecked compound; the poshest come with air-con and cable TV. Offers a friendly, German-Thai welcome, internet access and great sunset views of the beach from the attractive restaurant. ⑤
Bill Resort At the far southern end of the bay T077 424403, W www.billresortsamui.com. A friendly, efficient and orderly setup, crammed into a fragrant, overgrown garden with a decent-sized pool and Jacuzzi, on a pleasant stretch of beach

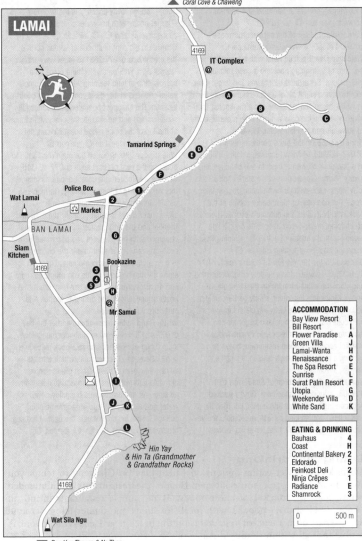

Coral Cove & Chaweng

LAMAI

4169

IT Complex @

A

B

C

Tamarind Springs ■

E **D**

F

1

Police Box

2

Wat Lamai ⚓

🎵 Market

BAN LAMAI

G

Siam
Kitchen

4169

Bookazine

3

Ⓢ

4

5

H

@

Mr Samui

✉

I

J **K**

L

*Hin Yay
& Hin Ta (Grandmother
& Grandfather Rocks)*

4169

⛩ Wat Sila Ngu

Ban Hua Thanon & Na Thon

ACCOMMODATION	
Bay View Resort	**B**
Bill Resort	**I**
Flower Paradise	**A**
Green Villa	**J**
Lamai-Wanta	**H**
Renaissance	**C**
The Spa Resort	**E**
Sunrise	**L**
Surat Palm Resort	**F**
Utopia	**G**
Weekender Villa	**D**
White Sand	**K**

EATING & DRINKING	
Bauhaus	**4**
Coast	**H**
Continental Bakery	**2**
Eldorado	**5**
Feinkost Deli	**2**
Ninja Crêpes	**1**
Radiance	**E**
Shamrock	**3**

0	500 m

and up the hill behind. Its widely varied, clean,
rooms and bungalows, most with air-con and hot
water, offer good value if you don't need much
elbow room. Fan ❸, air-con ❺–❾
Flower Paradise On the bay's northern headland
☎077 418059 or 089 288 8326, ⓦwww
.samuiroestiland.com. Just a short walk from the
beach, a friendly, well-run German-Swiss place in a
small but beautiful garden. All the attractive, well-
tended bungalows of varying sizes have mosquito

nets and hot water, and there's a good restaurant,
Röstiland (closed Mon), specializing in the
eponymous hash browns. Fan ❸–❹, air-con ❹
Green Villa On the access road to *White Sand*, at
the far southern end of the bay ☎077 424296,
ⓔresagreenvilla@hotmail.com. Quiet, French-run
operation set back from the beach in a spacious
garden among palm trees, with a small swimming
pool, clean, simple, en-suite bungalows with fans
(some with hot water) and grand, air-con villas with

281

TVs, fridges, hot-water bathtubs and open-air showers. Fan ❷–❸, air-con ❻

Lamai-Wanta East of the central crossroads ☎077 424550, ⓦwww.lamaiwanta.com. Welcoming, well-placed hotel with a seductive beachfront swimming pool and a good restaurant (see below). Set around trim lawns, the large, plain rooms have a slight air of a sanatorium, decorated in white, beige and dark wood in a minimalist Thai style, while the bungalows are a little more elegant; all have air-con and hot water. ❻–❼

Renaissance On the bay's northern headland ☎077 429300, ⓦwww.renaissancekohsamui.com. In a fine position with access to two beaches, this luxury Marriott resort presents a stark choice: long, lofty villas, each with its own plunge pool, in lush, frog-filled gardens, or far cheaper rooms at the back with balconies and outdoor jacuzzis. There's an enticing, many-tiered beachside pool, a spa, tapas bar, and a roster of activities including Thai massage and towel-folding classes. ❾

Sunrise On the Hin Yay Hin Ta access road ☎077 424433, ⓦwww.sunrisebungalow.com. Welcoming and clued-up establishment on the far southern end of the beach. In a quiet, shady garden amidst coconut palms, choose between clean fan rooms with cold-water bathrooms and larger air-con bungalows with hot water, cable TV and fridge. Internet access, a decent restaurant, books to borrow, a gym and, in high season, a small spa. Fan ❸, air-con ❻

Surat Palm Resort South of *Spa Resort* ☎077 418608, Ⓔkjorlux@yahoo.com. Tightly packed between the road, canal and beach, but friendly, well tended and shaded by lush vegetation. You've got three choices: small, neat, en-suite, wooden

huts – "bunga-lowly priced", as the brochure says – larger affairs with hot water on the beach or air-con rooms. Fan ❸–❺, air-con ❻

Utopia On the central stretch of Lamai, north of the crossroads ☎077 233113–4, ⓦwww.utopia-samui.com. Well-run, welcoming place on a narrow strip of land teeming with flowers, good value and reasonably quiet considering its central location. The cheapest bungalows have mosquito screens, fans and en-suite bathrooms, while those at the top of the price range boast air-con, hot water, TV and fridge. Fan ❹, air-con ❻

Weekender Villa Between the main road and the beach to the east of Ban Lamai ☎077 424116, ⓦwww.weekender-villa.com. Despite its location, this very well-maintained, homely, German-run establishment (not to be confused with *Weekender Hotel*) is quiet enough; the staff are friendly and the large, smart air-con bungalows, equipped with hot showers and decorated with contemporary art, shelter under the coconut trees in a small but spacious compound. There's a small swimming pool, an air-con massage room and an attractive beachside bar-restaurant that hosts bridge, chess and draughts nights. À la carte breakfast included. ❻

White Sand At the far southern end of the bay ☎077 424298, ⓦwww.samuibudgetbungalow .com. Long-established and laid-back place in a large, shady, sandy compound, which attracts plenty of long-term travellers. It offers simple, old-style huts with fans and mosquito nets, some en suite, as well as concrete bungalows with hot water and air-con, and one attractive bamboo cottage on the beach that gets the best of the sea breezes (no air-con). Fan ❶–❺, air-con ❹

Eating and drinking

There are far fewer eating options on Lamai than on Chaweng to tempt you away from your guest house kitchen. Besides the **restaurants** recommended below, there's a **market** of cheap foodstalls and simple restaurants inland on Highway 4169 that's popular with locals for lunch and dinner (closes around 8pm). Apart from a few bar-restaurants on the beach near *Lamai-Wanta*, Lamai's **nightlife** is all within spitting distance of the central crossroads.

Bauhaus North of the central crossroads. Barn-like complex sporting a bistro and a dance floor, with entertainment provided by big-screen TVs, pool tables and foam parties (Mon & Fri).

Coast *Lamai-Wanta*, east of the central crossroads ☎077 424550. Hip, open-sided restaurant by the hotel pool and beach, minimalist but mellow, with a menu that's half Thai, including tasty *kaeng matsaman kai* (B160), and half international fusion.

Continental Bakery North of the central cross-roads, near Highway 4169. Friendly, Swiss-run place

serving good breads, cakes, burgers, sandwiches and espressos, as well as all-day breakfasts ranging from French and American to Belgian (with pork steak, apparently). Daily 8am–8pm.

Eldorado Just west of the central crossroads. Highly recommended, good-value Swedish restaurant, serving a few Thai favourites, salads, steaks, pizzas and other international main courses, plus one or two indigenous specialities such as Swedish meatballs. All-you-can-eat barbecue on Wed evenings for B260.

Feinkost Deli next to *Continental Bakery*. Deli for meats, cheeses and own-baked breads, plus café-bar serving a wide selection of Western, mostly German food, including plenty of sausages, schnitzels and good pizzas, with German beer to wash it all down and apple strudel to finish you off.
Ninja Crêpes On Highway 4169, east of Ban Lamai. A branch of Chaweng's backpacker hotspot, a dependable, simple, cheap, 24hr café, with internet booths, serving basic Thai favourites, as well as crêpes and other Western food.
Radiance *The Spa Resort*, at the far north end of the beach. Excellent, casual, moderately priced

beachside restaurant, serving a huge range of mostly vegetarian Thai and international (including Mexican) dishes, plus raw and vegan food, as well as plenty of meat and marine offerings. The veggie "ginger nuts" stir-fry and *som tam* with spicy Thai sausage are excellent. A long menu of juices, smoothies and shakes includes a delicious lime juice with honey.
Shamrock North of the central crossroads. Popular Irish bar with pool tables and TV sports, which hosts lively cover bands and keeps Guinness and Kilkenny bitter on draught.

Listings

Bookshop Bookazine, selling English-language books, newspapers and magazines, on the main beachside drag.
Cookery classes Learn Thai cooking, take a market tour and eat your own-cooked lunch or dinner, on two- to four-person classes at Siam Kitchen on Route 4169 (3hr; B1200 including Lamai pick-ups; ☎086 109 1915, ⓦwww .siamkitchen.net).
Internet Among dozens of options on Lamai, a couple stand out. Mr Samui's art gallery and café, just south of the central crossroads, is a congenial choice offering good espresso coffee, or you could head for the unmissable, shiny IT Complex at the

north end of the bay, headquarters of website Sawadee, which offers fast internet and fierce air-con.
Meditation retreats Wat Suan Mokkh (see p.261) has recently branched out to offer five-day retreats at Dipabhavan, a hermitage in the hills above Lamai (ⓦwww.dipabhavan.com). Helped by farang co-ordinators, Suan Mokkh's abbot, Ajarn Poh, leads the retreats himself, which take place in English from the 22nd to the 27th of each month; pick-ups are laid on from *The Spa Resort*, *Utopia* and Wat Sila Ngu on the 21st for registration. For more information, contact Khun Siriwan at *Utopia* or on ☎081 892 3457.

The south and west coasts

Lacking the long, attractive beaches of the more famous resorts, the **south and west coasts** rely on a few charming, isolated spots with peaceful accommodation. Heading south from Lamai, you come first to the Muslim fishing village of **Ban Hua Thanon** and *Ban Hua Thanon Seafood*, a justly famous **restaurant** on Highway 4169, recommended in all the Thai food guides. A world away from Samui's slick resort restaurants, this rustic wooden shophouse with lovely outdoor tables on the water keeps its reasonably priced fish in tanks at the front. Recommended dishes include baked green mussels with lemon grass and excellent crispy, shredded prawn with mango salad. On Route 4170 a couple of kilometres down the coast, Kiteboarding Asia (☎081 591 4592–3, ⓦwww.kiteboardingasia.com; B4000 for one day, B11,000 for three), based at *Samui Orchid Resort*, offers instruction in **kiteboarding**, which is at its best here between December and February, as well as rentals. Don't be tempted by the pitiful aquarium at the same resort, where the tanks are barely bigger than the fish.

A kilometre further on is one of the island's most secluded hotels: founded as a private club on a quiet south-facing promontory, the *Laem Set Inn* (☎077 424393, ⓦwww.laemset.com; fan ❺, air-con ❽) now offers a wide range of elegant rooms and suites – some of them reassembled village houses, some with their own plunge pool – as well as an excellent restaurant, cookery courses, a spa, wi-fi, plenty of watersports and a scenically positioned swimming pool. The access road to the *Laem Set Inn* takes you past the nearby **Samui Butterfly Garden** (daily 8.30am–5.30pm; B170, children B120), opposite *Centara Villas*.

Here you can wander among artificial waterfalls and lush vegetation, on a net-covered, rocky hillside overlooking the sea, surrounded by dozens of brilliantly coloured lepidopterans.

The gentle but unspectacular coast beyond is lined with a good reef for snorkelling, which can be explored most easily from the fishing village of **Ban Bangkao**. There's also good snorkelling around **Ko Taen**, a short way offshore to the south: a five-hour boat trip from, for example, TK Tour (☎077 334052–3, ⓦwww.tktoursamui.com) in the next village to the west, **Ban Thongkrut**, including pick-up from your accommodation, snorkelling equipment and lunch on the long beach of the neighbouring island, Ko Mad Sum, will set you back B1100 per person (B1300 with kayaking).

About 5km inland, near **Ban Thurian**, the **Na Muang Falls** make a popular outing as they're not far off the round-island road (each of the two main falls has its own signposted kilometre-long paved access road off Route 4169). The lower fall splashes and sprays down a twenty-metre wall of rock into a large pool, while Na Muang 2, upstream, is a more spectacular, shaded cascade that requires a bit of foot-slogging from the car park (about 15min uphill).

On the west coast, the flat beaches are unexceptional but make a calm alternative when the northeast winds hit the other side of the island. At **Ban Taling Ngam**, the *Five Islands Gallery Café* lays on half-day **boat trips** to **Ko Si Ko Ha**, the heavily guarded islands just offshore where sea gypsies gather swifts' nests for bird's-nest soup (see p.418). Rounded off by a varied Thai lunch or dinner at its beachside restaurant, the package costs from B6050 for two people, including transfers.

Ko Pha Ngan

In recent years, backpackers have tended to move over to Ko Samui's fun-loving little sibling, **KO PHA NGAN**, 20km to the north, but the island still has a relatively simple atmosphere, mostly because the lousy road system is an impediment to the developers. With a dense jungle covering its inland mountains and rugged granite outcrops along the coast, Pha Ngan lacks the huge, gently sweeping beaches for which Samui is famous, but it does have plenty of coral to explore and some beautiful, sheltered bays: if you're seeking total isolation, trek out to **Hat Khuat** (**Bottle Beach**) on the north coast or the half-dozen pristine beaches on the east coast; **Thong Nai Pan** at the top of the east coast is not quite as remote, and offers a decent range of amenities and accommodation; while on the long neck of land at the southeast corner, **Hat Rin**, a pilgrimage site for ravers, is a thoroughly commercialized backpackers' resort in a gorgeous setting. Much of Pha Ngan's development has plonked itself on the south and west sides along the only coastal roads on the island, which fan out from **Thong Sala**, the capital; the unattractive south coast is hard to recommend, but the west coast offers several handsome sandy bays with great sunset views, notably **Hat Yao** and **Hat Salad**.

Pha Ngan's **bungalows** all have running water and electricity (on the remotest beaches, only in the evenings and from individual generators), and nearly all come with en-suite bathrooms. There are only a handful of luxury resorts, though plenty of places now offer air-con, especially on Hat Rin. The three hundred or so resorts generally have more space to spread out than on Ko Samui, and the cost of living is lower. The prices given on the following pages are standard for most of the year (though on Hat Rin they tend to vary with the phases of the moon), but in slack periods you'll be offered discounts (possible, roughly, in May, June, Oct & Nov), and at the very busiest times (especially Dec & Jan) Pha Ngan's bungalow owners are canny enough to raise the stakes. **Nightlife** is concentrated at Hat Rin, climaxing every month in a wild **full moon party** on the beach; a couple of smaller outdoor **parties** have now got in on the act, the Half Moon Festival (twice monthly, about a week before and after the full moon; ⓦwww.halfmoonfestival.com) and the monthly Black Moon Party (ⓦwww.fullmoon.phangan.info), both at Ban Tai.

There's no TAT office on Ko Pha Ngan, but a couple of free, widely available booklets provide regularly updated **information** about the island: *Phangan Info* (which has a particularly good website, on which you can book accommodation, at ⓦwww.phangan.info) and *Phangan Explorer* (ⓦwww.phanganexplorer.com).

Getting to Ko Pha Ngan

The most obvious way of getting to Ko Pha Ngan is on a **boat** from the **Surat Thani** area (but see also p.258 for boats from Chumphon); for contact details of **transport companies** in Surat, see p.264. Boat services fluctuate according to demand, but the longest-established ferry is the night boat from Ban Don pier in Surat Thani to Thong Sala, which leaves at 11pm every night (ⓉO77 284928 or 081 326 8973; 6hr; B300); tickets are available from the pier on the day of

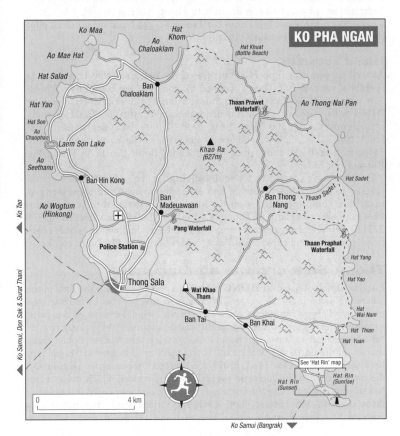

departure. From Don Sak to Thong Sala, there are six Raja vehicle ferries a day (on Pha Ngan ☎077 377452–3) and one Songserm Express Boat service a day (8am; on Pha Ngan ☎077 377704). Both the above charge B400, including bus transport to the pier from Surat Thani, with a total journey time of around four hours. **From Bangkok**, bus and train packages similar to those for getting to Ko Samui are available (see p.266), notably government buses from the Southern Terminal (first-class air-con 1 daily B750; VIP 1 daily B1050).

Two Songserm Express Boats a day do the 45-minute trip from Na Thon on **Ko Samui** to Thong Sala (B200). Two Seatran Discovery boats a day from the east end of Bangrak (on Samui ☎077 246086–8, Pha Ngan ☎077 238679, Ⓦwww.seatranferry.com) and three Lomprayah catamarans from Maenam (Samui ☎077 427765–6, Pha Ngan ☎077 238412, Ⓦwww.lomprayah.com) call in at Thong Sala after thirty minutes (B250), on their way to Ko Tao and Chumphon. From the centre of Bangrak, the *Haad Rin Queen* crosses four times a day to Hat Rin in under an hour (times have remained fairly constant over the years: 10.30am, 1pm, 4pm & 6.30pm; B200, or B250 including pick-up from Samui hotels; ☎077 484668 or 077 231069). If there are enough takers and the weather's good enough – generally reliable between roughly January and September – one small boat a day crosses from the pier in Ban Maenam at noon to Hat Rin (B150), before sailing up Ko Pha Ngan's east coast, via Hat Sadet and anywhere else upon demand, to Thong Nai Pan (B350).

For information about boats from **Ko Tao** to Ko Pha Ngan see p.297; all offer the same service in the return direction.

Island activities

As well as boat trips from Hat Rin (see p.292), organized **day-trips** include speedboat tours to Ang Thong National Marine Park (see p.268) from Thong Sala with Grand Sea (based on Ko Samui; Mon, Wed & Fri; B1600 a head, or B1800 with kayaking, plus B200 national park fee; ☎077 427001, Ⓦwww .grandseatours.com); and Safari Boat jaunts (B1000, including transfers and lunch; ☎077 238232, Ⓦwww.safariboat.info), which take in an elephant camp (optional rides B500) and boating to Hat Khom, Bottle Beach, Ao Thong Nai Pan and Hat Sadet.

The island isn't a great base for **scuba-diving**: getting to the best sites around Ko Tao involves time-consuming and expensive voyages, and there aren't as many dive companies here as on Ko Samui or Ko Tao – of those that exist, Phangan Divers on Hat Rin, Thong Nai Pan, Ao Mae Hat and Hat Yao (☎077 375117, Ⓦwww.phangandivers.com) is a PADI Five-Star centre, which offers frequent courses and trips to Sail Rock, halfway between Pha Ngan and Tao.

Thong Sala and the south coast

Like the capital of Samui, **THONG SALA** is a port of entrance and little more, where the incoming ferries, especially around midday, are met by touts sent to escort travellers to bungalows elsewhere on the island. In front of the piers, songthaews and jeeps to the rest of the island congregate by a dusty row of banks, supermarkets, travel agents and scuba-diving outfits, with a popular night market on the north side of the road. If you really need to **stay** in Thong Sala, head for *Pha Ngan Chai Hotel* (☎077 238109, Ⓦwww.pha-nganchai.com; ❹), the incongruous white high-rise overshadowing the piers, which makes a fair stab at international-standard features for visiting businesspeople and government officials, with air-con, hot water, TVs, fridges and, in some rooms, sea-view balconies, as well as a pool, free wi-fi and internet access.

Among many travellers' **restaurants** here, *Yellow Café*, on the corner in front of the main pier, a few doors up from *Pha Ngan Chai Hotel*, is a good, friendly choice with free wi-fi, serving tasty coffee, baguettes, baked potatoes and other Western meals; and there's a branch of *Nira's* (see p.291; daily 7am–6pm) south along the waterfront opposite the Seatran pier, offering bakery goods, deli sandwiches and Thai and Western main courses. The other Thong Sala restaurant that's worth knowing about is *Boat Ahoy* (☎077 238759), about 2km from the pier on the Hat Rin road, a complex of outdoor and air-con tables (and karaoke) specializing in seafood and salads, with plenty of vegetarian options; under the same management, *Somtum Inter* next door dishes up popular northeastern Thai food.

From Thong Sala, there's an easy excursion to the grandiosely termed Than Sadet–Ko Pha Ngan National Park (admission free), which contains **Pang (Phaeng) Waterfall**, Pha Ngan's biggest drop. The park headquarters and a simple canteen lie 4km northeast of Thong Sala off the road to Chaloaklam – if you don't have a bike, take a Chaloaklam-bound songthaew as far as Ban Madeuawaan, and then it's a one-kilometre-plus signposted walk east. The main fall – bouncing down in stages over the hard, grey stone – is a steep 250m walk up a forest path. The trail then continues for 300m to a stunning viewpoint overlooking the south and west of the island.

The long, straight **south coast** is well served by songthaews from Thong Sala, and is lined with bungalows, especially around **Ban Khai**, to take the overspill from nearby Hat Rin. It's hard to recommend staying here, however: the beaches are mediocre by Thai standards, and the coral reef that hugs the length of the shoreline gets in the way of swimming.

On a quiet hillside above **Ban Tai**, 4km from Thong Sala, **Wat Khao Tham** holds ten-day **meditation retreats** most months of the year (B4500 per person to cover food); the American and Australian teachers emphasize compassionate understanding as the basis of mental development. Space is limited (retreats are especially heavily subscribed Dec–March), so it's best to pre-register either in person or in writing; go to ⓦwww.watkowtahm.org for full details of rules and requirements and the schedule of retreats.

Thong Sala listings

Bookshop English-language books, magazines and newspapers at Bookazine on the south side of the main road to the pier.
Hospital The island's basic main hospital (☎077 377034 or 077 375103) lies 3km north of town, on the inland road towards Mae Hat. There's also a 24hr emergency rescue service, staffed by volunteers (☎077 377500, 077 377194 or 081 698 9493).
Internet Phangan Batik, set back on the west side of the old main street (turn south off the main pier road).

Police station 2km up the Ban Chaloaklam road ☎077 377114.
Post office About 500m from the pier on the old main street (Mon–Fri 8.30am–noon & 1–4.30pm, Sat 9am–noon).
Vehicle rental Motorbikes (B150–200 per day) and jeeps (B800–1000) from many places on the main road to the pier.

Hat Rin

HAT RIN is now firmly established as the major party venue in Southeast Asia, especially in the peak seasons of August, December and January, but every month of the year people flock in for the **full moon party** – something like *Apocalypse Now* without the war. The atmosphere created by thousands of folk mashing it up on a beautiful, moon-bathed beach, lit up by fireworks and fire-jugglers, ought to be enough of a buzz in itself, but unfortunately drug-related horror stories are common currency here, and many of them are true: dodgy Ecstasy, *ya baa* (Burmese-manufactured methamphetamines) and all manner of other concoctions put an average of two farangs a month into hospital for psychiatric treatment. The local authorities have started clamping down on the trade in earnest, setting up a permanent police box at Hat Rin, instigating regular roadblocks and bungalow searches, paying bungalow and restaurant owners to inform on travellers whom they've sold drugs to, and drafting in scores of police (both uniformed and plain-clothes) on full moon nights. It doesn't seem to have dampened the fun, only made travellers a lot more circumspect. Other **tips** for surviving the full moon are mostly common sense: leave your valuables in your resort's safe – it's a bad night for bungalow break-ins – and don't take a bag out with you; keep an eye on your drink to make sure it's not spiked; watch out for broken bottles on the beach; and do not go swimming while under the influence – there have been several deaths by drowning at previous full moon parties. In 2008, there were also several reports of unprovoked, late-night gang attacks in Hat Rin, especially around full moon night. Note that when the full moon coincides with an important **Buddhist festival**, the party is moved one night away to avoid a clash; check out Ⓦ www.fullmoon.phangan.info for details.

Hat Rin occupies the flat neck of Pha Ngan's southeast headland, which is so narrow that the resort comprises two back-to-back beaches, joined by transverse roads at the north and south ends. The eastern beach, usually referred to as **Sunrise**, or Hat Rin Nok (Outer Hat Rin), is what originally drew visitors here, a classic curve of fine white sand between two rocky slopes; there's still some coral off the southern slope to explore, though the water is far from limpid these days. This beach is the centre of Hat Rin's action, with a solid line of bars, restaurants and bungalows tucked under the palm trees. **Sunset** beach, or Hat Rin Nai (Inner Hat Rin), which for much of the year is littered with flotsam, looks ordinary by comparison but has plenty of quieter accommodation. Unfortunately, development between the beaches does no justice to the setting: it's ugly, cramped and chaotic, with new low-rise concrete shophouses thrown up at any old angle. Businesses here, concentrated around what's known as **Chicken Corner**, where the southern transverse road meets the road along

▲ Sunrise beach, Hat Rin

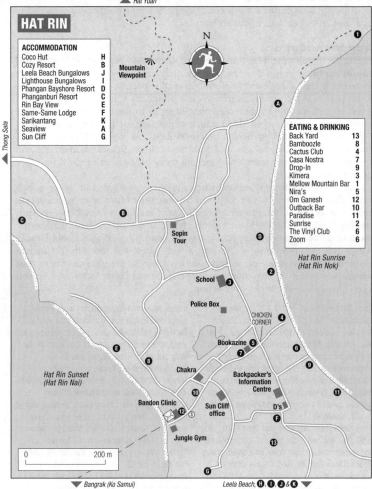

HAT RIN

ACCOMMODATION

Coco Hut	H
Cozy Resort	B
Leela Beach Bungalows	J
Lighthouse Bungalows	I
Phangan Bayshore Resort	D
Phanganburi Resort	C
Rin Bay View	E
Same-Same Lodge	F
Sarikantang	K
Seaview	A
Sun Cliff	G

EATING & DRINKING

Back Yard	13
Bamboozle	8
Cactus Club	4
Casa Nostra	7
Drop-In	9
Kimera	3
Mellow Mountain Bar	1
Nira's	5
Om Ganesh	12
Outback Bar	10
Paradise	11
Sunrise	2
The Vinyl Club	6
Zoom	6

the back of Sunrise, include supermarkets, overseas phone facilities, dozens of internet outlets, plenty of ATMs and bank currency-exchange booths, as well as outlets for more outré services such as bikini waxing and Playstation rental. Half-hearted attempts to tart up the large body of water in the middle of the headland with a few park benches and lights have been undermined by all-too-accurate signposts pointing to "Hat Rin Swamp".

Arrival

The awkwardness of **getting to Hat Rin** in the past helped to maintain its individuality, but this has changed now that the road in from Ban Khai has been paved. All the same, it's a winding, precipitous roller coaster of a route, covered by songthaews (B100) and air-con minibuses (B120–150) from Thong Sala – take care if you're driving a motorbike. The easiest approach of all, however, if you're coming from Ko Samui, or even Surat Thani, is on the *Haad Rin Queen* from Bangrak on Samui's north coast (see p.286): four boats a day cross to the pier on Sunset beach in under an hour.

Accommodation

For most of the year, Hat Rin has enough bungalows to cope, but on **full moon nights** over ten thousand revellers may turn up. Your options are either to arrive at least a day early (preferably several, especially during the Aug, Dec & Jan peak seasons – some resort owners even specify a minimum stay of up to seven nights); to forget about sleep altogether; or to hitch up with one of the many **party boats** (about B450 return per person, or B700 in a speedboat) organized through guest houses and restaurants on Ko Samui, especially at Bangrak and Bophut, which usually leave between 9pm and midnight and return around dawn; there's also generally transport by boat or car from other beaches on Pha Ngan.

Even at other times, staying on **Sunrise** is often expensive and noisy, though a few places can be recommended. On **Sunset**, the twenty or more resorts are laid out in orderly rows, and are especially quiet and inexpensive between April and June and in October. Many visitors choose to stay on the **headland** to the south of the main beaches, especially at white-sand, palm-fringed **Leela Beach**, which is a twenty-minute walk along a well-signposted route from Chicken Corner, on the west side of the promontory. At any of the places out here your bungalow is likely to have more peace and space and better views, leaving you a torchlit walk to the night-time action.

Coco Hut Leela Beach ☏077 375368, ⓦwww .cocohut.com. On a clean, quiet stretch of beach, this lively, efficiently run place is smart and attractive, with some traditional southern Thai elements in the architecture. On offer is a huge variety of accommodation, from rooms with fans and shared bathrooms to en-suite bungalows with air-con, fridges, wi-fi, TVs and DVDs, as well as an attractive pool, an adobe-style spa and internet access. Fan ❹, air-con ❽

Cozy Resort Northern transverse ☏089 770 2290. Pleasant staff and a range of smart concrete and white clapboard bungalows, on a broad, grassy slope set back from the road. Choose either fan and cold water or air-con and hot. One of the last places to fill at full moon and big discounts possible at other times. Fan ❹, air-con ❻

Leela Beach Bungalows Leela Beach ☏077 375094 or 081 995 1304, ⓦwww.leelabeach.com. A good, friendly and reliable budget choice with plenty of space under the palm trees and almost half of the white-sand beach to itself. Sturdy, well-built bungalows with mosquito nets and either cold or hot showers, or larger air-con cottages with hot water. Fan ❷–❹, air-con ❻

Lighthouse Bungalows On the far southwestern tip of the headland ☏077 375075, ⓦwww .lighthousebungalows.com. Phone for a boat pick-up from Sunset pier or Thong Sala, or do the 30min walk from Chicken Corner, the last section along a wooden walkway over the rocky shoreline. At this

friendly haven, fan-cooled wooden and concrete bungalows, sturdily built to withstand the wind and backed by trail-filled jungle, are priced according to size and comfort. The restaurant food is varied and tasty. Shared bathroom ❷, en-suite ❹–❺

Phangan Bayshore Resort In the middle of Sunrise ☏077 375227, ⓦwww.phanganbayshore .com. Hat Rin's first upmarket resort, a well-ordered, slightly institutional place, boasting 80m of beachfront. There's a large, kidney-shaped pool and a wide variety of close-knit villas, bungalows and rooms, with either air-con and hot water or fan and cold, on a green lawn shaded with palms. Fan ❹, air-con ❺

Phanganburi Resort Towards the north end of Sunset beach ☏077 375481–9, ⓦwww .phanganburiresort.net. Welcoming, luxury complex that encompasses three hotel blocks, dozens of bungalows, a spa and two very attractive pools in its extensive, beachside grounds. Decorated in a simple but smart Thai style, all the rooms have air-con, hot water, fridge, safety box and satellite TV. Substantial discounts on their website. ❽

Rin Bay View Near the pier on Sunset ☏077 375188. A good-value, friendly option in a central location, occupying a narrow strip of land – though not too tightly squeezed – and ornamented with flowers and trees. The air-con bungalows and rooms with mosquito screens, hot showers and balconies are a decent size and generally well maintained and clean. ❹

Same-Same Lodge Above Sunrise at the start of the road to Leela Beach ☎077 375200, ⓦwww .same-same.com. Well-run, welcoming and sociable Thai-Scandinavian spot. Above a popular bar-restaurant, clean, well-maintained and decent-sized rooms come with fan and cold showers or air-con and hot water. Fan ❸, air-con ❹

Sarikantang Leela Beach ☎077 375055–6, ⓦwww.sarikantang.com. Boutique resort with a swimming pool, a beachside spa and a good measure of style. Accommodation includes rooms with fans, verandas and hot-water bathrooms as well as chic, white-painted "deluxe" options with air-con, TVs, DVDs and separate outdoor sunken baths. ❺

Seaview At the quieter northern end of Sunrise ☎077 375160. Not to be confused with a copycat *Sea View* way out on the rocks beyond *Paradise*. On a big plot of shady land, this clean, orderly old-timer with a good restaurant offers air-con at the back, fans beachside, and en-suite bathrooms (with plans to install hot showers) throughout. Fan ❹, air-con ❺

Sun Cliff High up on the tree-lined slope above the south end of Sunset ☎077 375134 or 077 375463. Friendly place with great views of the south coast and Ko Samui, and a wide range of bright, well-maintained bungalows, some with large balconies, fridges, hot water and air-con. Fan ❷, air-con ❹

Eating

As well as good simple Thai food at some of the bungalows, Hat Rin sports an unnerving choice of **world cuisines** for somewhere so remote, and vegetarians are unusually well provided for.

Bamboozle Off the southern transverse, near Sunset pier. Among a wide variety of tasty Mexican food here, the chicken fajitas with all the trimmings (available as a good-value combo for two people, with margaritas) are especially good; plus pizzas and a short menu of tapas.

Casa Nostra On the southern transverse, opposite 7-Eleven. Excellent, tiny, Italian café-restaurant which prepares great pasta dishes – try the spaghetti bolognese – pizzas (whole or by the slice), espresso coffee, salads and plenty of other dishes for vegetarians, such as home-made cannelloni with ricotta and spinach, and a chocolate mousse to die for. Daily 2pm–midnight.

Kimera North of Chicken Corner. Italian-run restaurant offering everything from espresso and

chocolate *crostata* for breakfast, through sandwiches and antipasti, to a tasty *fritto misto* of deep-fried squid and prawns.

Nira's Near Chicken Corner. Justly popular restaurant and 24hr bakery. Around the clock it offers great croissants – sweet and savoury – cakes, quiches, sandwiches and coffees; from around 8am to 8pm, it operates like a food court in a Bangkok shopping centre, with different open kitchens rustling up burgers, hot dogs, pizzas and fish'n'chips, while more substantial Thai and Western main courses are available à la carte.

Om Ganesh On the southern transverse near the pier. Excellent, relaxing Indian restaurant with good thalis, biryanis, plenty of veggie dishes and breads, and cheerful service.

Nightlife

Nightlife normally begins at the south end of Sunrise at open-air dance halls such as the *Cactus Club* and *Drop-In*, which pump out mostly radio-friendly dance music onto low-slung candlelit tables and mats on the beach. Inland on the southern transverse, British-run *Outback Bar* is a lively meeting place with pool tables, big-screen sports, free wi-fi and well-received steak pies and the like. For somewhere to chill, head for *Mellow Mountain Bar*, which occupies a great position up in the rocks on the north side of Sunrise, with peerless views of the beach.

On **full moon night**, *Paradise* at the very southern end of Sunrise is the main party host, sometimes bringing in big-name international DJs. However, the mayhem spreads along most of Sunrise, fuelled by hastily erected drinks stalls and around a dozen major sound systems – listen out for psy-trance and driving techno at *Zoom* and *The Vinyl Club*, and house and drum'n'bass at *Sunrise* further up the beach. Next day, as the beach party winds down, *Back Yard* kicks off its afterparty at around eleven in the morning, with the best of the previous night's DJs; it's up the hill behind the south end of Sunrise off the path to Leela Beach.

Listings

Boat trips Several places on Hat Rin, such as Reggae Magic at *Cactus Club* (T 081 788 9143) and Sopin Tour on the northern transverse (T 077 375092), organize day-trips up the east coast and back, typically charging B700 (including simple lunch and snorkelling equipment) and taking in Mae Hat, Thong Nai Pan, Bottle Beach and Thaan Sadet.

Bookshops Bookazine, on the southern transverse, carries a decent line of new fiction and travel books, as well as magazines and newspapers. D's, next to the Backpackers Information Centre, is good for secondhand books.

Clinic Bandon International Hospital, a large private hospital on Ko Samui, runs a clinic on the southern transverse near the pier (T 077 375471–2).

Cookery courses *Same-Same Lodge* (see p.291) runs afternoon Thai cooking classes, including a market visit, lasting one (B900), three (B2500) or five (B4200) days.

Gym Jungle Gym (T 077 375115, W www.junglegym.co.th), near the pier, offers Thai boxing classes, a steam room, yoga and a juice bar.

Massages Chakra, in an alley off the southern transverse (T 077 375401, W www.islandwebs.com/thailand/chakra.htm), does the best massages in Hat Rin, and also runs massage courses.

Travel agent The excellent, English-Thai Backpackers Information Centre, based to the south of Chicken Corner (T 077 375535 or 089 471 7419, W www.backpackersthailand.com), is a very reliable and clued-up full-service travel agency – with a useful website – which can make bookings and give advice on local tours and travel throughout Thailand and Asia. Also acts as agents for Ko Pha Ngan's Lotus Diving and Ko Tao's Crystal Diving (with special deals available).

Vehicle rental Plenty of places on Hat Rin rent jeeps (B1000 per day) and motorbikes (from B150 per day). There have been lots of reports, however, of travellers being charged exorbitant amounts if they bring the vehicle back with even the most minor damage – at the very least, check the vehicle over very carefully before renting. *Sun Cliff* (see p.291), who have an office just off the southern transverse, is a reliable place for motorbikes, and won't try this scam.

The east coast

North of Hat Rin, the rocky, exposed **east coast** stretches as far as Ao Thong Nai Pan, the only substantial centre of development. No roads run along this coast, only a rough, steep, fifteen-kilometre trail, which starts from Hat Rin's northern transverse road (near *Thai House Bungalows*, partially waymarked with green painted dots as far as Hat Yuan) and runs reasonably close to the shore, occasionally dipping down into pristine sandy coves with a smattering of bungalows. From roughly January to September, one small boat a day runs via the east coast beaches from Hat Rin to Thong Nai Pan, having started its voyage across at Maenam on Ko Samui (see p.286). Otherwise there are ample longtails at Hat Rin that will take you up the coast – around B150 per person to Hat Thian, for example. See p.292 for information about organized day-trips by boat up this coast from Hat Rin.

Hat Yuan and Hat Thian

About ninety minutes up the trail, the adjoining small, sandy bays of Hat Yuan and Hat Thian have established a reputation as a quieter alternative to Hat Rin. A rough road has recently been bulldozed from Ban Kai, and the bays now sport about a dozen bungalow outfits between them. On **HAT YUAN**, *Barcelona* (T 077 375113; shared bathrooms ❶, en-suite ❸–❹) is a good budget choice, with plenty of space, great views and well-built accommodation either in clean, old-style huts or white bungalows with large verandas. The main operation on **HAT THIAN** is the *Sanctuary* (T 081 271 3614, W www.thesanctuarythailand.com; ❷–❾), which offers a huge range of basic and luxury en-suite bungalows and family houses, as well as dorm accommodation (B120), kayaking and good vegetarian meals, seafood and home-made bread and cakes. It also hosts courses in yoga, meditation and the like, has a branch of Jungle Gym (see above) and provides two kinds of treatment: the spa does massage, facials and beauty treatments, while the wellness centre goes in for fasting and cleansing.

Hat Sadet

Steep, remote **HAT SADET**, 12km up the trail from Hat Rin, has a handful of bungalow operations, sited here because of their proximity to **Thaan Sadet**, a boulder-strewn brook that runs out into the sea. The spot was popularized by various kings of Thailand – Rama V visited no less than fourteen times – who came here to walk, swim and vandalize the huge boulders by carving their initials on them; the river water is now considered sacred and is transported to Bangkok for important royal ceremonies. A rough track has been bulldozed through the woods above and parallel to Thaan Sadet to connect with the unpaved road from Thong Sala to Ao Thong Nai Pan. Best of the bungalows is the welcoming *Mai Pen Rai* (☎077 445090, ⓦwww.thansadet.com; ❸–❹), which has a variety of attractive, characterful accommodation with airy bathrooms (some with big upstairs terraces), either on the beach at the stream mouth or scattered around the rocks for good views; a jeep taxi leaves Thong Sala pier for the resort every day at 1pm (B150).

Ao Thong Nai Pan

AO THONG NAI PAN is a beautiful, semicircular bay backed by steep, green hills, which looks as if it's been bitten out of the island's northeast corner by a gap-toothed giant, leaving a tall hump of land dividing the bay into two parts, **Thong Nai Pan Noi** to the north, **Thong Nai Pan Yai** to the south. For non-guests it's worth making the climb up to *Panviman Resort* on the central outcrop, for the view from the restaurant perched over the cliff edge. With lovely, fine, white sand, the longer, more indented Thong Nai Pan Yai has marginally the better beach, but both halves of the bay are sheltered and deep enough for swimming. Thong Nai Pan is now developed enough for tourism to support a few internet shops, travel agents, dive outfits, bars, stand-alone restaurants, ATMs and a post office (on Thong Nai Pan Yai). A bumpy nightmare of a road, only partly paved, winds its way for 13km over the steep mountains from Ban Tai on the south coast to Thong Nai Pan: jeeps (B150 per person) connect with incoming and outgoing boats at Thong Sala every day. **Boat trips**, taking in Ao Mae Hat, Hat Khuat and Thaan Sadet, can be arranged through *White Sand*, for example (B700 per person, minimum ten people).

Accommodation

Dolphin At the quieter southern end of Thong Nai Pan Yai ☎077 238968, ✉kimgiet@hotmail.com. Popular, tranquil spot, overgrown with lush vegetation and with lots of comfortable salas to recline in. The large, very clean bungalows come with fans and en-suite bathrooms (the owners may upgrade some to air-con and hot water), and the beachfront restaurant, which serves good mostly Western breakfasts and lunches and great coffee, turns into a mellow tapas bar at night. The same family run the less atmospheric *Thai House* next door (☎077 445045), with smart wood and concrete, en-suite, fan-cooled bungalows set among flowers, at the same rates. ❸

Santhiya Thong Nai Pan Noi ☎077 428999, ⓦwww.santhiya.com. Extravagant, new, top-end

resort on a lush, hilly plot, where many guests arrive by speedboat transfer from Samui. Tons of golden teak have gone into the building of the villas and rooms, which are in a traditional Thai, occasionally kitsch style, with *bencharong* lamps, colourful paintings and fabrics; some boast outdoor bathrooms and their own large, infinity-edge pools with fine views. There's an impressive pool fed by a huge artificial waterfall beside a small private beach, divided by boulders from the main part of Thong Nai Pan Noi. Rates from B10,800. ❾

Star Huts Thong Nai Pan Noi ☎077 445085, ✉star_hut@hotmail.com. Probably the best budget choice on the northern beach: very clean, well-maintained wooden bungalows, with spacious, furnished balconies and air-con and hot water or fan and cold. The friendly owners dish up good food and offer internet access. Fan ❹, air-con ❺

White Sand Next door to *Dolphin* ☎077 445123. Friendly establishment in a colourful garden with a decent restaurant and smart, comfortable, concrete bungalows with en-suite bathrooms; the older, cheaper ones are by the beach. ❸

The north coast

The village of **BAN CHALOAKLAM**, on Ao Chaloaklam, the largest bay on the **north coast**, has long been a famous R&R spot for fishermen from all over the Gulf of Thailand, with sometimes as many as a hundred trawlers littering the broad and sheltered bay. As a tourist destination, it has little to recommend it save that it can easily be reached from Thong Sala, 10km away, by songthaew (B100) along a paved road. A handy, congenial spot for **lunch** on a round-island tour is *L'Oasi*, 1km south of the village on the main road (closed Sat). As well as burgers and barbecues, it serves up tasty Italian specialities and decent wine by the glass, in a pretty garden setting with a kids' playground.

Hat Khom has more to offer than Chaloaklam, a tiny cove dramatically tucked in under the headland to the east, with a secluded strip of white sand and good coral for snorkelling. Run by Thai rastas here, friendly *Coral Bay* (☎077 374245, ⓦwww.coral-bay-haad-khom.blogspot.com; ❶–❸) has plenty of space and great views on the grassy, flower-strewn promontory dividing Hat Khom from Ao Chaloaklam. The sturdy bungalows range from simple affairs with shared bathrooms and no fans to large pads with funky bathrooms built into the rock and fans (electricity evenings only); snorkelling equipment can be rented to make the most of Hat Khom's reef.

If the sea is not too rough, longtail boats run several times a day for most of the year from Ban Chaloaklam (east of the fishing pier; B100 per person or B400 per boat) to isolated **HAT KHUAT** (**BOTTLE BEACH**), the best of the beaches on the north coast, sitting between steep, jungle-clad hills in a perfect cup of a bay; you could also walk there along a testing trail from Hat Khom in around ninety minutes. Among a handful of resorts here, the best is *Smile Resort* (☎081 956 3133; ❸), which has a pleasant, quiet setting for its en-suite, fan-cooled bungalows, on a pretty flower-strewn hillside at the western end of the beach, and serves good Thai, Western and vegetarian food.

The west coast

Pha Ngan's **west coast** has attracted about the same amount of development as the forgettable south coast, but the landscape here is more attractive and varied, broken up into a series of long sandy inlets with good sunset views over the islands of the Ang Thong National Marine Park to the west; most of the bays, however, are sheltered by reefs which can keep the sea too shallow for a decent swim, especially between May and October. There's a paved coastal road up as far as Hat Salad, where it loops inland to meet the main inland road from Thong Sala via the hospital to Ao Mae Hat.

The first bay north of Thong Sala, Ao Wogtum (aka Hinkong), yawns wide across a featureless expanse that turns into a mud flat when the sea retreats behind the reef barrier at low tide. The nondescript bay of **AO SEETHANU** beyond is home to the excellent *Loy Fa* (☎077 377319, Ⓔloyfabungalow@yahoo.com; fan ❸, air-con ❻), a well-run, flower-strewn place that commands good views from its perch on top of Seethanu's steep southern cape, and offers decent snorkelling and swimming from its private beach below; bungalows are either on the hilltop or down on the beach, and come with fan and cold showers or air-con, hot water and minibar (some with TV); internet access and wi-fi are available.

Ao Chaophao

Continuing north, there's a surprise in store in the shape of **Laem Son Lake**, a tranquil stretch of clear water cordoned by pines; however, you should avoid swimming here, as the lake, site of a former tin mine, is considered toxic. Beyond, on the small, pretty bay of **AO CHAOPHAO**, *Seaflower* (℡077 349090, ℻077 349091; ❶–❹) is a quiet and congenial spot, set in a well-tended garden, with excellent veggie and non-veggie food. En-suite bungalows with their own bathrooms vary in price according to their size and age: the newer ones – more like cottages – have marble open-air bathrooms and big balcony seating areas. If you're feeling adventurous, ask the owner about the occasional three-day, two-night boat treks to Ang Thong National Marine Park (see p.268), which involve snorkelling, caving, catching your own seafood, and sleeping in tents or hammocks on the beach (B3500 per person, including food and soft drinks; minimum eight people). On a patch of grass behind *Seaflower*, the English-run *Village Green* pub-restaurant keeps the punters happy with a wide variety of breakfasts, great sandwiches (including the raid-the-pantry DIY option), and Thai and international (including Mexican) main courses, washed down with a big choice of drinks and cocktails; it also has a few well-equipped bungalows (℡077 349217, ⓦwww.villagegreen.phangan.info; fan ❸, air-con & hot water ❺).

Hat Yao

North of Chaophao, the long, gently curved, fine-sand beach of **HAT YAO** is gradually and justifiably becoming busier and more popular, with several stand-alone bars and restaurants, diving outfits, supermarkets, a bank currency-exchange booth, ATMs and jeep and bike rental. Among a nonstop line of bungalows here, a good budget bet is *Ibiza* (℡077 349121, ⓦwww.ibiza phangan.com; fan ❹, air-con ❺), a lively, central spot in a spacious garden with airy bungalows that run the full gamut, whether you're happy with a fan and cold water by the beach or want air-con and hot water. There's also internet access and an ATM, and they can arrange **boat trips** to Hat Salad, Mae Hat and Bottle Beach (B600 per person, including snorkels). On a broad, grassy bank behind the north end of the beach, English-run *Shiralea* has recently set up shop (℡080 719 9256, ⓦwww.shiralea.com; ❹). Spacious, very attractive thatched bungalows here come with hot water and fans; a pool and dive school are planned, as well as some air-conditioned and some cheaper (cold water) bungalows. Hat Yao's nicest upmarket spot is *Long Bay Resort*, with a long stretch of beach and spacious gardens towards the north end of the bay (℡077 349057–9, ⓦwww.longbay-resort.com; ❺–❾ including breakfast). Choose between small but smart bungalows and a range of large cottages, all with air-con and hot water. There's an attractive swimming pool, kayaks to rent and pricey internet access.

Hat Salad and Ao Mae Hat

To the north of Hat Yao, **HAT SALAD** is another pretty bay, sheltered and sandy, with good snorkelling off the northern tip. On the access road behind the beach is a rather untidy service village of shops, travel agents, bike and jeep rental outlets and internet offices. Among the dozen or so bungalow outfits, the congenial, family-friendly and well-run old-timer, ⚞ *Salad Hut*, stands out (℡077 349246, ⓦwww.saladhut.com; fan ❻, air-con ❼). Parallel to the beach-front behind a swimming pool, in a shady, colourful garden, are ten stylish bungalows done out in dark woods and white, with rattan furniture, day beds with axe cushions and large verandas. All come with hot water, minibar and TV, and a cooked breakfast at the chic bar-restaurant is included.

On the island's northwest corner, **AO MAE HAT** is good for swimming and snorkelling among the coral that lines the causeway to the tiny islet of Ko Maa. The broad, coarse-sand bay supports several bungalow resorts, notably the popular, friendly *Wang Sai Resort* by a shady stream at its south end (☎077 374238; ❷–❺). On a huge plot of land, most of the en-suite bungalows are set back from the beach and are generally priced according to size – the cheapest are up the slope behind, with great sunset views, while the most expensive are on the beach, with air-conditioning.

Ko Tao

KO TAO (Turtle Island) is so named because its outline resembles a turtle nose-diving towards Ko Pha Ngan, 40km to the south. The rugged shell of the turtle, to the east, is crenellated with secluded coves where one or two bungalows hide among the rocks. On the western side, the turtle's underbelly is a long curve of classic beach, **Hat Sai Ree**, facing **Ko Nang Yuan**, a beautiful Y-shaped group of islands offshore, also known as Ko Hang Tao (Turtle's Tail Island). The 21 square kilometres of granite in between is topped by dense forest on the higher slopes and dotted with huge boulders that look as if they await some Easter Island sculptor. It's fun to spend a couple of days exploring the network of rough trails, after which you'll probably know all 1100 of the island's inhabitants. Ko Tao is now best known as a venue for **scuba-diving**, with a wide variety of dive sites in close proximity; see the box on pp.298–299 for further details.

The island is the last and most remote of the archipelago that continues the line of Surat Thani's mountains into the sea. It served as a gaol for political prisoners from 1933 to 1947, then was settled by a family from Ko Pha Ngan. Now, there are around 120 sets of **bungalows** for visitors, just about enough to cope during the peak seasons of December to March and August, concentrated along the west and south sides; they include a small but rapidly growing number of upmarket resorts with such luxuries as air-con, hot water and swimming pools. There's a limited government supply of electricity, so some of it still comes from private generators – usually evenings only on the remotest beaches.

If you're just arriving and want to stay on one of the less accessible beaches, it might be a good idea to go with one of the touts who meet the ferries at Mae Hat, with pick-up or boat on hand, since at least you'll know their bungalows aren't full; otherwise call ahead, as even the remotest bungalows now have landlines or mobile phones and most owners come to market once a day (pick-ups are either free or B50–150 per person). Some resorts with attached scuba-diving operations have been known to refuse guests who don't sign up for diving trips or courses; on the other hand, many of the dive companies now have their own lodgings, available at a discounted price to divers. With a year-round customer base of divers – and resident dive instructors – more and more sophisticated Western **restaurants** and **bars** are springing up all the time, notably in Mae Hat and on Hat Sai Ree. For nightlife, your best bet is to watch out for posters advertising weekly and monthly parties around the island, which keep the crowds rotating.

The **weather** is much the same as on Pha Ngan and Samui (see p.266), but being that bit further off the mainland, Ko Tao feels the effect of the southwest monsoon more: June to October can have strong winds and rain, with a lot of debris blown onto the windward coasts.

Getting to Ko Tao

For details of boats **from Chumphon**, which is connected to Bangkok by train and bus, see p.258. The three main Chumphon–Ko Tao boat companies all offer through tickets from **Bangkok**; with Lomprayah (on Ko Tao ☏077 456176, ⓦwww.lomprayah.com), for example, this costs B850, including a VIP bus from Thanon Ram Bhuttri (☏02 629 2569–70), via **Hua Hin** (see p.244). It's better to buy a Bangkok–Tao through ticket direct from the boat company's office in the capital rather than from a travel agency, otherwise you're unlikely to get

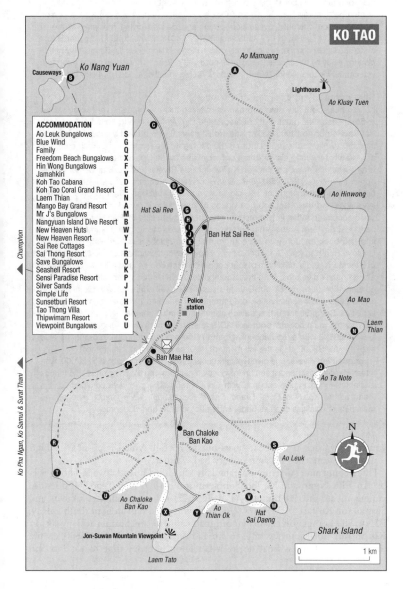

KO TAO

Ko Nang Yuan
Causeways B
Ao Mamuang
A
Lighthouse
Ao Kluay Tuen

ACCOMMODATION

Ao Leuk Bungalows	S
Blue Wind	G
Family	Q
Freedom Beach Bungalows	X
Hin Wong Bungalows	F
Jamahkiri	V
Koh Tao Cabana	D
Koh Tao Coral Grand Resort	E
Laem Thian	N
Mango Bay Grand Resort	A
Mr J's Bungalows	M
Nangyuan Island Dive Resort	B
New Heaven Huts	W
New Heaven Resort	Y
Sai Ree Cottages	L
Sai Thong Resort	R
Save Bungalows	O
Seashell Resort	K
Sensi Paradise Resort	P
Silver Sands	J
Simple Life	I
Sunsetburi Resort	H
Tao Thong Villa	T
Thipwimarn Resort	C
Viewpoint Bungalows	U

C
D E
F Ao Hinwong
Hat Sai Ree
G
H
I
J
K
L
Ban Hat Sai Ree

Chumphon

Ao Mao

Laem Thian
N

Police station
M

Ban Mae Hat
P O

Ko Pha Ngan, Ko Samui & Surat Thani

Q
Ao Ta Note

R

Ban Chaloke Ban Kao
S
Ao Leuk
N

T

U
Ao Chaloke Ban Kao
X
Y
Ao Thian Ok
V
Hat Sai Daeng
W
Shark Island

Jon-Suwan Mountain Viewpoint

Laem Tato

0   1 km

Scuba-diving off Ko Tao

Some of the best **dive sites** in Thailand are found off Ko Tao, which is blessed with outstandingly clear (visibility up to 35m), safe and relatively deep water close in to shore. On top of that, there's a kaleidoscopic array of coral species and other marine life, and you may be lucky enough to encounter whale sharks, barracudas, leatherback turtles and pilot whales. Diving is possible at any time of the year, with sheltered sites on one or other side of the island in any season – the changeover from southwest to northeast monsoon in November is the worst time, while visibility is best from April to July, in September (usually best of all) and October. Ko Tao supports a small, one-person recompression chamber, evacuation centre and general diving medicine centre at Badalveda in Mae Hat (☎077 456664 or 086 272 4618, ⓦwww.badalveda.com). Most of Ko Tao's dive centres, however, rely on the bigger chamber on Ko Samui, only ninety minutes away by speedboat (see p.269), but if you're keen to have help on the doorstep, you can buy insurance for Badalveda for B300 (six months) at your dive shop.

Dive companies, courses and trips

Ko Tao has about fifty **dive companies**, making this the largest dive-training centre in Southeast Asia; most of them are staffed by Westerners and based at Mae Hat, Hat Sai Ree or Ao Chaloke Ban Kao. You'll generally be offered discounted accommodation while you're diving (from B200 per night for a fan room, B500 air-con), but ask exactly how long it's for (three or four nights for an Openwater course), where it is and what it's like. Operators on Ko Tao include Crystal (PADI 5-Star Career Development Centre; ☎077 456106–7, ⓦwww.crystaldive.com), a large, lively, sociable outfit with a swimming pool, two big boats and a speedboat, offering courses in ten languages and the chance to buy videos of your dives; it provides a wide choice of good accommodation in two resorts, one on the north side of Mae Hat, and one on north Hat Sai Ree. At the other end of the scale are schools that are small, personal and laid-back (though with no compromising on safety) such as New Heaven on Chaloke Ban Kao (☎077 457045, ⓦwww.newheavendiveschool.com), which boasts of later starts and a maximum of four people on each course, and will take snorkellers along on their dive trips. Both these companies have a strong commitment to marine conservation (also check out Crystal's associated website ⓦwww.ecokohtao.com) and organize reef conservation programmes for qualified divers among many other activities. See p.58 for further advice about choosing a company.

By far the most popular **course**, PADI's four-day "Openwater" for beginners, costs around B9800 with a reputable dive centre. One-day introductions to diving are also available for B2000, as is the full menu of PADI courses, up to "Instructor".

For **qualified divers**, one dive typically costs B1000, a ten-dive package B7000, with fifteen-percent discounts if you bring your own gear. Among the more unusual offerings available are luxury live-aboards with Coral Grand Divers (ⓦwww.coralgranddivers.com) at the *Koh Tao Coral Grand Resort* (see p.303), while Crystal (see above) maintains specialities such as underwater photography and videography.

your money back if the boat turns out to be full, which is possible in high season, or is cancelled because of very bad weather.

Three companies currently operate daily scheduled boats between Thong Sala on **Ko Pha Ngan** and Ko Tao. Songserm (on Ko Tao ☎077 456274) does the voyage in around 90 minutes (1 daily; B250). Lomprayah (see above) and Seatran (on Ko Tao ☎077 456907–8) cover the ground in an hour (both 2 daily; B350). The Lomprayah catamaran originates at Maenam, Seatran at Bangrak, on **Ko Samui** (total journey time to Ko Tao on either 1hr 30min; B550), while the Songserm Express Boat docks at Na Thon (journey time to Ko Tao 3hr;

Main dive sites

Ko Nang Yuan Surrounded by a variety of sites, with assorted hard and soft corals and an abundance of fish: the **Nang Yuan Pinnacle**, a granite pinnacle with boulder swim-throughs, morays and reef sharks; **Green Rock**, a maze of boulder swim-throughs, caves and canyons, featuring stingrays and occasional reef sharks; **Twins**, two rock formations covered in corals and sponges, with a colourful coral garden as a backdrop; and the **Japanese Gardens**, on the east side of the sand causeway, which get their name from the hundreds of hard and soft coral formations here and are good for beginners and popular among snorkellers.

White Rock (Hin Khao) Between Hat Sai Ree and Ko Nang Yuan, where sarcophyton leather coral turns the granite boulders white when seen from the surface; also wire, antipatharian and colourful soft corals, and gorgonian sea fans. Plenty of fish, including titan triggerfish, butterfly fish, angelfish, clown fish and morays.

Shark Island Large granite boulders with acropora, wire and bushy antipatharian corals, sea whips, gorgonian sea fans and barrel sponges. Reef fish include angelfish, triggerfish and barracuda; there's a resident turtle, and leopard and reef sharks may be found as well as occasional whale sharks.

Hinwong Pinnacle At Ao Hinwong; generally for experienced divers, often with strong currents. Similar scenery to White Rock, over a larger area, with beautiful soft coral at 30m depth. A wide range of fish, including blue-spotted fantail stingrays, sweetlips pufferfish and boxfish, as well as hawksbill turtles.

Chumphon or **Northwest Pinnacle** A granite pinnacle for experienced divers, starting 14m underwater and dropping off to over 36m, its top covered in anemones; surrounded by several smaller formations and offering the possibility of exceptional visibility. Barrel sponges, tree and antipatharian corals at deeper levels; a wide variety of fish, in large numbers, attract local fishermen; barracudas, batfish, whale sharks (seasonal) and huge groupers.

Southwest Pinnacle One of the top sites in terms of visibility, scenery and marine life for experienced divers. A huge pyramid-like pinnacle rising to 6m below the surface, its upper part covered in anemones, with smaller pinnacles around; at lower levels, granite boulders, barrel sponges, sea whips, bushy antipatharian and tree corals. Big groupers, snappers and barracudas; occasionally, large rays, leopard and sand sharks, swordfish, finback whales and whale sharks.

Sail Rock (Hin Bai) Midway between Ko Tao and Ko Pha Ngan, emerging from the sand at a depth of 40m and rising 15m above the sea's surface. Visibility of up to 30m, and an amazing 10m underwater chimney (vertical swim-through). Antipatharian corals, both bushes and whips, and carpets of anemones. Large groupers, snappers and fusiliers, blue-ringed angelfish, batfish, kingfish, juvenile clown sweetlips and barracuda; a possible spot for sighting whale sharks and mantas.

B350). This Songserm boat originates at Don Sak, near **Surat Thani** (6hr to Ko Tao; B550); there's also a night boat from Surat Thani, departing at 11pm (℡077 284928 or 081 326 8973; 8hr; B550).

These services fluctuate according to demand, and in high season extra boats may appear. Voyages to and from Ko Tao may also be at the mercy of the weather at any time between June and January. Boat ticket prices fluctuate, too – for example, with so much competition between operators and routes, you'll currently find that leaving the island is a lot cheaper than the prices quoted above for getting there.

Information and island transport

There isn't a TAT office on Ko Tao, but the regularly updated and widely available free booklet, *Koh Tao Info*, is a useful source of **information**, along with its associated **website**, ⓦ www.kohtaoonline.com, which allows online accommodation booking.

You can **get around** easily enough on foot, but there are roads of sorts now to most of the resorts, though many are still very rough tracks, suitable for four-wheel drive only; motorbike **taxis** (from B60) and pick-ups (from B100 per vehicle plus B50 per person; rates go up at night, or for a 4WD to somewhere more remote) are available in Mae Hat. There are also **rental** mopeds (from B150 per day) and even a few jeeps (around B1400 per day). If you can, resist the temptation to rent a quad bike, or **ATV** – not only do they have a disproportionate number of accidents, but they're also very polluting. As on Ko Phangan, there have been lots of reports of travellers being charged exorbitant amounts if they bring the vehicle back with even the most minor damage – avoid the outfits in front of the main pier in Mae Hat, and rent from your bungalow or someone reliable like Mr J (motorbikes) or Save Shop (motorbikes and jeeps); for both see p.302.

Longtail-boat taxis are available at Mae Hat or through your bungalow, as are **round-island boat tours**, with stops for snorkelling and swimming (B550 per person in a longtail, B650 in a bigger boat, including lunch and pick-ups, or from around B1500 to hire your own boat for the day, for example through New Heaven dive school; see p.298); these take in snorkelling in the Japanese Gardens off Ko Nang Yuan, but you'll have to pay the B100 entrance fee if you set foot on the island to climb up to the viewpoint. Recommended operators include *AC Resort* on Hat Sai Ree (B650; ☎077 456197), who provide an informative and ecologically aware guide.

Eco Tao

With so many divers and other visitors coming to this tiny island, the pressures on the environment, both above and below the waterline, are immense. To minimize your impact, look out for the work of a community group, **Save Koh Tao**, which has been formed among concerned locals and resident Westerners, with a sub-group devoted to marine conservation (ⓦ www.marineconservationkohtao.com). Projects include a turtle-release programme, a campaign for septic tanks to stop waste water being run straight into the sea, and a bio-rock pilot project, an artificial reef, generated by passing an electric current through coral fragments, at Ao Thian Ok. Their monthly land and underwater clean-ups are given a big splash once a year, during the one- or two-day **Underwater Festival** in February or March, which involves mass beach-cleaning and fund-raising. At Mae Hat and on the main beaches, recycling bins are planned, as well as billboards listing businesses on the island that are involved with Save Koh Tao. Look out also for **Sabai Jai**, a free quarterly eco-travel magazine produced by the owner of Yakuzen Japanese Bath Village.

Much of what visitors can do to help is common sense: avoiding littering, recycling where possible and turning down plastic bags when you're shopping. The island suffers from a scarcity of water, with occasional droughts during the hot season after a poor rainy season, so conserve water whenever possible. In the sea, the main rule is not to touch the coral, which may mean avoiding snorkelling when the water is low from April to September – if in doubt, ask locally for advice, be careful and go out at high tide. Don't take away dead shells, and don't buy coral or shell jewellery. If you're feeling really keen, check whether your bungalow resort has a septic tank. And most dive schools have a Save Koh Tao donation box.

Mae Hat and around

All boats to Ko Tao dock at **MAE HAT**, a small, lively village in a pleasant, beachfront setting, which boasts the lion's share of the island's amenities. A paved high street heads straight up the hill from the main pier (eventually ending up in Ao Chaloke Ban Kao), with a narrower front street running at right angles, parallel to the seafront. Three of the ferry companies each have their own pier, Lomprayah and Songserm to the south of the main one, Seatran to the north.

Up a small hill on the southeast side of the village, inland from the Songserm pier, the delightful, eco-friendly **Yakuzen Japanese Bath Village** (daily except Wed 6–11pm, last admission 10pm; B700 1hr, B1000 1hr 30min; ☎084 837 3385) is highly recommended. Under the stars and the coconut palms here, you can relax in five landscaped bathing pools among the boulders, each set at a different temperature and made with different textures of rock and wood, and massage yourself with herbal compresses. There's also a tea lounge, an organic herb and fruit garden and a very good restaurant (see below).

Accommodation

The most characterful **accommodation** near Mae Hat is spread along the coast to the south.

Mr J's Bungalows Behind Mr J's supermarket, 5min walk north of Mae Hat ☎077 456066–7; and **Save Bungalows** near the Save Shop super-market on the village's front street just south of the piers ☎077 456347. If you just want functional, reliable, good-value accommodation, head for either of these very similar places, owned by the same family (see p.302). Large, clean, en-suite rooms (*Mr J's*) or bungalows (*Save*), with hot showers in some of the air-con offerings. Fan ❷, air-con ❺

Sai Thong Resort 40min walk south of Mae Hat (about B100 per person in a taxi-boat) ☎077 456868, ⓦwww.saithong-resort.com. In shady grounds spread between its own, private Sai Nual beach and the next small bay to the south, and popular with families, this resort provides a wide variety of en-suite bungalows – those by the beach are overpriced, but the "seaview" and "hillside" versions offer good value. Attractive, relaxing

restaurant serving Thai, Western and Burmese food, and internet, massages, kayaks and snorkels are available. Fan ❸–❻, air-con ❼

Sensi Paradise On the lower slopes of the headland just south of the village ☎077 456244, ⓦwww.kohtaoparadise.com. Charming resort in flower-covered grounds, offering a pretty beachside restaurant, free snorkelling equipment and some of the best upmarket accommodation on the island: well-designed wooden Thai-style cottages and villas with mini-bars, some with air-con and some with large terraces and open-air bathrooms. ❽

Tao Thong Villa 50min walk south of Mae Hat (about B100 per person in a taxi-boat) ☎077 456078. Sturdy, en-suite bungalows dotted around a rocky outcrop and the slope behind, with a breezy restaurant on the tiny, sandy isthmus in between. Plenty of shady seclusion and good snorkelling and swimming. Fan ❷, air-con ❺

Eating and drinking

Cappuccino 100m from the pier up the high street. French-run café that does a mean pain au chocolat and coffee, plus gourmet sandwiches, burgers and salads.

🏃 **Dirty Nelly's** Off the north side of the high street near the main pier. Helpful, Irish-managed pub, which has decent Guinness on tap, a pool table, big-screen sports, a varied

menu of very good food and occasional live bands.

🏃 **Kakureya** Yakuzen Japanese Bath Village (see above) ☎087 936 2160 or 084 837 3385. Small, relaxing and thoroughly authentic Japanese restaurant, serving the best food on the island. Don't miss the excellent tasting set as a starter, which you might follow with delicious, lightly grilled tuna and seaweed salad. If you're a fan of *ramen* noodles, get there early – the chef only makes two servings a day. Daily except Wed 6–10pm.

La Matta High street, beyond *Cappuccino*. Delicious pizzas in scores of varieties, tasty home-made pastas, *panini* and a few Italian meat and fish dishes, as well as espresso coffees and home-made limoncello.

Tukta about 2km out on the Chaloke Ban Kao road. Relaxing, cheap restaurant – open-sided with a few garden tables – serving a wide choice of tasty Thai food, including a good *kaeng matsaman* with chicken.

Whitening 200m south of the main pier down the front street. Congenial, mellow and chic bar-restaurant, with a great deck and relaxing beach tables overlooking the bay. It dishes up some very tasty and creative Thai and Western food, as well as mean cocktails.

Listings

Banks Siam City Bank, up the high street on the left, with an ATM and Western Union facilities; and at the crossroads hard by the main pier, a Krung Thai Bank currency-exchange booth with an ATM.

Books B-Books up the high street on the right sells secondhand and new books and international newspapers.

Health Mae Hat has a small government health centre (halfway up the high street, turn right) plus several private clinics and pharmacies.

Internet Prasit Service, up the high street on the left, has a good reputation both as a travel agent and for internet access.

Police station 5min walk north of Mat Hat, on the narrow road towards Hat Sai Ree (☎077 456631).

Post office At the top of the village (turn left), near the start of the main paved road to Ban Hat Sai Ree, with poste restante facilities.

Supermarket and travel agency 5min walk north of Mae Hat, at the top of a small rise opposite the primary school, you'll find the head office of Ko Tao's all-purpose fixer, and all-round character, Mr J. Here you can rent motorbikes, recycle batteries, buy and sell secondhand books, even borrow money. Mr J's family runs another supermarket and travel agency in Mae Hat, Save Shop, south of the Songserm pier.

Watersports MV Watersports (☎077 456065 or 087 264 2633, ⓦwww.kohtaowatersports.com), south of the piers on the front street opposite *Save Bungalows*, is one of several places on the island that rents kayaks (B100 per hr, two-person B150 per hr), as well as offering sailing rental and tuition, windsurfer rental and tuition, wakeboarding and water-skiing.

Hat Sai Ree

To the north of Mae Hat, beyond a small promontory, you'll find **Hat Sai Ree**, Ko Tao's only long beach. The strip of white sand stretches for 2km in a gentle curve, backed by a smattering of coconut palms and around twenty bungalow resorts. A narrow, mostly paved track runs along the back of the beach to the village of Ban Hat Sai Ree, paralleled by the main road further inland. **Rock climbing** and bouldering, including courses for beginners, are offered by Goodtime Adventures, based at the *Narakaan Hotel* on the southern half of the beach (☎087 275 3604, ⓦwww.gtadventures.com); they also organize abseiling, hiking and mountain biking, as well as pub crawls and booze cruises.

Around the northerly end of the beach spreads **BAN HAT SAI REE**, a burgeoning village of supermarkets, clinics, pharmacies, travel agents, internet outlets, a Siam City Bank currency-exchange booth with an ATM, restaurants and bars. **Yoga** classes are held twice a day at *Blue Wind Bungalows* (not Sun; B300; ☎084 440 6755, ⓔshambhalayogaa@yahoo.co.nz), with reiki massages available on request. Inland, there's a branch of B-Books (see above) in Sairee Plaza on the main road from Mae Hat, while at the east end of the village, on the road towards Ao Hinwong, is Monsoon **gym** (☎089 866 4511), which offers *muay thai* classes.

Accommodation

Blue Wind Two doors north of *Sunsetburi Resort* ℡077 456116, ✉bluewindwadear@hotmail.com. Good restaurant (see below) and a variety of smart, well-kept, en-suite rooms and bungalows, some with hot water and a few with air-con and TV, scattered about a shady compound. Fan ❷, air-con ❻

Koh Tao Cabana Far north end of beach ℡077 456504–5, ⓦwww.kohtaocabana.com. Welcoming, rustic-chic luxury resort on a long beach frontage, backed by pleasant lawns that are dotted with elegant day beds. All the thatched, air-con rooms (at the lower end of this price range) feature open-air bathrooms with hot water: choose between round, adobe-style villas up the slope behind the beach and stilted cottages on the headland, some with fantastic views. A spa, swimming pool, pool villas and wi-fi are planned. ❾

Koh Tao Coral Grand Resort North of Ban Hat Sai Ree ℡077 456431–4, ⓦwww.kohtaocoral .com. Welcoming luxury beachfront development with a dive school, where the sandstone-pink octagonal cottages with polished coconut-wood floors and large, attractive bathrooms gather – some a little tightly – around a pretty, Y-shaped pool; all have hot water, TV and air-con. Breakfast included. ❽

Sai Ree Cottages Towards the midpoint of the beach, 20min walk from Mae Hat ℡077 456126, ℱ077 456558. In a large, beautiful, flower-strewn garden, the full spectrum of digs, all en suite and well maintained, from primitive huts to sturdy bungalows, many with hot water, some with air-con. Kayaks for rent and excellent grub. Fan ❷–❺, air-con ❺–❻

Seashell Resort Next door to *Sai Ree Cottages* ℡077 456271, ⓦwww.diveseashell.com. In a spacious, tidy compound, a friendly, well-run place with a dive school and a popular seafood restaurant (a swimming pool is planned); it offers traditional massage and massage courses, as well as very smart, sturdy, en-suite bungalows, either with fans or with air-con, hot water, fridge and TV. Fan ❹, air-con ❻

Silver Sands Ban Hat Sai Ree ℡077 456603–6, ⓦwww.silver-sands-resort.com. Congenial resort on a narrow but lush and shady strip of land, where the bungalows are clean and well kept. The cheapest are simple wooden affairs well off the beach, while the beachside air-con cottages with hot water command top dollar (some of the fan rooms also have hot showers). Internet access and snorkels to rent. Chic, new air-con rooms done out in black and primary colours are on the drawing board. Fan ❷–❹, air-con ❻

Simple Life Ban Hat Sai Ree ℡077 456142, ⓦwww.simplelifedivers.com. Good beachfront choice with a dive school, offering comfortable, en-suite, fan-cooled bungalows, great food, notably fresh, barbecued fish, and a lively beach bar. ❸

Sunsetburi Resort Ban Hat Sai Ree, next door to *Simple Life* ℡077 456266, ℱ077 456101. On a narrow but tree-lined strip of land with a beachside swimming pool, modern, concrete cottages with TVs and minibars, many with air-con and some with the luxury of hot water. Fan ❹, air-con ❺–❽

Thipwimarn Resort North of Hat Sai Ree, opposite Ko Nang Yuan ℡077 456409, ⓦwww .thipwimarnresort.com. Stylish, eco-friendly upscale spot with a spa, which tumbles down a steep slope, past an elevated, infinity-edge swimming pool, to its own small beach. Dotted around the hillside, smart, thatched, whitewashed villas, most with hot water, enjoy a fair measure of seclusion, satellite TV, minibars and fine sunset views; in one or two, you have the option of keeping the air-con off, at a cheaper rate. ❽

Eating and drinking

Blue Wind Two doors north of *Sunsetburi Resort* (see above). Very good beachside restaurant serving up home-made breads, cakes, croissants, and fruit shakes, as well as Indian and Thai food, home-made pasta and other Western meals.

Lotus Bar On the beach near *Papa's Tapas*. Raucous, very popular late-night haunt for drinking and dancing,

New Heaven Deli & Bakery On the beach road on the south side of the village. Stylish spot offering great home-baked breads and cakes, as well as sandwiches, salads, ice cream and booster juices. Daily 7.30am–8pm.

Papa's Tapas On the beach road on the south side of the village ℡077 457020. The Swedish chefs here, one of Tao's few attempts at a gourmet restaurant, can be a bit hit-and-miss, though their tuna sashimi with vegetable tempura is very good. Contemporary tapas and good house wine are also available, and there's a mellow lounge with sheesha pipes. Daily 6–11pm.

Ko Nang Yuan

One kilometre off the northwest of Ko Tao, **KO NANG YUAN**, a close-knit group of three tiny islands, provides the most spectacular beach scenery in these parts, thanks to the causeway of fine white sand that joins up the islands. You can easily swim off the east side of the causeway to snorkel over the Japanese Gardens, which feature hundreds of hard and soft coral formations. Boats from the Lomprayah pier in Mae Hat, just south of the main pier, run back and forth twice a day (B150 return), but note that rules to protect the environment here include banning visitors from bringing cans, plastic bottles and fins with them, and day-trippers are charged B100 to land on the island; alternatively, it's B550 for an all-in day-trip, including boat transfers, buffet lunch and island fee (snorkels B50 extra). Transfers from and to Mae Hat are free for people staying at the *Nangyuan Island Dive Resort* (T077 456088–93, W www.nangyuan.com; fan ❻, air-con ❼–❾), which makes the most of its beautiful location, its bungalows, all with en-suite bathrooms and fridges, some with hot water, spreading over all three islands.

The north and east coasts

The lone bay on the north coast, **Ao Mamuang** (Mango Bay), is a beautiful, tree-clad bowl, whose shallow reef is a popular stop on snorkelling day-trips, though there's little in the way of a beach. The attractive bar-restaurant of *Mango Bay Grand Resort* spreads its large deck over the rocks here (T077 456948–9, W www.mangobaykohtao.com; fan ❻, air-con ❼–❽; breakfast and transfer included). Its well-appointed, colourful, heavily varnished wooden bungalows on stilts all come with hot water, and some have air-con and TV.

The sheltered inlets of the east coast, most of them containing one or two sets of bungalows, can be reached by boat, pick-up or four-wheel-drive. The most northerly inhabitation here is at **Ao Hinwong**, a deeply recessed, limpid bay strewn with large boulders and great coral reefs, which has a particularly remote, almost desolate air. Nevertheless, the bay's most spacious resort, *Hin Wong Bungalows* (T077 456006 or 081 229 4810; ❷), is welcoming and provides good, en-suite accommodation on a steep, grassy slope above the rocks, in wooden bungalows with mosquito nets and large bathrooms. It has a nice waterside deck in front of its restaurant and rents out kayaks and snorkels. In the middle of the coast, the dramatic tiered promontory of **Laem Thian** shelters a tiny beach and a colourful reef on its south side. With the headland to itself, *Laem Thian* (T077 456477 or 081 083 5186, E pingpong_laemthian@hotmail .com; fan ❷–❹, air-con ❺) has a secluded, castaway feel, offering comfy wooden bungalows, some with open-air bathrooms, and rooms in an incongruous hotel-style block; the layout of the resort isn't particularly appealing, but it's friendly and well maintained. The food's decent, and kayaks, snorkels and round-island boat trips (B650 per person, minimum four people) are on offer.

Laem Thian's coral reef stretches down towards **Ao Ta Note**, a horseshoe inlet sprinkled with boulders and plenty of coarse sand, with excellent snorkelling just north of the bay's mouth. The pick of the half-dozen resorts here is *Family* (*Ta Note Bay Dive Resort*; T077 456757–8; fan ❹, air-con ❼), with a dive centre and plenty of well-designed, en-suite wooden bungalows with solar-powered hot water, set among thick bougainvillea, some enjoying large verandas and views out towards Ko Pha Ngan and Ko Samui. Snorkelling equipment is available at the resort, while the *Black Tip Dive Resort* (T077 456488, W www .blacktipdiving.com) offers kayaking, wakeboarding and snorkelling trips. The last bay carved out of the turtle's shell, **Ao Leuk**, has a well-recessed beach and

Underwater Thailand

Dip your head beneath the surface of the Andaman Sea or the Gulf of Thailand and a whole new world of outrageous shapes and colours opens up. The figures speak for themselves: together these two tracts play host to over 850 species of open-water fish, more than 100 species of reef fish and some 270 species of hard coral. On these pages we highlight just a few of the most fascinating examples, so you'll know more about what you're seeing while out diving or snorkelling.

Coral

Coral reefs are living organisms composed of a huge variety of marine life forms, which provide a habitat for hundreds of species of fish, but the foundation of every reef is its **stony coral** constructions such as **boulder, cabbage patch, cave, mushroom, bushy staghorn** and **brain coral**. Though seemingly inanimate, stony coral is actually composed of colonies of polyps – minuscule invertebrates which feed on plankton, generally depend on algae and direct sunlight for photosynthesis, and extract calcium carbonate (limestone) from sea water in order to reproduce. The polyps use this calcium carbonate to build new skeletons outside their bodies – an asexual reproductive process known as budding – and this is how a reef is formed. It's an extraordinarily slow process, with colony growth averaging between 0.5cm and 2.8cm a year.

Fleshy, plant-like **soft coral**, such as **dead man's fingers** and **elephant's ear**, is also composed of polyps, but has flaccid internal skeletons built from protein rather than calcium. The lack of an external casing means the polyps' vivid colours are much more visible and, as they do not depend on direct sunlight, they flourish at greater depths, swaying with the currents and using tentacles to trap micro-organisms.

Horny coral, or **gorgonians**, like **sea whips** and **sea fans**, are a cross between stony and soft coral, while **sea anemones** have the most obvious, and poisonous, tentacles of any member of the coral family, using them to trap fish and other large prey.

Cabbage coral ▲

Soft corals and a school of pygmy sweepers ▼

Thailand's top diving spots

▶▶ **Ko Tao** Boasting a dozen great spots in deep, clear water close in to shore – at least some of which can be accessed all year round – "Turtle Island" has established itself as Southeast Asia's largest dive-training centre.

▶▶ **Ko Similan** National park archipelago that's rated as one of the best and most varied diving destinations in the world. Prolific reefs dominate the east-facing coasts while the west is all granite boulders, caves and tunnels. Visibility extends to 30m and the cast of celebrity visitors includes white-tip sharks, barracuda, giant lobster, enormous tuna and whale sharks.

▶▶ **Ko Phi Phi** Fringing reefs of hard and soft corals that descend to 35m, plus wrecks and varied marine life mean there's plenty here for both snorkellers and divers, all within easy reach of Phi Phi's hotels, nightlife and beautiful beaches.

▶▶ **Hin Daeng and Hin Muang** Two spectacular, and challenging, reef walls that attract lots of reef fish and pelagics. Hin Muang, at well over 50m, is the deepest drop in Thailand and reliable for stingrays, manta rays, tuna, jacks, silvertip sharks and whale sharks.

▶▶ **Ko Lipe** Around forty sites, most of them nearby in the undisturbed Ko Tarutao National Park, notable for their colourful diversity of topography, (including wrecks) of corals, both hard and soft, and of species, including rare surgeonfish, sailfish and demon stingers.

▶▶ **Ko Surin and Richelieu Rock** The shallow reefs around the awesomely beautiful Surin islands offer the best snorkelling in the country: plentiful sea anemones, flamboyant giant clams, spectacular coral gardens and countless species of reef fish. The nearby sunken pinnacle at Richelieu Rock is considered the country's premier dive site, famed for its manta rays and whale sharks.

▲ Hard corals

▼ Manta ray

Angelfish ▲

Surgeonfish ▼

Parrotfish ▼

Reef fish

The algae and plankton that accumulate around coral colonies attract a catalogue of fish known collectively as **reef fish**. Most are small in stature, with vibrant and exotically patterned skins for camouflage against the coral, and flattened bodies, broad tails and specially adapted fins for easy manoeuvring around the tiniest of reef crannies.

Butterfly fish are typically well designed: named for the butterfly-like movements of their thin, flat, yellow-white-and-black bodies, they can swim backwards, and some also have elongated snouts for nosing into crevices; a number even sport eye-like blotches near the tail to confuse predators.

Members of the similarly well-fashioned **angelfish** family include the **emperor angelfish**, with its luscious tangerine and blue stripes, which makes an audible clicking sound when disturbed and can grow up to 30cm in length.

The **moorish idol** is easily recognizable by the long pennant fin that trails from its dorsal fin, and by its pronounced snout and dramatic bands of colour.

There are approximately one hundred different species of **surgeonfish**, each with its own distinctive markings, but they all share the feature that gives them their name – a sharp blade on either side of their tail-base that becomes erect when antagonized and can inflict serious damage.

Among the most impressive reef fish that school are the huge shoals of silvery **fusilierfish**, which move as one, changing direction in an eyecatching flash of rippling silver.

Some reef fish, among them the ubiquitous **parrotfish**, eat coral. With the help of a bird-like beak, which is in fact several teeth fused together, the parrotfish scrapes away at the coral, leaving characteristic white scars, and then grinds the fragments down with another set of back teeth – a practice reputedly responsible for the erosion of a great deal of Thailand's reef.

Anemonefish are so called because, having covered themselves in the sea anemone's mucus, they are able to move amongst and gain protection from the anemone's venomous tentacles, which would paralyse other fish on contact. Since the movie *Finding Nemo* came out, their most famous species, the **clown anemonefish**, is generally just referred to as "Nemo".

Equally as predictable as sightings of anemonefish is the presence of cleaner fish, or **cleaner wrasse**, on the edges of every shoal of reef fish. Streamlined, with a long snout and jaws that act like tweezers, a cleaner fish spends its days picking parasites off the skins of other fish, such as the normally voracious **grouper fish** – a symbiotic relationship essential to both parties.

The commonly sighted **coral hind** is a close but more colourful relative of the grouper and is often found among bushy staghorn coral.

Larger, less frequently spotted visitors to Thailand's offshore reefs include the **moray eel**, whose elongated jaws of viciously pointed teeth make it a deadly predator; it hunts mainly at night and often holes up in coral caves during the day.

The similarly be-fanged **barracuda** can grow to two metres and is the world's fastest-swimming fish.

▲ Clown anemonefish

▼ Moray eels

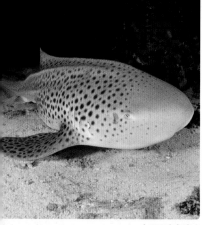

Leopard shark ▲

Sharks and rays

Passive **leopard sharks** and the more excitable **white-tip reef sharks** are quite common off the Andaman coast reefs, but you'd have to be lucky to encounter a **whale shark**, which, at up to 18m long, is the largest fish in the world.

It is sometimes possible to swim with a **manta ray**, whose extraordinary flatness, strange wing-like fins, and massive size – up to 6m across and weighing some 1600kg – make it an astonishing presence.

Turtles

Occasionally seen paddling around reef waters, turtles come in four local species, all of them endangered: the green, the leatherback, the Olive Ridley and the hawksbill. The loggerhead turtle also once swam in Thai waters, until the constant plundering of its eggs rendered it locally extinct.

Of the remaining four species, the **green turtle** is the commonest, a mottled brown creature named not for its appearance but for the colour of the soup made from its flesh. Adults weigh up to 180kg and are herbivorous, subsisting on sea grass, mangrove leaves and algae.

The **leatherback**, encased in a distinctive ridged shell, is the world's largest turtle, weighing in at between 250kg and 550kg; it eats nothing but jellyfish.

The small **Olive Ridley** weighs up to 50kg and feeds mainly on shrimps and crabs.

Named for its peculiar beak-like mouth, the **hawksbill** is prized for its spectacular carapace (the sale of which was banned by CITES in 1992); it weighs up to 75kg and lives off a type of sea sponge.

Whale shark ▲

Hawksbill turtle ▼

Invertebrates

Thailand's reefs support countless species of **invertebrates**, including spiral-feathered **Christmas-tree worms**, also sometimes evocatively known as bottle-brush worms, which embed their lower bodies in coral heads; all sorts of multi-celled, multi-hued **sponges**, both encrusting and free-standing; neon-bright squamose giant clams, which burrow into the reef, exposing only their soft, flamboyantly coloured mantle; and a thousand-plus species of hermaphroditic, shell-less mollusc known as **nudibranchs** or sea slugs, which come in an arresting array of patterns and shapes and live in shallow waters.

Of the reef's numerous spiny echinoderms, the commonest **sea urchins**, which also tend to live in shallow areas near shore, are those with evil-looking black spines up to 35cm in length, though some varieties are covered in short, blunt spines or even excruciatingly painful flower-like pincers.

The magnificent **crown-of-thorns starfish** is also protected by highly venomous spines, which sheath the twenty or so "arms" that extend from a body that can measure up to 50cm in diameter. Disastrously for many reefs, the crown-of-thorns starfish feeds on coral, laying waste to as much as fifty square centimetres of stony coral in a 24-hour period. The much more benign **feather stars** also have multiple feather-like arms arranged in star formations and come in many versions; they feed at night, crawling along reef surfaces with the help of tiny jointed limbs, or cirri, to sway in the current.

Though hideous, the **sea cucumber**, which looks like a large slug and lies

▲ Crown-of-thorns starfish

▼ Coral off Ko Tao

half-buried on the sea bed, is quite harmless. Deceptively slothful in appearance, sea cucumbers are constantly ingesting and excreting so much sand and mud that the combined force of those in a three-square-kilometre area can together redistribute one million kilogrammes of sea-bed material a year.

Large jellyfish with a jackfish in its tentacles ▲

Lionfish ▼

Banded sea snake ▼

Biters and stingers

Thailand is home to 25 species of **sea snake**, whose tails are flattened to act as an efficient paddle in water. Most sea snakes are venomous, though not aggressive. Of the poisonous ones, the commonest and most easily recognized is the banded sea snake, which is silvery grey with thirty to fifty black bands and a slightly yellow underside at its front end. It grows to 1.5m and inhabits shallow coastal waters, coming onto land to lay its eggs.

Other harmful creatures to be avoided include the highly camouflaged seabed-dwelling **stonefish** and **scorpionfish**, both of whom can be very hard to spot but have extremely poisonous spines which are dangerous when trodden on. The magnificent **lionfish** should also be admired from afar as its impressive plumes are poisonous if brushed against, as are the tentacles of the **jellyfish**. The **blue-spotted ray** or **stingray** has two venomous spines on its long tail with which it lashes out when threatened; as it tends to bury itself with almost complete disguise in the mud or sand near reefs, it can be a particular hazard to unwary divers. Another thing to be wary of is so-called **fire coral** (not actually a true coral but a coral-like brownish encrustation), which is found in shallow waters on the edge of the reef and is covered in a mass of tiny, fuzz-like tentacles that can inflict a painful burn.

▲ Ao Hinwong, Ko Tao

water that's deep enough for good swimming and snorkelling, featuring hard and soft coral gardens. It's home to the en-suite wooden bungalows and large family rooms at *Ao Leuk Bungalows* (☎077 456692; ❸–❺), which enjoy plenty of space and shade, either in the palm grove behind the beach or up the hill to the south. If there happens to be no room here, don't worry – the same friendly family own the bay's other two resorts, its taxis and the beachfront bar, where snorkels and kayaks are available.

The south coast

The southeast corner of the island sticks out in a long, thin mole of land, which points towards Shark Island, a colourful diving and snorkelling site just offshore; the headland shelters the sandy beach of **Hat Sai Daeng** on one side if the wind's coming from the northeast, or the rocky cove on the other side if it's blowing from the southwest. Straddling the headland is *New Heaven Huts* (☎087 933 1329, ✉newheavenhut@yahoo.com; ❸–❹), a laid-back, well-equipped place with a good kitchen and snorkelling equipment, whose pleasantly idiosyncratic en-suite bungalows enjoy plenty of elbow room and good views. Overlooking **Ao Thian Ok**, the next bay along on the south coast, is the same family's *New Heaven Resort* (☎077 456462, ⓦwww.newheavenkohtao.com; fan ❻, air-con ❼–❽), with a scenic restaurant and attractive bungalows. On a beautiful deck perched high on the eastern flank of the Laem Tato headland, classic Thai dishes, including seafood specialities, are dished up in the evening, simpler fare at lunch-time; the bungalows, on a tree-covered slope running down to a private sandy beach, feature large bathrooms and verandas with great views, and include family and air-con rooms. The remote, rocky coastline between Hat Sai Daeng and Ao Thian Ok provides the spectacular location for a luxurious **spa resort**, *Jamahkiri* (call ☎077 456400–1 for reservation and pick-up; free hourly shuttle from their Mae Hat office, next to *Café del Sol* on Mae Hat Square; ⓦwww .jamahkiri.com; from B8000, including breakfast; ❾), which offers saunas, body wraps, massages, facials and other beauty treatments. There's also a panoramic bar-restaurant, a dive centre, a tiered swimming pool and a fitness centre, as well as opulent, secluded rooms, in a chic mix of Thai and Western design, with red silk furnishings, air-con, hot water, satellite TVs and mini-bars.

The deep indent of **Ao Chaloke Ban Kao** is protected from the worst of both monsoons, and consequently has seen a fair amount of development, with several dive resorts taking advantage of the large, sheltered, shallow bay. Behind the beach are clinics, ATMs, bike rental shops, bars and restaurants. Among them is *Koppee*, a lovely little **bakery-café** on the main road near the centre of the beach (daily 7.30am–7pm), with books and magazines to browse and reasonably priced **internet** access. It rustles up tasty gourmet sandwiches on a choice of breads, salads, all-day breakfasts, as well as a good choice of drinks and sweet treats. Opposite, at New Heaven dive school, run by the same family, drop-in **yoga** classes are held daily between 5.30 and 7pm (B200).

Two **accommodation** options stand out from the crowd here. Run by a friendly bunch, *Viewpoint Bungalows* (T077 456666 or 077 456777, Wwww .kohtaoviewpoint.com; ❺–❻) sprawl along the western side of the bay and around the headland beyond, with great sunset views; architect-designed in chic Balinese style, they boast rock bathrooms, lovely polished hardwood floors, mosquito nets and attractive verandas. There are also a couple of tasty air-con villas with their own infinity-edge pools (❾; B10,000 per night), as well as kayaks and snorkels to explore the reef just offshore.

On the east side of the bay, *Freedom Beach Bungalows* (T077 456596; fan ❸–❹, air-con ❻) offers a mix of old-style, blue-painted, en-suite huts with sturdy corrugated roofs and small verandas, and smart, new bungalows with fan or air-con and hot water; they dot a spacious slope that leads down to a lovely decked bar on the idyllic white sand of **Freedom Beach**, a secluded palm-lined spot carved out of the Laem Tato headland. Rough signposts will lead you beyond the bungalows for a fifteen-minute walk, the last stretch up a steep hillside to **Jon-Suwan Mountain Viewpoint**, which affords fantastic views, especially at sunset, over the neighbouring bays of Chaloke Ban Kao and Thian Ok and across to Ko Pha Ngan and Ko Samui.

Nakhon Si Thammarat and around

NAKHON SI THAMMARAT, the south's second-largest town, occupies a blind spot in the eyes of most tourists, whose focus is fixed on Ko Samui, 100km to the north. Nakhon's neglect is unfortunate, for it's an absorbing place: the south's major pilgrimage site and home to a huge military base, it's relaxed, self-confident and sophisticated, well known for its excellent cuisine and traditional handicrafts. The stores on Thanon Thachang are especially good for local nielloware (*kruang tom*), household items and jewellery, elegantly patterned in gold or silver often on black, and *yan lipao*, sturdy basketware made from intricately woven fern stems of different colours. Nakhon is also the best place in the country to see how Thai shadow plays work, at Suchart Subsin's workshop, and the main jumping-off point for towering **Khao Luang National Park** and its beautiful waterfall, **Krung Ching**.

The town is recorded under the name of Ligor (or Lakhon), the capital of the kingdom of Lankasuka, as early as the second century, and classical dance-drama, *lakhon*, is supposed to have been developed here. Well placed for trade with China and southern India (via an overland route from the port of Trang, on the Andaman Sea), Nakhon was the point through which the Theravada form of Buddhism was imported from Sri Lanka and spread to Sukhothai, the capital of the new Thai state, in the thirteenth century.

Known as *muang phra*, the "city of monks", Nakhon is still the religious capital of the south, and the main centre for **festivals**. The most important of these are the **Tamboon Deuan Sip**, held during the waning of the moon in the tenth lunar month (either Sept or Oct), and the **Hae Pha Khun That**, which is held several times a year, but most importantly on Maha Puja (February full moon; see also p.54) and on Visakha Puja (May full moon; see p.54). The purpose of Tamboon Deuan Sip is to pay homage to dead relatives and friends; it is believed that during this fifteen-day period all *pret* – ancestors who have been damned to hell – are allowed out to visit the world, and so their relatives perform a merit-making ceremony in the temples, presenting offerings from the first harvest to ease their suffering. A huge ten-day fair takes place at Thung Talaat park on the north side of town at this time, as well as processions, shadow plays and other theatrical performances. The Hae Pha Khun That also attracts people from all over the south, to pay homage to the relics of the Buddha at Wat Mahathat. The centrepiece of this ceremony is the Pha Phra Bot, a strip of yellow cloth many hundreds of metres long, which is carried in a spectacular procession around the chedi.

Arrival and information

Nakhon's **bus terminal** and **train station** are both fairly centrally placed, though the **airport** (☎075 369546), served daily by Nok Air (☎1318 or 02 900 9955, ⓦwww.nokair.com), is about 20km northwest of the city off the Surat Thani road; air-con minibuses (B80 per person) or taxis (B300) meet arriving flights to ferry passengers to the centre of town (on departure, you can catch a minibus to the airport at the *Thai Hotel*). **Air-con minibus** offices around town include one for Ko Samui (via the Don Sak ferry) about 1km north of the centre on the right-hand side of Thanon Ratchadamnoen near Wat Pradu; others are marked on our map. For getting around Nakhon, small blue **share-songthaews** ply up and down Thanon Ratchadamnoen for B12 a ride.

TAT has an office in a restored 1920s government officers' club on Sanam Na Muang (daily 8.30am–4.30pm; ☎075 346515–6, ⓔtatnksri@tat.or.th). Klickzone in Bovorn Bazaar on Thanon Ratchadamnoen is a good place for **internet** access. Decent, cheap **massages** are available at Wat Sala Meechai, a traditional medicine centre out beyond the National Museum on Thanon Ratchadamnoen (☎075 446136; B120 per hr).

Accommodation

Nakhon has no guest houses or traveller-oriented **accommodation**, but the best of its hotels offer very good value in all price ranges.

Bue Loung (Bua Luang) Hotel 1487/19 Soi Luang Muang, Thanon Chamroenwithi ☎075 341518, ⓕ075 342977. Friendly and central but reasonably quiet; gets the thumbs-up from visiting sales reps, with a choice of fan and cold water or air-con and hot water in basic double or twin rooms, most with cable TV. Fan ❶, air-con ❷

Grand Park Hotel 1204/79 Thanon Pak Nakhon ☎075 317666–75, ⓦwww.grandparknakhon.com. If you're looking for something more upmarket in the centre of town, this place, set back a little from the busy road, is worth considering – it's large, stylish and bright, with air-con, hot water, TV and

minibar in every room, and staff are cheery and attentive. ❹

🚶 **Nakorn Garden Inn** 1/4 Thanon Pak Nakhon ☎075 313333, ⓕ075 342926. A rustic but sophisticated haven in a three-storey, red-brick building overlooking a tree-shaded courtyard. Large, attractive rooms come with air-con, hot water, cable TV and mini-bars. ❸

Thai Hotel 1375 Thanon Ratchadamnoen ☎075 341509, ⓦwww.thaihotel-nakorn.com. Formerly top of the range in Nakhon – and still boasting some of the trappings, such as liveried doorman – this large institutional high-rise is now offering good value on its clean, reliable rooms, with fans and cold water or air-con and cold or hot water, all with cable TV. ❷

Twin Lotus About 3km southeast of the centre at 97/8 Thanon Patanakarn Kukwang ☎075 323777, Ⓦwww.twinlotushotel.net. Gets pride of place in Nakhon – though not for its location; sports five bars and restaurants, a large, attractive outdoor swimming pool, a spa and a health club. ❻

The Town

The **town plan** is simple, but puzzling at first sight: it runs in a straight line for 7km from north to south and is rarely more than a few hundred metres wide, a layout originally dictated by the availability of fresh water. The modern centre for businesses and shops sits at the north end around the landmark **Tha Wang intersection**, where Thanon Neramit meets Thanon Ratchadamnoen. To the south, centred on the elegant, traditional mosque on Thanon Karom, lies the old Muslim quarter; south again is the start of the old city walls, of which few remains can be seen, and the historic centre, with the town's main places of interest now set in a leafy residential area.

Wat Mahathat

Missing out **Wat Mahathat** would be like going to Rome and not visiting St Peter's, for the Buddha relics in the vast chedi make this the south's most important shrine. In the courtyard inside the temple cloisters, which have their main entrance facing Thanon Ratchadamnoen, about 2km south of the modern centre, row upon row of smaller chedis, spiked like bayonets, surround the main chedi, the sixty-metre-tall **Phra Boromathat**. This huge, stubby Sri Lankan bell supports a slender, ringed spire, which is in turn topped by a shiny pinnacle said to be covered in 600kg of gold leaf. According to the chronicles, relics of the Buddha were brought here from Sri Lanka two thousand years ago by an Indian prince and princess and enshrined in a chedi. It's undergone plenty of face-lifts since: an earlier Srivijayan version, a model of which stands at one corner, is encased in the present twelfth-century chedi. The most recent restoration work, funded by donations from all over Thailand, rescued it from collapse, although it still seems to be leaning dangerously to the southeast. Worshippers head for the north side's vast enclosed stairway, framed by lions and giants, which they liberally decorate with gold leaf to add to the shrine's radiance and gain some merit.

The **Viharn Phra Kien Museum** (hours irregular, but usually daily 9am–5pm; free), which extends north from the chedi, is an Aladdin's cave of bric-a-brac, said to house fifty thousand artefacts donated by worshippers, ranging from ships made out of seashells to gold and silver models of the Bodhi Tree. At the entrance to the museum, you'll pass the Phra Puay, an image of the Buddha giving a gesture of reassurance. Women pray to the image when they want to have children, and the lucky ones return to give thanks and to leave photos of their chubby progeny.

Outside the cloister to the south is the eighteenth-century **Viharn Luang**, raised on elegant slanting columns, a beautiful example of Ayutthayan architecture. The interior is austere at ground level, but the red coffered ceiling shines with carved and gilded stars and lotus blooms. In the spacious grounds on the viharn's south side, cheerful, inexpensive stalls peddle local handicrafts such as shadow puppets, bronzeware and basketware.

The National Museum

Ten minutes' walk south again from Wat Mahathat, the **National Museum** (Wed–Sun 9am–noon & 1–4pm; B30; Ⓦ www.thailandmuseum.com) houses a small but diverse collection, mostly of artefacts from southern Thailand. In the prehistory room downstairs, look out for the two impressive ceremonial bronze kettledrums dating from the fifth century BC, one of them topped with chunky frogs (the local frogs are said to be the biggest in Thailand and a prized delicacy).

Also on the ground floor are some interesting Hindu finds, including several stone lingams from the seventh to ninth centuries AD and later bronze statues of Ganesh, the elephant-headed god of wisdom and the arts. Look out especially for a vivacious, well-preserved bronze of Shiva here, dancing within a ring of fire on the body of a dwarf demon, who holds a cobra symbolizing stupidity. Among the collections of ceramics upstairs, you can't miss the seat panel from Rama V's barge, a dazzling example of the nielloware for which Nakhon is famous – the delicate animals and landscapes have been etched onto a layer of gold which covers the silver base, and then picked out by inlaying a black alloy into the background. The nearby exhibition on local wisdom includes interesting displays on Buddhist ordinations and weddings, and on *manohra*, the southern Thai dramatic dance form.

The shadow puppet workshop

The best possible introduction to *nang thalung*, southern Thailand's **shadow puppet theatre**, is to head for Ban Nang Thalung Suchart Subsin, 110/18 Soi 3, Thanon Si Thammasok, ten minutes' walk east of Wat Mahathat (☏075 346394). In this atmospheric compound, Suchart Subsin, one of the south's leading exponents of *nang thalung*, and his son, Wathee, have opened up their

---

Shadow puppets

Found throughout southern Asia, **shadow puppets** are one of the oldest forms of theatre, featuring in Buddhist literature as early as 400 BC. The art form seems to have come from India, via Java, to Thailand, where it's called *nang*, meaning "hide": the puppets are made from the skins of water buffalo or cows, which are softened in water, then pounded until almost transparent, before being carved and painted to represent the characters of the play. The puppets are then manipulated on bamboo rods in front of a bright light, to project their image onto a large white screen, while the story is narrated to the audience.

The grander version of the art, **nang yai** – "big hide", so called because the figures are life-size – deals only with the *Ramayana* story (see p.113). It's known to have been part of the entertainment at official ceremonies in the Ayutthayan period, but has now almost died out. The more populist version, **nang thalung** – *thalung* is probably a shortening of the town name, Phatthalung (which is just down the road from Nakhon), where this version of the art form is said to have originated – is also in decline now: performances are generally limited to temple festivals, marriages, funerals and ordinations, lasting usually from 9pm to dawn. As well as working the sixty-centimetre-high *nang thalung* puppets, the puppet master narrates the story, impersonates the characters, chants and cracks jokes to the accompaniment of flutes, fiddles and percussion instruments. Not surprisingly, in view of this virtuoso semi-improvised display, puppet masters are esteemed as possessed geniuses by their public.

At big festivals, companies often perform the *Ramayana*, sometimes in competition with each other; at smaller events they put on more down-to-earth stories, with stock characters such as the jokers Yor Thong, an angry man with a pot belly and a sword, and Kaew Kop, a man with a frog's head. Yogi, a wizard and teacher, is thought to protect the puppet master and his company from evil spirits with his magic, so he is always the first puppet on at the beginning of every performance.

In an attempt to halt their decline as a form of popular entertainment, the puppet companies are now incorporating modern instruments and characters in modern dress into their shows, and are boosting the love element in their stories. They're fighting a battle they can't win against television and cinemas, although at least the debt owed to shadow puppets has been acknowledged – *nang* has become the Thai word for "movie".

workshop to the public, including a small museum of puppets dating back as far as the eighteenth century, and, for a small fee (around B100 per person), they'll usually be able to show you a few scenes from a shadow play in the small open-air theatre. You can also see the intricate process of making the leather puppets and can buy the finished products as souvenirs: puppets sold here are of much better quality and design than those usually found on southern Thailand's souvenir stalls.

The Phra Buddha Sihing shrine

In the chapel of the provincial administration complex on Thanon Ratchadam-noen sits the **Phra Buddha Sihing** statue (Mon–Fri 8.30am–noon & 1–4.30pm), which according to legend was magically created in Sri Lanka in the second century. In the thirteenth century it was sent by ship to the king of Sukhothai, but the vessel sank and the image miraculously floated on a plank to Nakhon. Two other images, one in the National Museum in Bangkok, one in Wat Phra Singh in Chiang Mai, claim to be the authentic Phra Buddha Sihing, but none of the three is in the Sri Lankan style, so they are all probably derived from a lost original. Although similar to the other two in size and shape, the image in Nakhon has a style unique to this area, distinguished by the heavily pleated flap of its robe over the left shoulder, a beaky nose and harsh features, which sit uneasily on the short, corpulent body. The image's plumpness has given the style the name *khanom tom* – "banana and rice pudding".

Eating and drinking

Nakhon is a great place for inexpensive **food**, not least at the busy, colourful night market on Thanon Chamroenwithi near the *Bue Loung Hotel*.

Hao Coffee In the Bovorn Bazaar, Thanon Ratchad-amnoen. Popular place modelled on an old Chinese-style coffee shop, packed full of ageing lamps, clocks and other antiques. Offers a wide selection of inexpensive Thai dishes, cakes, teas and coffees, including Thai filter coffee and delicious iced cappuccinos. Daytime only.

Hua Thale Thanon Pak Nakhon, opposite the *Nakorn Garden Inn* (no English sign). The town's best restaurant, renowned among locals for its excellent, varied and inexpensive seafood, and almost reason in itself to come to Nakhon. Plain and very clean, with an open kitchen and the day's catch displayed out front, and relaxing patio tables and an air-con room at the back. Recommended dishes include a superb *yam plaa duk foo*, shredded and deep-fried catfish with a mango salad dip, whole baked fish and king prawns, and *hoy maleang poo op mordin*, large green mussels

in a delicious herb soup containing lemon grass, basil and mint. Daily 3.30–9.30pm.

Khanom Jiin Muangkorn Thanon Panyom, near Wat Mahathat. Justly famous, inexpensive outdoor restaurant dishing up one of the local specialities, *khanom jiin*, noodles topped with hot, sweet or fishy sauce served with *pak ruam*, a platter of crispy raw vegetables. Lunchtimes only.

Krua Nakhon (Krour Nakorn) In the Bovorn Bazaar, Thanon Ratchadamnoen. A great place to sample southern food, buffet-style in a big, rustic pavilion, with good *khanom jiin* and other very cheap local dishes: *kaeng som*, a mild yellow curry; *kaeng tai plaa*, fish stomach curry; *khao yam*, a delicious southern salad of rice and vegetables; and various *khanom wan*, coconut milk puddings. Breakfast and lunch only.

Rock 99 Bovorn Bazaar. Bar-restaurant with live bands on Wed, Fri & Sat and outdoor tables.

Khao Luang National Park

Rising to the west of Nakhon Si Thammarat and temptingly visible from all over town is 1835-metre-high **Khao Luang**, southern Thailand's highest mountain. A huge **national park** (B200), with its headquarters to the south of the summit near Karom Waterfall (☏075 391240 or 075 391218, ⍐www.dnp .go.th), encompasses Khao Luang's jagged green peaks, beautiful streams with numerous waterfalls, tropical rainforest and fruit orchards. The mountain is also the source of the Tapi River, one of the peninsula's main waterways, which flows into the Gulf of Thailand at Surat Thani. **Fauna** here include macaques, musk deer, civets, binturongs, as well as more difficult to see Malayan tapirs, serows, tigers, panthers and clouded leopards, plus over two hundred bird species. There's an astonishing diversity of **flora** too, notably rhododendrons and begonias, dense mosses, ferns and lichens, plus more than three hundred species of both ground-growing and epiphytic orchids, some of which are unique to the park. The best time to visit is after the rainy season, from January onwards, when there should still be a decent flow in the waterfalls, but the trails will be dry and the leeches not so bad. However, the park's most distinguishing feature for visitors is probably its difficulty of access: main roads run around the 570-square-kilometre park with spurs into some of the waterfalls, but there are no roads across the park and very sparse public transport along the spur roads. Only **Krung Ching Waterfall**, one of Thailand's most spectacular, really justifies the hassle of getting there.

Before heading off to Khao Luang, be sure to drop into Nakhon's TAT office for a useful park **brochure**, with a sketch map and sketchy details of the walking routes to Krung Ching waterfall and to the peak itself. For the latter, which begins at Ban Khiriwong on the southeast side of the park and involves two nights camping on the mountain, contact the Ban Khiriwong Ecotourism Club (☎075 533113), who can arrange a trek to the peak, including meals and guides, between January and June, as well as homestays in the village. Irregular **songthaews** on the main roads around the park and to Ban Khiriwong congregate on Thanon Klong Tha south of the *Bue Loung Hotel* in Nakhon. Air-conditioned **minibuses with drivers** are available from Noi Tub Tim Tours on Thanon Paniet (☎075 345371; B1500 per day plus petrol).

Krung Ching

A trip to **Krung Ching**, a nine-tier waterfall on the north side of the park, makes for a highly satisfying day out, with a mostly paved nature trail taking you through dense, steamy jungle to the most beautiful, third tier. The easiest way to **get there** from Nakhon with your own transport is to head north on Highway 401 towards Surat Thani, turning west at Tha Sala on to Highway 4140, then north again at Ban Nopphitam on to Highway 4186, before heading south from Ban Huai Phan on Highway 4188, the spur road to Ban Phitham and the Krung Ching park office, a total journey of about 70km. Public song-thaews run from Nakhon to Ban Huai Phan in about an hour, but you'd then have to do a deal with the driver to take you the extra 13km to the park office. Two- to forty-person **bungalows**, most with hot water, are available at the park office (B600–4000); camping is free if you bring your own tent. There's also a **campsite** and a canteen, where food needs to be ordered in advance.

The shady four-kilometre **trail** to the dramatic main fall is very steep in parts, so you should allow four hours at least there and back. On the way you'll pass giant ferns, including a variety known as *maha sadam*, the largest fern in the world, gnarled banyan trees, forests of mangosteen and beautiful, thick stands of bamboo. You're bound to see colourful birds and insects, but you may well only hear macaques and other mammals. At the end, a long, stepped descent brings you to a perfectly positioned wooden platform with fantastic views of the forty-metre fall; here you can see how, shrouded in thick spray, it earns its Thai name, Fon Saen Ha, meaning "thousands of rainfalls".

Travel details

Trains

All through trains stop at Surat Thani, Chumphon, Hua Hin and Nakhon Pathom.

Ban Krud to: Bangkok (3 daily; 5hr 30min–7hr 30min); Chumphon (6 daily; 2hr); Hat Yai (2 daily; 8hr 30min–10hr 30min); Nakhon Si Thammarat (1 daily; 10hr); Surat Thani (5 daily; 4hr–5hr 30min); Trang (1 daily; 10hr).

Cha-am to: Bangkok (5 daily; 3hr 10min–3hr 50min); Chumphon (3 daily; 5–7hr); Hat Yai (1 daily; 13hr 30min); Hua Hin (5 daily; 30min); Prachuap Khiri Khan (3 daily; 2hr).

Chumphon to: Bangkok (12 daily; 7hr–9hr 30min); Butterworth (Malaysia; 1 daily; 14hr); Hat Yai (6 daily; 7hr–8hr 30min); Nakhon Si Thammarat (2 daily; 7hr); Surat Thani (11 daily; 2hr 5min–4hr); Trang (2 daily; 7hr).

Hua Hin to: Bangkok (12 daily; 4–5hr); Butterworth (Malaysia; 1 daily; 17hr 30min); Chumphon (13 daily; 3hr 30min–5hr 20min); Hat Yai (5 daily; 10hr 30min–12hr 30min); Nakhon Si Thammarat (2 daily; 12hr); Prachuap Khiri Khan (11 daily; 1hr 30min); Surat Thani (11 daily; 5hr 40min–8hr); Trang (2 daily; 12hr).

Nakhon Si Thammarat to: Bangkok (2 daily; 15–16hr); Hat Yai (2 daily; 4–5hr).

Phetchaburi to: Bangkok (11 daily; 2hr 45min–3hr 45min); Chumphon (10 daily; 4hr–6hr 30min); Hat Yai (4 daily; 11hr 30min–13hr 30min); Hua Hin (12 daily; 1hr); Nakhon Si Thammarat (2 daily; 12–13hr); Prachuap Khiri Khan (11 daily; 2–3hr); Surat Thani (8 daily; 6hr 45min–9hr); Trang (1 daily; 13hr).

Prachuap Khiri Khan to: Bangkok (11 daily; 5–7hr); Chumphon (11 daily; 2hr–3hr 30min); Hat Yai (4 daily; 9–11hr); Nakhon Si Thammarat (2 daily; 10hr 30min); Surat Thani (8 daily; 4hr 30min–6hr); Trang (1 daily; 11hr).

Pranburi to: Bangkok (3 daily; 5hr 30min); Chumphon (2 daily; 4hr 30min); Hat Yai (1 daily; 12hr 30min); Prachuap Khiri Khan (3 daily; 1hr).

Surat Thani (Phunphin) to: Bangkok (10 daily; 9–12hr); Butterworth (Malaysia; 1 daily; 11hr 15min); Hat Yai (7 daily; 4hr 30min–6hr); Nakhon Si Thammarat (2 daily; 4hr 30min); Trang (2 daily; 4hr 30min).

Buses

Cha-am to: Bangkok (every 40min; 2hr 45min–3hr 15min); Hua Hin (every 20–30min; 35min); Phetchaburi (every 20–30min; 50min).

Chumphon to: Bangkok (roughly hourly; 7–9hr); Hat Yai (4 daily; 7hr 30min); Hua Hin (hourly; 3hr 30min–4hr 30min); Phuket (4 daily; 7hr); Prachuap Khiri Khan (6 daily; 2–3hr); Ranong (roughly hourly; 2hr); Surat Thani (roughly hourly; 3hr 30min).

Hua Hin to: Bangkok (from Baw Khaw Saw: at least hourly; 4hr; from Thanon Srasong: every 40min; 3hr); Cha-am (every 20–30min; 35min); Chumphon (hourly in the morning, fewer in the afternoon; 3hr 30min–4hr 30min); Hat Yai (4 daily; 10hr); Krabi (3 daily; 9hr); Phetchaburi (every 20–30min; 1hr 30min); Phuket (7 daily; 9hr); Prachuap Khiri Khan (every 30min; 1hr 30min–2hr); Pranburi (from Thanon Srasong: every 20min; 40min; from Baw Khaw Saw hourly; 30min); Surat Thani (4 daily; 7hr).

Ko Pha Ngan to: Bangkok (Southern Terminal; 2 daily; 14hr).

Ko Samui to: Bangkok (Southern Terminal; 8 daily; 13hr); Hat Yai (2 daily; 7hr); Krabi (3 daily; 7hr); Nakhon Si Thammarat (2 daily; 4hr); Phuket (1 daily; 8hr).

Nakhon Si Thammarat to: Bangkok (Southern Terminal; 19 daily; 12hr); Hat Yai (16 daily; 3hr 30min); Ko Samui (2 daily; 4hr); Krabi (2 daily; 4hr); Phatthalung (7 daily; 2hr); Phuket (7 daily; 6hr); Ranong (1 daily; 6hr); Surat Thani (21 daily; 2hr 30min).

Phetchaburi to: Bangkok (every 40min; 2hr 15min); Cha-am (every 20–30min; 50min); Hua Hin (every 20–30min; 1hr 30min).

Prachuap Khiri Khan to: Bangkok (every 30min; 4–5hr); Chumphon (6 daily; 2–3hr); Hua Hin (every 30min; 1hr 30min–2hr); Phetchaburi (every 30min; 3hr–3hr 30min); Pranburi (every 30min; 1hr–1hr 30min).

Pranburi to: Bangkok (every 40min; 3hr 30min); Hua Hin (every 20min; 30–40min).

Surat Thani to: Bangkok (Southern Terminal; 10 daily; 10–12hr); Chumphon (roughly hourly; 3hr 30min); Hat Yai (10 daily; 5hr); Khao Sok (11 daily; 2hr 30min); Krabi (23 daily; 3–4hr); Nakhon Si Thammarat (21 daily; 2hr 30min); Phang Nga (10 daily; 3hr 30min); Phatthalung (10 daily; 5hr); Phuket (14 daily; 5–6hr); Phunphin (every 10min; 40min); Ranong (10 daily; 4–5hr).

Flights

Hua Hin to: Bangkok (Suvarnabhumi; 2 daily; 50min).

Ko Samui to: Bangkok (Suvarnabhumi; 20 daily; 1hr–1hr 30min); Chiang Mai (2 weekly; 2hr 30min); Hong Kong (5 weekly; 3hr); Krabi (3 weekly; 50min); Kuala Lumpur, Malaysia (2 weekly; 2hr);

Pattaya (1 daily; 1hr); Phuket (2 daily; 50min); Singapore (1 daily; 1hr 45min).
Nakhon Si Thammarat to: Bangkok (Don Muang; 3 daily; 1hr 5min).

Surat Thani to: Bangkok (Don Muang 2 daily with Thai Airways, Suvarnabhumi 2 daily with Air Asia; 1hr 15min).

Southern Thailand:
the Andaman coast

CHAPTER 4   # Highlights

✳ **Island idylls** Tranquillity rules
on the uncommercial islands
of Ko Phayam, Ko Ra, Ko Yao
Noi and Ko Jum. See p.328,
p.334, p.380 & p.419

✳ **Ko Surin and Ko Similan**
Remote island chains offering
the finest snorkelling and
diving. See p.336 & p.348

✳ **Khao Sok National Park**
Sleep in a treehouse or on a
lake, and wake to the sound
of hooting gibbons.
See p.337

✳ **Phuket Old Town** Handsome
Sino-Portuguese architecture
and some of the most

interesting dining on the
island. See p.355

✳ **Sea-canoeing in Ao Phang
Nga** The perfect way to
explore the limestone karsts
and hidden lagoons of this
spectacular bay. See p.386

✳ **Rock-climbing** Even novices
can get a bird's-eye view
of the Railay peninsula's
fabulous coastal scenery.
See p.408

✳ **Ko Lanta Yai** The "island
of long beaches", plus an
atmospheric Old Town.
See p.423

▲ The view from Ko Yao Noi

Southern Thailand: the Andaman coast

SOUTHERN THAILAND: THE ANDAMAN COAST

As Highway 4 switches from the east flank of the Thailand peninsula to the **Andaman coast** it enters a markedly different country: nourished by rain nearly all the year round, the vegetation down here is lushly tropical, with forests reaching up to 80m in height, and massive rubber, palm-oil and coconut plantations replacing the rice and sugar-cane fields of central Thailand. Sheer limestone crags spike every horizon and the translucent Andaman Sea laps the most dazzlingly beautiful islands in the country, not to mention its finest **coral reefs**. This is of course the same sea whose terrifyingly powerful **tsunami** waves battered the coastline in December 2004, killing thousands and changing countless lives and communities forever. The legacies of that horrific day are widespread, for more on which see p.344, but all the affected holiday resorts have been re-built, with the tourist dollar now arguably more crucial to the region's well-being than ever before.

The **cultural mix** along the Andaman coast is also different. Many southern Thais are Muslim, with a heritage that connects them to Malaysia and beyond. This is also the traditional province of nomadic *chao ley*, or sea gypsies, many of whom have now settled but still work as boat captains and fishermen. The commercial fishing industry, on the other hand, is mostly staffed by immigrants – legal and not – from neighbouring Burma, just a few kilometres away along the northern Andaman coast.

The attractions of the northern Andaman coast are often ignored in the race down to the high-profile honeypots around Phuket and Krabi, but there are many quiet gems up here, beginning with the low-key little sister islands of **Ko Chang** (quite different from its larger, more famous East Coast namesake) and **Ko Phayam**, where the hammocks and paraffin lamps offer an old-style travellers' vibe that's harder to find further south. Awesome, world-class reefs draw snorkellers and divers to the remote National Park island chains of **Ko Surin** and **Ko Similan**, with many choosing to base themselves at the mainland beach resort of **Khao Lak**, though homestay programmes around **Khuraburi** offer an interesting alternative. Inland, it's all about the jungle – with twenty-first-century amenities – at the enjoyable **Khao Sok National Park**, where accommodation is on rafts on the lake and treehouses beneath the limestone crags.

Tourism begins in earnest on **Phuket**, Thailand's largest island and the region's major resort destination for families, package tourists and novice divers; its

SOUTHERN THAILAND: THE ANDAMAN COAST

BURMA

Chumphon

KRA ISTHMUS

Kraburi

St Matthew's Island

Kaw Thaung

Ranong

Saphan Pla

Nam Tok Ngao

Lang Suan

GULF OF THAILAND

Ko Chang

Pha To

Ko Phayam

Kapoe

Ko Surin Nua

Ban Talae Nok

Ko Surin Tai

Tung Nang Dam

ANDAMAN SEA

Ko Ra

Khuraburi

Ko Phra Thong

KHAO SOK NATIONAL PARK

Cheow Lan Lake

Surat Thani

Phunphin

Ratchabrap Dam

Khao Sok National Park Headquarters

Ban Ta Khun

Ko Kho Khao

Takua Pa

Phanom

Sai Rung Falls

Khao Lak

Ko Similan

Thap Lamu

Sa Nang Manora Forest Park

Thep Phut

Phang Nga

Thai Muang

Ao Luk

Khokkloi

Ao Phang Nga

Laem Sak

Ko Yao Noi

Ao Thalen

Talat Kao

Khao Phanom

Krabi

Nua Klong

Khlong Thom

Phuket

Ko Yao Yai

Ao Nang

Phuket Town

Laem Kruat

Ban Huay Nam Khao

Ko Jum

Ban Hua Hin

Bo Muang

Ko Phi Phi

Ko Lanta Noi

Ko Racha Yai

Ko Lanta Yai

Ko Racha Noi

Nakhon Si Thammarat

Trang

N

0 — 40 km

shopping and entertainment facilities are second to none, but the high-rises and hectic consumerism dilute the Thai-ness of the experience. There's Thai life in spades across on the quiet rural island of **Ko Yao Noi**, scenically located within spectacular **Ao Phang Nga**, whose scattered karst islets are one of the country's top natural wonders, best appreciated from a sea-canoe. The Andaman coast's second hub is **Krabi** province, rightly famous for its turquoise seas and dramatic islands. Flashiest of these is the flawed but still handsome **Ko Phi Phi**, with its great diving, gorgeous beaches and high-octane nightlife. Mainland and mainstream, **Ao Nang** can't really compete, but is at least close to the majestic cliffs and superb rock-climbing of the **Railay** peninsula at **Laem Phra Nang**. Offshore again, there's horizon-gazing aplenty at mellow, barely developed **Ko Jum** and the choice of half a dozen luxuriously long beaches, and plentiful resort facilities, at **Ko Lanta Yai**.

Unlike the Gulf coast, the Andaman coast is hit by the **southwest monsoon**, which usually generally lasts from the end of May until at least the middle of October. During this period heavy rain and high seas render some of the outer islands inaccessible, but conditions aren't usually severe enough to ruin a holiday on the other islands, or on the mainland, and you'll get tempting discounts on accommodation. Some bungalows at the smaller resorts shut down entirely during low season (highlighted in the text), but most beaches keep at least one place open, and some dive shops lead expeditions year-round.

There is no rail line down the Andaman coast, but many travellers take the **train** from Bangkok to the Gulf coast and then nip across by bus; most direct **buses** from the capital travel south overnight. The faster option is to arrive by plane: both Phuket and Krabi have international **airports**, and there are domestic airports at Trang, not far from Ko Lanta in the deep south, and Ranong.

Ranong and around

Thailand's Andaman coast begins at **Kraburi**, where, at kilometre-stone 545 (the distance from Bangkok), a signpost welcomes you to the **Kra Isthmus**, the narrowest part of peninsular Thailand. Just 44km separates the Gulf of Thailand from the Andaman Sea's Chan River estuary, and Burmese border, here. Though a seemingly obvious shortcut for shipping traffic between the Indian Ocean and the South China Sea, avoiding the 1500-kilometre detour via the Strait of Malacca, the much-discussed **Kra Canal** project has yet to be realized, despite being on the table for over three hundred years.

Seventy kilometres south of the isthmus, the channel widens out at the provincial capital of **Ranong**, which thrives on its proximity to Burma. Thai tourists have been coming here for years, to savour the health-giving properties of the local spring water, but foreign travellers have only quite recently discovered it as a useful departure-point for the alluring nearby little islands of **Ko Chang** and **Ko Phayam**. The other reason to stop off in Ranong is to make a visa-run to the Burmese town of **Kaw Thaung**.

Ranong is the capital of Thailand's wettest province, which soaks up over 5000mm of rain every year – a fact you'll undoubtedly experience first hand if you linger in the region. The landscape to the south of Ranong town is particularly lush, and any journey along Highway 4 will whizz you between waterfall-streaked hills to the east and mangrove swamps, rubber plantations and casuarina groves to the west; much of this coastal strip is preserved as **Laem Son National Park**.

Ramong Governor's Cemetery ▲ ▲ Andaman Club Pier ▲ Chumphon

RANONG

0 ──────── 350 m

First Governor's House

ACCOMMODATION
Asia Hotel C
Bangsan B
Suta House
  Bungalows A
Tinidee Hotel D

THANON RATTPHIMIT
THANON DUPKHADI
Police Station

EATING
Pon's Place 2
Sophon's Hideaway 1

THANON RUANGRAT
A-One Diving

THANON LUWANG
THANON PHETKASEM
THANON CHONRAU
4

Kay Kai

THANON KAMLANGSAP
Coffee House
THANON KAMLANGSAP

THANON PHOEM PHON

Night Market
Stadium

N

& Saphan Pla
Hot Springs

CAT
Bangkok Bank
Bookshop
THANON THA MUANG
THANON PHETKASEM

TRANSPORT
Songthaews (to Saphan Pla,
  the bus station, etc) A
VIP buses to Bangkok B
Ranong Bus Station C

Ranong Town

Despite being the soggiest town in the country, **RANONG** has a pleasing buzz about it, fuelled by the mix of Burmese, Thai, Chinese and Malay inhabitants. It's a prosperous town, the lucrative nineteenth-century tin-mining concessions now replaced by a thriving fishing industry centred around the port of Saphan Pla, 5km southwest of town, and its scores of fishing boats and fish-processing factories staffed mainly by notoriously poorly treated Burmese workers. As with most border areas, there's also said to be a flourishing illegal trade in amphetamines, guns and labour, not to mention the inevitable tensions over international fishing rights, which sometimes end in shoot-outs, though the closest encounter you're likely to have will be in the pages of the *Bangkok Post*.

A stroll along the town centre's main road, **Thanon Ruangrat**, brings its history and geography to mind. The handsome, if faded, shopfront architecture bears many of the hallmarks of nineteenth-century Sino-Portuguese design (see p.356), with its arched "five-foot" walkways shading sidewalk pedestrians, pastel paintwork and shuttered windows. Chinese goods fill many of the shops – this is a good place to stock up on cheap clothes too – and many signs are written in the town's three main languages: Thai, Chinese and curly Burmese script.

Arrival and transport

All Andaman-coast **buses** travelling between Bangkok or Chumphon and Khuraburi, Takua Pa, Phuket or Krabi stop briefly at Ranong's **bus station** on Highway 4 (Thanon Phetkasem; ☎077 811548), 1500m southeast of the central market. If coming from Khao Sok or Surat Thani, you'll usually need to change buses at Takua Pa, though there is also a private minibus service from and to **Surat Thani** (hourly 7am–3pm; 3hr; B190). There is a direct government bus service from **Chumphon** (2–3hr), as well as a faster private minibus service (hourly 6am–5pm; 2hr; B120), so **from Bangkok** it's often more comfortable to take a night **train** to Chumphon and then change on to a bus or minibus. Alternatively, Air Asia currently operates Bangkok **flights** in and out of Ranong airport, which is 20km south of Ranong on Highway 4; taxis between the airport and town cost B150 per person or B200 from the Saphan Pla piers.

City songthaews shuttle across and around Ranong, most of them starting from the Thanon Ruangrat market, close to town-centre hotels. Many have their destinations written in English on the side, and most charge B10–15 per ride. Several songthaews pass Ranong bus station, including the # 2 (red), which runs to the Thanon Ruangrat hotels and day market, and the #6, which beetles between the bus station and the port area at Saphan Pla, 5km to the southwest (for boats to Ko Chang, Ko Phayam and Kaw Thaung); another songthaew runs direct from the market on Thanon Ruangrat to the Saphan Pla port area.

Information

The best source of **tourist information** in town is the ever helpful Pon at *Pon's Place* restaurant and tour agency, 129 Thanon Ruangrat (daily 7.30am–9pm; ☎081 597 4549, ⓦ www.ponplace-ranong.com), where you can also organize a visa run to Burma and back, arrange tours of the local area, book accommodation on Ko Chang and Ko Phayam, rent bicycles, motorbikes and cars, and buy air, bus and (Chumphon) train tickets. Should you want to fix a **diving** trip before heading out to the islands, Ko Phayam's A-One Diving has its main office in town at 256 Thanon Ruangrat (☎077 832984, ⓦ www.a-one-diving.com; see p.330) and runs liveaboards to the Surin islands from the end of October to the end of April.

Coffee House at 116 Thanon Ruangrat is a **postal agent** (Mon–Fri 7am–1pm & 3–7pm, Sat & Sun 7am–6pm); the **Ranong Hospital** is at 11 Thanon Kamlangsap (☎077 812630); the police station is on Thanon Dupkhadi (☎077 811173); and the **immigration office**, for visa extensions, is out at Saphan Pla (see p.323), across the road from the Thai Farmers Bank (daily 8.30am–6pm).

Accommodation

Most travellers stop over in Ranong for just one night, but there's a reasonable spread of **accommodation** to choose from. At the bottom of the ladder is *Bangsan* (no phone; ❶) whose eight thin-walled cubicles are very bare bones, share bathrooms and mostly have no windows; it's above the retro, Sixties-styled *TV Bar* at 225 Thanon Ruangrat. Some of the en-suite fan rooms at the typical Chinese–Thai *Asia Hotel* (☎077 811113; fan ❶–❷, air-con ❸) only cost a bit more but are large, airy and spruce for the price and there's air-con if you want it; the hotel is painted pale blue inside and out and is just south of the market at 39/9 Thanon Ruangrat. Set 100m off the same road, the very popular *Suta House Bungalows* (☎077 832707; ❸) is an unusual find in a city, with its row of small but well-maintained air-con bungalows, all of them with clean tiled floors, built-in beds and cable TV and wi-fi. They're set round a small yard, with car parking, a little bar-coffee shop and a restaurant. The top digs in town are at the modern, good-value high-rise *Tinidee Hotel @ Ranong*, a ten-minute walk from the market at 41/144 Thanon Tha Muang (℗077 835240, ⓦwww .tinidee-ranong.com; ❻). Its air-con rooms all come with bathtubs fed by the local mineral water and there's also a spa and swimming pool.

Around the town

Though there's little in Ranong to warrant a sightseeing tour, it can be fun to follow the crowds of domestic tourists in their quest for the medicinal and stress-relieving properties of Ranong's famously pure **geothermal springs** (daily 8am–5pm). They're the focus of forested Raksawarin Park, about 3km east of the Thanon Ruangrat market and accessible on songthaew #2 or by motorbike taxi. At the park you can sip the potable 65°C water, or paddle in one of the three mineral spa pools, but for a more leisurely soak, cross the road to the jacuzzis at the Siam Hot Spa Ranong (daily 6.30am–10pm; ℗077 813551), which also offers inexpensive spa, massage and steam treatments (from B200, reservations advisable).

Ranong's history is closely associated with its most famous son, Khaw Soo Cheang, a poor Hokkien Chinese emigrant turned tin baron who became the first governor of Ranong province in 1854; he is still so esteemed that politicians continue to pay public homage at his grave, and his descendants bear the respected aristocratic surname "na Ranong" ("of Ranong"). Little now remains of Khaw Soo Cheang's house, but in its grounds, west off Thanon Ruangrat on the northern edge of town, stands a Khaw clan shrine and small museum, the **First Governor's House** (Nai Khai Ranong; daily 9am–4.30pm; free). Follow either road running north from near the First Governor's House, in the direction of the Andaman Club pier, for about 4km to reach his burial site at the **Ranong Governor's Cemetery**, where Chinese-style horseshoe-shaped graves and a series of symbolic stone statues stand proud at the foot of the grassy hill; songthaews from the Thanon Ruangrat market should get you there in about fifteen minutes.

If you haven't had enough of water features, you could make a trip out of town to the impressive **Nam Tok Ngao**, an enormous waterfall 12km south of Ranong, which cascades almost all the way down the eastern hillside in full view of Highway 4. It's part of Nam Tok Ngao National Park (ⓦwww.dnp .go.th/National_park.asp; B100). Any south-bound bus will drop you there. Another enjoyable day out would be to head into the interior for a day's organized rafting at **Pha To**, 51km east of Ranong, off Route 4006 to Chumphon (see p.259); Runs n' Roses tours and accommodation at Pha To (ⓦwww.runsnroses.com) can be booked through Ranong tour agencies.

Eating and drinking

Ranong's ethnic diversity ensures a tasty range of **eating** options, and a stroll up Thanon Ruangrat takes you past Muslim foodstalls and Chinese pastry shops as well as a small but typically Thai night market. A bigger night market convenes at dusk just east of the CAT phone office off Thanon Phoem Phon. *Pon's Place* at 129 Thanon Ruangrat opens at 7.30am and is the obvious place for farang-style breakfast, free wi-fi and as much local information as you care to gather. A lively and enjoyable venue for dinner is *Sophon's Hideaway* at Thanon Ruangrat, where Thai families and expats congregate for the wide-ranging menu, which includes sour 'n spicy fish curry, fried pork spare ribs and ostrich steaks (mostly B90–150); the cheapish beer and friendly staff are also a plus and there's international sports on the TV, a pool table and free wi-fi. This stretch of Thanon Ruangrat, down to the Thanon Luwang junction, is also abuzz after dark with urbane little local **bars** that keep reinventing themselves.

Ko Chang

Not to be confused with the much larger Ko Chang off Thailand's east coast (see p.207), Ranong's **KO CHANG** is a forested little island about 5km offshore, whose car-free, ultra laid-back, roll-your-own vibe more than compensates for the less than perfect beaches. The pace of life here is very slow, and for the relatively small number of tourists who make it to the island the emphasis is strongly on kicking back and chilling out – bring your own hammock and you'll fit right in. Those in search of (slightly) livelier scenes head across the water to sister-island Ko Phayam. Most islanders make their living from fishing and from the rubber, palm and cashew nut plantations that

KO CHANG

N

▲ Ranong

Ao Ko

Ko Plai

Ko Bonsai

Army Base

A

C

B

1

D
E Om Tao

Aladdin Dive Safari

Ao Yai

F

G

Wat Pah Ko Chang

Minimarket

Minimarket

2

Rainy-season Pier

Ao Chao Ley

3

4

H

I

5

J

K

M L

N

373m

Saphan Hin

Ao Daddaeng

Ao Kai Tao

National Park Ranger Station

Ao Lek

Ao Siad (Ao Lek)

O

◀ Ko Phayam

EATING & DRINKING

Air Bar	5
Bakery	4
Nice View	1
Sunshine Restaurant	2
Thai Bar	3

ACCOMMODATION

Cashew Resort	F
Chang Tong	I
Eden	E
Full Moon	K
Golden Bee	H
Hornbill	B
Ko Chang Resort	J
Koh Chang Contex	C
Little Italy	G
Long Beach	D
Mama's Bungalows	N
N&X	O
Sawasdee Resort	L
Sea Eagle	A
Tadang Bay	M

0 approximate 1 km

Ko Phayam ▼ ▼ Ranong

dominate the flatter patches of the interior. The beaches are connected by tracks through the trees and there are only sporadic, self-generated supplies of electricity for a few hours each evening.

The best of Ko Chang's beaches are on the west coast, and of these the longest, nicest and most popular is **Ao Yai**. The tiny bays to the north and south mostly hold just one set of bungalows each and are good for getting away from it all, though access to Ao Yai is easy enough if you don't mind the hike. About halfway between the west and east coasts, a crossroads bisects Ko Chang's only **village**, a tiny settlement that is home to most of the islanders and holds just a few shops, restaurants and a clinic. Signs at the *Sunshine Restaurant* direct you south to Saphan Hin (3km) and Ao Lek (5km); follow the unsigned northern route for a concrete path to the northern pier (used by boats during the wet season).

Nearly all the bungalows on Ko Chang **close** down from about mid-May until mid- or late October, when the island is subjected to very heavy rain, the beaches fill with flotsam, paths become dangerously slippery and food supplies dwindle with no ice available to keep things fresh. Many bungalow staff relocate to the mainland for this period, so you should phone ahead to check first.

Getting to Ko Chang

Boats to Ko Chang leave from the Islands Pier in **Saphan Pla**, 5km south of Ranong's town centre and accessed by **songthaews** from the Thanon Ruangrat market (red; #3; 20min; B15) and the bus station (#6; 20min; B15). The songthaews drop you on the main road through Saphan Pla, from where it's about 500m to the pier and its minimarket and dive shop. Alternatively, *Pon's Place* charges B50 per person for transfers from the town centre to the pier itself.

From about mid-October to mid-May there are three daily **boat departures** to Ko Chang's Ao Yai beach (currently 9.30am, noon & 2pm; 1hr; B150), but ask at Ranong information centres for the latest schedules. You'll be dropped as close as possible to your intended bungalow, which for the little bays north of Ao Yai usually means *Contex*. If heading for Saphan Hin or Ao Siad, you'll probably be put on the Ko Phayam boat (see p.330) instead. The easiest and cheapest option **from Ko Phayam** is to use the thrice weekly daytrippers' boat run by *Ko Chang Resort*, which returns from Ko Phayam village pier around 2pm (currently Mon, Wed & Fri; B150); a charter from Ko Phayam costs about B1500 per boat. During the **rainy months** of June through October there are only three boats a week from Ranong to Ko Chang (currently Mon, Wed & Sat from Ranong, returning from Ko Chang on Mon, Wed & Fri), and they only travel as far as the island's east coast, a three-kilometre walk from Ao Yai.

During the tourist season, there's at least one morning boat from Ko Chang **back to Saphan Pla**, generally about 7.30am, and another one at about 1.30pm; ask at your bungalows the day before. Taxis meet the boats at Saphan Pla and charge B50 per person to town or the bus station; songthaews charge just B15 but you have to walk 500m to the main road to flag them down.

Island practicalities

Most of the **bungalow** operations are simple wooden-plank or woven bamboo constructions, comprising just a dozen huts and a small restaurant each. Though they nearly all have their own generators (which usually only operate in the evenings), some stick to candles and paraffin lamps so you might appreciate having a torch. None have fans. As internet access is limited on the island, few bungalow owners check their email more than once a fortnight during high season. For general **information** on the island see ⓦ www.kohchang-ranong.com.

Part of Ko Chang's charm is its lack of commercial activity. There are, however, tiny **minimarkets** selling basic necessities at *Cashew Resort*, *Golden Bee* and behind the khlong on Ao Yai; and at *Sunshine Restaurant*, beside the crossroads in the heart of the island. The crossroads is also where you'll find the island **clinic**. *Cashew* and *Ko Chang Resort* can both do **overseas phone calls** and **internet access**, and *Cashew Resort* can also arrange bus tickets, Ranong–Bangkok flights, and speedboat charters to Ranong.

The German-Dutch-run **dive shop** Aladdin Dive Safari (℡077 820472, and at the Islands Pier in Saphan Pla ℡077 813698, Ⓦwww.aladdindivesafari.com) is based at *Cashew Resort* and from late October through mid-May teaches PADI dive courses and runs liveaboards that take in all the top local dive sites: Ko Surin, Ko Bon, Ko Tachai, Ko Similan, and Richelieu Rock (from B18,900 for four days excluding equipment and national park fees). *Air Bar* at *Ko Chang Resort* is one of several places that run **fishing**, **snorkelling and camping trips** to local islands including Ko Kham, which is famed for its beautiful beaches and reefs. Om Tao on Ao Yai holds morning Hatha **yoga** classes and afternoon qigong.

Ao Yai (Long Beach) and Ao Daddaeng

Effectively divided in two by a khlong, the main cross-island track, and the stumps of a long wooden pier, **Ao Yai**, or **Long Beach**, enjoys a fine view of the brooding silhouette of Burma's St Matthew's Island, which dominates the western horizon. The 800-metre-long stretch of Ao Yai that runs north from the khlong is the most attractive on the island, nice and wide even at high tide, and especially good for kids. South of the khlong, the beach is very narrow at high tide, but when the water goes out you have to walk a longish distance to find any depth. Further south still, around a rocky headland, tiny secluded gold-sand **Ao Daddaeng** (Tadang) is sandwiched between massive boulders and holds just a few bungalows: reach it via a five-minute footpath from behind *Tadang Bay Bungalows*.

A narrow concrete road connects central Ao Yai with the mangrove-filled little harbour on the east coast, a distance of around 1700m that can be walked in under half an hour. The western end of the road begins beside the island's only temple, **Wat Pah Ko Chang**, whose bot and monks' quarters are partially hidden amongst the trees beside the beach, with a sign that asks tourists to dress modestly when in the area and not to swim or sunbathe in front of it.

Accommodation

Cashew Resort ℡077 820116, Ⓔcashew_resort@hotmail.com. The longest-running accommodation on the island, and also the largest, *Cashew* feels like a tiny village, with its forty en-suite bungalows spread among the cashew trees along 700m of prime beachfront, and returnees personalizing their bungalows like mini homes. It's exceptionally good value: all bungalows enjoy both a sea view and some privacy, they're well maintained, built from either wood or brick, and some have big glass windows. The resort offers the most facilities on the island, including wi-fi, internet access, foreign exchange, Visa and MasterCard capability, an overseas phone service, and a pool table. ❶–❸

Chang Tong ℡084 846 1198, Ⓦwww.kohchang -ranong.com. The cheapest wood and bamboo bungalows at this friendly spot are very basic, though they're all en suite and are well spaced beneath the shoreside trees; pay a bit more for newer, slightly better appointed ones. ❶–❷

Full Moon ℡077 820130, Ⓔfamilymoon99 @hotmail.com. Though simple, the attractive wooden en-suite bungalows here are well designed and a cut above many others on Ao Yai. Prettily painted and with cute stencilwork on doors and bathrooms, they are comfortable, modern and have an inviting personality. ❶–❸

Ko Chang Resort ℡081 896 1839, Ⓦwww .kohchangandaman.com. Occupying a fabulous spot high on the rocks right over the water, the best of the en-suite wooden bungalows here have fine sea views from their balconies; the bamboo ones are set further back beside the path. Interiors are very rudimentary but the decks are huge. Also has a big, more luxurious family bungalow. You can swim below the rocks at low tide, or the more reliable beach is just a couple of minutes' scramble to south or north. There's internet on site, plus a tattoo parlour and the very chilled *Air Bar.* ❶–❺

Little Italy ☎084 851 2760, ⓔdaniel060863 @yahoo.it. This tiny Italian-Thai-run outfit has just two attractive bungalows set in a secluded garden of paperbark trees 100m inland from *Cashew Resort*, behind their recommended Italian garden restaurant. Bungalows are two storey, with exceptionally clean, smartly tiled papaya-coloured bathrooms downstairs and Thai-style bamboo-walled sleeping quarters upstairs, with varnished wood floors and big decks. One of the few places to keep both its bungalows and restaurant open all year. ❷–❸

Long Beach ☎087 280 8213, ⓔlongbeach bungalowkohchang@yahoo.co.th. At the far northern end of Ao Yai, this popular spot offers a choice of en-suite bungalows, the best of which are the large, robust wooden ones on the seafront; the smaller, cheaper, older ones are just one row behind. Open all year. ❷–❸

🛶 **Mama's Bungalows** 5min walk south over the headland from Ao Yai, on Ao Daddaeng ☎077 820180, ⓔmamasbungalows@yahoo.com. The ten attractive, well-maintained wooden bungalows here come in two sizes, all of them with decent bathrooms. They're built in a pretty flower garden staggered up the hillside; a couple are on the beach and the uppermost ones overlook the bay from the edge of a rubber plantation. Lighting is by paraffin lamps. The restaurant serves generous portions of good food, including many German specialities. Very popular, so book ahead. ❶–❷

Sawasdee Resort ☎081 803 0946, ⓔsawasdeekohchang@yahoo.com. This welcoming place at the far southern end of Ao Yai is a little pricier than many but more style conscious too and tends to attract slightly older, less hammock-bound guests. The nine thoughtfully designed wooden bungalows are not fancy but all have exceptionally good bathrooms (tiled floors, colour-washed walls, sinks and showers). The food is recommended too. Because of wave erosion a sea wall has been built around the garden, which mars the view a little, though the water is still just a couple of steps away. ❷–❸

Eating and drinking

Bungalow **restaurants** that stand out include *Cashew Resort* for its fresh bread; *Sawasdee* for its fish with tamarind sauce and its *matsaman* curries; and *Mama's* for its huge breakfasts and home-cooked south-German specialities. Italian-run *Little Italy* makes deliciously authentic sauces for its pasta – Sicilian-style succo, carbonara, arrabbiata (B100–230) – and serves them year-round in its peaceful garden 100m inland from *Cashew* (see above). There's also the very charming *Bakery*, in a tiny forest clearing about 300m inland from *Golden Bee*, where you sit at low tables under the trees and sample the home-made bread, cakes, yoghurt, sandwiches and teas.

A couple of low-key but funky little beach **bars** tempt the slightly more active beachbums out of their hammocks: *Thai Bar*, between the khlong and *Golden Bee*, puts on occasional parties, while fairy-lit *Air Bar*, in a scenic position on the rocks alongside *Ko Chang Resort*, plays cool music and stirs cheap cocktails and is a prime spot for hornbill-spotting at sunset.

The rest of the island

North of Ao Yai, the crenellated coast reveals a series of tiny bays occupied by just one set of bungalows apiece. The gritty gold-sand beaches are secluded and feel quite remote, accessible only via a track through forest and rubber plantations. Even if you don't want to base yourself up here, you can do an enjoyable **loop** around the northern bays in well under three hours from Ao Yai. Alternatively, you could make use of the Ranong boats, which charge about B50 for any hop up or down the west coast.

Following **the track** inland from *Eden*, a ten-minute walk north brings you to the top of the first of several hills (a reliable place to get a mobile phone signal) and the barbed-wire perimeters of a military camp, established here to monitor activity along the (maritime) Thai–Burma border. Ten minutes further on, *Nice View* restaurant and bungalows are aptly named: perched atop an outcrop with glorious panoramas over the unfolding little bays and islets beyond, it's a perfect spot to break for lunch or a drink. It's another twenty minutes to *Sea Eagle* (you need to go via the beach at *Hornbill* before returning inland), the last of the northern bay bungalows, beyond which a ten-minute walk up and over the next hill takes you to the edge of the northeast-facing fishing village, an unprepossessing place complete with incongruous Christian church. This is **Ao Ko**, which is linked by road to the east coast's rainy season pier, and also to Ao Yai.

Ao Siad, at the southern end of the island, is even more isolated, though there are several bungalow outfits fronting the sandy shore here. It's sometimes known as Ao Lek, though the real **Ao Lek** is the mangrove-lined bay fifteen minutes' walk to the northeast, on the other coast. The Ranong–Ko Phayam boat service makes a stop off Ao Siad (Ranong–Ko Chang boats do not; see p.330), but to get anywhere else you'll need to negotiate a ride in a longtail if staying here. The alternative is to walk, either from Ao Daddaeng or from the village. From Ao Daddaeng, a clear path takes you south, in about an hour, to **Ao Kai Tao**, a pretty beach and site of the national park ranger station. From Ao Kai Tao the route then follows an indistinct path across the saddle between two hills and along a creek bed to reach east coast Ao Lek (this takes another hour), after which it's fifteen minutes south to Ao Siad. Coming **from the village**, you follow the signed track from the *Sunshine Restaurant* crossroads south to Ao Lek and then on to Ao Siad; it's 5km and should take about two hours.

Accommodation

Hornbill North around two headlands from Ao Yai, about 35min walk ☏077 870240, 66_hornbill@hotmail.com. Set amongst the trees fronting their own little gold-sand bay, the ten unobtrusive en-suite bungalows here are constructed to different designs, some of them extremely comfortable, and all enjoy sea views. The food here has a good reputation and the owner is very welcoming. It lives up to its name, as majestic black-and-white hornbills are a common sight. Opens earlier than many, in September, and has internet access and boat trips. ❶–❷

Koh Chang Contex 25min walk from northern Ao Yai ☏087 827 2874. Located in its own peaceful little bay, which is good for snorkelling and fine for swimming except at low tide, this place has seventeen wood, bamboo and concrete huts, some of them very large and all with generous decks and their own bathrooms. Some occupy elevated spots on the rocks, others are scattered around a garden just above the beach. ❶–❸

N&X 10min walk south of Ao Siad and at least a 2hr walk from either Ao Daddaeng or from the inland village. Occupying its own tiny bay, isolated even from remote Ao Siad, this place offers ten good en-suite bungalows ranged up the shorefront hillside. ❶–❸

Sea Eagle About 40min walk from Ao Yai ☏082 289 0683, ⓦwww.seaeaglebangkalo.com. The sole occupants of the longest and widest of the northern bays, which is graced by an attractive band of gold sand, the seven dark green-painted, en-suite bamboo bungalows here are set among trees just back from shore. They have comfy deck furniture for soaking up the sea views and there are kayaks for rent and a beach volleyball net. ❷

Ko Phayam

The diminutive kangaroo-shaped island of **KO PHAYAM** offers fine white-sand beaches and coral reefs and is home to around five hundred people, most of whom either make their living from prawn, squid and crab fishing, or from growing cashew nuts, *sator* beans, coconut palms and rubber trees. Many

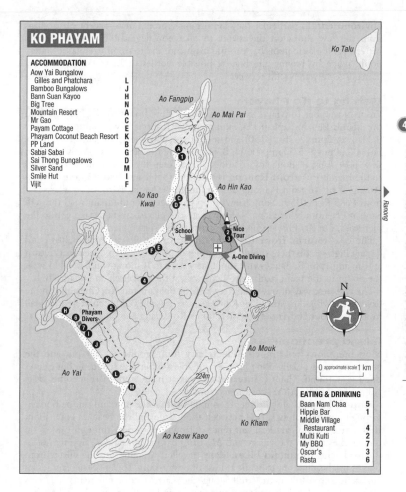

KO PHAYAM

ACCOMMODATION

Aow Yai Bungalow	
Gilles and Phatchara	L
Bamboo Bungalows	J
Bann Suan Kayoo	H
Big Tree	N
Mountain Resort	A
Mr Gao	C
Payam Cottage	E
Phayam Coconut Beach Resort	K
PP Land	B
Sabai Sabai	G
Sai Thong Bungalows	D
Silver Sand	M
Smile Hut	I
Vijit	F

Ko Talu

Ao Fangpip

Ao Mai Pai

Ranong

Ao Hin Kao

Ao Kao
Kwai

School

Nice
Tour

A-One Diving

N

Phayam
Divers

Ao Mouk

0 approximate scale 1 km

Ao Yai

224m

Ko Kham

Ao Kaew Kaeo

EATING & DRINKING

Baan Nam Chaa	5
Hippie Bar	1
Middle Village	
Restaurant	4
Multi Kulti	2
My BBQ	7
Oscar's	3
Rasta	6

islanders live in Ko Phayam's only **village**, behind the pier on the northeast coast, which connects to other corners of the island by a network of concrete roads and rutted tracks. The bays either side of the village have a couple of nice places to stay, but the main beaches and accommodation centres are on the west coast, at **Ao Yai** and **Ao Kao Kwai**. A motorbike taxi service covers all routes, but no journey is very great as the island measures just five by eight kilometres at its widest points.

Because of the roads, Ko Phayam has a livelier and slightly more developed feel than neighbouring Ko Chang, underlined by a low-key beach-bar scene – all hand-painted signs and driftwood sculptures – and the presence of a significant number of foreigners who choose to spend six or more months here every year. Some expats even take up the **rainy-season** challenge, staying on through the downpours and rough seas that lash the island from June to October, but a number of bungalows close down during this time and staff take refuge in Ranong. As the island gets more popular, residents and expats are beginning to try and forestall the inevitable negative impact on the island's

environment. In particular they are urging visitors not to accept plastic bags from the few shops on the island, to take non-degradable rubbish such as batteries and plastic items back to the mainland, and to minimize plastic water-bottle usage by buying the biggest possible bottles or better still creating a demand for a water-refill service.

Getting to Ko Phayam

From November to May there are two daily slow **boats** to Ko Phayam from the Islands Pier in Saphan Pla, 5km south of Ranong town centre (currently 9.30am & 2pm; 2–3hr; B150) and several speedboat services (currently 10am, noon, 2.30pm & 5.30pm; 40min; B350). During the rainy season only the 2pm slow boat runs; Ranong information centres keep the latest timetables. Access to the Islands Pier **from Ranong** is either by songthaew (red #3 from Thanon Ruangrat or #6 from Ranong bus station; both 20min, B15), or by share-taxi from *Pon's Place* (B50). Songthaews drop passengers on the main road through Saphan Pla, from where it's a 500m walk to the pier; share-taxis take you to the pier itself. On Ko Phayam, all boats arrive at the village pier.

The boat **returns from Ko Phayam** to Saphan Pla at about 8.30am and during high season there should be another departure at 2pm; speedboats return at 9am and 1pm. To flag down a songthaew back to Ranong you'll need to walk the 500m to the main road; share-taxis wait at the pier itself and charge B50.

The cheapest way of travelling between Ko Phayam and **Ko Chang** is on the day-trippers' boat organized by *Ko Chang Resort* (see p.325); a chartered longtail from Nice Tour and Travel costs B1500 to Ko Chang and takes 45 minutes.

Island practicalities

Most bungalows only provide **electricity** from around 6 to 11pm and the cheapest rooms usually don't have a fan. Unless otherwise stated, all bungalows open year-round. There is **internet access** at many and wi-fi at some. *Baan Nam Chaa* on the Ao Yai road rents **books**.

Motorbike taxis always meet incoming boats at the pier and can be booked through any bungalow; a ride between the village and the beaches costs about B80. There are no cars. You can rent your own motorbike through outlets on the beaches and in the village and *My BBQ* bar on central Ao Yai, just west of the road, rents **mountain bikes**. Many travellers heading into the village from one of the beaches opt to **walk** at least one way: from Ao Yai's *Smile Hut* it's an enjoyable seven-kilometre stroll along the narrow concrete road than cuts through the cashew plantations, with the possibility of stopping for a breather at the aptly named *Middle Village Restaurant*. From southern Ao Kao Kwai to the village takes less than an hour.

A-One Diving (℡077 824303, ⊛www.a-one-diving.com), based in the village, teaches PADI **dive** courses and runs liveaboards to Ko Surin, Richelieu Rock and Ko Similan (from B13,900 for three days) and to Burma Banks and the Mergui archipelago. On Ao Yai, Phayam Divers at *Phayam Lodge* offers a similar deal (℡084 849 9766, ⊛www.phayamlodge.com). *Mr Gao* on Ao Kao Kwai (℡077 870222, ⊛www.mr-gao-phayam.com) runs two-day **snorkelling** trips to Ko Surin at B4000 per person including accommodation in national park tents. Most bungalows can arrange fishing and snorkelling day-trips for B1500 per boat.

The village and around

The tiny cluster of homes and shops that constitute Ko Phayam's only **village** are within a few minutes' walk of the pier. There are a few little general stores here, plus a 24-hour minimarket, several restaurants and a **clinic**. North a little way up the shoreline stands the island **temple**, with its circular viharn resting on a huge concrete lotus flower at the end of its own pier.

Oscar's bar (daily 7am–late, ℡084 842 5070), just north of the pier-head, is a good source of island **information**, rents motorbikes, sells speedboat tickets, charters speedboats to Ranong airport and other islands, and takes people wakeboarding in the village bay. It serves breakfasts and Thai and European standards but is most famous for its partially open-air **bar**, which is the focal point of the expat social scene (customers who can't make it home are invited to crash out at the adjacent *Hangover Hut*). Nearby *Multi Kulti* is the place to go for multi-grain sandwiches, and there are some cheap Thai *som tam* places too. **Tour agent** Nice Tour and Travel (℡089 651 5177, ⓦwww.kohphayamisland .com) **changes money** and does Visa cash advance, sells bus, train, airline and speedboat tickets, can arrange boat hire and fishing tours, and offers **internet** access and an **international phone service**; it also sells creative Nepalese clothing and handicrafts.

Accommodation

Most people choose to **stay** at the west-coast beach centres, but there are a couple of nice little hideaways within easy reach of the village and its facilities. On their own little beach five minutes' walk south, *Sabai Sabai* (℡087 895 4653, Ⓔsabaisabai_thailand@yahoo.com; ❶–❷) has five wooden, solar-powered bungalows, all with 24-hour electricity and all but one en suite; cute, stylish touches give them a modern look. There's a cool lounge area, regular movie nights and other events, plus internet access and Nintendo Wii. Fronting a small beach about ten minutes' walk north from the village, *PP Land* (℡081 678 4310, Ⓦppland.cabanova.de; ❸) is a cut above many places to stay on the island, with its tasteful, green-painted shaggy thatched bungalows, pretty furnishings, polished wood floors inside and out, nice bathrooms, and big comfy decks. There's internet, wi-fi and homemade ice cream too, plus 24-hour electricity, safety boxes in the rooms and bicycles and motorbikes for rent.

Ao Yai

Ko Phayam's main beach is the three-kilometre-long **Ao Yai** on the southwest coast, a wide and handsome sweep of silvery white sand that curves quite deeply at its northern and southern ends into rocky outcrops that offer some snorkelling possibilities. The shore is pounded by decent waves that are fun for boogie-boarding and pretty safe; the sunsets are quite spectacular too. For the moment Ao Yai's bungalow operations are mostly widely spaced along the shoreline, and much of the forest behind the beach is still intact. You're more than likely to see — and hear — some of the resident black-and-white hornbills at dawn and dusk, along with many white-bellied sea eagles, and sightings of crab-eating macaques are also common.

Accommodation and eating

When it comes to **eating**, *Silver Sand* bungalows does famously tasty yellow seafood curries and *Bamboo* makes authentic spaghetti pesto. The invitingly hippyish *Ban Nam Chaa* on the Ao Yai road (Mon–Sat 8am–5pm) makes its own bread and cakes, dreams up unusual salads, Indian and Burmese curries, and stocks plenty of weird teas. Many bungalow operations on Ao Yai, including the long-running *Rasta*, also host laid-back little **beach-bar shacks** which put on fireshows and occasional parties.

Aow Yai Bungalow Gilles and Phatchara ☎075 870216, ⓔgilles_phatchara@hotmail.com. Established by a French-Thai couple, this was the first set of bungalows on the island and remains one of the most popular, especially with return guests. The 22 good-quality bungalows are dotted around an extensive garden of flowers, fruit trees and palms and come in various styles, with price depending on size. There's wi-fi and internet access, snorkels for rent and bus tickets for sale. ❷—❹

Bamboo Bungalows ☎077 820012, ⓦwww .bamboo-bungalows.com. Ao Yai's liveliest accommodation is Israeli-Thai managed and very traveller savvy, with internet access and free wi-fi, plus kayak, motorbike and boogie-board rental, currency exchange and overseas phone services. Its 39 bungalows and handful of tents (with proper mattresses) are set under the trees in a well-tended flower garden and range from luxuriously large chalets with 24hr electricity and pretty furnishings to characterful shell-studded concrete bungalows and a choice of bamboo and wood huts. Tents ❶, bungalows ❷—❻

Bann Suan Kayoo ☎089 819 8782, ⓦwww .gopayam.com. There's a genuinely warm welcome from the island-family owners here and the peaceful location at the far northern end of the bay appeals particularly to solo travellers looking for quiet. Choose between simple thatched bamboo huts nicely spaced along the shoreline and with decent beds and en-suite bathrooms, or slightly sturdier ones with tin roofs and bigger decks, the latter set within a grassy shorefront garden with floral hedges. Closed May–Oct. ❶—❸

Big Tree ☎087 893 7075. Another lovely quiet spot, removed from the main action at the far southern end of the bay, and set near the eponymous tree and above a rocky point that offers some snorkelling. The thirteen bamboo, wood and concrete bungalows are a good size, with price depending on size and location, though nearly all of them have a direct sea view and some have commanding panoramas from atop a small rise. Closed during the rainy season. ❶—❹

Phayam Coconut Beach Resort ☎089 920 8145, ⓦwww.koh-phayam.com. Occupying a great spot in the centre of the bay and run by a Ko Phayam family, the 25 good-value bungalows here are of a high standard, each set in its own tiny garden. Choose between small bamboo en-suite huts through larger wood or bamboo versions to big concrete bungalows at the top end. Also rents kayaks. ❷—❹

Smile Hut ☎081 810 7252, ⓦwww.smilehutthai .com. Like *Bamboo*, this is very popular with travellers. The 35 split-bamboo huts are simple but en suite and are spread among the shorefront trees, with the slightly cheaper versions set one row behind. Has internet access. ❷—❸

Ao Kao Kwai and around

The northwest coast is scalloped into **AO KAO KWAI**, a name that's pronounced locally as **Ao Kao Fai** and translates as **Buffalo Bay**; from the cliffside midway along the bay you can see how the two halves of the beach curve out into buffalo-like horns. The southern half of Ao Kao Kwai is subject to both very low and very high tides, which makes it unreliable for swimming, but the northern stretch, from *Sai Thong* and *Mr Gao* bungalows onwards, is exceptionally pretty, secluded between outcrops with decent swimming at any tide, and none of the big waves that characterize Ao Yai. Ao Kao Kwai is particularly popular both with long-stay guests and returnees, so you might want to book your accommodation in advance. Both *Sai Thong* and *Mr Gao* have reputations for very good Thai **food**, and *Hippie Bar* has occasional parties.

North of *Mountain Resort* at the northern end of Ao Kao Kwai, a thirty-minute walk brings you to the pretty little sandy beach at **Ao Fangpip** (also spelt Ao Kwang Pib), which is the best spot on the island for snorkelling. There's also some snorkellable reef at **Ao Hin Kao** on the northeast coast.

Accommodation

Mountain Resort ☎086 144 7208. Managed by a welcoming family, the five bungalows here vary in size but they're comfortable, en suite and have screened doors. They're set in a lovely grassy garden at the peaceful, northernmost end of the beach, under palms and among bougainvillea and hibiscus. The concrete road ends about 1km before *Mountain Resort*, so the last stretch is via a potholed dirt track (or you can walk via the beach instead). ❸

Mr Gao ☎077 870222, ⓦwww.mr-gao
-phayam.com. Located on the best stretch of
the beach, this is one of the most famous and
popular spots, a well-established operation comprising just ten well-designed bungalows, in assorted
sizes and luxury, set in a lovingly tended garden of
shrubs and bamboos. All have good bathrooms and
generous decks and most have polished wood floors,
screened windows and thoughtfully furnished
interiors. There is internet access here and free wi-fi,
and it's open all year. ❷–❸
Payam Cottage ☎085 222 1847, ⓦwww
.payamcottage.com. More resort-like in style and
facilities than others on Ko Phayam, with 24hr
electricity, the option of air-con, a kids' play area,
and a swimming pool in the pipeline. Bungalows

are tastefully furnished and built in angled rows
across a central garden to give each one some sort
of sea view. Internet access and free wi-fi. Fan ❺,
air-con ❻
Sai Thong Bungalows ☎080 141 1231,
ⓔsaithong_ranongth@yahoo.com. Friendly, local
setup that shares the same pretty stretch of beach
with *Mr Gao* and has just five good-quality rattan
huts, each furnished with a thick mattress, a
mosquito net and its own well-appointed
bathroom. ❷
Vijit ☎077 834082, ⓦwww.kohpayam-vijit.com.
This long-running outfit is very popular. Some of the
26 bungalows are designed for families and they're
all reasonably spacious. Has currency exchange,
kayak, motorbike and bicycle rental. ❷–❸

Khuraburi and Ko Surin

The small town of **Khuraburi**, 110km south of Ranong on Highway 4, is the
main departure point for the magnificent national park island chain of **Ko
Surin**, a group of five small islands around 60km offshore, just inside Thai
waters. Much closer to Khuraburi are the islands of **Ko Ra** and **Ko Phra
Thong**, which offer empty beaches and decent snorkelling and bird-watching,
or there's the chance to participate in typical village life at **homestays** in
mainland coastal communities.

Khuraburi

Most travellers use the town of **KHURABURI** as a staging post en route to or
from the Surin islands: the main pier for boats to the islands is just 7.5km away,
and Khuraburi's tour agents sell boat tickets and offer transport to the pier, plus
there is accommodation in town. Though lacking in famous attractions, the
local area is nonetheless scenic, both offshore and inland: with an afternoon or
more to spare, you could either rent a motorbike, mountain bike or kayak to
explore it independently, or charter a motorbike taxi or longtail boat.

Khuraburi is also the headquarters of the community-based tourism initiative
Andaman Discoveries (☎087 917 7165, ⓦwww.andamandiscoveries.com),
which runs a recommended **homestay programme** in several local villages.
It was established after the tsunami to help the area's many devastated fishing
communities get back on their feet and has since developed a range of stimulating packages featuring all sort of village jobs and activities, from soap-making
and batik design to rubber-tapping and roof-thatching; a typical, all-inclusive
three-day stay costs from B5400 per person. The office is just east off the
highway, up the soi beside the police box, across from Tom & Am Tour.

Practicalities

The commercial heart of Khuraburi is a 500-metre strip of shops and businesses
either side of Highway 4 and most **buses** travelling along Highway 4 between
Bangkok/Chumphon/Ranong and Takua Pa/Khao Lak/Phuket stop here. Bus
passengers are usually met by staff from Tom & Am Tour (☎086 272 0588,
ⓔtom_am01@yahoo.co.th), which runs boats to Ko Surin and rents **tents**
(B100 per day), bedding sets (B30 per day) and snorkel sets (B50 per day) for

Ko Surin (all cheaper than National Park prices) as well as bicycles and motor-bikes. Nearby Sabina Tour (℡081 737 5801, ⓦwww.sabinatour.com) is a good operator of boats to Ko Surin and has two offices in central Khuraburi and another at the pier. For details of transport to Ko Surin see p.336. *Boon Piya Resort* (see below) rents kayaks and motorbikes and can arrange snorkelling trips to Ko Ra and Ko Phra Thong; and Indian Ocean Adventures (ⓦwww .diverichelieurock.com) runs twice-weekly liveaboard **dive trips** out of Khuraburi to Ko Tachai, Ko Surin and Richelieu Rock (three days; B12,450).

Set alongside the river at the northern end of town, about 250m north of the bus drop, *Tararin* (℡076 491789; fan ❷, air-con ❸) is a cute, rustic-style place with just a handful of simple but appealing en-suite wooden and concrete **bungalows** overlooking the water, plus an attractive riverside restaurant and eating deck. The pristine concrete bungalows at the motel-style *Boon Piya Resort* (℡081 752 5457; ❸–❹), 150m north of the bus drop, are better appointed, if rather tightly packed, and all have fan or air-con and powerful showers; they're the usual choice of sales reps and NGOs. The poshest accommodation in the area are the attractive wooden chalets at *Khuraburi Greenview Resort* (℡076 401400, ⓦwww.kuraburigreenview.co.th; ❻–❼), 12km south of Khuraburi, beneath a range of forested hills alongside Highway 4, at kilometre-stone 739. Rooms are air-conditioned and there's wi-fi, a swimming pool and spa; the hotel also does (expensive) speedboat day-trips and transfers to Ko Surin.

At night, many people **eat** at one of the night markets near the bus drop, where the roti stall is a particular favourite, flipping out a constant pile of sizzling *roti mataba* (chicken) and *roti kluay* (banana), and *Krua Pakarang* does excellent-value seafood from 4pm. The morning market (daily from 5am) across from *Boon Piya* is the place to stock up on food for the Surin islands, but the best place for fresh coffee is next door but one to *Boon Piya* at the *Friends de Sea* **internet** café (daily 8am–9pm). Popular *Cucina Andaburi*, beside the bridge and *Tararin*, is a welcoming spot for farang food and a favourite hangout of resident NGOs.

Ko Ra and Ko Phra Thong

Chief among Khuraburi's local maritime attractions are the **islands** of Ko Ra and Ko Phra Thong, both of them accessible by chartered longtail from the Khuraburi pier (B2500 per day including snorkel gear and transfers from town). Hilly, forested **Ko Ra** (measuring about 10km north to south and 3km across) sits just off Khuraburi pier's mangrove-lined estuary and is graced with intact rainforest full of towering trees, hornbills and wild, empty beaches. The island is home to some two dozen Moken and *Mai Thai* people (see opposite) plus just one place to stay, the rather special American-Thai run ⚟ *Ko Ra Ecolodge* (℡089 867 5288, ⓦwww.thaiecolodge.com; ❺). The *Ecolodge* fronts a curve of bronze sand on the north coast, with magnificent views to the Khuraburi hills, but its star feature is its wild, forty-acre, forest garden. Filled with screw palms, red-barked *samet daeng* trees, dipterocarps and over seventeen epiphytic orchids, the private forest is crossed by trails and home both to a rich bird life, especially sunbirds and oriental pied hornbills, and to monitor lizards, crab-eating macaques and dusky langurs. Accommodation is in eighteen plain but spacious rooms in split-bamboo longhouses just back from the shore, communal meals are taken in the beach-side *sala* and there's a genuine focus on community and environmental projects; the *Ecolodge* also runs the Thai arm of Reefcheck NGO (see p.67). There are kayak rental and trips, plus hiking, snorkelling and diving, in particular to the nearby Surin islands (B4900 for two dives) and Richelieu Rock. A longtail transfer to the *Ecolodge* from Khuraburi costs B250 per person (20min).

The chao ley: Moken and Urak Lawoy

Sometimes called sea gypsies, the **chao ley** or *chao nam* ("people of the sea" or "water people") have been living off the seas around the west coast of the Malay peninsula for hundreds of years. Some still pursue a traditional nomadic existence, living in self-contained houseboats known as **kabang**, but many have now made permanent homes in Andaman coast settlements in Thailand, Burma and Malaysia. Dark-skinned and sometimes with an auburn tinge to their hair, the *chao ley* of the Andaman Sea are thought to number around five thousand, divided into five groups, with distinct lifestyles and dialects.

Of the different groups, the **Urak Lawoy**, who have settled on the islands of Ko Lanta, Ko Jum, Ko Phi Phi, Phuket and Ko Lipe, are the most integrated into Thai society. They came north to Thailand from Malaysia around two hundred years ago (having possibly migrated from the Nicobar Islands in the Indian Ocean some two centuries prior) and are known as *Mai Thai*, or "New Thai". Thailand's Urak Lawoy have been recognized as Thai citizens since the 1960s, when the late Queen Mother granted them five family names, thereby enabling them to possess ID cards and go to school. Many work on coconut plantations or as fishermen, while others continue in the more traditional *chao ley* **occupations** of hunting for pearls and seashells on the ocean floor, attaching stones to their waists to dive to depths of 60m with only an air-hose connecting them to the surface; sometimes they fish in this way too, taking down enormous nets into which they herd the fish as they walk along the sea bed. Their agility and courage make them good bird's-nesters as well (see box, p.418).

The **Moken** of Thailand's Ko Surin islands and Burma's Mergui archipelago probably came originally from Burma and are the most traditional of the *chao ley* communities. Some still lead remote, itinerant lives, and most are unregistered as Thai citizens, and own no land or property, but are dependent on fresh water and beaches to collect shells and sea slugs to sell to Thai traders. They have extensive knowledge of the plants that grow in the remaining jungles on Thailand's west-coast islands, using eighty different species for food alone, and thirty for medicinal purposes.

The *chao ley* are **animists**, with a strong connection both to the natural spirits of island and sea and to their own ancestral spirits. On some beaches they set up totem poles as a contact point between the spirits, their ancestors and their shaman. The sea gypsies have a rich **musical heritage** too. The Moken do not use any instruments as such, making do with found objects for percussion; the Urak Lawoy, on the other hand, due to their closer proximity to the Thai and Malay cultures, are excellent violin- and drum-players. During community entertainments, such as the Urak Lawoy's twice-yearly full-moon **festivals** on Ko Lanta (see p.436), the male musicians form a semicircle around the old women, who dance and sing about the sea, the jungle and their families.

Building a new boat is the ultimate expression of what it is to be a *chao ley*, and tradition holds that every newly married couple has a *kabang* built for them. But the complex art of constructing a seaworthy home from a single tree trunk, and the way of life it represents, is disappearing. In Thailand, where **assimilation** is actively promoted by the government, the truly nomadic flotillas have become increasingly marginalized, and the number of undeveloped islands they can visit unhindered gets smaller year by year. The 2004 tsunami further threatened their cultural integrity: when the waves destroyed the Moken's boats and homes on Ko Surin, they were obliged to take refuge on the mainland, where some were encouraged by mission-aries to convert from their animist religion. Though the Moken have since returned to the Surin islands, inappropriate donations and the merging of two villages have exacerbated family rivalries and caused divisions that may prove lethal to their traditional way of life.

Immediately to the south of Ko Ra, about one kilometre off the Khuraburi coast, **KO PHRA THONG** (Golden Buddha Island) also has some lovely beaches, the nicest of which, on the west coast, is 10km long and blessed with fine gold sand. This is the site of the *Golden Buddha Beach Resort* (T081 892 2208, Wwww.goldenbuddharesort.com; ⑧–⑨), a tasteful complex of 25 individually styled wooden Thai-style homes, sleeping two to six. The resort is ninety minutes' boat ride from the pier and offers kayaking, diving and occasional yoga retreats plus a spa and clubhouse.

Ko Surin

Spectacularly varied and unusually shallow reefs, a palette of awesomely clear turquoise waters and dazzling white sands, and dense forests of lofty diptero-carps combine to make the islands of Mu **Ko Surin** National Park (open Nov 16–May 15; B400/200 entry fee for a week; Wwww.dnp.go.th/National_park.asp) one of the must-visit destinations in south Thailand. It's very much an outdoors experience, with the bulk of accommodation in national park tents, no commerce on the islands at all, and twice-daily snorkelling the main activity. Many tour operators run snorkelling and diving day-trips from Khuraburi and Ranong, and there are diving live-aboards too, but independent travel is also recommended.

The most beautiful and easily explored of the reefs are those off the two main islands in the group, Ko Surin Nua (north) and Ko Surin Tai (south), which are separated only by a narrow channel. **Surin Nua**, slightly the larger at about 5km across, holds the national park headquarters, visitor centre and park accom-modation. Across the channel, **Surin Tai** is the long-established home of a community of **Moken** *chao ley* (see p.335), who these days mostly make their living as longtail boatmen for snorkellers staying on Surin Nua. Their recent history has been an unhappy one: not only were their settlements destroyed in the 2004 tsunami, but the aid and outside intervention that followed has changed the community forever, amalgamating two villages, building new homes too close together and introducing various modern-day vices. Some tour companies take visitors on a walk around the village on Ao Bon and up the hill behind it, but unless you are able to hire an English-speaking Moken guide it's a dispiriting experience; if you do visit, you'll at least be making a positive contribution if you buy one of the woven-pandanus-leaf souvenirs the villagers make. One of the Moken traditions that does persist is the new year celebration that's held every April, during Songkhran, when *chao ley* from nearby islands (including those in Burmese waters) congregate here and, among other rites, release several hundred turtles into the sea, a symbol of longevity.

Practicalities

Because the islands are so far out at sea, Ko Surin is closed to visitors from mid-May to mid-November, when monsoon weather renders the sixty-kilometre trip a potentially suicidal undertaking. During the rest of the year, most visitors either do **snorkelling day-trips** to the islands from Khuraburi or Ko Ra (around B2500), join a multi-day snorkel trip from *Mr Gao* on Ko Phayam, or opt for live-aboard **dive trips** out of Khao Lak, Phuket, Ranong, Ko Chang or Ko Phayam, the majority of which also take in nearby Richelieu Rock, considered to be Thailand's top dive site (see p.371).

Independent travel to Ko Surin is highly recommended however, as this gives you the chance to base yourself on the islands and explore the countless different reefs over several days. During the season, **boats** to Ko Surin depart from Khuraburi pier, 7.5km northwest of Khuraburi town; agencies in the town sell tickets and provide free transfers to the pier. The national park's slow boat departs the pier daily at 9am and returns from Ko Surin at 1pm (2–3hr; B1200 return); private speedboats depart at 9am and leave Ko Surin about 2.30pm (1hr 15min; B1600 return). Once on the islands, there's an efficient system of **boat hire** for access to the reefs: longtails depart twice a day from the campsites to four different reefs and charge B80 per person for about two hours. You can also charter your own for B2000. Snorkel sets cost B80 per day and there's kayak rental too.

All island **accommodation** is on Surin Nua and is provided by the national park. On the beach at **Ao Chong Khad**, near the park headquarters and pier, you have the choice between expensive en-suite national park bungalows (●) and either renting a national park tent (B300–450 per day) or pitching your own (available for rent in Khuraburi) for B80 per day; bedding sets cost B60 per day. The nicer campsite, with tents and pitches but no bungalows, is at **Ao Mai Ngam**, reached via a two-kilometre trail from headquarters or by longtail. Both campsites have bathrooms, lockers (B30 per day) and dining rooms where meals are served at fixed times three times a day (B80–200); many people take their own supplies from Khuraburi instead. Bungalows need to be booked in advance either through the National Parks website (Ⓦwww.dnp.go.th/National_park .asp) or at the Khuraburi pier office (Ⓣ076 491378), but tents should be available on spec except during public holidays and long weekends.

Khao Sok National Park

Most of the Andaman coast's highlights are, unsurprisingly, along the shoreline, but the stunning jungle-clad karsts of **KHAO SOK NATIONAL PARK** (Ⓦwww.dnp.go.th/National_park.asp) are well worth heading inland for. Located about halfway between the southern peninsula's two coasts and easily accessible from Khao Lak, Phuket and Surat Thani, the park has become a popular stop on the travellers' route, offering a number of easy trails, a bit of amateur spelunking and some scenic rafthouse accommodation on **Cheow Lan Lake**. Much of the park, which protects the watershed of the Sok River and rises to a peak of nearly 1000m, is carpeted in impenetrable rainforest, home to gaurs, leopard cats and tigers among others – and up to 155 species of bird. The limestone crags that dominate almost every vista both on and away from the lake are breathtaking, never more so than in the early morning: waking up to the sound of hooting gibbons and the sight of thick white mist curling around the karst formations is an experience not quickly forgotten.

The park has two centres: the **tourist village** that has grown up around the park visitor centre and trailheads, and the dam, 65km further east, at the head of **Cheow Lan Lake**. Most visitors stay in the tourist village and organize their lake trips from there, but it's also feasible to do one or more nights at the lake first.

Arrival and information

Khao Sok, its tourist village and Cheow Lan Lake are all north off Highway 401, which is served by frequent **buses**: all services between the junction town of **Takua Pa**, 40km south of Khuraburi, and Surat Thani come this way, as do some Surat Thani services to and from Khao Lak and Phuket as well. Coming from Bangkok, Hua Hin or Chumphon, take a Surat Thani-bound bus as far as the Highway 401 junction, about 20km before Surat Thani, and change onto one for Takua Pa. If coming direct from Surat Thani, note that there have been complaints about the tourist **minibus** services to Khao Sok that leave at or after

KHAO SOK NATIONAL PARK

0 250 m

Sip-et Chan Falls

Ton Koi Falls

Bang Laen River

National Park
Visitor Centre

Khao Sok
Track & Trail

Jungle
Mania

Our Jungle House

Funky
Monkey

Minimarket

Morning Mist
Minimarket

Jungle
Huts

Sok River

Smiley

Thai Massage

Minimarket

Treetops
Jungle Safari

N

Minimarket

Wat Tham Phanturat

Bus stop

Bus stop

401

Takua Pa

Ban Ta Khun, Cheow Lan Lake & Surat Thani

EATING

Thai Garden 1
Thai Herb
  Restaurant 2

ACCOMMODATION

Art's Riverview Jungle Lodge	E
Bamboo House	A
Elephant Hills	F
Khao Sok Green Mountain View	G
Khao Sok Rainforest Resort	D
Morning Mist Resort	C
Nung House	B

3pm: despite advertising a door-to-door service, they reputedly dump their passengers at an affiliated guest house on the Khao Sok access road, delaying their arrival until after dark. See p.341 for transport services from Surat Thani train station direct to the lake.

The access road to the tourist village and trailheads is at kilometre-stone 109 on Highway 401, where guest-house staff meet all passengers and **offer free lifts** to their accommodation, the furthest of which is 3km from the main road.

The tourist village offers all essential services – minimarkets, **internet**, laundry, massage and **motorbike rental** – but there's **no ATM** here. Khao Sok Track & Trail does currency exchange, has overseas phone services and sells bus, boat, plane and train tickets.

Moving on from Khao Sok

Onward bus connections from Khao Sok are frequent (see p.438), or you can make use of the minibus services organized by Track & Trail, including to Krabi (2hr; B300), Surat Thani train station at Phunphin (1hr 45min; B250), Ko Samui (3hr; B500), Trang (4hr 30min; B520) and Penang (12hr; B750). Jungle Mania sells tickets on the overnight VIP government bus to Bangkok's Southern Bus Terminal (12hr; B1000).

Accommodation and eating

The bulk of the budget **accommodation** is scenically sited beneath the karsts near the park visitors' centre, but despite the edge-of-the rainforest location, it can get noisy of an evening, with the sound systems at some backpacker bars pitched against the chattering of the cicadas. There are quieter, more remote alternatives further east, including the deluxe tented camp run by *Elephant Hills* as part of a package booked from southern beach resorts (℡076 381703, ⓦ www.elephant-hills.com), and rafthouses on the lake (see p.341). Some guest houses (not listed here) can make life difficult for guests who choose not to book park trips through them. For **food**, *Thai Herb Restaurant* at *Morning Mist Resort* serves exceptionally tasty and inventive spicy *yam* salads and other Thai classics plus fresh sapodilla and tamarind juices; staff grow much of their own produce and run popular cooking classes (from B800). *Thai Garden* also does great Thai food, including vegan and gluten-free dishes, set dinners (from B240), very good stir-fried red curry with chilli, basil and pork, and delicious fresh coconut shakes.

Art's Riverview Jungle Lodge ℡086 479 3234, ⓦ krabidir.com/artsriverviewlodge /index.htm. Popular place, with 35 bungalows nicely located away from the main fray, surrounded by jungle and mostly enjoying pretty river views. The cheaper bungalows are spacious, tastefully designed wooden affairs, with shutters and a deck; the deluxe versions are bigger still and attractively furnished, and there are treehouse-style bungalows and family ones too. All rooms have fans and mosquito nets. ❹–❻

Bamboo House ℡081 787 7484, ⓦ krabidir.com /bamboohouse/index.htm. One of the first guest houses in the park and run by members of the park warden's family. The simple, en-suite, bamboo huts here are the cheapest in this part of the park and there are also stilted wooden huts, concrete versions, and a couple of treehouses. Also has a swimming platform in the river. ❶–❹

Khao Sok Green Mountain View 1500m north from km 106.5 ℡087 263 2481, ⓔ green _mountain_view@yahoo.co.th. In a very quiet spot far from almost everyone else, this is a great budget option if you want a remote location. The seven good-quality bamboo and wood bungalows are all en suite and have some nice touches, with pretty open-roofed bathrooms, fans, mosquito nets, decks and hammocks. They sit on the edge of a rubber plantation on the other side of the karsts from the main accommodation area.

There's free transport to the park village or you can walk to *Our Jungle House* across the river in 15min and on to the park headquarters in another 25. ❷–❸

Khao Sok Rainforest Resort ℡077 395135, ⓦ khaosokrainforest.com. This welcoming place has five spectacularly sited "mountain view" bungalows – set high on a jungle slope and affording unsurpassed karst views – plus seven others at ground level, overlooking the river. Interiors are decent enough if a bit faded and all rooms are en suite. ❸

Morning Mist Resort ℡089 971 8794, ⓦ khaosokmorningmistresort.com. Built within a profuse riverside garden that's filled with carefully tended tropical blooms and a big herb garden that supplies the excellent restaurant and cooking school, this well-run place offers ten large, immaculate rooms in variously styled bungalows, all with hot water and either river, mountain or garden view. It's nicely set up for families, with some rooms sleeping up to four, plus lots of space for kids to play in. ❸–❺

Nung House ℡077 395147, ⓦ www.nunghouse .com. Friendly place run by the park warden's son and his family, with fourteen very good huts set around an attractive grassy garden full of rambutan trees. Choose between simple bamboo constructions with en-suite facilities, brick and concrete bungalows, and treehouses. ❷–❸

The park: trails and tours

The B200 national park **entrance fee** (B100 for kids or with a student card) is payable at the checkpoint (6am–6pm) close to the visitor centre and is valid for 24 hours; you'll have to pay again at the lake if you arrive more than 24 hours later. The checkpoint office and **visitor centre** (daily 8am–6pm; ☎077 395155) both supply a small sketch map of the park and trails, and the latter also has a small display about flora and fauna, but the best introduction to Khao Sok is the **guidebook** *Waterfalls and Gibbon Calls* by Thom Henley (see p.485), which is available at some Khao Sok minimarkets and bungalows. Take plenty of water as Khao Sok is notoriously humid.

The trails

Seven of the park's nine **trails** branch off the clearly signed route that runs west of the park headquarters and visitor centre, along the Sok River. The first 3.5km constitute the **interpretative trail** described in *Waterfalls and Gibbon Calls*, an unexceptional ninety-minute one-way trail along a broad, road-like track. Most people continue to **Ton Kloi waterfall**, 7km from headquarters (allow 3hr each way), which flows year-round and tumbles into a pool that's good for swimming. En route, signs point to **Bang Liap Nam waterfall** (4.5km from headquarters), which is a straightforward hike; and **Tan Sawan waterfall** (6km from headquarters), which involves wading along the river bed for the final kilometre and should not be attempted during the rainy season. The trail to the rather spectacular eleven-tiered **Sip-et Chan waterfall**, which shoots off north from the park headquarters and follows the course of the Bang Laen River, is no longer much used and can be quite indistinct. Though the falls are only 4km from headquarters, there's a fair bit of climbing on the way, plus half a dozen river crossings, so you should allow three hours each way.

Guided treks and tours

The vast majority of visitors choose to join a **guided trek** at some point during their stay in the park. Though the trails are waymarked and easy to navigate alone, the guided experience alerts you to details you'd certainly miss on your own – the claw marks left by a sun-bear scaling a tree in search of honey, for example, or the medicinal plants used for malarial fevers and stomach upsets – and is both fun and inexpensive; prices are fixed but exclude the national park entrance fee. The usual **day trek** (B750–900) goes to Ton Kloi waterfall, and from December to March there's also a special route that takes in the blooming of the world's second-biggest flower, the **rafflesia kerrii**, a rather unprepossessing brown, cabbage-like plant whose enormous russet-coloured petals unfurl to a diameter of up to 80cm. Short after-dinner **night safaris** along the main park trails (B600 for 2hr) are also popular, not least because they're good for spotting civets, mouse deer and slow loris and, if you're exceptionally lucky, elephants and clouded leopards as well. You get to stay out in the jungle on the **overnight camping trips** (B2000), usually around Tan Sawan falls; for details of day and overnight trips to Cheow Lan Lake, see p.342. The most reputable and long-serving **guides** are those booked through *Bamboo House*, *Nung House* and *Khao Sok Rainforest Resort* and at Jungle Mania (☎087 270 0938, ✉khaosokjunglemania@gmail.com).

Any guest houses can also arrange **elephant-rides** (2hr; B850) and fix you up with equipment and transfers for **tubing** and **canoeing** trips along the Sok River (B375/750).

Cheow Lan Lake

Dubbed Thailand's Guilin because of its photogenic karst islands, forested inlets and mist-clad mountains encircling jade-coloured waters, the vast 28-kilometre-long **Cheow Lan Lake** (also known as **Ratchabrapa Dam** reservoir; B200 national park entry fee) is Khao Sok's most famous feature and the most popular destination for guided tours. It was created in the 1980s when the Khlong Saeng river was dammed to power a new hydro-electricity plant, and its forested shores and hundred-plus islands now harbour abundant birdlife, as well as some primates, most easily spotted in the very early morning. Tours generally combine a trip on the lake with a wade through the nearby flooded cave system and a night on a floating rafthouse. The lake is 65km from Khao Sok's accommodation area, and can only be explored by longtail boat tour, arranged either from Khao Sok or from Ratchabrapa Dam.

For many people, the highlight of their lake excursion is the adventurous three-hour trek to and through the 800-metre-long horseshoe-shaped **Nam Talu cave**, a five-minute boat ride from the national park rafthouses, or about an hour's boat ride from the dam. The **trek** is not for everyone, however, as the cave section entails an hour-long wade through the river that hollowed out this tunnel: it's slippery underfoot and pitch black and there will be at least one twenty-metre section where you have to swim. When the river level is high there will be longer swims. Never attempt the cave without an authorized park guide and heed any closure signs posted because of high water levels and strong currents; in October 2007 a flash flood caused nine fatalities here and the park authorities are now stricter. Wear sandals with decent grip and request (or take) your own torch.

Lake practicalities

Access to the lake is via the town of **Ban Ta Khun**, 50km east of Khao Sok on the Takua Pa–Surat Thani bus route, Route 401, from where it's 12km north to the dam. Many travellers book their tour of the lake from their Khao Sok

▲ Rafthouses on Cheow Lan Lake

accommodation, in which case all transport is included, but if coming from Surat Thani or Phang Nga, you could do the lake first. There's a regular **minibus service** from Surat Thane's Phunphin train station to and from the dam (every 2hr; 1hr) or you could take the normal Surat Thani–Takua Pa bus service (see p.337), alight at Ban Ta Khun and get a motorbike taxi to the dam. The Australian-Thai-run Limestone Lake Rainforest Tours (☏078 954476, ⓦwww.limestonelaketours.com) offers a big range of **lake-based tours**, including a two-hour trip (B1800 per boat) and a full-day trip with optional overnight in a rafthouse (from B2500/3500 per person for up to three people, excluding park entry fee, or cheaper with larger groups). Khao Sok guest houses charge B1500 for a day-trip and B2500 for overnighters. It's also possible to simply turn up at the dam and hire a boat for around B2000.

On overnight trips to the lake, **accommodation** is either in tents in the jungle or at rafthouses on the lake. There are both private and national park rafthouses moored at various scenic spots around the lake shore, mostly around an hour's boat ride from the dam. All rafthouse huts are rudimentary bamboo structures with nets and mattresses, offering fabulous lake views from your pillow. If you've arranged your own boat transport, you can fix accommodation at any of the lake's rafthouses for B500 per person including three meals. Jungle Yoga runs yoga retreats at the remote *500 Rai Lake* rafthouses from November to April (ⓦwww.jungleyoga.com). Part of the appeal of a night in a rafthouse is the **dawn safari** the next morning, when you've a good chance of seeing langurs, macaques and gibbons on the lakeshore; some tours include this option, or you can usually borrow a kayak from your accommodation and paddle around the shore yourself.

Khao Lak

Handily located just an hour north of Phuket International Airport, and some 30km south of Takua Pa, **KHAO LAK** has established itself as a thriving, mid-market beach resort with plentiful opportunities for diving and snorkelling, easy access to the supreme national park reefs of Ko Similan, and a style that is determinedly unseedy. It lacks sophistication, and is mostly a bit pricey for backpackers, but is ideal for families and extremely popular with Scandinavian tourists. High season here runs from November to April, when the weather and the swimming are at their best and the Similan Islands are open to the public; during the rest of the year, Khao Lak quietens down a lot – and becomes much cheaper too.

The area usually referred to as Khao Lak is in fact a string of beaches west off Highway 4. **Khao Lak** proper is the southernmost and least developed, 5km from the most commercial part of the resort, **Nang Thong**, which throngs with shops, restaurants, dive centres and countless places to stay, both on the beachfront and inland from Highway 4. North again about 3km (5min by taxi or a 45-min walk up the beach) is lower-key, slightly more youthful **Bang Niang**, a lovely long stretch of golden sand that's backed by a developing tourist village whose network of sois is away from the highway and feels more enticing than its neighbour. Removed from all this commerce, **Laem Pakarang**, 12km further up the coast, is where you find the area's most exclusive accommodation.

There is, thankfully, little obvious evidence these days of the area's devastating experience during the December 2004 **tsunami**, when the undersea earthquake off Sumatra sent a series of murderous waves on to Khao Lak's shores

▲ **A** , *Laem Pakarang, Bang Sak, Takua Pa & Surat Thani*

KHAO LAK, NANG THONG & BANG NIANG

0 ___ 1 km

Bang Niang River

Bang Niang

See inset below left

❶ **Book Tree**

Chong Fah Falls

Nang Thong

THANON NANG THONG

See inset below right

CHAT HAT BANG NIANG

EATING & DRINKING

813 Degree Bar	5
Dive In	11
Everyday House	1
Fisherman Bar	9
Happy Snapper	6
Jai	8
Khao Lak Seafood	7
Khao Niaw	2
Phu Khao Lak Seafood	12
Song's Bar	4
Stempfer Café	10
Takieng	3

Khao Lak-Lam Ru National Park Headquarters

Police

National Park Bungalows

Tong Pling Falls

ACCOMMODATION

Amsterdam Resort	G
Ayara Villas	D, E & H
Fair House	F
La Flora	I
Jai	L
Khao Lak Banana	P
Khao Lak Green Beach	M
Khao Lak Seafood Family House	K
Nang Thong Bay Resort	N
Phu Khao Lak Resort	O
Poseidon Bungalows	B
Sanuk Bungalows	C
The Sarojin	A
Tiffy's Cafe	J

N

Khao Lak

Khao Lak Merlin

4

❶ **B**

▼ *Phang Nga, Phuket & Krabi*

BANG NIANG

Bang Niang Beach

CHAT HAT BANG NIANG

❶ **C**

❶ **E** ❶ **D** ❶ **G**

❶ **H**

Sanuk Bakery ❶ **F**

Yoga Studio

Book Tree ❶ **I**

❶ **4** ❶ **2** ❶ **5**

Bang Niang Market

Tsunami Museum

Police Boat Memorial

❶ **3**

Bang Niang River

0 ___ 500 m

NANG THONG

❶ **J** **Sea Dragon Dive Centre**

Krathom Khao Lak Clinic

❶ **6** ❶ **K**
❶ **7**
❶ **8** ❶ **L**

❶ **9** **Khao Lak Land Discovery**

❶ **M**

Nang Thong Supermarket

Police Box

❶ **N**

THANON NANG THONG

❶ **10** **IQ Dive**

Volunteer Teaching

SOI BANG LA ON

❶ **O** ❶ **11**

❶ **12** ❶ **P**

0 ___ 500 m

343

(and the rest of the Andaman coast; see box below), vaporizing almost every shorefront home and hotel here and killing thousands. Nang Thong quickly became the centre of a huge reconstruction effort, with thousands of volunteers arriving to help, and rebuilding was mostly completed within a couple of years,

After the tsunami

The **Boxing Day tsunami** hit Thailand's Andaman coast just after 9.30am on December 26, 2004. The first place to suffer significant damage was Phuket, and the next two hours saw village after resort get battered or decimated by the towering waves thundering in from the Sumatra faultline, 1000km away. The entire coastline from Ranong to Satun was affected, but not all of it with the same intensity: the worst-hit province was Phang Nga, where 4200 people were recorded dead or missing, many of them in the resort of Khao Lak; over 2000 suffered a similar fate on Ko Phi Phi; and more than 900 died on the beaches of Phuket, especially on Patong and Kamala. There were 8212 fatalities in all, a third of them holidaymakers. Another 6000 people were made homeless and some 150,000 lost their jobs, mostly in the tourism and fishing industries. By the end of that day, nearly a quarter of a million people in a dozen countries around the Indian Ocean had lost their lives in the worst natural disaster in recorded history.

Many homes, shops and hotels were quite swiftly rebuilt, but the emotional and social **legacy** of the tsunami endures and most residents along the Andaman coast have a story of terror and bereavement to tell. It's no surprise that many survivors are now afraid of the sea: fearing ghosts, some longtail boatmen won't motor solo past where villages once stood, and hundreds of hotel staff have since sought new jobs in the northern city of Chiang Mai, as far from the sea as they could go.

Immediately after the tsunami, many were surprised when then prime minister Thaksin Shinawatra declined offers of **aid** from foreign governments. But help poured in instead from the Thai government and from royal foundations and local and foreign NGOs and individuals. Of the many **projects** established to help support and rebuild affected communities, the majority have now completed their task; others have evolved into longer-term NGO ventures, including an English-teaching programme in Khao Lak (see p.348), and the community-based tourism company Andaman Discoveries in Khuraburi (see p.333).

Generosity and altruism were not the only responses to the disaster, however. Almost every tsunami-affected community talks of **dishonourable practice** and **corruption**, experiences which have caused bitterness and rifts. Many allegations concern donated money and goods being held back by the local leaders charged with distributing them, and in some cases big business interests muscled in on land deemed "ownerless" because the paperwork had been lost to the waves. Most small businesses had no insurance, and government **compensation** was inconsistently awarded and invariably lacking. In a country where most family enterprises scrape by season to season, it's sobering to contemplate the number of tsunami victims who simply picked up and started over.

Determined not to be caught unawares again, in the unlikely event of Thailand being struck by a second tsunami, the government has created a **tsunami early-warning system** that relays public announcements from towers all the way down the Andaman coast. They have also mapped out evacuation routes, flagged by innumerable "Tsunami Hazard Zone" signs in all the big resorts. For their part, Phuket authorities have remodelled stretches of Ao Patong's beachfront as a building-free zone, creating a park that doubles as a tsunami **memorial**. Krabi officials now require all new buildings to be constructed at least 30m inland from a high-tide boundary, and they even forbid the use of sunloungers below that point. In Khao Lak, a beached police boat has become an eloquent memorial: it rests where it was hurtled by the wave, two kilometres inland, on the other side of the highway.

though for many survivors recovery will probably take a lifetime. Inland from the highway at Bang Niang, a **beached police boat** has become a memorial to the extraordinary power of the tsunami waves – it was propelled up here, 2km inland, while patrolling the waters in front of *La Flora* resort. A tiny Tsunami Museum (daily 9am–6.30pm; donation) occupies a nearby shop but merely presents a rather dry summary of the facts; for the human story you need to read Erich Krauss' *Wave of Destruction* (see p.483).

Arrival, transport and information

Khao Lak is just 70km north of **Phuket airport** (1hr, B1700–2200 by taxi; see p.352). All **buses** running from Phuket to Takua Pa and Ranong (and vice versa), as well as some of its Surat Thani services, pass through Khao Lak and can drop you anywhere along Highway 4; coming from Krabi or Phang Nga you may need to change buses in **Khokkloi**. When it comes to moving on, the VIP overnight bus to Bangkok costs B1000 and takes twelve hours. There's also an **air-con tourist minivan** service that runs at least daily to Krabi/Ao Nang (2hr 30min; B370), with boat connections to Ko Lanta and Ko Phi Phi; to Trang (5hr; B650); and to Penang (12hr; B950).

In the Khao Lak area, a few public **songthaews** shuttle between Nang Thong and Bang Niang, charging B10–20, but mostly they act as private **taxis** instead and charge B100 or more. Many hotels can rent **motorbikes**, and rental **cars** are available through tour operators; Budget also has an agent on the soi down to *Nang Thong Resort* (T076 443454, Wwww.budget.co.th). *Khao Lak Seafood* rents **bicycles**.

Nang Thong offers plenty of **shopping**, mainly for clothes, souvenirs and handicrafts, with countless tailors and opticians too. Book Tree, in far northern Nang Thong, stocks new and secondhand books plus magazines, newspapers and art cards, and also serves coffee; it has a small branch on Chai Hat Bang Niang too. The **Bang Niang market** convenes beside the highway (Mon, Wed & Sat pm) and is a fun spot for a browse through stalls selling everything from hot food and fresh vegetables to clothes and household items. There's **internet** access, ATMs and tour agents aplenty in both Nang Thong and Bang Niang, as well as several clinics.

Accommodation

There's no really cheap accommodation in Khao Lak, but plenty of options from ❹ and up.

Laem Pakarang

The Sarojin 12km north of Khao Lak T076 427905, Wwww.thesarojin.com. With a staff-to-guest ratio of two to one and a style and attitude that exude understated, unpretentious class, this is the top place to stay around Khao Lak. The 56 sleek, tastefully simple rooms are discreetly sited around the wide beachfront garden and stunning square turquoise swimming pool. It's an obvious honeymoon choice, with a policy of no under-12s, a range of excursions designed for two, and private candlelit tables on the beach. There are complimentary Hobie Cats (sailing catamarans), kayaks and mountain bikes, and a spa. Published rates from $429 but discount packages always available. ❾

Bang Niang

Amsterdam Resort Soi 3 T081 857 5881, Wwww.khaolak-resorts.com. Just 200m inland from the beach, this Dutch-run little complex of red-brick bungalows and rooms offers some of the cheapest accommodation in Bang Niang. Bungalows vary in size and have either fans or air-con; some have hot water. Also has internet and wi-fi, cycle rental and a tour desk. ❸–❺

Ayara Villas T076 486 4788, Wwww.ayara -villas.com. An attractive upper-mid range option, spread over three different compounds. At the top end are beachfront villas right on the sand; many others are terraced bungalows just a few metres from the sea, and the rest are in a three-storey building overlooking the pool, with ground-floor rooms enjoying direct pool access. Interiors are air-con and nicely furnished with dark wood in contemporary style and all have kitchenettes. ⑧—⑨

Fair House ☏089 473 7985. Currently one of the cheapest place to stay in Bang Niang, with its handful of neat, fan-cooled concrete bungalows and rooms widely spaced around a garden set back from the highway, about 1km walk from the beach. ❸

La Flora ☏076 428000, ⓦwww.lafloraresort.com. The 138 rooms at this upscale beachfront hotel are all furnished in elegant contemporary Asian style, with day beds, stylish bathrooms and balconies. The cheaper ones are in three-storey hotel wings, some with direct access to the freeform swimming pool; you pay extra for stand-alone villas, many of which enjoy direct sea views. There's also an infinity pool and a kids' pool, plus a spa, mountain bike and kayak rental and wi-fi. ⑨

Sanuk Bungalows ☏076 486800, ⓦwww .sanukresort.com. Dinky little group of five comfortable and spacious brick bungalows in a small garden with its own tiny pool, just 100m from the beach. Bungalows come with either fan or air-con and all have fridges and kitchenettes but there are no staff or other facilities on site. Check in via the office next to the Sanuk Bakery on the main access road from the highway. ❺

Nang Thong

Jai ☏076 485390, ⓔjai_bungalow@hotmail.com. A busy, family-run place that fills up fast not least because it offers some of the cheapest accommodation in Khao Lak. The fifteen good-quality en-suite concrete bungalows are fan cooled and are dotted around a scruffy little yard behind the excellent restaurant, quite close to the highway and about 600m from the beach. ❸

Khao Lak Banana Soi Bang La On ☏076 485889, ⓦwww.khaolakbanana.com. Dozens of thoughtfully designed banana-coloured, fan and air-con bungalows packed into a garden of banana trees and tropical flowers. All have a safety box, TV, wi-fi and fridge and there's a tiny swimming pool. ❺

🏃 **Khao Lak Green Beach** ☏076 485845, ⓦwww.greenbeach.de. The attractive design and shorefront location of the bungalows here make this a good-value option, and the staff are great too. The forty cream-painted chalet-style bungalows have air-con, polished wood floors, pretty furnishings, nice bathrooms and a fridge. Price mainly depends on location: some are right

on the shore and none are more than a few metres away. ❻

Khao Lak Seafood Family House Soi Noen Thong ☏076 485318, ⓦwww.khaolakseafood .com. The large, good-quality bungalows here are set well back from the road in a garden behind the eponymous restaurant. The fan ones are especially good value for Khao Lak: roomy and nicely designed with good bathrooms; air-con rooms in a couple of two-storey blocks are also available. It's a family business and very popular with returning guests and long stayers. Fan ❹, air-con ❺

Nang Thong Bay Resort ☏076 485088, ⓦwww .nangthong.com. Well priced considering its on-the-beach location, this popular, long-established place offers smartly maintained air-con bungalows that are well spaced around the shorefront garden and mostly enjoy sea views, plus some hotel-style rooms. There's a sea-view swimming pool and restaurant as well. Prices drop by fifty percent May–Oct. ❻—❼

🏃 **Phu Khao Lak Resort** ☏076 485141, ⓦwww.phukhaolak.com. There is a luxurious amount of space at this well-run place, where the thirty large, spotlessly clean bungalows sit prettily amid a grassy lawned park-style coconut plantation. Fan rooms have tiled floors and hot-water bathrooms; air-con ones have picture windows and quite stylish interiors. There's a swimming pool, good restaurant and wi-fi in the lounge-library. About 500m walk from the beach. Fan ❹, air-con ❻

Tiffy's Cafe ☏084 051 4138. The cheapest beds in the area are the bunks in the six-person dorm here, behind the restaurant. B80 per person.

Khao Lak

Poseidon Bungalows ☏076 443258, ⓦwww .similantour.com. Seven kilometres south of central Nang Thong, surrounded by rubber plantations and set above a sandy shore of wave-smoothed rocks just north of the Thai navy's private beach, this Swedish–Thai-run guest house is both a quiet place to hang out for a few days and a long-established organizer of snorkelling expeditions to the Similan islands (see p.348). All fifteen bungalows are en suite and fan cooled, with generous amounts of space and balconies, some enjoying sea views; also has internet access and motorbike rental. Get off the bus at the *Poseidon* sign between kilometre-stones 53 and 54, then phone for a pick-up or walk 1km. Closed May–Oct. ❺

Day-trips and other activities

Aside from diving and snorkelling trips to Ko Similan (see box below), there are several other attractions within day-tripping distance of Khao Lak, including a number of local **waterfalls**. Of these, Sai Rung (Rainbow Falls) about 16km north of Nang Thong in Bang Sak, is the most satisfying. Others include Tong Pling, across from the *Merlin* resort in Khao Lak; Nam Tok Lumphi, about 20km south of Khao Lak; and Chong Fah Falls, located less than 5km east of Bang Niang, but subject to a B100 entry fee because it's part of Khao Lak–Lam Ru National Park (⊛www.dnp.go.th/National_park.asp), whose headquarters is on the headland between Nang Thong and Khao Lak beaches.

One of the best, though not the cheapest, local **tour operators** is the reputable Khao Lak Land Discovery (☎076 485411, ⊛www.khaolakland discovery.com), whose excursions include elephant riding (from B1600), kayaking around Ao Phang Nga (B3200) and trekking, canoeing and elephant-riding in Khao Sok National Park (B2800). The Green Biking Club in Bang Niang runs interesting **guided mountain-bike trips** around rural and coastal Khao Lak (from B1850; ☎076 443211, ⊛www.greenbikingclub.com) and rents mountain bikes for B150 per day.

Everyday House restaurant at the north end of Nang Thong teaches morning **cooking courses** (B1000), there's Hatha **yoga** at The Yoga Studio on the Bang Niang beach access road (Mon–Sat 11am) and **Thai boxing** courses and bouts

---

Diving and snorkelling around Khao Lak

Khao Lak is the closest and most convenient departure point for **diving and snorkelling trips** to the national park islands of **Ko Similan** (see p.348), which can be reached in three to four hours on a live-aboard or other large boat or in two hours in a much less comfortable speedboat. The islands are currently only open from approximately November through April and all divers have to pay a one-off national park fee of B400 plus a B200 a day diving fee, usually on top of dive-trip prices. **Local Khao Lak dives** are generally possible year round, especially the highly rated **wreck** of a tin-mining boat near Bang Sak, which is especially rich in marine life such as ghost pipefish, moray eels, scorpion fish, nudibranchs and yellow-tail barracuda. All Khao Lak dive shops also teach PADI **dive courses**, with the last two days of the Openwater course often done on location in the Similans; for advice on choosing a dive shop see p.58.

IQ Dive Nang Thong ☎076 485614, ⊛www.iq-dive.com. Swiss–Thai-run PADI Five-Star Instructor Development Centre that specializes in one-day dive trips to the Similans, on a big dive boat (B4500 plus equipment; B2700 for snorkellers). Their Openwater courses costs B18,700 with two days spent diving the Similans.

Poseidon At *Poseidon Bungalows*, 7km south of central Nang Thong, in Khao Lak (see opposite) ☎076 443258, ⊛www.similantour.com. Highly recommended three-day live-aboard snorkelling trips to the Similans (B7900). Current departures are twice weekly on Tuesdays and Fridays, from the end of October to the end of April.

Sea Dragon Dive Center Nang Thong ☎076 485420, ⊛www.seadragondivecenter .com. Highly recommended PADI Five-Star IDC dive centre which has three live-aboard boats – including budget and deluxe options – running frequent three-day trips to the Similans and Ko Bon (from B11,800 including equipment), and four-day trips to the Similans, Surin islands, Ko Bon, Ko Tachai and Richelieu Rock (from B21,200). Snorkellers get one-third off. Also offers local wreck and other dives (B2200) that operate year-round, as do most of their PADI dive courses: the one-day Discover Scuba costs B2000 (or B7100 at the Similans), and the four-day Openwater is B9800 or B22,400 on a live-aboard.

at the Khao Lak Boxing Stadium just north of Bang Niang (☎089 589 3108, ⓦwww.khaolakboxing.com).

The organization **Volunteer Teaching in Thailand** (ⓦwww.volunteer teacherthailand.org; see also p.67) is based on Soi Bang La On and welcomes willing visitors to help teach English to local kids and adults, a need that's especially pressing given that an estimated eighty percent of Khao Lak's English speakers died in the tsunami.

Eating and drinking

Though farang food dominates the **restaurant** scene, there's good, cheap, authentic Thai cuisine here too. The **nightlife** scene is mellow, convivial and much influenced by dive-staff regulars. Several places host live music nights, given more of a Thai accent in Bang Niang.

Bang Niang

813 Degree Bar With its wooden tables and rustic, Thai-country vibe, this cheap, welcoming and enjoyably local bar-restaurant is a fun place to listen to live Thai music, mostly rock, at its liveliest after 10pm.

Khao Niaw Very good northeastern Thai food at deliciously cheap prices (from B50).

Song's Bar Another country-style Thai pub, with wooden tables, candles in bottles and plenty of foliage, this is Bang Niang's most famous nightlife venue and a favourite with dive staff. There's live music nightly but the biggest draw is the twice-weekly *kathoey* cabaret, a glamorously and hilariously camp production (Tues & Fri eve).

Takieng Authentic Thai food, including good *tom yum kung* and exceptional seafood hotplates, at reasonably authentic Thai prices (B60–180).

Nang Thong

Dive In Soi Bang La On. Owner and chef Sunny cooks up a storm here and is a favourite with expats, locals and returning tourists. She does all sorts of Thai food (B60–320), and her highlights include a deliciously aromatic *matsaman* curry, *khanom jiin* Phuket-style noodles with fish and red curry, deep-fried fish topped with mango,

roast duck with orange sauce and rotis with yellow chicken curry.

Fisherman Bar Lively and genial watering hole that serves cocktails very cheaply during its extended happy hour (midday–8pm), holds regular barbecues and sometimes has live music.

Happy Snapper Khao Lak's most famous dive-staff hangout is chilled and pleasant, with a folksy lounge ambience, live reggae, pop and blues most nights from 10.30pm – plus the occasional open-mike session – and a drinks menu that runs to over a hundred cocktails. Daily 8.30pm–1am.

Jai Deservedly popular for its many different curries (from B60), including *kaeng phanaeng* and *matsaman*, its seafood and its *tom yam kung*.

Khao Lak Seafood Very popular, unpretentious place to sample the local catch; most dishes B60–200.

Phu Khao Lak Seafood Well-known and good-value restaurant attached to the bungalows of the same name serving exceptionally good Thai food from a menu that stretches to over a hundred dishes. Everything from red, yellow and green curries (B80–200) to seafood platters.

Stempfer Café European-run café serving eight different set breakfasts, fresh coffees, hot chocolate, lots of cakes and bread, plus salads and a few hot dishes.

Ko Similan

Rated as one of the world's best spots for both above-water and underwater beauty, the eleven islands at the heart of the Mu **KO SIMILAN** National Park (ⓦwww.dnp.go.th/National_park.asp; B400/200; closed approximately mid-May to mid-Nov) are among the most exciting **diving** destinations in Thailand. Massive granite boulders set magnificently against turquoise waters give the islands their distinctive character, but it's the thirty-metre visibility that draws the divers. The underwater scenery is nothing short of overwhelming here: the reefs teem with coral fish, and you'll also see turtles, manta rays, moray eels, jacks, reef sharks, sea snakes, red grouper and quite possibly white-tip sharks, barracuda, giant lobster and enormous tuna.

The **islands** lie 64km off the mainland and include the eponymous Ko Similan chain of nine islands as well as two more northerly islands, Ko Bon and Ko Tachai, which are both favoured haunts of manta rays and whale sharks and are halfway between the Similan chain and the islands of Ko Surin. The Similans are numbered north–south from nine to one and are often referred to by number: Ko Ba Ngu (number nine), Ko Similan, Ko Hin Posar (aka Hin Huwagralok), Ko Payoo, Ko Ha, Ko Miang (number four), Ko Pahyan, Ko Pahyang and Ko Hu Yong. The national park headquarters and accommodation is on Ko Miang and there's also a campsite and restaurant on Ko Similan. Ko Similan is the largest island in the chain, blessed with a beautiful, fine white-sand bay and impressive boulders; Ko Miang has two pretty beaches, twenty minutes' walk apart; Ko Hu Yong has an exceptionally long white-sand bay and is used by **turtles** for egg-laying from November to February.

Such beauty has not gone unnoticed and the islands are extremely popular with day-trippers from Phuket and Khao Lak, as well as with divers and snorkellers on longer live-aboard trips. This has caused the inevitable congestion and environmental problems and the Similan reefs have been damaged in places by anchors and by the local practice of using dynamite in fishing. National parks authorities have responded by banning fishermen and enforcing strict regulations for tourist boats, including **closing the islands** during the monsoon season, from mid-May to mid-November, though there is talk of a shorter closure in future.

Practicalities

Most travel agents in Khao Lak, Phuket and Phang Nga sell snorkelling **packages** to Ko Similan, both day-trips (from B2900/1450) and overnight (from B3900/1950), featuring at least four island stops. The majority of these trips carry quite large groups and use fast boats that depart from **Thap Lamu pier**, about 8km south of central Khao Lak, 90km north of Phuket town, at about 8am and get to their first island stop, Ko Ba Ngu, in under two hours. They depart the islands at around 3pm. Independent travellers wanting to stay on the island for a few days can usually use these **boats** for transfers, with the chance of a discount if joining the boat at Thap Lamu pier rather than being picked up from one of the resorts. Companies offering this service include Medseye Travel and Tours (℡076 486796, ⓦwww.similanthailand.com) and Jack Similan (℡076 443205, ⓦwww.jacksimilan.com), both of which have offices at the Thap Lamu pier. If travelling independently, you'll need to use Ko Similan longtail boats to travel **between the islands** and to explore different reefs: prices are fixed and cost B150–300 per person, depending on the distance.

Limited **accommodation** is available on Ko Miang, in the shape of national park bungalows (❺–❻) and tents (❸), and there's a campsite on Ko Similan too; both islands also have a restaurant. Accommodation should be booked ahead, either at the national parks office near Thap Lamu pier (℡076 595045) or online (ⓦwww.dnp.go.th/National_park.asp), as facilities can get crowded with tour groups, especially on weekends and holidays.

Overcrowding is a growing problem at the Similans and the best way to escape this is to join a small-scale **live-aboard** diving or snorkelling trip to the islands; they usually last two to five days and cost from B11,800 inclusive for divers, or from B8000 for snorkellers. The best and cheapest live-aboard trips run out of Khao Lak, the closest mainland resort to the Similans (see p.347);

Phuket is another popular springboard, and you can also do them from Ko Chang and Ko Phayam.

Phuket

Thailand's largest island and a province in its own right, **PHUKET** (pronounced "Poo-ket") has been a prosperous region since the nineteenth century, when Chinese merchants got in on its tin-mining and sea-borne trade, before turning to the rubber industry. It remains the wealthiest province in Thailand, with the highest per-capita income, but what mints the money nowadays is **tourism**: with an annual influx of visitors that tops five million, Phuket ranks second in popularity only to Pattaya, and the package-tour traffic has wrought its usual transformations. Thoughtless tourist developments have scarred much of the island, and the trend is upmarket, with very few budget possibilities (expect to shell out up to twice what you'd pay on the mainland for accommodation, food and transport), but many of the beaches are still strikingly handsome, resort facilities are second to none, and the offshore snorkelling and diving is exceptional. Away from the tourist hubs, many inland neighbourhoods are clustered round the local mosque – 35 percent of Phuketians are **Muslim**, and there are said to be more mosques on the island than Buddhist temples; though the atmosphere is generally as easy-going as elsewhere in Thailand, it's especially important to dress with some modesty outside the main resorts, and to not sunbathe topless on any of the beaches.

Phuket's capital, Muang Phuket or **Phuket town**, is on the southeast coast, 42km south of the Sarasin Bridge causeway to the mainland. Though it's the most culturally stimulating place on Phuket, most visitors pass straight through the town on their way to the **west coast**, where three resorts corner the bulk of the trade: high-rise **Ao Patong**, the most developed and expensive, with an increasingly seedy nightlife; the slightly nicer, if unexceptional, **Ao Karon**; and adjacent **Ao Kata**, the smallest of the trio. If you're after a more peaceful spot, aim for the seventeen-kilometre-long national park beach of **Hat Mai Khao**, its more developed neighbour **Hat Nai Yang**, or one of the smaller alternatives at **Hat Nai Thon** or **Hat Kamala**. Most of the other west-coast beaches are dominated by just a few upmarket hotels, specifically **Hat Nai Harn**, **Ao Pansea** and **Ao Bang Tao**; the southern and eastern beaches are better for seafood than swimming but also run boats to other islands such as **Ko Racha Yai**.

As with the rest of the Andaman coast, the sea around Phuket is at its least inviting during the **monsoon**, from June to October, when the west-coast beaches in particular become quite rough and windswept. At any time of year, beware the strong **undertow** and heed any red warning flags; in the first nine months of 2008 there were twenty fatalities in the water and over a hundred rescues by helpful bystanders: there is currently no official lifeguard service on the island. Some stretches of Phuket's coast were very badly damaged by the December 2004 **tsunami** (see box, p.344), which caused significant loss of life and destroyed a lot of property. Reconstruction was swift, however, and a first-time visitor to the island is now unlikely to notice any major post-tsunami effect.

There's a wide-ranging **website** about Phuket, ⓦ www.phuket.com, which is particularly good for discounted accommodation; for a detailed historical and cultural **guide** to the island, it's hard to better Oliver Hargreave's impressive *Exploring Phuket & Phi Phi* (Within Books).

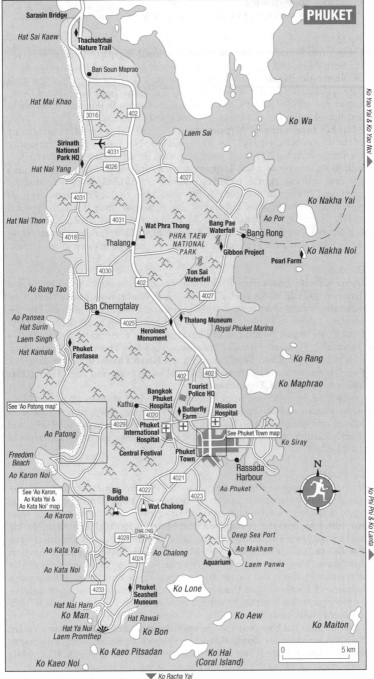

PHUKET

Sarasin Bridge

Hat Sai Kaew

Thachatchai Nature Trail

● Ban Soun Maprao

Hat Mai Khao

3016

402

Ko Wa

Laem Sai

Sirinath National Park HQ

4031

4026

Hat Nai Yang

Ko Yao Yai & Ko Yao Noi ▶

4027

Hat Nai Thon

4031

Ko Nakha Yai

4031

4018

Wat Phra Thong

Bang Pae Waterfall

PHRA TAEW NATIONAL PARK

Ao Por

Bang Rong ●

Thalang ●

Gibbon Project

Ko Nakha Noi

4030

Ton Sai Waterfall

Pearl Farm

402

Ao Bang Tao

4027

Ban Cherngtalay ●

4025

Thalang Museum

Royal Phuket Marina

Ao Pansea

Hat Surin

Laem Singh

Heroines' Monument

Hat Kamala

Phuket Fantasea

Ko Rang

402

402

Ko Maphrao

See 'Ao Patong map'

Bangkok Phuket Hospital

Tourist Police HQ

Ao Patong

Kathu ●

4020

Butterfly Farm

Mission Hospital

4029

Phuket International Hospital

Ko Siray

Freedom Beach

Central Festival

See Phuket Town map

Ao Karon Noi

Phuket Town

See 'Ao Karon, Ao Kata Yai & Ao Kata Noi' map

Big Buddha

4022

● Rassada Harbour

4021

Ao Phuket

Ao Karon

Wat Chalong

4023

Ao Kata Yai

4028

CHALONG CIRCLE

Deep Sea Port

Ao Makham

Ao Kata Noi

4024

Ao Chalong

4233

Aquarium

Laem Panwa

Phuket Seashell Museum

Ko Lone

Hat Nai Harn

Ko Man

Hat Rawai

Ko Aew

Ko Maiton

Hat Ya Nui

Laem Promthep

Ko Bon

N

Ko Phi Phi & Ko Lanta ▶

Ko Kaeo Pitsadan

Ko Hai (Coral Island)

0   5 km

Ko Kaeo Noi

▼ *Ko Racha Yai*

Getting to Phuket

Phuket is very well served by flights, buses and ferries, but there's no rail link.

By air

Quite a few airlines operate direct **international flights** to Phuket (see p.19). Between them, Thai Airways, Air Asia, Bangkok Airways and Nok Air run up to 27 **domestic flights** a day between Bangkok and Phuket, while Bangkok Airways connects Phuket with Pattaya and Ko Samui, and Phuket-based Destination Air (☎076 328638, ⓦwww.destinationair.com) operates seaplanes to and from Ko Phi Phi, Ko Lanta, Ko Mook and Khao Lak.

Phuket International Airport (☎076 327230–79) is near the northern tip of the island, between Hat Mai Khao and Hat Nai Yang, 32km northwest of Phuket town. It has ATMs, currency exchange, hotel booking and tourist information counters plus a **left-luggage** service (daily 6am–10pm; B60 per item per day) and **car rental**, including Avis (☎076 351243, ⓦwww.avisthailand .com) and Budget (☎076 205396, ⓦwww.budget.co.th). Taxis transport most passengers to the beaches, but there's also an **airport bus** that runs approximately hourly to the bus station in Phuket town, via Thalang (Mon–Fri 6.30am–8.30pm, Sat, Sun & hols 8.30am–8.30pm; B85; 1hr); as it doesn't serve the beaches, you'll need to change on to the songthaews in town to reach those.

By bus

Direct **air-con buses** from Bangkok to Phuket leave from the Southern Bus Terminal and take about twelve hours to reach Phuket town's bus station; most make the journey overnight, departing from mid-afternoon onwards. There is no train service to Phuket, but you could book an overnight sleeper train to Surat Thani, about 290km east of Phuket, and take a bus from there to Phuket (about 5hr). There are plenty of buses between **Surat Thani** and Phuket, some of which run via **Khao Sok**, **Takua Pa** and **Khao Lak**; in the other direction, there are frequent services from **Krabi**, via **Phang Nga**, and from **Trang**, **Hat Yai** and **Nakhon Si Thammarat**.

Nearly all buses to and from Phuket use the **bus station** (☎076 211480) at the eastern end of Thanon Phang Nga in Phuket town, from where it's a ten-minute walk or a short tuk-tuk ride to the town's central hotel area, and slightly further to the Thanon Ranong departure-point for songthaews to the beaches.

By boat

If you're coming to Phuket from Ko Phi Phi, Ko Lanta or Ao Nang, the quickest and most scenic option is to take the **boat**. During peak season, up to three ferries a day, plus a speedboat or two, make the trip to and from **Ko Phi Phi**, docking at **Rassada Harbour** on Phuket's east coast; during low season, there's at least one ferry a day in both directions. Travellers from **Ko Lanta** (service available Nov–May only) may have to change boats at **Ao Nang** (Nov–May only) or Ko Phi Phi. Fixed-fare **taxis** meet the ferries at Rassada Harbour and charge B50 per person for transfers to Phuket town hotels, and B500–600 per three-person car to the major west-coast beaches or the airport (leave plenty of extra time if you have a flight to catch as boats are notoriously tardy).

Ferries from **Ko Yao Noi** and the **speedboat** service from Ao Nang via Ko Yao Noi terminate at **Bang Rong** on Phuket's northeast coast. Songthaews shuttle between Bang Rong and Phuket town (7am–4pm; 90min; B35), while **taxis** charge B500 to the airport, B700 to Patong and B2000 to Khao Lak.

Moving on from Phuket

For durations and frequencies on all major routes, see Travel details, p.438.

By air

The cheapest way for solo travellers to **get to the airport** is by the airport bus from Phuket town bus station (at least every 90min Mon–Fri 5.30am–6.30pm, Sat & Sun 7am–6.30pm; 1hr; B85; ☎076 232371). From the beaches, most people use taxis organized by their hotel instead – about B500 for the hour's ride from Patong or Karon. See p.359 for **airline offices** on Phuket.

By bus

The TAT office in Phuket town keeps up-to-date bus timetables. In addition to the government bus services (see opposite), there are fast private minibus services **to Surat Thani** from outside the *Montri Hotel* on Thanon Montri in Phuket town (every 2hr 7am–5pm; 4hr 30min; B180) and to **Nakhon Si Thammarat** from opposite *Baan Suwantawe* on Thanon Dibuk (hourly 6am–4pm; 7hr; B300). Some hotels can also arrange minibus transport to **Butterworth** in Malaysia (B1200).

By boat

Ferries to **Ko Phi Phi**, **Ao Nang** and **Ko Lanta** depart from Rassada Harbour (see opposite). Tickets bought in advance should include transfers from your hotel. Ferries to **Ko Yao Noi** leave from Bang Rong (see p.380); the **speedboat** service to Ao Nang via Ko Yao Noi also leaves from Bang Rong.

Island transport

Although the west-coast beaches are connected by road, to get from one beach to another by **public transport** you nearly always have to go back into Phuket town; songthaews run regularly throughout the day from Thanon Ranong in the town centre to the coast and cost B25–40. **Tuk-tuks and taxis** do travel directly between major beaches, but are notoriously overpriced (there are almost no metered taxis on the island), charging around B100 from Kata to Karon or B250 between Patong and Karon; Phuket TAT issues a list of price guidelines but you'll likely end up paying at least twenty percent on top of that. For transport within resorts, the cheapest option is to make use of the public songthaews where possible, or to hail a **motorbike taxis** where available (from B20). Many tourists rent their own **motorbike** or moped, which are widely available, but be warned that there are a very sobering average of 10,000 motorbike injuries a year on Phuket, and about a hundred fatalities; it makes sense to obey the compulsory helmet law, which is anyway strictly enforced in most areas of Phuket, with flouters subject to a B500 fine.

Phuket town

Though it has plenty of hotels and restaurants, **PHUKET TOWN** (Muang Phuket) stands distinct from the tailor-made tourist settlements along the beaches as a place of tangible history and culture. Most visitors hang about just long enough to jump on a beach-bound songthaew, but you may find yourself returning for a welcome dose of real life; there's plenty to engage you in a stroll through the small but atmospherically restored heart of the Old Town, along with many idiosyncratic cafés and art shops, several notable restaurants and some of the best sarong and handicraft shops on the island. If you're on a tight budget, the town can make a more affordable base than the beaches, and certainly works well as an overnight transit point between the islands and the bus station or airport.

PHUKET TOWN

0   200 m

Khao To Sai

Police Station

THANON NAKHON

Khao Rung

THANON KAEW SIMBU

THANON YAOWARAT

THANON CHUMPHON

N

Provincial Court

THANON DAMRONG

THANON THUNG KA

THANON SU THAI

THANON NANSON

THANON MAE LUAN

THANON SATORN (SUI)

THANON YAOWARAT

THANON THEPKASATRI

Minibuses to Nakhon Si Thammarat
2 ★

A

THANON VICHIT SONGKHRAM

THANON PATIPAT

THANON KRABI

Phuket Thaihua Museum 1

THANON DIBUK

Shrine of Serene Light

3
D 4
SOI ROMANEE
@

★ Minibuses to Surat Thani

Ban Boran Textiles
Thai Airways

E 5
THANON
6
THALANG

i TAT

Bus Station

Songthaews to beaches

Wat Jui Tui

THANON RANONG

8

South Wind Books

Radsada Hand Made

7

Goonet

THANON PHANG NGA

THANON MONTRI

F

THANON TILOK UTHIT 2

THANON PHATTANA

SOI PHUTORN

Ban Boran 9

Phuket Center
THANON RATSADA

Thavorn Hotel

Phuket Reminder

THANON BANGKOK

10

11

THANON TAKUA PA

The Books @

THANON TAKUA PA

SOI SURIN

SOI TALING CHAN

THANON BANGKOK

Clock Tower

G

THANON CHANA CHAROEN

Boots

THANON PHUKET

SOI TILOK UTHIT 1

Ocean Department Store

Paradise Cinema

Phuket Ruam Phaet Hospital ✚

Robinson

THANON LONGSIMPAI

Night Market

THANON KRA

12

Immigration Office ▼

EATING & DRINKING

Aroon	6
China Inn Café	5
Dibuk Restaurant	1
Ka Jok See	11
Kanasutra	9
La Gaetana	12
Lemongrass	2
Natural Restaurant (Thammachat)	10
On On Café	7
Ruamjai Vegetarian Restaurant	8
Soi Romanee Bars	3 & 4

ACCOMMODATION

Baan Suwantawe	C
Crystal Inn Hotel	G
Old Town Hostel	B
On On Hotel	E
Royal Phuket City	F
Sino House	A
Thalang 37 Guest House	D

Accommodation

As befits this heritage town, there are some interesting places to stay, and more opportunities to meet other (solo) travellers than at the beaches.

Baan Suwantawe 1/10 Thanon Dibuk ☏076 212879, ⓦwww.baansuwantawe.co .th. Offering four-star rooms at two-star prices, this apartment-style hotel is designed with long-stay residents in mind but is also exceptionally comfortable for tourists. The huge, pleasantly decorated air-con rooms all have a balcony overlooking the small swimming pool and come with TV, broadband, fridge and kettle. There's no restaurant or hotel services but the front desk is helpful and the location very handy for TAT and the Old Town. ⑤

Crystal Inn Hotel 2/1–10 Soi Surin, Thanon Montri ☏076 256789, ⓦwww.phuketcrystalinn.com.

Surprisingly stylish and contemporary cream- and dark-wood decor makes this small, 54-room downtown hotel an inviting and good-value option. All rooms have air-con and there's internet downstairs. Good discounts if you forego breakfast. ⑤

On On Hotel 19 Thanon Phang Nga ☏076 211154. This attractive, colonial-style 1920s building is a long-running travellers' favourite, mainly because the rooms are so cheap. They're pretty basic, with very thin walls, holes in the floorboards and ancient plumbing, but they're adequate and there are lots of them; the cheapest share bathrooms, the most expensive have air-con.

There's internet access and a tour agent in the lobby. Shared bathroom ❶, en suite ❷, air–con ❷ **Royal Phuket City** 154 Thanon Phang Nga ☎076 233333, ⓦwww.royalphuketcity.com. Large, high-rise business hotel, with swimming pool, spa, gym, business centre and light, bright, comfortable air-con rooms, most of them with fine views over the city and all with broadband. ❼

Sino House 1 Thanon Montri ☎076 232494, ⓦwww.sinohousephuket.com. Beautifully styled with Chinoiserie artefacts and elegant flourishes, the apartment-style rooms in this striking Art Deco building are huge and light and all come with air-con, complimentary wi-fi, coffee-making facilities and breakfast. There's a restaurant and the Raintree Spa on site, plus some tour services, but no pool. ❼

Thalang 37 Guest House 37 Thanon Thalang ☎076 214225, ⓔthalang37@gmail.com, ⓦwww .thalangguesthouse.com. Housed in a 1940s, Sino-Portuguese, wood-floored former shophouse in one of the Old Town's most attractive streets, this place is fairly simple but full of character, traveller-friendly and good value. The thirteen fan and air-con rooms are large and en suite – the best of them are up on the rooftop, affording unusual panoramic views. It's very popular, so phone or email to book ahead (website reservations don't work); if it's full the owner has slightly cheaper overspill rooms at the less interesting *Old Town Hostel* (☎076 258272, ⓔothostel@gmail.com; ❷–❸), nearby at 42 Thanon Krabi, which mostly have no window or private bathroom. Rates at both include breakfast. ❷–❸

The Old Town

Phuket town's most interesting features are clustered together in the **Old Town** conservation zone (ⓦwww.lestariheritage.net/Phuket), a grid of streets between Thanon Dibuk and Thanon Rat Sada whose historic colonial-style **Sino–Portuguese shophouses** date back to the nineteenth century, the former homes of emigrant Chinese merchants from Penang, Singapore and Melaka. Modern-day residents have put a lot of effort into restoring these handsome old neighbourhoods and there's an engagingly bohemian style to a number of the businesses here. The Phuket Old Town Foundation publishes the excellent free **Phuket Town Treasure Map**, available all over the Old Town, and also stages the **Old Town Festival** just before Chinese New Year (sometime between Jan & March). For more on Sino-Portuguese architecture, see the box on p.356.

Some of the Old Town's most elegant buildings line the western arm of **Thanon Thalang**, where a dozen signboards – including at *Thalang Guest House* at no. 37 (see above), and outside the *China Inn Café* at no. 20 (see p.357) – highlight the special features worth an upward or sideways glance: pastel-coloured doors and shutters, elaborate stucco mouldings, ornate wooden doors, and the distinctively arched "five-foot walkways" that link them. Further east along Thanon Thalang there's more of an Islamic emphasis, with many old-style shops selling fabric and dressmaking accessories, including lots of good-value sarongs from Malaysia and Indonesia, and *roti* restaurants such as *Aroon* (see p.357). The road's former red-light alley, **Soi Romanee**, has also been given a major multi-coloured facelift and these days buzzes come sundown with arty little bars, while on nearby **Thanon Dibuk** the doors and window shutters of *Dibuk Restaurant* at no. 69 display intricate wooden and gold-leaf fretwork. You'll find other renovated Sino-Portuguese buildings on **Thanon Yaowarat**, and on **Thanon Ranong** (where the Thai Airways office occupies a fine old mansion), **Thanon Phang Nga** (especially the *On On Hotel*) and **Thanon Damrong**, whose town hall, just east of the Provincial Court, stood in for Phnom Penh's US embassy in the film *The Killing Fields*.

West across Yaowarat from Thanon Thalang at 28 Thanon Krabi, the 1930s' Neoclassical-style former school – complete with grand columns, stucco decoration, shuttered windows and central light well – has been turned into the **Phuket Thaihua Museum** (Tues–Fri 1–8pm, Sat & Sun 9am–8pm; free).

Some of the old school desks are still in situ, and the pedagogic tradition continues through the Mandarin Language School upstairs, but the focus of the museum's excellent displays, videos and historic photos is on the role and traditions of Phuket's main immigrant groups, namely the Chinese and mixed-race Baba (Malay–Chinese) communities who arrived to work in the island's burgeoning tin-mining industry.

There's a much quainter, mustier whiff of the past contained within the wood-panelled lobby of Thanon Rat Sada's *Thavorn Hotel*, whose museum-like reception area and adjacent rooms, signed as the **Phuket History Corner**, are filled with faded photos of historic Phuket, plus a jumble of posters, typewriters and other everyday objects dating from the late nineteenth and early twentieth centuries, most of it amassed by the Thavorn family. Entry is free and non-guests are welcome to admire the eclectic collection, some of which also spills over into the hotel's streetside *Collector Pub*.

Old Town Sino-Portuguese architecture

As Chinese immigrant merchants got rich on tin-mining profits so they started building homes. Though the very richest commissioned enormous mansions, a number of which survive in Phuket town today, the vast majority bought themselves eminently practical terraced **shophouses** at the heart of the merchant district. Phuket's Old Town retains south Thailand's finest examples, some of which are open to the public, but there are also intact, if less well-conserved shophouse neighbourhoods in many other southern cities, including Ranong and Takua Pa.

Shophouse design followed a standard prototype favoured by the mixed-race Chinese–Malay ("Baba", or "Straits Chinese") immigrants from Melaka and other parts of the Malay Peninsula. It's a style now widely dubbed **Sino-Portuguese** because Melakan architecture of the time was itself strongly influenced by the territory's Portuguese former colonists, though it also incorporates traits from Dutch and Anglo-Indian colonial architecture. Although some features have evolved with changing fashions the basic look is still recognizably mid-nineteenth century.

Because streetside space was at a premium, shophouses were always long and thin, with narrow frontages, recessed entrances and connecting porches that linked up all the way down the block to make shady, arched colonnades known as **five-foot walkways**, ideal for pedestrians and shoppers. The front room was (and often still is) the business premises, leaving the rest of the two-or three-storey building for living. A light-well behind the front room encouraged natural ventilation and sometimes fed a small courtyard garden at its base, and the household shrine would always occupy a prominent and auspicious position. Outside, the hallmark features that make the neighbourhoods so striking today include pastel-painted **louvred windows** that might be arched or rectangular and perhaps topped by a pretty glass fantail, lacquered and inlaid wooden doors, fancy gold-leaf fretwork, detailed **stucco mouldings** and perhaps Neoclassical pilasters.

▲ Sino-Portuguese doorway, Phuket Town

The spiritual heritage of Phuket's Chinese immigrants is kept very much alive by their descendants who maintain many shrines around town, including **Saeng Tham**, the tiny **Shrine of Serene Light** (daily 8.30am–noon & 1.30–5.30pm), which is accessed via a soi through the narrow archway next to South Wind Books on Thanon Phang Nga, and whose roof is decorated with intensely coloured ceramic figurines of dragons, carp and sages in bright blues, greens and reds. The extraordinary spectacle of the annual Vegetarian Festival (see p.358) is the most public expression of the community's religious beliefs.

Phuket Butterfly Garden

Kids usually enjoy the **Phuket Butterfly Garden and Insect World** (daily 9am–5pm; B300, kids B150; ☏076 210861, ⓦwww.phuketbutterfly.com), located a couple of kilometres beyond the northern end of Thanon Yaowarat at 71/6 Soi Paneang in Ban Sam Kong, whose thousands of butterflies of some twenty indigenous species flit around the prettily landscaped grounds; there's also a silk museum documenting the amazingly industrious short life of the silkworm, plus scorpions, tarantulas and other notorious creepies. There's no public **transport** to the butterfly farm, but a tuk-tuk from the town centre should cost around B150 return; if you reserve ahead by phone or internet you can get transport between town or beach hotels and the Butterfly Garden for an extra B50–150 per person.

Eating and drinking

Phuket town has much the largest concentration of good Thai **food** on the island, well worth making the trip for. Unlike Thais in most other parts of the country, Phuketians like to breakfast on **noodles** rather than rice; spindly white *khanom jiin* noodles, made with rice-flour and ladled over with one of several different fiery, soupy curry sauces, are a local speciality and served at some of the restaurants listed below.

Aroon Thanon Thalang. Very popular cheap Muslim café that serves *roti* (chapatti-style pancakes) with egg, curry or *mertabak* (mutton) plus several unusual southern Thai dishes from Pattani, including *khao yam Pattani*, a steamed rice dish mixed with shredded greens, roasted coconut and fish. Dishes B12–40. Mon–Sat 7am–6pm, Sun 7am–2pm.

China Inn Café 20 Thanon Thalang. This beautifully renovated heritage house and courtyard garden would be reason enough to stop by for a meal, but the menu (B120–250) is also enticing, both for its classy Thai and Mediterranean dishes, including delicious mozzarella salad, its spicy Thai salads, and its tamarind and rambutan juice. Streetside, the gallery shop displays Asian antiques, textiles and one-off artefacts. Mon–Wed 11am–6pm, Thurs–Sat 11am–11pm.

🏃 **Ka Jok See** 26 Thanon Takuapa ☏076 217903. A Phuket institution, housed in a charmingly restored traditional shophouse (unsigned), next to *Kanasutra*, this place serves fabulous Thai food and fosters a fun, sociable atmosphere. Mains are sophisticated and beautifully presented – their *goong sarong*, individual

shrimps bound in a crisp-noodle wrap, is famous island-wide. Dishes are pricey at around B300, but always come with a free starter and dessert. By about 10pm there is jiving between courses as staff take the lead and encourage locals and expats to have a boogie. Reservations are essential. Tues–Sun 6pm–1am.

Kanasutra 18 Thanon Takuapa. Contemporary Indian restaurant with a tandoori oven, serving everything from sheesh kebab to prawn vindaloo (mostly B160–360). Mon–Sat 11am–3pm & 6–11pm, Sun 6–11pm.

La Gaetana 352 Thanon Phuket ☏076 250523. Inviting Italian-Thai restaurant whose menu includes home-made pasta with some great sauces, a special house fish stew, outstanding home-made ice creams (the durian ice cream is an acquired taste but worth the plunge) and good-value wine by the glass. Most mains cost around B220. Mon, Tues & Fri noon–2pm & 6pm–late, Thurs, Sat & Sun 6pm–late.

Lemongrass 2/9 Thanon Dibuk. Good, authentic, mid-priced Thai food (mostly B80) is the hallmark of this popular, unpretentious, al fresco restaurant that's especially recommended for its fish dishes, numerous curries, and mountain-fern, wing bean and banana-flower salads. Daily 5pm–1am.

Natural Restaurant (Thammachat) 62/5 Soi Putorn ⓦwww.naturalrestaurant -phuket.com. There are plenty of reasons to linger over dinner at this rambling, informal, hugely popular, plant-wreathed restaurant, not least the two hundred different choices on the menu, and the affordable prices (B80–120). Highlights include fried sea bass with chilli paste, fried chicken with Muslim herbs, soft-shelled crab with garlic and pepper, and spicy Phuket bean salad. Tues–Sun 10.30am–11.30pm.

On On Café Thanon Phang Nga. Sociable spot for cheap farang-style meals, especially breakfasts,

including good banana pancakes, fry-ups and fresh coffee. Mon–Sat 7am–8pm.

Ruamjai Vegetarian Restaurant 219 Thanon Ranong. Cheap and simple vegan canteen where for B25 or B30 you get two main-course servings from the trays of stir-fries and curries plus a plate of brown rice. Daily 7am to about 8pm.

Soi Romanee This artfully restored soi connecting Dibuk and Thalang roads shows off its handsome new pastel paintwork and stuccoed Old Town facades with half a dozen little café-bars whose seating spills out on to the pavement for ultimate architectural appreciation. From November to April, there's free live jazz on the street on the last Sunday evening of the month.

Shopping

Unless otherwise stated all listed Phuket Town **shops** are closed on Sundays. The Books (daily 9am–9pm) on Thanon Phuket is the best source of new English-language **books** on the island; South Wind Books on Thanon Phang Nga (Mon–Sat 9am–7pm, Sun 10am–3pm) has a big range of secondhand books and Bo(ok)hemia at 61 Thanon Thalang (1–10pm) has a small, eclectic stock, plus secondhand DVDs, coffee, wi-fi and occasional film screenings. Ban Boran Textiles, at 51 Thanon Yaowarat, specializes in **clothes** made from the handspun cotton of north and northeast Thailand, and the shops on eastern Thanon Thalang keep a phenomenal range of well-priced sarongs mostly of Burmese, Malaysian and Indonesian designs. For high-street fashions, there's Robinson department store on Thanon Tilok Uthis 1, and Ocean Department

---

Ngan Kin Jeh: the Vegetarian Festival

For nine days every October or November, at the start of the ninth lunar month (see ⓦwww.phuketvegetarian.com for exact dates), the celebrations for **Ngan Kin Jeh** – the Vegetarian Festival – set the streets of Phuket buzzing with processions, theatre shows and food stalls, culminating in the unnerving spectacle of men and women parading about with steel rods through their cheeks and tongues. The festival marks the beginning of **Taoist Lent**, a month-long period of purification observed by devout Chinese all over the world, but celebrated most ostentatiously in Phuket, by devotees of the island's five Chinese temples. After six days' abstention from meat (hence the festival's name), alcohol and sex, the white-clad worshippers flock to their local temple, where drum rhythms help induce a trance state in which they become possessed by spirits. As proof of their new-found transcendence of the physical world they skewer themselves with any available sharp instrument – fishing rods and car wing-mirrors have done service in the past – before walking over red-hot coals or up ladders of swords as further testament to their otherworldliness. In the meantime there's singing and dancing and almost continuous firework displays, with the grandest festivities held at Wat Jui Tui on Thanon Ranong in Phuket town.

The ceremony dates back to the mid-nineteenth century, when a travelling Chinese opera company turned up on the island to entertain emigrant Chinese working in the tin mines. They had been there almost a year when suddenly the whole troupe – together with a number of the miners – came down with a life-endangering fever. Realizing that they'd neglected their gods, the actors performed elaborate rites, and most were soon cured. The festival has been held ever since, though the self-mortification rites are a later modification, possibly of Hindu origin.

Store nearby, but for the biggest brand names, including Esprit, Lacoste and Jim Thompson silk, you need to head out to the glitzy **Central Festival shopping plaza** on the bypass at the western edge of town, at the big intersection of roads to Phuket town, Ao Patong, and Ao Chalong; there's a free shuttle bus from *Royal Phuket City* hotel, or Patong- and Chalong-bound songthaews can drop you close by. Downtown, the two most fruitful shopping roads for **handicrafts** and **antiques** are Thanon Yaowarat and Thanon Rat Sada. On Thanon Rat Sada, Radsada Hand Made at no. 29 sells textiles, carved wooden textile hangers, mango-wood vases and silver jewellery, while Soul of Asia at no. 37 specializes in quality Southeast Asian antiques, fine art and furniture. Ocean Department Store's more mass-market souvenir stalls are also worth a browse.

Listings

Airlines Bangkok Airways ☎076 225033; Dragon Air ☎1800 700707 toll free from Phuket, or 02 2630367 from elsewhere; Firefly ☎076 239980; Korean Air ☎076 328540; Malaysia Airlines ☎076 213749; Nok Air ☎076 351464; Silk Air ☎076 304018–20; Thai Airways ☎076 360444.

Cinemas English-language blockbusters are shown throughout the day and evening at the Paradise Multiplex next to Ocean Department Store on Thanon Tilok Uthis 1 and the SF Coliseum inside the Central Festival shopping plaza on the bypass road.

Dentists At Phuket International Hospital and Bangkok Hospital Phuket; see "Hospitals", below.

Hospitals Phuket International Hospital (☎076 249400, emergencies ☎076 210935, ⓦwww .phuketinternationalhospital.com), north of Central Festival shopping centre on Highway 402, just west of Phuket town, is considered to have Phuket's best facilities, including an emergency department, an ambulance service and private rooms. Reputable alternatives include Bangkok Hospital Phuket, on

the northwestern edge of town just off Thanon Yaowarat at 2/1 Thanon Hongyok Uthis ☎1719 or 076 245425, ⓦwww.phukethospital.com, and the Mission Hospital (aka Phuket Adventist Hospital), on the northern outskirts at 4/1 Thanon Thepkasatri ☎076 237220–5, emergencies ☎076 237227, ⓦwww.missionhospitalphuket.com. See map on p.351 for locations.

Immigration office At the southern end of Thanon Phuket, in the suburb of Saphan Hin ☎076 221905; Mon–Fri 8.30am–4.30pm, Sat 8.30–noon.

TAT 191 Thanon Thalang (daily 8.30am–4.30pm ☎076 212213, ✉tatphket@tat.or.th).

Telephones For international calls use the CAT phone office on Thanon Phang Nga (daily 8am–8pm).

Tourist Police For all emergencies, call the tourist police on the free, 24hr phone line ☎1155, or visit them during office hours at their office just north of Tesco Lotus on the northwest edge of town, on Route 402.

Hat Mai Khao

Phuket's longest and quietest beach, the seventeen-kilometre **HAT MAI KHAO**, unfurls along the island's upper northwest coast, beginning some 3km south of the Sarasin Bridge causeway and ending just north of the airport (34km from Phuket town). It's a beautiful piece of casuarina- and palm-shaded coastline, minimally developed and protected in part as **Sirinath National Park** (ⓦwww.dnp.go.th/National_park.asp) because of the few giant marine turtles that lay their eggs here between October and February. Also within the national park is the **Thachatchai Nature Trail**.

Accommodation on Hat Mai Khao is predominantly five star: an enclave of half a dozen luxury hotels is elegantly spaced behind the sloping shoreline towards the north end of the beach, accessed by an all-but private road served by electric buggies, with guests welcome to use any neighbouring facilities. All the resorts have several swimming pools as the undertow here can be fierce and unpredictable: the *JW Marriott Phuket Resort and Spa* (☎076 338000, ⓦwww .jwmarriottphuket.com; ❾) has three, plus a water slide, a well-equipped children's pavilion, good sports facilities and extensive landscaped lawns that all help make it a favourite with families. In contrast, the sharp, Sino-modern

architecture of the villa compounds at *Sala Phuket* (℡076 338888, ⓦwww
.salaphuket.com; published rates from $490; ❾) – all done out in cool creams and
silver, with colour-coordinated planting and the occasional lacquered screen –
attract mainly couples, especially honeymooners, who enjoy the style and privacy,
especially of the pool villas. There's an enticing open-air seafront lounging area
here too, with deliciously squishy sofas, plus a rooftop terrace. Though the trend
on Hat Mai Khao is indisputably upmarket, it is still possible to enjoy this glorious
beach on a smaller budget, at *Mai Khao Beach Bungalows* (℡081 895 1233,
ⓦmaikhaobeach.wordpress.com; ❹, tents ❶; closed May–Oct), whose four
simple en-suite fan bungalows, and four tents, sit just behind the shore beneath
thinly planted coconut palms hung with hammocks, some 3km south down the
beach from *Sala Phuket*. There's a restaurant and motorbike rental here too, but
not much else. Easiest access to *Mai Khao Beach Bungalows* is by long-distance bus
to or from Phuket town: ask to be dropped in Ban Soun Maprao, a road junction
just north of kilometre-stone 37 on Highway 402, from where you can phone
the bungalows for a pick-up, 2km west.

Thachatchai Nature Trail

Snaking through the mangroves at Phuket's northern tip, 700m south of the
Sarasin Bridge exit to the mainland, the **Thachatchai Nature Trail** (dawn to
dusk; free) aims to introduce visitors to life in a mangrove swamp. It's run by
the Sirinath National Park and is located east off Highway 402; any bus travelling between Phuket town and the mainland should drop you at the sign. The
six-hundred-metre **trail** follows a raised wooden walkway that loops through a
patch of coastal mangrove swamp. Informative English-language boards
describe the flora and fauna: you can't fail to spot the swarms of fiddler crabs
scuttling around the muddy roots, and the "bok-bok" sound that you can hear
above the roar of the distant highway is the noise the mangrove-dwelling
shrimps make when they snap their pincers as they feed – they're the ones that
give the distinctive taste to the green papaya salad, *som tam*.

Hat Nai Yang

The long curved sweep of **HAT NAI YANG**, 5km south of Hat Mai Khao
and 30km north of Phuket town, is partly under the protection of Sirinath
National Park and has only fairly low-key development, with plentiful shade
from the feathery casuarinas and cajeput trees that run half the length of the bay,
a dozen seafood restaurant shacks, and a tiny, low-rise tourist village of transport
rental outlets, a few accommodation options, an ATM, a massage pavilion, and
the inevitable tailors' shops. The beach is clean and good for swimming at the
southern end, and there's a reasonable, shallow **reef** about 1km offshore (10min
by longtail boat) from the Sirinath National Park headquarters, which are a
fifteen-minute walk north of the tourist village. From May to September there's
also kiteboarding here, care of Kiteboarding Asia (ⓦwww.kiteboardingasia
.com). The Thachatchai Nature Trail is quite nearby (see above).

Hat Nai Yang is just 2km south of the **airport**, B150 by taxi. An infrequent
songthaew service (B35; 1hr 45min) runs between Phuket town and Hat Nai
Yang via the airport.

Accommodation

Accommodation is pleasingly limited on Hat Nai Yang, though not aimed at
budget travellers. Best of the lot is the luxurious *Indigo Pearl* (℡076 327006,
ⓦwww.indigo-pearl.com; ❾), whose rooms and villas look on to attractively
landscaped plantation-style gardens that run down to the southern end of the

beachfront road; facilities include a meandering lagoon-like salt-water swimming pool, a dive shop, an inventively programmed activities centre, a spa and kids' playground. Interiors are designed to evoke Phuket's tin-mining history, with metallic colour schemes, polished cement floors and a penchant for industrial art, but the look is softened by very comfortable furniture, generous balconies and plenty of greenery. Nearby *Nai Yang Beach Resort* (☎076 328300, ⓦwww .naiyangbeachresort.com; ❽–❾) is a good upper-mid-range alternative, its cosy, modern, whitewashed air-con rooms fitted with attractive dark-wood furniture and ranged in two- and three-storey wings around pretty tropical gardens; there are three swimming pools, and wi-fi throughout.

Eating and drinking
Nai Yang is locally famous for its shorefront **restaurant**-shacks that serve mostly barbecued seafood (and the odd wood-fired pizza), both on mats under the trees during the daytime and at tables on the sand, candlelit and exceptionally tranquil at night; *Mama Mia* is a favourite and gets consistently good reviews. For a really top-notch romantic dinner, however, you can't top the intimate, black-painted *sala* at ✻ *Black Ginger*, inside the *Indigo Pearl* hotel (reservations advisable on ☎076 327006). Highlights from the very classy menu here include the Phuket lobster with red coconut curry, supremely creamy *phanaeng* curries (from B290), fresh Vietnamese-style rice-flour pancakes stuffed with shrimps, coriander and herbs, and indulgent set meals of four or more courses (from B1500 for two). Of the several little beach **bars**, *The Beach Club*, at the southern end of the bay, makes a cool, relaxed place for a drink in its low-slung track-side chairs or on one of its day beds with triangular cushions on the beach.

Hat Nai Thon
The next bay south down the coast from Hat Nai Yang is the small but perfectly formed five hundred-metre-long gold-sand **HAT NAI THON**, with good snorkelling at reefs a brief longtail ride offshore. Shops, hotels and restaurants line the inland side of its narrow little shorefront road, but there's still a low-key, village-like atmosphere here; most visitors rent their own transport as songthaews don't make the detour from the highway and taxis are thin on the ground. The cheapest rooms are upstairs above *Tienseng* restaurant (☎081 535 0512; fan ❹, air-con ❺), with some sea views. *Naithonburi Beach Resort* (☎076 318700, ⓦwww.naithonburi.com; ❽–❾) is huge, with 229 posh air-con rooms in a U-shaped complex enclosing an enormous pool, some of them with direct pool access, but it doesn't dominate. About 2km south over the southern headland, occupying secluded cliffside land that runs down to its own gorgeous little bay of white sand and turquoise water, *Andaman White Beach Resort* (☎076 316300, ⓦwww.andamanwhitebeach.com; ❾) offers luxurious rooms and villas with unsurpassed views, including some designed for families, plus a swimming pool.

Ao Bang Tao
Relandscaped from a former tin-mining concession, complete with lagoons, parkland, an outdoor sports centre, an eighteen-hole golf course and an impressive eight-kilometre shorefront, **AO BANG TAO** is dominated by the vast, upscale *Laguna Phuket*, a gated "integrated resort" of six luxury hotels and their all-encompassing facilities. It's a world away from the thrust and hustle of Patong and a popular choice for families, with no need to leave the *Laguna* village, though beware of the undertow off the coast here, which confines many guests to the hotel pools. There's free transport between the hotels, and (for a

minimal fee) day pass access to all hotel facilities, which include thirty restaurants and five spas plus a shopping centre, tennis and badminton courts, riding stables, watersports, and abseiling and rock-climbing at the Camp Laguna kids' activity centre.

All *Laguna Phuket* **hotels** are in the top price bracket but try ⓦwww .lagunaphuket.com for discounted rates. The family-oriented *Allamanda Laguna* (ⓣ076 362700, ⓦwww.allamanda.com; ❾) comprises 150 apartment-style suites with kitchenette and separate living area; while the exclusive *Banyan Tree Phuket* (ⓣ076 324374, ⓦwww.banyantree.com; ❾) offers villas in private gardens and the gloriously indulgent, award-winning, Banyan Tree spa.

Half-hourly **songthaews** (B25; 1hr 15min) cover the 24km from Phuket town to Ao Bang Tao, or there are resort shuttle buses and on-site car rental.

Hat Surin and Ao Pansea

South around Laem Son headland from Ao Bang Tao, handsome little **HAT SURIN** is a favourite weekend getaway for sophisticated Phuketians and a big draw for expats, who inhabit the ever expanding forest of condo developments inland from the small, pretty beach. The shorefront gets very crowded, however, packed with sunloungers and beach restaurants, so it can be hard to appreciate the setting. Eating and shopping facilities cater to the upmarket clientele and beachfront dining and drinking is the main pastime. Things are much quieter on Hat Surin's northern bay, **AO PANSEA**, which is divided from the main beach by a rocky promontory. **Songthaews** travel the 24km between Phuket town and Hat Surin, via Hat Kamala, approximately every half-hour and cost B25. Taxis to and from Patong charge B500.

Accommodation on Hat Surin is no bargain, but just across the small park from the beach you'll find large, attractive and stylish rooms at both *Surin Bay Inn*, above a restaurant at 106 Thanon Hat Surin (ⓣ076 271601, ⓦwww .surinbayinn.com; ❼), and *Benyada Lodge*, at nearby no. 103 (ⓣ076 271261, ⓦwww.benyadalodge-phuket.com; ❼–❽); both have in-room air-con, wi-fi, TV and fridge, and *Benyada* has a rooftop terrace and bar. North around the rocks, **Ao Pansea** is secluded from the riff-raff and is a favourite haunt of royalty and Hollywood stars, who stay in the butler-staffed pavilions at the *Amanpuri* (ⓣ076 324333, ⓦwww.amanresorts.com; ❾; rates start at US$700). Sharing this effectively private white-sand hideaway is the delightful, and slightly more reasonably priced *The Chedi Phuket* (ⓣ076 324017, ⓦwww .ghmhotels.com; ❾; rates from B17,000 but specials often available), whose 108 generously proportioned, Bali-style thatched villas are set within a lushly planted hillside palm grove that drops down to the shore.

Among the many restaurants on and behind Hat Surin proper, sophisticated seafront *Taste* (Tues–Sun midday till late; ⓦwww.tastesurinbeach.com) serves great seafood – steamed red snapper with lobster-dill white wine sauce; *moules marinières* (B195–395) – while the beachside lounge bar at *The Catch Beach Club* is the fashionable place to go after sundown, with its illuminated palm trees, resident DJs and very well-stocked bar; though it's open during the day, the food is very pricey and you have to pay an exorbitant B1500 rental for a sunlounger if you're not a guest at *Twinpalms Resort*. Inland, inside the Surin Plaza shopping complex, expats dining out for a special occasion come to famously elegant *Silk* (ⓣ076 271702, ⓦwww.silkphuket.com), which specializes in top-of-the range Thai cuisine (B195–450) such as rose-apple salad with poached prawns, *goong sarong* (prawns wrapped in Phuket-style noodles) and pan-fried snow fish with lemon grass.

Bookings for all the following **Phuket day-trips and activities** can be made through any tour agent and should include return transport from your hotel. For details of dive operators in Phuket, see p.370. Other **sights** worth checking out, especially for kids, include the Phuket Butterfly Garden and Insect World in Phuket town (see p.357), the Aquarium on Laem Panwa (p.377), the Shell Museum in Rawai (p.376), the Big Buddha near Chalong (p.377), the Dino Park on Karon (p.371) and the Gibbon Rehabilitation Project near Thalang (p.379). Avoid any tour that features Ko Siray (Ko Sireh), the island across the narrow channel from Phuket town, which merely encourages tour-bus passengers to gawp at Phuket's largest and longest-established indigenous *chao ley* community; for more on the *chao ley* see p.335.

Activities and days out

Bicycle touring Full- and half-day guided mountain-bike rides into Phuket's rural hinterlands with Action Holidays Phuket (℡076 263575, ⊛www.biketoursthailand .com; full day from B2400/kids B2200).

Deep-sea fishing Day-trips and overnight charters with Andaman Hooker (℡076 282036, ⊛www.phuket.com/fishing/andaman.htm); and Harry's Fishing Adventures (℡076 340418, ⊛www.harrysfishing-phuket.com).

Elephant trekking Award-winning, conservation-conscious Siam Safari runs Four-in-One tours featuring their hillside elephant camp plus rubber tapping, buffalo-cart racing and a sail on a Burmese junk (from B2250, kids B1550; ℡076 280116, ⊛www .siamsafari.com).

Harley-Davidson Tours Famous local HD nut Nicky, owner of Patong's *Nicky's Handlebar* Harley bar and shop (see p.369), leads riders on a 330km ride around adjacent Phang Nga province. B7500 or B10,500 for rider plus pillion, including bike rental, lunch and dinner (℡076 345770).

Sea-canoeing Sunset, one- and two-day expeditions in sea kayaks around the spectacular limestone karsts of Ao Phang Nga, or in Khao Sok National Park, for around B3000–3500 per person per day. There are dozens of companies but two with the best reputations are John Gray's Sea Canoe (℡076 254505, ⊛www.johngray -seacanoe.com) and Paddle Asia (℡076 240952, ⊛paddleasia.com).

Thai cookery courses Different daily classes at Phuket Thai Cookery School east of Phuket town on Ko Siray (B2500; ℡076 252354, ⊛www.phuket-thaicookeryschool .com); and at many hotels, including, most famously, every Saturday and Sunday at *Mom Tri's Boathouse* hotel on Ao Kata Yai (B2200 for one day, or B3500 for both days; ℡076 330015, ⊛www.boathousephuket.com).

Thai culture and wildlife tours Full-day "Thai Life" tours that include market and temple visits, Buddhist merit-making, a cooking class and craft and rubber production. Can be combined with the Gibbon Rehabilitation project (see p.379). B1500 with Plan to Phuket (℡081/691 1955).

Nights out

Phuket FantaSea ℡076 385111, ⊛www.phuket-fantasea.com. Enjoyable, hi-tech mega-spectacular staged at the enormous FantaSea entertainments complex in Kamala and featuring high-wire trapeze acts, acrobatics, pyrotechnics, illusionists, comedy and traditional dance – plus a depressing baby elephant circus. Fri–Wed 9pm; B1500 for adults and kids or B1900/1700 including the unexciting pre-show dinner.

Phuket Simon Cabaret ℡076 342011, ⊛www.phuket-simoncabaret.com. Famously flamboyant extravaganza starring a troupe of outré transvestites. It's all very Hollywood – a little bit risqué but not at all sleazy – and popular with tour groups and families. Nightly 7.30pm & 9.30pm at the Simon Theatre just south of Patong; B700/500.

Hat Kamala and Laem Singh

With its cheerfully painted houses and absence of high-rises, the small, village-like tourist development at **HAT KAMALA** is low-key and mid-market, sandwiched between the beach and the predominantly Muslim town of Ban Kamala, about 300m west of the main Patong-Surin road, 6km north of Patong and 26km northwest of Phuket town. Accommodation, shops, restaurants and other tourist services are mostly clustered either side of shoreside Thanon Rim Had (also spelt Rim Hat) which, despite its limited choice, is a much pleasanter place to browse than the big resorts. The beach gets prettier and quieter the further north you go, away from Thanon Rim Had, with restaurant shacks renting sunloungers along most of its course. A stretch of this area is backed by the Muslim cemetery, so it's particularly important to respect local sensibilities and avoid going topless.

Kamala was very badly hit by the 2004 **tsunami**, which killed many residents and wiped out the beachfront school, the temple and countless homes and businesses. Though extensive rebuilding has extinguished most of the physical scars, a copper sculpture in the park opposite *Print Kamala* bears witness to the devastation, and a volunteer English-teaching programme at the school (see p.67), aims to help rebuild some of the young lives affected.

The Phuket FantaSea entertainments complex (see box, p.363) is about 1km northeast of Hat Kamala on the main Patong-Surin road. Just beyond, a couple of steep paths lead west off the main road and down to **Laem Singh** cape, a pretty little sandy cove whose picturesque combination of turquoise water and smooth granite boulders makes it one of Phuket's finest. It's good for swimming and very secluded, plus there's a decent patch of shade throughout the day.

The cheapest way to get to Hat Kamala is by **songthaew** from Phuket town (every 30min, 1hr 15min; B30). Tuk-tuks charge B300 from Patong.

Accommodation

Hat Kamala is popular with long-stay tourists, and several **hotels** offer rooms with kitchenettes; there's also a preponderance of small-scale places.

Benjamin Resort 83 Thanon Rim Had, opposite the school at the southerly end of the beachfront road ☎076 385147, ⊛www.phuketdir.com /benjaminresort. Set right on the beach and about the best and friendliest deal in Kamala, this block of 37 air-con rooms lacks character but couldn't be closer to the sea. Although views are obstructed from all but the most expensive rooms, the spacious interiors are almost identical and all have fridge, TV, hot water and breakfast included, plus use of sunloungers out front. ❸—❻

Coconut Garden Soi Police Station ☎081 477 3331, ⊛www.coconutgarden.se. The best thing about the dozen good-sized but unexceptional concrete air-con bungalows here are their location on the nicer northerly stretch of the central beach. ❼

Kamala Dreams 74/1 Thanon Rim Had ☎076 279131, ⊛www.kamaladreams.net. Epitomizing all the best things about Kamala, this is a really nice, small hotel set right on the shore, in the middle of the tourist village. Its eighteen rooms are large and furnished in contemporary style, and all have air-con, TVs, a kitchenette and a large balcony overlooking the pool and the sea. ❼

Malinee House 75/4 Thanon Rim Had ☎076 385094, ⊛www.malineehouse.com. Very friendly, traveller-oriented guest house in the middle of the tourist village, with internet access and the Jackie Lee travel agency downstairs, and jut eight large, comfortably furnished and cheerfully painted air-con rooms upstairs, all of them with balconies. ❺

Print Kamala Resort 74/8 Thanon Rim Had ☎076 385396, ⊛www.printkamalaresort.net. The best accommodation here is in a village-like complex of very generously sized bungalows, connected via stilted walkways around a tropical Bali-style garden. The bungalows all have prettily furnished air-con bedrooms plus separate living rooms, and capacious, shaded decks. The pricier ones are detached. The hotel also has some less interesting, but more expensive, rooms in a hotel wing, and a large pool. ❽—❾

Eating and drinking

The most famous **restaurant** in Kamala is Australian-run *Rockfish* at the *Kamala Beach Estate* hotel (☎076 279732, ⓦwww.rockfishrestaurant.com), which enjoys an island-wide reputation for great food, mostly Asian fusion and seafood dishes such as tiger prawns in tamarind sauce, blue crab and mango salad and lemon grass pannacotta (B200–700); you also get lovely views from its southern headland location. Otherwise, most people eat on the beach, especially at the restaurant shacks that pretty much line the shore all the way north from opposite *Print Kamala*; seafood is the big seller here, and you can bury your feet in the sand. For a seaside **drink** with a reggae vibe try *Yellow Bar*, just before the cemetery, done out with Rasta colour schemes and driftwood decor.

Ao Patong

The busiest and most popular of all Phuket's beaches, **AO PATONG** – 5km south of Ao Kamala and 15km west of Phuket town – is vastly over-developed and hard to recommend. A congestion of high-rise hotels, tour agents and souvenir shops disfigures the beachfront road, tireless touts are everywhere, and hostess bars and strip joints dominate the nightlife, attracting an increasing number of single Western men to the most active scene between Bangkok and Hat Yai. On the plus side, the broad, three-kilometre-long beach offers good sand and plenty of shade beneath the parasols and there are hundreds of shops and bars plus a surprising number of good restaurants to keep you busy after dark.

Transport

For transport from and to the **airport** and the **ferry port**, see p.352. **Song-thaews** from Phuket town (every 15min 6am–6pm; 20min; B20) approach Patong from the northeast, driving south along one-way Thanon Raja Uthit Song Roi Phi (Thanon Raja Uthit 200) then circling back north along beach-front Thanon Thavee Wong (also one-way) via the *Patong Merlin*, where they wait to pick up passengers for the return trip. A **tuk-tuk** or **taxi** from Patong to Ao Karon will set you back at least B200.

National/SMT **car rental** (☎076 340608, ⓦwww.nationalcarrental.co.th) has a desk inside the *Holiday Inn*, the local Budget agent is at the nearby *Patong Merlin* (☎076 292389, ⓦwww.budget.co.th), or you can rent jeeps and motor-bikes from any transport tout on Thanon Thavee Wong.

Information

Most of the **tour agents** and **dive operators** have offices on the southern stretch of Thanon Thavee Wong: see the box on p.363 for a roundup of available day-trips and activities, and the box on p.370 for diving details.

There are **post offices** on Thanon Thavee Wong (daily 11am–7pm) and Thanon Raja Uthit Song Roi Phi (Mon–Fri 8.30am–4.30pm, Sat & Sun 9.30am–noon) and the Patong branch of Phuket's **Immigration** office (for visa extensions; Mon–Fri 10am–noon & 1–3pm; ☎076 340477) is next to *Sala Bua* restaurant on Thanon Thavee Wong.

Accommodation

It's hard to find much **accommodation** under ❺ in Patong, and there are no backpacker places, but upper-end hotels are reasonable value and all have excellent facilities.

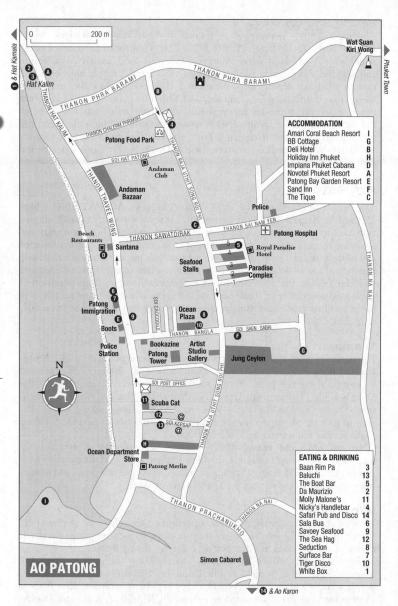

ACCOMMODATION

Amari Coral Beach Resort	I
BB Cottage	G
Deli Hotel	B
Holiday Inn Phuket	H
Impiana Phuket Cabana	D
Novotel Phuket Resort	A
Patong Bay Garden Resort	E
Sand Inn	F
The Tique	C

EATING & DRINKING

Baan Rim Pa	3
Baluchi	13
The Boat Bar	5
Da Maurizio	2
Molly Malone's	11
Nicky's Handlebar	4
Safari Pub and Disco	14
Sala Bua	6
Savoey Seafood	9
The Sea Hag	12
Seduction	8
Surface Bar	7
Tiger Disco	10
White Box	1

AO PATONG

Amari Coral Beach Resort 104 Thanon Traitrang ☏076 340106, ⓦwww.amari.com. Occupying its own secluded little beach on a headland at the southernmost end of the bay, this upmarket Thai chain hotel offers contemporary-chic rooms with generous sea-view balconies, plus two swimming pools, romantic spa facilities, tennis courts and

several restaurants. The views are exceptional and the location peaceful but convenient; as it's ranged up a slope it's not ideal for guests with mobility problems. ⑨

BB Cottage 17/21 Soi Saen Sabai ☏076 342948, ⓔpppropt@loxinfo.co.th. A rare thing indeed in Patong: 29 lowish-budget bungalows dotted around a peaceful green oasis of a garden, beneath the shadow of the sprawling Jung Ceylon centre and hotel. Admittedly, interiors are plain – though they are large, have TVs and fridges, and some have kitchenettes – and there are no verandas, but they're kept very clean, there's a sense of space and you're close to the nightlife yet a little bit secluded. Staff are friendly and guests can also use a nearby swimming pool. Fan ⑤, air-con ⑤—⑥

Deli Hotel (formerly Shamrock Park Inn) 31 Thanon Raja Uthit Song Roi Phi ☎076 340991. Friendly, good-value three-storey hotel at the northern end of the resort with 28 pleasant, well-maintained and cheerily painted air-con rooms, half of them with balconies and all with TVs, fridges, wi-fi and safety box. Unlike many places it doesn't raise its rates for Christmas and New Year. ④

Holiday Inn Phuket 86/11 Thanon Thavee Wong ☎076 340608, ⓦwww.phuket.holiday-inn.com. Reliable, upmarket chain hotel that offers smart, contemporary rooms just across the road from the beach, in two differently styled wings, and fosters an informal, unpretentious atmosphere. The poshest Busakorn villa rooms have their own interconnected plunge-pools and there are also large pools for each wing, plus several restaurants and an interesting programme of daily activities. The hotel makes a big effort to be family-friendly, with special "kidsuites" for children, an all-day kids' club and a teens' club and two children's pools. Also offers wheelchair-accessible rooms. ⑨

Impiana Phuket Cabana 94 Thanon Thavee Wong ☎076 340138, ⓦwww.impiana.com. Located right on the beach and in the heart of the resort, the very tastefully designed air-con cabanas here are set around a garden and smallish swimming pool; also has a kids' pool and a spa. ⑨

Novotel Phuket Resort Thanon Phra Barami/Thanon Hat Kalim ☎076 342777, ⓦwww.novotel phuket.com. Luxurious and relaxing chain hotel built on the hillside above Kalim Bay, the quieter, northern end of the resort, a 10min walk or a free shuttle ride to Patong's main beach and shops, but very close to some of the best restaurants. Occupying sloping landscaped tropical gardens and offering exceptional high-level sea views, it's especially popular with families as it offers heaps of activities as well as a kids' club plus a multi-level swimming pool. ⑨

Patong Bay Garden Resort 33/1 Thanon Thavee Wong ☎076 340297, ⓦwww.patongbaygarden .com. Lively, mid-sized 71-room hotel set right on the beach, with the top "studio" rooms having uninterrupted sea views, quite unusual in central Patong. Other rooms look out on the small shore-front pool or have no view at all. Rooms are quite elegantly furnished and all have air-con and TV. ⑨

Sand Inn 171 Soi Saen Sabai ☎076 340275, ⓦwww.sandinnphuket.com. Thirty well-appointed air-con rooms, a little on the compact side, but maintained to a good standard in the ideal location for nightlife, just east off bar-packed Thanon Bangla. There's TV in all rooms, a *Euro Café* bakery downstairs, and use of a small swimming pool just a few metres up the soi. ⑤—⑥

The Tique 29 Thanon Sawatdirak ☎076 297023, ⓦwww.thetique.com. Tiny urban-chic boutique inn, where the 22 air-con rooms are cleverly designed in retro-neutral, bachelor-pad colour schemes and all have flatscreen TVs, wi-fi, and a petite balcony. There's a small jacuzzi pool on the fourth-floor roof terrace and rates include breakfast, high-tea, and a weekend glass of wine at cocktail hour. ⑦—⑧

Eating

Much of the **food** on Patong is dire, but in among the disastrous little cafés advertising everything from Hungarian to Swedish "home cooking" you'll find a few genuinely reputable, long-running favourites. Phone numbers are given where reservations are advisable. For cheapish food on the beach, head for the half dozen little restaurants under the shorefront trees just north of the *Impiana* hotel. For well-priced Thai fast food, there are the regional speciality stalls at the *Food Haven* foodcentre in Jung Ceylon, the *Patong Food Park* night market that sets up around 5pm towards the northern end of Thanon Raja Uthit Song Roi Phi, and the row of seafood stall-restaurants further south, opposite the *Royal Paradise Hotel* complex.

Baan Rim Pa Across from the *Novotel* on Thanon Hat Kalim ☎076 340789, ⓦwww .baanrimpa.com. One of Phuket's most famous fine-dining restaurants, this is an elegant spot that's beautifully set in a teak building on a clifftop overlooking the bay, with tables also on its sea-view terrace. Known for its classic "Royal Thai" cuisine

(mains B250–500), including banana blossom salad, creamy duck curry and fried tiger prawns with tamarind sauce, as well as for its cellar of more than 270 wines. Live jazz in the *Piano Bar*.

Baluchi Inside the *Horizon Beach Hotel* on Soi Kepsap. One of Patong's better Indian restaurants, specializing in North Indian cuisine and tandoori dishes – Rogan josh kashmiri lamb, tandoori prawns – with most mains costing B200–400.

Da Maurizio Across from the *Novotel* on Thanon Hat Kalim ☎076 344079, ⓦwww.damaurizio.com. Superior Italian restaurant in a stunning location set over the rocks beside the sea. Serves authentic home-made pasta and antipasti (capellini with scallops, prosciutto-wrapped goat's cheese), fabulous seafood (Phuket lobsters, local kingfish with wild mushroom sauté), and a good wine list. Main dishes from B450.

Sala Bua 41 Thanon Thavee Wong ☎076 340138, ⓦwww.sala-bua.com. Fabulously stylish, breezy, beach-view restaurant attached to the *Impiana Phuket Cabana* hotel. The innovative, pricey, Pacific Rim menu (B300–1900) includes Cajun-style red snapper, local rock-lobster lasagne, Australian tenderloin steaks and sweet sushi rolls filled with green mango, sticky rice and orange sauce.

Savoey Seafood 136 Thanon Thavee Wong. Cavernous and unatmospheric but very popular for its huge selection of locally caught fish and seafood (dishes from B180), particularly Phuket lobster, cooked to Thai, Chinese and Western recipes.

The Sea Hag inland from *Zen* Japanese restaurant on Soi Dr Wattana. The same chef has been cooking great seafood here for over a decade and this is where expat hoteliers come for a good Patong feed. Fish and seafood cooked any number of Thai-style ways for B180–380.

White Box Thanon Hat Kalim, 1.5km north of the *Novotel* ☎076 346271, ⓦwww.whiteboxphuket .com. This chic, sophisticated waterside restaurant and bar, strikingly designed as a modernist cube with panoramic picture windows, is a magnet for visiting celebs and style-conscious expats. The very expensive menu (B320–1350) mixes Thai and Mediterranean flavours – grilled Phuket lobster with mint and ginger, beef carpaccio, red curry with roasted duck – and the rooftop sofas are ideal for a pre- or post dinner drink. Daily 5pm–1am.

Nightlife and entertainment

After dark, everyone heads to pedestrianized Thanon Bangla for their own taste of Patong's notorious **nightlife** and the road teems with a cross-section of Phuket tourists, from elderly couples and young parents with strollers, to glammed-up girlfriends and groups of lads. The big draw for the more innocent onlookers is Thanon Bangla's Soi Crocodile, better known as Soi Katoey, or "Trannie Alley", where pouting, barely clad transvestites jiggle their implants on podiums at the mouth of the soi and pose for photos with giggling tourists (B200 a shot). But the real action happens further down the many bar-filled sois shooting off Thanon Bangla, where open-air bar-beers and neon-lit go-go clubs

▲ Songthaew on Thanon Thavee Wong, Ao Patong

packed with strippers and goggle-eyed punters pulsate through the night. The pick-up trade pervades most bars in Patong, and though many of these joints are welcoming enough to couples and female tourists, there are a few alternatives, listed below, for anyone not in that kind of mood.

The **gay** entertainment district is concentrated around the Paradise Complex, a network of small sois and dozens of bar-beers in front of *Royal Paradise Hotel* on Thanon Raja Uthit Song Roi Phi: see ⓦgaypatong.com for events listings, including dates for the regular local street parties plus details of the Gay Pride festival, which is usually held in early February.

If you're looking for something else to do with yourself (or your kids) in the evening, check out the nearby transvestite Simon Cabaret, or the spectacular show at Phuket FantaSea (see box, p.363).

(see box, p.363)

The Boat Bar Soi 5, Paradise Complex, off Thanon Raja Uthit Song Roi Phi. Long-running, very popular gay bar and disco, with two cabaret shows nightly after midnight. Daily from 9pm.

Molly Malone's 94/1 Thanon Thavee Wong. Genial Thai-Irish pub chain that serves draught Guinness and Kilkenny, shows international sports TV, stages live music from 9pm Mon–Sat and has a small beer garden and no overt hostess presence. Daily from 10am.

Nicky's Handlebar Thanon Raja Uthit Song Roi Phi. Harley Davidson themed bar, headquarters and rental outlet run by the man who organizes famous Harley tours from Phuket (see p.363). Daily 10am–1am.

Safari Pub and Disco Just beyond the southern edge of Patong, between Simon Cabaret and the *Le Meridien* hotel at 28 Thanon Sirirat. Decked out as a jungle theme park, complete with waterfalls and five different bars, this is a fun and hugely popular late-night party place. Two bands play nightly from around 9pm, and DJs spin everything from 80s disco to current techno, but it only really gets going once most other venues have shut at about 2am.

Seduction Soi Happy, off Soi Bangla. Currently the favourite venue for partying couples and others not looking for freelance company, this two-storey bar and disco has fairly classy lounge areas, a decent-sized dance floor, hi-tech lighting and a catholic music policy. Free until midnight, after which the B300 entry includes two drinks. Nightly from 10pm.

Surface Bar Top floor, *La Flora Resort Patong*, 39 Thanon Thavee Wong. The perfect place for a sophisticated sundowner, enjoyed from the comfort of enormous sofas on the hotel's wide rooftop terrace. Expansive ocean views and a sea breeze as well. Daily 4–11pm.

Tiger Disco 49 Thanon Bangla. By midnight, the upstairs disco in this unashamedly kitsch complex of bar-beers and go-go bars is packed with a mixed crowd of tourists, freelancers and punters. You can't miss the entrance, with its huge moulded jungle trees and rocks, plus the trademark larger-than-life tiger sculptures. It's just as unsubtle inside, where the pole dancers wear tiger outfits. B250 entry includes two drinks. Nightly from 9pm.

Shopping

Though you can't move for **shops** in downtown Patong, by far the best, and least hectic, place to browse is the enormous **Jung Ceylon** shopping centre on Thanon Raja Uthit Song Roi Phi, whose refreshingly tasteful and spacious design includes fountains and plaza seating plus countless shops and restaurants. Brand-name concessions include an Apple reseller and Sports World, plus there are branches of Robinsons Department Store and South Wind secondhand books, the That's Siam Thai handicrafts emporium in the basement, close by a massage centre, and a seven-screen **cinema** as well. Bookazine on Thanon Bangla carries a good range of English-language **books** and magazines, and the cavernous The Artist Studio Gallery on Thanon Raja Uthit Song Roi Phi, with another branch on Thanon Thavee Wong (ⓦphuketdir.com/theartiststudio) is as good a place as any on Phuket to buy **paintings**.

Ao Karon

AO KARON, Phuket's second resort, after Patong, is very much a middle-of-the-road destination. Far less lively, or congested, than Patong, but more commercial and less individual than the smaller beaches, it's the domain of affordable guest houses and package-tour hotels and appeals chiefly to mid-budget tourists, many of them from Scandinavia. The 2.5-kilometre-long **beach** is graced with squeaky soft golden sand and is completely free of developments, though there's very little natural shade; an embankment screens most of the southern half of the beach from the road running alongside, but north of the *Hilton* the road is more often in view and parts of the shore back on to lagoons and wasteland. The **undertow** off Ao Karon is treacherously strong

Diving and snorkelling off Phuket

The reefs and islands within sailing distance of Phuket rate among the most spectacular in the world, and **diving and snorkelling** trips are both good value and hugely popular. Many trips operate year-round, though some of the more remote islands and reefs become too dangerous to reach during part or all of the monsoon season, roughly June to October.

Dive shops and trips

All the dive **shops** listed below are established and accredited PADI Five-Star Instructor Development Centres; they teach courses, organize dive trips and rent equipment. See also p.58 for general advice on choosing a dive shop and other relevant diving information. Prices range from an average B3300 for a one-day introductory **diving course** to B12,000–15,000 for the four-day Openwater course, including equipment. **Day-trips** to the closest of the dive sites listed below, including at least two dives, cost B3100–3900, while multi-day **live-aboard** cruises to the more distant top-rated reefs of Ko Similan and Ko Surin, Hin Daeng and Hin Muang, and the Mergui archipelago cost around B33,000 for four days, including sixteen dives and full board but excluding equipment and national park fees.

There are **recompression chambers** at Phuket International Hospital and Bangkok Hospital Phuket, both in Phuket town and detailed on p.359, and at Wachira Hospital, Soi Wachira, Thanon Yaowarat, Phuket town (T076 211114).

Dive Asia 24, Thanon Karon, Kata/Karon headland, Ao Karon T076 330598, and 623 Thanon Patak, Karon Circle, Ao Karon T076 396199, W www.diveasia.com.

Marina Divers Next to *Marina Phuket Resort* at 45 Thanon Karon, Ao Karon T076 330272, W www.marinadivers.com.

Santana 49 Thanon Thavee Wong, Ao Patong T076 294220, W www.santanaphuket .com.

Scuba Cat 94 Thanon Thavee Wong, Ao Patong T076 293120, W www.scubacat .com.

Snorkelling trips

The most popular snorkelling destination from Phuket is **Ko Phi Phi** (see p.412). All travel agents sell mass-market day-trips there, on huge ferries with capacities of a hundred plus; prices average B1500, or B1200 for children and include snorkelling stops at Phi Phi Leh and Phi Phi Don, snorkel rental and a seafood lunch. Smaller speedboat trips to Ko Phi Phi are usually worth the extra money to avoid the big groups; those run by Offspray Leisure (B2950/2250; T076 281375, W www .offsprayleisure.com) get good reviews. Speedboat snorkel trips to **Ko Racha Yai** are also widely sold (B2000/1400; see p.378), while day-trips to the remote but beautiful **Ko Similan** islands start from B2900/1450 (see p.348). Many of the dive companies listed welcome snorkellers on board their day-trips, and sometimes on the live-aboards too, for a discount of about thirty percent.

during the monsoon season from June to October, so you should heed the warning signs and flags and ask for local advice – fatalities are not uncommon. The tiny bay just north of Ao Karon – known as **Karon Noi** or Relax Bay – is almost exclusively patronized by guests of the *Le Meridien* hotel, but non-guests are quite welcome to swim and sunbathe here.

For inland entertainment, there's the Dino Park **mini-golf** (daily 10am–midnight; B240, kids B180, or B120/90 without the golf), next to *Marina Phuket Resort* on the Kata/Karon headland, which is part of a pseudo-prehistoric theme

Andaman coast dive and snorkel sites

Anemone Reef About 22km east of Phuket. Submerged reef of soft coral and sea anemones starting about 5m deep. Lots of fish, including leopard sharks, tuna and barracuda. Usually combined with a dive at nearby Shark Point. Unsuitable for snorkellers.

Burma Banks About 250km northwest of Phuket; only accessible on live-aboards from Khao Lak and Phuket. A series of submerged "banks", well away from any land mass and very close to the Burmese border. Only worth the trip for its sharks. Visibility up to 25m.

Hin Daeng and **Hin Muang** 56km southwest of Ko Lanta (see box, p.428). Hin Daeng is an exceptional reef wall, named after the red soft corals that covered the rocks, with visibility up to 30m. One hundred metres away, Hin Muang also drops to 50m and is good for stingrays, manta rays, whale sharks and silvertip sharks. Visibility up to 50m. Because of the depth and the current, both places are considered too risky for novice divers who have logged fewer than twenty dives. Unsuitable for snorkellers.

King Cruiser Near Shark Point, between Phuket and Ko Phi Phi. Dubbed the *Thai Tanic*, this became a wreck dive in May 1997, when a tourist ferry sank on its way to Ko Phi Phi. Visibility up to 20m, but hopeless for snorkellers because of the depth and collapsed sections make it dangerous for any but the most experienced divers.

Ko Phi Phi 48km east of Phuket's Ao Chalong. Visibility up to 30m. The most popular destination for Phuket divers and snorkellers. Spectacular drop-offs; good chance of seeing whale sharks. See p.412.

Ko Racha Noi and **Ko Racha Yai** About 33km and 28km south of Phuket's Ao Chalong respectively. Visibility up to 40m. Racha Yai is good for beginners and for snorkellers; at the more challenging Racha Noi there's a good chance of seeing manta rays, eagle rays and whale sharks. See p.378.

Ko Rok Nok and **Ko Rok Nai** 100km southeast of Phuket, south of Ko Lanta (see box, p.428). Visibility up to 18m. Shallow reefs that are excellent for snorkelling.

Ko Similan 96km northwest of Phuket; easiest access from Khao Lak. One of the world's top diving spots. Visibility up to 30m. Leopard sharks, whale sharks and manta rays, plus caves and gorges. Usually closed approximately mid-May to mid-Nov. See p.348.

Ko Surin 174km northwest of Phuket; easiest access from Khuraburi, or from Ko Chang and Ko Phayam. Spectacular and varied shallow reefs of soft and hard corals that are particularly good for snorkelling. Closed mid-May to mid-Nov. See p.336.

Richelieu Rock Just east of Ko Surin (see p.336), close to Burmese waters. A sunken pinnacle that's famous for its whale sharks. Considered by many to be Thailand's top dive spot.

Shark Point (Hin Mu Sang) 24km east of Phuket's Laem Panwa. Protected as a marine sanctuary. Visibility up to 10m. Notable for soft corals, sea fans and leopard sharks. Often combined with the *King Cruiser* dive and/or Anemone Reef; unrewarding for snorkellers.

park comprising a dinosaur restaurant and an erupting "volcano". For day-trip attractions elsewhere on Phuket see the box on p.363.

Transport and orientation

Ao Karon is 5km south of Patong and 20km southwest of Phuket town. For transport to and from the **airport** and **ferry ports** see p.352. **Songthaews** from Phuket town (every 20min; 30min; B25) arrive in Karon via Thanon Patak, hitting the beach at the northern end of Ao Karon and then driving south along beachfront Thanon Karon, continuing over the headland as far as *Kata Beach Resort* on Ao Kata Yai. To catch a songthaew back into town, just stand on the other side of the road and flag one down. Transport touts throughout the resort rent motorbikes and jeeps.

Karon's main **shopping and eating areas**, with all the usual resort facilities, are grouped around the *Centara Hotel* on the northern curve of Thanon Patak; along and around Thanon Luang Pho Chuain, location of the Kata Plaza enclave of accommodation, restaurants and bars; and along Thanon Taina (sometimes referred to as Kata Centre). The local branch of Bookazine, for new books and foreign newspapers, is across from the Thanon Taina junction on the Kata-Karon headland.

Accommodation

Like Patong, Karon does little to attract budget travellers, but there's a bit more space here and a decent selection of inviting **accommodation** in the mid-range and upper brackets.

Casa Brazil 9 Soi 1, Thanon Luang Pho Chuain ☏076 396317, ⓦwww.phuket.com /casa-brazil. Appealingly arty little hotel, designed in Santa Fe style, with adobe-look walls, earth-toned paintwork, and funky decor and furnishings. The 21 rooms are comfortable and nearly all have air-con. Choose rooms at the back for a rare green and peaceful view of Karon's hilly backdrop, best enjoyed from the French windows and private balconies. Rates include breakfast and there's wi-fi. ❻

Le Meridien On Ao Karon Noi (also known as Relax Bay), north of Ao Karon ☏076 370100, ⓦwww.lemeridien.com. This huge hotel complex has the tiny bay all to itself and boasts an amazing breadth of facilities, including nine restaurants, two lagoon-style swimming pools (with islands), a spa, squash and tennis courts, a climbing wall and private woods. It's a good choice for kids, with reliable babysitting services, a kids' club and lessons in everything from windsurfing and water polo to Thai cookery. ❾

Lucky Guest House 110/44–45 Thanon Taina, Kata Centre ☏076 330572, ⓔluckyguesthouse kata@hotmail.com. Reasonable value place offering unusually large, bright en-suite rooms in a low-rise block (the best have balconies) and some rather plain but very clean semi-detached bungalows on land further back; there's a refreshing sense of space here that's at a premium on this road packed with shops, bars and restaurants. Fan ❸, air-con ❹

Marina Phuket Resort 47 Thanon Karon, far southern end of Ao Karon, on the Karon/Kata headland ☏076 330625, ⓦwww.marinaphuket .com. Enjoying both a very central location, backing on to the beach and just steps from restaurants and shops, and a luxuriously spacious and secluded tropical garden, this is a good upper-end choice. Accommodation is in air-con cottages – Garden View options are old-fashioned and plain, but Jungle View versions are very appealing – and there's a pool, wi-fi and the prettily located *On the Rock* restaurant. ❾

The Old Phuket Soi Aroona Karon, 192/36 Thanon Karon ☏076 396353, ⓦwww.theoldphuket.com. The Sino Wing at this attractive, peacefully secluded heritage-conscious hotel is designed to evoke Sino-Portuguese shophouse architecture. Its rooms are both pretty and modern, with coloured glass window panels and East Indies-style wooden doors; the "terrace deluxe rooms" have garden shower rooms and their own little front garden. Furnishings in the Serene Wing are much more contemporary and minimalist and many of its rooms have direct access to the lagoon-like pool. Also has a gym, a large grassy lawn and wi-fi throughout. ❾

Pineapple Guesthouse Karon Plaza, off Patak and Luang Pho Chuain roads ☏076 396223, ⓦwww .pineapplephuket.com. Good-value British-Thai-run guest house offering seventeen sprucely kept, tiled-floor rooms, all with air-con, fridges, wi-fi and hot water, plus a ten-bed mixed dorm at B200 a bed, with lockers and several fans. The downstairs restaurant serves full English breakfasts and the guest house is surrounded by other expat bars and restaurants in the enclave known as Karon Plaza (not to be confused with the Karon Plaza market stalls at the north end of Karon

beachfront). Discounts sometimes available to walk-in guests. ④–⑤

Prayoon Bungalows Behind the stadium, off Thanon Karon; access via *Andaman Seaview* ☎076 396196. Long-established family-run place with just seven large, comfortable, old-style fan bungalows, all with verandas and good bathrooms, widely spaced under the trees around a big, sloping garden just 150m or so off the beach. ④

Eating and drinking

Karon's choice of **restaurants** is underwhelming, lacking either the big-name restaurants of Patong or the authenticity of Phuket town.

Most of the Thanon Taina **bars** are small places: *Blue Fin* is typical, and hosts happy hours 3–6.30pm daily. Though go-go bars haven't arrived yet, clusters of outdoor bar-beers with hostess service are popping up at a depressing rate.

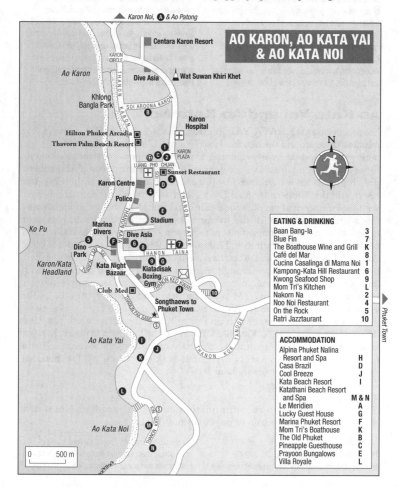

EATING & DRINKING

Baan Bang-la	3
Blue Fin	7
The Boathouse Wine and Grill	K
Café del Mar	8
Cucina Casalinga di Mama Noi	1
Kampong-Kata Hill Restaurant	6
Kwong Seafood Shop	9
Mom Tri's Kitchen	L
Nakorn Na	2
Noo Noi Restaurant	4
On the Rock	5
Ratri Jazztaurant	10

ACCOMMODATION

Alpina Phuket Nalina Resort and Spa	H
Casa Brazil	D
Cool Breeze	J
Kata Beach Resort	I
Katathani Beach Resort and Spa	M & N
Le Meridien	A
Lucky Guest House	G
Marina Phuket Resort	F
Mom Tri's Boathouse	K
The Old Phuket	B
Pineapple Guesthouse	C
Prayoon Bungalows	E
Villa Royale	L

Baan Bang-la 6 Soi Patak, off Thanon Patak. The seafood here has a good reputation and there are also pizzas, pasta dishes and Thai cuisine on the menu too. Dining is mostly al fresco in Thai *salas* set around a pretty little garden. Mains B180–300.

Café del Mar Thanon Taina. An inviting, hip little bar serving margaritas, daiquiris and the rest.

Cucina Casalinga di Mama Noi Karon Plaza off Thanon Patak and Thanon Luang Pho Chuian. Expats, dive staff and Italian tourists fill this place at lunch and dinnertime, savouring the home-from-home taste of the excellent, mid-priced, pizzas and pasta.

Kampong-Kata Hill Restaurant Access via a steep ramp off Thanon Karon. Quality Thai and seafood dishes and fancy Thai-style decor set this place apart and ensure it always gets a good crowd. Its curries – red, green, dry and country-style – are especially good and come in all permutations (B120–180). It also serves reasonably priced imported wine by the glass. Daily 5pm–midnight.

Kwong Seafood Shop 114 Thanon Taina. Unassuming but very popular family-run institution that's famous for its well-priced fresh fish and seafood cooked to order; most dishes B120. Daily 11am–11pm.

Nakorn Na Karon Plaza Off Thanon Patak/Thanon Luang Pho Chuian. In among the sports bars, bar-beers and rooms for rent in Karon Plaza are a couple of "art bars" run by cool local creative types, including this invitingly bohemian little place, all driftwood and found objects, with live music nightly from 9pm and a dreadlocked, reggae vibe. Nightly from 7pm.

Noo Noi Restaurant Soi 1, Thanon Luang Pho Chuian. Small, simple, family-run café, in front of the family home, that deserves a mention for determinedly continuing to dish out Thai standards (mainly fried rice and noodle dishes, from B35) at exceptionally cheap prices, despite the inflated rates charged by most other similar places. Daily 8am–10pm.

On the Rock In the grounds of *Marina Phuket Resort*, Kata/Karon headland. Occupying a fine spot above the rocks at the southern end of Ao Karon, this open-air restaurant serves especially good baskets of grilled and deep-fried seafood, baked mussels and mixed seafood satay. Especially romantic at night. Main dishes B150–600. Daily 8am–11pm.

Ao Kata Yai and Ao Kata Noi

Broad, curving **AO KATA YAI** (Big Kata Bay; see map, p.373) is only a few minutes' drive around the headland from Karon (17km from Phuket town), but both prettier and safer for swimming, thanks to the protective rocky promontories at either end. It's also a good distance from the main road. The northern stretch of Kata Yai is overlooked by the unobtrusive buildings of the *Club Med* resort, and the southern by *Kata Beach Resort*: in between the soft sand is busy with sunloungers and the occasional drink and fruit stall. The rest of the accommodation, and the bulk of the tourist village, with its restaurants, bars, tour operators and many shops, fans out eastwards from the walled *Club Med* compound, up to the main road, Thanon Patak. Beyond the southern headland, **AO KATA NOI**'s (Little Kata Bay) smaller white-sand bay feels secluded, being at the end of a no-through road, but is very popular and filled with loungers and parasols. Kata Noi has its own low-key but rather charmless cluster of businesses, including an ATM and minimarket, though it's dominated by the various sections of the enormous *Katathani* hotel.

Most **songthaews** from Phuket go first to Karon, then drive south past *Club Med* and terminate beside *Kata Beach Resort* on the headland between Kata Yai and Kata Noi (B30; returning songthaews depart approx every 20min 6am–4.40pm). To get to Kata Noi, continue walking over the hill for about ten minutes, or take a tuk-tuk for about B100.

Accommodation

There is no really cheap **accommodation** on Kata Yai, and Kata Noi is now the all-but-exclusive domain of one luxurious hotel.

Alpina Phuket Nalina Resort and **Spa** 7/1 Thanon Ked Kwan, **Kata Yai** ☎076 370999, ⓦwww.phuketnalina.com.Very pleasant hotel with comfortable, tastefully Thai-style rooms and a surprisingly quiet location that's close to shops and restaurants and about 10min walk from the beach.

A free shuttle also runs guests to the hotel's private beach club in front of *Club Med*. Rooms have generous balconies overlooking the freeform pool and the hills beyond, with some enjoying direct pool access; suites and private pool villas are enormous. Also has a spa, several restaurants and wi-fi throughout. ❾

Cool Breeze 225 Thanon Kok Tanode, **Kata Yai** ☎076 330484, ⓦwww.phuketindex.com /coolbreezebungalows. Though one of the cheapest places in Kata, for your money you get a spacious private bungalow, plus a view of sorts from the terrace (either of the distant sea or of the hilltop Big Buddha in profile), the sixteen bungalows being ranged steeply up the hillside, in a grassy palm-and shrub-filled garden. Interiors are nothing fancy but good value and are sufficiently far above the narrow, noisy road. Fan ❹, air-con ❺

Kata Beach Resort Thanon Kata, **Kata Yai** ☎076 330530, ⓦwww.katagroup.com. This huge 275-room, four-storey hotel occupies a great spot right on the edge of the southern end of Kata Yai's white-sand beach. It has a big, shorefront swimming pool and restaurant, a palm-shaded seaside garden, a kids' pool and lots of watersports facilities, so it's popular with families; some rooms also have direct pool access, and some have sea views Also runs Thai cooking and fruit-carving classes. ❾

Katathani Beach Resort and Spa 14 Thanon Kata Noi ☎076 330124, ⓦwww.katathani.com. The various wings and offshoots of the enormous and luxurious *Katathani* now occupy almost the entire shoreline of small, secluded Kata Noi. The beachfront all-suite Thani wing has the prime position, with the narrow lawn dropping seamlessly onto the white sand; all rooms here have sea-view balconies. Across the effectively private, no-through road, the garden-view Bhuri wing has a distinc-tively contemporary look and its rooms too are very deluxe. There's broadband throughout and a shuttle service to town and to Patong. The hotel has six restaurants, six swimming pools and a spa, plus tennis courts, a games room, a dive shop and a kids' playground. ❾

Mom Tri's Boathouse Thanon Kok Tanode, **Kata Yai** ☎076 330015, ⓦwww.boathousephuket.com. Exclusive beachfront boutique hotel, designed by the architect owner in graceful, understated classical Thai style, with just 38 elegantly furnished sea-front rooms, a reputation for classy service, and a famously top-notch restaurant. All rooms have free wi-fi, there's a pool and weekend cooking classes. Also has some even more luxurious suites and studios at *Villa Royale*, a "gourmet hotel" set in landscaped tropical gardens above Kata Noi. Advance booking essential. ❾

Eating

Kata Yai's *The Boathouse Wine and Grill* (☎076 330015, ⓦwww.boathouse phuket.com) is one of the best-known **restaurants** on Phuket, not least for its famously extensive, award-winning wine list. Its French-Thai menu is also highly rated, offering, among many other interesting choices, pan-roasted beef with *tom yam* sauce and seared sea scallops on risotto with black truffle sauce (mains B410–1900, degustation menus from B1650). The beachside terrace and dining room, attached to the boutique hotel of the same name, enjoy fine views and there are Thai cooking classes here every weekend (see above). Sister restaurant *Mom Tri's Kitchen*, part of the *Villa Royale* hotel complex above Kata Noi, is also well regarded, specializing in Thai-European fusion fine dining. Also worth making the effort for is *Ratri Jazztaurant*, reached by a vertiginous but short climb (or by road) east off Thanon Patak (daily from 5.30pm). This rather sophisticated eyrie makes a panoramic spot for cocktails at sundown, with high-level views across Kata, plenty of squishy sofas to sink into and a good if pricey menu of Thai food (B220–500), including *matsaman* and Indian-Thai curries, and blue-shell crab stuffed with pork and served with plum sauce. The in-house jazz band plays nightly from about 8.30pm and is worth lingering for.

Hat Nai Harn, Hat Ya Nui and Laem Promthep

The favourite beach of the many expats who live in nearby Rawai, **HAT NAI HARN**, 18km southwest of Phuket town, is an exceptionally beautiful curved bay of white sand backed by a stand of casuarinas and plenty of foodstalls but only minimal development. It does get crowded with parasols and loungers, however, and during the monsoon the waves here are huge. The beach is dominated by a luxurious **hotel**, *The Royal Phuket Yacht Club* (T076 380200, Wwww.pura-varna.com; ⑨), whose rooms are raked up the hill and all have living-room sized balconies to make the most of the fine sea views. There's slightly cheaper accommodation next door at the well-sited though architec- turally unexciting *All Seasons Naiharn Phuket* (T076 289327, Wwww .allseasons-naiharn-phuket.com; ⑧–⑨), which offers contemporary styled concrete row rooms with ocean or garden view and a decent-sized pool just over the narrow road from the shore.

Follow the coastal road 2km south around the lumpy headland and you reach the tiny roadside beach of **Hat Ya Nui**, which gets a surprising number of visitors despite being so small and right next to the admittedly quiet road. There are coral reefs very close to shore, though the currents are strong, and kayaks and sunloungers for rent. Two hundred metres uphill from the beach the friendly and very pleasant *Nai Ya Beach Bungalow* (T076 238179; ⑤; closed May–Oct) has attractive, en-suite, fan-cooled bamboo bungalows in a garden that's nicely shaded by cashew nut trees and enjoys high-level sea views.

The rugged, wind-blasted, grassy flanked headland of **Laem Promthep**, 1km beyond Hat Ya Nui, marks Phuket's southernmost tip, jutting dramatically – and photogenically – into the deep blue of the Andaman Sea. The cape is one of the island's top beauty spots and at sunset, busloads of tour groups get shipped in to admire the spectacle; Thais pay their respects at the Hindu shrine here, offering elephant figurines in honour of the enshrined four-headed god Brahma and his elephant mount, Erawan. You can escape the crowds by following the trail along the ridge and down to the rocks just above the water.

Songthaews from Phuket town (every 30min; 45min; B40) go to Nai Harn, via Rawai, but for Hat Ya Nui and Laem Promthep you have to do the lengthy climb round the promontory on foot. Taxis from Patong cost about B500.

Hat Rawai

Phuket's southernmost beach, **HAT RAWAI**, was the first to be exploited for tourist purposes, but, half a century on, the hoteliers have moved to the far more appealing sands of Kata and Karon, leaving Rawai to its former inhabitants, the Urak Lawoy *chao ley* ("sea gypsies"; see p.335), and to an expanding expat population. Most visitors are here for the many al fresco **seafood restaurants** along Thanon Viset's beachside promenade, the best and most famous of which is *Salaloy* (daily 10am–10pm), towards the northern end, whose highlights include inexpensive fried fish with turmeric, and omelette topped with baby oysters. Nearby *Nikita's* (daily 10am till late) is a standout among the many expat-favoured café-bars in the area, not least for the horizon-gazing potential from its peaceful tables on the sand (candle-lit at night) and for the well-priced cocktails, wines by the glass and fresh coffees.

Aside from its seafront restaurants, Rawai's chief attraction is the **Phuket Seashell Museum** (daily 8am–6pm; B100), 1500m north of the beach on Highway 4024, which displays some two thousand species of shell, including 380 million-year-old fossils, giant clams, and a 140-carat gold pearl.

Songthaews from Phuket town pass through Rawai (35min; B30) on their way to and from Nai Harn.

Ao Chalong, the Big Buddha and Phuket Aquarium

North of Rawai, the sizeable offshore island of Ko Lone protects the broad sweep of **AO CHALONG**, where many a Chinese fortune was made from the huge quantities of tin mined in the bay. These days, Ao Chalong is the main departure point for dive excursions and fishing trips, and for speedboats to other islands, including Ko Racha Yai, which leave from Chalong Pier, east of the roundabout known as Chalong Circle, or Chalong Ha Yaek. **Songthaews** from Phuket town charge B25.

For islanders, Chalong is important as the site of **Wat Chalong** (8km southwest of Phuket town, on Thanon Chao Fa Nok, aka Route 4022; the Phuket–Karon songthaew passes the entrance), Phuket's loveliest and most famous temple, which enshrines the statue of revered monk Luang Pho Saem, who helped resolve a violent rebellion by migrant Chinese tin-miners in 1876. Elsewhere in the temple compound, the Phra Mahathat chedi is believed to contain a relic of the Buddha.

With your own transport, a visit to Wat Chalong combines well with an uphill pilgrimage to the newly erected **Big Buddha of Phuket**, officially Phra Buddha Mingmongkol Eaknakakeeree (daily dawn to dusk; free; Ⓦwww .mingmongkolphuket.com), a towering 45-metre statue atop Khao Nakkerd that dominates many island vistas, including from Kata Yai to the southwest, and is easily spotted from aeroplane windows. Made of concrete but faced with glistening white-marble tiles, the eastward-looking Buddha boasts enormous proportions: he sits on a lotus flower that's nearly 25m across and even his individual hair curls measure almost a metre each. Views from the base of the statue extend east over Ao Chalong to hilly Ko Lone beyond, while western panoramas take in Kata Noi; it's a popular sunset-viewing spot. **Access** to the Big Buddha is via the very steep and winding six-kilometre Soi Jao Fa 51, signed west off Thanon Chao Fa Nok (West), a couple of kilometres south of Wat Chalong, or 1km north of Chalong Circle. Taxis from Kata, a thirty-minute drive away, charge B800 for the return trip.

Ao Chalong tapers off eastwards into **Laem Panwa**, at the tip of which you'll find the **Phuket Aquarium** (daily 8.30am–4.30pm; B100, kids B50), 10km south of Phuket town and accessible by frequent songthaews from the market (B25). Run by the island's Marine Research Centre, it's not a bad primer for what you might see on a reef and has walk-through tunnels, a touch pool where you can interact with sea cucumbers and sea stars and a feeding show (Sat & Sun 11am).

Accommodation and eating

Though there's no special reason to **stay** in this part of the island, you might make an exception for alternative, traveller-oriented *Shanti Lodge* (Ⓣ076 280233, Ⓦwww.shantilodge.com; ④–⑤), 1500m south down Thanon Chao Fa Nok from Wat Chalong (or 500m north of the Big Buddha turn-off) on Soi Bangrae; the Phuket-Karon songthaew can drop you close by. It's set in a relaxing garden, with salt-water swimming pool and predominantly vegetarian restaurant, and has fan and air-con doubles with or without private bathrooms, some of them wheelchair accessible, and family rooms.

A good reason to dawdle on your way to or from the islands is the prospect of a blowout seafood meal at the classy, long-running *Kan Eang @ Pier* (daily 10.30am–11pm), one of Phuket's most famous **restaurants**, which is handily, and scenically, sited at the mouth of Chalong Pier. The big draw here is of course the seafood, the best of it barbecued old-style on burning coconut husks (from B1200 per kg of crabs, oysters, prawns, cuttlefish and the rest); deep-fried seaweed with shrimps and chilli sauce is also good and the *hawy mok* (fish curry steamed in a banana leaf) is exceptional. Sister restaurant *Kan Eang 2*, north up the beach, enjoys a similarly good reputation.

Ko Racha Yai

Graced with a couple of awesome white-sand beaches, crystal-clear turquoise water and several well-stocked reefs, the tiny island of **KO RACHA YAI** (**Ko Raya Yai**), 23km south off Ao Chalong, is a popular day-tripping destination (B2000/1400 including hotel transfers, lunch and snorkelling equipment) but is also an enjoyable place to stay for a night or two. Easiest independent access, from November through April, is to join the morning day-trippers' **speedboats** which depart Chalong Pier at 9am and return from the island at about 3pm (45min; B1000 per person one way or B1400 return including Phuket hotel transfers). Longtails from Hat Rawai (1hr 30min) cost about B2500 to charter.

The island measures just 3km by 3km and its beaches are small, so can get crowded with day-trippers. Handsome, deep-cut **Ao Batok** (Patok) is the main docking point, while two minutes' walk over the hill from beside *Bungalow Raya Resort*, north-facing **Ao Siam** is the longest and prettiest bay on the island and still largely backed by coconut palms; it's only really good for swimming at high tide, however. About fifteen minutes' walk due east of Ao Batok, **Ao Ter** has good snorkelling both on the shoreline, where the reef is uninteresting but the fish quite spectacular in range and number, and about 100m offshore, where there are two dive sites, including a small wreck. Further down the east coast, there's even less of a beach at **Ao Kon Kare**, though you can swim here, and its reefs are rewarding for snorkelling and diving. Exploring the interior is also fun; tracks crisscross through palm groves and a couple of hamlets, with plenty of wilderness still in evidence and occasional stands of cashew and jackfruit, mango and tamarind trees, even a few water buffaloes and some resident metre-long iguanas.

Accommodation and eating

Cheapest **accommodation** is at *Raya Seaview Bungalow* (☎081 397 5141; ❺; closed May–Oct), up on Ao Siam's western cliff, which has pretty en-suite bamboo bungalows, all with fans, mosquito nets and some sort of view. The *Jungle Bar* at the eastern end of the beach does barbecues and occasional live music. On Ao Batok, there are en-suite, fan-cooled bamboo bungalows at *Bungalow Raya Resort* (☎076 383136, ⓦrayaresort.net; ❻), a couple of which offer unbeatable views over the sparkling sea, plus an attractively sited, if pricey, restaurant. Neighbouring *The Racha* (☎076 355455, ⓦwww.theracha.com; ❾) occupies the main section of the beach with its elegant white-cube and slate-roof buildings, its ultra-luxurious villas and its infinity pool, spa and restaurants.

Northeast Phuket

There's not a great deal for tourists along Phuket's northeast coast. The swanky new **Phuket Royal Marina** caters to yachties and those who can afford the waterfront condo lifestyle, while the mangrove-fringed natural harbour at **Bang Rong** is the departure point for boats to Ko Yao Noi and a speedboat service to Ao Nang, plus chartered longtail tours around the karst islands of western Ao Phang Nga (B3000–5000; see p.386). Inland, there's cultural interest at the museum in **Thalang**, and **rescued gibbons** to visit in **Khao Phra Taew Forest Reserve**.

Thalang and around

As the only official introduction to Phuket's rich and intriguing history, **Thalang National Museum** (daily 9am–4pm; B30; ⓦwww.thailandmuseum .com) doesn't really match up to the task, but taken in conjunction with the privately funded Thaihua Museum in Phuket town, the picture starts to flesh out. Displays include some interesting exhibits on the local tin and rubber industries, accounts of some of the more colourful folkloric traditions and photos of the masochistic feats of the Vegetarian Festival (see box, p.358). The museum is on Route 4027, 200m east of the landmark **Heroines' Monument**, which stands in the centre of the Tha Rua junction, 12km north of Phuket town on Highway 402. The monument commemorates the repulse of the Burmese army by the widow of the governor of Phuket and her sister in 1785; together they rallied the island's womenfolk who, legend has it, frightened the Burmese away by cutting their hair short and rolling up banana leaves to look like musket barrels – a victory that's celebrated every March 13–15 with a monks' ordination ceremony and processions. All mainland-bound traffic and all **songthaews** between Phuket and Hat Surin and Hat Nai Yang pass the monument.

Eight kilometres north of the Heroines' Monument, just beyond the crossroads in the district town of **THALANG**, stands **Wat Phra Thong**, one of Phuket's most revered temples on account of the power of the Buddha statue it enshrines. The solid gold image is half-buried and no one dares dig it up for fear of a curse that has struck down excavators in the past. After the wat was built around the statue, the image was encased in plaster to deter would-be robbers.

Khao Phra Taew Forest Reserve and the Gibbon Project

The minor road east of the Thalang intersection takes you to the visitor centre of **KHAO PHRA TAEW WILDLIFE PARK AND FOREST RESERVE**, 3km away. Several paths cross this small hilly enclave, leading you through the forest habitat of macaques and wild boar, but the most popular features of the park are the Gibbon Rehabilitation Project and the Ton Sai and Bang Pae waterfalls, which combine well as a day-trip (or on a tour, see p.363). The Gibbon Project is located about 10km northeast of the Heroines' Monument, off Route 4027. **Songthaews** from Phuket town, more frequent in the morning, will take you most of the way: ask to be dropped off at Bang Pae (a 40min drive from town) and then follow the signed track for about 1km to get to the project centre. You can get drinks and snacks at the foodstall next to the Rehabilitation Centre, and the route to the waterfalls is signed from here.

The Gibbon Rehabilitation Project

Phuket's forests used to resound with the whooping calls of indigenous white-handed lar gibbons, but they make such charismatic pets that they were poached to extinction on the island by the mid-1980s. The lar is now an endangered species, and in 1992 it became illegal in Thailand to keep them as pets, to sell them or to kill them. Despite this, you'll come across a depressing number of pet gibbons on Phuket, kept in chains by bar and hotel owners as entertainment for their customers. The **Gibbon Rehabilitation Centre** (daily 9am–4pm, last tour at 3.15pm; national park entry B200, kids 100; ⓦwww.gibbonproject.org) aims to reverse this state of affairs, first by rescuing as many pet gibbons as they can, and then by resocializing and re-educating them for the wild before finally releasing them back into the forests. It is apparently not unusual for gibbons to be severely traumatized by their experience as pets: not only will they have been taken forcibly from their mothers, but they may also have been abused by their owners.

Visitors are welcome at the project, which is centred in the forests of Khao Phra Taew Reserve, protected as a "non-hunting area", close to Bang Pae waterfall, but because the whole point of the rehab project is to minimize the gibbons' contact with humans, you can only admire the creatures from afar. There's a small exhibition here on the aims of the project, and the well-informed volunteer guides will fill you in on the details of each case and on the idiosyncratic habits of the lar gibbon (see p.479 for more about Thailand's primates). Should you want to become a **project volunteer** yourself, adopt a gibbon, or make a donation, you can email the project centre.

Bang Pae and Ton Sai waterfalls

If you follow the track along the river from the Gibbon Project, you'll soon arrive at **Bang Pae Falls**, a popular picnic and bathing spot, ten to fifteen minutes' walk away. Continue on the track for another 2.8km (about 1hr 30min on foot) and you should reach **Ton Sai Falls**: though not a difficult climb, the route is unsigned and indistinct, is steep in places and rough underfoot. There are plenty of opportunities for cool dips in the river en route. Once at Ton Sai you can either walk back down to the Khao Phra Taew Reserve access road and try to hitch a ride back home, or return the way you came.

Ko Yao Noi

Located in an idyllic spot on the edge of Phang Nga bay, almost equidistant from Phuket, Phang Nga and Krabi, the island of **KO YAO NOI** enjoys magnificent maritime views from almost every angle and makes a refreshingly tranquil getaway. Measuring about 12km at its longest point, it's home to some four thousand islanders, the vast majority of them Muslim, who earn their living from rubber and coconut plantations, fishing and shrimp-farming. Tourism here is low key, not least because the beaches lack the wow factor of more sparkling nearby sands, and visitors are drawn instead by the rural ambience and lack of commercial pressures. Nonetheless, there's decent swimming off the east coast at high tide, and at low tide too in a few places, and plenty of potential for kayaking and rock-climbing. Most tourists stay on the east side, which has the bulk of the accommodation, at **Hat Tha Khao**, **Hat Klong Jaak (Long Beach)**, **Hat Pasai** and **Laem Sai**. Exploring the interior is a particular pleasure, either via the barely trafficked round-island road as it runs through tiny villages and the island's diminutive town, **Ban Tha Khai**, or via the trails that crisscross the forested interior, where you've a good chance of encountering monkeys as well as cobras and even pythons, not to mention plenty of birds, including majestic oriental pied hornbills.

Getting to Ko Yao Noi

There are three mainland departure points for **boats** to Ko Yao Noi – from Phuket, Krabi's Ao Thalen, and Phang Nga – plus a speedboat service from Ao Nang. Ko Yao Noi **taxis** meet all arriving boats and charge B70–100 per person for transfers to accommodation.

The most common route is **from Bang Rong** on Phuket's northeast coast (approximately hourly 7.30am–5pm; 1hr 10min; B120), which is served,

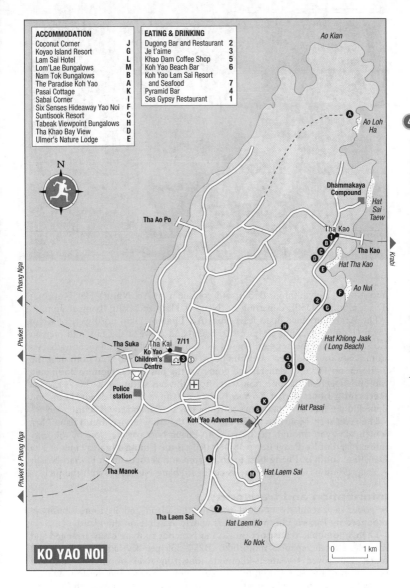

ACCOMMODATION

Coconut Corner	J
Koyao Island Resort	G
Lam Sai Hotel	L
Lom'Lae Bungalows	M
Nam Tok Bungalows	B
The Paradise Koh Yao	A
Pasai Cottage	K
Sabai Corner	I
Six Senses Hideaway Yao Noi	F
Suntisook Resort	C
Tabeak Viewpoint Bungalows	H
Tha Khao Bay View	D
Ulmer's Nature Lodge	E

EATING & DRINKING

Dugong Bar and Restaurant	2
Je t'aime	3
Khao Dam Coffee Shop	5
Koh Yao Beach Bar	6
Koh Yao Lam Sai Resort and Seafood	7
Pyramid Bar	4
Sea Gypsy Restaurant	1

KO YAO NOI

mornings only, by songthaews from Phuket town's Thanon Ranong market (8.30–11am; 90min; B35); a taxi to Bang Rong from town or the main beaches costs about B500. Bang Rong boats dock at Tha Manok or Tha Suka on Ko Yao Noi's southwest coast, depending on the tide. Returning **to Bang Rong**, boats depart Tha Manok every one to two hours from 7.15am to 4.40pm; songthaews meet incoming boats for transfers to Phuket town, or the taxi service charges B500 to Phuket airport, B700 to Patong and B2000 to Khao Lak. The Green Planet **speedboat** service also connects Bang Rong with Ko

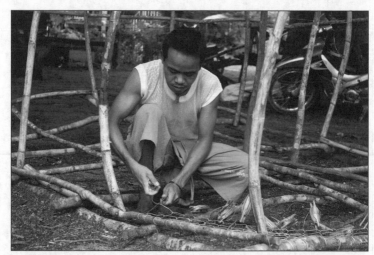

▲ Making fish traps, Ko Yao Noi

Yao Noi (1 daily; 30min; B350), and continues to **Ao Nang**'s Hat Nopparat Thara (30min; B350), departing Ao Nang at 11am and Bang Rong at 3pm.

The **Krabi** province boats leave from **Ao Thalen**, 33km northwest of Krabi town (10am, 1pm, 3pm & 4pm; 1hr; B120) and arrive at the Tha Kao pier on Ko Yao Noi's northeast coast. There's also a 5pm speedboat (B200). Songthaews from Krabi town connect with the boats, leaving an hour before from near the 7-Eleven on Thanon Maharat and going via the bus station (45min; B50); only the 5pm speedboat connection starts from the bus station, not the 7-Eleven. **Returning boats** depart Ko Yao Noi at 7.30am, 8.30am, 9.30am, 11am and 2pm and are met by songthaews to Krabi bus station and town centre.

The most scenic journey to Ko Yao Noi is the daily service from Phang Nga, which takes you through the heart of Ao Phang Nga, passing close by the stilt-house island of Ko Panyi (see p.387). It departs the **Phang Nga** bay pier at Tha Dan, 9km south of Phang Nga town, at 1pm and **returns** from Ko Yao Noi at 7.30am (90min; B200); songthaews connect Phang Nga town with the pier.

Information and transport

A good, free, regularly updated **map** of the island and its tourist business, produced by Pakorn Photo Classics, is widely available on the island.

There's no public **transport** on Ko Yao Noi, but taxis are easily arranged and most hotels can organize motorbike (B250–350 per day) and bicycle (B200) rental. The paved seventeen-kilometre-long ring road around the southern two-thirds of the island is quite manageable on a bicycle, but the four-wheel-drive track up to *Paradise* on the northeast coast is notoriously challenging, especially for motorbikes. Koh Yao Adventures on Pasai (☎076 597553, ⓦwww.kohyaoadventures.com) leads **bicycle tours** around neighbouring big-sister island Ko Yao Yai (B2500); they can also book **buses to Bangkok** via Phuket or Krabi and transport to Ko Samui.

Activities and day-trips

Kayaking around the coast is a very enjoyable pastime, and the dozens of tiny islands visible from eastern shorelines make enticing destinations for experienced paddlers; kayaks can be rented through Ko Yao Noi hotels for about B150 per hour and guided kayaking trips around Ao Phang Nga cost B2700–3500. For a really special kayaking experience, contact Koh Kayak Expeditions at *Coconut Corner* on Hat Pasai (☎0879 294320, ❀www.kayakthailand.com), who rent out their good-quality kayaks fully equipped for self-guided overnight expeditions that can last anything from 24 hours to a month (B1200 per single or B1800 per tandem per 24hr, including camping equipment plus an itinerary and maps).

Every hotel sells **snorkelling** trips to Ko Hong and other islands in Ao Phang Nga (B2300), but **diving** trips and courses are the speciality of Koh Yao Dive and Marine Sports (❀www.kohyaodiver.com), based at *Lom'Lae* and with branches in Laem Sai, at *Paradise* and at *Dugong Bar and Restaurant*. Dives to the reefs around Phuket and Phi Phi cost B3600–4600 and the Openwater course is B16,800.

Ko Yao Noi is fast becoming a respected destination for **rock-climbers**, who appreciate the fresh sites and uncrowded routes compared to the hectic scene at nearby Ton Sai and Railay. There are over a hundred bolted routes on the island, from beginner level to advanced (5 to 8A), established by the American and Thai climbers who run The Mountain Shop at *Sea Gypsy Restaurant* in Ban Tha Khao (☎083 969 2023, ❀www.themountainshop.org). Many routes are over water and accessible only by boat, or at the least via a hike off the dirt track to *Paradise* hotel. There's also a climbing wall at *Paradise*, along with a branch office and equipment rental; on Long Beach, ask at *Khao Dam Coffee Shop*. Prices range from B2500 for a half-day's climb to B10,000 for a three-day skills' course; climbing is possible year-round but from May to October operates only out of *Paradise*.

There's also guided **bird-watching** with Thailand Bird Watching (❀www.thailandbirdwatching.com; B3500 per half day) based at *Ulmer's Nature Lodge* on Hat Tha Khao – Ko Yao Noi has some 150 resident species – and **yoga and meditation**, also at *Ulmer's* (B100 per class or B3000 for an all-inclusive three-day retreat).

Hat Tha Khao and Hat Sai Taew

The most northerly of the main eastern beaches is **HAT THA KHAO**, site of a small village, **BAN THA KHAO**, with a couple of shops and restaurants, the pier for boats to and from Krabi, and the cheapest and most backpacker-oriented bungalows on the island. It's also the closest point to Ko Yao's nicest beach, so-called **Temple Beach** or **Hat Sai Taew**, 2km away, whose pretty, gold-sand shore is great for swimming at any tide. However, it's backed by private land that belongs to the Dhammakaya Foundation, a popular Buddhist sect, and is unsigned and a bit tricky to find. From Tha Khao pier, head inland and take the first right behind the shops, walk alongside the khlong and its sheltered marina, over the bridge, then via the faint trail over the hill to the beach. Or just kayak there from the pier.

Accommodation and eating

All the **bungalows** have **restaurants**, but for a change of scene there's also *Sea Gypsy Restaurant* (Nov–April only), near the pier, which has a small bar and serves à la carte Thai food as well as family-style dinners nightly for anyone who books earlier in the day.

Nam Tok Bungalows ☎087 292 1102. Set back from the beach, beside a khlong, a 5min walk south from the Tha Khao ferry pier, this ultra laid-back set of bungalows is one of the cheapest places to stay on the island. The budget options are spacious and comfortable wooden huts, with cute garden bathrooms and hammocks on the deck, encircling a small garden full of flowers and a fishpond; the more luxurious ones have hot water. *Nam Tok's* manager, Danny, takes guests on camping trips to Ko Pak Bia (B5000 per boat) and also arranges massage and healing sessions with locally famous masseur Bao. ③–⑤

Suntisook Resort ☎089 781 6456, ⓦwww .suntisookkohyao.com. Run by a couple of former teachers and their genial son E, *Suntisook's* nine bungalows are nicely spaced around a garden and mostly come with TVs, fridges and good bathrooms. They're all a bit different but each has a deck and a hammock and some have air-con and three beds. Discounts often available. ④–⑦

Tha Khao Bay View ☎086 942 0812. You have to climb a fair few steps up the cliffside to reach the simple but comfortably appointed en-suite bungalows here but the bay views from the hammocks on their decks are well worth it, and the restaurant enjoys the same panoramic outlook. ③–④

Ulmer's Nature Lodge ☎084 848 5112, ⓦwww .thailandbirdwatching.com. Occupying a peaceful spot on the edge of the mangroves, down a track at the far southern end of the bay, *Ulmer's Nature Lodge* is establishing itself as a centre for bird-watching and yoga, though of course anyone is welcome to stay at its five shoreside bungalows, all of which are en suite. ③

Hat Klong Jaak (Long Beach) and Hat Pasai

A couple of kilometres south of Hat Tha Khao, **HAT KLONG JAAK**, more commonly referred to as **Long Beach**, is the site of the longest-running and best-known tourist accommodation and the liveliest places to eat and drink. The beach is indeed long, around 1500m from the northern end to *Sabai Corner* on the southern headland. Much of it is rocky and all but unswimmable at low tide, except in front of *Koyao Island Resort*, the smoothest stretch. The seaward views are glorious from every angle, however, taking in the many lovely islets of eastern Ao Phang Nga. A minute's walk south from *Sabai Corner* and you're on **HAT PASAI**, a rather pretty little beach, with some shade, plus several bungalows, restaurant-bars and a tiny shop.

Accommodation

Coconut Corner ☎076 454221, ⓦwww .kohyaotravel.com. Offering some of the cheapest and most traveller-friendly accommodation on the island, in simple en-suite bungalows set around a small garden just across the road from the northern end of Hat Pasai beach. It's just a few minutes' walk from *Pyramid Bar* on Long Beach and has internet access, bicycle and motorbike rental. ③

Koyao Island Resort ☎076 597474, ⓦwww .koyao.com. This lovely, stylish resort occupies the best part of the beach and comprises just fifteen chic, thatched, fan-cooled cottage compounds, all of them with separate living areas, huge bathrooms, and sliding doors that give access to the spacious garden and its fine bay views. There's a swimming pool and spa, internet access and a restaurant serving expensive European food. ⑨

Pasai Cottage ☎076 597064, ⓦwww .kohyaotravel.com. The ten bamboo cottages here, just across from Pasai's beach but away from the road, have unexpectedly tasteful interiors, folding glass doors and prettily tiled bathrooms. ④

Sabai Corner ☎081 892 1827, ⓦwww.sabai cornerbungalows.com. Occupying Long Beach's rocky southern point, this long-established,

Italian-Thai, laid-back little outfit has ten thought-fully designed wooden bungalows, all with fans, nets and rustic bathrooms, plus decks and hammocks. They're dotted along a rise between the road and the beach, under cashew and jackfruit trees. Internet access, bicycle and a good restaurant on site. ④–⑥

Six Senses Hideaway Yao Noi ☎076 418500, ⓦwww.sixsenses.com. Extraordinarily luxurious and expensive retreat, hidden in its own little bay and accessed by a private road. The huge villas are designed in natural-chic style, mostly wood and thatch, but all come with private pool, expansive sun deck and personal staff. Rates from B45,500. ⑨

Tabeak Viewpoint Bungalows ☎089 590 4182, ⓦwww.kohyaotravel.com. Two hundred metres inland, on a cross-island track, this Japanese-Thai-run place has large, well-outfitted, fan-cooled, wood and bamboo bungalows, all with polished wood floors and French windows and balconies that give commanding views of the islands. The Thai owner is a community policeman and enthusiastic fisherman and an excellent source of island information. ⑤

Eating and drinking

Island expats congregate at the tiny Swiss-Thai **café**, the *Khao Dam Coffee Shop* (daily 8am–6pm; Nov–April only), about 200m north of *Sabai Corner*, drawn both by its invitingly chilled vibe and by the fresh coffees, delicious banana-chocolate muffins, home-made bread, sandwiches and salads. You can ask here about rock-climbing and can also buy the cloth bags painted by the kids at Children's Centre in Thai Khai. Next door, *Pyramid Bar* is another famous island meeting place, with its pool table, sports TV and extensive **bar** menu; it's at its liveliest on Friday nights when half the island turns up for the very enjoyable weekly sets by island musicians (8.30pm till late). *Koh Yao Beach Bar*, at the southern end of Hat Pasai, also puts on live music nights in high season, and serves good seafood through the week. North up Long Beach, opposite *Koyao Island Resort*, *Dugong Bar and Restaurant* occupies a beautiful barn-like structure built from recycled wood by its batik artist and dive instructor owner and serves good Thai food, cocktails and the rest.

Laem Sai

Beyond Hat Pasai, tiny **HAT LAEM SAI** is often known simply as **Hat Lom'Lae**, after the appealing Thai-Canadian *Lom'Lae Bungalows* (T076 597486, Wwww.lomlae.com; ❼, family houses ❾; closed May–Sept) which sits on the shore. It's a beautiful, secluded haven, backed by ricefields and rubber plantations and enjoying stunning bay views from its palm-fringed beach and grassy garden. The eight attractive, wooden, fan-cooled bungalows are widely spaced and have sliding doors, decks and hammocks to capitalize on the vistas. Some have additional upstairs loft beds, and there are two-bedroom family houses as well. Kayaks, bikes and motorbikes are available for rent and there's a dive shop and cooking classes.

A few hundred metres west from the *Lom'Lae* turn-off, about 3km from Tha Kai, another side-road takes you down towards **Laem Sai pier**, along a coast that has no real beach but is scenically dotted with houses on stilts, fishing platforms, dozens of longtails and some inviting views of Ko Yao Noi's larger twin, Ko Yao Yai, just across the channel. A British father-and-daughter team run the *Lam Sai Hotel* here, a two-storey block of just eight good-quality tiled rooms, all with TVs and balconies and use of the swimming pool (T0847 463861, Wwww .lamsaihotel.com; fan ❹, air-con ❻). What really sets them apart is that both are **muay thai boxers**; they run training sessions at their sea-view Ko Yao Noi Gym here (B250 for a two-hour drop-in class or B2000 for a week of classes) and during high season stage monthly fights open to the public (Wwww.phuket -krabi-muaythai.com). About 1.5km further down the road, beyond where the paving stops, *Koh Yao Lam Sai Resort and Seafood* is a great place for a **seafood lunch**, and there's a nice little beach 300m east further around the rocks.

Ban Tha Kai and north

The island's commercial and administrative centre is **BAN THA KAI**, inland from the main piers on the southwest coast. This is where you'll find the post office, bank with **exchange** counter, hospital, police station (T089 590 4182), obligatory 7-Eleven shop with **ATM** (which sometimes runs out of money), as well as a couple of **internet** centres, the main market and several roti stalls; at the crossroads, the welcoming *Je t'aime* **restaurant** is especially good for locally caught fish and seafood and has occasional live music.

Visitors are very much encouraged to drop by the **Ko Yao Children's Community Centre** (Mon–Wed 4.30–6.30pm, Sat & Sun 8.30am–4.30pm;

@www.koyao-ccc.com), at the western end of town, an NGO that aims to help improve the English-language and computer skills of island children and adults; the kids also paint and sell cloth shopping bags to support environmental projects on Ko Yao Noi. You can also experience a little of island family life for yourself in Ban Tha Kai, which runs a **homestay** community-based tourism project involving twenty local families (from B2000 per person for an all-inclusive two-day programme; ℡086 942 7999, @www.kohyao-cbt.com).

The road running **north from Tha Kai**'s 7-Eleven is particularly scenic, taking you through several hamlets with their mosques and latex-pressing mangles, and past ricefields and their resident buffaloes, framed by mangroves in the middle distance, sea eagles hovering overhead, and the rounded hills of nearby islands in the background. At a junction about 3km from Thai Khai, the northbound road soon turns into a horrible track leading to Ao Loh Ha, while veering right will take you over the hill and down to Tha Khao on the east coast, about 4km away.

Within a couple of kilometres, the northbound road to **AO LOH HA**, Ko Yao Noi's northernmost beach, turns into rough, four-wheel-drive-only track which finally ends at the deluxe thatched rooms and villas of *The Paradise Koh Yao* (℡081 892 4878, @www.theparadise.biz; ❾). The beach here is a picture, and there's a huge pool, an outdoor spa and a climbing wall.

Ao Phang Nga

Embraced by Phuket to the west and the Krabi mainland to the east, the extraordinary seascape of Ao Phang Nga is the Andaman coast's most spectacular natural attraction, fringed with mangroves and dotted with hundreds of sculptural limestone karst outcrops. This is Thailand's own version of Vietnam's world-famous Ha Long bay, reminiscent too of Guilin's scenery in China, and much of it is now preserved as **national park** (entry B200; @www.dnp.go.th /National_park.asp). The bay is thought to have been formed about twelve thousand years ago when a dramatic rise in sea level flooded the summits of mountain ranges, which over millions of years had been eroded by an acidic mixture of atmospheric carbon dioxide and rainwater. Some of these karst islands have been further eroded in such a way that they are now hollow, hiding secret lagoons or *hongs* that can only be accessed at certain tides and only by kayak (see *Ao Phang Nga* colour section). The main *hong* islands are in the **western** and **eastern** bay areas – to the west or east of Ko Yao Noi, which sits roughly midway between Phuket and Krabi. But the most famous scenery is in the **central bay** area, which boasts the biggest concentration of karst islands, and the weirdest rock formations.

Exploring the bay

There are several **departure points** for tours of the bay and several ways of seeing its many attractions. The most rewarding, and generally the most expensive option, is to join a **sea-canoeing** trip (either guided or self-paddle), which enables you to get inside the *hongs* and, unhampered by a grinding engine, also means you've the best chance of spotting the wildlife that lives both inside and around the karst islands. Most sea-canoeing tours use large support boats carrying groups of up to thirty people; they can be arranged from any resort in Phuket, at Khao Lak, at all Krabi beaches and islands, and on Ko Yao Noi (see relevant resort accounts for details and prices), but the itinerary is usually determined by your departure point, with Phuket trips focusing on the western bay and Krabi tours concentrating on the eastern half. Most tours of the central bay are either in large **tour boats** booked out of Phuket or Krabi, which generally feature snorkelling and beach stops rather than kayaking, or in inexpensive, small-group **longtail boats** that depart from Phang Nga town, Phuket and Ko Yao Noi. The bay is very popular so be prepared for crowds at almost every stop.

The central bay

On tours of the **central bay**, the standard itinerary follows a circular or figure-of-eight route, passing extraordinary karst silhouettes that change character with the shifting light – in the eerie glow of an early morning mist it can be a breath-taking experience. Some of the formations have nicknames suggested by their weird outlines – like **Khao Machu** (**Marju**), which translates as "Pekinese Rock". Others have titles derived from other attributes – **Tham Nak** (or Nark, meaning Naga Cave) gets its name from the serpentine stalagmites inside; **Ko Thalu** (Pierced Cave) has a tunnel through it; and a close inspection of **Khao Kien** (Painting Rock) reveals a cliff wall decorated with paintings of elephants, monkeys, fish, crabs and hunting weapons, believed to be between three thousand and five thousand years old.

Ao Phang Nga's most celebrated features, however, earned their tag from a movie: the cleft **Khao Ping Gan** (Leaning Rock) and its tapered outcrop **Khao Tapu** (Nail Rock) are better known as **James Bond Island**, having starred as Scaramanga's hideaway in *The Man with the Golden Gun*. Every boat stops off here so tourists can pose in front of the iconic rock – whose narrowing base is a good example of how wave action is shaping the bay; the island crawls with seashell and trinket vendors.

The central bay's other major attraction is **Ko Panyi**, a Muslim village built almost entirely on stilts around the rock that supports the mosque. Nearly all boat tours stop here for lunch, so you're best off avoiding the pricey seafood restaurants around the jetty, and heading instead towards the islanders' foodstalls near the mosque. You can enjoy a more tranquil Ko Panyi experience by joining

▲ Ao Phang Nga

one of the overnight tours from Phang Nga town (see p.389), which include an evening meal and guest-house accommodation on the island – and the chance to watch the sun set and rise over the bay; you can also rent a kayak from the jetty and go exploring yourself.

At some point on your central-bay tour you should pass several small brick **kilns** on the edge of a mangrove swamp, which were once used for producing charcoal from mangrove wood. You'll also be ferried beneath **Tham Lod**, a photogenic archway roofed with stalactites that opens onto spectacular limestone and mangrove vistas.

The western bay: Ko Panak and Ko Hong

The main attraction of **the western bay** is **Ko Panak**, whose limestone cliffs hide secret tunnels to no less than five different **hongs** within its hollowed heart. These are probably Ao Phang Nga's most spectacular hidden worlds, the pitch-black tunnel approaches infested by bats and the bright, roofless *hongs* an entire other world, draped in hanging gardens of lianas and miniature screw pines and busy with cicadas and the occasional family of crab-eating macaques. Western-bay tours also usually take in nearby **Ko Hong** (different from the Ko Hong in the eastern bay), whose exterior walls are coated with encrusting sponges and busy with tiny crabs, while the dark, interior passageways light up with bioluminescent plankton and lead to a series of cave-lagoons.

The eastern bay: Ko Hong, Ao Thalen and Ao Luk

The principal *hong* island in the **eastern bay**, known both as **Ko Hong** and **Ko Lao Bileh**, lies about midway between Krabi's Hat Klong Muang beach and the southeast coast of Ko Yao Noi. The island is fringed by white-sand beaches and exceptionally clear aquamarine waters that make it a popular snorkelling destination. The island's actual *hong* lacks the drama of Ao Phang Nga's best *hongs* because it's not fully enclosed or accessed via dark tunnels as at Ko Panak, but it is pretty, full of starfish, and tidal, so can only be explored at certain times.

The eastern bay's other big attractions are the mangrove-fringed inlets along the mainland coast between Krabi and Phang Nga, particularly around **Ao Luk** and **Ao Thalen** (sometimes Ao Talin or Talane), though the latter can get very crowded with tour groups. Trips around here take you through complex networks of channels that weave through the mangrove swamps, between fissures in the limestone cliffs, beneath karst outcrops and into the occasional cave. Many of these passageways are *hongs*, isolated havens that might be up to 2km long, all but cut off from the main bay and accessible only at certain tides. The **Ban Bor Tor** (or Ban Bho Tho) area of Ao Luk bay is especially known for **Tham Lod**, a long tunnel hung with stalagmites and stalactites whose entrance is obscured by vines, and for nearby **Tham Phi Hua Toe**, whose walls display around a hundred prehistoric cave-paintings, as well as some interestingly twisted stalactite formations.

Phang Nga town and around

Friendly if unexciting little **PHANG NGA TOWN**, beautifully located under looming limestone cliffs edged with palm groves midway between Phuket and Krabi, serves mainly as a point from which to organize budget longtail trips around the spectacular karst islands of Ao Phang Nga (see *Ao Phang Nga* colour section). But there are also several caves and waterfalls nearby, accessible either on cheap tours run by every Phang Nga tour operator, or by motorbike, and you can also arrange trips to Ko Similan and Ko Surin.

Arrival and information

Phang Nga has good **bus** connections: all Krabi-bound services from Phuket and Takua Pa make a stop at the bus station (☎076 412014) on Thanon Phetkasem, located towards the northern end of this long, thin town; if you're heading to or from Khao Sok, it's usually fastest to change buses in Takua Pa. There are also useful services from Phang Nga to Surat Thani, with the 10.30am bus going direct to Ko Samui, and to Trang. Taxis from Phang Nga to **Phuket airport** cost B1100, to Khao Lak B1200 and to Khao Sok B1600. The pier for **boats** around Ao Phang Nga, and to Ko Yao Noi, is at Tha Dan, 9km south of town and served by songthaews that pass the bus station (B25).

There's no official **tourist information**, but the several tour operators inside the bus station compound are helpful and will store your baggage for a few hours; they also sell bus and boat tickets.

If you turn right (north) out of the bus station onto Thanon Phetkasem, you'll find **banks**, with exchange counters and ATMs and several **internet** centres. Most other municipal facilities are further south down Thanon Phetkasem: the **police station** (☎076 430390) and immigration office (☎076 412011) are about 500m south of the bus station, off Soi Thungchedi, the **telephone office** is another 100m south of them, and Phang Nga Hospital (☎076 412034) and the **post office** are over 2km south of the bus station.

Accommodation

Phang Nga's best budget **hotels** are within 250m of the bus station, on the bus station side of Thanon Phetkasem. First up, on the right-hand side as you turn right out of the bus station, is *Phang Nga Guest House* at no. 99/1 (☎076 411358; fan ❷, air-con ❸–❹), which has clean and comfortable en-suite rooms, though few have anything but a brick-wall view. The old-style, fastidiously maintained *Thawisuk Hotel* at no. 77 (☎076 412100; fan ❶, air-con ❸) has very clean and bright fan rooms, a couple of huge air-con options, and a rooftop terrace. The best accommodation in town is at *Phang Nga Inn* (☎076 411963, ✉phang-ngainn@hotmail.com; ❸–❹), a converted family home that's clearly signed to the left of the bus station, about 250m away, at 2/2 Soi Lohakji, just off Thanon Phetkasem. Its fourteen rooms have beautiful polished wood floors and attractive furnishings and are equipped with air-con, hot water, wi-fi and TVs; a couple have no windows, however.

Tours of Ao Phang Nga

The most popular budget tours of Ao Phang Nga are the **longtail-boat trips** run by tour operators based inside Phang Nga bus station. Competition between these outfits is fierce and the itineraries they offer are almost identical (see p.387), so it's best to get recommendations from other tourists fresh from a bay trip, especially as reputations fluctuate with every change of staff. To date the one that's remained most constant is Mr Kean Tour (☎076 430619); next door but one is Sayan Tour (☎076 430348, ⓦwww.sayantour.com). Both offer half-day tours of the bay (daily at about 8.30am & 2pm; 3–4hr) costing B500 per person (minimum four people), as well as full-day extensions, which last until 4pm and cost B800, including lunch; take the 8.30am tour to avoid seeing the bay at its most crowded. All tours include a chance to swim in the bay, and most offer the option of an hour's canoeing around Ko Thalu as well, for an extra B300.

All tour operators also offer the chance to **stay** overnight at their own guest house on **Ko Panyi**. This can be tacked onto the half- or full-day tour for an extra B250 (departures at 8am, 2pm & 4pm); dinner, accommodation, and morning coffee are included in the price. In 2010 Mr Kean will also offer an interesting-sounding alternative overnight programme on his home island of **Ban Mai Phai**, a much less commercial version of Ko Panyi; the B1200 fee should include food and accommodation, plus cycle and kayak use and the chance to trek and go rock-climbing.

Around Phang Nga town

One of the most famous caves near Phang Nga town is **Tham Phung Chang**, or **Elephant Belly Cave**, a natural 1200-metre-long tunnel through the massive 800-metre-high wooded cliff that towers over the Provincial Hall, about 4km west of the town centre. With a bit of imagination, the cliff's outline resembles a kneeling elephant, and the hollow interior is, of course, its belly. It's possible to travel through the elephant's belly to the other side of the cliff and back on organized two-hour excursions that involve wading, rafting and canoeing along the freshwater stream, Khlong Tham, that has eroded the channel. Any Phang Nga tour operator can arrange this for you, or you can organize it yourself at the desk in the car park in front of the cliff (afternoons are quieter) for B500. To get to the cave entrance yourself, exit Phang Nga along the Phuket–Krabi highway and watch for signs – and a large statue of an elephant – on the north side of the road, before the highway forks right for Phuket and left for Krabi.

Another quite popular local attraction is **Sa Nang Manora Forest Park** (free entry), 9km north of the bus station, with a hiking trail plus several water-falls with swimmable pools. Tour agencies will take you there for about B350; with your own transport, continue north through town along Thanon Phetkasem for about 5km, until you pick up signs for the park.

Eating

For **eating**, locals rate *Duang* as the best Thai food in town; it's been going thirty years and serves especially good *kaeng som* (sour and very spicy fish curry) from its tiny premises (unsigned in English) across the road from the bus station, between the Kaisorn (Thai Farmers) and Bangkok banks. *Bismilla* (Sat–Thurs 8.30am–10pm), left about 100m from the bus station at no. 247, has an English menu and does a reasonable if pricey range of beef, chicken and shrimp dishes (B80–120) as well as Western breakfasts. There's also a basic Thai vegetarian canteen (*raan ahaan jeh*; daily 6.30am until about 2pm), about 50m further on. For a great Thai breakfast, go left 20m from the bus station and cross the road to find the corner coffee shop *Kafeh* (no English sign but look for the picture of a coffee cup; daily 6am–8pm) at 180/2 Thanon Phetkasem, across from Soi Langkai. Fill your tray with assorted Thai *khanom* at B5 apiece – banana-leaf parcels of sticky rice laced with sweet coconut milk and stuffed with banana, mango or other delights – then order from the selection of hot and cold coffees and watch Thai breakfast TV with everyone else.

Krabi town and around

The estuarine town of **KRABI** is both provincial capital and major hub for onward travel to some of the region's most popular islands and beaches, including Ko Phi Phi, Ko Lanta, Ao Nang, Klong Muang and Laem Phra Nang (Railay). So efficient are the transport links that you don't really need to stop here, but it also makes an appealing base, strung out along the west bank of the Krabi estuary, with mangrove-lined shorelines to the east, craggy limestone outcrops on every horizon, and plenty of guest houses. The beaches of **Ao Nang** (p.398) and **Railay** (p.404) are both within 45 minutes of town, and other nearby attractions include the **mangrove swamps** and **Ko Klang** peninsula across the estuary, the dramatically sited Tiger Cave Temple at **Wat Tham Seua** and **Khao Phanom Bencha National Park**. For details of organized **day-trips in the Krabi area**, including snorkelling and kayaking excursions, see the box on p.400.

Krabi is at its busiest during high season, from November to February, a period that officially begins with the annual **Krabi Berk Fah Andaman festival**, a week of festivities featuring parades and outdoor concerts, and climaxes at Loy Krathong, the nationwide festival celebrated in late October or early November.

Arrival

Krabi International **airport** (℡075 636541-2) is just off Highway 4, 18km east of Krabi town, 35km from Ao Nang, and served by international Air Asia **flights** from Kuala Lumpur and by domestic flights from Bangkok with Thai Airways and Air Asia, and from Ko Samui with Bangkok Airways. An airport shuttle bus runs to Krabi town at B100 per person and Ao Nang for B150, or there are fixed-price taxis at B350 per car to Krabi town and port and B600–900 to Ao Nang (30min) and Klong Muang. For car rental see p.395.

Numerous long-distance buses run to Krabi's **bus terminal**, which is 5km north of the town centre in the suburb of Talat Khao, beside Highway 4. A frequent songthaew service shuttles between the bus station and Thanon Maharat in the town centre, or a motorbike taxi will cost you B50. Air-con and VIP **buses** from Bangkok depart from the capital's Southern Bus Terminal,

Moving on from Krabi

Onward tickets are best bought through Krabi town tour agents, who keep current timetables. For details of songthaew transport to local beaches and nearby attractions, see opposite.

By air

Any hotel or travel agent can arrange transport to Krabi **airport**: taxis cost B350 per car or there's a shuttle bus timed for all departing flights at B100 per person. For local airline office phone numbers see p.395.

By ferry and longtail

Ferries to Ko Phi Phi, Ko Lanta and Ko Jum leave from the airport-style terminal at **Krabi Passenger Port** (sometimes referred to as Tha Khlong Jilad; ☏075 620052), a couple of kilometres southwest of Krabi town centre (if staying in Ao Nang, however, see p.399 for ferries from there, which also run to Phuket). Ferry tickets bought from tour operators in town should include a free transfer to Krabi Passenger Port, though any Ao Nang-bound songthaew will also drop you there on request (about 10min). At the time of writing, ferries **to Ko Phi Phi** depart daily at 10am and 3pm (2hr; B450), with extra services at 9am and 1pm during peak periods. Ferries **to Ko Lanta**, via **Ko Jum**, only run from mid-October to mid-May, departing at 11am (2hr 30min; B450); during the rest of the year, or if you miss the ferry, you need to go by minivan or songthaew (see below).

Longtail boats for **East Railay** on Laem Phra Nang (45min; B1500 per boat or B150 per person if there are 8–10 passengers) leave on demand from the town-centre piers at Tha Chao Fa on Thanon Kong Ka and nearby on Thanon Utrakit.

Boats **to Ko Yao Noi** leave from the pier at Ao Thalen, which is 33km northwest of Krabi town and served by songthaews that depart from near the 7-Eleven on Thanon Maharat (see p.382).

By bus and minivan

Government buses to all major destinations depart from the **bus terminal**, 5km out of town in Talat Kao (☏075 611804), which is served by frequent songthaews from the town centre.

Several **private companies** offer supplementary bus services to some of the same destinations, tickets for which are sold by Krabi tour agents. For long-distance services, for example to Bangkok, government buses have a better, safer, more reliable reputation (see p.30); this particularly applies to private buses that go direct to Bangkok's Khao San Road. But useful private **minivan** services include those to **Surat Thani**, which depart from Maharat Soi 5 (hourly 7.30am–4.30pm; 2hr; B150), and to **Nakhon Si Thammarat**, which leave from Thanon Utrakit, across from the TAT office (approximately hourly 7.30am–4pm; 3hr; B180), as well as to **Penang** (2 daily; 9hr; B750) and **Langkawi** (daily; 11hr; B800). Tour agents also sell combination bus and train tickets **to Bangkok** via Surat Thani and through tickets to Ko Samui and Ko Pha Ngan.

Air-con **minivans to Ko Lanta** depart year-round from a shop on Thanon Maharat Soi 6 (hourly 7am–5pm; 2hr; B200–300 depending on drop-off point on Ko Lanta).

mainly in the late afternoon or evening, and take about twelve hours to reach Krabi; see p.30 for warnings about the private buses direct from Thanon Khao San. A more comfortable alternative is to take the overnight **train** from Bangkok to Surat Thani and then change on to one of the frequent air-con buses or minivans to Krabi (hourly; 2hr). There are also frequent bus services from Phuket, Phang Nga, Takua Pa (for Khao Sok) and Trang.

Information

Krabi's **TAT office** (daily 8.30am–4.30pm; ☎075 622163, ✉tatkrabi@tat.or.th) is beside the river on Thanon Utrakit at the northern edge of the town centre. Don't confuse this with the tourist information office run by the ferry operator PP Family, which is down on Thanon Kong Ka; you can get information here, but it may be partisan. Any of the town's numerous **tour agents** will fill you in on the many organized day-trip options (see p.400), sell you bus, boat, train and air tickets, and fix you up with a room on one of the beaches – a service that's worth considering for your first night or two, particularly during the notoriously oversubscribed Christmas–New Year period. Recommended agents include Krabi Friendly Tour & Travel, currently at 13/6 Thanon Chao Fa but likely to relocate to larger premises nearby (☎075 612558, ✿www.krabicarhire.com), and Krabi Brilliant Travel at 2/1 Thanon Kong Ka (☎075 620819, ✉orawan16@hotmail.com).

If you're spending some time in this region, it's worth buying a copy of *Krabi: Caught in the Spell – A Guide to Thailand's Enchanted Province*, expat environmentalist Thom Henley's lively and opinionated **book** about Krabi people, islands and traditions (see p.485).

Local transport

Most of the public **songthaew** services to local beaches, towns and attractions leave from outside the 7-Eleven just south of the Soi 8 intersection on Thanon Maharat (see map, p.391); they usually circulate around town and along Thanon Utrakit before heading out. Unless otherwise stated, most run at least twice an hour from dawn till noon, and then less frequently until dusk. Useful destinations include **Ao Nang**, via Krabi Passenger Port on request, and **Klong Muang**; and, via the bus station, **Ao Thalen** (5 daily), **Nua Klong** and **Ao Luk**.

Accommodation

During the busiest season, from December to February, it's worth reserving **accommodation** ahead if you can.

Chan-Cha-Lay 55 Thanon Utrakit ☎075 620952, ✿www.chanchalay.com. With its stylish blue-and-white theme throughout, funky bathrooms, white-painted wooden furniture and blue shutters, this is the most charming and arty place to stay in Krabi. The en suites in the garden come with fan or air-con and are by far the nicest option; rooms in the main building share bathrooms and some don't have windows. Shared bathroom ➋, en suite fan ➌, air-con ➍

Hello KR Mansion 52/1 Thanon Chao Fa ☎075 612761, ✉chaina_ans@hotmail.com. There are lots of rooms at this traveller-oriented five-storey hotel so it's a good place to try during busy periods.

Choose between pretty decent fan and air-con rooms, with or without private bathroom; the uppermost ones have panoramic views. Also has a rooftop bar, internet access and wi-fi downstairs, and motorbike rental. Fan ➊, en suite ➋, air-con ➌

K Guest House 15–25 Thanon Chao Fa ☎075 623166, ✿www.krabidir.com /kguesthouse. Deservedly popular and well run, in a peaceful but central spot, this long, timber-clad row house has attractive upstairs rooms with wooden floors, panelled walls and streetside balconies. Also offers some cheaper rooms with shared bathroom downstairs and at the back. Shared bathroom ➋, en suite ➌, air-con ➍

Krabi River Hotel 73/1 Thanon Kong Ka ☏075 612321, ⓦwww.krabiriverhotel.com. Occupying a scenic spot beside the estuary on the southern edge of Krabi town, a few minutes' walk south of Tha Chao Fa pier, this place offers high-standard air-con rooms, the best of which have big river-view balconies; the smaller, cheaper ones look onto the wall of the adjacent hotel. There's riverside eating area too. ④, river view ⑤

Kyo Ngean ("Nern") Chao Fa Mansion 2 25/1 Thanon Chao Fa, ☏075 621111, ⓔkyo-ngean@hotmail.com. Great-value little mansion-style hotel with very clean and well-appointed rooms, all of them with air-con, TVs, free wi-fi, fridge, duvets, hot water and balconies; some on the upper floors have long-range river views. Staff are friendly but don't speak much English. ④

Lipstic 20–22 Soi 2, Thanon Maharat ☏075 612392, ⓔkayanchalee@hotmail.com. Good

budget option above an Italian restaurant but tucked away off the street. Rooms are simple but well priced; some have windows and others have private bathrooms, but only the air-con ones have both. Fan ①, air-con ③

Maritime Park and Spa Resort 2km north of town off Thanon Utrakit ☏075 620028, ⓦwww .maritimeparkandspa.com. Beautifully located upper-end hotel, set beside the limestone karsts and mangroves of the Krabi River. Rooms are a little old fashioned but have fine views over the extensive landscape grounds and lake. Has a big pool and a spa, and shuttles into Krabi town and Ao Nang. ⑧–⑨

Swallow 31 Soi 4, Thanon Maharat ☏075 612464. Tiny six-roomed guest house that's kept spotlessly clean and is a good budget option. All rooms have windows and fans; the cheapest share bathrooms. No advance booking. Shared bathroom ①, en suite ②

The Town

Krabi town has no unmissable sights, but is small enough for a pleasant stroll around its main landmarks. Its chief attraction is its setting and a good way to appreciate this is to follow the paved **riverside walkway** down to the fishing port, about 800m south of Tha Chao Fa; several hotels capitalize on the views here, across to mangrove-ringed Ko Klang, and towards the southern end the walkway borders the municipal Thara Park.

Inland, in the centre of town, you can't fail to notice the bizarre sculptures of hulking **anthropoid apes** clutching two sets of traffic lights apiece at the Thanon Maharat/Soi 10 crossroads. They are meant to represent Krabi's most famous ancestors, the tailless *Siamopithecus oceanus*, whose forty-million-year-old remains were found in a lignite mine in the south of the province and are believed by scientists to be among the earliest examples worldwide of the ape-to-human evolutionary process.

It's also hard to miss the striking white walls of the minimalist new bot at the town-centre temple, **Wat Kaew Korawaram** (Grovaram), approached via a grand naga staircase west off Thanon Maharat, opposite Soi 6. The interior murals depict traditional scenes, including Jataka episodes from the lives of the Buddha, but are spiced up with some modern twists – including warring hairy foreigners on either side of the door.

Just across Thanon Isara from Wat Kaew Korawaram's extensive compound, **Krabi Museum of Contemporary Art** (Tues–Sat 10am–1pm & 2–5pm, Sun 11am–1pm & 2–4.30pm; free) stages changing exhibitions of modern paintings by artists from the Krabi area and beyond.

Eating

Krabi has plenty of traveller-oriented **restaurants**, but there's also inexpensive al fresco dining at the **night markets** on riverside Thanon Kong Ka and on Maharat Soi 10. The **Walking Street night bazaar** on Soi 8 (Fri, Sat & Sun 5–10pm) also brims with excellent foodstalls, as well as an entertainments stage and trinket and craft stalls.

Bai Toey Next to *Thara Guesthouse* on Thanon Kong Ka. Good place for a sundowner with pleasing river views and great seafood, especially spicy mussels salad. Most dishes B60–180.

Good Dream 83 Thanon Utrakit. A great place for breakfast: mega fry-ups (B170), continental sets, muesli and fruit and a great deal more, all served with fresh coffee. There's free wi-fi and internet access for customers too.

Hong Ming Vegetarian Food Thanon Pruksa Uthit. Typical unpretentious Chinese-Thai veggie café serving meat-substitute curries and stir-fries at B25–30 for two servings over rice. Mon–Sat 9am–5pm.

Ko Tung 36 Thanon Kong Ka. Though it looks nothing much, this little Thai restaurant is always packed with locals and tourists savouring the excellent, good-value, southern-style seafood. Special highlights include the sweet mussels (*hawy wan*), baked crab, and mushroom, long bean and shrimp *yam* salads. Most dishes B60–80.

May and Mark Soi 2 Thanon Maharat. Early hours, home-baked bread, fresh coffee and full-English fry-ups make this a popular spot for breakfast. Also does tacos, sandwiches, cheese and tuna melts (B160) and pizzas. Daily 6.30am–9.30pm.

Muslim Restaurant Thanon Pruksa Uthit. Filling rotis (flat fried breads) served with a choice of curry sauces, from B15. Daily 7am–7pm.

Pizzeria Firenze Thanon Kong Ka. Authentic Italian dishes, including twenty different thin-crust pizzas (from B150), pastas, ice creams, tiramisu and imported wines. Daily 11am–10pm.

Ruen Mai About 2km north of the town centre at 315/5 Thanon Maharat. Popular with locals and well regarded, this inviting, artfully planted garden restaurant is well worth making the effort to get to. Among the many highlights of its mostly Thai menu (B60–180), standouts include the perfectly spiced *tom yam kung* with satisfyingly large prawns, juicy deep-fried ribs, and fried butterfish with tamarind and ginger. Daily 11am–9pm.

Listings

Airlines Local offices are all based at the airport: Air Asia ☎075 701 5514; Bangkok Airways ☎075 701608–9; Thai Airways ☎075 701591–3.

Bookshops The Books, next to Vogue Department Store on Thanon Maharat, is good for new English-language books, and the well-stocked Pakarang on Thanon Utrakit buys and sells secondhand books.

Car rental Budget (☎075 636171, ⓦwww.budget.co.th) and Avis (☎075 691941, ⓦavisthailand.com) have desks at the airport, or try Krabi Friendly in town (☎075 612558, ⓦwww.krabicarhire.com; see p.393).

Hospitals Krabi Hospital is about 1km north of the town centre at 325 Thanon Utrakit (☎075 611202) and also has dental facilities, but the

better hospital is considered to be the private Muslim hospital, Jariyatham Ruam Phet Hospital (☎075 611223), which is about 3km north of town at 514 Thanon Utrakit and has English-speaking staff.

Immigration office Currently on Thanon Utrakit (Mon–Fri 8.30am–4.30pm; ☎075 611097) but may move to Krabi Passenger Port.

Police For all emergencies, call the tourist police on the free, 24hr phone line ☎1155, or contact the local branch of the tourist police in Ao Nang on ☎075 637208. Krabi police station is at the southern end of Thanon Utrakit ☎075 611222.

Telephones The CAT phone office is about 2km north of the town centre on Thanon Utrakit (Mon–Fri 8am–8pm, Sat & Sun 8.30am–4.30pm).

Mangrove tours and Ko Klang

A boat trip through the eerily scenic **mangrove**-lined channels of the Krabi estuary is a fun way to gain a different perspective on the area. As well as a close-up view of the weird creatures that inhabit the swamps (see *Ao Phang Nga* colour section), you'll get to visit a riverside cave or two and can choose whether or not to stop on the Ko Klang peninsula. **Tours** are best organized directly with the longtail boatmen who hang around Krabi's two piers (B500 per boat per hr), but can also be arranged through most tour agents.

The estuary's most famous features are the twin limestone outcrops known as **Khao Kanab Nam**, which rise a hundred metres above the water from opposite sides of the Krabi River near the *Maritime Park and Spa Resort* and are so distinctive that they've become the symbol of Krabi. One of the twin karsts hides caves, which can be explored – many skeletons have been found here over the centuries, thought to be those of immigrants who got stranded by a flood before reaching the mainland.

Ko Klang

Most of Krabi's longtail boatmen come from **Ko Klang**, the mangrove-encircled peninsula just across the channel from Tha Chao Fa and Tha Thara Park. On a two-hour mangrove tour you can choose to stop off on the peninsula for a visit, or you can go there yourself, on one of the public longtail **boats** that shuttle across throughout the day, both from Tha Chao Fa (B20; 10min) and Tha Thara Park (B20; 3min). You can also stay there in Ban Ko Klang as part of a **homestay** programme, which features batik-making, rice-farming and trips to local islands, and can be booked locally through the English-speaking co-ordinator Khun Supranee (☏089 475 0495) or in advance as part of a package with Tell Tale Travel (ⓦ www.telltaletravel.co.uk).

The predominantly Muslim peninsula is home to three small **villages** housing a total of around four thousand people, most of whom earn their living from tourism and fishing. The island is no great beauty but therein lies its charm, offering the chance to experience a little of typical southern-Thai life. The homestays have bicycles and motorbikes for rent or you can take your own over on the Tha Thara Park longtail; there's about 12km of paved road on the island. You can swim off Ko Klang's long, wild southwestern **beach**, from where you also get an excellent view of the distinctive profiles of all the famous local **islands** – Laem Phra Nang (30min boat ride away), Ko Poda (45min), Bamboo Island, Ko Phi Phi (2hr) and Ko Jum; any Ko Klang boatman will take you out there for the same price as from Krabi town.

Wat Tham Seua and Khao Phanom Bencha

Spectacularly situated amid limestone cliffs within a tropical forest, **Wat Tham Seua** (Tiger Cave Temple) is a famous meditation temple of caves, wooded trails and panoramic viewpoints, about 10km northeast of Krabi town. Infrequent **songthaews** from Krabi town go as far as Nua Klong (20min; B20), from where you'll need to either take a motorbike taxi or walk the final 2km. Bear in mind that as Wat Tham Seua is a working monastery, visitors are required to wear respectable dress (no shorts or sleeveless tops for men or women).

Wat Tham Seua's abbot is a renowned teacher of Vipassana meditation, and some of his educational tools are displayed in the main **bot**, on the left under the cliff overhang, in the main temple compound. Though these close-up photos of human entrails and internal organs may seem shockingly unorthodox, they are there as reminders of the impermanence of the body, a fundamental tenet of Buddhist philosophy; the human skulls and skeletons dotted around the rest of the compound serve the same purpose. Beyond the bot, follow the path past the nuns' quarters to reach the pair of steep **staircases** that scale the 600-metre-high cliffside. The first staircase is long (1272 steps) and very steep,

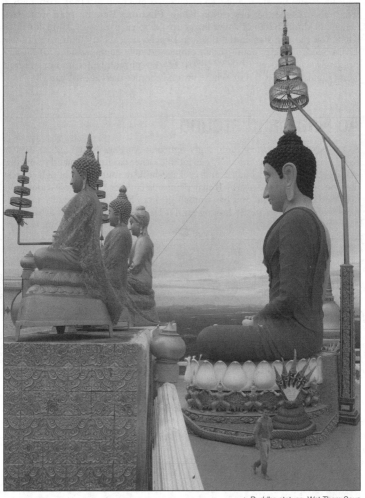

▲ Buddha statues, Wat Tham Seua

and takes about an hour to climb, but the vista from the summit is quite spectacular, affording fabulous views over the limestone outcrops and out to the islands beyond. There's a huge seated Buddha image and chedi at the top, and a few monks' cells hidden among the trees. The second staircase, next to the large statue of the Chinese Goddess of Mercy, Kuan Im, takes you on a less arduous route down into a deep dell encircled by high limestone walls. Here the monks have built themselves self-sufficient meditation cells (*kuti*) in and around the rocky crannies, linked by paths through the lush ravine: if you continue along the main path you'll eventually find yourself back where you began, at the foot of the staircase. The valley is home to squirrels and monkeys as well as a pair of remarkable trees with overground **buttress roots** over 10m high.

With your own transport, you could combine a visit to Wat Tham Seua with a meander around the scenic backroads and a plunge into **Huay Toh Falls**, a five-tiered cascade that lies within **Khao Phanom Bencha National Park** (dawn till dusk; B200; ⓦwww.dnp.go.th/National_park.asp), 25km north of Krabi. You can also **stay** in the Phanom Bencha area, about 10km north of Wat Tham Seua, in the tranquil garden cabins and fully equipped tents of *Phanom Bencha Mountain Resort* (☎075 660501, ⓦwww.phanombenchamountainresort .com; cabins ❹, tents B300), whose grounds border the national park.

Ao Nang and around

AO NANG (sometimes confusingly signed as Ao Phra Nang), 22km west of Krabi town, is a busy, continually expanding, rather faceless mainland resort that mainly caters for mid-budget and package-holiday tourists. Although it lacks the fine beaches of the nearby Railay peninsula (an easy 10min boat-ride away), it is less claustrophobic, and has a much greater choice of restaurants and bars, masses of shopping (mostly beachwear, DVDs and souvenirs), plus a wealth of

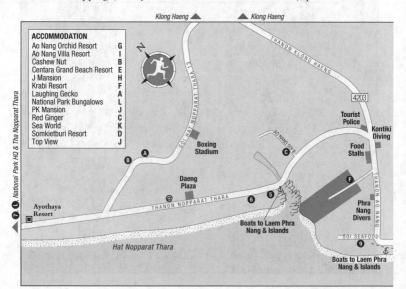

dive shops, day-tripping and snorkelling possibilities and other typical resort facilities. Adjacent **Hat Nopparat Thara**, part of which comes under the protection of a national marine park, is prettier, and divided into two separate beaches by a khlong. The uncrowded, two-kilometre-long **eastern beach** is effectively linked to Ao Nang by a conurbation of accommodation and shops, but the **western beach**, sometimes known as **Hat Ton Son**, across the khlong, is an altogether quieter and more beautiful little enclave, accessible only via longtail or a circuitous back road. Fifteen kilometres drive west of Ao Nang, **Hat Klong Muang** is no great shakes as a beach but does have some attractive four- and five-star accommodation.

Arrival, transport and information

Ao Nang has no proper transport terminals of its own so most long-distance journeys entail going **via Krabi town** (see p.391). The cheapest onward connection **to Ao Nang** is by **songthaews**, which run regularly throughout the day from Krabi town centre, ferry port and bus station (every 10min; 45min; B50) and pass eastern Nopparat Thara en route. Alight at the Nopparat Thara national park T-Junction and car park for longtails across the narrow khlong **to the western beach** (B20–50) or, with your own transport, follow the Klong Muang road until signs direct you off it. There's also a songthaew service from Krabi town **to Klong Muang**. Taxis charge about B500 from Krabi to Ao Nang.

Frequent longtail boats shuttle back and forth from Ao Nang's central beach-front to West Railay and Ao Ton Sai on **Laem Phra Nang**, departing when full (10min; B80, or B100 plus after dark), while from November to May there's a daily ferry service from Tha Nopparat Thara, near the national park visitors' centre, to **Ko Phi Phi Don** (2hr 30min), **Ko Lanta** (2hr 30min) and **Phuket** (3hr); transfers from Ao Nang hotels are included in the ticket price. The Krabi **songthaews** are useful for nipping between Ao Nang, Hat Nopparat Thara and town; **motorbikes** and **jeeps** are available for rent throughout the resort; and there are **kayaks** on the beach in front of *The Last Café* (B100–150 per hr),

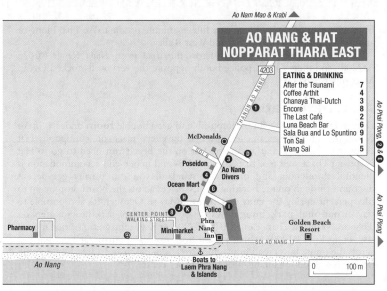

Ao Nam Mao & Krabi ▲

AO NANG & HAT NOPPARAT THARA EAST

4203

EATING & DRINKING

After the Tsunami	7
Coffee Arthit	4
Chanaya Thai-Dutch	3
Encore	8
The Last Café	2
Luna Beach Bar	6
Sala Bua and Lo Spuntino	9
Ton Sai	1
Wang Sai	5

THANON AO NANG

Ao Phai Plong ② & ⑤ ▲

Ao Phai Plong ▲

McDonalds

SOI 8

Poseidon

Ao Nang Divers

Ocean Mart

Police

CENTER POINT WALKING STREET

Phra Nang Inn

Pharmacy

Minimarket

Golden Beach Resort

@

SOI AO NANG 17

Boats to Laem Phra Nang & Islands

Ao Nang

0   100 m

Snorkelling and other day-trips around Krabi

Any tour agent in Krabi town, Ao Nang, Klong Muang or Railay can set you up on these **snorkelling** and other **day-trips**; prices usually include transport from your accommodation.

Multi-island snorkelling trips

By far the most popular organized outings from Krabi, Ao Nang and Laem Phra Nang are the **snorkelling trips** to nearby islands. The main **islands** in question are Ko Poda, Ko Tub and Chicken Island, all of them less than half an hour's longtail ride from Ao Nang or Railay. There are various permutations, offered by numerous companies, including the number of islands you visit (usually three, four or five) and whether you go in a longtail boat or speedboat, but in all cases you should be prepared to share the experience with dozens, even hundreds of others, because pretty much everyone congregates at the same spots. It's a lot more fun than it sounds though – so long as you're not expecting a solitary experience.

One of the best and cheapest **tours** is the four-island longtail trip run by Green Planet (℡075 637488); it's professionally run, uses 22-person boats, and is a bargain at B450 including national park entry fee, packed lunch and snorkel set. The more private alternative is to organize your own boat trip with the **longtail boatmen** on Ao Nang waterfront. Their prices are fixed, but don't include snorkelling equipment, lunch or the B100 national park fee: for the return trip to either Ko Poda, Ko Tub or Chicken Island (8am–4pm), they charge B300 per person, minimum six people; for Ko Hong (see p.388) or Bamboo Island (near Ko Phi Phi; see p.412) it's B1700/3800 per boat per half/full day. Krabi town is quite a bit further from the islands so its boatmen charge B500 per hour per boat.

From some angles, one of the pinnacles on **Chicken Island** does indeed look like the scrawny neck and beaky head of a chicken. There's decent snorkelling off its coast, with a fair range of reef fish and quite a lot of giant clams, though most of the reef is either bleached or dead. Its dazzlingly white-sand northeastern shore, which has a food stall, toilets and kayak rental, is connected to the islets of **Ko Tup** by a sandbank, which is walkable at low tide – quite a striking sight as you arrive to see

from where, in calm seas, it's an easy fifteen-minute paddle to Ao Phai Plong or about 45 minutes to Ao Ton Sai and West Railay.

The **tourist police** are based across the road from *Krabi Resort* (℡075 637208), and there's also a police booth opposite the very well-stocked Ocean Mart supermarket.

Accommodation

During high season, it's almost impossible to get a double **room** under ➍ in Ao Nang, though there is one exceptional travellers' place on contiguous Hat Nopparat Thara east. For a bamboo hut on the beach you need to go to Hat Nopparat Thara west (see map, p.396). Mid- and upper-end accommodation is plentiful throughout and of a high standard; you can usually get decent discounts through online booking agents. Prices across the board drop by up to fifty percent during the rainy season, from May to October. It's also possible to stay in **national park bungalows** beside the national park headquarters on Thanon Nopparat Thara east (℡075 637200, Ⓦwww.dnp.go.th/National_park .asp; bungalows B1000), which is 2km from Ao Nang's main facilities but just across the (quite busy) road from a nice stretch of beach and a five-minute walk from the seafood restaurants near the visitors' centre.

other visitors seemingly walking on water. Nearby **Ko Poda**, which sits directly in front of the Ao Nang beachfront, is encircled by lovely white-sand beaches and clear turquoise water. There's a restaurant here and plenty of shade under the casuarina trees, so this is the typical lunch stop; sandwich-selling boats dock here too. Though you might get three hundred people lunching on the shore here at any one time, it's big enough to cope. Some itineraries also feature **Ao Phra Nang** and its cave, on the Laem Phra Nang (Railay) peninsula (see p.407), and this is the one to avoid unless you enjoy scrambling for your metre of sand on this overrun little bay.

Activities and day-trips

Cycle rides Half- and full-day rides into the Krabi countryside, or to Khao Phanom Bencha falls or Khlong Tom's Emerald Pool. With Krabi Eco Cycle (℡081 607 4162, Ⓦwww.krabiecocycle.com), from B1000, kids B800 inclusive.

Elephant trekking Nosey Parker's Elephant Trekking (℡075 612258, Ⓦwww.krabidir.com/noseyparkers), 7km north of Ao Nang, has a good reputation. From B800, kids B400 for an hour's trek along the river and elephant bathing.

Horseriding Beach rides from B750 per hour (kids B500), lessons B450 per hour and trips into the countryside from B1800 with Swiss-Thai run Krabi Nature Horse Riding (℡081 085 9627, Ⓦwww.krabi-horse-riding.com) east of Ao Nang at Ao Nam Mao.

Rock-climbing On Ton Sai and Railay (see p.408).

Sea canoeing Guided and self-paddle trips around the spectacular karst islands and secret lagoons of Ao Phang Nga, usually focusing on Ao Luk, Ao Thalen and Ko Hong in the eastern bay (see p.386); B900–2100. Dozens of companies offer this, including the local branch of south Thailand's most famous kayaking outfit, John Gray's Sea Canoe (℡076 528839, Ⓦwww.seacanoe.net), and Sea Kayak Krabi (℡075 630270, Ⓦwww.seakayak-krabi.com).

Thai cookery lessons Krabi Thai Cookery School runs morning and afternoon courses (daily 9am–1pm & 2–6pm; B1300/1000 including transport; ℡081 979 0677, Ⓦwww.thaicookeryschool.net).

Ao Nang and Hat Nopparat Thara east

Inexpensive and moderate

Cashew Nut Soi Hat Nopparat Thara 13 ℡075 637560. Twenty-two good, sturdy en-suite brick and concrete bungalows with fan or air-con ranged around a peaceful garden full of cashew trees 5min walk from Hat Nopparat Thara east. Family-run and peaceful. Price depends on the size. Fan ❹, air-con ❺

J Mansion Off Thanon Ao Nang ℡075 695128, Ⓦwww.jmansionaonang.com. The best-known and most popular of the mini-hotels in Ao Nang's travellers' enclave, this place has large, very good, fan and air-con rooms, all with satellite TVs, safety boxes and wi-fi. Most have high-level views, some of which extend to the green-clad cliffs behind. The rooftop terrace also has a panoramic outlook. ❹–❺

Laughing Gecko Soi Hat Nopparat Thara 13 ℡081 270 5028, Ⓦwww.laughinggecko thailand.com. Perhaps the last of the old-style

bungalows left in the Ao Nang area, this is an easy-going and exceptionally traveller-friendly haven run by a Thai-Canadian couple. Choose from a range of simple bamboo huts set around a garden dotted with cashew trees: the cheapest beds are in a nine-person dorm (B150), or there are private rooms with shared bathrooms, en-suite huts and three-room bamboo houses for five. Also has internet access and nightly all-you-can-eat Thai buffets (B150), with live music. The owners are opening a second guest house in the same style – with swimming pool – under the same name, closer to the national park visitors' centre at Hat Nopparat Thara Soi 4 (see map, p.396). Shared bathroom ❷, en suite ❸, family house ❺

PK Mansion and **Top View** Off Thanon Ao Nang ℡075 637431, Ⓦkrabidir.com/pkmansion. Offering rates similar to its budget-oriented neighbours, *PK Mansion* and its adjacent, slightly pricier, sister hotel, *Top View*, have a range of mostly very good quality rooms, with hot-water bathrooms, fan or air-con, wide balconies (with green or partial sea views), TVs and fridges. Reservations advisable. Fan ❹–❺, air-con ❺–❻

Sea World Off Thanon Ao Nang ☎075 637388, ✉seaworld999@hotmail.com. Sometimes offered at rates slightly cheaper than its neighbours on the backpackers' soi, rooms here have good facilities but can be shabbier than the competition. Most have safety boxes and the choice of fan or air-con; some also enjoy good views, mostly green ones to the karsts inland, though a few look towards the sea. Fan ❸–❹, air-con ❹–❻

Expensive

Ao Nang Orchid Resort 141 Thanon Ao Nang ☎075 638445, ⊛www.aonangorchid-resort.com. This medium-sized but well-appointed hotel is good value for Ao Nang. Choose from rooms in the hotel wing, where the nicest overlook the pool and karst mountains beyond (rather than those with "city" views), or go for stand-alone villas with direct access to the lagoon pool. Interiors are chic and attractive, rooms and bungalows all have decks and safes, many have hardwood floors. Wi-fi in some areas. ❽–❾

Ao Nang Villa Resort 113 Thanon Ao Nang ☎075 637270, ⊛www.aonangvilla.com. A very popular hotel whose grounds run onto the beachfront walkway. The 157 upscale, air-con rooms are contained within several low-rise wings, a few of them enjoying a sea view, but most overlooking the garden or the bigger of the resort's two pools. ❽–❾

Centara Grand Beach Resort and Villas Krabi Ao Phai Plong ☎075 637789, ⊛www.centara hotelsresorts.com. Ao Nang's top hotel has the secluded sandy bay of Ao Phai Plong all to itself, but is just a 20min walk (up and over the cliff) from the resort's shops and restaurants or a few minutes by longtail boat. Designed to sit almost seamlessly against the forested crags behind, there's a lovely green feel here and seaward vistas are also beautiful. Nearly all rooms in the four-storeyed hotel buildings and detached villas have sea views. Interiors are modern and generous with sun-balconies and shaded outdoor daybeds; all have bathtubs, TVs and wi-fi. There's a big pool, a dive centre, gym and spa. ❾

Krabi Resort Ao Nang ☎075 637030, ⊛www .krabiresort.net. Set in a vast tropical garden that runs right down to the western end of Ao Nang beach, this is the oldest resort in Ao Nang, and one of the more old-fashioned. Air-con bungalows are staggered in rows back from the shoreline and are comfortable if not especially contemporary consid-ering the price, though it's about the only place in central Ao Nang where you have the sea right on

your doorstep. It also has more modern luxury villas and rooms in a main, low-rise building. ❽–❾

Red Ginger Ao Nang Soi 8 ☎075 637999, ⊛www.redgingerkrabi.com. Located between the two beaches and a short walk from central Ao Nang shops, this contemporary Sino-Thai hotel has jut 63 rooms, some of them duplexes, set round a saltwater pool. Lines are clean and simple with modern Chinese styling and it all feels bright and upbeat. ❽–❾

Somkietburi Resort Thanon Ao Nang ☎075 637990, ⊛www.somkietburi.com. Guests here enjoy one of the most delightful settings in Ao Nang, with the 26 rooms and swimming pools surrounded by a feral, jungle-style garden that's full of hanging vines and lotus ponds. Rooms are perfectly pleasant but nothing special; all have air-con and TV, and there's a spa. ❼–❽

Hat Nopparat Thara west

Emerald Bungalows ☎081 956 2566. There's some very comfortable accommodation here, in forty big, brightly painted and stylishly furnished en-suite wooden bungalows, widely spaced around a shady shorefront garden and all with at least partial sea views, huge decks, and either fan or air-con. Also has a good restaurant and a bar. Usually closed May–Aug, but phone to check. Fan ❺, air-con ❼

Long Beach Bungalow 600m west from khlong ☎089 777 5853, ✉ampoeiing@gmail.com. Most of the accommodation at this small place is in very simple bamboo huts set round a grassy lawn, with nothing more than a platform bed and a mosquito net (no fans), though some are en suite. Also has a couple more solid seafront rooms. Nightly family-style dinners, cooking classes, snorkelling trips and motorbike rental. ❷–❸

PAN Beach At the westernmost end of the beach, about 700m walk from the khlong ☎089 866 4373, ⊛www.panbeachkrabi.com. Fifteen sturdy, simply furnished wooden bungalows in two sizes and styles, each with screened windows, fans and bathrooms, set just back from the shore around a lawn. Also has motorbikes for rent and organizes local boat trips. ❹

Hat Klong Muang

Sheraton Krabi Beach Resort ☎075 628000, ⊛www.sheraton.com/krabi. Unusually for a top-notch beachfront hotel, the *Sheraton* Krabi does not boast of its sea views because the entire low-rise resort has been built amongst the mangroves and alongside a khlong; the result is refreshingly green and cool – and full of birdsong. The sandy shore – the nicest in Klong Muang – is anyway just a few steps away, accessed via a series of wooden walkways, and there's a seafront lawn for lounging. Rooms are large, sleek and very comfortable; there's a big pool, a spa and water-sports centre, plus, weather permitting, nightly films on the outdoor movie screen. **⑨**

The beaches

Ao Nang's central beach is unexceptional and busy with longtail traffic; the nicer stretch is east beyond *Phra Nang Inn*, accessed by the sidewalk that takes you all the way along the shore to the appropriately named *The Last Café*, a very pleasant spot for a shady drink. En route you'll pass a crowd of two-dozen **massage** huts set out under the trees, charging a standard B300 per hour. Follow the wooden walkway from beyond *The Last Café* and scale the steps up and over the headland to reach, in about ten minutes, the beach at diminutive **Ao Phai Plong**, which is the sole province of the luxurious *Centara Grand* hotel.

Immediately west of Ao Nang, beyond the headland occupied by *Krabi Resort* but reached by simply following the road (on foot or in one of the frequent Krabi-bound songthaews), **Hat Nopparat Thara east** is long and pretty, though the road runs unscreened alongside it. Its eastern hinterland is developing fast with hotels and restaurants, but the other end, close to the T-junction with Route 4202, is the site of the Hat Nopparat Thara – Mu Ko Phi Phi **national park headquarters** and accommodation. Here too is the **tsunami memorial**, *Hold Me Close* by Louise Bourgeois (2005), a broken, roofless, wood-slatted corncob structure enclosing two pairs of hands, joined, prayer like and pleading, extending from a lumpy sea. At low tide it's almost impossible to swim on this beach, but the sands come alive with thousands of starfish and hermit crabs, and the view out towards the islands is glorious; you can walk to the nearest outcrop at low water. The **national park visitor centre** is across Route 4202, beside the khlong and its sheltered marina and jetty, Tha Nopparat Thara, which is the departure point for Ao Nang ferry services to Phuket, Phi Phi and Ko Lanta, as well as for longtails to the western beach. The visitor centre's car park is famous for its **seafood restaurants**, and Krabi residents also like to picnic under the shorefront casuarina trees here.

Hat Nopparat Thara west has a quite different atmosphere from its eastern counterpart: just a handful of small bungalow hotels and a few private residences share its long swathe of peaceful casuarina- and palm-shaded shoreline, making it a great place to escape the crowds and commerce of other Krabi beaches. The views of the karst islands are magnificent, though swimming here is also tide-dependent. Without your own transport you can only get here by longtail across the narrow but deep khlong beside the national park visitor's centre, but with a car or bike you can arrive via the very quiet back road that snakes through the mangroves from the Klong Muang road to the edge of the bungalow properties.

Diving

Ao Nang is Krabi's main centre for **dive shops**, with a dozen or more outlets, the most reputable of which include Kon-Tiki (☏075 637826, ⓦwww.kontiki -thailand.com), Phra Nang Divers (☏075 637064, ⓦwww.phranangdivers .com), and Poseidon (☏075 637263, ⓦwww.poseidon-diving.com), all of whom have a price agreement and mostly offer the same programmes. Diving with Ao Nang operators is possible year-round, with some dive staff claiming that off-season diving is more rewarding, not least because the sites are much less crowded. Most one-day **dive trips** head for the area round Ko Phi Phi and include dives at Shark Point and the "King Cruiser" wreck dive (see p.370) for B3400 including two tanks; the Ko Ha island group, near Ko Lanta, is also popular and costs about the same (see p.428). Two dives in the Ao Nang area – at Ko Poda and Ko Yawasam – average B2700 (B1500 for snorkellers). PADI dive courses start at B5500 for the introductory Discover Scuba day, or B14,900 for the Openwater. The nearest recompression chambers are on Phuket (see p.370); check to see that your dive operator is insured to use one of them. See Basics, p.58, for general information on diving in Thailand.

Eating, drinking and entertainment

Eating and drinking options in Ao Nang are not sophisticated and there are few places that stand out from the crowd. At weekends, locals flock to the **seafood restaurants** in the national park visitors' centre car park on Hat Nopparat Thara, or buy fried chicken from nearby stalls and picnic on mats under the shorefront trees. In central Ao Nang, there are cheap hot-food stalls on the road outside *Krabi Resort*, and handcarts selling Muslim **roti** pancakes (filled with milk, banana or chocolate) pitch up all over the resort. The **bar** scene is mainly focused around Ao Nang Center Point Walking Street, a U-shaped passageway behind the beachfront shops that's packed with makeshift little bars and their flirty staff.

The *muay thai* **boxing** stadium, 2km west out of Ao Nang, near the *Laughing Gecko* guest house on Soi Nopparat Thara 13, stages heavily promoted twice-weekly bouts in high season (Mon & Fri 9pm; B1000).

After the Tsunami National park visitors' centre car park, Hat Nopparat Thara. Hugely popular with locals, expats and visiting Thais for its reasonably priced fresh seafood and shellfish (B60–180). Daily 11am–9pm.

Coffee Arthit Thanon Ao Nang. A really good place for breakfast, with its big menu of set breakfasts including vegetarian full English, a range of breads, croissants and fresh coffees. Daily from 7.30am.

Chanaya Thai-Dutch Thanon Ao Nang. With its fairy lights, trailing plants and wooden tables, this invitingly atmospheric place always gets a good crowd. The menu is mostly European – T-bone steaks done various ways, ostrich steaks, asparagus, ham and cheese bake – and there are tempting set dinners rounded off with Dutch apple pie and cream. Most mains B180; sets from B600.

Encore Ao Nang Centerpoint Walking Street. Nightly live music from 10pm – and a pool table – draws decent-sized crowds to this bar decorated with pictures of rock stars. 4pm–1am.

The Last Café Soi Ao Nang 17. Set under the cliffs on the sand at the far easternmost end of the beach, this is an especially nice spot for a beer at sunset.

Luna Beach Bar Beachside, eastern end of Hat Nopparat Thara. Beach bar with live music and several small bar-beers within the same compound whose main attraction is its late hours: it generally keeps going well after the central Ao Nang bars have shut.

Sala Bua and Lo Spuntino Soi Seafood. Enjoying great sea views especially at sunset, this is a two-in-one restaurant with two chefs. One does the Thai dishes under *Sala Bua*, including excellent *phanaeng* curries and seafood (mostly B120–150), while the other cooks authentic Italian – pizzas from B200, plus tiramisu and sambuca liquors to follow – for *Lo Spuntino*.

Ton Sai 150m north of *McDonalds* on Thanon Ao Nang. Home-style Thai cooking is the calling card at this bamboo-shack family-run restaurant. The curries are delicious, there's plenty of seafood and you can get almost any dish cooked to order. Most mains B60–80.

Wang Sai Beside the bridge at the eastern end of Thanon Nopparat Thara. Large, long-running seafood place right on the beach. Mains B80–200.

Laem Phra Nang: Railay and Ton Sai

Seen from the close quarters of a longtail boat, the combination of sheer limestone cliffs, pure white sand and emerald waters around the **LAEM PHRA NANG** peninsula is spectacular – and would be even more so without the hundreds of other admirers gathered on its four beaches. The peninsula (often known simply as **Railay**) is effectively a tiny island, embraced by impenetrable limestone massifs that make road access impossible – but do offer excellent, world-famous **rock-climbing**; transport is by boat only, from Krabi town or, most commonly, from nearby Ao Nang. It has four beaches within ten minutes' walk of each other: **Ao Phra Nang** graces the southwestern edge, and is flanked by **East and West Railay**, just 500m apart; **Ao Ton Sai** is beyond West Railay, on the other side of a rocky promontory. Almost every patch of buildable land fronting East and West Railay has been taken over by bungalow resorts, and development is creeping up the cliffsides and into the forest behind. But at least high-rises don't feature, and much of the construction is hidden among trees or set amid prettily landscaped gardens. Accommodation is at a premium and not cheap, so the scene on West and East Railay, and Ao Phra Nang, is predominantly holidaymakers on short breaks rather than backpackers. The opposite is true on adjacent Ao Ton Sai, Krabi's main travellers' hub and the heart of the rock-climbing scene.

Arrival and information

Laem Phra Nang is only accessible by **boat** from Krabi town, Ao Nam Mao, Ao Nang and Ko Phi Phi. Longtail boats to Laem Phra Nang depart from the

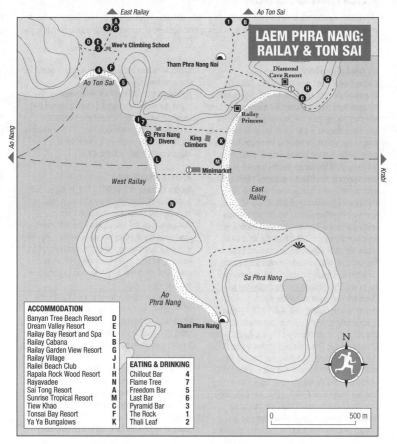

LAEM PHRA NANG: RAILAY & TON SAI

ACCOMMODATION
Banyan Tree Beach Resort	D
Dream Valley Resort	E
Railay Bay Resort and Spa	L
Railay Cabana	B
Railay Garden View Resort	G
Railay Village	J
Railei Beach Club	I
Rapala Rock Wood Resort	H
Rayavadee	N
Sai Tong Resort	A
Sunrise Tropical Resort	M
Tiew Khao	C
Tonsai Bay Resort	F
Ya Ya Bungalows	K

EATING & DRINKING
Chillout Bar	4
Flame Tree	7
Freedom Bar	5
Last Bar	6
Pyramid Bar	3
The Rock	1
Thali Leaf	2

0   500 m

Krabi riverfront (45min; B150 per person, minimum 8 people, or B1500 when chartered), leaving throughout the day as soon as they fill up. Depending on the tide, all Krabi boats land on or off East Railay, so you may have to wade; they do run during the rainy season, but the waves make it a nerve-wracking experience, so you're advised to go via Ao Nang instead. Coming back there are at least five scheduled boats between 9.30am and 5.30pm, and others on demand. **Ao Nang** is much closer to Laem Phra Nang, and longtails run from the beachfront here to West Railay and Ao Ton Sai (10min; B80, or B100 after 6pm) all year round. Boats between Ao Ton Sai and West Railay cost B50. During high season there should also be daily ferries from Ao Nang via West Railay to **Ko Phi Phi** (2hr 30min), **Ko Lanta** (2hr 30min) and **Phuket** (3hr); if not, you'll need to transfer to Ao Nang yourself.

There are tour agencies and shops selling beach essentials on each beach, and you can **change money** at many bungalow operations, though rates can be up to ten percent lower than at the Krabi banks; you'll find ATMs at *Viewpoint Bungalows* on East Railay and at the minimarket behind *Railay Bay*. **Internet access** is widely available.

Accommodation

Because demand is so high, from November to March it's often hard to get a **room** on spec on West or East Railay, though you should have more luck on Ao Ton Sai.

West Railay

Railay Bay Resort and Spa ☎075 622570, ⓦwww.krabi-railaybay.com. There's a huge range of rooms here, on land that runs down to both East and West Railay, plus two swimming pools and a spa. The cheapest are in small, old-style but spruce bungalows, and there are also some comfortable, more modern rooms in a two-storey hotel block, but the pick of the bunch are the private, walled compounds of the "Privacy cottages", with outdoor jacuzzi and a very spacious bedroom. ⑧–⑨
Railay Village Resort and Spa ☎075 622578, ⓦwww.railayvillagekrabi.com. Occupying very pretty gardens in between the two beaches, with nowhere more than 300m from the West Railay shore, the style here is elegant tropical, in white-washed spa villas and pool-access hotel rooms, all roofed in low-impact wooden tiles, with wooden floors and Thai furnishings completing the look. There are two pools and a spa. ⑨
Railei Beach Club ☎086 685 9359, ⓦwww .raileibeachclub.com. Unusual compound of 21 charming fan-cooled private houses, built of wood in idiosyncratic Thai style and rented out by their owners. One-, two- and three-bed houses are available, all well spaced, and there are a couple of cheaper private rooms; most have kitchen facilities and there's wi-fi throughout. The compound is only minimally screened from the beach, so seafront houses get good views but may lack privacy and bear the brunt of the noisy longtail

traffic. Minimum stays of three nights or seven in Dec and Jan. ⑦–⑨
Rayavadee ☎075 620740, ⓦwww.rayavadee .com. The supremely elegant two-storey spiral-shaped pavilions here are set in a beautifully landscaped compound bordering all three beaches. It's all very exclusive – as it should be at a staggering B22,300 a night. ⑨

East Railay

Railay Cabana ☎084 057 7167. In a tree-filled amphitheatre of majestic karst cliffs, a 5min walk from *Princess Resort* or *Diamond Cave Bungalows*, on the track to Ton Sai, this friendly family-run place offers simple bamboo bungalows with thick mattresses, fans and bathrooms. It's a lovely quiet spot, away from the East Railay crassness. Staff can help transport luggage from the pier. ③
Railay Garden View Resort ☎085 888 5143, ⓦwww.railaygardenview.com. This place really stands out for it simple rustic-chic style, great high-level views over the mangroves and sea beyond, and green surrounds in a garden of jackfruit, banana and papaya trees. The twenty fan-cooled bungalows, built from good-quality split–bamboo, are widely spaced and on stilts, with colour-washed cold-water bathrooms, wooden floored bedrooms and decks, and plenty of triangular cushions for lounging. The drawback is that it's up a steep stairway beyond the far north end of East Railay,

accessed via a short walkway beyond *The Last Bar*, about 15min walk from West Railay. ⑤–⑥

Rapala Rock Wood Resort ☏075 622586. Climb a steep flight of stairs to reach the 31 rough-hewn timber huts here, which are among the cheapest on Railay, set in rows around a scruffy garden high above the beach, with some enjoying dramatic karst views from their verandas. The very cheapest rooms are in the handful of basic terraced bamboo huts with shared facilities, but most are in simple bungalows with decent private bathrooms. There's also a nice communal deck among the treetops, and a restaurant that serves Indian food. ③–④

🏃 **Sunrise Tropical Resort** ☏075 622599, ⓦwww.sunrisetropical.com. The most stylish of the affordable hotels on the cape offers just forty rooms, most in elegantly designed air-con bungalows, and some in a couple of two-storey buildings, all with Thai furnishings and generously spacious living areas, set around a landscaped tropical garden with a small pool. Wi-fi throughout. ⑦–⑧

Ya Ya Bungalows ☏075 622593, ⓦyaya-resort.com. This idiosyncratic place has some of the cheapest accommodation on Railay and is built almost entirely of wood, with most of the 86 fan and air-con rooms contained in a series of sturdy, quite well-designed, three-storey wooden buildings. They all have verandas and en-suite bathrooms, but soundproofing is not great and most rooms are quite dark. Fan ④–⑤, air-con ⑦

Ao Ton Sai

Banyan Tree Beach Resort ☏089 470 8532. Built in a line under the trees, the 36 bungalows here come in two types: standard bamboo and wooden versions with mosquito nets and bathrooms, or nicer mint-green clapboard chalets with comfortable beds and good bathrooms. ②–④

Dream Valley Resort ☏089 589 2230, ⓦwww.dreamvalleyresortkrabi.com. The 85 bungalows here are ranged discreetly amongst the trees running far back towards the cliff-face, offering a range of good-quality accommodation in various categories, from split-bamboo huts with fans and bathrooms through to air-conditioned villas, the best of which are the premier accommodation on Ao Ton Sai. Fan ④–⑤, air-con ⑥–⑦

Sai Tong Resort 400m along the track to East Railay ☏081 079 6583. This friendly, good-value little place offers cheap, woven-bamboo huts with nets, fans and bathrooms beside the track, and bigger, more comfy, cute-looking split bamboo ones, also en suite and with nets, fans and proper beds. ②

Tiew Khao 250m along the track to East Railay. The rudimentary bamboo huts here are ranged up the hillside beside the track, with the uppermost ones enjoying fine high-level views of the karst wall beyond. They're the cheapest on Ao Ton Sai: all of them share bathrooms and facilities comprise nothing more than a mattress and a veranda. ①

Tonsai Bay Resort ☏075 660511, ⓦwww.tonsaibay.co.th. With its large, widely spaced and plain but comfortable air-con bungalows, each one boasting huge glass windows and a big deck from which to soak up the pretty location in a grove of trees about 200m back from the shore, this is one of the top places to stay on Ao Ton Sai. The fan options nearer the beach are overpriced and within earshot of the all-night *Freedom Bar*. Fan ⑤, air-con ⑦

The beaches

The loveliest and most popular beach on the cape is **WEST RAILAY**, with its gorgeous white sand, crystal-clear water and impressive karst scenery at every turn. The best of the peninsula's bungalow hotels front this shoreline, and longtail boats from Ao Nang pull in here too, so it gets crowded. Follow any of the tracks inland, through the resort developments, and within a few minutes you reach **EAST RAILAY** on the other coast, whose mangrove swamps and muddy shore make it unsuitable for swimming; boats from Krabi town dock here. Accommodation on this side is a bit cheaper, and there's more variety in price too, though – aside from a couple of gems – it's mostly an uncomfortable mix of uninspired, low-grade developments and unsubtle bars with names like *Skunk* and *Stone*. Depressingly, much of East Railay's hinterland is despoiled by trash and building rubble, but inland it's another story, with a majestic amphitheatre of forested karst turrets just ten minutes' walk away, on the back route to Ao Ton Sai.

Continue south along East Railay's shoreline, past *Sunrise Tropical Resort*, to pick up the walkway to the diminutive, cliff-bound beach at **AO PHRA NANG** (also called **Hat Tham Phra Nang**). Though exceptionally pretty, the bay can be hard to appreciate beneath the trinket sellers and crowds of day-trippers who are deposited here in their hundreds, by boats that pollute the coastal waters. Better to visit before 10am or after 4pm if you can. The walkway from East Railay winds between the super-lux *Rayavadee* hotel and the lip of a massive karst before emerging at the beach beside **Tham Phra Nang**, or **Princess Cave**. The beach and cave, and indeed the peninsula, are named for this princess (*phra nang* means "revered lady"), whom the local fisherfolk believe lives here and controls the fertility of the sea. To encourage large catches, red-tipped wooden phalluses are left as offerings to her at the cave entrance. Buried deep inside the same cliff is **Sa Phra Nang** (**Princess Lagoon**), which is accessible only via a steep 45-minute descent that starts halfway along the walkway. You'll need proper shoes for it, as slippery descents and sharp rocks make it hard in flip-flops or bare feet. After an initial ten-minute clamber, negotiated with the help of ropes, the path forks: go left for a panoramic view over East and West Railay, or right for the lagoon. (For the strong-armed, there's the third option of hauling yourself up ropes to the top of the cliff for a bird's-eye view.) Taking the right-hand fork, you'll pass through the tropical dell dubbed "big tree valley" before eventually descending to the murky lagoon.

The beach at **AO TON SAI**, north across the oyster rocks from West Railay, is not the prettiest, prone to murk and littered with rocks that make it impossible to swim at low tide. But its orange-and-ochre-striped cliffs are magnificently scenic, dripping with curlicues and turrets that tower over a central tree-filled bowl and host scores of challenging rock climbs. Most of the accommodation here is aimed at climbers and travellers, and is well hidden several hundred metres back from the shore, scattered within the remains of a forest and along the track that, beyond *Sai Tong*, takes you to East Railay in about twenty minutes. The vibe here is green and comradely, with climbers doing their thing during the day and partying at the several chilled bars after dark. At low tide you can pick your way over the razor-sharp rocks from West Railay, while at high tide you either need to swim or get a longtail, or walk over the hill from East Railay.

Climbing and kayaking

Ton Sai and Railay are Thailand's biggest **rock-climbing** centres, attracting thousands of experienced and novice climbers every year to the peninsula's seven hundred bolted routes, which range in difficulty from 5a to 8c (see Ⓦwww.railay.com for a full rundown). Of the many climbing **schools** that rent out equipment and lead guided climbs, the most established include King Climbers (Ⓣ075 662096, Ⓦwww.railay.com/railay/climbing/climbing_king _climbers.shtml), at *Ya Ya* on East Railay, and Wee's Climbing School (Ⓦwww .weesclimbingschool.com) on Ton Sai. A typical half-day introduction costs B1000, or B1800 for a full day, and equipment is B2400 per day for two people. If you don't need instruction, King Climbers' *Route Guide* gives you all the route information you need. Unaided over-water climbing on cliffs and outcrops out at sea, known as **deep-water soloing**, with no ropes, bolts or partner, is also becoming a big thing around here and can be arranged through most climbing schools for about B1000.

Kayaking around this area is also very rewarding – you can get to Ao Nang in less than an hour; kayaks cost B200 per hour to rent. For details of kayaking trips around spectacular Ao Phang Nga, and **snorkelling** trips to nearby islands, including Ko Poda and Chicken Island, see the box on p.400. For **diving**, contact the branch of Phra Nang Divers in Flame Tree Plaza on West Railay (Ⓦwww.phranangdivers.com) and see p.412 for information on nearby sites.

Eating and drinking

It's hard to get excited about most of the unexceptional **restaurants** on East and West **Railay**, but *Flame Tree*, on the seafront at West Railay, has a slightly more varied menu than many – including cashew nut salad and mushroom steak – and does a tempting "Thai tapas" set for four (B395 per person) featuring, among other dishes, *tom yam*, fishcakes, *matsaman* curry and bananas in coconut milk. Located in the middle of the spectacular cliff-lined basin on the track to Ton Sai, ten minutes' walk from both East and West Railay, *The Rock* is worth a visit for its views alone, but luckily its food is also good, mostly seafood and Thai curries, and in the reasonable B80–120 range. There's no shortage of traveller-style **bars,** especially on East Railay, with their fire-juggling and chillums; *Last Bar*, at the far end, has a pretty deck jutting out over the water.

On **Ton Sai**, *Pyramid Bar* is busy day and night with climbers scoffing the fresh coffees, tuna and cheese melts, salads and ciabatta sandwiches; it also hosts occasional DJ parties. In the evenings, *Thali Leaf*, opposite *Tiew Khao* on the East Railay track, serves Indian curries and lassies on sumptuous silky cushions. Beachfront *Freedom Bar* and *Chillout Bar* both hold regular all-nighters and full-moon parties.

Ko Phi Phi Don

About 40km south of Krabi, the island of **KO PHI PHI DON** looks breathtakingly handsome as you approach from the sea, its classic arcs of pure white sand framed by dramatic cliffs and lapped by water that's a mouthwatering shade of turquoise. A flat sandy isthmus connects the hilly east and west halves of the island, scalloped into the much photographed symmetrical double bays of Ao Ton Sai and Ao Loh Dalum. The vast majority of the tourist accommodation is squashed in here, as is the island's kicking nightlife, with just a few alternatives scattered along eastern coasts. Phi Phi's few indigenous islanders mostly live in the northeast.

▲ Ao Loh Dalum, Ko Phi Phi Don

KO PHI PHI DON

Ko Yung (Mosquito Island)

Ko Mai Pai (Bamboo Island)

Laem Tong

Chao Lay Village

Ao Loh Lanaa

Camel Island

Ao Nui

Ao Loh Bakao

Hat Pak Nam

Hat Rantee

Viewpoint

Ao Toh Ko

Ao Yongkasem

See Inset map above

Ao Loh Dalum

Ao Ton Sai

Laem Hin

Ao Loh Moodii

Ma Prao

Hat Yao (Long Beach)

Ao Poh

Ao Wang Long

N

0   1 km

▼ Phuket & Ko Phi Phi Leh   ▼ Krabi

TON SAI VILLAGE

Viewpoint ▲

Long Beach ▶

Ao Loh Dalum

Police

Aswindum Boxing Stadium

Phi Phi Hospital

Ao Ton Sai

Laem Hin

EATING & DRINKING	
Carpe Diem	10
Cosmic	5
Garlic 1992	3
Hippies Bar	9
Ibiza Bar	2
Le Grand Bleu	6
Madame Restaurant	4
Mama's	7
Mojito Bar	1
Papaya	5
Pee Pee Bakery	8
Reggae Bar	4
Rolling Stoned	5

ACCOMMODATION	
Ao Poh The Last Paradise	X
Ao Toh Ko Beach Resort	S
Bay View Resort	M
The Beach Resort	W
Gypsy Village	I
Holiday Inn Resort Phi Phi Island	O
Long Beach Bungalows	V
Phi Phi Andaman Legacy	L
Phi Phi Hill Resort	Y
Phi Phi Hotel	H
Ph Phi Inn	G
Phi Phi Island Cabana Hotel	F
Phi Phi Island Village Beach Resort and Spa	P
Phi Phi Natural Resort	N
Phi Phi Paradise Pearl Resort	T
Phi Phi Relax Beach Resort	Q
Phi Phi Villa Resort	K
PP Casita	C
PP Nice Beach Resort	J
Rantee Beach Resort	R
The Rock	E
Tropical Garden	D
US Guest House	B
Viewpoint Bungalows	A
Viking Nature Resort	U

4

SOUTHERN THAILAND: THE ANDAMAN COAST

Such beauty, however, belies the island's turbulent recent history. By the early 1990s, Phi Phi's reputation as a tropical idyll was bringing huge crowds of backpackers to its shores, and the beaches began to lose their looks under the weight of unrestricted development and non-existent infrastructure. The problem worsened after uninhabited little sister island **Ko Phi Phi Leh** – under national marine park protection on account of its lucrative bird's-nest business (see box, p.418) – gained worldwide attention as the location for the movie *The Beach* in 1999, adding day-trippers, package-tourists and big hotels to the mix on Phi Phi Don. Then, in December 2004, the **tsunami** struck (see p.344). As a five-metre-high wave crashed in from the north, over the hotels, restaurants and hundreds of sunbathers on Ao Loh Dalum, a three-metre-high wave from the south hurtled in across the ferry dock and tourist village at Ao Ton Sai. The waves met in the middle, obliterating seventy percent of all buildings on the sandy flats, uprooting scores of trees, and killing two thousand. The rest of the island was barely affected.

Volunteers and donations poured in to help the island back on its feet, and though the rebuild was dogged by much political wrangling, the Phi Phi of today thrives much as it ever did, firmly re-established as the must-see destination on almost any trip to southern Thailand. Unfortunately, few of the pre-tsunami **problems** have been properly resolved – in part because tsunami survivors were desperate to make a new start as fast as they could. The island is now once again floundering under unregulated, unsightly and unsustainable development, with inadequate rubbish disposal and a plague of overpriced accommodation, at its most acute around the Ton Sai–Loh Dalum hub. The noise pollution from the untrammelled outdoor bars and clubs is an additional turn-off for some – though it is a fun place to party, and there are enough more remote escapes for a peaceful stay too.

All boats dock in **Ao Ton Sai**, from where it's a short walk to the main accommodation centres – in **Ton Sai village**, at **Laem Hin**, the next little stretch of sand to the east, and on **Ao Loh Dalum**, the still gorgeous, deeply curved bay across the isthmus. **Hat Yao**, another fine beach just a short boat ride away, is also very popular. To escape the crowds you need to aim for one of the smaller bays further north: **Ao Poh**, **Hat Toh Ko** and **Ao Rantee** are all good for budget breakaways, while **Hat Pak Nam**, **Ao Loh Bakao** and **Laem Tong** are pricier and more luxurious.

Getting to Ko Phi Phi Don

Ferries to Ko Phi Phi Don run year-round from **Krabi** (at least twice daily; currently 10am & 3pm, returning from Phi Phi at 9am & 2pm; 2hr; B450) and **Phuket** (currently 8.30am & 2.30pm, returning from Phi Phi at 9am & 2.30pm; 1hr 30min–2hr 30min; B450–600). Extra services are put on during peak periods, and there's also a high-season speedboat service from Phi Phi to Phuket (5pm; 45min; B800). From November to May, you can also reach Phi Phi by daily ferries from **Ao Nang**, via **West Railay** (departing Ao Nang at 9am, returning from Phi Phi at 3.30pm; 2hr 30min; B400), and from **Ko Lanta Yai** (departing Ko Lanta at 11am and returning from Phi Phi at 9am; 1hr 30min; B450). Tour agents in Phuket, Ao Nang, Krabi town and Ko Lanta all organize snorkelling day-trips to Phi Phi Don and Phi Phi Leh. For longer, overland journeys from Ko Phi Phi, any tour agent in Ton Sai can sell you bus tickets, usually via Krabi town, or train tickets, via Krabi and Surat Thani.

Touts and bungalow staff always meet the ferries; if you've pre-booked **accommodation** your luggage will be transported in a handcart. As demand frequently outstrips supply on Phi Phi, if you haven't made a reservation, it's

Snorkelling, diving and rock-climbing off Ko Phi Phi

Ko Phi Phi and nearby islets have famously varied reefs, which make for excellent and very popular **diving and snorkelling**. There's decent **rock-climbing** here too, though it doesn't compare to Railay.

Snorkelling

There's some great **snorkelling** around Phi Phi's shallow fringing reefs, most rewardingly at strikingly beautiful, uninhabited **Ko Mai Pai (Bamboo Island)**, off Phi Phi Don's northeast coast, where much of the reef lies close to the surface, and at nearby **Ko Yung (Mosquito Island)**, with its spectacular, steep-sided drop. Phi Phi Don has its own worthwhile reefs too, including at west-coast **Ao Yongkasem**, within kayaking distance of Ao Loh Dalum, but the tranquil waters of **Ao Maya** (Maya Bay, *The Beach* beach) on Phi Phi Leh are more famous, and a lot more crowded (see p.418).

Outings to these and other reefs are easily arranged as part of an **organized tour** (B450–800 including equipment) or by **hiring your own longtail** boatman at the pier (B1500/3000 per boat per half/ full-day), the latter far preferable to the largest tour boats, whose groups of forty-plus trippers inundate the reefs. **Overnight camping trips** to Bamboo Island or Maya Bay are a neat way of avoiding the big crowds, offering late-afternoon snorkelling and kayaking rounded off with a barbecue on the beach; they usually depart Phi Phi about 4pm and return the next day at 10am, charging B1900.

Diving

Offering visibility touching 30m, a great diversity of healthy hard and soft corals, and potential encounters with white-tip sharks, moray eels and stingrays, the diving around Ko Phi Phi is the best in the region and the usual destination of dive boats from Ao Nang and Phuket, as well as, of course, from Phi Phi itself. Highlights include the gorgonian sea fans, barracudas, manta rays and even whale sharks at **Ko Bidah Nok** and **Ko Bidah Nai**, the mass of leopard sharks at **Hin Bidah**, and the *King Cruiser* **wreck** (see p.370).

worth using the agents' booking service at the pier head, where pictures and – genuine – room prices for hotels in all categories are posted for easy browsing; staff then call ahead to secure your room, and might even carry your bag there. Be warned though that rooms are very expensive on Phi Phi, and often poorly maintained. We've quoted rates for high season, which runs from November to April, but most places slap on a thirty- to fifty-percent surcharge during Christmas and New Year and, conversely, will discount up to fifty percent in quiet periods between May and October.

Island practicalities

From Ao Ton Sai you can catch a **longtail** to any of the other beaches, or use the **paths** across the steep and at times rugged interior. There are only a few short motorbike tracks and one **road**, from the back of Ton Sai village to *The Beach* on Long Beach, which takes around forty minutes on foot. You could also get about by **kayak** (B200 per hr), which is the perfect way to explore the limestone cliffs and secluded bays, without the roar of an accompanying longtail or cruise ship.

Ton Sai village has all the essential services, including **ATMs** and **exchange** counters run by national banks (daily 7am–10pm), scores of **internet** centres, and bicycle rental (B100 per 3hr). The island's only health centre, **Phi Phi Hospital** (℡081 270 4481), is at the western end of Ao Ton Sai, and there's a **police** box (℡081 536 2427) next to the *Apache Bar* on the track to Laem Hin.

There are at least twenty **dive shops** on Phi Phi, the majority of them in Ton Sai, and though they all stick to a price agreement there are variations in professionalism. It's important to check credentials and equipment (see p.58) and to ask about the dive boat: some places use longtails rather than the much more comfortable, better-equipped proper dive boats. Also note that it is considered risky for a novice diver with fewer than twenty dives under their belt to dive at distant Hin Daeng and Hin Muang (see p.428), due to the depth and the current; the most reputable dive shops will only take Advanced Divers there. Recommended Ton Sai dive shops include Visa Diving (☏075 601157, ⓦwww.visadiving.com) and Moskito (☏075 601154, ⓦwww .moskitodiving.com), both on the main track to the pier, and Viking Divers, on the cross-island soi inland from *Chao Koh Phi Phi Lodge* (☏081 719 3375, ⓦwww .vikingdiversthailand.com). There are also small dive centres on Hat Yao, Ao Loh Bakao and Laem Tong.

Prices for **day-trips** including two tanks, equipment and lunch start at B2500. **Dive courses** cost B3400 for the introductory Discover Scuba day, B12,900 for the certificated four-day Openwater course, and B10,400 for a two-day Advanced course. The nearest recompression chambers are on Phuket (see p.370); check to see that your dive operator is insured to use one of them.

Rock-climbing

Phi Phi's topography is a gift for **rock-climbers** and both Cat's (☏081 787 5101) and Spidermonkey (☏075 819384, ⓦwww.spidermonkeyclimbing.com) in the village offer climbing instruction and equipment rental. Prices average B10000/1500 for a half-/full-day's instruction. The main climbing area is just to the west of Ao Ton Sai, and includes the Ton Sai Tower and the Drinking Wall, with thirty routes from grades 5 to 7a. A newer attraction is **cliff-jumping**, offered by several tour agencies and featuring jumps of up to 18m off a Phi Phi Don cliff.

Ton Sai village, Ao Loh Dalum and Laem Hin

Ton Sai village is a hectic warren of a place, both strangely old-fashioned with its alley traffic of bicycles and push carts, its tidy fresh market tucked away in the middle and its squalid shanty town and stinky sewers hidden along the edges, and of course bang up to date, the narrow lanes bursting with state-of-the-art dive shops, raucous bars and trendy boutiques.

West of the pier, **Ao Ton Sai** beach is an attractive little retreat under the limestone karsts, though it gets busy for a couple of hours around lunchtime and you're not far from the longtail moorings. Most people simply head for **Ao Loh Dalum** instead, less than 300m north across the narrow isthmus, which looks astonishingly pretty at high tide, with its glorious curve of powder-white sand beautifully set off by pale blue water; it's a different story at low-water, however, as the tide goes out for miles. Sun-loungers and parasols line the shore here and you can try parasailing and waterskiing in the bay. There's a small Tsunami Memorial Park of carefully tended shrubs, epitaphs and photos at the eastern end.

The **viewpoint** that overlooks eastern Ao Loh Dalum affords a magnificent panorama over the twin bays and every evening a stream of people makes the steep fifteen-minute climb up the steps for sunset shots; early morning is also photogenic, and the shop at the "Topview" summit, set within a pretty tropical garden, serves coffee as well as cold drinks. From the viewpoint you can descend the rocky and at times almost sheer paths to the trio of little east-coast bays at Ao Toh Ko, Ao Rantee (Lanti), and Hat Pak Nam, each of which takes about thirty minutes.

East along the coast from the Ton Sai pier, about ten minutes' walk down the main lane, is the promontory known as **Laem Hin**, beyond which lies a small beach and bungalows that enjoy a little more space. Inland, there are island homes and a mosque.

Accommodation

Ton Sai **hotels** are the least good value on the island and almost none, however expensive, is out of earshot of the thumping all-night beats cranked up by the various bars and clubs; bring some heavy-duty earplugs if you're not planning to party every night.

Ton Sai village and Ao Loh Dalum

Phi Phi Hotel ☎075 60023, ⓦgeocities.com /pphotel. One of the biggest hotels in Ton Sai, with a range of mid-market air-con rooms in low-rise buildings just inland from the pier. At the top-end you get some sort of sea view, either over Ton Sai or Loh Dalum, while the cheapest have no window at all. There's a small pool on site. ⑥–⑦

Phi Phi Inn ☎081 797 2088, ⓔphiphi_inn @hotmail.com. Small, sparklingly clean, all-air-con little hotel right next to *Phi Phi Hotel*, where all fifteen rooms have TVs, safety boxes and balconies, though only the upstairs ones have the chance of a view and also enjoy more privacy. ⑥

Phi Phi Island Cabana Hotel ☎075 601170, ⓦwww.phiphi-cabana.com. The views from the contemporary rooms at this large, imposing hotel are breathtakingly lovely. Most look out across the scoop of Ao Loh Dalum and its framing cliffs, and ground-floor ones have direct access to the sand. There's a huge pool too. On the minus side, the hotel lacks atmosphere, has a cavernous restaurant and some rooms are affected by late-night club noise. Reception is west of the pier on Ton Sai. ⑨

PP Casita ☎075 601214, ⓦgeocities.com /pphotel. Just inland from Ao Loh Dalum, this place is designed as its own little village, comprising eighty dinky buttermilk clapboard cabanas built on stilts and connected by wooden walkways that sit above a tropical garden. Interiors are on the small side but good, with air-con, platform beds, TV, wi-fi and nice tiled bathrooms. The drawback is that the cabanas are tightly packed and outdoor seating is on the walkway, making it a sociable place, but not very private or quiet. Noise from the nearby *Ibiza Bar* can also be a problem. Also has more spacious rooms in a hotel block and a pool. ⑦

PP Nice Beach Resort ☎081 894 5164. The location here is rather lovely, almost at the westernmost end of Ton Sai, under the shadow of the cliff wall just beyond the harbour area; the sand is gorgeously white and the sea a pretty blue, though you may feel inundated by day-trippers at

lunchtime. It's family run and has fairly simple fan bungalows and better quality air-con ones made from bamboo and wood. Fan ⑥, air-con ⑦

The Rock ☎081 607 897. Traveller-oriented hangout offering the cheapest beds on the island, in two mixed-sex fourteen- and sixteen-bed dorms (B250 per bed); bunk beds are crammed in, but there are fans and lockers. Also has a few singles and doubles with shared bathrooms. ④

Tropical Garden ☎081 968 1436, ⓦwww .thailandphiphitravel.com. The good-sized rough-timber fan and air-con huts here are mostly built on stilts up the side of an outcrop, beyond the turn-off for the path to the viewpoint. The better ones have a breezy veranda (though not much of a view) and there's a refreshing amount of greenery around, plus a tiny pool, despite being surrounded by other accommodation. Also has some cheap rooms in the main wooden building above the restaurant; their walls are thin but all have a window and pleasant decor. ④–⑥

US Guest House ☎087 278 7906, ⓔjo_uspp @hotmail.com. This two-storey block of sixteen functional en-suite fan rooms has the look and feel of an urban guest house, and offers some of the cheaper rooms in the area. Interiors aren't bad at all and there's a long shared deck with seating beside the narrow lane. It's close by the base of the viewpoint access steps. ④

Viewpoint Bungalows ☎075 601200, ⓦwww .phiphiviewpoint.com. Strung out across and up the cliffside at the far eastern end of Ao Loh Dalum, these fifty bungalows enjoy great views out over the bay, though interiors tend towards the cheap and flimsy and the all-night *Ibiza Bar* is too near to ignore. Facilities include a scenically sited restaurant, a couple of bars, a tour desk and a small, idyllically situated bayview pool and *Mojito Bar*. Fan ⑥, air-con ⑦–⑨

Laem Hin

Bay View Resort Yao ☎075 601127, ⓦwww .phiphibayview.com. The draw at the seventy large, air-con bungalows here is their prime location:

they're set high on the cliffside at the far eastern end of Laem Hin beach, strung out along the ridge almost as far as Hat Yao. All have massive windows and decks to enjoy the great views and there's a pool here too. Be prepared for lots of steps though. ❽–❾

Gypsy Village ☎075 601045, ⓦwww.ppgypsy village.com. The 25 plain and pretty shabby pink-painted concrete bungalows here are relatively cheap, but they're all en suite and are set round a big dry lawn about 150m down the track between the mosque and *Phi Phi Andaman Legacy*. ❹

Phi Phi Andaman Legacy ☎075 601106, ⓦwww.phiphiandamanlegacy.com. Set in a secluded enclosure just a few metres back from

the beach, the rather old-fashioned bungalows here are arranged in a square around a large lawn and small central swimming pool, while the 36 more modern rooms occupy a three-storey hotel building at the back. All rooms are air-con and come with TVs, hot water and safety boxes. ❼–❽

Phi Phi Villa Resort ☎075 601100, ⓦwww .phiphivillaresort.com. The best of the many options at this outfit are the huge air-con family cottages occupying the front section of the prettily landscaped garden, near the small pool. Also available are smaller air-con bungalows. Just a few steps from *Carpe Diem* so handy for on-the-doorstep drinks and fireshows. ❽–❾

Eating

Ton Sai is the best place to eat on the island, offering everything from bakery cafés to seafood **restaurants**, as well as cheap Thai curry-and-rice stalls.

Cosmic Well-priced home-made pasta (B130) and pizzas at two locations.
Garlic 1992 Cheap Thai food, especially curries and soups served with extra coconut milk straight from the fresh coconut. Mostly B70.
Le Grand Bleu Classy place close to *Phi Phi Hotel* serving a French-inspired menu (B270–350) that includes lots of fresh seafood, duck fillet with mango, sirloin steak and changing dishes of the day. Daily from 6pm.
Madame Restaurant Deservedly popular for its curries – *kaeng phanaeng*, *matsaman* green and red – mostly B80. Also does thin-crust pizzas and a decent vegetarian selection, and shows nightly movies.

Mama's Indulge yourself from the cabinet of tempting cakes, and make use of the free wi-fi at the same time or come for a leisurely seafood dinner of mackerel steak with mash or prawns in peanut sauce. Daily 11am–3pm & 6–11pm.
Papaya One of the best of several village-style kitchens whose authentic and reasonably cheap Thai standards, including noodle soups, *phat thai* (B60), fried rice dishes and fiery curries, makes it very popular with locals and dive staff.
Pee Pee Bakery The obvious place for breakfast, with its different blends of real coffee, set breakfasts (from B80) and piles of freshly baked croissants, Danish pastries, home-made breads, cakes and cookies. Has two branches. Daily 7am–8pm.

Drinking and entertainment

Ton Sai **nightlife** is young and drunken, involving endless buckets of Sansom and red bull, dance music played until dawn, and fire-juggling shows on the beach. Most of the bars offer a pretty similar formula, so it's often the one-off events and happy hours that make the difference.

The **Aswindum Thai Boxing Stadium** and training camp (ⓦphiphias windumresort.com), inland on the track between Laem Hin's mosque and *The Rock*, stages regular bouts of *muay thai* (Mon, Tues & Fri 9.30pm; B700–1000).

Carpe Diem Opposite *PP Villa* at Laem Hin. There's cushion seating on the upper terrace here, nightly fire shows from around 10pm and dancing on the beach. Also serves food from morning till late.
Hippies Bar Across from *PP Andaman* on Laem Hin. Hugely popular place with a chilled-out sea-view and on-the-beach bar and restaurant that shows nightly movies at 8pm, followed by fire shows some time after 10pm, and hosts regular half-moon parties. You can learn fire-juggling here yourself every afternoon.

Ibiza Bar On the beach at Loh Dalum. Very loud and very late on-the-sand bar that keeps punters entertained almost till sunrise with its booming sound system, DJs spinning mostly house and techno, fire shows and the rest.
Mojito Bar Poolside at *Viewpoint Bungalows* on Ao Loh Dalum. The best place for a cocktail or three in Ton Sai, with unsurpassed sea and sunset views, good music, very genial hosts and an especially irresistible mango daiquiri. Daily 2–10pm.

Reggae Bar In the heart of the village, on the soi that runs north beside *Chao Koh Phi Phi Lodge*. A Phi Phi institution that's been running for years in various incarnations. These days it arranges regular amateur *muay thai* bouts in its boxing ring – "beat up your friend and win free buckets" – and has pool tables and a bar around the sides. Even has reggae karaoke.

Rolling Stoned Centre of the village. Lively bar with nightly gigs from the in-house Thai cover band.

Long Beach (Hat Yao) and Ao Por

With its deluxe sand and large reefs packed with polychromatic marine life just 20m offshore, **HAT YAO** (Long Beach) is considered the best of Phi Phi's main beaches, but it's lined with hotels so gets very busy. For food you've only got hotel restaurants, but there's also the beachside *Buddha Bar*, which has fireshows and keeps serving till about 2am. The tiny bays to either side, within ten minutes' walk of Hat Yao, are much quieter and support just one set of bungalows apiece.

UK-run Long Beach Divers (Ⓦwww.longbeachdivers.com) at *Long Beach* runs all the same **dive** trips and courses as shops in the village and offers discounted stays at *Long Beach Bungalows* for dive students.

Longtail **boats** do the ten-minute shuttle between Hat Yao and Ao Ton Sai (B100 per person, or B150 after dark), but at low tide it's also possible to **walk** between the two in half an hour, via the coast in front of *Bay View Resort* on Laem Hin and then via *Viking*. The island's single **road** follows an inland route to *The Beach* from *The Rock* junction in the village, passing the post-tsunami housing project and Water Hill reservoir en route; it's a hot, hilly and unshaded forty-minute walk.

Accommodation

Ao Poh The Last Paradise ☏084 861 7630, ⓔao_poh_resort@hotmail.com. A 10min walk over the forested headland from behind *The Beach* and *Phi Phi Hill*, the pretty little white-sand bay of Ao Poh has just a dozen rudimentary bamboo bungalows. The cheapest have neither fan nor private bathroom, the most expensive are en suite. ❸–❹

The Beach Resort ☏075 618268, Ⓦwww .phiphithebeach.com. Currently the poshest option on Hat Yao, this place has a throng of large, timber-clad chalets built on stilts up the hillside, with the tallest, most deluxe ones enjoying commanding views of Phi Phi Leh. Interiors are fairly upscale, with air-con and liberal use of wood for flooring and wall panels. There's wi-fi and a small beach-front pool. ❽–❾

Long Beach Bungalows ☏086 470 8984, ⓔlongbeach@gmail.com. The first choice of most budget travellers, this fairly cheap, well-located and long-running option has dozens of tightly packed huts for rent. At the bottom end you get ultra-simple bamboo huts, many of which contain nothing more than a bed, a fan and a mosquito net, though some also have their own bathrooms. The slightly better ones are sturdier wooden huts and many of these are right on the shorefront. Shared bathroom ❸, en suite ❹, beachfront ❺

Phi Phi Hill Resort ☏075 618203, Ⓦwww .phiphihill.com. The fifty mint-green wooden cabins here occupy a glorious spot high above the beach, overlooking the far eastern end of Hat Yao. With fine sunrise or sunset views, depending on your location, and plenty of breeze, the only off-putting factor here is the one hundred steps that connect the resort with the beach below (though there is a pulley system for luggage). Rooms are simply furnished and come with fan or air-con. Fan ❹, air-con ❺–❻

Phi Phi Paradise Pearl Resort ☏075 601246, Ⓦwww.phiphiparadisepearl.com. The 25 bungalows at this efficiently run place are fairly well spaced along the western half of the beach, with none more than a few steps from the shore. Interiors are unremarkable but perfectly comfortable and all have air-con. There's internet access here, plus a tour counter and book exchange. ❼–❽

Viking Nature Resort ☏075 819399, Ⓦwww .vikingnatureresort.com. Tucked away on and above two private little coves just west of Hat Yao, with easy access via a rocky path, this is a very stylish take on classic Thai beach-bungalow archi-tecture. It's nearly all wood and bamboo here, with no air-con or hot water and in some cases no private bathroom either, but interiors that are styled with Asian boho-chic artefacts. The most glamorous accommodation is in the enormous, high-level, two- to four-bedroom "Makmai" tree houses, with their massive living-room decks overlooking the bay. Cheaper alternatives range from smaller en-suite tree houses to simple huts with shared facilities. There's a stylish lounge and dining area on the beach, with wi-fi. Shared bathroom ❹, en suite ❻–❼, Makmai ❾

Ao Toh Ko, Hat Rantee and Hat Pak Nam

Travellers wanting to escape the crowds around Ton Sai and Hat Yao without spending a fortune head for the trio of little bays midway along the east coast: Ao Toh Ko, Hat Rantee (Lanti) and Hat Pak Nam. Longtail transfers cost about B100 per person from Ao Ton Sai, or you can reach the bays inland, via steep forest trails that run from the Viewpoint above Ao Loh Dalum (see p.413) and take half an hour to walk. At **AO TOH KO**, it's the exceptionally welcoming family who run ⚓ *Ao Toh Ko Beach Resort* (☎081 537 0528, ✉tohkobeach @gmail.com; ❸–❹, family ❼) who keep people staying and returning – and they're great cooks too. The 32 bungalows here have the beach all to themselves and some sit right over the sea on the rocks to the south. They come in a range of styles, but are all good and comfortable. with fans and private bathrooms. At low tide you can walk to **HAT RANTEE** in five minutes, where *Rantee Beach Resort* (☎087 472 8192; ❹) has simple en-suite bamboo huts in the middle of the palm- and casuarina-fringed white-sand bay; there's great snorkelling at the reef right off the beach too. *Phi Phi Relax Beach Resort* (☎089 725 4411, ⓦphiphirelaxbeach.com; ❻–❽) on **HAT PAK NAM** offers the most comfortable, and expensive, though still rustic, accommodation, in fifteen attractive, en-suite thatched bamboo bungalows in among the beachfront trees.

Ao Loh Bakao and Laem Tong

Far removed from the hustle of Ao Ton Sai and its environs, the beautiful, secluded northern beaches at Ao Loh Bakao and Laem Tong are the domain of just a few upscale resorts. Access is usually by hotel boat from Ao Ton Sai (generally B150–200 per person on arrival but as much as B2000 per boat thereafter) or by chartering your own longtail (about B800 per boat); it's forty minutes to Ao Loh Bakao and a further fifteen minutes north to Laem Tong.

The plush, air-conditioned chalets at *Phi Phi Island Village Beach Resort and Spa* (☎075 628999, ⓦwww.ppisland.com; ❾) have the gorgeous eight-hundred-metre-long white-sand beach and turquoise waters of **AO LOH BAKAO** all to themselves. It's a popular honeymoon spot, and a lovely location for anyone looking for a quiet, comfortable break. The thatched, split-bamboo bungalows are designed in traditional Thai style and furnished with character and elegance. There's a good-sized pool and spa centre in the prettily landscaped tropical gardens, as well as a dive centre and kayak rental. If you tire of these sands, and the hotel restaurants, there's a cluster of reasonably priced local restaurants behind the resort, and you can walk to the long, semi-circular beach at **Ao Loh Lanaa**, across on the west coast, in ten minutes, or to Laem Tong in half an hour.

Almost right at Phi Phi's northernmost tip, **LAEM TONG** is busier and more commercial than Loh Bakao, with several upmarket resorts along its white-sand shores, and views across to nearby Bamboo and Mosquito islands. The beach is home to a group of Urak Lawoy *chao ley* "sea gypsies" (see p.335), whose village is next to the *Holiday Inn*; all longtail boat tours and transfers are run by Laem Tong's *chao ley* co-operative. At the southern end of the beach, *Holiday Inn Resort Phi Phi Island* (☎075 627300, ⓦwww.phiphi-palmbeach.com; ❾) offers 76 air-conditioned bungalows set in graceful gardens of tidy lawns and flowering shrubs plus a swimming pool, dive centre and spa. Up at the northern

Bird's-nesting

Prized for its aphrodisiac and energizing qualities, **bird's-nest soup** is such a delicacy in Taiwan, Singapore and Hong Kong that ludicrous sums of money change hands for a dish whose basic ingredients are tiny twigs glued together with bird's spit. Collecting these nests is a lucrative but life-endangering business: sea swifts (known as edible-nest swiftlets) build their nests in rock crevices hundreds of metres above sea level, often on sheer cliff-faces or in cavernous hollowed-out karst. **Nest-building** begins in January and the harvesting season usually lasts from February to May, during which time the female swiftlet builds three nests on the same spot, none of them more than 12cm across, by secreting an unbroken thread of saliva, which she winds round as if making a coil pot. **Gatherers** will only steal the first two nests made by each bird, prising them off the cave walls with special metal forks. This in theory allows the bird to build a final nest and raise her chicks in peace. Gathering the nests demands faultless agility and balance, skills that seem to come naturally to the *chao ley*, whose six-man teams bring about four hundred nests down the perilous bamboo scaffolds each day, weighing about 4kg in total. At a market rate of up to $2000 per kilo, so much money is at stake that a government franchise must be granted before any collecting commences, and armed guards often protect the sites at night. The *chao ley* seek spiritual protection from the dangers of the job by making offerings to the spirits of the cliff or cave at the beginning of the season; in the Viking Cave, they place buffalo flesh, horns and tails at the foot of one of the stalagmites.

In recent years, entrepreneurs in Ban Laem, near Phetchaburi, across on south Thailand's Gulf Coast, have started competing with the *chao lay* – by constructing **sea swift condominiums** and trying to attract the swiftlets that frequent the attic of the nearby temple. The theory is that by constructing windowless concrete towers they can mimic the Andaman Sea caves – complete with cool dark interiors, droppings-smeared walls and swiftlet soundtracks on continuous replay – entice the birds in to build their nests, and harvest them with ease. To date, the main beneficiary seems to have been the company that builds these ugly towers, as the local swiftlet population suddenly has an awful lot of new accommodation to choose from.

end, the cheaper, old-style air-con rooms and wooden chalets at *Phi Phi Natural Resort* (℡075 613010, ⓦwww.phiphinatural.com; ⑧–⑨) are scattered around an extensive tropical shorefront garden, with pool, that stretches along the coast to the next tiny uninhabited bay.

Ko Phi Phi Leh

More rugged than its twin, Ko Phi Phi Don, and a quarter the size, **KO PHI PHI LEH** is the number-one day-tripping destination from Phi Phi Don, twenty minutes' north, and a feature of all snorkelling tours out of Phuket and Ao Nang. It is very scenic indeed, and world famous, following its starring role in the film *The Beach,* so expect huge crowds, a plethora of discarded polystyrene lunch boxes, and a fair bit of damage to the reefs from the carelessly dropped anchors of tourist and fishing boats. The best way to appreciate the island is probably on one of the overnight camping and snorkelling trips from Phi Phi Don (see p.412).

Most idyllic of all the island's bays is **Ao Maya** on the southwest coast, where the water is still and very clear and the coral extremely varied; **Ao Phi Leh**, an almost completely enclosed east-coast lagoon of breathtakingly turquoise water, is also beautiful. Nearby, the **Viking Cave** gets its misleading name from the scratchy wall-paintings of Chinese junks inside, but more interesting than this 400-year-old graffiti is the **bird's-nesting** that goes on here: rickety bamboo scaffolding extends hundreds of metres up to the roof of the cave, where intrepid *chao ley* harvesters spend the day scraping the unfeasibly valuable nests made by tiny sea-swifts off the rockface for export to specialist Chinese restaurants all over the world.

Ko Jum

Situated halfway between Krabi and Ko Lanta Yai, **KO JUM** (whose northern half is also known as **Ko Pu**) is the sort of laid-back spot that people come to for a couple of days, then can't bring themselves to leave. Though there's plenty of accommodation on the island, there's nothing more than a handful of beach bars for evening entertainment, and little to do during the day except try out the half-dozen west-coast beaches and read your book under a tree. The beaches may not be pristine, and are in some places unswimmably rocky at low tide, but they're mostly long and wild, and all but empty of people. Nights are also low key: it's paraffin lamps and starlight after about 11pm at those places that are off the main grid, and many don't even provide fans as island breezes are sufficiently cooling.

The island is home to around three thousand people, the majority of them Muslim, though there are also communities of *chao ley* sea gypsies on Ko Jum (see p.335), as well as Buddhists. The main village is **Ban Ko Jum,** on the island's southeastern tip, comprising a few local shops and small restaurants, one of the island's three piers for boats to and from Laem Kruat on the mainland, and a beachfront school. It's about 1km from the village to the southern end of the island's most popular beach, the appropriately named **Long Beach**. Long Beach is connected to **Golden Pearl Beach**, which sits just south of **Ban Ting Rai**, the middle-island village that's about halfway down the west coast. North of Ban Ting Rai, a trio of smaller, increasingly remote beaches at **Ao Si, Ao Ting Rai**, and **Ao Luboa** complete the picture. The island's third village, **Ban Ko Pu,** occupies the northeastern tip, about 5km beyond Ban Ting Rai, and has another Laem Kruat ferry pier. Many islanders refer to the north of the island, from Ban Ting Rai upwards, as Ko Pu, and define only the south as Ko Jum. Much of the north is made inaccessible by the breastbone of forested hills, whose highest peak (422m) is Khao Ko Pu.

Very high winds and heavy seas mean that Ko Jum becomes an acquired taste from May through October, so most tourist accommodation **closes** for that period: exceptions are highlighted in the text.

Getting to Ko Jum

During high season, usual access to Ko Jum is via the Krabi–Ko Lanta **ferries** (1hr 30min–2hr from Krabi, or about 45min from Ko Lanta; B400; see p.352 for times). Ko Jum bungalows send longtails out to meet the ferries as they make two stops off the west coast: coming from Krabi, stop one is for the *Ko Pu* bungalows (on Ao Ting Rai and Ao Luboa) and the second, "Ko Jum", stop is for *Ao Si, Golden Pearl* and *Long Beach* bungalows. When it comes to moving on, you can also charter a longtail from Ko Jum direct to Ko Phi Phi for about B2000: the trip takes a couple of hours.

In the **rainy season** you have to travel to Ko Jum **overland**, and an increasing number of visitors now use this route year-round; some bungalow operators, for example, offer transfers from Krabi airport using this route (about B600 per car to Laem Kruat). Coming from Krabi town, you first need to take a **songthaew** to **Nua Klong**, and then another one to **Laem Kruat** (allow two hours in total, though it's only about 40km). **Boats** run from Laem Kruat to all three east-coast "village" piers on Ko Jum, from where a motorbike taxi with sidecar

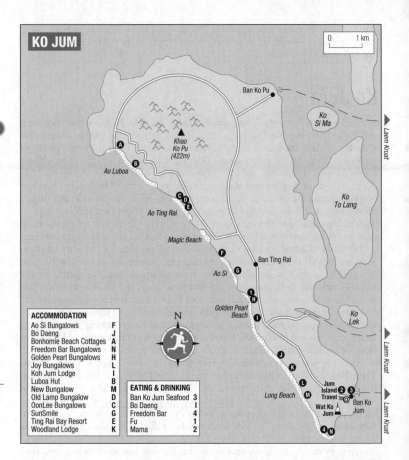

should transfer you to your bungalow for B50 per person. Timetables are a little vague: boats **to Ban Ko Jum** depart Laem Kruat between 1pm and 3pm, and return from Ko Jum about 7.30am (1hr; B70); boats to **Mu 2, east of Ban Ting Rai**, depart Laem Kruat in the afternoon until 5pm, and return from Ko Jum at 7.30am & 1.30pm (50min; B60); boats to **Ban Ko Pu** depart Laem Kruat about every two hours between 9am and 5.30pm, and return from Ban Ko Pu between 7am and 8.30am (45min; B50).

Island practicalities

Most bungalows can arrange **kayak** and **motorbike** rental. They will also organize **day-trips**, as will tour agencies in Ban Ko Jum, for example to Ko Phi Phi, Bamboo Island and Mosquito Island (B800–1500 per person or about B4000 per boat), or around Ko Jum (B1500 per boat). Many offer guided hikes up Khao Ko Pu (B500 per half day, or more from southern accommodation), and *OonLee* does a trip to Khlong Thom hot spring on the mainland (B1500 per person). Blue Juice Dive (☎086 997 9197, ✉bluejuicedivers@gmail.com; also has branch in Krabi town) at *Woodland Lodge* on Long Beach runs **diving trips** to Phi Phi (B3900) and diving courses (Discover Scuba B4900; Openwater B14,900).

There's no ATM on the island, but you can **change money** at Jum Island Travel next to the pier in Ban Ko Jum and *Koh Jum Lodge* on Long Beach does Visa cash advances. There's **internet** access in Ban Ko Jum and, evenings only, at one or more of the hotels on almost every beach. Ban Ko Jum also has a couple of shops selling beachwear and basic necessities. The island **medical centre** is on the road just south of *Golden Pearl* bungalows, beyond the southern edge of Ban Ting Rai. For a comprehensive **guide** to life on the island and pictures of all the bungalow operations, see ⓦ www.kohjumonline.com.

Long Beach, Golden Pearl Beach and Ban Ko Jum

LONG BEACH (sometimes known as **Andaman Beach**) is the main backpackers' beach and is indeed long – at around 2.5km – with large chunks of the shoreline still uncultivated, backed with trees and wilderness, and well beyond sight of the island road. From *New Bungalow* towards the southern end it's a twenty-minute walk into Ban Ko Jum village.

At its northern end, Long Beach segues into **GOLDEN PEARL BEACH**, which is about 750m/fifteen minutes' walk north up the beach from *Bo Daeng*, 5km by road from Ban Ko Jum and 1km south of Ban Ting Rai. Like Long Beach, it also has only a few bungalow outfits along its curving shoreline, though these are close by the island road.

Accommodation
Accommodation on Long Beach is in three clusters, each about fifteen minutes' walk apart.

Long Beach
Bo Daeng ☎ 081 494 8760. This funky, ultra cheap and ultra basic travellers' classic is run by a famously welcoming charismatic island *chao ley* family and has legendary food. The rudimentary bamboo huts come with or without private bathrooms – the latter are among the very cheapest on the island, but all have nets and electricity during the evening. Open all year. ❶
Freedom Bar Bungalows ☎ 085 792 8130. Just a handful of rustic-contemporary bamboo bungalows way off on their own at the southernmost point, occupying an unparalleled spot on a tiny rocky promontory, with awesome 360-degree sea views and as yet no neighbours. The bungalows are enormous and beautifully simple, with loads of space for hammocks and chairs on the deck, plus nice partly al-fresco bathrooms. There are no real hotel facilities, just the staff at its sister outfit, the ultra laid-back *Freedom Bar* itself. ❻
Joy Bungalows ☎ 075 618199, ⓦ www.kohjum -joybungalow.com. This is the longest running and most famous place to stay on the island, though not necessarily the friendliest. It has a big spread of accommodation set in a grove of trees behind the shorefront, the majority of them smart wooden bungalows in various sizes and proximity to the sea, plus some cheap bamboo ones and a

two-bedroom house. None has electricity, so it's paraffin lamps all round at night. ❸–❼
New Bungalow ☎ 075 618116, ⓔ nbkohjum @hotmail.com. The two-dozen differently styled bungalows at this friendly, long-established place include a few cheapie bamboo ones with and without private bathrooms, a couple of treehouses with idyllic sea views and shared bathrooms, plus some plain, en-suite wooden huts. ❶–❹
Woodland Lodge ☎ 081 893 5330, ⓦ www .woodland-koh-jum.tk. Welcoming, peaceful spot owned by a UK-Thai couple and one of the few places on the island to stay open year round. Its large, attractive bungalows are widely set beneath the trees of its shorefront garden and all have good bathrooms; the doubles have platform beds, varni-shed wooden floors and deep shady decks, while the bigger ones are designed for families. Nearly all of them enjoy sea views between the trees. ❸–❺

Golden Pearl Beach
Golden Pearl Bungalows ☎ 075 618131. The nineteen simple woven-bamboo huts here are set within a coconut grove across the road from the shore; the budget ones are the cheapest on the island and have neither fans nor private bathrooms, but the en-suite versions are also a very good price. ❶–❸

Koh Jum Lodge ☎089 921 1621, ⓦwww
.kohjumlodge.com. French run, and one of the most
upscale places on the island, with just sixteen
thatched wooden chalets designed in charming
rustic-chic style. Thoughtfully constructed to make
the most of the island breezes, they have doors
onto the veranda to avoid the need for air-con, low
beds and elegantly simple furniture. All the
bungalows can sleep up to five small kids as well
as two adults. The resort has a small pool, internet
access, a TV and DVD area, a massage service and
a restaurant. Minimum stay one week. ❾

Eating and drinking

All the bungalows do **food**, but for a really outstanding Thai meal, at some of
the cheapest prices on the island, you should join the (often lengthy) queue at
🍴 *Bo Daeng* on **Long Beach**, whose highlights include baked fish, vegetable
tempura, curries and coconut shakes. *Joy* does pizzas and fresh coffee, *Woodland*
makes delicious curries, and *New* has newspapers to read while you wait for
your meal. **Ban Ko Jum** is good for cheap village food, including Thai breakfasts from 5am at *Mama*, but the big name here is the very popular and very
good B*an Ko Jum Seafood* (Nov–May daily 10am–10pm), whose tables occupy
a scenically sited jetty near the pier, and enjoy fine view across the mangrove
channel. Among its big menu of fresh seafood cooked any number of ways, the
juicy fat prawns barbecued with honey are a standout, and their crab and lobster
dishes are famous too.

Many people round off the night with a **drink** around the camp fire at easy-
going *Freedom Bar*, right down the bottom end of Long Beach. The *Fu* beach
bar on Golden Pearl holds occasional full-moon parties.

Ao Si

Around the rocky headland from Golden Pearl Beach, accessible in ten minutes
at low tide or quite a bit further by road, long and beautifully uncluttered **AO
Si** is good for swimming. In about the middle of the beach sits *SunSmile* (☎086
280 4811; ❸), whose eleven blue-roofed concrete bungalows all enjoy sea views
and are kept very clean, with tiled floors, good beds, fans and decent bathrooms.
Ao Si's northern headland is the sole province of Scottish-run *Ao Si Bungalows*
(☎081 747 2664, ⓔreena.aosi@hotmail.com; ❸–❹); its eight woven-bamboo,
en-suite bungalows are built on piles up the side of the cliff and have wraparound verandas for soaking up the commanding views of the bay and the
southern half of the island. A big troupe of monkeys makes its home here too.
A ten-minute walk through the rubber trees from the uppermost of *Ao Si's*
bungalows brings you to Magic Beach, just south of Ao Ting Rai.

Ban Ting Rai, Khao Ko Pu and Ao Ting Rai

The road begins to climb as soon as you leave Golden Pearl Beach, taking you
up through the ribbon-like village of **Ban Ting Rai**, pretty with bougainvillea
and wooden houses, and location of a few small restaurants and noodle shops.
Khao Ko Pu which rises in the distance is, at 422m, the island's highest
mountain and home to macaques who sometimes come down to forage on the
rocks around the northern beaches; guided treks up the eastern flank to the
summit take about an hour and reward you with fine 360-degree panoramas
encompassing the entire island, the mainland and the outer islands.

The little bay of **AO TING RAI**, sometimes known as **Hat Kidon**, has some
nice places to stay, and good snorkelling off its shore, with reef to explore and
plenty of fish. At low tide it's too rocky for swimming though, when you'll need
either to pick your way over the rocks, rent a kayak, or walk south 500m along
the coastal road, to get to the little sandy crescent known as **Magic Beach**,

which is swimmable at any tide. You can walk to Ao Ting Rai from Ao Si in about twenty minutes along the coast road.

The southernmost **accommodation** on Ao Ting Rai is at the very popular *Ting Rai Bay Resort* (☎087 277 7379; ⓦwww.tingrai.com; ❸–❺), where sixteen nicely designed wooden bungalows are ranged up the sloping shorefront on stilts, most offering fine views from capacious decks (especially the "honeymoon" ones). Interiors have fans, four-poster style beds, and plenty of attention to detail. The food here is also good and there's internet access and onward transport tickets. Next door, *Old Lamp Bungalow* (☎089 876 8572, ⓦwww .oldlampbungalows.com; ❸) has a dozen surprisingly spacious bungalows made from coconut wood, secreted among the trees, and designed with thoughtful, practical touches; most have nice garden bathrooms and all of them have big wooden beds. There's fresh wholewheat bread baked daily too. North again, French-Thai *OonLee Bungalows* (☎087 200 8053, ⓦwww.koh-jum-resort .com; ❸–❺; phone ahead for a pick-up from your landing point; open all year) is a small, enthusiastically run and well-liked place with nine bungalows in various styles, plus a four-bed family bungalow. The wooden bungalows have plenty of storage, appealing bathrooms and sea-view verandas. Bungalows are stacked up the cliffside here, so there are quite a lot of steps; there's a stylish upper-level lounge area and restaurant, and a bar and massage area at beach level, plus free kayaks, bicycles and snorkels for guests. *OonLee* offers lots of organized **activities** and tours, including guided treks up Khao Ko Pu, fishing trips, day-trips to Ko Lola off Long Beach, round-island tours and trips to Ko Phi Phi.

Ao Luboa

Ko Jum's peaceful northernmost beach, **AO LUBOA**, feels remote. It's accessed chiefly by a loop in the main island road that circles the northeastern slopes of Khao Ko Pu and terminates at the north end of the bay, though the steeply undulating coast road from Ao Ting Rai can also be walked (in about 45min from *OonLee*) or ridden on a motorbike with good brakes. Like Ao Ting Rai, Ao Luboa's shorefront reef gets exposed at low tide, making it impossible to swim, though at high water things are fine and it's anyway a supremely quiet, laid-back beach with just a few **bungalows**. The friendly *Luboa Hut* (☎081 959 4576, ⓦwww.luboahut2008.com; ❷–❹) has nine en-suite bamboo and wooden bungalows with sea view and electricity (but no fans) in a well shaded spot under shoreside trees; many of them are roomy and good quality, some have extra beds or sofas and all have mosquito nets. The owners do kayak and motorbike rental and have internet. At the far northern end of the beach, *Bonhomie Beach Cottages* (☎086 788 7585, ⓦwww.bonhomiebeach.com; ❸–❹) has ten very large, attractively designed en-suite wooden chalets, many with sea view; price depends on proximity to the sea.

Ko Lanta Yai

Although **KO LANTA YAI** can't compete with Phi Phi's stupendous scenery, the thickly forested 25-kilometre-long island has the longest beaches in the Krabi area – and plenty of them. There's decent snorkelling and diving nearby, plus caves to explore, elephant trekking and kayaking, so many tourists base themselves here for their entire holiday fortnight. The island is especially popular with families, in part because of the local laws that have so far prevented jet-skis, beachfront parasols and girlie bars from turning it into another Phuket,

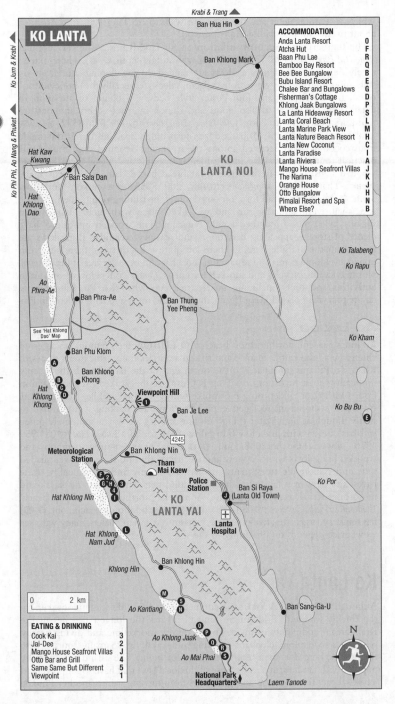

KO LANTA

Krabi & Trang ▲
Ban Hua Hin ●
Ban Khlong Mark ●

Ko Jum & Krabi ◀
Ko Phi Phi, Ao Nang & Phuket ◀

ACCOMMODATION

Anda Lanta Resort	O
Atcha Hut	F
Baan Phu Lae	R
Bamboo Bay Resort	Q
Bee Bee Bungalow	B
Bubu Island Resort	E
Chalee Bar and Bungalows	G
Fisherman's Cottage	D
Khlong Jaak Bungalows	P
La Lanta Hideaway Resort	S
Lanta Coral Beach	L
Lanta Marine Park View	M
Lanta Nature Beach Resort	H
Lanta New Coconut	C
Lanta Paradise	I
Lanta Riviera	A
Mango House Seafront Villas	J
The Narima	K
Orange House	J
Otto Bungalow	H
Pimalai Resort and Spa	N
Where Else?	B

Hat Kaw Kwang
Ban Sala Dan ●

Hat Khlong Dao

KO LANTA NOI

Ko Talabeng
Ko Rapu

Ao Phra-Ae

Ban Phra-Ae ●
Ban Thung Yee Pheng ●

Ko Kham

See 'Hat Khlong Dao' Map

Ban Phu Klom ●
Ⓐ
Ban Khlong Khong ●
Ⓑ
Ⓒ
Ⓓ
Hat Khlong Khong

Viewpoint Hill
❶
Ban Je Lee ●

Ko Bu Bu
Ⓔ

4245

Meteorological Station
Ban Khlong Nin ●
Tham Mai Kaew

Ⓕ❷
Ⓖ Ⓗ ❸
Ⓐ
Ⓘ
Hat Khlong Nin

Police Station
Ban Si Raya Ⓙ (Lanta Old Town)

Ko Por

Ⓚ

Ⓛ
Hat Khlong Nam Jud

KO LANTA YAI

Lanta Hospital

Khlong Hin
Ban Khlong Hin ●

Ⓜ
Ban Sang-Ga-U ●
Ⓝ ❺
Ao Kantiang

Ⓞ
Ⓟ
Ao Khlong Jaak
Ⓠ
Ⓡ
Ⓢ
Ao Mai Phai

National Park Headquarters
Laem Tanode

N

0   2 km

EATING & DRINKING

Cook Kai	3
Jai-Dee	2
Mango House Seafront Villas	J
Otto Bar and Grill	4
Same Same But Different	5
Viewpoint	1

though resort facilities are expanding fast. Lanta is also rapidly being colonized by Scandinavian expats, with villa homes and associated businesses popping up all over the place, at a pace that not all islanders are happy about. The majority of Ko Lanta Yai's ten thousand indigenous residents are mixed-blood descendants of Muslim Chinese-Malay or animist *chao ley* ("sea gypsy") peoples, most of whom supported themselves by fishing and cultivating the land before the tourist boom brought new jobs, and challenges.

One of those challenges is that the **tourist season** is quite short, with the weather and seas at their calmest and safest from November to April; the main ferries don't run outside that period, and some hotels close, though most do stay open and offer huge discounts. The short money-making window, however, means that accommodation prices on Ko Lanta fluctuate more wildly than many other south Thailand destinations (see p.427).

The local *chao ley* name for Ko Lanta Yai is *Pulao Satak*, "Island of Long Beaches", an apt description of the string of beaches along the **west coast**, each separated by rocky points and strung out at quite wide intervals. Broadly speaking, the busiest and most mainstream beaches are in the north, within easy reach of the port at **Ban Sala Dan**: **Hat Khlong Dao** is the family beach and **Ao Phra-Ae** the longer and more beautiful. The middle section has variable sands but some interesting places to stay, at **Hat Khlong Khong**, **Hat Khlong Nin** and **Hat Khlong Nam Jud**. Southerly **Ao Kantiang** is reliable for swimming year-round and marks the end of the made road; beyond here **Ao Khlong Jaak** and **Ao Mai Phai** are a little harder to get to and so feel more remote. Lanta Yai's mangrove-fringed **east coast** has no real tourist development but is both good for kayaking and culturally interesting because of the traditional homes in **Lanta Old Town**. North across the narrow channel from the port at Ban Sala Dan, Lanta Yai's sister island of **Ko Lanta Noi** has Ko Lanta's administrative offices and several small villages but no tourist accommodation. The rest of the Ko Lanta archipelago, which comprises over fifty little islands, is mostly uninhabited.

Every March Ko Lanta Yai celebrates its rich ethnic heritage at the **Laanta Laanta Festival**, which is held over three days in Lanta Old Town and features both traditional and modern music and dance, countless specialist foodstalls and crafts for sale (check ⓦlantaoldtown.com for dates and specifics). Traditional *chao ley* rituals are celebrated on Ko Lanta twice a year, on the full moons of the sixth and eleventh lunar months (usually June and Oct/Nov; see p.436).

Moving on from Ko Lanta Yai

From mid-October to mid-May, there are **ferries** at least once a day, more during peak periods, to **Krabi** via **Ko Jum**; to **Ao Nang** via **West Railay**; to **Ko Phi Phi**; and to **Phuket**. See p.426 for durations and fares.

There are also daily boats in high season **to Ko Hai, Ko Mook, Trang** (Hat Yao pier) and **Ko Lipe** (B1500; 5hr 30min), with a mooted extension to Langkawi in Malaysia (6hr 30min), all with Tigerline (☎081 092 8800, ⓦwww.tigerlinetravel.com); and a faster service with Satun Pakbara Speedboat (☎074 783 643, ⓦwww.tarutaolipeislnd.com), which gets to Lipe in three hours (B1800) and also makes a stop on Ko Bulon Lae. You can also make use of the day-trippers' snorkelling boats operated by Garden Hill (☎075 684042, ⓦwww.lantaislandtours.com) and Petpailin (☎075 667033) for transfers to Ko Hai, Ko Mook and **Ko Kradan**. See p.448 for details on all Trang province boats.

Most Ko Lanta tour agents can fix you up with an onward bus or air ticket **to Bangkok** or elsewhere and some can also organize train tickets, though this will take several days and cost quite a bit extra. Several also offer **visa-run** day-trips by minivan to Satun for about B1200.

▲ Beach bar on Ao Phra-Ae

Getting to Ko Lanta Yai

The principal mainland gateways to Ko Lanta are Krabi, Phuket and Trang, all of which have good long-distance bus services, and **airports**; Trang also has a train station. See relevant accounts for travel information.

From approximately mid-October to mid-May there are **ferries** at least once a day, more during peak periods, to Ko Lanta Yai **from Krabi** (2hr 30min; B450), via **Ko Jum** (about 1hr; B450); from **Ko Phi Phi** (1hr 30min; B300), with connections from **Phuket** (4hr 30min; B750); and from **Ao Nang** (2hr 30min; B450) via West **Railay** (2hr; B450). In high season here are also speedboat services to Ko Lanta from **Trang** and the islands of **Ko Hai, Ko Mook, Ko Lipe** and **Ko Bulon Lae**, for details of which, see individual island accounts and p.448. All ferries dock at Ban Sala Dan and are met by bungalow touts who usually transport you to the beach of your choice for free. If you need to use the motorbike sidecar taxi service instead, be warned that drivers will try and charge arrivals way over the normal fares quoted below; walk 250m from the pier head to the main road to get a ride at more reasonable rates.

The alternative to the ferries is the **overland route** to Ko Lanta Yai – essential during the **rainy season** but increasingly popular at any time of year. This is the route used by minivans from **Krabi town** (hourly; 2hr; B200–300 depending on which beach you get dropped at); by taxis from **Krabi airport** (about B2500 per car); by minivans from **Trang** (4 daily; 3hr); and by anyone bringing their **own vehicle**. Access is via Ban Hua Hin on the mainland, 75km east of Krabi, from where a small ferry crosses to Ban Khlong Mark on Ko Lanta Noi, after which there's a seven-kilometre drive across to Lanta Noi's southwest tip, then another ferry over the narrow channel to the car-ferry port on Ko Lanta Yai's northeastern coast; both ferries run approximately every twenty minutes from about 7am to 10pm.

Island practicalities

There's no public **transport** on the island, but motorbikes are widely available for rent and there are jeeps too. A fleet of **motorbike sidecar taxis**, with drivers in numbered vests, operates out of Ban Sala Dan and will go pretty much anywhere on the island, though they usually need to be phoned (by staff at hotels or restaurants) for pick-ups from anywhere outside Sala Dan. Lanta has its share of scamming taxi-drivers, so bear in mind the following approximate rates for rides out of Sala Dan: B40 to Hat Khlong Dao, B60 to Ao Phra-Ae, B80 to Hat Khlong Kong, or about B50 between the above.

Most bungalows will **change money**, though you'll get the best rates at the bank in Ban Sala Dan, where there are also a couple of **ATMs**; there are also ATMs beside the road at most of the beaches. Many bungalows offer international telephone services for guests, and there's **internet** access on every beach. The post office is in Lanta Old Town. Nearly every beach has a clinic, there's a larger **health centre** in Ban Sala Dan (Mon–Fri 4.30–8.30pm, Sat & Sun 8.30am–4.30pm) and the rather basic island hospital is in Lanta Old Town (℡075 697017), though for anything serious you'll need to go to Phuket. There's a **police** box in Sala Dan (℡075 684657) but the police station is in Lanta Old Town (℡075 697085).

For details on **snorkelling**, **diving**, **kayaking** and **day-trips** on Ko Lanta, see the box on p.428. During high-season there are **yoga** classes in Ban Sala Dan and at *Cha Ba* bungalows on Khlong Dao, but the most famous teacher is at *Relax Bay* on Ao Phra-Ae (B400/90min).

Ko Lanta Yai is extremely popular during high season (Nov–Feb), when it's worth either booking your first night's **accommodation** in advance or taking up the suggestions of the bungalow touts who ride the boats from the mainland. A confirmed booking also means you should get free transport from the port to your hotel. Accommodation **pricing** on Ko Lanta is disconcertingly flexible and alters according to the number of tourists on the island: bungalow rates can triple between mid-December and mid-January, while during the rainy season between May and October rates are vastly discounted. The rates we've quoted are for the beginning and end of high season (generally Nov to early Dec & late Jan to April).

Ban Sala Dan

During high season, direct boats from Krabi and Phi Phi arrive at the T-shaped fishing port and tourist village of **BAN SALA DAN**, on the northernmost tip of Ko Lanta Yai. Pretty much everything you'll need is here, from beachwear shops and minimarkets to banks with currency **exchange** and ATMs, tour agents and dive shops. The weekly Sunday market sets up south of the Health Centre and sells cheap clothes, household goods and hot food.

The old part of the village, strung out along the waterside, facing sister island Ko Lanta Yai across the narrow channel, retains its charming old wooden houses built on piles over the water. Many of these have been turned into attractive jetty **restaurants**, perfect for whiling away a breezy hour with views of marine activity. *Ko Lanta Seafood* on the left-hand arm of the T is the oldest restaurant in town and the most highly rated – its seafood is great, worth braving the service which is lackadaisical at best. Also near here is *Baan Café* (Sat–Thurs 7am–5pm) which does home-baked breads, rolls and cakes. Along the right-hand arm of the T, *Bai Fern* does inexpensive Thai food, while *Catfish* also sells art cards and has the best selection of **secondhand books** on Ko Lanta, including Thai novels in translation and Thai dictionaries and language books. Though it doesn't share the atmospheric location, *Kocha* opposite Lanta Diver on the main road is popular with locals for its excellent taste and cheap prices, especially beef in oyster sauce and *mii krop* (crispy noodles) with crispy pork (B50–60).

Any Lanta tour agent can sort you out with **day-trips** and activities.

Snorkelling trips

The best and most popular **snorkelling** is at the islands of **Ko Rok Nai** and **Ko Rok Nok**, 47km south of Ko Lanta; these forested twins are graced with stunning white-sand beaches and accessible waterfalls and separated by a narrow channel full of fabulous shallow reefs. Also hugely popular is the **"four island"** snorkelling trip that takes in the much nearer islands off Trang – the enclosed emerald lagoon on **Ko Mook** (Ko Muk; p.450), plus nearby **Ko Hai** (Ko Ngai), **Ko Cheuak** (Ko Chuk) and **Ko Kradan** (see pp.448–452 for island descriptions) – but these sites get very crowded. Another option is the day-trip to **Phi Phi Don**, Phi Phi Leh and Bamboo Island (see p.412). The trips are typically on large **speedboats** which hold about thirty people, and cost B1800 for adults or B900 for kids under 12, including lunch, snorkel mask, and national park entry fee. One of the main operators is Lanta Garden Hill Speed Boat (℡075 684042, www.lantaislandtours.com), and their trips can be booked through any agent on Ko Lanta. For a smaller, much more personal experience, contact Sun Island Tours (℡087 891 6619, www.lantalongtail.com), whose various **longtail trips**, to the four islands, around Ko Lanta, and to Lanta's eastern islands (including an overnight camping option), come very highly rated and cost B1500.

Diving

The **reefs** around Ko Lanta are quieter and in some cases more pristine than those round Phi Phi and Phuket, and excellent for seeing whale sharks. The **diving season** runs from November to April, though a few dive shops continue to run successful trips from May to August. All dive boats depart from Ban Sala Dan, and nearly all dive courses are taught either in Sala Dan or on Hat Khlong Dao, though there are dive shops on every beach.

Some of Lanta's best **dive sites** are located between Ko Lanta and Ko Phi Phi, including the soft coral at **Ko Bidah**, where you get lots of leopard sharks, barracuda and tuna. West and south of Lanta, the **Ko Ha** island group offers four different dives on each of its five islands, including steep drop-offs and an "underwater cathedral"

Hat Khlong Dao

Long and gently curving **HAT KHLONG DAO** is known as "the family beach", both for its plentiful mid-range accommodation, and for its generous sweep of flat sandy shoreline that's safe for swimming and embraced by protective headlands. Despite being developed to capacity, it's broad enough never to feel overcrowded, the sunsets can be magnificent, and the whole is framed by a dramatic hilly backdrop. It's also the nearest resort to the facilities and ferries of Ban Sala Dan, about half an hour's walk away, or 2–3km by road. The beach also has its own minimarkets and transport outlets, shoreside and along the main road.

Accommodation

There are a couple of budget-oriented places to stay on Hat Khlong Dao, but the emphasis is on accommodation for families and others looking for air-conditioned comfort. See map, p.430.

Cha-Ba Bungalows ℡075 684118, www .krabidir.com/chababbungalows/index.htm. There's plenty of kitsch creativity at this idiosyncratic complex of bungalows, restaurant and art gallery, set among bright blue Flintstone walls and archways and oversized concrete sculptures. The fifteen en-suite fan and air-con bungalows are simple and flimsy, but cute, decorated with loud retro-look fabrics and wallpapers. Air-con ones come with TVs, fridges, safety boxes and hot water. Fan ❸–❺, air-con ❻ and other caves; visibility is often very good. Much further south, about 56km from Ko Lanta, there's a fifty-metre wall at spectacular **Hin Daeng** and **Hin Muang**, plus a good chance of seeing tuna, jacks, silvertip sharks, manta rays and even whale sharks. See the descriptions of Andaman coast dive sites on p.370 for more on some of these reefs.

Ko Lanta's best **dive shops** include the German-run Ko Lanta Diving Centre, on the main road into Ban Sala Dan, with a branch office at *Lanta Island* hotel on central Hat Khlong Dao (⊤075 668065, ⊛www.kolantadivingcenter.com); and the Swedish-owned, PADI Five-star Instructor Development Centre, Lanta Diver, also on the main road into Ban Sala Dan, and with branch offices at *Relax Bay* near Hat Khlong Dao and at *Ozone Bar* on Ao Phra-Ae (⊤087 891 4141, ⊛www.lantadiver.com). They charge B2600–3100 for **two dives**, excluding equipment, and B1500 for accompanying snorkellers, with discounts if you do three consecutive days. Diving **courses** average out at B13,500 for the four-day Openwater course, or B10,500 for the two-day Advanced course. The nearest recompression chambers are located on Phuket (see p.370); check to see that your dive operator is insured to use one of them, and see Basics, p.58, for more information on diving in Thailand.

Kayaking

There are several rewarding **kayaking** destinations, rich in mangroves and caves, around Ko Lanta Yai's east coast and around Ko Lanta Noi and its eastern islands, including **Ko Talabeng** and **Ko Bubu**; a few companies also offer kayak-snorkel trips to the four islands described above. Trips can be arranged through tour operators in Ban Sala Dan, and on most beaches, for B750–1200 per person (kids B550–600).

Day-trips inland

Ko Lanta's biggest inland attraction is the **Tham Mai Kaew caves** (see p.435). Though it's not much more than a trickle, the **waterfall** inland from Ao Khlong Jaak is another fairly popular spot, and can be reached from the bay by walking along the course of the stream for about two hours. Alternatively join one of the tours that combine visits to the caves and the waterfall with an **elephant-ride** (from B700/500).

Costa Lanta ⊤075 684630, ⊛www.costalanta .com. You're either going to love or hate this ultra-brutal minimalist grouping of 22 polished-grey concrete boxes, each module containing an unadorned bedroom all in grey and white and a similarly styled bathroom. The setting is less than magnificent – a dry, plain garden bisected by greenish khlongs – but there's a biggish pool, a striking bar-restaurant and DVD players in every room. ➒

Hans ⊤075 684152, ⊛www.krabidir.com /hansrestaurant. By far the cheapest place on this beach, with fifteen huts ranged along a narrow strip of garden behind the shorefront restaurant in the heart of the beach. Choose between very simple, rickety bamboo bungalows with mosquito nets and bathrooms, and better-furnished wooden versions with screened windows. All bungalows are wi-fi accessible. Closed from early April to Oct. ➌–➍

Kaw Kwang Beach Resort At the northernmost end of Khlong Dao ⊤081 979 6959,

⊛www.lanta-kawkwangresort.com. Welcoming, family-run outfit of 61 good-value (for Lanta) rooms occupying a huge area of beachfront land between the headland's two shores. There are many options here, from cheap, decent, old-style en-suite wood and concrete huts among the trees above the shore, through bigger, beachside air-con bungalows, family bungalows and hotel-style rooms. Has a pool and wi-fi in some rooms. Open all year with fifty-percent discounts from June–Oct. Fan ➌–➍, air-con ➏–➑

The Noble House ⊤075 668096, ⊛www .lantanoblehouse.com. Appealingly small-scale, Swiss-run place where the 23 inviting fan and air-con bungalows have big glass windows and bathtubs. They're set in facing rows, in a pretty shrub-filled garden, mostly around the little swimming pool. Also has a few rooms in a couple of small two-storey blocks. Fan ➎, air-con ➐

Southern Lanta Resort ⊤075 684175, ⊛www .southernlanta.com. One of the biggest hotels on the beach, offering dozens of very spacious air-con bungalows set at decent intervals around a garden of shrubs, clipped hedges and shady trees. There's a good-sized swimming pool too and wi-fi throughout. Popular with families and package tourists. ➐

Eating and drinking

Restaurant tables fill the shoreline in the evening, illuminated with fairy lights and lanterns, which lends a nice mellow atmosphere. The formula is very similar at most of them, with fresh seafood barbecues the main attraction during the season. *Costa Lanta*'s sea-view daybeds and plump bolsters are the most sophisticated venue, and a good reason to linger over the pricey but very good menu, especially its lemon grass martinis and the sea bass steamed in banana leaves. Down at the far southern end of the beach, *Slow Down* is all about keeping the family happy, with its special kids' menu (and quite limited but reasonably priced Thai-European adult version), enormous ice creams, cushion seating in a converted longtail boat and, most importantly, its volleyball net within sight of adult dining areas.

Clusters of little beach **bars** serve cocktails on deckchairs and cushions, often with a campfire to gather round and chillout music. One of the most genial is *Indian Bar*, next to *Cha-Ba Bungalows*, where the host, easily spotted by his trademark Sioux-style feather headdress, makes a mean cocktail and does good fire-juggling shows.

Ao Phra-Ae (Long Beach)

With its lovely long parade of soft, white sand, calm and crystal-clear water that's good for swimming and shady fringe of casuarina trees, **AO PHRA-AE** (also known as **Long Beach**) is strikingly beautiful and the best of Lanta's many long beaches. There's a little more variety and character among the accommodation options here than at Khlong Dao, a couple of kilometres to the north, and quite

Ko Phi Phi & Ao Nang ▲   Ko Jum & ▲ Krabi

BAN SALA DAN, HAT KHLONG DAO & AO PHRA-AE

➊ Police
➋
➌
➍

✚ Health Centre

Kaw Kwang Ⓐ   Ⓑ

Ⓒ

Ⓓ

▶ Car Ferry

Hat Khlong Dao

N

Ⓔ

Ⓕ
➎

➏

0   500 m

Ⓖ
➐ Ⓗ
Ⓘ
Ⓙ
➑ ✚
Ⓚ

Ao Phra-Ae (Long Beach)

➒

➓
⑪
Ⓛ

Ⓜ

Hat Khlong Khong ▼

EATING & DRINKING

Baan Café	3
Bai Fern	2
Catfish	2
Costa Lanta	B
Indian Bar	5
Klapa Klum	8
Kocha	4
Ko Lanta Seafood	1
Moonwalk Bar	11
Out to Lunch	7
Ozone Bar	7
Red Snapper	10
Sayang Beach Resort	H
Slow Down	6
Thai Cuisine	9

ACCOMMODATION

Cha-Ba Bungalows	F
Costa Lanta	B
Hans	D
Kaw Kwang Beach Resort	A
Lanta LD Beach	H
Lanta Marina Resort	L
Lanta Palm Beach	J
Layana	K
The Noble House	C
Relax Bay Resort	M
Sayang Beach Resort	G
Somewhere Else	I
Southern Lanta Resort	E

a development of shops, with ATM, restaurants and tour agents along the main road. The main stretch of the beach is divided from the southern rocky extremity by a shallow, easily wadeable khlong; *Lanta Marina Resort* marks the southern reaches of the beach and is about half an hour's walk along the beach from *Sayang* at the northern end. Phra Ae's budget enclave clusters along a network of sandy tracks behind the *Ozone Bar*.

Accommodation

Accommodation is marked on the map opposite.

4

Lanta LD Beach (formerly Sandy Beach) ⊕075 684548, ⓦwww.sandybeachlanta.com. In a grassy lot just behind *Somewhere Else* and the beach bars, 100m from the sea, this place offers cheapish en-suite bamboo bungalows with fans and mosquito nets, plus more robust concrete alternatives with either fans or air-con, TVs and hot water. ④–⑤

🏃 **Lanta Marina Resort** ⊕075 684168, ⓔlanta_marina_resort@yahoo.com. At the far southern end of Ao Phra-Ae, inland from a rocky point, this friendly little place has just thirteen shaggily thatched wood-and-split-bamboo bungalows angled towards the sea, connected by a wooden walkway that circles a small lawn. Huts vary in size but all have nice beds, well-designed bathrooms, high palm-leaf rooves, fans and wi-fi access. ④

Lanta Palm Beach ⊕075 684406, ⓦwww.lantapalmbeachresort.com. A busy, central and popular spot that has a range of different bungalows within stumbling distance of several beach bars. Cheapest are the handful of bamboo huts with bathrooms, good beds and mosquito nets that enjoy a full view of the sea. The forty pricier concrete bungalows set back from the shore, within a garden of neat clipped hedges, and come with fan or air-con and in varying degrees of luxury. Has internet access. Fan ③, air-con ④–⑥

🏃 **Layana** ⊕075 607100, ⓦwww.layanaresort.com. Located plumb in the middle of the beautiful beach, this is currently the top spot on Ao Phra-Ae and one of the best and most liked on the whole island, not least for its calm ambience (the hotel has a no-under-18s policy) and attentive service. Its fifty air-con rooms occupy chunky, two-storey villas designed in modern-Thai style and set around a tidy beachfront

garden of lawns and mature shrubs; the priciest have sea views. There's a gorgeous shorefront salt-water infinity pool, a spa, dive centre and plenty of day-trip activities, plus wi-fi throughout. ⑨

Relax Bay Resort ⊕075 684194, ⓦwww.relaxbay.com. Sharing its own tiny bay south around the next rocky point (and quite a hike) from *Lanta Marina*, with just one other set of bungalows, the style of this French-managed place is affordable rustic chic. Accommodation is in forty tastefully simple thatched bungalows, all with large sea-view decks and beds for three. Choose between fan and air-con. Also has a luxury African-safari style "romantic" en-suite tent on stilts. There's a pool, and yoga classes during high season (see p.427). Open all year. Fan ⑤, air-con ⑥–⑧

🏃 **Sayang Beach Resort** ⊕075 684156, ⓦwww.sayangbeach.com. Very welcoming, family-run, mid-range place whose thirty fan and air-con bungalows are nicely spaced beneath the palm trees in the expansive shorefront grounds. Some bungalows are designed for families and there's also a beachfront suite. Prices include buffet breakfasts and there's a very good restaurant here too. Fan ⑤, air-con ⑥–⑧

Somewhere Else ⊕081 536 0858. Located in the heart of the liveliest part of Ao Phra-Ae, with beach bars left, right and seaward, this is one of the main travellers centres on the beach, with the cheapest rooms, and correspondingly hectic. It has just sixteen spacious, unusually designed hexagonal bungalows made of tightly woven bamboo and with pretty bathrooms. Price depends on the size. The drawback is that most are close together and lack a sense of privacy, though many have sea views. ③–④

Eating and drinking

Most of Ao Phra-Ae's most interesting **restaurants** are along the main road, while down on the beach you get small, mellow **bars**.

Klapa Klum Near *Lanta Palm* bungalows. There are bamboo love-booths and private seating areas at this beachfront bar plus happy hours (6–8pm), cheap cocktails all night long and weekly on-the-beach parties.

Moonwalk Bar One of the livelier spots on the far southern beach, with cushion seating on a beautifully sited deck that offers good sea views and breezes, weekly parties with fireshows and music that's mostly trance and techno, barbecues and discounted beer until sunset.

Out to Lunch Next to *Ozone*. Accurately named, this is indeed a good place for lunch, right on the beach and with a range of breads and fillings: paninis and baguettes (mostly B140) topped or filled with imported cheeses – mozzarella, edam, cheddar – and cold meats. Also does burgers and salads.

Ozone Bar On the beach, near *Somewhere Else* bungalows. One of the most famous bars on the beach, especially for its weekly beach parties, which usually draw a lively crowd.

Red Snapper On the main road, inland from *Lanta Marina* bungalows at the southern end of Phra-Ae. Tapas and creative European cuisine are the hallmarks of this highly rated Dutch-run restaurant and bar, where the mid-priced menu changes every couple of months. Daily from 6pm.

Sayang Beach Resort On the beach, at *Sayang Beach Resort*. This is a lovely spot for dinner, with tables set out under shoreside casuarinas strung with fairy lights. The kitchen here has a tandoori oven and serves a long menu of authentic Indian dishes, including sheesh, masalas and dhal, as well as Thai and Western food, plus fresh seafood nightly and a big veggie menu. Mains B70–220.

🍴 **Thai Cuisine** On the main road, inland from *Layana*. Very popular, outdoor place that serves some deliciously authentic Thai food (B60–180), from thick *matsaman* curries to fiery *kway tiaw phat kii maew* (drunkard's fried noodles, so called because the liberal use of chilli is meant to sober you up). Also has plenty of seafood plus some more unusual choices including a surprisingly delicious rice fried with banana. Daily from 6pm.

Hat Khlong Khong

The luxuriously long beach at **HAT KHLONG KHONG**, 2km south of Ao Phra-Ae's *Relax Bay Resort*, is peppered with rocks and in most parts only really swimmable at high tide, though the snorkelling is good. Another big draw is the traveller-oriented bungalows, among them the most creatively designed places to stay on the island. There are several funky little **beach-bars** too, with the inevitable "special" mushroom omelettes on the menu.

Accommodation

🍴 **Bee Bee Bungalow** ☏081 537 9932, ✉beebeepiya02@hotmail.com, 🌐www .diigii.de/sugarbeebee. A special, friendly place that stands out for its thirteen highly individual huts, each one a charmingly idiosyncratic experiment in bamboo architecture. All the bungalows are simple but comfortably furnished, given style with batik fabric flourishes, and have fans, mosquito nets and partially open-air bathrooms; some have an upstairs room as well. Closed early May to mid-Oct; unlike most other places on the beach it keeps its prices constant throughout the season. ❸–❹

🍴 **Fisherman's Cottage** ☏081 476 1529, 🌐www.fishermanscottage.biz. This quiet, low-key chummy place at the southern end of the beach has just eleven thatched-roof and concrete bungalows, each with big windows, quite spartan one-off beach-modern interiors – whitewashed concrete, nutty mural artworks, splashes of strong colour – mosquito nets, fans and good bathrooms. Free wi-fi throughout. Closed mid-may to Oct. ❹

Lanta Riviera ☏075 667043, 🌐www.lantariviera .net. There are rows and rows of good, standard-issue, comfortably furnished fan and air-con concrete bungalows here, plus a few rooms in a two-storey building, set among shady beds of shrubs and flowers at the far northern end of the beach. Many of the rooms sleep three so it's popular with families. Also has a small pool near the shore. Fan ❹, air-con ❺–❼

Lanta New Coconut ☏081 537 7590, ✉newcoconut@hotmail.com. A range of options here, including sturdy wooden bungalows with fan, plus stone and concrete versions with TVs and hot water and the option of fan or air-con. ❸–❺

Where Else? ☏081 536 4870, 🌐www.lanta -where-else.com. As you might expect from the name, this charming collection of 22 bungalows has a laid-back vibe and lots of personality, though it's more of a party place than *Bee Bee*. The artfully and individually designed bamboo and coconut-wood bungalows all have fans, mosquito nets and open-air bathrooms filled with plants, and there are shell mobiles, driftwood sculptures and pot plants all over the place. The pricier bungalows are larger and nearer the sea, and some even have bamboo sunroofs and turrets. ❸–❻

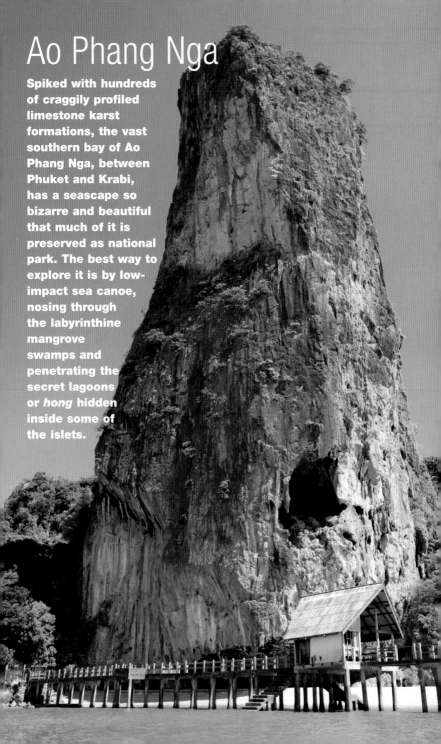

Ao Phang Nga

Spiked with hundreds of craggily profiled limestone karst formations, the vast southern bay of Ao Phang Nga, between Phuket and Krabi, has a seascape so bizarre and beautiful that much of it is preserved as national park. The best way to explore it is by low-impact sea canoe, nosing through the labyrinthine mangrove swamps and penetrating the secret lagoons or *hong* hidden inside some of the islets.

Karst islands ▲

Entering a *hong* ▼

Khao Tapu ▼

Secret lagoons

Hong are the *pièce de résistance* of Ao Phang Nga: invisible to any passing boat, these hidden tidal lagoons are roofless caves enclosed within seemingly impenetrable limestone outcrops, accessible via murky tunnels that can only be navigated at certain tides in sea canoes small enough to slip beneath and between low-lying overhangs.

Like the islands themselves, the *hong* ("rooms" in Thai) have taken millions of years to form, with the softer limestone hollowed out from the side by the pounding waves, and from above by the wind and the rain. Eventually, when the *hong's* roof collapsed and the two hollows met, the interior of the karst formation was able to receive sufficient light to support its own ecosystem, around and above the tidal lagoon.

The most spectacular *hong* lie within the island of **Ko Panak**, in the western bay, where limestone cliffs hide tunnels to no fewer than five different tidal lagoons. Other commonly visited *hong* include **Ko Hong**, also in the western bay, and **Ko Lao Bileh** (also sometimes known as Ko Hong) in the eastern bay.

The world inside these collapsed cave systems is an extraordinary one, protected from the open bay by a turreted ring of cliff faces hung with vertiginous **prehistoric-looking gardens** of upside-down cycads, twisted bonsai palms, lianas, miniature screw pines and tangled ferns. And as the tide withdraws, the *hong's* resident creatures emerge to forage on the muddy floor, among them fiddler crabs, mudskippers, dusky langurs and crab-eating macaques, with white-bellied sea eagles often hovering overhead.

Viewed from the intimate proximity of a sea canoe, a *hong* island's **exterior walls** reveal an equally fascinating ecosystem. Red, yellow and orange encrusting sponges flourish along the tide-line, interspersed with oyster shells and primitive eight-valved molluscs known as chitons – all of which provide good camouflage for the scuttling red, blue and black crabs.

Tours of the bay

The bay covers some four hundred square kilometres of coast between Phuket and Krabi.

The main *hong* islands are in the **western bay** area, near Phuket, and in the **eastern bay** area, between Ko Yao Noi and Krabi.

The islands with the most photogenic silhouettes, on the other hand, are concentrated in the **central bay** area, near the town of Phang Nga. This is where you'll find so-called **James Bond Island**, whose twin outcrops, Khao Ping Gan and Khao Tapu, served as Scaramanga's lair in the movie *The Man with the Golden Gun*. Also in the central bay is the famously quaint stilt-village island of **Ko Panyi**, one of only relatively few inhabited islands in Ao Phang Nga.

Tours of the bay, by tour boat, longtail or sea canoe, can be arranged from any resort on **Phuket**, from **Ko Yao Noi**, **Khao Lak** or **Phang Nga town**, and from any of the Krabi beaches and islands: **Krabi town**, **Ao Nang**, **Laem Phra Nang** or **Ko Phi Phi**; see relevant accounts for details and prices.

All the main areas of the bay are extremely popular so don't expect a solitary experience; one good way to escape the crowds is to go on an **overnight self-guided paddle** from Ko Yao Noi.

▲ White-bellied sea eagle

▼ Ao Phang Nga

▼ Fishing from a longtail boat

Mangrove roots ▲

Crab-eating macaque ▼

Mangrove mazes

Mangroves have colonized the mud flats inside most *hong*, but the biggest and creepiest **mangrove swamps** are those that fringe the mainland coastline of the central and eastern bay areas, particularly around **Phang Nga town**, **Ao Thalen** and **Ao Luk**. Here, hundreds of mangrove-clogged inlets are just begging to be explored, their labyrinthine networks of tidal channels harbouring further clandestine worlds, which, like *hong*, are only really accessible to canoeists, and only at certain tides.

At high tide only the upper branches of the various species of mangrove are visible, most of them thick with the glossy, dark-green leaves designed to excrete excess salt. But as the tide recedes, the swamps become ever more unearthly, their exposed **aerial roots** forming a tangled mass of knotted archways above the muddy sea floor. These roots absorb oxygen and are crucial to the mangrove's breathing apparatus, but they also serve a wider purpose, trapping silt and thus gradually reclaiming land from the sea, and buffering shorelines from erosion and tropical storms, as was highlighted during the 2004 tsunami. Their ecological importance isn't appreciated by all, however, and mangrove forests across Thailand are threatened by encroaching prawn farms and commercial charcoal producers.

Mangrove swamps host an intriguing cast of creatures, among them the **mudskipper**, a specially adapted fish that can absorb atmospheric oxygen on land as long as it keeps its skin damp; the **fiddler crab**, named after the male's single outsized reddish claw; and every crustacean's nemesis, the sea-loving **crab-eating macaque**.

Hat Khlong Nin

About 4km south of Hat Khlong Khong the road forks at kilometre-stone 13, at the edge of the village of **Ban Khlong Nin**. The left-hand, east-bound arm runs across to Ko Lanta Yai's east coast, via the caves and viewpoint (see p.435). The right-hand fork is the route to the southern beaches and continues southwards along the west coast for 14km to the southern tip.

Just beyond the junction, the little enclave of bungalows, restaurants, bars and tour agents at **HAT KHLONG NIN** lend this beach more of a village atmosphere than the northern beaches. The beach itself is lovely: long and sandy and good for swimming, and free of visible commercial tat; although the road runs close alongside it, the traffic is pretty light. There are several reasonably priced places to stay here, with the cheapest beds in some hotels located in separate little garden compounds on the inland side of the road, and a low-key collection of shoreside bar-restaurants with plenty of character and mellow vibes.

There's a minimarket, **ATM** and clinic at the Ban Khlong Nin junction, and *Atcha Hut* has a **hammam** steam room. Taxis to Sala Dan should cost about B80 per person and you can walk the 3km to the Tham Mai Kaew caves from Khlong Nin in about an hour.

Accommodation

Atcha Hut ☏089 470 4607, ✉juneto14@hotmail .com. A truly individual, alternative spot at the northern end of the beach, where a couple of adobe caravanserai-style dormitory buildings have B150 beds, the cheapest singles on the island, each in their own little concrete, open-sided cubbyhole, screened by a curtain. Also has six dinky, en-suite wooden bungalows and a hammam and massage service. ❸

Chalee Bar and Bungalows ☏087 685 0080. Cute, homely place of just half-a-dozen simple, rickety but en-suite fan-cooled bamboo bungalows, all with decks and shell mobiles, set in a pretty little sandy garden that's right by the road but also right on the shore. Also has four even more basic rooms, sharing a bathroom, above the restaurant. ❶–❷

Lanta Nature Beach Resort ☏075 662560, ⓦwww.lantanaturebeachresort.com. In the cluster of concrete bungalow operations right on the beach at the southern end of Khlong Nin, this one has rows of cream-and-lilac painted fan and air

concrete huts, with spacious tiled interiors. There are even bigger, cheaper bungalows in a garden inland, across the road. Fan ❹–❻, air-con ❺–❼

Lanta Paradise ☏075 662569, ⓦwww .lantaparadiseresort.com. Though the shorefront concrete bungalows here are packed uncomfortably close together, they feel spacious inside; they lack style and are plain but are all air-con, and there's a pool here too. There are cheaper fan bungalows in a garden across the road. Fan ❸, air-con ❺–❼

Otto Bungalow ☏084 051 7180, ✉otto_lanta @hotmail.com. Run by the same people behind the *Bar and Grill* 300m south along the beach, there are just four shorefront A-frame cabins here, with thatched roofs, concrete walls, mosquito nets and fans. Also has an air-con room in a converted bus, beside the small swimming pool, plus a deluxe air-con beachside villa. The drawback is it's right by the road. Fan ❹, air-con ❻

Eating and drinking

A dozen or so mellow little beachfront **bar–restaurants** make inviting places to while away a few hours, day or night, with mats and cushions on the sand, tables under the shade of the spiky shoreside pandanus trees, and appropriately chilled sounds. *Jai-Dee*, in the northerly cluster, has a lovely shady deck, internet access and free wi-fi, a massage service and a good menu of Thai curries and sandwiches. Larger, more formal, beach-view *Otto Bar and Grill*, serves seafood and Thai and European dishes, while *Cook Kai* restaurant, diagonally north across the road from *Nice Beach* bungalows, does hearty portions of all the Thai classics, plus famous hotplate dishes including sizzling squid with garlic and pepper, for B80–170.

Hat Khlong Nam Jud

Just over 1km south of Hat Khlong Nin, the road passes the two tiny little bays known as **HAT KHLONG NAM JUD**. The northerly one is the domain of *The Narima* (℡075 662668, Ⓦwww.narima-lanta.com; ❼–❽), a very quiet but welcoming, elegantly designed, environmentally conscious resort of 32 posh but unadorned thatch-roofed bamboo bungalows set in three rows in a palm-filled garden. The bungalows all have polished wood floors, verandas with sea view, and fans as well as air-con (but no TV); there's also a three-tiered pool (with kids' level), a spa and a dive centre, and staff rent out jeeps.

A brief scramble around the rocky point to the south, the next tiny cove is rocky in parts but enjoys a swimmable beach and one set of bungalows, *Lanta Coral Beach* (℡075 62535; fan ❸–❹, air-con ❺; closed May–Oct). The twenty good-sized plain but very clean bamboo and concrete huts here are scattered among the palms (some of which are hung with hammocks) and come with fan or air-con.

Ao Kantiang

The secluded cove of **AO KANTIANG**, some 7km beyond Hat Khlong Nam Jud, is an impressively long curve, backed by jungle-clad hillsides and dominated by one luxury hotel, which keeps the southern half of the beach in pristine condition. Unusually for Lanta, the bay is protected enough to be good for swimming year-round, and there's some coral at the northern end; snorkelling and fishing trips are easily arranged. The small but lively roadside village covers most necessities, including tours, onward transport, motorbike rental and internet access. There's also a clinic a little further south, between *Kantiang Bay View* and *Pimalai*. Wherever you're staying on Ao Kantiang, it's well worth heading down to *Same Same But Different*, a tranquil haven of a **restaurant** on the beach to the south of *Pimalai*, where the tables are set beneath a tangled growth of shrubs and vines, surrounded by shell-mobiles and driftwood sculptures; it's run by the man behind the renowned *Ruen Mai* restaurant in Krabi, and the mid-priced menu of mainly Thai and seafood dishes is of a similarly high standard.

The thirty or so **bungalows** at the buzzing *Lanta Marine Park View* (℡081 956 2935, Ⓦwww.lantamarine.com; fan ❹, air-con ❺–❼) are ranged up the slope at the northern end of the beach: steps lead down to the shore. The best of the bungalows, though pricey, are great value as they're on stilts and enjoy glorious bay views from their balconies and glass-fronted interiors, and the furnishings are chic and modern. The cheap fan-cooled bamboo bungalows sit further back and are plain and not especially interesting for the price. There's also a small cliffside bar affording great views, plus internet access and a tour agency. Down at sea level, the southern end of Ao Kantiang is the province of one of Ko Lanta's poshest hotels, the *Pimalai Resort and Spa* (℡075 607999, Ⓦwww.pimalai.com; ❾; published rates from B11,500), which spreads over such an extensive area that guests are shuttled around in golf buggies. All rooms are luxuriously and elegantly designed in contemporary style, and there's a delightful spa, a swimming pool and dive centre. However, only the more expensive accommodation gets a sea view (the walled beach villas are particularly stunning). From November to April, guests are transferred direct to the resort by boat, landing at the *Pimalai*'s private floating jetty.

Ao Khlong Jaak and Ao Mai Phai

The paved road terminates at the *Pimalai* boundary at the southern end of Ao Kantiang, so from here to Lanta's southern tip, about 4km away, access is via a steeply undulating, rutted and potholed track that's either dusty or muddy depending on the season – take care on a motorbike as it's extremely challenging. The next bay south of Ao Kantiang is **AO KHLONG JAAK**, site of the lively, buzzing *Anda Lanta Resort* (T075 665018, Wwww.andalanta.com; ❼–❽), which offers two-dozen well-furnished, well-maintained air-con bungalows and rooms (with wi-fi) set around the shorefront garden and swimming pool. It's popular with families and has kayaks and plenty of day-tripping options, though be prepared for a long drive if you want to go to the village facilities of Ban Saladan, for example. Sharing the bay, but right at the other end, convivial, traveller-oriented *Khlong Jaak Bungalows* (T075 665016; ❸–❹) has fan-cooled bamboo huts nicely located by the sea, plus some less interesting concrete air-con boxes, and a few rooms in a building at the back of the plot. The staff do regular beach barbecues and rent motorbikes.

South around the headland from *Klong Jaak Bungalows*, western Lanta plays its final card in the shape of handsome white-sand **AO MAI PHAI**, a peaceful getaway because of its remote position on the unmade road. There's good coral close to shore here, but this makes it too rocky for low-tide swimming, when you'll need to kayak up to Ao Klong Jaak instead. At the northern end of the bay, the welcoming and very popular Thai-Danish *Bamboo Bay Resort* (T075 665023, Wwww.bamboobay.net; fan ❹, air-con ❻–❼) offers 21 concrete bungalows, with fan or air-con, stepped up the cliffside above the headland, plus a few just across the narrow road. Nearly all have great sea views and interiors are spacious and of a high standard. Its *pièce de resistance* is its idyllically sited deck restaurant and bar, which jut out over the rocks just above the water. Occupying the centre of the bay, the tastefully camp *Baan Phu Lae* (T081 201 1704, Wwww.baanphulae.net; fan ❺, air-con ❻; closed May to mid-Oct) manages to combine a whiff of Bangkok sophistication with laid-back island charm. Its nine fan-cooled bamboo bungalows are stylishly simple and nearly all enjoy direct sea views; the four air-con rooms high above the shore are less interesting. The most luxurious of the trio on this beach is *La Lanta Hideaway Resort* (T087 883 9966, Wwww.lalaanta .com; ❼–❾) at the far southern end; it's very well liked for its attentive staff and comfortable wooden-floored villas – all with air-con, DVD players, low beds and wi-fi – built to a cosy, village-style layout, around two pools and a beachfront garden.

The interior and the east coast

Although the **east coast** lacks decent beaches, it's got plenty of other attractions, including an impressive series of caves at **Tham Mai Kaew**, a jaw-droppingly great **view over islands and coastlines** at the viewpoint (worth an early rise), an atmospheric neighbourhood in **Lanta Old Town**, and cultural interest at its museum. The tiny island of Ko Bubu is also reached from here. Access to the east coast is easy as the road is good: it starts at the Ban Klong Nin junction halfway down the west coast at kilometre-stone 13. Alternatively, most tour agencies offer guided day-trips covering this area.

Tham Mai Kaew caves

The myriad chambers at **Tham Mai Kaew caves**, some of which you can only just crawl into, are Ko Lanta's biggest inland attraction. They are filled with stalactites and interesting rock formations, and there's a creepy cave pool too, as well as the inevitable bats. Access to the cave, 3km from the Khlong Nin junction, is regulated by the local family who first properly explored the cave system in the 1980s: they now act as caretakers and guides, in conjunction with the national park authorities, and charge B200 for a two-hour tour (elephant rides, longer cave tours, and overnight jungle treks are also available). Most of Thailand's countless caves are underwhelming and certainly not worth B200, but this is one of the better ones, not least because the caretakers have resisted stringing it with electric lights so you're left to wonder both at what you catch with your torch and at what you don't see. Among its star features are crystallized waterfalls, fossils and ammonites embedded in the cave walls and overhangs, stalagmites and stalactites young and old and a tangible sense of there being endless passageways to explore. In the rainy season it's a more slippery, challenging experience, with some wading likely and the option of a dip in the wet-season-only lagoon. Even in the dry season it's moderately arduous and best done in sensible shoes and clothes you're happy to get grubby in. If you don't have your own transport, a motorcycle taxi costs about B200 each way from Khlong Dao or Ao Phra-Ae.

The viewpoint

Three kilometres beyond the turn-off to the caves, the eastbound road drops down over the central spine of hills and you pass *Viewpoint* café (daily 6am–9pm), where nearly everyone stops for a drink and a gawp at the stunning panorama. The **view over the east coast** is glorious, encompassing the southeast coast of mangrove-fringed Ko Lanta Noi, dozens of islets – including Ko Bubu and Ko Por – adrift in the milky blue sea, and the hilly profile of the mainland along the horizon. It's an unbeatable spot for a sunrise breakfast.

Lanta Old Town (Ban Si Raya)

Once back down at sea level, follow the east-coast road (Route 4245) south for a few kilometres to reach, at kilometre-stone 20, the seductively atmospheric little waterfront settlement of **LANTA OLD TOWN** (ⓦwww .lantaoldtown.com), officially known as **Ban Si Raya**. Ko Lanta's oldest town, it began life as a sheltered staging post for ships sailing between China and Penang and served as the island's administrative capital from 1901 to 1998. The government offices have since moved to Ko Lanta Noi, and Ban Sala Dan has assumed the role of harbour, island gateway and commercial hub, so Ban Si Raya has been left much as it was a century ago, with its historic charm intact. There's little more to the Old Town than its peaceful main street, which runs right along the coast and is lined with traditional, hundred-year-old sea- and wind-blasted wooden homes and shops, many of them constructed on stilted jetties over the sea, their first-floor overhangs shading the pavements and plant-filled doorways. The Chinese shrine midway down the street is evidence of the town's cultural mix: Ban Si Raya is home to a long-established Buddhist Chinese-Thai community as well as to Muslims and, in its southern neighbourhood, communities of animist Urak Lawoy *chao ley* ("sea gypsies").

The **Urak Lawoy** *chao ley* (see box, p.335) are thought to have been Ko Lanta's first inhabitants, perhaps as long as five hundred years ago, living along the shoreline during the monsoon season and setting off along the coast again when the winds abated. They have now settled permanently in their own villages on the island, including at **Ban Sang-Ga-U**, 4km to the south of the Lanta Old Town; other Urak Lawoy living elsewhere in the Andaman Sea, around Trang and beyond, consider Ko Lanta their capital and will always stop at Sang-Ga-U when making a journey. One of the accessible elements of Urak Lawoy culture is their **music**, an interesting fusion of far-flung influences, featuring violins (from the Dutch East Indies), drums (from Persia), and gongs (from China), as well as singing, dancing and ritual elements. A good time to hear their music is at one of their twice-yearly three-day full-moon **festivals**, or at the Laanta Lanta Festival (see p.425).

There's an attempt to introduce the cultures of Ban Si Raya's three distinct but peaceable communities at the **Koh Lanta Community Museum** (daily 9am–5pm; B40), which is housed in the attractive 1901 wooden building that used to serve as the local district office, across the small grassy park from the pier and parking lot. Archive photos and the odd English-language caption describe the main occupations for the communities, including fishing, trading and making charcoal from mangrove wood; there's also a fair bit on post-tsunami projects and an interesting video in which villagers air their concerns about the recent explosion in tourism on the island and the effect that the influx of incomers and investors is having on traditional lifestyles and livelihoods.

Practicalities

As an additional incentive to linger among the wooden architecture of main street there are several browsable **shops** selling batik sarongs and souvenirs, plus the charming Hammock House (ⓦwww.jumbohammock.com), whose amazing range of hammocks include ones woven by people of the endangered Phi Tong Luang tribe of northern Thailand. South across the bridge from the pier, Sun Island Tours sells watercolours of Ko Lanta and modern batik sarongs, as well as doing longtail boat tours (see p.428).

There are several enticing **restaurants** in the old town too: the dining area at locally popular *Kroua Lanta Yai Seafood* is on a jetty over the seafront, while sophisticated little *Mango House Seafront Villas, Bar and Café* is all done out in stylish dark wood and does burgers, salads and sandwiches. Its waterside **rooms** (ⓣ086 948 6836, ⓦwww.bestofkolanta.com; ❼) are delightful and would make an attractive and unusual Ko Lanta base. Three stilted century-old wooden buildings, one of them a former charcoal store, have been charmingly converted into guest homes that can each sleep three; interiors are furnished in fishing-village chic, with elegant contemporary bathrooms, fans, TV, free wi-fi and kitchenette. The big draw though is the large waterside deck, which affords fine views of seven islands. Enjoying a similarly mesmerizing view are the three guest-house rooms at nearby *Orange House* (ⓣ083 104 3109, ⓦwww.lantamarineservices.com; ❹–❺), which also does boat trips, charters and transfers.

There's **internet** access and wi-fi on the main street plus an **ATM**, and a fuel station on the edge of town. The hourly Krabi minibus service starts from and terminates in Lanta Old Town.

Ko Bubu

If you really want to get away from everything, the minuscule, wooded island of **Ko Bubu**, with a radius of just 500m, is the place to head for. There's little to do here other than enjoy the pretty beach, swing in a hammock and stroll the round-island trail. Ko Bubu is 7km northeast off Lanta Old Town and is the sole preserve of *Bubu Island Resort* (ⓣ075 618066; B400–1000; closed May–Oct), which has just fifteen en-suite bungalows and a restaurant. It's twenty minutes' chartered **longtail** ride (B200 per person) from Lanta Old Town.

Travel details

Buses

Cheow Lan Lake (Ratchabrapa Dam, Khao Sok) to: Phunphin (Surat Thani train station; every 2hr; 1hr).

Khao Lak to: Khao Sok (9 daily; 1hr 30min); Phuket (20 daily; 2hr 30min); Ranong (8 daily; 2hr 30min–3hr); Surat Thani (9 daily; 3hr 30min); Takua Pa (18 daily; 30min).

Khao Sok to: Khao Lak (9 daily; 1hr 30min); Surat Thani (every 90min; 2hr); Takua Pa (every 90min; 50min).

Khuraburi to: Khao Lak (5 daily; 1hr 45min); Phuket (5 daily; 3hr 30min–4hr); Ranong (5 daily; 2hr); Takua Pa (5 daily; 1hr);

Krabi to: Bangkok (10 daily; 12hr); Hat Yai (13 daily; 4–5hr); Ko Lanta (hourly; 2hr); Nakhon Si Thammarat (at least hourly; 3hr); Phang Nga (at least hourly; 2hr); Phattalung (7 daily; 3hr); Phuket (at least hourly; 4hr); Ranong (4 daily; 5hr); Satun (2 daily; 5hr); Sungai Kolok (3 daily; 9hr); Surat Thani (at least hourly; 2hr); Takua Pa (4 daily; 3hr 30min–4hr 30min); Trang (at least hourly; 2–3hr).

Phang Nga to: Bangkok (5 daily; 11hr); Krabi (at least hourly; 1hr 30min–2hr); Phuket (at least hourly; 1hr 30min–2hr 30min); Surat Thani (5 daily; 4hr); Takua Pa (at least hourly; 1hr); Trang (at least hourly; 3hr).

Phuket to: Bangkok (34 daily; 10–14hr); Chumphon (20 daily; 6hr 30min); Hat Yai (24 daily; 7hr); Khao Lak (17 daily; 2hr 30min); Khao Sok (13 daily; 3–4hr); Khuraburi (17 daily; 3hr 30min–4hr); Krabi (27 daily; 3hr–4hr 30min); Nakhon Si Thammarat (8 daily; 7hr); Phang Nga (27 daily; 1hr 30min–2hr 30min); Phattalung (20 daily; 6hr); Ranong (17 daily; 5hr 30min); Satun (5 daily; 7hr); Sungai Kolok (3 daily; 11hr); Surat Thani (13 daily; 4hr 30min); Takua Pa (17 daily; 2hr 30min–3hr); Trang (20 daily; 5–6hr).

Ranong to: Bangkok (12 daily; 9hr); Chumphon (hourly; 2–3hr); Hat Yai (3 daily; 5hr); Khao Lak (6 daily; 3hr 45min); Khuraburi (6 daily; 2hr); Krabi (5 daily; 5hr); Phang Nga (5 daily; 4hr); Phuket (6 daily; 5hr 30min); Surat Thani (10 daily; 3–5hr); Takua Pa (6 daily; 3hr).

Takua Pa to: Bangkok (10 daily; 12–13hr); Khuraburi (at least 8 daily; 1hr); Krabi (at least 4 daily; 3hr); Phang Nga (hourly; 1hr); Phuket (hourly; 3hr); Ranong (5 daily; 3hr 30min–4hr); Surat Thani (11 daily; 3hr 15min).

Ferries

Ao Nang to: Ko Lanta Yai (Nov–May 1 daily; 2hr 30min); Ko Phi Phi Don (Nov–May 1 daily; 2hr 30min); Phuket (Nov–May 1 daily; 3hr).

Khuraburi to: Ko Surin (Nov–May 1–2 daily; 1hr 15min–3hr).

Ko Chang to: Ranong (June–Oct 3 weekly; Nov–May 2 daily; 1hr).

Ko Jum to: Ko Lanta Yai (mid-Oct to mid-May 1–2 daily; 1hr); Krabi (mid-Oct to mid-May 1–2 daily; 1hr 30min); Laem Kruat (at least 4 daily; 45min–1hr).

Ko Lanta Yai to: Ao Nang (Nov–May 1 daily; 2hr 30min); Ko Phi Phi Don (Nov–May 1–2 daily; 1hr 30min); Krabi (mid-Oct to mid-May 1–2 daily; 2hr 30min); Phuket (Nov–May 1–2 daily; 4hr 30min).

Ko Phayam to: Ranong (1–4 daily; 40min–3hr).

Ko Phi Phi Don to: Ao Nang and West Railay (Nov–May 1 daily; 2hr 30min); Ko Lanta Yai (Nov–May 1–2 daily; 1hr 30min); Krabi (2–4 daily; 2hr); Phuket (at least 2 daily; 1hr 30min–2hr 30min).

Ko Yao Noi to: Krabi (Ao Thalen; 5 daily; 1hr); Phang Nga (daily; 90min); Phuket (8 daily; 1hr 10min).

Krabi to: Ko Jum (mid-Oct to mid-May 1–2 daily; 1hr 30min–2hr); Ko Lanta Yai (mid-Oct to mid-May 1–2 daily; 2hr 30min); Ko Phi Phi Don (2–4 daily; 2hr); Ko Yao Noi (departs Ao Thalen; 5 daily; 1hr).

Laem Kruat to: Ko Jum (at least every 2hr; 45min–1hr).

Phang Nga (Tha Dan) to: Ko Yao Noi (daily; 90min).

Phuket to: Ao Nang (Nov–May 1 daily; 2hr); Ko Lanta Yai (Nov–May 1 daily; 4hr 30min); Ko Phi Phi Don (2–3 daily; 1hr 30min–2hr 30min); Ko Yao Noi (hourly; 1hr 10min).

Ranong to: Ko Chang (June–Oct 3 weekly; Nov–May 3 daily; 1hr); Ko Phayam (1–4 daily; 40min–3hr).

Thap Lamu (Khao Lak) to: Ko Similan (Nov–May 1 daily; 2hr).

Flights

Krabi to: Bangkok (up to 6 daily; 1hr 20min); Ko Samui (3 weekly; 50min).

Phuket to: Bangkok (up to 27 daily; 1hr 20min); Ko Samui (2 daily; 55min); Pattaya/ U-Tapao (1–2 daily; 1hr 35min–2hr 55min).

Ranong to: Bangkok (3 weekly; 1hr 5min).

The deep south

CHAPTER 5

Highlights

* **Nature Resorts** Not-for-profit resorts, great tours and nice people, at Ban Chao Mai, on Ko Mook and Ko Libong. See p.447, p.451 & p.453

* **Ko Hai** A variety of good resorts for all budgets and gorgeous views. See p.448

* **Tham Morakhot** Ko Mook's Emerald Cave, with its inland beach at the base of a natural chimney, is best visited by kayak. See p.450

* **Ko Sukorn** For a glimpse of how islanders live and an outstanding beach resort. See p.453

* **Ko Tarutao National Marine Park** A largely undisturbed haven – bar fast-developing Ko Lipe – of beautiful land- and seascapes. See p.455

▲ Boat on Ko Mook

The deep south

The frontier between Thailand and Malaysia carves across the peninsula six degrees north of the equator, but the cultures of the two countries shade into each other much further north. According to official divisions, the southern Thais – the *thai pak tai* – begin around Chumphon, and as you move further down the peninsula you'll see ever more sarongs, yashmaks and towering mosques, and hear with increasing frequency a staccato dialect that baffles many Thais. Here too, you'll come across caged singing doves outside many houses, as well as strange-looking areas spiked with tall metal poles, on which the cages are hung during regular cooing competitions; and you'll spot huge, hump-backed Brahma bulls on the back of pick-up trucks, on their way to bullfights (in the Thai version, beast is pitted against beast, and the first to back off is the loser). In Trang and Phatthalung provinces, the Muslim population is generally accepted as being Thai, but the inhabitants of the southernmost provinces – Satun, Pattani, Yala, Narathiwat and most of Songkhla – are ethnically more akin to the Malays: most of the 1.5 million followers of Islam here speak Yawi, an old Malay dialect. To add to the ethnic confusion, the deep south has a large urban population of Chinese, whose comparative wealth makes them stand out sharply from the Muslim farmers and fishermen.

Travel warning

Because of the ongoing **violence** in the deep south (see p.443), all major Western governments are currently advising people **not to travel** to or through Songkhla, Pattani, Yala and Narathiwat provinces, unless essential; following on from this, insurance companies are refusing to cover travel in these areas. The four provinces encompass the city and transport hub of **Hat Yai** and several of the main border crossings to Malaysia: by rail from Hat Yai (and Bangkok) to Butterworth via Padang Besar and to Sungai Kolok; and by road from Hat Yai via Sadao, from Yala via Betong, and down the east coast to Kota Bharu.

The routes to Sungai Kolok, Betong and Kota Bharu pass through particularly volatile territory, with martial law declared in Pattani, Yala and Narathiwat provinces; however, **martial law** is not in effect in Hat Yai itself or the districts of Songkhla province through which the Bangkok–Butterworth rail line or the Hat Yai–Sadao road pass.

The provinces of Trang and **Satun** are not affected, and it's still perfectly possible to continue overland via Satun: by air-con minibus from nearby Ban Khuan to Kangar, or by ferry from Thammalang to Kuala Perlis or the Malaysian island of Langkawi (see p.461); or by boat from Ko Lipe to Langkawi (see p.447). For up-to-the-minute advice, consult your government travel advisory (see p.51).

The touristic interest in the deep south is currently all over on the beautiful **west coast**, where sheer limestone outcrops, pristine sands and fish-laden coral stretch down to the Malaysian border. The spread of tourism outwards from Phuket has been inching its way south towards **Trang** and **Satun** for some time now, but they remain largely undeveloped. Along Trang's mainland **coast**, there's a thirty-kilometre stretch of attractive beaches, dotted with mangroves and impressive caves that can be explored by sea canoe, but the real draw down here is the offshore **islands**, which offer gorgeous panoramas and beaches, great snorkelling and at least a modicum of comfort in their small clusters of resorts. An added attraction is the recently introduced, scheduled boat services which have set up the intriguing possibility of **island-hopping**: it would now be possible to work your way down from Phuket as far as Penang without setting foot on the peninsula.

As well as the usual bus services, the area covered in this chapter is served by flights and trains to Trang. The deep south is also the territory of **share-taxis**, which connect towns for about twice the fare of ordinary buses. The cars leave when they're full, which usually means six passengers, and sometimes a long wait, though there's always the option of buying up extra seats if you're in a hurry. They are a quick way of getting around and you should get dropped off at the door of your journey's end. A more recent – and now much more successful – phenomenon, run on almost exactly the same principles at similar prices, is **air-conditioned minibuses**; on these you'll be more comfortable, with a seat to yourself, and most of the various ranks publish a rough timetable – though the minibuses also tend to leave as soon as they're full.

Some history
The central area of the Malay peninsula first entered Thai history when it came under the rule of Sukhothai, probably around the beginning of the fourteenth century. Islam was introduced to the area by the end of that century, by which time Ayutthaya was taking a firmer grip on the peninsula. **Songkhla** and **Pattani** then rose to be the major cities, prospering on the goods passed through the two ports across the peninsula to avoid the pirates in the Straits of Malacca between Malaysia and Sumatra. More closely tied to the Muslim Malay states to the south, Pattani began to **rebel** against the central power of Ayutthaya in the sixteenth century, but the fight for self-determination only weakened Pattani's strength. The town's last rebellious fling was in 1902, after which it was definitively and brutally absorbed into the Thai kingdom, while its allies, Kedah, Kelantan and Trengganu, were transferred into the suzerainty of the British in Malaysia.

During World War II the **Communist Party of Malaya** made its home in the jungle around the Thai border to fight the occupying Japanese. After the war they turned their guns against the British colonialists, but having been excluded from power after independence, descended into general banditry and racketeering around Betong. The Thai authorities eventually succeeded in breaking up the bandit gangs in 1989 through a combination of pardons and bribes, but the stability of the region soon faced disruption from another source, a rise in **Islamic militancy**. Armed Muslim resistance to the Thai state had fluctuated at a relatively low level since the 1960s, but in early 2004 the violence escalated dramatically. Since then, there have been thousands of deaths on both sides in the troubles, and barely a day goes by without a fatal incident of one kind or another. The insurgents have viciously targeted Buddhist monks, police, soldiers, teachers and other civil servants, as well as attacking a train on the Hat Yai–Sungai Kolok line and setting off bombs in marketplaces, near tourist hotels and bars and at Hat Yai airport. Increasingly, they have attacked other Muslims who are seen to be too sympathetic to the Thai state. Writing the militants off as bandits, the authorities have stirred up hatred – and undermined moderate Muslim voices – by reacting violently, notably in crushing protests at Tak Bai and the much-revered Krue Se Mosque in Pattani in 2004, in which a total of over two hundred alleged insurgents died. Meanwhile, the army has "subcontracted" much of its work to rangers, untrained village militias, thus inflaming the situation further and deepening the ethnic divide. In 2005, the government announced a **serious state of emergency** in Pattani, Yala and Narathiwat provinces, and imposed **martial law** here and in southeastern parts of Songkhla province. This, however, has exacerbated economic and unemployment problems in what is Thailand's poorest region.

A large part of the problem is that a wide variety of shadowy groups – with names like the Pattani Islamic Mujahideen, the Barisan Revolusi Nasional-Coordinate and New Pulo – are operating against the government, generally working in small cells at village level without central control. Rather than religious issues, the most likely causes of their militancy seem to be disempowerment and resentment towards not only Thais but also the remote and corrupt Muslim elite. However, it's unclear exactly who they are or what they want and, faced with such shifting sands, all attempts to broker a ceasefire have failed.

Trang town

TRANG (also known as Taptieng) is gradually developing as a popular jumping-off point for backpackers drawn south from the crowded sands of Krabi to the pristine beaches and islands of the nearby coast. The town, which prospers on rubber, oil palms, fisheries and – increasingly – tourism, is a sociable place whose wide, clean streets are dotted with crumbling, wooden-shuttered houses. In the evening, restaurant tables sprawl onto the main Thanon Rama VI and Thanon Sathanee, and during the day, many of the town's Chinese inhabitants hang out in the cafés, drinking the local filtered coffee. Trang's Chinese population makes the **Vegetarian Festival** at the beginning of October almost as frenetic as Phuket's (see box, p.358) – and for veggie travellers it's an opportunity to feast at the stalls set up around the temples.

Arrival and information

Nok Air (℡075 212229, at the airport) and One-Two-Go (see p.33) run daily **flights** between Bangkok and Trang airport, which is connected to Trang town 3km to the north by B90 air-conditioned minibuses, operated by, for example, World Travel, 25/2 Thanon Sathanee (℡075 214010–1). Two overnight **trains** from the capital run down a branch of the southern line to Trang. **Buses** arrive at the terminal on Thanon Huay Yod, to the north of the centre, including an air-conditioned service between Satun and Phuket four times daily; many buses also make a stop near the central clocktower. Most **air-conditioned**

minibus services have their own offices, as marked on our map, while those for Pak Bara can be found at Andrew Tour travel agency opposite the station (☎075 216110, ⓦwww.andrewlipe.com), those for Ban Saladan on Ko Lanta, KK Travel next door (☎075 211198). **Share taxis** for Pak Bara and Satun congregate on Thanon Ratsada, out on the southeast side of town, for Krabi opposite the bus station.

The best **travel agency** in town is Trang Island Hopping Tour, directly opposite the station at 28/2 Thanon Sathanee (☎075 211457 or 085 888 0898, ⓦwww.trang-islands.com). This well-organized outfit offers a huge range of services, including accommodation booking on any island, boat trips, island and mainland transfers and **car rental** (with or without driver; B1200–1600 per day), as well as one-day treks inland and excursions to waterfalls and **Tham Le** (also known as Khao Kob), a dramatic inland system of caverns accessed by boat. The friendly staff are a great source of impartial information on the area, and their office makes a good first stop in town. Libong Travel, 59/1 Thanon Tha Klang (☎075 214676, ⓦwww.libong-travel.com), offer longer treks and two-night camping trips out to Ko Rok (see p.428) at weekends. **Dive** outfits include Sea Moth at 212/5 Thanon Wisetkul (☎075 225968, ⓦwww.seamoth .com). **Motorbikes** can be rented at *Wunderbar* (see p.446; B150 per day).

TAT have a **tourist office** on Thanon Wisetkul (daily 8.30am–4.30pm; ☎075 215867–8, ⓔtattrang@tat.or.th). **Internet** access is available at, among others, *Wunderbar* and Gigabyte opposite the *Koh Teng Hotel* on Thanon Rama VI.

Accommodation

Trang's **hotels** are handily concentrated along Thanon Rama VI.

Koh Teng Hotel 77–79 Thanon Rama VI ☎075 218622 or 075 218148. Characterful 1940s Chinese hotel offering large, clean en-suite rooms, some with cable TV and air-con, above a popular restaurant and coffee shop, serving southern Thai and Chinese food and Western breakfasts. Fan ➊, air-con ➋

Only for You Contact Ani's jewellery shop, 285 Thanon Ratchadamnoen ☎081 397 4574. Quiet, fan-cooled house with a rear terrace, kitchen and cold-water bathroom, 5min walk from the shop. The owners are a good source of information on the area. B1000 for three nights (minimum), B1500 per week.

Sri Trang Hotel 22 Thanon Sathanee ☎075 218122, ⓦwww.sritranghotel.com. Welcoming, recently converted hotel offering spacious rooms with some colourful decorative touches, free wi-fi,

hot water, TVs and fridges. Air-con in all but one room. Internet access. ➌

Thumrin Hotel Thanon Rama VI ☎075 211011–4, ⓦwww.thumrin.com. Formerly the top hotel in town, now offering international-standard facilities – air-con, hot water, TV, wi-fi and internet access – at bargain prices, in a high-rise block above its popular bakery-cum-coffee shop. ➌

Thumrin Thana Hotel 69/8 Thanon Huay Yod ☎075 211211, ⓦwww.thumrin.com. The best hotel in town, though not in the same league as the *Anantara* on the coast (see p.446). Spacious, well-equipped rooms, a pool and health club, wi-fi and internet access. ➐

Trang Hotel 134/2–5 Thanon Wisetkul ☎075 218944, ⓕ075 218451. Good, welcoming, moderately priced choice, with large, comfortable twin rooms with air-con, hot water and TV. ➌

Eating and drinking

Trang's streets are dotted with dozens of traditional cafés, which serve up gallons of **kopii** (local filtered coffee) accompanied by various tidbits and light meals. Most famous of these is the local delicacy, **muu yaang**, delicious barbecued pork, which is generally eaten for breakfast. At the excellent **night market**, around the back of the city hall on Thanon Ruenrom, you can try another tasty southern dish, *khanom jiin*, soft noodles topped with hot, sweet or fishy sauces and eaten with crispy greens.

Fatimah Thanon Sathanee. Simple, pink-awninged restaurant that's especially popular in the evenings. Buffet of southern halal curries all day, tasty *pat thai* (3–11pm), *kopii* and tea.

See Far Lifestyle 37 Thanon Phattalung ☏075 210139. Excellent, inexpensive restaurant with a varied menu of carefully prepared dishes, specializing in healthy cuisine – fruit and veg sorbets, brown rice – and local food, such as *tom som plakapong*, a light, refreshing soup of sea bass, mushrooms and cumin, and *kao yok*, a Chinese-style dish of steamed pork with taro found only in Trang.

Sin-o-cha Next to the station at 25/25–26 Thanon Sathanee. Very popular, updated traditional café: *kopii* with Thai and Western cakes and main courses, or espresso, various teas, Western breakfasts, and even baguettes and ciabattas. Daily 7am–7pm.

Wang Jaa Thanon Huay Yod, near the Hat Yai minibus office. Simple café open for breakfast and lunch, that's renowned for its *muu yaang*, but also serves *salapao* (Chinese buns), dim sum and, of course, *kopii*.

Wunderbar Bottom end of Thanon Rama VI, near the station ☏075 214563, ⓦwww .wunderbar-trang.com. Multi-purpose farang bar-restaurant that serves a wide selection of drinks (including wine), Thai food, and salads, burgers, pizzas and other Western favourites. Also acts as a travel agent, especially for island bookings, and offers internet and reasonably priced overseas calls.

The Trang coast

From **PAK MENG**, 40km due west of Trang town, down to the mouth of the Trang River runs a thirty-kilometre stretch of lovely beaches, broken only by dramatic limestone outcrops. Air-conditioned **minibuses** (roughly every 30min; 45min; B60) run from Thanon Tha Klang in Trang to Pak Meng (as well as to Ban Chao Mai in the south; see opposite), but if you want to explore the whole coastline, you'll need to **rent** a motorbike or car in Trang.

Although it has a fine outlook to the headlands and islands to the west, the beach at Pak Meng itself is not the most attractive on the coast, becoming a rather muddy strip of sand at low tide. At other times, however, it offers quiet, calm swimming, and there's always the possibility of a meal at one of the many tree-shaded foodstalls and restaurants that line the back of the beach. The nicest place **to stay** is *Lay Trang Resort*, a stone's throw from the pier at the far north end of the beach (☏075 274027–8, ⓦwww.laytrang.com; ❹–❺); ranged around a large, peaceful garden, its smart brick rooms come with cold-water bathrooms, air-con and TV, while the bungalows boast fridges and hot water, and it has a pleasant, reasonably priced **restaurant** that's locally renowned for its seafood. Another good, more central restaurant is the popular and helpful *Yok Yor*, less than a kilometre south of the main T-junction where the Trang road hits the beachfront road, which offers carefully presented dishes of fish and seafood under the seaside casuarinas.

Immediately south of Pak Meng's beach is the white sand of **Hat Chang Lang**, famous for its oysters, which shelters at its north end the finest luxury hotel in the province, *Anantara Si Kao* (☏075 205888, ⓦwww.anantara.com; ❾). The low-rise blocks of stylish bedrooms with large balconies, including seven pool suites, are set behind a line of casuarina trees, and facilities encompass a beautiful, large pool, Italian and international restaurants, a fitness centre, and a spa and wellness centre overseen by an Indian naturopathic doctor. Watersports on offer include diving, kayaking, windsurfing and sailing, and there's a huge range of other activities laid on, notably yoga, cooking and Thai-language lessons and some interesting local tours. The hotel also has its own beach club and restaurant on the main strand on Ko Kradan (see p.451), reached by daily boat transfer.

Three kilometres further on is the turning for the headquarters of the **Hat Chao Mai National Park** (entry B200; ☏075 213260, ⓦwww.dnp.go.th), which covers 230 square kilometres, including parts of Ko Mook and Ko

Kradan. At the headquarters there's a simple café as well as bungalows and rooms for two to six people (B800–1500), or you can rent a two-person tent to pitch under the casuarinas at the back of the sandy beach (B270 including bedding). From the headquarters a short trail leads to the south end of the beach and a viewpoint partway up a karst pinnacle, from which you can see Ko Mook and occasionally dugongs in the bay below.

Four kilometres south of Hat Chang Lang, beyond Kuantunku, the pier for Ko Mook, is **Hat Yong Ling**. This quiet and attractive convex beach, which shelters a national park ranger station, is probably the nicest along this stretch of coast, with a large cave which you can swim into at high tide or walk into at low tide. Immediately beyond comes **Hat Yao**, which runs in a broad five-kilometre white-sand strip, backed by casuarina trees and some simple restaurants.

Next up is **BAN CHAO MAI** (also called **Ban Hat Yao**), a straggle of houses on stilts, which exists on fishing, especially for crabs. Roughly half-hourly air-conditioned **minibuses** (B60) from Thanon Tha Klang in Trang via Hat Yao take about an hour to reach Ban Chao Mai, from whose harbour boats run regularly across to Ko Libong. By the harbour, ⚓ *Had Yao Nature Resort* (☎075 207934 or 081 894 6936, ⓦwww.trangsea.com; fan ❸, air-con ❹) is a well-managed, non-profit resort, where your custom will go towards helping local people and the environment (see p.64). The same people own *Libong Nature Beach Resort* (see p.453), *Ko Mook Nature Beach Resort* (see p.451), and an organic farmstay on Highway 4 between Trang and Krabi, where in the low season you can learn to make aloe vera soap, jam and shampoo. Dorm beds in the large house cost B300, and there are also some fan-cooled rooms with shared bath, as well as nicer air-con rooms and bungalows, some with hot water and/or balconies over the canal. The breezy, waterside **restaurant** serves up Western breakfasts, vegetarian food and excellent squid and other seafood dishes; for exploring nearby beaches, **bikes** can be rented for B100 per day, and snorkelling equipment, internet and wi-fi are available. The owners organize tours to the local islands, including highly recommended dugong-watching trips to Ko Libong (available from Ban Chao Mai; see p.452), and through the mangroves to the nearby cave of **Tham Chao Mai**; inside are impressively huge rock pillars and a natural theatre, its stage framed by rock curtains. Tham Chao Mai can be visited on a guided and fully insured trip by longtail and canoe (B1200 per person, including lunch; minimum four people) or you can rent a **kayak** (B800–1200 per day) and guide yourself through the mangroves with a map and torch.

The Trang and Satun islands

Generally blessed with blinding white beaches, great coral and amazing marine life, the islands off the coast of Trang and Satun provinces have managed, mostly with just a handful of resorts on each, to cling onto some of that illusory desert-island atmosphere which better-known places like Phuket and Samui lost long ago. Indeed, islands such as **Ko Hai** and **Ko Kradan** support no permanent settlements other than the bungalow concerns, while on **Ko Tarutao** and **Ko Adang** in the far south, the peace and quiet is maintained by the national parks department; at the other end of the scale, however, nearby **Ko Lipe** is developing at its own merry pace and now boasts over twenty resorts, as well as a substantial *chao ley* village (see p.335). **Access** from a variety of mainland ports is described in the accounts below, but what sets this area apart are the enticing opportunities for **island-hopping**, thanks to regular boat services in the tourist season out of Ko Lanta. Scheduled services are provided by Tigerline, with its office on Thanon Sathanee in Trang (☎075 590489, ⓦwww.tigerlinetravel .com), which operates daily ferries between Lanta and Lipe (1 daily; about 5hr; B1500) via Ko Hai, the village on Ko Mook, Ban Chao Mai on the mainland and Ko Lao Liang (on request); and by Satun Pakbara Speedboat Club (Lanta ☎075 684283, Pak Bara ☎074 783643–5, Lipe ☎074 750388, ⓦwww .tarutaolipeisland.com), which sails from Lanta to Lipe (1 daily; about 3hr; B1900) via Ko Hai, Hat Farang on Ko Mook and Ko Bulon Lae once daily in season, with onward services to the Malaysian island of Langkawi. Meanwhile, day-trip boats from Ko Lanta to Ko Hai, Ko Mook and Ko Kradan will drop you at, or transfer you between, any of the islands: Garden Hill (☎075 684042, ⓦwww.lantaislandtours.com) sends out a speedboat every day in season (B500 between Ko Hai and Hat Farang on Ko Mook, for example) while Petpailin (☎075 667033) has a bigger, slower ferry (B400 for the same leg). Resorts such as *Ko Hai Seafood* also put together longtail transfers, which can work out the cheapest option if there are enough takers.

Accommodation on the islands, much of which is mid-priced, is now often fully booked at the very busiest times. Most of the resorts open year round, though in practice many can't be reached out of season (roughly June–Oct) due to treacherous seas. It's sensible to get in touch ahead of time to check whether the resort you're interested in is open or has vacancies, and in many cases to arrange transfers from Trang; many of the resorts maintain offices in Trang town to make this easier.

If you just fancy a day exploring some of the islands, any travel agent in Trang can book you on a **boat trip** (mid-Oct to mid-May only) to Ko Kradan, the Emerald Cave on Ko Mook, and other small nearby islands for snorkelling, for B1050 per person including admission to Hat Chao Mai National Park, packed lunch and soft drinks. More active types might well be tempted by *Lao Liang Resort* (ⓦwww.laoliangresort.com; ❽; closed May to mid-Oct), the only habitation on **Ko Lao Liang**, beautiful, twin desert islands to the west of Ko Sukorn that can be reached on the Tigerline ferry. All-in costs include meals, kayaks, snorkelling gear and camping in luxury tents; diving, rock-climbing, yoga and snorkelling tours are extra. **Scuba-diving** is also available on Ko Hai, Ko Mook, Ko Libong and Ko Lipe, while Paddle Asia run **sea-kayaking** trips around the Trang and Tarutao islands (see p.61).

Ko Hai (Ko Ngai)

KO HAI (also known as **KO NGAI**), 16km southwest of Pak Meng, is the most developed of the Trang islands, though it's still decidedly low-key. The island's action, such as it is, centres on the east coast, where half a dozen resorts enjoy a dreamy panorama of jagged limestone outcrops, whose crags glow pink and blue against the setting sun, stretching across the sea to the mainland behind. The gently sloping beach of fine, white sand here runs unbroken for over 2km (though at low tide, swimming is not so good at the northern end, which is scattered with dead coral), and there's some good snorkelling in the shallow, clear water off the island's southeastern tip. For the best snorkelling in the region, the resorts run **boat trips** every day in high season (from B250 per person at *Coco Cottage*, for example) to Ko Cheuak and Ko Maa, just off Ko Hai to the east, where you can swim into caverns and explore a fantastic variety of multi-coloured soft and hard coral; it's also possible to add Ko Mook's Emerald Cave to these trips. As well as all manner of transfers to other islands, the resorts also offer day-trips to the popular snorkelling and diving site of Ko Rok (see p.428), 30km southwest in the Mu Ko Lanta National Park (from B700 per

▲ Ko Hai

person by longtail, B1300 by speedboat, at *Coco Cottage*), while *Seafood* does overnighters on Ko Rok for B2300 per person.

Ko Hai's resorts lay on **boats** for their guests from Pak Meng, charging from B300 per person in a longtail (45min–1hr), B450 per person in a speedboat (20min), fed by transfers from Trang town or airport for B150 (some also offer pick-ups from Krabi airport). Otherwise, you can book a minibus-and-longtail transfer from Trang town (daily in season; B450) through agents such as Trang Island Hopping Tour (see p.445). Hat Chao Mai National Park maintains a booth at Pak Meng pier, where you'll be charged B200 entrance fee (if the rangers have bothered to show up for work). **Snorkelling equipment** (B100 per day at *Coco Cottage*, for example) and **kayaks** (around B700 per day for a two-seater) can be rented at most of the resorts. Towards the southern end of the beach, *Fantasy Resort* has a well-organized **dive shop**, the German-run Rainbow Divers (☎075 206962, ⓦwww.rainbow-diver.com; Nov–April).

Accommodation

Ko Hai now has the whole gamut of **accommodation**, from simple, en-suite bamboo bungalows to swanky, air-con cottages.

Coco Cottage Towards the northern end of the beach ☎089 724 9225 or 087 898 6522, ⓦwww.coco-cottage.com. Charming, helpful and family-friendly resort in a grassy palm grove, where the stylish, thatched wooden bungalows sport verandas, mosquito nets and outdoor bathrooms with wooden basins and bamboo showers. Very good restaurant and beach bar, internet access, occasional yoga courses and a particularly wide range of boat trips and transfers at cheap prices. Breakfast included. Fan ❻–❼, air-con ❽

Ko Hai Paradise Resort Ao Kauntong on the south coast ☎075 203024, ⓦwww .kohhaiparadise.com; Trang office at

The Meeting Point restaurant opposite the station ☎075 216420. With a tranquil bay all to themselves, the simple en-suite bungalows at this friendly resort are sheltered by tall palms in spacious, grassy grounds. The food's good and the long, white-sand beach slopes down towards some great coral for snorkelling right in front of the resort. The resort has opened sporadically over the last couple of years, tending to operate only at the height of the high season. ❸–❺

Ko Hai Seafood Near the centre of the beach, north of *Villa* ☎081 538 0980 or 081 367 8497. Large, well-built, thatched bungalows with wall fans, mosquito screens and well-equipped bathrooms, in a single row parallel to the beach. Substantial discounts in shoulder season. Breakfast included. ⑥

Koh Ngai Villa Near the centre of the main beach ☎075 203263 or 086 279 4487, ⓦwww .kohngaivillathai.com; Trang office opposite the station ☎075 210496. Friendly, old-style beach resort with plenty of space. Simple, well-organized bamboo bungalows boast verandas and small toilets, or you could opt for a large room with two double beds in a concrete longhouse or a smart concrete bungalow with air-con, or even a two-person tent (B300, including bedding). Breakfast included with most rooms. Fan ❸–❺, air-con ❻

Thanya South end of the beach ☎075 206965–7, ⓦwww.kohngaithanyaresort.com. A large, very attractive beachside swimming pool with jacuzzis is the main draw here. As well as 24hr air-con, hot water and fridges, the villas feature verandas, big

French windows and lots of polished teak, while the restaurant has a varied menu of Thai food, including some interesting seafood dishes. Just opened at the time of research, but looks promising: a spa is planned, though prices may rise. Breakfast included. ❼–❽

Thapwarin Resort Towards the northern end of the main beach, next to *Coco Cottage* ☎081 894 3585, ⓦwww.thapwarin.com; Trang office at 140/2 Thanon Rongrien ☎075 218153. Welcoming, shady resort, where you can choose between well-appointed bamboo and rattan cottages with outdoor bathrooms, and large, very smart, beach-front wooden bungalows boasting air-con as well as miniature gardens in their spacious bathrooms; all have hot showers. There's internet access, a massage spa, beach bar and good restaurant, serving Thai and Western food and espresso coffee. Breakfast included. Fan ❼, air-con ❽–❾

Ko Mook

KO MOOK, about 8km southeast of Ko Hai, supports a comparatively busy fishing village on its eastern side, around which – apart from the sandbar that runs out to the very pricey *Sivalai Resort* – most of the beaches are disappointing, reduced to dirty mud flats when the tide goes out. However, across on the island's west coast lies beautiful **Hat Farang**, with gently shelving white sand, crystal-clear water that's good for swimming and snorkelling, and gorgeous sunsets.

The island's main source of renown is **Tham Morakhot** (part of Hat Chao Mai National Park and closed July–Sept), the stunning "Emerald Cave" further north on the west coast, which can only be visited by boat, but shouldn't be missed. An eighty-metre swim through the cave – 10m or so of which is in pitch darkness – brings you to a *hong* (see p.386) with an inland beach of powdery sand open to the sky, at the base of a spectacular natural chimney whose walls are coated with dripping vegetation. Chartering your own longtail is preferable to taking one of the big day-trip boats that originate on Lanta or Pak Meng: if you time it right, you'll get the inland beach all to yourself, an experience not to be forgotten. It's also easy enough to **kayak** there from Hat Farang (from B100 per hr from *Sawaddee/Mookies*), and at low tide you can paddle right through to the inland beach: buoys mark the cave entrance, from where a tunnel heads straight back into the rock; about halfway along, there's a small, right-hand kink in the tunnel which will plunge you briefly into darkness, but you should soon be able to see light ahead from the *hong*. Mid-afternoon is often a good time to paddle off on this trip, after the tour boats have left and providing the tide is right. If you fancy a **boat trip** to the cave and Kradan, Chuak and Ma islands in one day, take your custom to *Ko Mook Nature Beach Resort*, where tours are fully insured and licensed and the revenue (B1500 per person; twenty-percent discount for guests) goes to help local people. Meanwhile, *Rubber Tree* put together three-day, two-night trips to Ko Rok for B4000 per person (minimum six people).

The easiest way to **get to Ko Mook** is to book a minibus-and-boat package to Hat Farang through a travel agent in Trang, which costs B350, including the thirty-minute longtail ride. Otherwise, there's a pretty reliable public boat (B60) at around midday to Ko Mook's village from Kuantunku pier, 8km south of Pak Meng, between Hat Chang Lang and Hat Yong Ling; Ban Chao Mai air-con minibuses from Trang (see p.446) will usually detour to Kuantunku if asked (around B100 per person from Trang); once landed at the village, you're left with a thirty-minute walk or B50 motorbike-taxi ride over to Hat Farang.

There's an English-run **dive shop** at *Charlie's Resort* on Hat Farang, Princess Divers (Ⓦwww.divekohmook.com; Nov–early May), offering PADI courses from Bubblemaker up to Divemaster, local dives including a World War II wreck off Ko Kradan and the rock pinnacle of Hin Nok, and trips by speedboat to sites such as Ko Rok, Hin Daeng and Hin Muang.

Accommodation

Most of Hat Farang is unfortunately occupied by the disappointing *Charlie's Resort*, while there are rumours that the Centara hotel chain will take over what's left from *Sawaddee*. However, *Rubber Tree* and *Mookies* make the best of the attractive, shady slopes behind the beach, while *Ko Mook Nature Beach Resort* is away on the east side of the island near the village.

Ko Mook Nature Beach Resort Recently opened branch of the non-profit *Had Yao Nature Resort*, which promotes conservation and sustainable tourism (see p.447; ☏089 647 7030). On the south-facing shore of the sandbar that ends at *Sivalai Resort*, two-person tents with mosquito screens, beds, tables, lights and fans, sharing cold-water bathrooms (B150–200, or B100 with your own tent). Bicycles, kayaks, snorkels, internet and wi-fi available. There are also imminent plans for eco-friendly villas for long stays (minimum one week), each with a kitchen, living room, TV, hot water and air-con. ❻
Mookies ☏087 275 6533. Welcome to the "tentalows": comfortable tents, each pitched under a semi-permanent shelter with a bed, table, light, fan and mosquito screens. Shared toilets and hot showers. Good, inexpensive Thai and Western food at the popular, often raucous,

Thai-Australian bar-restaurant. Free pick-ups from the village. At the lower end of this price range. ❷
Rubber Tree ☏081 270 4148, Ⓦwww .mookrubbertree.com; or contact *Sea Breeze* restaurant in front of the station in Trang ☏075 215972. On a well-tended, landscaped slope that's also a working rubber plantation, fan bungalows with cold-water bathrooms and crisp, white linen, or spacious, smartly designed air-con versions with rubber-wood furniture and hot showers. Breakfast included. Fan ❹, air-con ❻
Sawaddee ☏075 207964–5, Ⓔsawaddee resort64@yahoo.com; or contact *Wunderbar* in Trang (see p.446). Laid-back, old-style, concrete or stilted wooden bungalows parallel to the beach, which enjoy en-suite bathrooms, plenty of shade and largely uninterrupted sea views. Internet access. At the lower end of this price range. ❹

Ko Kradan

About 6km to the southwest of Ko Mook, **KO KRADAN** is the remotest of the inhabited islands off Trang, and one of the most beautiful, with crystal-clear waters. On this slender triangle of thick jungle, the main beach is a long strand of steeply sloping, powdery sand on the east coast, with fine views of Ko Mook, Ko Libong and the karst-strewn mainland, and an offshore reef to the north with a great variety of hard coral; such beauty, however, has not escaped the attention of the day-trip boats from Ko Lanta, who turn the beach into a lunchtime picnic ground most days in summer. From a short way north of the *Anantara's* beach club (see p.446), towards the south end of this beach, a path across the island will bring you after about fifteen minutes to Sunset Beach, another lovely stretch of fine, white sand in a cove; a branch off this path at *Paradise Lost* (see p.452) leads to a beach on the short south coast, which enjoys good reef snorkelling (also about 15min from the *Anantara* beach club).

Practicalities

Minibus-and-longtail **transfers** from Trang town (daily in season; B450) can be booked through agencies such as Trang Island Hopping Tour (see p.445). Kradan's best-value **accommodation** option is the American-run *Paradise Lost* (☎089 587 2409, Ⓔkokradan@yahoo.com; ④–⑤), in the middle of the island, roughly halfway along the path to Sunset Beach. In a grassy, palm-shaded grove, it offers simple, clean, thatched rattan bungalows with shared bathrooms or larger, wooden affairs (either en suite or sharing), as well as an open-sided dorm with mosquito nets and fans (B250 per person), kayaks, snorkels and good Thai and Western food. By far the best of several mostly forgettable resorts on the east coast is *Seven Seas* (☎075 203389–90, Ⓦwww.sevenseasresorts.com; ⑨ breakfast included), which adds a surprising splash of contemporary luxury to this remote spot. Behind a small, black, infinity pool, the large bungalows and rooms with outdoor warm-water bathrooms are stylishly done out in greys and whites, and sport air-con, wi-fi, fridges, TVs and DVDs. At the south end of the main beach there's a Hat Chao Mai National Park ranger station, with a few tents to rent (B200–300 for two to three people, including bedding; contact the park's headquarters for information; see p.446).

Ko Libong

The largest of the Trang islands with a population of six thousand, **Ko Libong** lies 10km southeast of Ko Mook, opposite Ban Chao Mai on the mainland. Less visited than its northern neighbours, it's known mostly for its wildlife, although it has its fair share of golden beaches too. Libong is one of the most significant remaining refuges in Thailand of the **dugong**, a large marine mammal similar to the manatee, which feeds on sea grasses growing on the sea floor – the sea-grass meadow around Libong is reckoned to be the largest in Southeast Asia. Sadly, dugongs are now an endangered species, traditionally hunted for their blubber (used as fuel) and meat, and increasingly affected by fishing practices such as scooping, and by coastal pollution which destroys their source of food. The dugong has now been adopted as one of fifteen "reserved animals" of Thailand and is the official mascot of Trang province.

Libong is also well known for its migratory **birds**, which stop off here on their way south from Siberia, drawn by the island's food-rich mud flats (now protected by the Libong Archipelago Sanctuary, which covers the eastern third of the island). For those seriously interested in ornithology, the best time to come is during March and April, when you can expect to see brown-winged kingfishers, masked finfoots and even the rare black-necked stork, not seen elsewhere on the Thai–Malay peninsula.

As well as tours of local islands, *Libong Nature Beach Resort* runs award-winning, day-long **boat trips around Libong** itself (B1200 per person, including lunch, in a group of four or more; twenty percent discount for guests), which are safe, insured and licensed with TAT, and staffed by local sea gypsies who know the dugong well. As well as visiting a *chao ley* village, these give you the chance to kayak into the sanctuary to observe the rare birds and to snorkel at the sea-grass beds – with, they reckon, an eighty percent chance of seeing a dugong.

Practicalities

You can arrange a direct **boat** transfer from Ban Chao Mai (see p.447) to *Libong Nature Beach Resort* for about B1000 per boat. Alternatively, public longtails depart daily year-round from Ban Chao Mai when full (most frequent in the morning and around lunchtime; B50 per person), arriving twenty minutes later at Ban Phrao on Ko Libong's north side. From here motorbike taxis (B100) transport you across to the fishing village of **Ban Lan Khao** on the south-western coast, where the island's handful of resorts occupy a long, thin strip of golden sand. At low tide here, the sea retreats for hundreds of metres, exposing rock pools that are great for splashing about in but not so good for a dip.

By far the best of the island's **resorts** is *Libong Nature Beach Resort*, which is run by the same charitable foundation that operates the *Had Yao Nature Resort* (see p.447; ☏075 207934 or 081 894 6936, Ⓦwww.trangsea.com; ❹–❺). Its neat, en-suite bungalows, all with wi-fi and some with hot water and air-con, stretch back from a secluded part of the beach, a ten-minute walk south of Ban Lan Khao, and there's another sheltered cove a further five minutes' walk (or kayak) to the south. There's a good restaurant attached too, with internet access, and mountain bikes and snorkelling gear are available to rent. Guided or unguided treks into the national park jungle behind the resort include a three-hour walk to a good viewpoint at the southwestern end of the island. There's a **dive shop** at *Libong Beach Resort* on the north side of Ban Lan Khao (☏086 297 9747, Ⓦwww.jollyrogerdive.com).

Ko Sukorn

A good way south of the other Trang islands, low-lying **Ko Sukorn** lacks the white-sand beaches and beautiful coral of its neighbours, but makes up for it with its friendly inhabitants, laid-back ambience and one excellent resort; for a glimpse of how islanders live and work, this is the place to come.

The lush interior is mainly given over to rubber plantations, interspersed with rice paddies, banana and coconut palms; the island also produces famously delicious watermelons, which are plentiful in March and April. Hat Talo Yai, the main **beach** – 500m of gently shelving brown sand, backed by coconut palms – runs along the southwestern shore. It's here you'll find the outstanding ⚐ *Sukorn Beach Bungalows* (represented in Trang by Trang Island Hopping Tours, see p.445; ☏075 207707, Ⓦwww.sukorn-island-trang.com; fan ❹–❺, air-con ❺–❼, breakfast included), one of the few Trang resorts that's reliably accessible all year round (discounts of up to fifty percent are available in low season). The clued-up and congenial Thai-Dutch duo who run the place are keen to keep the resort low-key and quiet (no children under 7), and work with the locals as much as possible, something that's reflected in the friendly welcome you get all over the island. Attractively decorated and well-designed bungalows and rooms – all spotlessly clean and with en-suite bathrooms, most with hot water – are set around a lush garden dotted with deckchairs and umbrellas, and there's an excellent, well-priced **restaurant**. At the resort, you can access the internet (including wi-fi), make overseas calls, exchange money and get a good massage, and you're free to paddle around in kayaks.

Boat excursions from the resort include trips out to Ko Lao Liang and Ko Takieng, which are part of the Mu Ko Phetra National Marine Park, for some excellent snorkelling. These run nearly every day from November to May; at other times of year, the sea is sometimes calm enough but you're usually restricted to fishing trips – and to looking round the island itself, which, at thirty square kilometres, is a good size for exploring. The resort offers **guided tours** (B250 per person), or it has motorbikes (B300 per day) and mountain bikes (half-day B150) for rent, as well as a handy map that marks all the sights, including the three villages and seafood market.

A songthaew-and-boat **transfer to the island** (B175 per person), via the public ferry from Laem Ta Sae, leaves Trang Island Hopping Tours daily at 11.30am and takes a couple of hours, or you can arrange a private transfer. The resort can also organize pricey longtail-boat transfers to or from any of the nearby islands, and can even put together very appealing, five-night island-hopping packages (from B11,000 per person).

The best of the rest of the island's handful of resorts is the friendly and peaceful *Ko Sukorn Cabana* (☏089 724 2326, Ⓦwww.sukorncabana.com;

fan ❹–❺, air-con ❺–❻, breakfast included), offering stilted bungalows with attractive bathrooms and large, well-appointed log cabins on a secluded beach to the north of Hat Talo Yai. Day-trips to Lao Liang and Takieng, kayaks, motor-bikes, internet and wi-fi are also available; private transfers from Trang can be arranged for B2100 all-in.

Ko Bulon Lae

The scenery at tiny **KO BULON LAE**, 20km west of Pak Bara in Satun province, isn't as beautiful as that generally found in Ko Tarutao National Park just to the south, but it's not at all bad: a two-kilometre strip of fine white sand runs the length of the casuarina-lined east coast, while *chao ley* fishermen make their ramshackle homes in the tight coves of the rest of the island. A reef of curiously shaped hard coral closely parallels the eastern beach, while **White Rock** to the south of the island has beautifully coloured soft coral and equally dazzling fish. **Snorkelling** gear, as well as **boats** for trips to White Rock and around the island (around B1700 per boat for 4–5hr), can be rented at *Pansand* resort, while *Bulone* has **kayaks**.

Ferries for Ko Bulon Lae currently leave Pak Bara (see p.454) daily at about 1.30pm (1hr 30min; B350 one way, B500 return). As there's no pier on Bulon Lae, the inter-island boats are met by longtails to transfer visitors to shore (B50). Boats return from Bulon Lae to Pak Bara at around 9am.

Accommodation

The island's **resorts** are open roughly from mid-October to early May. The largest and best of them is *Pansand* on the east-coast beach (☎074 728132 or 083 1726812, ⓦwww.pansand-resort.com; Trang office at First Andaman Travel, 82–84 Thanon Wisetkul ☎075 218035; ❺–❻ breakfast included), where large, smart cottages come with verandas, cold-water bathrooms and plenty of room to breathe. On the beach side of the shady, well-tended grounds, there's a sociable restaurant serving up good seafood and other Thai dishes; internet access is also available, and wi-fi is planned. The best of several cheaper resorts is friendly *Bulone* (☎081 897 9084 or 086 960 0468, ⓦwww .bulone-resort.net; ❸–❺), a huge grassy compound under the casuarinas at the north end of the main beach. En-suite accommodation ranges from airy, bamboo-walled bungalows to large, white, clapboard affairs, and be sure to eat

---

En route to Bulon Lae, Tarutao and Lipe: Pak Bara

The main port for Bulon Lae, Tarutao and Lipe is **PAK BARA**, towards the north end of Satun province. **From Trang**, Andrew Tour (see p.445; in Pak Bara ☎074 783459) offer direct air-con minibuses to Pak Bara (2 daily, more in high season; 1hr 30min–2hr); otherwise you'll need to take a Satun-bound bus (2hr–2hr 30min) or a share-taxi from Thanon Ratsada (1hr 30min) to the inland town of **Langu** and change there to a red songthaew for the ten-kilometre hop to the port. Andrew Tour also lay on one air-con minibus a day all the way through **from Krabi** in high season (4hr). Frequent buses, air-con minibuses and taxis **from Satun** make the fifty-kilometre trip to Langu.

If you need a place **to stay** in Pak Bara, try *Bara Guesthouse* (☎089 654 2801; ❷), 200m before the pier on the west side of the main road, which offers large but slightly gloomy, tiled, concrete rooms with their own bathrooms in a garden running down to the sea. There are no banks on the Tarutao islands or Bulon Lae, but Krung Thai Bank send a minibus to Pak Bara pier every day in high season, with an on-board **ATM** and currency exchange facilities.

at the restaurant, which features a small selection of tasty Italian favourites, as well as internet access.

Ko Tarutao National Marine Park

The unspoilt **KO TARUTAO NATIONAL MARINE PARK** is probably the most beautiful of all Thailand's accessible beach destinations. Occupying 1400 square kilometres of the Andaman Sea in Satun province, the park covers 51 mostly uninhabited islands, of which three are easy to reach from the mainland and offer accommodation for visitors. Site of the park headquarters, **Ko Tarutao** offers a variety of government-issue accommodation and things to do, while **Ko Adang** is much more low-key and a springboard to some excellent snorkelling. Home to a population of around a thousand *chao ley*, tiny **Ko Lipe** is something of a frontier maverick, attracting ever more travellers with one dazzling beach, twenty or so private bungalow resorts and a rough-and-ready atmosphere. The port of **Pak Bara** (see p.454) is the main jumping-off point for the park, and houses a **national park visitor centre** (☎074 783485, ⓦwww.dnp.go.th), set back on the left just before the pier, where you can gather information and book a room on Tarutao or Adang before boarding your boat.

The park's forests and seas support an incredible variety of **fauna**: langurs, crab-eating macaques and wild pigs are common on the islands, which also shelter several unique subspecies of squirrel, tree shrew and lesser mouse deer; among the hundred-plus bird species found here, reef egrets and hornbills are regularly seen, while white-bellied sea eagles, frigate birds and pied imperial pigeons are more rarely encountered; and the park is the habitat of about 25 percent of the world's tropical fish species, as well as dugongs, sperm whales, dolphins and a dwindling population of turtles.

The park amenities on Adang, though not on Tarutao, are officially closed to tourists in the monsoon season from mid-May to mid-November (the exact dates vary from year to year). Many of the resorts on Ko Lipe close at this time too, and the frequency of the ferry service is reduced. Accommodation is especially likely

ACCOMMODATION			EATING & DRINKING		
	Castaway	**B**	Pattaya Song	**C**	Kafair	**4**
Bundhaya	**F**	Daya	**D**	Porn	**A**	Café Lipe	**3**	Pattaya Song	**C**
Blue Tribes	**F**	Family	**E**		Flour Power Bakery	**1**	Pooh's	**2**

to get full around the three New Years (Thai, Chinese and Western), when it's best to book national park rooms in advance in Bangkok (see p.40).

The prime **diving sites** in the park, served by several dive shops on Ko Lipe, are to the west of Ko Tarutao, around Ko Klang, Ko Adang, Ko Rawi and Ko Dong, where encounters with reef and even whale sharks, dolphins and stingrays are not uncommon. **Snorkelling gear** can be rented at Pak Bara or on Ko Adang for around B50 per day, and is widely available from the private bungalow outfits or dive shops on Ko Lipe.

Ferries

Ferry services into the park seem to change by the year, due to competition between the boat companies and local politicking. For up-to-date **information**, call the Pak Bara National Park Visitor Centre or contact Koh Lipe Thailand.com (see p.458). There is no pier on Adang or Lipe, so boats anchor in the channel between the islands or off Hat Pattaya, where they're met by **longtails** (B50 to any beach on Lipe or B100 to the Adang park station). The pier at Ao Pante on Tarutao is inaccessible at low tide, when longtails (B30) shuttle people to shore.

Among ferry and speedboat companies from **Pak Bara**, the most reliable are currently Adang Sea Ferry (℡074 783338 or 081 609 2604, Ⓦwww .adangseatour.com) and Lipeh Speedboat Co. (℡089 464 7816, Ⓦwww .lipehferry-speedboat.com), who each run at least one daily service year-round. In high season, the former has sailings at around 11am and 1.30pm for Ao Pante on Ko Tarutao (1hr; B350 one way, B600 return), before continuing to Ko Adang and Ko Lipe (from Pak Bara: 3hr; B500 one way, B900 return); the latter operates faster boats at 11.30am and 1.30pm to Adang/Lipe (1hr 30min; B650 one way, B1200 return), which usually stop at Ao Pante (30min; B350 each way). With either company, a return ticket to Adang/Lipe will allow you to stop off at Tarutao. Satun Pakbara Speedboat Club (see p.448; in Pak Bara ℡074 783643–5) also covers this route in high season. There have also been services in the past from Thammalang pier, 10km south of Satun town, which may possibly reappear; for island-hopping boats from Ko Lanta, see p.448.

Speedboats operate **between Ko Lipe and Langkawi**, the large Malaysian island to the southeast, at least twice a day in high season (1hr; B1200), including those operated by Satun Pakbara Speedboat Club (see p.448). A temporary Thai immigration post is set up at *Bundhaya Resort* on Lipe's Hat Pattaya to cover this route, and there are plans to extend its hours to cater for three weekly boats in low season.

Ko Tarutao

The largest of the national park's islands, **KO TARUTAO** offers the greatest natural variety: mountains covered in semi-evergreen rainforest rise steeply to a high point of 700m; limestone caves and mangrove swamps dot the shoreline; and the west coast is lined with perfect beaches for most of its 26-kilometre length.

Boats will drop you off at **Ao Pante**, on the northwestern side of the island, where the admission fee (B200) is collected and where the **park headquarters** is situated. Here you'll find the only shop on the island, selling basic supplies, as well as a visitor centre, a library and a **restaurant**. The **bungalows** (B1000 per bungalow sleeping four people, or B600 for a twin room), which are spread over a large, quiet park behind the beach, are for the main part national park standard issue with cold-water bathrooms, but there are also some basic mattress-on-floor four-person rooms in **longhouses**, sharing bathrooms (B500 per room). Two/three-person **tents** can be rented for B225 per night (plus B50 per person for bedding). The visitor centre can arrange **transport** by car to several of the island's beaches, as detailed below; transfers to the same places by boat cost at least twice as much, though you may be tempted by a **round-island boat trip** for B3000.

Behind the settlement, the steep, half-hour climb to **To-Boo cliff** is a must, especially at sunset, for the view of the surrounding islands and the crocodile's-head cape at the north end of the bay. A fun ninety-minute boat trip (B500 per boat; contact the visitor centre to book) can also be made near Ao Pante, up the canal which leads 2km inland from the pier, through a bird-filled mangrove swamp, to **Crocodile Cave** – where you're unlikely to see any of the big snappers, reported sightings being highly dubious.

A half-hour walk south from Ao Pante brings you to the two quiet bays of **Ao Jak** and **Ao Molae**, fringed by coconut palms and filled with fine white sand; the latter now sports some **bungalows** (from B600 for an en-suite twin room), tents for rent and a small restaurant. Transfers by car from Ao Pante to Ao Molae are free if you're staying here, B200 per car otherwise. Beyond the next headland lies **Ao Sone** (which gets its name from the casuarina trees that fringe the beach), where a pretty freshwater stream runs past the ranger station at the north end of the bay, a good place for peaceful camping; bungalows and a restaurant may be built here in the future. Transfers to Ao Sone from Ao Pante cost B400 per car, or else it's a two-hour walk. The main part of the bay is a three-kilometre sweep of flawless sand, with a one-hour trail leading up to Lu Du Waterfall at the north end, a ninety-minute trail to Lo Po Waterfall in the middle and a mangrove swamp at the far south end.

On the east side of the island, **Ao Taloh Wow** is a rocky bay with a ranger station, shop and campsite, connected to Ao Pante by a twelve-kilometre road (B600 per car transfer) through old rubber plantations and evergreen forest. Beyond Taloh Wow, a trail (5hr return) cuts through the forest to **Ao Taloh Udang**, a sandy bay on the south side where you can pitch a tent. Here the remnants of a penal colony for political prisoners are just visible: the plotters of two failed coup attempts – including the author of the first English–Thai dictionary and a grandson of Rama VII – were imprisoned here in the 1930s before returning to high government posts. The ordinary convicts, who used to be imprisoned here and at Ao Taloh Wow, had a much harsher time, and during World War II, when supplies from the mainland dried up, prisoners and guards ganged together to turn to piracy. This turned into a lucrative business, which was not suppressed until 1946 when the Thai government asked the British in Malaysia to send in three hundred troops. Pirates and smugglers still occasionally hide out in the Tarutao archipelago, but the main problem now is illegal trawlers fishing in national park waters.

Ko Adang

At **KO ADANG**, a wild, rugged island covered in tropical rainforest 40km west of Ko Tarutao, the park station is at **Laem Sone** on the southern shore, where the beach is steep and narrow and backed by a thick canopy of pines. There are **rooms** in bamboo longhouses (B400 per room sleeping four), **bungalows** sleeping up to eight people (B600–1800), and two/three-person **tents** can be rented (B150 per night). There's a **restaurant** here, too.

The half-hour climb to **Sha-do** cliff on the steep slope above Laem Sone gives good views over Ko Lipe to the south, while about 2km west along the coast from the park station, a twenty-minute trail leads inland to the small **Pirate Waterfall**. You can rent **longtail boats** (as well as snorkels and masks) through the rangers for excellent snorkelling trips to nearby islands such as Ko

Rawi and Ko Jabang (around B1500–2500 for up to ten people, depending on how far you want to go).

Ko Lipe

KO LIPE, 2km south of Adang, makes a busy contrast to the other islands. A small, flat triangle, it's covered in coconut plantations and inhabited by *chao ley*, with shops, a school and a health centre in the village on the eastern side. By rights, such a settlement shouldn't be allowed within the national park boundaries, but the *chao ley* on Lipe are well entrenched: Satun's governor forced the community to move here from Phuket and Ko Lanta between the world wars, to reinforce the island's Thai character and prevent the British rulers of Malaya from laying claim to it. More recently, a diverse influx of tourists – Westerners and Thais, families and backpackers – has been enticed here by the gorgeous beach of **Hat Pattaya**, a shining crescent of squeaky-soft white sand with an offshore reef to explore on its eastern side, as well as by the relaxed, anything-goes atmosphere and mellow nightlife. Many of Lipe's *chao ley* have now sold their beachfront land to Thai-Chinese speculators from the mainland, who have increased the island's capacity to nearly two thousand guest rooms – with further developments, including spas and swimming pools, planned. Lipe's main drag is a paved path between the eastern end of Hat Pattaya and the village, lined with tattoo parlours, shops advertising guitars for rent and even a small, so-far-unoccupied mall. The other island path that's most likely to be useful is from *Daya Resort* at the west end of Pattaya across to Sunset beach in around ten minutes.

The best **travel agent** and source of **information** on the island, including a good, regularly updated **website**, is Koh Lipe Thailand.com (☎089 464 5854 or 081 541 4489, ⓦwww.kohlipethailand.com), which currently has three outlets on the path between Hat Pattaya and the village, with the main one hard by the beach. On offer are accommodation bookings (including on the website), transport tickets, **internet** access (B3 per minute), **currency exchange** and **snorkelling trips** to the best sites around the islands on the west side of Ko Adang (B550–650 per person). On the east side of *Porn Resort* on Sunset beach is Canadian-run Sabye Sports (☎081 897 8725, ⓦwww.sabye-sports.com), Lipe's oldest **dive shop**, which offers daily trips and PADI courses from Discover Scuba up to Divemaster, as well as specialities such as photography, naturalist and deep diving. Sabye also does snorkel rental (B150 per day including fins) and trips (B750 per person including lunch). **Mountain bikes** can be rented, for example, from the shop opposite *Pooh's* (see opposite) for B300 per day.

Accommodation

The majority of Lipe's bungalows are on **Hat Pattaya**, the prettiest but most crowded beach on the island. *Porn Resort* has **Sunset** beach on the northwest side to itself, a shady, attractive spot with good views of Ko Adang. Several resorts have set up shop on **Sunrise**, on the east side near the village, an exposed, largely featureless beach that gives access to some good snorkelling around Ko Gra.

If you get stuck for somewhere to stay, you could try *Pooh's* (☎074 750345, ⓦwww.poohlipe.com; ❸) or *Café Lipe* (☎086 969 9472, ⓦwww.cafe-lipe .com; ❹), which both have a few **rooms** behind their restaurants (see opposite).

Bundhaya Hat Pattaya ☎074 750248–9, ⓦwww .bundhayaresort.com; offices at Pak Bara pier and 66/24 Thanon Sathanee, Trang ☎075 219802. Over a hundred comfortable but tightly packed units, ranging from deluxe family bungalows with air-con, hot water and fridges down to basic, en-suite, fan rooms. Wide array of facilities including a popular restaurant, currency exchange, kayak rental and massages; a spa is planned, and perhaps a fitness centre. Breakfast included. ❻–❾

Blue Tribes Hat Pattaya ☎083 654 0316, ⓦwww.bluetribeslipe.com. Congenial spot with very spacious, well-spread bungalows in lovely dark wood, sporting attractive tiled bathrooms; some are two-storied with a balcony and chillout room/extra bedroom upstairs. Mediterranean restaurant planned. ⑤–⑥

Castaway Sunrise ☎ 083 138 7472, ⓦ www .castaway-resorts.com. Airy, thatched, two-storey villas with well-equipped, cold-water bathrooms, ceiling fans and a certain amount of style, mostly bestowed by the distinctive red Indonesian hardwood that they're made from. On a sandy patch with a dive shop, a mellow, multi-tiered bar-restaurant and a massage spa; kayaks and snorkels for rent. ⑥

Daya Hat Pattaya; book through Koh Lipe Thailand .com (see opposite). *Chao ley*-owned resort with over thirty colourful rooms and bungalows in a large, shady, flower-strewn garden, ranging from simple bamboo huts to clapboard bungalows in a great position on the beach. ②–⑤

Family (Mit's) Hat Pattaya ☎ 084 633 8332. Good-value, *chao ley*-owned resort, offering basic but sturdy wooden, en-suite bungalows with mosquito nets, in plenty of space and under a little shade, behind a simple, popular restaurant. ③

Pattaya Song Hat Pattaya ☎ 074 728034, ⓦ www.pattayasongresort.com. Italian-run resort, the oldest on the beach (the name means "Pattaya no. 2"), where plain, en-suite bamboo or concrete bungalows are strung out behind the beach or in a lovely location up on a steep promontory with great views of the bay; kayaks for rent.

Porn Sunset ☎ 087 394 4972 or 084 691 8743. Attractive, welcoming and well-run spot in a pleasant, spacious setting under the trees on the beach. Well-designed bungalows come with verandas, mosquito nets and en-suite bathrooms, or there are two-person tents for rent (B200), which might be useful while waiting for a bungalow to become free. Internet access planned. ④

Eating and drinking

Besides the **eating places** reviewed below, there are about half a dozen largely indistinguishable resort restaurants on Hat Pattaya, such as *Daya*, that lay out seafood barbecues and tables on the beach at night. Pattaya supports a similar number of **beach bars**, with low candlelit tables sprawled on the sand and names like *Time to Chill*. The *Navy Club* at the far east end of Pattaya – actually a jerry-built bar with a few wooden benches – is the best spot for a quiet, reasonably priced beer watching the sun set.

Café Lipe Hat Pattaya. Eco-conscious, solar-powered place that rustles up communal Thai dinners if booked in advance, as well as home-made bread and muesli.

Flour Power Bakery Sunset, under the trees behind Sabye Sports. Delicious home-made brownies, apple pies, cookies and iced coffee, as well as sandwiches and other Western and Thai dishes. Daily 7am–5.30pm.

Kafair 100m from Hat Pattaya on the paved trail to Sunrise. Mellow, welcoming café serving deli sandwiches, breakfasts, chicken biryani and good espressos, using coffee from Doi Chang in northern Thailand. Internet access and wi-fi planned.

Pattaya Song Hat Pattaya. Not the best location, set back a little from the sand, but in the evenings they do great home-made pastas, pizzas and bruschetta.

Pooh's On the paved trail between Sunrise and Hat Pattaya. Well-run and welcoming bar-restaurant that's a popular hive of activity, with an attached travel agency and dive school (ⓦ www.lotusdive .com). On offer are great Thai and Western food, including a wide choice of breakfasts and espresso coffees, internet access, big-screen DVDs and live music in the evenings; also has a new bakery, two doors away.

Satun town

Nestling in the last wedge of Thailand's west coast, the remote town of **SATUN** is served by just one road, Highway 406, which approaches through forbidding karst outcrops. Set in a green valley bordered by limestone hills, the town is leafy and relaxing but not especially interesting: the boat services to and from Kuala Perlis and Langkawi in Malaysia are the main reason for foreigners to come here.

If you find yourself with time on your hands in Satun, it's worth seeking out the **National Museum** (Wed–Sun 9am–4pm; B30) on Soi 5, Thanon Satun Thani, on the north side of the centre. It's memorable, as much as anything else, for its setting, in the graceful **Kuden Mansion**, which was built in British colonial style, with some Thai and Malay features, by craftsmen from Penang, and inaugurated in 1902 as the Satun governor's official residence. The exhibits and audiovisuals in English have a distinctive anthropological tone, but are diverting enough, notably concerning Thai Muslims, the *chao ley* on Ko Lipe, and the **Sakai**, a dwindling band of nomadic hunter-gatherers who still live in the jungle of southern Thailand.

Practicalities

Satun's new **bus station** is far to the southeast of the centre on the new bypass, but Hat Yai and non-air-con Trang buses make a stop at the 7-Eleven on Thanon Satun Thani in both directions; incoming air-con buses from Phuket via Trang (4 daily) will set you down further north on the same road by the *Wangmai* hotel; and you can book tickets in advance at the central Baw Khaw Saw office on Thanon Hatthakam Sueksa. **Share-taxis** and **air-con minibuses** have a variety of bases in town, as marked on our map (minibuses for Langu use the bus station). **Internet access** and overseas calls are available at Satun Cybernet, 136 Thanon Satun Thani. From her restaurant next to the *Sinkiat Thani Hotel* at 48 Thanon Bureewanit, On Kongnual (℡074 730469 or 081 097 9783, ℗onmarch13 @hotmail.com) offers **motorbike** (B150 per day) and **car rental** (B1200 per day), as well as local **tourist information**. The other good fixer in town is Bon Satarat at Andaman Trips, 68 Soi 6, Thanon Satun Thani (℡074 722988 or 086 287 6745, ℗andamantrips@hotmail.com), who can provide local tours and transfers.

Your best bet for budget **accommodation** is *On's Guest House*, 1km north of the centre at 49 Thanon Kuhaprawed – contact On at her restaurant (see above). In a leafy part of town, the airy wooden house shelters four clean fan rooms (❶) sharing a toilet and hot shower, a kitchen and a spacious living area. Just on the west side of the centre at 4 Thanon Saman Pradit, *Rian Thong* (℡074 711036; ❶) is a decent budget **hotel** with friendly owners, where some of the clean, large, en-suite rooms overlook the canal. Moving upmarket as far as Satun will go, the nearby *Sinkiat Thani*, 50 Thanon Bureewanit (℡074 721055–8, ℗sinkiathotel@hotmail.com; ❹), offers large, carpeted bedrooms with air-con, hot water, fridges and good views over the surrounding countryside.

On's (The Living Room) bar-restaurant (see opposite) offers a wide array of Western **food**, including good breakfasts and sandwiches, a short menu of typical Thai dishes, wi-fi and internet access. For a meal in the evening, however, you can't do much better than the lively and popular night market, north of the centre on the west side of Thanon Satun Thani, or try *Ko Ho*, on Thanon Saman Pradit opposite the Chinese temple, a cheap, busy, friendly restaurant that serves tasty Thai and Chinese food, including plenty of fish, seafood and salads.

Hat Yai

Travelling to or through **HAT YAI**, the biggest city in the region, is currently **not recommended** because of the troubles in the south (see p.441). To be honest you're not missing much, but as it's a major transport axis, we've provided a few, rudimentary practicalities and a map of the city, in case you get stuck there.

The **TAT office** is at 1/1 Soi 2, Thanon Niphat Uthit 3 (daily 8.30am–4.30pm; ☏074 243747 or 074 238518, ⊜tatsgkhl@tat.or.th). The **tourist police** have an office just south of here on Thanon Niphat Uthit 3 (☏074 246733 or 1155). The three central Niphat Uthit roads are known locally as sai neung, sai sawng and sai saam.

The **train station** is on the west side of the centre at the end of Thanon Thamnoon Vithi; the **bus terminal** is far to the southeast of the centre on Thanon Kanchanawanit, while the new **air-con minibus terminal** at Talat Kaset is about 5km west of town towards the airport, both leaving you with a songthaew ride to the centre. The helpful Cathay Tour (☏074 235044, ⊜cathay_ontours@hotmail.com), a **travel agency** on the ground floor of the guest house of the same name, handles onward flight, bus, share taxi and air-con minibus bookings, both within Thailand and into Malaysia.

Accommodation

Cathay Guest House 93 Thanon Niphat Uthit 2 ☏074 243815, ⊜cathay_ontours@hotmail.com. This friendly place in the heart of town has long been Hat Yai's main travellers' hub; the café acts as a sociable meeting-place, and the rooms have en-suite cold-water bathrooms. ❶

Lee Gardens Plaza Hotel 29 Thanon Prachatipat ☏074 261111, ⊛www.leeplaza.com. Characterless but good-value. Central upmarket option with great views of the city from its four hundred comfortable rooms. Facilities include a fitness centre, a rooftop pool and a 33rd-floor panoramic restaurant. ❻

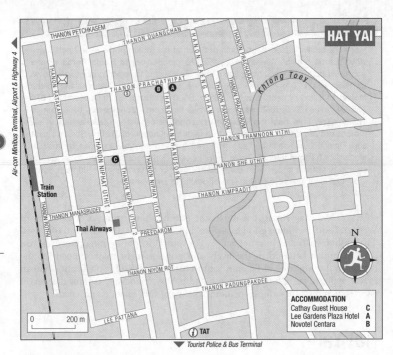

Air-con Minibus Terminal, Airport & Highway 4

HAT YAI

THANON PETCHKASEM

THANON DUANGCHAN

THANON SAENG CHAN

THANON PRACHARAK

Khlong Toey

THANON RATAKARN

THANON PRACHATHIPAT

THANON PRACHAROM

THANON PARADON

THANON SANEHANUSORN

THANON THAMNOON VITHI

THANON SHE UTHIT

Train
Station

THANON NIPHAT UTHIT 1

THANON NIPHAT UTHIT 3

THANON KIMPRADIT

THANON HOTRAI

THANON MANASRUDEE

THANON NIPHAT UTHIT 2

Thai Airways

PREEDAROM

N

THANON NIYOM ROT

THANON PADUNGPAKDEE

0   200 m

LEE PATTANA

ACCOMMODATION
Cathay Guest House   C
Lee Gardens Plaza Hotel A
Novotel Centara   B

(i) TAT

▼ Tourist Police & Bus Terminal

Novotel Centara 3 Thanon Sanehanusorn ☎ 074 352222, ⊛ www.centarahotelsresorts .com. Luxury hotel in a good location next to the Central Department Store, with spa, fitness centre, sauna, swimming pool and Thai, Chinese and Japanese restaurants. Substantial discounts often available on their website. ❽

Travel details

Trains

Trang to: Bangkok (2 daily; 15–16hr).

Buses

Satun to: Bangkok (5 daily; 16hr); Phuket (4 daily; 7hr); Trang (every 30min; 2hr 30min–3hr).

Trang to: Bangkok (11 daily; 12–14hr); Krabi (roughly every 30min; 2hr); Phuket (hourly; 5hr); Satun (every 30min; 2hr 30min–3hr).

Flights

Trang to: Bangkok (2 daily; 1hr 30min).

Contexts

Contexts

History

Thailand's history is complex and fascinating, but what follows can be only a brief account of the major events in the country's past. For more detailed coverage, get hold of a copy of David Wyatt's excellent *Thailand: A Short History* (see p.484).

Early history

The region's first distinctive civilization, **Dvaravati**, which encompassed city-states in central and northern Thailand, was established around two thousand years ago by an Austroasiatic-speaking people known as the Mon. One of its mainstays was Theravada Buddhism, which had been introduced to Thailand during the second or third century BC by Indian missionaries. In the eighth century, peninsular Thailand to the south of Dvaravati came under the control of the **Srivijaya** empire, a Mahayana Buddhist state centred on Sumatra, which had strong ties with India.

From the ninth century onwards, both Dvaravati and Srivijaya Thailand succumbed to invading **Khmers** from Cambodia, who took control of north-eastern, central and peninsular Thailand. They ruled from Angkor and left dozens of spectacular temple complexes throughout the region. By the thirteenth century, however, the Khmers had overreached themselves and were in no position to resist the onslaught of a vibrant new force in Southeast Asia: the **Thais**. The earliest traceable history of the Thai people picks them up in southern China around the fifth century AD, when they were squeezed by Chinese and Vietnamese expansionism into sparsely inhabited northeastern Laos. Their first significant entry into what is now Thailand seems to have happened in the north, where, some time after the seventh century, the Thais formed a state known as Yonok. Theravada Buddhism spread to Yonok via Dvaravati around the end of the tenth century, which served not only to unify the Thais themselves, but also to link them to the wider community of Buddhists.

By the end of the twelfth century, they formed the majority of the population in Thailand, then under the control of the Khmer empire. The Khmers' main outpost, at Lopburi, was by this time regarded as the administrative capital of a land called "Syam".

Sukhothai and Ayutthaya

Some time around 1238, Thais in the upper Chao Phraya valley captured the main Khmer outpost in the region at **Sukhothai** and established a kingdom there. When the young Ramkhamhaeng came to the throne around 1278, he seized control of much of the Chao Phraya valley, and over the next twenty years gained the submission of most of Thailand under a complex tribute system.

Although the empire of Sukhothai extended Thai control over a vast area, its greatest contribution to the Thais' development was at home, in cultural and political matters. A famous inscription by Ramkhamhaeng, now housed in the Bangkok National Museum, describes a prosperous era of benevolent rule, and it is generally agreed that Ramkhamhaeng ruled justly according to Theravada Buddhist doctrine. A further sign of the Thais' growing self-confidence was the invention of a new script to make their tonal language understood by the non-Thai inhabitants of the land.

After the death of Ramkhamhaeng around 1299, however, his empire fell apart, and **Ayutthaya** became the capital of the Thai empire. Soon after founding the city in 1351, the ambitious King Ramathibodi united the principalities of the lower Chao Phraya valley, which had formed the western provinces of the Khmer empire. When he recruited his bureaucracy from the urban elite of Lopburi, Ramathibodi set the style of government at Ayutthaya, elements of which persist to the present day. The elaborate etiquette, language and rituals of Angkor were adopted, and, most importantly, so was the concept of the ruler as *devaraja* (divine king).

The site chosen by Ramathibodi for an international port was the best in the region, and so began Ayutthaya's rise to prosperity, based on exploiting the upswing in trade in the middle of the fourteenth century along the routes between India and China. By 1540, the Kingdom of Ayutthaya had grown to cover most of the area of modern-day Thailand. Despite a 1568 invasion by the Burmese, which led to twenty years of foreign rule, Ayutthaya made a spectacular comeback, and in the seventeenth century its foreign trade boomed. In 1511, the Portuguese had become the first Western power to trade with Ayutthaya, while a treaty with Spain in 1598 was followed by similar agreements with Holland and England in 1608 and 1612 respectively. European merchants flocked to Thailand, not only to buy Thai products, but also for the Chinese and Japanese goods on sale there.

In the mid-eighteenth century, however, the rumbling in the Burmese jungle to the north began to make itself heard again. After an unsuccessful siege in 1760, February 1766 saw the **Burmese** descend upon the city for the last time. The Thais held out for over a year but, finally, in April 1767, the city was taken. The Burmese savagely razed everything to the ground, led off tens of thousands of prisoners to Burma and abandoned the city to the jungle.

From Taksin to Rama III

Out of this lawless mess emerged **Phraya Taksin**, a charismatic general, who was crowned king in December 1768 at his new capital of **Thonburi**, on the opposite bank of the river from modern-day Bangkok. Within two years, he had restored all of Ayutthaya's territories and, by the end of the next decade, had brought Cambodia and much of Laos into a huge new empire.

However, by 1779 all was not well with the king. Taksin was becoming increasingly irrational and sadistic, and in March 1782 he was ousted in a coup. Chao Phraya Chakri, Taksin's military commander, was invited to take power and had Taksin executed.

With the support of the Ayutthayan aristocracy, Chakri – reigning as **Rama I** (1782–1809) – set about consolidating the Thai kingdom. His first act was to move the capital across the river to what we know as Bangkok, on the more defensible east bank. Borrowing from the layout of Ayutthaya, he built a new royal palace and impressive monasteries in the area of Ratanakosin within a defensive ring of two (later expanded to three) canals. In the palace temple, Wat Phra Kaeo, he enshrined the talismanic Emerald Buddha, which he had snatched during his campaigns in Laos. Trade with China revived, and the style of government was put on a more modern footing: while retaining many of the features of a *devaraja*, he shared more responsibility with his courtiers, as a first among equals.

The peaceful accession of Rama I's son as **Rama II** (1809–24) signalled the establishment of the Chakri dynasty, which is still in place today. This Second Reign is best remembered as a fertile period for Thai literature; indeed, Rama II himself is renowned as one of the great Thai poets.

By the reign of **Rama III** (1824–51), the Thais were starting to get alarmed by British colonialism in the region. In 1826, Rama III was obliged to sign the

Burney Treaty, a limited trade agreement with the British, by which the Thais won some political security in return for reducing their taxes on goods passing through Bangkok.

Mongkut and Chulalongkorn

Rama IV, commonly known to foreigners as **Mongkut** (in Thai, *Phra Chom Klao*; 1851–68), had been a Buddhist monk for 27 years when he succeeded his brother. But far from leading a cloistered life, Mongkut had travelled widely throughout Thailand, and had taken an interest in Western learning, studying English, Latin and the sciences. Realizing that Thailand would be unable to resist the military might of the British, the king reduced import and export taxes, allowed British subjects to live and own land in Thailand and granted them freedom of trade under the Bowring Treaty. Within a decade, similar agreements had been signed with France, the United States and a score of other nations. Thus, by skilful diplomacy the king avoided a close relationship with just one power, which could easily have led to Thailand's annexation.

Mongkut's son, **Chulalongkorn**, took the throne as Rama V (1868–1910) at the age of only fifteen, but was well prepared by an excellent education which mixed traditional Thai and modern Western elements – provided by Mrs Anna Leonowens, subject of *The King and I*. One of his first acts was to scrap the custom by which subjects were required to prostrate themselves in the presence of the king. In the 1880s, he began to restructure the government to meet the country's needs, setting up a host of departments – for education, public health, the army and the like – and bringing in scores of foreign advisors to help with everything from foreign affairs to rail lines.

Throughout this period, however, the Western powers maintained their pressure on the region. The most serious threat to Thai sovereignty was the Franco–Siamese Crisis of 1893, which culminated in the French sending gunboats up the Chao Phraya River to Bangkok. Flouting numerous international laws, France claimed control over Laos and made other outrageous demands, which Chulalongkorn had no option but to agree to. During the course of his reign, the country was obliged to cede almost half of its territory, and forewent huge sums of tax revenue in order to preserve its independence. However, by Chulalongkorn's death in 1910, the frontiers were fixed as they are today.

The end of absolute monarchy and World War II

Chulalongkorn was succeeded by a flamboyant, British-educated prince, **Vajira-vudh** (Rama VI, 1910–25), and by the time the young and inexperienced **Prajadhipok** – 76th child of Chulalongkorn – was catapulted to the throne as Rama VII (1925–35), Vajiravudh's extravagance had created severe financial problems, which were exacerbated by the onset of the Great Depression.

On June 24, 1932, a small group of middle-ranking officials, dissatisfied with the injustices of monarchical government and led by a lawyer, **Pridi Phanomyong**, and an army major, Luang Phibunsongkhram (**Phibun**), staged a coup with only a handful of troops. Prajadhipok weakly submitted to the conspirators, and a hundred and fifty years of **absolute monarchy** in Bangkok came to a sudden end. The king was sidelined to a position of symbolic significance, and in 1935 he abdicated in favour of his ten-year-old nephew, Ananda, then a schoolboy living in Switzerland.

Phibun emerged as prime minister after the decisive elections of 1938, and a year later officially renamed the country Thailand ("Land of the Free") – Siam, it was argued, was a name bestowed by external forces, and the new title made it clear that the country belonged to the Thais rather than the economically dominant Chinese.

The Thais were dragged into **World War II** on December 8, 1941, when, almost at the same time as the assault on Pearl Harbor, the Japanese invaded the east coast of peninsular Thailand, with their sights set on Singapore to the south. The Thais at first resisted fiercely, but realizing that the position was hopeless, Phibun quickly ordered a ceasefire.

The Thai government concluded a military alliance with Japan and declared war against the United States and Great Britain in January 1942, probably in the belief that the Japanese would win. However, the Thai minister in Washington, Seni Pramoj, refused to deliver the declaration of war against the US, and, in cooperation with the Americans, began organizing a resistance movement called Seri Thai. Pridi Phanomyong, now acting as regent to the young king, secretly coordinated the movement, smuggling in American agents and housing them in Bangkok. By 1944, Japan's defeat looked likely, and in July, Phibun, who had been most closely associated with them, was forced to resign by the National Assembly.

Postwar upheavals

With the fading of the military, the election of January 1946 was the first one contested by organized political parties. Pridi became prime minister, a new constitution was drafted, and the outlook for democratic, civilian government seemed bright. Hopes were shattered, however, on June 9, 1946, when King Ananda was found dead in his bed, with a bullet wound in his forehead. Three palace servants were hurriedly tried and executed, but the murder has never been satisfactorily explained. Pridi resigned as prime minister, and in April 1948, Phibun, playing on the threat of communism, took over the premiership again.

As **communism** developed its hold in the region with the takeover of China in 1949 and the French defeat in Indochina in 1954, the US increasingly viewed Thailand as a bulwark against the red menace. Between 1951 and 1957, when its annual state budget was only about $200 million a year, Thailand received a total of $149 million in American economic aid and $222 million in military aid.

Phibun narrowly won a general election in 1957, but only by blatant vote-rigging and coercion. After vehement public outcry, General Sarit, the commander-in-chief of the army, overthrew the new government in September the same year. Believing that Thailand would prosper best under a unifying authority, Sarit set about re-establishing the monarchy as the head of the social hierarchy and the source of legitimacy for the government. Ananda's successor, **Bhumibol** (Rama IX), was pushed into an active role, while Sarit ruthlessly silenced critics and pressed ahead with a plan for economic development.

The Vietnam War and the democracy movement

Sarit died in 1963, whereupon the military succession passed to General Thanom. His most pressing problem was the **Vietnam War**. The Thais, with the backing of the US, quietly began to conduct military operations in Laos, to which North Vietnam and China responded by supporting anti-government insurgency in Thailand. By 1968, around 45,000 US military personnel were on Thai soil, which became the base for US bombing raids against North Vietnam and Laos. The effects of the American presence were profound. The economy swelled with dollars, and hundreds of thousands of Thais became reliant on the Americans for a living, with a consequent proliferation of prostitution – centred on Bangkok's infamous Patpong district – and corruption.

Moreover, the sudden exposure to Western culture led many to question traditional Thai values and the political status quo.

Poor farmers in particular were becoming increasingly disillusioned with their lot, and many turned against the Bangkok government. At the end of 1964, the Communist Party of Thailand and other groups formed a broad left coalition which soon had the support of several thousand insurgents in remote areas of the northeast and the north. By 1967, a separate threat had arisen in southern Thailand, involving Muslim dissidents and the Chinese-dominated Communist Party of Malaysia.

Thanom was now facing a major security crisis, and in November 1971 he imposed repressive military rule. In response, **student demonstrations** began in June 1973, and in October as many as 500,000 people turned out at Thammasat University in Bangkok to demand a new constitution. Clashes with the police ensued on October 14, during which over 350 people were reported killed, but elements in the army, backed by King Bhumibol, refused to provide enough troops to crush the uprising. Later that day, Thanom was forced to resign and leave the country.

In a new climate of openness, **Kukrit Pramoj** formed a coalition of seventeen elected parties and secured a promise of US withdrawal from Thailand, but his government was riven with feuding. In October 1976, the students demonstrated again, protesting against the return of Thanom to Bangkok. This time there was no restraint: supported by elements of the military and the government, the police and reactionary students launched a massive assault on Thammasat University. On October 6, hundreds of students were brutally beaten, scores were lynched and some even burnt alive; the military took control and suspended the constitution.

"Premocracy"

Soon after, the military-appointed prime minister, Thanin Kraivichien, forced dissidents to undergo anti-communist indoctrination, but his measures seem to have been too repressive even for the military, who forced him to resign in October 1977. General Kriangsak Chomanand took over, and began to break up the insurgency with shrewd offers of amnesty. He in turn was displaced in February 1980 by **General Prem Tinsulanonda**, backed by a broad parliamentary coalition. Untainted by corruption, Prem achieved widespread support, including that of the monarchy. Overseeing a period of rapid economic growth, Prem maintained the premiership until 1988, with a unique mixture of dictatorship and democracy sometimes called **Premocracy**: although never standing for parliament himself, Prem was asked by the legislature after every election to become prime minister. He eventually stepped down because, he said, it was time for the country's leader to be chosen from among its elected representatives.

The 1992 demonstrations and the 1997 constitution

The new prime minister was indeed an elected MP, Chatichai Choonhavan. He pursued a vigorous policy of economic development, but this fostered widespread corruption. Following an economic downturn and Chatichai's attempts to downgrade the political role of the military, the armed forces staged a bloodless coup on February 23, 1991, led by Supreme Commander Sunthorn and General Suchinda, the army commander-in-chief, who became premier.

When Suchinda reneged on promises to make democratic amendments to the constitution, hundreds of thousands of ordinary Thais poured onto the streets around Bangkok's Democracy Monument in **mass demonstrations** between

May 17 and 20, 1992. Suchinda brutally crushed the protests, leaving hundreds dead or injured, but was then forced to resign when King Bhumibol expressed his disapproval in a ticking-off that was broadcast on world television.

Elections were held in September, with the **Democrat Party**, led by Chuan Leekpai, a noted upholder of democracy and the rule of law, emerging victorious. Chuan was succeeded in turn by Banharn Silpa-archa – nicknamed by the local press "the walking ATM", a reference to his reputation for buying votes – and General Chavalit Yongchaiyudh. The most significant positive event of the latter's tenure was the approval of a **new constitution** in 1997. Drawn up by an independent drafting assembly, its main points included: direct elections to the senate, rather than appointment of senators by the prime minister; acceptance of the right of assembly as the basis of a democratic society and guarantees of individual rights and freedoms; greater public accountability; and increased popular participation in local administration. The eventual aim of the new charter was to end the traditional system of patronage, vested interests and vote-buying.

Tom yam kung: the 1997 economic crisis

In February 1997 foreign-exchange dealers began to mount speculative attacks on the **baht**, alarmed at the size of Thailand's private foreign debt – 250 billion baht in the unproductive property sector alone, much of it accrued through the proliferation of prestigious skyscrapers in Bangkok. Chavalit's government defended the pegged exchange rate, spending $23 billion of the country's formerly healthy foreign-exchange reserves, but at the beginning of July was forced to give up the ghost – the baht was floated and soon went into free-fall. Thailand was forced to seek help from the **IMF**, who in August put together a $17-billion **rescue package**, coupled with severe austerity measures.

In November, the inept Chavalit was replaced by Chuan Leekpai, who immediately took a hard line in following the IMF's advice, which involved maintaining cripplingly high interest rates to protect the baht and slashing government budgets. Although this played well abroad, at home the government encountered increasing hostility from its newly impoverished citizens – the downturn struck with such speed and severity that it was dubbed the **tom yam kung crisis**, after the searingly hot Thai soup. Chuan's tough stance paid off, however, with the baht stabilizing and inflation falling back, and in October 1999 he announced that he was forgoing almost $4 billion of the IMF's package.

Thaksin and recent upheavals

The general election of January 2001 was the first to be held under the 1997 constitution, which was intended to take the traditionally crucial role of money, especially for vote-buying, out of politics. However, this election coincided with the emergence of a new party, Thai Rak Thai (TRT; "Thai Loves Thai"), formed by one of Thailand's wealthiest men, **Thaksin Shinawatra**, an ex-policeman who had made a personal fortune from government telecommunications concessions.

TRT duly won the election but, instead of a move towards greater democracy, as envisaged by the new constitution, Thaksin's government seemed to represent a full-blown merger between politics and big business, concentrating economic power in even fewer hands. Furthermore, the prime minister began to apply commercial and legal pressure, including several lawsuits, to try to silence critics in the media and parliament, and to manipulate the Senate and supposedly independent institutions such as the Election Commission. As his standing became more firmly entrenched, he rejected constitutional reforms designed to rein in his power – famously declaring that "democracy is only a tool" for achieving other goals.

Thaksin did, however, maintain his profile as a populist reformer by carrying through nearly all of his controversial election promises. He issued a three-year loan moratorium for perennially indebted farmers and set up a one-million-baht development fund for each of the country's seventy thousand villages – though many villages used the money to cover past debts, rather than creating projects for the future as intended. To improve public health access, a standard charge of B30 per hospital visit was introduced nationwide. However, too little was invested in the health service to cope with the increased demand.

Despite a sharp escalation of violence in the Islamic southern provinces in early 2004 (see p.443), but bolstered by his high-profile response to the tsunami on December 26, 2004 (see p.344), Thaksin breezed through the February 2005 election, becoming the first Thai prime minister to win an outright majority at the polls. The prospect of such a one-party state, however, alarmed a wide spectrum of opposition. When Thaksin's relatives sold their shares in the family's Shin Corporation in January 2006 for £1.1 billion, without paying tax, tens of thousands of mostly middle-class Thais flocked to Bangkok to take part in protracted but peaceful demonstrations, under the umbrella of the **People's Alliance for Democracy** (**PAD**). After further allegations of corruption and cronyism, in September Thaksin, while on official business in the United States, was ousted by a military government in a benign **coup**.

Thaksin set up home in London, but in May 2007 his party, TRT, was found guilty of electoral fraud and dissolved. Undeterred, his supporters formed the People's Power Party (PPP), which despite its ill-concealed opposition to the royalist-military elite, won the December 2007 general election; its leader, Samak Sundaravej, an irascible, right-wing TV chef, openly confessed to being a proxy for Thaksin. In response, the PAD – its trademark yellow shirts (the colour of the king) now firmly established – stepped up its mass protests, eventually occupying the government's offices for several months. Meanwhile, the merry-go-round of court cases continued, including the disqualification of Samak from political office – only to be replaced as prime minister by Thaksin's brother-in-law. Thaksin was finally convicted *in absentia* of corruption and, as a fugitive from justice, was refused a visa extension by the UK.

Matters came to a head in November and December 2008: the PAD seized and closed down Bangkok's Suvarnabhumi and Don Muang airports; the ruling People's Power Party was declared illegal, which persuaded the yellow shirts to lift their sit-in; and Puea Thai, the PPP's swift reincarnation, was unable to form a new coalition government. Instead, led by the young, charismatic **Abhisit Vejjajiva**, who was born in Newcastle-upon-Tyne and educated at Eton and Oxford, the Democratic Party jumped into bed with the Friends of Newin (aka the Bhumjaithai Party), formerly staunch supporters of Thaksin, to take the helm. At the time of writing, however, the divisions between the pro- and anti-Thaksin camps have not been resolved. Thaksin's supporters, now red-shirted and organized into the UDD (United Front for Democracy against Dictatorship), have taken their turn to hold mass protests; in April 2009 they forced the ASEAN (Association of Southeast Asian Nations) summit in Pattaya to be embarrassingly abandoned and closed down central Bangkok for several days before being dispersed by the army. Meanwhile the PAD, who have blotted their copybook internationally by advocating a part-elected, part-appointed system of government for Thailand to try to minimize corruption, are talking about forming a political party.

Religion: Thai Buddhism

O
ver 85 percent of Thais consider themselves **Theravada Buddhists**, followers of the teachings of a holy man usually referred to as the Buddha (Enlightened One), though more precisely known as Gautama Buddha to distinguish him from lesser-known Buddhas who preceded him. Theravada Buddhism is one of the two main schools of Buddhism practised in Asia, and in Thailand it has absorbed an eclectic assortment of animist and Hindu elements.

Islam is the biggest of the minority religions in Thailand, practised by between five and ten percent of the population. Most Muslims live in the south, especially in the Deep South provinces of Yala, Pattani and Narithiwat, along the Malaysian border, whose populations are over seventy percent Muslim. The separatist violence in this region has caused great tension between local Buddhist and Muslim communities, which have traditionally co-existed peacefully; it has not, however, obviously affected inter-faith relationships elsewhere in Thailand. The rest of the Thai population comprises Mahayana Buddhists, Hindus, Sikhs, Christians and animists.

The Buddha: his life and beliefs

Gautama Buddha was born in Nepal as **Prince Gautama Siddhartha** in either the sixth or seventh century BC. At his birth, astrologers predicted that he would become either a famous king or a celebrated holy man, depending on which path he chose. Much preferring the former, the prince's father forbade the boy from leaving the palace grounds, and set about educating Gautama in all aspects of the high life. Most statues of the Buddha depict him with elongated earlobes, which is a reference to this early pampered existence, when he would have worn heavy precious stones in his ears.

The prince married and became a father, but at the age of 29 he flouted his father's authority and sneaked out into the world beyond the palace. On this fateful trip he encountered successively an old man, a sick man, a corpse and a hermit, and thus for the first time was made aware that **pain and suffering** were intrinsic to human life. Contemplation seemed the only means of discovering why this was so – and therefore Gautama decided to leave the palace and become a Hindu ascetic.

For several years he wandered the countryside leading a life of self-denial and self-mortification, but failed to come any closer to the answer. Eventually concluding that the best course of action must be to follow a "Middle Way" – neither indulgent nor overly ascetic – Gautama sat down beneath the famous riverside bodhi tree at Bodh Gaya in India, facing the rising sun, to **meditate** until he achieved enlightenment. For 49 days he sat cross-legged in the "lotus position", contemplating the causes of suffering and wrestling with temptations that materialized to distract him. Most of these were sent by **Mara**, the Evil One, who was finally subdued when Gautama summoned the earth goddess **Mae Toranee** by pointing the fingers of his right hand at the ground – the gesture known as **Calling the Earth to Witness**, or *Bhumisparsa Mudra*, which has been immortalized by thousands of Thai sculptors. Mae Toranee wrung torrents of water from her hair and engulfed Mara's demonic emissaries in a flood, an episode that's also commonly reproduced, most famously in the statue in Bangkok's Sanam Luang.

Temptations dealt with, Gautama soon came to attain **enlightenment** and so become a Buddha. As the place of his enlightenment, the **bodhi tree** (or bo tree) has assumed special significance for Buddhists: not only does it appear in many Buddhist paintings, but there's often a real bodhi tree (*Ficus religiosa*) planted in temple compounds as well. In addition, the bot is nearly always built facing either a body of water or facing east (preferably both).

The Buddha preached his **first sermon** in a deer park in India, where he characterized his doctrine, or **Dharma**, as a wheel. From this episode comes the early Buddhist symbol the Dharmachakra, known as the Wheel of Law, which is often accompanied by a statue of a deer. Thais celebrate this first sermon with a public holiday in July known as **Asanha Puja**. On another occasion 1250 people spontaneously gathered to hear the Buddha speak, an event remembered in Thailand as **Maha Puja** and marked by a public holiday in February.

For the next forty-odd years the Buddha travelled the region converting non-believers and performing miracles. One rainy season he even ascended into the **Tavatimsa heaven** (Heaven of the 33 gods) to visit his mother and to preach the doctrine to her. His descent from this heaven is quite a common theme of paintings and sculptures, and the **Standing Buddha** pose of numerous Buddha statues comes from this story.

The Buddha "died" at the age of eighty on the banks of a river at Kusinari in India – an event often dated to 543 BC, which is why the **Thai calendar** is 543 years out of synch with the Western one, so that the year 2010 AD becomes 2553 BE (Buddhist Era). Lying on his side, propping up his head on his hand, the Buddha passed into **Nirvana** (giving rise to another classic pose, the **Reclining Buddha**), the unimaginable state of nothingness which knows no suffering and from which there is no reincarnation. Buddhists believe that the day the Buddha entered Nirvana was the same date on which he was born and on which he achieved enlightenment, a triply significant day that Thais honour with the **Visakha Puja** festival in May.

Buddhists believe that Gautama Buddha was the five-hundredth incarnation of a single being: the stories of these five hundred lives, collectively known as the **Jataka**, provide the inspiration for much Thai art. Hindus also accept Gautama Buddha into their pantheon, perceiving him as the ninth manifestation of their god Vishnu.

The spread of Buddhism

After the Buddha entered Nirvana, his **doctrine** spread relatively quickly across India, and probably was first promulgated in Thailand in about the third century BC. His teachings, the *Tripitaka*, were written down in the Pali language – a derivative of Sanskrit – in a form that became known as **Theravada**, or "The Doctrine of the Elders".

By the beginning of the first millennium, a new movement called **Mahayana** (Great Vehicle) had emerged within the Theravada school, attempting to make Buddhism more accessible by introducing a pantheon of **bodhisattva**, or Buddhist saints, who, although they had achieved enlightenment, postponed entering Nirvana in order to inspire the populace. Mahayana Buddhism spread north into China, Korea, Vietnam and Japan, also entering southern Thailand via the Srivijayan empire around the eighth century and parts of Khmer Cambodia in about the eleventh century. Meanwhile Theravada Buddhism (which the Mahayanists disparagingly renamed "Hinayana" or "Lesser Vehicle") established itself most significantly in Sri Lanka, northern and central Thailand and Burma.

Buddhist doctrine and practice

Central to Theravada Buddhism is a belief in **karma** – every action has a consequence – and **reincarnation**, along with an understanding that craving is at the root of human suffering. The ultimate aim for a Buddhist is to get off the cycle of perpetual reincarnation and suffering and to instead enter the blissful state of non-being that is **Nirvana**. This enlightened state can take many lifetimes to achieve so the more realistic goal for most is to be reborn slightly higher up the karmic ladder each time. As Thai Buddhists see it, animals are at the bottom of the karmic scale and monks at the top, with women on a lower rung than men.

Living a good life, specifically a life of "pure intention", creates good karma, and Buddhist doctrine focuses a great deal on how to achieve this. Psychology and an understanding of human weaknesses play a big part. Key is the concept of *dukka*, which holds that **craving is the root cause of all suffering** or, to put it simplistically, human unhappiness is caused by the unquenchable dissatisfaction experienced when one's sensual, spiritual or material desires are not met. Accepting the truth of this is known as the **Four Noble Truths** of Buddhism. The route to enlightenment depends on a person being sufficiently detached from earthly desires so that *dukka* can't take hold. One acknowledges that the physical world is impermanent and ever-changing, and that all things – including the self – are therefore not worth craving. A Buddhist works towards this realization by following the **Eightfold Path**, or **Middle Way**, that is by developing a set of highly moral personal qualities such as "right speech", "right action" and "right mindfulness". Meditation is particularly helpful in this.

A devout Thai Buddhist commits to the **five basic precepts**, namely not to kill or steal, to refrain from sexual misconduct and incorrect speech (lies, gossip and abuse) and to eschew intoxicating liquor and drugs. There are **three extra precepts** for special *wan phra* holy days and for those laypeople including foreign students who study meditation at Thai temples: no eating after noon, no entertainment (including TV and music) and no sleeping on a soft bed; in addition, the no sexual misconduct precept turns into no sex at all.

Making merit

Merit-making in popular Thai Buddhism has become slightly skewed, so that some people act on the assumption that they'll climb the karmic ladder faster if they make bigger and better offerings to the temple and its monks. However, it is of course the purity of the intention behind one's merit-making (*tham bun*) that is fundamental.

Merit can be made in many ways, from giving a monk his breakfast to attending a Buddhist service or donating money and gifts to the neighbourhood temple, and most **festivals** are essentially communal merit-making opportunities. Between the big festivals, the most common days for making merit and visiting the temple are **wan phra** (holy days), which are determined by the phase of the moon and occur four times a month. One of the more bizarre but common merit-making activities involves **releasing caged birds**: worshippers buy tiny finches from vendors at wat compounds and, by liberating them from their cage, prove their Buddhist compassion towards all living things. The fact that the birds were free until netted earlier that morning doesn't seem to detract from the ritual. In riverside and seaside wats, fish or even baby turtles are released instead.

For an insightful introduction to the philosophy and practice of Thai Buddhism, see ⑩www.thaibuddhism.net. Details of Thai temples that welcome foreign students of Buddhism and meditation are on p.57.

The monkhood

It's the duty of Thailand's 200,000-strong **Sangha** (monkhood) to set an example to the Theravada Buddhist community by living a life as close to the Middle Way as possible and by preaching the Dharma to the people. The life of a monk (*bhikkhu*) is governed by 227 precepts that include celibacy and the rejection of all personal possessions except gifts.

Each day begins with an **alms round** in the neighbourhood so that the laity can donate food and thereby gain themselves merit, and then is chiefly spent in meditation, chanting, teaching and study. As the most respected members of any community, monks act as teachers, counsellors and arbiters in local disputes, and sometimes become spokesmen for villagers' rights. They also perform rituals at cremations, weddings and other events, such as the launching of a new business or even the purchase of a new car. Many young boys from poor families find themselves almost obliged to become either a *dek wat* (temple boy) or a **novice monk** because that's the only way they can get accommodation, food and, crucially, an education. This is provided free in exchange for duties around the wat, and novices are required to adhere to ten rather than 227 Buddhist precepts.

Monkhood doesn't have to be for life: a man may leave the Sangha three times without stigma and in fact every Thai male (including royalty) is expected to **enter the monkhood** for a short period, ideally between leaving school and marrying, as a rite of passage into adulthood. Thai government departments and some private companies grant their employees paid leave for their time as a monk, but the custom is in decline as young men increasingly have to consider the effect their absence may have on their career prospects. Instead, many men now enter the monkhood for a brief period after the death of a parent, to make merit both for the deceased and for the rest of the family. The most popular time for temporary ordination is the three-month Buddhist retreat period – **Pansa**, sometimes referred to as "Buddhist Lent" – which begins in July and lasts for the duration of the rainy season. (The monks' confinement is said to originate from the earliest years of Buddhist history, when farmers complained that perambulating monks were squashing their sprouting rice crops.)

Monks in contemporary society

Some monks have acquired such a reputation for bringing wisdom and good fortune to their followers that they have become national gurus; others have extended their role as village spokesmen to become influential social and environmental activists. Though this kind of involvement in the secular world has not met with unanimous approval, far more disappointing to the laity are those monks who **flout the precepts** of the Sangha by succumbing to the temptations of a consumer society, flaunting Raybans, Rolexes and Mercedes (in some cases actually bought with temple funds), chain-smoking and flirting, even making pocket money from predicting lottery results and practising faith-healing. With so much national pride and integrity riding on the sanctity of the Sangha, any whiff of a deeper scandal is bound to strike deep into the national psyche. Cases of monks involved in drug-dealing, gun-running, even rape and murder have prompted a stream of editorials on the state of the Sangha and the collapse of spiritual values at the heart of Thai society. The inclusivity of the monkhood – which is open to just about any male who wants to join – has been highlighted as a particularly vulnerable aspect, not least because donning saffron robes has always been an accepted way for criminals, reformed or otherwise, to repent of their misdeeds.

Interestingly, back in the late 1980s, the influential monk Phra Bodhirak (Photirak) was defrocked after criticizing what he saw as a tide of decadence infecting Thai Buddhism. He now preaches his ascetic code of anti-materialism through his breakaway **Santi Asoke** sect, famous across the country for its cheap vegetarian restaurants, its philosophy of self-sufficiency and for the simple blue farmers' shirts worn by many of its followers.

Women and the monkhood

Although the Theravada Buddhist hierarchy in some countries permits the ordination of **female monks**, or *bhikkhuni*, the Thai Sangha does not. Instead, Thai women are officially only allowed to become **nuns**, or *mae chii*, shaving their heads, donning white robes and keeping eight rather than 227 precepts. Their status is lower than that of the monks and they are chiefly occupied with temple upkeep rather than conducting religious ceremonies.

However, the progressives are becoming more vocal, and in 2002 a Thai woman became the first of several to break with the Buddhist authorities and get **ordained** as a novice *bhikkhuni* on Thai soil. Thailand's Sangha Council, however, still recognizes neither her ordination nor the temple, Watra Songdhammakalyani in Nakhon Pathom, where the ordination took place. The Watra (rather than Wat) is run by another Thai *bhikkuni*, Dhammananda Bhikkhuni, the author of several books in English about **women and Buddhism** and of an informative website, ⓦwww.thaibhikkhunis.org.

Hindu deities and animist spirits

The complicated history of the area now known as Thailand has made Thai Buddhism a confusingly syncretic faith, as you'll realize when you enter a Buddhist temple compound to be confronted by a statue of a Hindu deity. While regular Buddhist merit-making insures a Thai for the next life, there are certain **Hindu gods and animist spirits** that many Thais – sophisticated Bangkokians and illiterate farmers alike – also cultivate for help with more immediate problems; and as often as not it's a Buddhist monk who is called in to exorcize a malevolent spirit. Even the Buddhist King Bhumibol employs Brahmin priests and astrologers to determine auspicious days and officiate at certain royal ceremonies and, like his royal predecessors of the Chakri dynasty, he also associates himself with the Hindu god Vishnu by assuming the title Rama IX – Rama, hero of the Hindu epic the *Ramayana*, having been Vishnu's seventh manifestation on earth.

If a Thai wants help in achieving a short-term goal, like passing an exam, becoming pregnant or winning the lottery, he or she will quite likely turn to the **Hindu pantheon**, visiting an enshrined statue of Brahma, Vishnu, Shiva or Ganesh, and making offerings of flowers, incense and maybe food. If the outcome is favourable, the devotee will probably come back to show thanks, bringing more offerings and maybe even hiring a dance troupe to perform a celebratory *lakhon chatri*. Built in honour of Brahma, Bangkok's Erawan Shrine is the most famous place of Hindu-inspired worship in the country.

Spirits and spirit houses

Whereas Hindu deities tend to be benevolent, **spirits** (or *phi*) are not nearly as reliable and need to be mollified more frequently. They come in hundreds of varieties, some more malign than others, and inhabit everything from trees, rivers and caves to public buildings and private homes – even taking over people if they feel like it.

So that these *phi* don't pester human inhabitants, every building has a special **spirit house** (*saan phra phum*) in its vicinity, as a dwelling for spirits ousted by the building's construction. Usually raised on a short column to set it at or above eye-level, the spirit house must occupy an auspicious location – not, for example, in the shadow of the main building. It's generally about the size of a dolls' house and designed to look like a wat or a traditional Thai house, but its ornamentation is supposed to reflect the status of the humans' building, so if that building is enlarged or refurbished, the spirit house should be improved accordingly. And as architects become increasingly bold in their designs, so modernist spirit houses are also beginning to appear, especially in Bangkok where an eyecatching new skyscraper might be graced by a spirit house of glass or polished concrete. **Figurines** representing the relevant guardian spirit and his aides are sometimes put inside, and daily offerings of incense, lighted candles and garlands of jasmine are placed alongside them to keep the *phi* happy – a disgruntled spirit is a dangerous spirit, liable to cause sickness, accidents and even death. As with any religious building or icon in Thailand, an unwanted or crumbling spirit house should never be dismantled or destroyed, which is why you'll often see damaged spirit houses placed around the base of a sacred banyan tree, where they are able to rest in peace.

The coastal environment

Spanning some 1650km north to south, Thailand lies in the heart of Southeast Asia's tropical zone, its southern border running less than seven degrees north of the Equator. Coastal Thailand's climate is characterized by high temperatures and even higher humidity, a very fertile combination which nourishes a huge diversity of flora and fauna in the tropical rainforests, mangrove swamps and coral reefs that constitute the region's main habitats.

The habitats

Some of Thailand's most precious habitats are protected as **national park**, including the steamy jungles of Khao Sok; the coastal mud flats of Khao Sam Roi Yot and the expansive lagoons of Thale Noi, both of which are favourite haunts of migrating birds; and the island shorelines and reefs of Ko Surin, Ko Similan, plus parts of Ko Phi Phi, Ko Lanta, Ko Tarutao, Ang Thong, Ko Samet and the Ko Chang archipelago.

Tropical rainforests

Thailand's **tropical rainforests** occur in areas of high and prolonged rainfall in the southern peninsula, most accessibly in the national parks of Khao Sok, Tarutao and Khao Luang. Some areas contain as many as two hundred species of tree within a single hectare, along with a host of other flora. Characteristic of a tropical rainforest is the multi-layered series of **canopies**. The uppermost storey sometimes reaches 60m, and will often have enormous buttressed roots for support; beneath this, the dense canopy of 25–35m is often festooned with climbers and epiphytes such as ferns, lianas, mosses and orchids; then comes an uneven layer 5–10m high consisting of palms, rattans, shrubs and small trees. The forest floor in tropical rainforests tends to be relatively open and free of dense undergrowth because the upper three layers shade much of the light.

The family **Dipterocarpaceae** dominate these forests, a group of tropical hardwoods prized for their timber – and as nesting sites for hornbills and lookout posts for gibbons. Also very common are the many different species of **epiphytes**, plants that usually grow on other plants, but aren't parasitic, obtaining their nutrients from the atmosphere instead, and from decaying plant and animal matter. Among the most famous, and most beautiful, epiphytes are Thailand's countless species of wild **orchids**, many of them gratifyingly common in the forest and prized as houseplants in the West, including the golden spiky petalled *Bulbophyllum picturatum*, the bright yellow members of the genus *Dendrobium*, the flame-red *Ascocentrum curvifolium*, and the blue *Vanda coerulea*.

For the early years of its life, the **strangling fig** (*Ficus* sp) is also an epiphyte, often using a dipterocarp as host while it drops its distinctive lattice of roots to the ground. It can then feed normally, so well in fact that, after many years, the fig's roots and crown completely enshroud the support tree and hasten its death. As the host decomposes, it leaves a hollow but structurally sound strangling fig. Strangling figs are excellent places to observe birds and mammals, particularly when in fruit, as they attract hornbills, green pigeons, barbets, gibbons, langurs and macaques.

Mangrove swamps and coastal forests

Mangrove swamps are an important habitat for a wide variety of marine life (including 204 species of bird, 74 species of fish and 54 types of crab) but, as with much of Thailand's inland forest, they have been significantly degraded by encroachment, as well as by large-scale prawn farming. Huge swathes of Thailand's littoral used to be fringed with mangrove swamps, but now they are mainly found only along the west peninsular coast, between Ranong and Satun, though Chanthaburi's Ao Khung Kraben is a notable east-coast exception. On Phuket, the Thachatchai Nature Trail leads you on a guided tour through a patch of mangrove swamp, but an even better way of **exploring the swamps** is to paddle a kayak through the mangrove-clogged inlets and island-lagoons of Ao Phang Nga, for more on which see the colour section on Ao Phang Nga, and p.386. Not only do mangrove swamps harbour a rich and important eco-system of their own, but they also help prevent coastal erosion; in certain areas of the tsunami-hit Andaman coast intact mangrove forest absorbed some of the waves' impact, protecting land and homes from even worse damage.

Nipa palms share the mangrove's penchant for brackish water, and these stubby-stemmed palm trees grow in abundance in the south, though commercial plantations are now replacing the natural colonies. Like most other species of palm indigenous to Thailand, the nipa is a versatile plant that's exploited to the full: alcohol is distilled from its sugary sap, and its fronds are woven into roofs (especially for beach huts and village homes), sticky-rice baskets and chair-backs.

The hardy **coconut palm** is also very tolerant of salty, sandy soil, and is equally useful. On islands such as Ko Kood, it's the backbone of the local economy, with millions of coconuts harvested every month for their milk, their oil-producing meat (copra), and their fibrous husks or coir (used for making ropes, matting, brushes and mattress stuffing); the palm fronds are woven into roof thatching and baskets, and the wood has an attractive grain.

Casuarinas (also known as she-oaks or ironwoods) also flourish in sandy soils and are common on beaches throughout Thailand; fast-growing and tall (up to 20m), they are quite often planted as wind-breaks. Though its feathery profile makes it look like a pine, it's actually made up of tiny twigs, not needles.

The wildlife

Thailand lies in an exceptionally rich "transition zone" of the Indo-Malayan realm, its forests, mountains and national parks attracting wildlife from both Indochina and Indonesia. In all, Thailand is home to three hundred species of mammal (36 of which are considered to be endangered) and 971 species of bird (42 of them endangered). For a guide to Thailand's spectacular array of **marine species**, see the *Underwater Thailand* colour section.

Mammals

In the main national parks like Khao Sok, the animals you're most likely to encounter – with your ears if not your eyes – are **primates**, particularly macaques and gibbons.

The latter are responsible for the distinctive hooting that echoes through the forests. Chief noise-maker is the **white-handed** or **lar gibbon**, a beige- or black-bodied, white-faced animal whose cute appearance, intelligence and dexterity unfortunately make it a popular pet. The poaching and mistreatment of lar gibbons has become so severe that a special Gibbon Rehabilitation Project has been set up in Phuket (see p.379).

Similarly chatty, macaques hang out in gangs of twenty or more. The **long-tailed** or **crab-eating macaque** lives in the lowlands, near rivers, lakes and coasts, including around Ao Phang Nga, Krabi, Ko Tarutao, Ang Thong and Khao Sam Roi Yot. It eats not only crabs, but mussels, other small animals and fruit, transporting and storing food in its big cheek pouch when swimming and diving. The **pig-tailed macaque**, named for its short curly tail, excels at scaling tall trees, a skill which has resulted in many of the males being captured and trained to pick coconuts.

Commonly sighted on night treks in Khao Sam Roi Yot, the **civet** – species of which include the common palm and small Indian – is a small mongoose-type animal which hunts smaller mammals in trees and on the ground; it's known in the West for the powerful smell released from its anal glands, a scent used commercially as a perfume base. Far more elusive is the **Indochinese tiger**, which lives under constant threat from both poachers and the destruction of its habitat by logging interests, both of which have reduced the current population to probably fewer than one hundred; it's thought that some still live in Khao Sok, however. Khao Sok is also potentially one of the easier places to encounter wild, small-eared Asian **elephants**, of which around two thousand now remain in Thailand.

Birds

Even if you don't see many mammals on a trek through a national park, you're certain to spot a satisfying range of birds. The **hornbill** is the most majestic, easily recognizable from its massive, powerful wings (the flapping of which can be heard for long distances) and huge beak surmounted by a bizarre horny casque. The two most commonly spotted species in Thailand are the plain black-and-white **oriental pied hornbill**, frequently sighted on the little islands of Ko Phayam and Ko Chang in Ranong province, among other places, and the flashier **great hornbill**, whose monochromic body and head are broken up with jaunty splashes of yellow. Thailand is also home to the extremely rare **Gurney's pitta**, found only in Khlong Thom national park, inland from Ko Lanta.

Coastal areas attract storks, egrets and herons, and Thale Noi Waterbird Park and the mud flats of Khao Sam Roi Yot are breeding grounds for the large, long-necked **purple heron**. The magnificent **white-bellied sea eagle** haunts the Thai coast, nesting in the forbidding crags around Ao Phang Nga, Krabi and Ko Tarutao and preying on fish and sea snakes. The tiny **edible nest swiftlet** makes its eponymous nest – the major ingredient of the luxury food, bird's-nest soup – in the limestone crags, too; for more on these swiftlets and their nests see p.418.

For exhaustive information on specific **bird-watching** locations throughout Thailand see ⊛www.thaibirding.com; for guided birding tours contact Thailand

---

The gecko

Whether you're staying on a beach or in a town, chances are you'll be sharing your room with a few **geckos**. These pale-green tropical lizards, which are completely harmless to humans and usually measure a cute four to ten centimetres in length, mostly appear at night, high up on walls and ceilings, where they feed on insects. Because the undersides of their flat toes are covered with hundreds of microscopic hairs that catch at even the tiniest of irregularities, geckos are able to scale almost any surface, including glass, which is why you usually see them in strange, gravity-defying positions. The largest and most vociferous gecko is known as the **tokay** in Thai, named after the disconcertingly loud sound it makes. Tokays can grow to an alarming 35cm but are welcomed by most householders, as they devour insects and mice; Thais also consider it auspicious if a baby is born within earshot of a crowing tokay.

Bird Watching (@www.thailandbirdwatching.com) and for bird-watching guidebooks see p.485.

Snakes

Thailand is home to around 175 different species and subspecies of **snake**, 56 of them dangerously venomous. Death by snakebite is not common, however, but all provincial hospitals should keep a stock of serum, produced at the Snake Farm in Bangkok.

Found everywhere and highly venomous, the two-metre, nocturnal, yellow-and-black-striped **banded krait** is one to avoid, as is the shorter but equally poisonous **Thai** or **monocled cobra**, which lurks in low-lying humid areas and close to human habitation and sports a distinctive "eye" mark on its hood. The other most widespread poisonous snake is the sixty-centimetre **Malayan pit viper**, which has an unnerving ability to camouflage its pinky-brown and black-marked body. The **mangrove snake** lives in the humid swamps south of Chumphon: arboreal, nocturnal and mildly venomous, it can grow to about 2.5m and is black with thin yellow bands.

Environmental issues

Thailand's rapid economic growth has had a significant effect on its environment. Huge new infrastructure projects, an explosion in real-estate developments and the constantly expanding tourist industry have all played a part, and the effects of the subsequent **deforestation** and pollution have been felt nationwide. Such was the devastation caused by floods and mud slides in Surat Thani in 1988 that the government banned commercial logging the following year, though land continues to be denuded for other purposes. There is also the endemic problem of "influence" so that when a big shot wants to clear a previously pristine area for a new property development, for example, it is virtually impossible for a lowly provincial civil servant to reject their plan, or money. Thailand lost nine percent of its forest cover between 1990 and 2005 (2005 figures show just over 28 percent of Thailand's total land area as forested).

Though flooding has always been a feature of the Thai environment, crucial to the fertility of its soil, and its worst effects obviated by the stilted design of the traditional Thai house, in recent times far more dangerous **flash floods** have recurred with depressing frequency every year, most dramatically around the northern town of Pai in 2005, where many homes and guest houses were washed away, and along the Mekong River in 2008. More mundanely there is now an almost annual inundation of certain riverside town centres, and of roads and railways, particularly along the Gulf coast. The link between deforestation and flash floods is now disputed, though encroaching cement and tarmac on Thai flood plains surely play a part, as does the clogging of exit channels by garbage and other pollutants, and of course climate change.

Reefs and shorelines

A number of Thailand's **coral reefs** – some of which are thought to be around 450 million years old – are being destroyed by factors attributable to tourism, most significantly the pollution generated by coastal hotels with inadequate sewage systems. Longtail boats that anchor on reefs, souvenirs made from coral, and the use of harpoon guns by irresponsible dive leaders all have a cumulative effect, dwarfed however by the local practice of using dynamite to gather fish, including reef fish for sale to aquariums.

The 2004 **tsunami** also caused significant damage to coastal and marine environments the length of the Andaman coast. Reefs close to shore were crushed by debris (furniture, machinery, even cars) and buried under displaced soil; the sea was temporarily polluted by extensive damage to sewage systems; and tracts of shorefront farmland were rendered unusable by salt water.

National parks

Although Thailand has since the 1970s been protecting some of its natural resources within **national parks**, these have long been caught between commercial and conservationist aims, an issue which the government addressed in 2002 by establishing a new National Park, Wildlife and Plant Conservation Department (DNP; ⊛www.dnp.go.th), separate from the Royal Forestry Department and its parent Ministry of Agriculture.

With 103 national parks across the country, plus 26 national marine parks, as well as various other protected zones, over thirteen percent of the country is now, in theory at least, protected from encroachment and hunting (a high proportion compared to other nations, such as Japan at 6.5 percent, and the US at 10.5 percent).

However, the **touristification** of certain national parks endures; Ko Phi Phi and Ko Samet in particular have both suffered irreversible environmental damage as a direct result of the number of overnight visitors they receive. While most people understand that the role of the national parks is to conserve vulnerable and precious resources, the dramatic hike in entrance fees payable by foreigner visitors to national parks – from B20 up to B200 in 2000 and up again to B400 for a few special parks – was greeted with cynicism and anger, not least because there is often little sign of anything tangible being done on site with the money.

Books

We have included publishers' details for books that may be hard to find outside Thailand, though some of them can be ordered online through ⓦ www.dcothai .com. Other titles should be available worldwide.

Culture and society

Michael Carrithers *The Buddha: A Very Short Introduction.* Accessible account of the life of the Buddha, and the development and significance of his thought.

Philip Cornwel-Smith and John Goss *Very Thai.* Why do Thais decant their soft drinks into plastic bags, and how does one sniff-kiss? Answers and insights aplenty in this intriguingly observant, fully illustrated guide to contemporary Thai culture.

James Eckardt *Bangkok People.* The collected articles of a renowned expat journalist, whose encounters with a varied cast of Bangkokians – from construction-site workers and street vendors to boxers and political candidates – add texture and context to the city.

Sandra Gregory with Michael Tierney *Forget You Had A Daughter: Doing Time in the "Bangkok Hilton" – Sandra Gregory's Story.* The frank and shocking account of a young British woman's term in Bangkok's notorious Lard Yao prison after being caught trying to smuggle 89 grammes of heroin out of Thailand.

Sebastian Hope *Outcasts of the Islands: The Sea Gypsies of Southeast Asia.* Unusual insight into the lives of the *chao ley* people from a British traveller who spent several months in various sea gypsy communities.

Erich Krauss *Wave of Destruction: One Thai Village and its Battle with the Tsunami.* A sad and often shocking, clear-eyed account of what Ban Nam Khen went through

before, during and after the tsunami. Fills in many gaps left unanswered by news reports at the time.

Father Joe Maier *Welcome To The Bangkok Slaughterhouse: The Battle for Human Dignity in Bangkok's Bleakest Slums.* Catholic priest Father Joe shares the stories of some of the Bangkok street kids and slum-dwellers that his charitable foundation has been supporting since 1972 (see p.64).

Cleo Odzer *Patpong Sisters.* An American anthropologist's funny and touching account of her life with the prostitutes and bar-girls of Bangkok's notorious red-light district.

James O'Reilly and Larry Habegger (eds) *Travelers' Tales: Thailand.* Absorbing anthology of contemporary writings about Thailand, by Thailand experts, social commentators, travel writers and first-time visitors.

Phra Peter Pannapadipo *Little Angels: The Real-Life Stories of Twelve Thai Novice Monks.* A dozen young boys, many of them from desperate backgrounds, tell the often poignant stories of why they became novice monks. For some, funding from the Students Education Trust (p.64) has changed their lives.

Phra Peter Pannapadipo *Phra Farang: An English Monk in Thailand.* Behind the scenes in a Thai monastery: the frank, funny and illuminating account of a UK-born former businessman's life as a Thai monk.

Pasuk Phongpaichit and Sungsidh Piriyarangsan *Corruption and Democracy in Thailand.* Fascinating academic study, revealing the nuts and bolts of corruption in Thailand and its links with all levels of political life, and suggesting a route to a stronger society. Their sequel, a study of Thailand's illegal economy, *Guns,* *Girls, Gambling, Ganja,* co-written with Nualnoi Treerat, makes equally eye-opening and depressing reading.

William Warren *Living in Thailand.* Luscious gallery of traditional houses, with an emphasis on the homes of Thailand's rich and famous; seductively photographed by Luca Invernizzi Tettoni.

History

William Stevenson *The Revolutionary King.* Fascinating biography of the normally secretive King Bhumibol, by a British journalist who was given unprecedented access to the monarch and his family. The overall approach is fairly uncritical, but lots of revealing insights emerge along the way.

William Warren *Jim Thompson: the Legendary American of Thailand.* The engrossing biography of the ex-intelligence agent, art collector and Thai silk magnate whose disappearance in Malaysia in 1967 has never been satisfactorily resolved.

David K. Wyatt *Thailand: A Short History.* An excellent, recently updated treatment, scholarly but highly readable, with a good eye for witty, telling details. Good chapters on the story of the Thais before they reached what's now Thailand, and on recent developments.

Art and architecture

Steve Van Beek *The Arts of Thailand.* Lavishly produced and perfectly pitched introduction to the history of Thai architecture, sculpture and painting, with superb photographs by Luca Invernizzi Tettoni.

Sumet Jumsai *Naga: Cultural Origins in Siam and the West Pacific.* Wide-ranging discussion of water symbols in Thailand and other parts of Asia, offering a stimulating mix of art, architecture, mythology and cosmology.

Steven Pettifor *Flavours: Thai Contemporary Art.* Takes up the baton from Poshyananda (see below) to look at the newly invigorated art scene in Thailand from 1992 to 2004, with profiles of 23 leading lights, including painters, multimedia and performance artists.

Apinan Poshyananda *Modern Art in Thailand.* Excellent introduction which extends up to the early 1990s, with very readable discussions on dozens of individual artists, and lots of colour plates.

William Warren and Luca Invernizzi Tettoni *Arts and Crafts of Thailand.* Good-value large-format paperback, setting the wealth of Thai arts and crafts in cultural context, with plenty of attractive illustrations and colour photographs.

Natural history and travel guides

Ashley J. Boyd and Collin Piprell
Diving in Thailand. A thorough guide
to 84 dive sites, plus general introductory sections on Thailand's
marine life, conservation and
photography tips.

Oliver Hargreaves *Exploring Phuket
& Phi Phi: From Tin to Tourism*.
Fascinating, thoroughly researched
guide to the Andaman coast's big
touristic honeypots; especially good
on Phuket's history.

🏃 **Thom Henley** *Krabi: Caught
in the Spell – A Guide to
Thailand's Enchanted Province* (Thai
Nature Education, Phuket). Highly
readable features and observations
on the attractions and people of
south Thailand's most beautiful

region, written by an expat
environmentalist.

**Boonsong Lekagul and Philip D.
Round** *Guide to the Birds of Thailand*.
Unparalleled illustrated guide to
Thailand's birds. Worth scouring
secondhand sellers for.

Craig Robson *A Field Guide to the
Birds of Thailand*. Expert and beautifully illustrated guide to Thailand's top
950 bird species, with locator maps.

Eric Valli and Diane Summers
The Shadow Hunters. Beautifully
photographed photo-essay on the
birds'-nest collectors of southern
Thailand, with whom the authors
spent over a year, together scaling the
phenomenal heights of the sheer
limestone walls.

Literature

Alastair Dingwall (ed) *Traveller's
Literary Companion: Southeast Asia*.
A useful though rather dry reference,
with a large section on Thailand,
including a book list, well-chosen
extracts, biographical details of
authors and other literary notes.

🏃 **Chart Korbjitti** *The Judgement*
(Howling Books). Sobering
modern-day tragedy about a good-
hearted Thai villager who is
ostracized by his hypocritical neighbours. Contains lots of interesting
details on village life and traditions
and thought-provoking passages on
the stifling conservatism of rural
communities. Winner of the S.E.A.
Write award in 1982.

🏃 **Rattawut Lapcharoensap**
Sightseeing. This outstanding
debut collection of short stories by
a young Thai-born author now
living overseas highlights big,
pertinent themes – cruelty,
corruption, racism, pride – in its

neighbourhood tales of randy
teenagers, bullyboys, a child's
friendship with a Cambodian
refugee, a young man who uses
family influence to dodge the draft.

Nitaya Masavisut (ed) *The S.E.A.
Write Anthology of Thai Short Stories and
Poems* (Silkworm Books, Chiang Mai).
Interesting medley of short stories and
poems by Thai writers who have won
Southeast Asian Writers' Awards,
providing a good introduction to the
contemporary literary scene.

S.P. Somtow *Jasmine Nights*. An
engaging and humorous rites-of-
passage tale, of an upper-class boy
learning what it is to be Thai.
*Dragon's Fin Soup and Other Modern
Siamese Fables* is an imaginative and
entertaining collection of often
supernatural short stories, focusing
on the collision of East and West.

🏃 **Khamsing Srinawk** *The Politi-
cian and Other Stories*. A collec-

tion of brilliantly satiric short stories, full of pithy moral observation and biting irony, which capture the vulnerability of peasant farmers in the north and northeast, as they try to come to grips with the modern world. Written by an insider from a peasant family, who was educated at Chulalongkorn University, became a hero of the left, and joined the communist insurgents after the 1976 clampdown.

Thailand in foreign literature

Dean Barrett *Kingdom of Make-Believe*. Despite the clichéd ingredients – the Patpong go-go bar scene, opium smuggling in the Golden Triangle, Vietnam veterans – this novel about a return to Thailand following a twenty-year absence turns out to be a rewardingly multi-dimensional take on the farang experience.

John Burdett *Bangkok 8*. Riveting Bangkok thriller that takes in Buddhism, plastic surgery, police corruption, the *yaa baa* drugs trade, hookers, jade-smuggling and the spirit world.

Alex Garland *The Beach*. Gripping cult thriller (later made into a film, shot partly on Ko Phi Phi Leh) that uses a Thai setting to explore the way in which travellers' ceaseless quest for "undiscovered" utopias inevitably leads to them despoiling the idyll.

Andrew Hicks *Thai Girl*. A British backpacker falls for a reticent young beach masseuse on Ko Samet but struggles with age-old cross-cultural confusion in this sensitive attempt at a different kind of expat novel.

Michel Houellebecq *Platform*. Sex tourism in Thailand provides the nucleus of this brilliantly provocative (some would say offensive) novel, in which Houellebecq presents a ferocious critique of Western decadence and cultural colonialism, and of radical Islam too.

Christopher G. Moore *God Of Darkness*. Thailand's best-selling expat novelist sets his most intriguing thriller during the economic crisis of 1997 and includes plenty of meat on endemic corruption and the desperate struggle for power within family and society.

Food and cookery

Vatcharin Bhumichitr *The Taste of Thailand*. Another glossy introduction to this eminently photogenic country, this time through its food. The author runs a Thai restaurant in London and provides background colour as well as about 150 recipes adapted for Western kitchens.

Jacqueline M. Piper *Fruits of South-East Asia*. An exploration of the bounteous fruits of the region,

tracing their role in cooking, medicine, handicrafts and rituals. Well illustrated with photos, watercolours and early botanical drawings.

David Thompson *Thai Food*. Comprehensive, impeccably researched celebration of the cuisine, with over 300 recipes, by the owner of the first Thai restaurant ever to earn a Michelin star.

Language

Language

Thai

T hai belongs to one of the oldest families of languages in the world, Austro-Thai, and is radically different from most of the other tongues of Southeast Asia. Being tonal, Thai is extremely difficult for Westerners to master, but by building up from a small core of set phrases, you should soon have enough to get by. Most Thais who deal with tourists speak some English, but once you stray off the beaten track you'll probably need at least a little Thai. Anywhere you go, you'll impress and get better treatment if you at least make an effort to speak a few words.

Distinct dialects are spoken in the north, the northeast and the south, which can increase the difficulty of comprehending what's said to you. **Thai script** is even more of a problem to Westerners, with 44 consonants and 32 vowels. However, street signs in touristed areas are nearly always written in Roman script as well as Thai, and in other circumstances you're better off asking than trying to unscramble the swirling mess of symbols, signs and accents. For more information on transliteration into Roman script, see the box in this book's introduction.

Among **language books**, *Thai: The Rough Guide Phrasebook* covers the essential phrases and expressions in both Thai script and phonetic equivalents, as well as dipping into grammar and providing a menu reader and fuller vocabulary in dictionary format (English–Thai and Thai–English). Probably the best pocket dictionary is Paiboon Publishing's (Ⓦwww.ThaiLao.com) *Thai-English, English-Thai Dictionary*, which lists words in phonetic Thai as well as Thai script, and features a very handy table of the Thai alphabet in a dozen different fonts.

The best **teach-yourself course** is the expensive *Linguaphone Thai* (including six cassettes), which also has a shorter, cheaper beginner-level PDQI version (with four CDs). *Thai for Beginners* by Benjawan Poomsan Becker (Paiboon Publishing) is a cheaper, more manageable textbook and is especially good for getting to grips with the Thai writing system; you can also buy accompanying CDs to help with listening skills, or get the whole thing in CD-ROM format. For a more traditional textbook, try Stuart Campbell and Chuan Shaweevongse's *The Fundamentals of the Thai Language*, which is comprehensive, though hard going. G.H. Allison's *Easy Thai* is best for those who feel the urge to learn the alphabet. The **website** Ⓦwww.thai-language. com is an amazing free resource, featuring a searchable dictionary of over 40,000 Thai words, complete with Thai script and audio clips, plus a guide to the language and forums.

Pronunciation

Mastering **tones** is probably the most difficult part of learning Thai. Five different tones are used – low, middle, high, falling, and rising – by which the meaning of a single syllable can be altered in five different ways. Thus, using four of the five tones, you can make a sentence from just one syllable: "mái mài mâi ma˘i" meaning "New wood burns, doesn't it?" As well as the natural difficulty in becoming attuned to speaking and listening to these different tones, Western efforts are complicated by our habit of denoting the overall meaning of a sentence by modulating our tones – for example, turning a statement into a question through a shift of stress and tone. Listen to native Thai speakers and you'll soon begin to pick up the different approach to tone.

The pitch of each tone is gauged in relation to your vocal range when speaking, but they should all lie within a narrow band, separated by gaps just big enough to differentiate them. The **low tones** (syllables marked `` ` ``), **middle tones** (unmarked syllables), and **high tones** (syllables marked ´) should each be pronounced evenly and with no inflection. The **falling tone** (syllables marked ^) is spoken with an obvious drop in pitch, as if you were sharply emphasizing a word in English. The **rising tone** (marked ˇ) is pronounced as if you were asking an exaggerated question in English.

As well as the unfamiliar tones, you'll find that, despite the best efforts of the transliterators, there is no precise English equivalent to many **vowel and consonant sounds** in the Thai language. The lists below give a simplified idea of pronunciation.

Vowels

a	as in dad		e	as in pen
aa	has no precise equivalent, but is pronounced as it looks, with the vowel elongated		eu	as in sir, but heavily nasalized
			i	as in tip
			ii	as in feet
ae	as in there		o	as in knock
ai	as in buy		oe	as in hurt, but more closed
ao	as in now		oh	as in toe
aw	as in awe		u	as in loot
ay	as in pay		uu	as in pool

Consonants

r	as in rip, but with the tongue flapped quickly against the palate – in everyday speech, it's often pronounced like "l"		k	is unaspirated and unvoiced, and closer to "g"
			p	is also unaspirated and unvoiced, and closer to "b"
kh	as in keep		t	is also unaspirated and unvoiced, and closer to "d"
ph	as in put			
th	as in time			

General words and phrases

Greetings and basic phrases

When you speak to a stranger in Thailand, you should generally end your sentence in *khráp* if you're a man, *khâ* if you're a woman – these untranslatable politening syllables will gain goodwill, and are nearly always used after *sawàt dii* (hello/goodbye) and *khàwp khun* (thank you). *Khráp* and *khâ* are also often used to answer "yes" to a question, though the most common way is to repeat the verb of the question (precede it with *mâi* for "no"). *Châi* (yes) and *mâi châi* (no) are less frequently used than their English equivalents.

Hello	sawàt dii	What's your name?	khun chêu arai?
Where are you going?	pai năi? (not always meant literally, but used as a general greeting)	My name is...	phŏm (men)/ diichăn (women) chêu...
		I come from...	phŏm/diichăn maa jàak...
I'm out having fun/ I'm travelling	pai thîaw (answer to pai năi, almost indefinable pleasantry)	I don't understand	mâi khào jai
		Do you speak English?	khun phûut phasăa angkrìt dâi măi?
		Do you have...?	mii...măi?
Goodbye	sawàt dii/la kàwn	Is...possible?	...dâi măi?
Good luck/cheers	chôhk dii	Can you help me?	chûay phŏm/ diichăn dâi măi?
Excuse me	khăw thâwt		
Thank you	khàwp khun	(I) want...	ao...
It's nothing/it doesn't matter	mâi pen rai	(I) would like to...	yàak jà...
		(I) like...	châwp...
How are you?	sabai dii reŭ?	What is this called in Thai?	níi phasăa thai rîak wâa arai?
I'm fine	sabai dii		

Getting around

Where is the...?	...yùu thîi năi?	south	tâi
How far?	klai thâo rai?	east	tawan àwk
I would like to go to...	yàak jà pai...	west	tawan tòk
		near/far	klâi/klai
Where have you been?	pai năi maa?	street	thanŏn
		train station	sathàanii rót fai
Where is this bus going?	rót níi pai năi?	bus station	sathàanii rót mae
		airport	sanăam bin
When will the bus leave?	rót jà àwk mêua rai?	ticket	tŭa
		hotel	rohng raem
What time does the bus arrive in...?	rót theŭng...kìi mohng?	post office	praisanii
		restaurant	raan ahăan
Stop here	jàwt thîi nîi	shop	raan
here	thîi nîi	market	talàat
there/over there	thîi nâan/thîi nôhn	hospital	rohng pha-yaabaan
right	khwăa	motorbike	rót mohtoesai
left	sái	taxi	rót táksîi
straight	trong	boat	reua
north	neŭa	bicycle	jàkràyaan

Accommodation and shopping

How much is...?	...thâo rai/kìi bàat?	How much is a room here per night?	hâwng thîi nîi kheun lá thâo rai?
I don't want a plastic bag, thanks	mâi ao thŭng khráp/ khâ	Do you have a cheaper room?	mii hâwng thùuk kwàa măi?

Can I/we look at the room?	duu hâwng dâi măi?		cheap/expensive	thùuk/phaeng
			air-con room	hăwng ae
I/We'll stay two nights	jà yùu săwng kheun		ordinary room	hăwng thammadaa
			telephone	thohrásàp
Can you reduce the price?	lót raakhaa dâi măi?		laundry	sák phâa
			blanket	phâa hòm
Can I store my bag here?	fàak krapăo wái thîi nîi dâi măi?		fan	phát lom

General adjectives

alone	khon diaw		easy	ngâi
another	ìik…nèung		fun	sanùk
bad	mâi dii		hot (temperature)	ráwn
big	yài		hot (spicy)	phèt
clean	sa-àat		hungry	hiŭ khâo
closed	pìt		ill	mâi sabai
cold (object)	yen		open	pòet
cold (person or weather)	năo		pretty	sŭay
			small	lek
delicious	aròi		thirsty	hiŭ nám
difficult	yâak		tired	nèu-ay
dirty	sokaprok		very	mâak

General nouns

Nouns have no plurals or genders, and don't require an article.

bathroom/toilet	hăwng nám		foreigner	fàràng
boyfriend or girlfriend	faen		friend	phêuan
			money	ngoen
food	ahăan		water/liquid	nám

General verbs

Thai verbs do not conjugate at all, and also often double up as nouns and adjectives, which means that foreigners' most unidiomatic attempts to construct sentences are often readily understood.

come	maa		go	pai
do	tham		sit	nâng
eat	kin/thaan khâo		sleep	nawn làp
give	hâi		walk	doen pai

Numbers

zero	sŭun		four	sìi
one	nèung		five	hâa
two	săwng		six	hòk
three	săam		seven	jèt

eight	pàet	twenty-two, twenty-three...	yîi sìp săwng, yîi sìp săam...
nine	kâo		
ten	sìp	thirty, forty, etc	săam sìp, sìi sìp...
eleven	sìp èt	one hundred, two hundred...	nèung rói, săwng rói...
twelve, thirteen...	sìp săwng, sìp săam...		
twenty	yîi sìp/yiip	one thousand	nèung phan
twenty-one	yîi sìp èt	ten thousand	nèung mèun

Time

The commonest system for telling the time, as outlined below, is actually a confusing mix of several different systems. The State Railway and government officials use the 24-hour clock (9am is *kâo naalikaa*, 10am *sìp naalikaa*, and so on), which is always worth trying if you get stuck.

1–5am	tii nèung–tii hâa	hour	chûa mohng
6–11am	hòk mohng cháo– sìp èt mohng cháo	day	wan
		week	aathít
noon	thîang	month	deuan
1pm	bài mohng	year	pii
2–4pm	bài săwng mohng– bài sìi mohng	today	wan níi
		tomorrow	phrûng níi
5–6pm	hâa mohng yen– hòk mohng yen	yesterday	mêua wan níi
		now	diăw níi
7–11pm	nèung thûm– hâa thûm	next week	aathít nâa
		last week	aathít kàwn
midnight	thîang kheun	morning	cháo
What time is it?	kìi mohng láew?	afternoon	bài
How many hours?	kìi chûa mohng?	evening	yen
How long?	naan thâo rai?	night	kheun
minute	naathii		

Days

Sunday	wan aathít	Thursday	wan pháréuhàt
Monday	wan jan	Friday	wan sùk
Tuesday	wan angkhaan	Saturday	wan săo
Wednesday	wan phút		

Food and drink

Basic ingredients

kài	chicken	ahăan thalay	seafood
mŭu	pork	plaa	fish
néua	beef, meat	plaa dùk	catfish
pèt	duck	plaa mèuk	squid

493

kûng	prawn, shrimp	puu	crab
hŏy	shellfish	khài	egg
hŏy nang rom	oyster	phàk	vegetables

Vegetables

makĕua	aubergine	taeng kwaa	cucumber
makĕua thêt	tomato	phrík yùak	green pepper
nàw mái	bamboo shoots	krathiam	garlic
tùa ngâwk	bean sprouts	hèt	mushroom
phrík	chilli	tùa	peas, beans or
man faràng	potato		lentils
man faràng thâwt	chips	tôn hŏrm	spring onions

Noodles

ba miì	egg noodles	kwáy tiăw/	rice noodles/egg
kwáy tiăw	white rice noodles	ba miì rât	noodles fried in
(sên yaì/sên lék)	(wide/thin)	nâ (mŭu)	gravy-like sauce with
khanŏm jiin nám	noodles topped with		vegetables (and
yaa	fish curry		pork slices)
kwáy tiăw/ ba	rice noodle/egg	miì kràwp	crisp fried egg noodles
miì haêng	noodles fried with		with small pieces of
	egg, small pieces of		meat and a few
	meat and a few		vegetables
	vegetables	phàt thai	thin noodles fried with
kwáy tiăw/ba	rice noodle/egg		egg, bean sprouts
miì nám (mŭu)	noodle soup, made		and tofu, topped with
	with chicken broth		ground peanuts
	(and pork balls)	phàt siyú	wide or thin noodles
			fried with soy sauce,
			egg and meat

Rice

khâo	rice	khâo nâ kài/pèt	chicken/duck served
khâo man kài	slices of chicken		with sauce over rice
	served over	khâo niăw	sticky rice
	marinated rice	khâo phàt	fried rice
khâo mŭu daeng	red pork	khâo kaeng	curry over rice
	with rice	khâo tôm	rice soup (usually for
			breakfast)

Curries and soups

kaeng phèt	hot, red curry	kaeng sôm	tamarind soup
kaeng phánaeng	thick, savoury curry	tôm khà kài	chicken, coconut and galangal soup
kaeng khǐaw wan	green curry		
kaeng mátsàman	rich muslim-style curry, usually with beef and potatoes	tôm yam kûng	hot and sour prawn soup
kaeng karìi	mild, indian-style curry	kaeng jèut	mild soup with vegetables and usually pork
hàw mòk thalay	seafood curry soufflé		
kaeng liang	peppery vegetable soup		

Salads

lâap	spicy ground meat salad	yam plaa mèuk	squid salad
		yam sôm oh	pomelo salad
nám tòk	grilled beef or pork salad	yam plaa dùk foo	crispy fried catfish salad
sôm tam	spicy papaya salad	yam thùa phuu	wing-bean salad
yam hua plee	banana flower salad	yam wun sen	noodle and pork salad
yam néua	grilled beef salad		

Other dishes

hâwy thâwt	omelette stuffed with mussels	néua phàt krathiam phrík thai	beef fried with garlic and pepper
kài phàt bai kraprao	chicken fried with holy basil leaves	néua phàt nám man hâwy	beef in oyster sauce
kài phàt nàw mái	chicken with bamboo shoots	phàt phàk bûng fai daeng	morning glory fried in garlic and bean sauce
kài phàt mét mámûang	chicken with cashew nuts	phàt phàk ruam	stir-fried vegetables
kài phàt khǐng	chicken with ginger	pàw pía	spring rolls
kài yâang	grilled chicken	plaa nêung páe sá	whole fish steamed with vegetables and ginger
khài yát sài	omelette with pork and vegetables		
kûng chúp paêng thâwt	prawns fried in batter	plaa ràt phrík	whole fish cooked with chillies
mǔu prîaw wǎan	sweet and sour pork	plaa thâwt	fried whole fish
		sàté	satay
		thâwt man plaa	fish cake

Thai desserts (khanŏm)

khanŏm beuang	small crispy pancake folded over with coconut cream and strands of sweet egg inside
khâo lăam	sticky rice, coconut cream and black beans cooked and served in bamboo tubes
khâo niăw daeng	sticky red rice mixed with coconut cream
khâo niăw thúrian/ mámûang	sticky rice mixed with coconut cream and durian/mango
klûay khàek	fried banana
lûk taan chêum	sweet palm kernels served in syrup
săngkhayaa	coconut custard
tàkôh	squares of transparent jelly (jello) topped with coconut cream

Drinks (khreûang deùm)

bia	beer
chaa ráwn	hot tea
chaa yen	iced tea
kaafae ráwn	hot coffee
kâew	glass
khúat	bottle
mâekhŏng (or anglicized Mekong)	thai brand-name rice whisky
klûay pan	banana shake
nám mánao/sôm	fresh, bottled or fizzy lemon/orange juice
nám plào	drinking water (boiled or filtered)
nám sŏdaa	soda water
nám taan	sugar
kleua	salt
nám yen	cold water
nom jeùd	milk
ohlíang	iced black coffee
thûay	cup

Ordering

I am vegetarian/vegan	Phŏm (male)/ diichăn (female) kin ahăan mangsàwirát/jeh
Can I see the menu?	Khăw duù menu nóy?
I would like…	Khăw…
with/without…	Sài/mâi sài…
Can I have the bill please?	Khăw check bin?

Glossary

Amphoe District.

Amphoe muang Provincial capital.

Ao Bay.

Apsara Female deity.

Avalokitesvara Bodhisattva representing compassion.

Avatar Earthly manifestation of a deity.

Ban Village or house.

Bang Village by a river or the sea.

Bencharong Polychromatic ceramics made in China for the Thai market.

Bhumisparsa mudra Most common gesture of Buddha images; symbolizes the Buddha's victory over temptation.

Bodhisattva In Mahayana Buddhism, an enlightened being who postpones his or her entry into Nirvana.

Bot Main sanctuary of a Buddhist temple.

Brahma One of the Hindu trinity – "The Creator". Usually depicted with four faces and four arms.

Celadon Porcelain with grey-green glaze.

Changwat Province.

Chao ley/chao nam "Sea gypsies" – nomadic fisherfolk of south Thailand.

Chedi Reliquary tower in Buddhist temple.

Chofa Finial on temple roof.

Deva Mythical deity.

Devaraja God-king.

Dharma The teachings or doctrine of the Buddha.

Dharmachakra Buddhist Wheel of Law (also known as Wheel of Doctrine or Wheel of Life).

Doi Mountain.

Erawan Mythical three-headed elephant; Indra's vehicle.

Farang Foreigner/foreign.

Ganesh Hindu elephant-headed deity, remover of obstacles and god of knowledge.

Garuda Mythical Hindu creature – half-man half-bird; Vishnu's vehicle.

Gopura Entrance pavilion to temple precinct (especially Khmer).

Hamsa Sacred mythical goose; Brahma's vehicle.

Hanuman Monkey god and chief of the monkey army in the Ramayana; ally of Rama.

Hat Beach.

Hin Stone.

Hinayana Pejorative term for Theravada school of Buddhism, literally "Lesser Vehicle".

Ho trai A scripture library.

Indra Hindu king of the gods and, in Buddhism, devotee of the Buddha; usually carries a thunderbolt.

Isaan Northeast Thailand.

Jataka Stories of the Buddha's five hundred lives.

Khaen Reed and wood pipe; the characteristic musical instrument of Isaan.

Khao Hill, mountain.

Khlong Canal.

Khon Classical dance-drama.

Kinnari Mythical creature – half woman, half bird.

Kirtimukha Very powerful deity depicted as a lion-head.

Ko Island.

Ku The Lao word for prang; a tower in a temple complex.

Laem Headland or cape.

Lakhon Classical dance-drama.

Lak muang City pillar; revered home for the city's guardian spirit.

Lakshaman/Phra Lak Rama's younger brother.

Lakshana Auspicious signs or "marks of greatness" displayed by the Buddha.

Lanna Northern Thai kingdom that lasted from the thirteenth to the sixteenth century.

Likay Popular folk theatre.

Longyi Burmese sarong.

Luang Pho Abbot or especially revered monk.

Maenam River.

Mahathat Chedi containing relics of the Buddha.

Mahayana School of Buddhism now practised mainly in China, Japan and Korea; literally "the Great Vehicle".

Mara The Evil One; tempter of the Buddha.

Mawn khwaan Traditional triangular or "axe-head" pillow.

Meru/Sineru Mythical mountain at the centre of Hindu and Buddhist cosmologies.

Mondop Small, square temple building to house minor images or religious texts.

Moo/muu Neighbourhood.

Muang City or town.

Muay thai Thai boxing.

Mudra Symbolic gesture of the Buddha.

Mut mee Tie-dyed cotton or silk.

Naga Mythical dragon-headed serpent in Buddhism and Hinduism.

Nakhon Honorific title for a city.

Nam Water.

Nam tok Waterfall.

Nang thalung Shadow-puppet entertainment, found in southern Thailand.

Nielloware Engraved metalwork.

Nirvana Final liberation from the cycle of rebirths; state of non-being to which Buddhists aspire.

Pak Tai Southern Thailand.

Pali Language of ancient India; the script of the original Buddhist scriptures.

Pha sin Woman's sarong.

Phi Animist spirit.

Phra Honorific term – literally "excellent".

Phu Mountain.

Prang Central tower in a Khmer temple.

Prasat Khmer temple complex or central shrine.

Rama/Phra Ram Human manifestation of Hindu deity Vishnu; hero of the Ramayana.

Ramakien Thai version of the Ramayana.

Ramayana Hindu epic of good versus evil: chief characters include Rama, Sita, Ravana, Hanuman.

Ravana see Totsagan.

Reua hang yao Longtail boat.

Rishi Ascetic hermit.

Rot ae/rot tua Air-conditioned bus.

Rot thammadaa Ordinary bus.

Sala Meeting hall, pavilion, bus stop – or any open-sided structure.

Samlor Three-wheeled passenger tricycle.

Sanskrit Sacred language of Hinduism; also used in Buddhism.

Sanuk Fun.

Sema Boundary stone to mark consecrated ground within temple complex.

Shiva One of the Hindu trinity – "The Destroyer".

Shiva lingam Phallic representation of Shiva.

Soi Lane or side road.

Songkhran Thai New Year.

Songthaew Public transport pick-up vehicle; means "two rows", after its two facing benches.

Takraw Game played with a rattan ball.

Talat Market.

Talat nam Floating market.

Talat yen Night market.

Tambon Subdistrict.

Tavatimsa Buddhist heaven.

Tha Pier.

Thale Sea or lake.

Tham Cave.

Thanon Road.

That Chedi.

Thep A divinity.

Theravada Main school of Buddhist thought in Thailand; also known as Hinayana.

Totsagan Rama's evil rival in the Ramayana; also known as Ravana.

Tripitaka Buddhist scriptures.

Trok Alley.

Tuk-tuk Motorized three-wheeled taxi.

Uma Shiva's consort.

Ushnisha Cranial protuberance on Buddha images, signifying an enlightened being.

Viharn Temple assembly hall for the laity; usually contains the principal Buddha image.

Vipassana Buddhist meditation technique; literally "insight".

Vishnu One of the Hindu trinity – "The Preserver". Usually shown with four arms, holding a disc, a conch, a lotus and a club.

Wai Thai greeting expressed by a prayer-like gesture with the hands.

Wang Palace.

Wat Temple.

Wiang Fortified town.

Yaksha Mythical giant.

Yantra Magical combination of numbers and letters, used to ward off danger.

Small print and

Index

A Rough Guide to Rough Guides

Published in 1982, the first Rough Guide – to Greece – was a student scheme that became a publishing phenomenon. Mark Ellingham, a recent graduate in English from Bristol University, had been travelling in Greece the previous summer and couldn't find the right guidebook. With a small group of friends he wrote his own guide, combining a highly contemporary, journalistic style with a thoroughly practical approach to travellers' needs.

The immediate success of the book spawned a series that rapidly covered dozens of destinations. And, in addition to impecunious backpackers, Rough Guides soon acquired a much broader and older readership that relished the guides' wit and inquisitiveness as much as their enthusiastic, critical approach and value-for-money ethos.

SMALL PRINT

These days, Rough Guides include recommendations from shoestring to luxury and cover more than 200 destinations around the globe, including almost every country in the Americas and Europe, more than half of Africa and most of Asia and Australasia. Our ever-growing team of authors and photographers is spread all over the world, particularly in Europe, the US and Australia.

In the early 1990s, Rough Guides branched out of travel, with the publication of Rough Guides to World Music, Classical Music and the Internet. All three have become benchmark titles in their fields, spearheading the publication of a wide range of books under the Rough Guide name.

Including the travel series, Rough Guides now number more than 350 titles, covering: phrasebooks, waterproof maps, music guides from Opera to Heavy Metal, reference works as diverse as Conspiracy Theories and Shakespeare, and popular culture books from iPods to Poker. Rough Guides also produce a series of more than 120 World Music CDs in partnership with World Music Network.

Visit www.roughguides.com to see our latest publications.

Rough Guide travel images are available for commercial licensing at www.roughguidespictures.com

Rough Guide credits

Text editor: Alice Park
Layout: Jessica Subramanian
Cartography: Animesh Pathak, Swati Handoo
Picture editor: Sarah Cummins
Production: Rebecca Short
Proofreader: Margaret Doyle
Cover design: Chloë Roberts
Photographer: Martin Richardson and Karen Trist
Editorial: Ruth Blackmore, Andy Turner, Keith Drew, Edward Aves, Lucy White, Jo Kirby, James Smart, Natasha Foges, Róisín Cameron, Emma Traynor, Emma Gibbs, Kathryn Lane, Christina Valhouli, Monica Woods, Mani Ramaswamy, Harry Wilson, Lucy Cowie, Helen Ochyra, Amanda Howard, Lara Kavanagh, Alison Roberts, Joe Staines, Peter Buckley, Matthew Milton, Tracy Hopkins, Ruth Tidball; **Delhi** Madhavi Singh, Karen D'Souza, Lubna Shaheen
Design & Pictures: **London** Scott Stickland, Dan May, Diana Jarvis, Mark Thomas, Nicole Newman, Emily Taylor; **Delhi** Umesh Aggarwal, Ajay Verma, Ankur Guha, Pradeep Thapliyal, Sachin Tanwar, Anita Singh, Nikhil Agarwal, Sachin Gupta
Production: Vicky Baldwin

Cartography: **London** Maxine Repath, Ed Wright, Katie Lloyd-Jones; **Delhi** Rajesh Chhibber, Ashutosh Bharti, Rajesh Mishra, Jasbir Sandhu, Karobi Gogoi, Alakananda Bhattacharya, Deshpal Dabas
Online: **London** George Atwell, Faye Hellon, Jeanette Angell, Fergus Day, Justine Bright, Clare Bryson, Aine Fearon, Adrian Low, Ezgi Celebi, Amber Bloomfield; **Delhi** Amit Verma, Rahul Kumar, Narender Kumar, Ravi Yadav, Debojit Borah, Rakesh Kumar, Ganesh Sharma, Shisir Basumatari
Marketing & Publicity: **London** Liz Statham, Niki Hanmer, Louise Maher, Jess Carter, Vanessa Godden, Vivienne Watton, Anna Paynton, Rachel Sprackett, Libby Jellie, Laura Vipond, Vanessa McDonald; **New York** Katy Ball, Judi Powers, Nancy Lambert; **Delhi** Ragini Govind
Manager India: Punita Singh
Reference Director: Andrew Lockett
Operations Manager: Helen Phillips
PA to Publishing Director: Nicola Henderson
Publishing Director: Martin Dunford
Commercial Manager: Gino Magnotta
Managing Director: John Duhigg

SMALL PRINT

Publishing information

This fourth edition published November 2009 by
Rough Guides Ltd,
80 Strand, London WC2R 0RL
14 Local Shopping Centre, Panchsheel Park, New Delhi 110017, India
Distributed by the Penguin Group
Penguin Books Ltd,
80 Strand, London WC2R 0RL
Penguin Group (USA)
375 Hudson Street, NY 10014, USA
Penguin Group (Australia)
250 Camberwell Road, Camberwell, Victoria 3124, Australia
Penguin Group (Canada)
195 Harry Walker Parkway N, Newmarket, ON, L3Y 7B3 Canada
Penguin Group (NZ)
67 Apollo Drive, Mairangi Bay, Auckland 1310, New Zealand
Cover concept by Peter Dyer.

Typeset in Bembo and Helvetica to an original design by Henry Iles.
Printed and bound in Singapore
© Paul Gray and Lucy Ridout, 2009
Maps © Rough Guides
No part of this book may be reproduced in any form without permission from the publisher except for the quotation of brief passages in reviews.
512pp includes index
A catalogue record for this book is available from the British Library
ISBN: 978-1-84836-091-4

The publishers and authors have done their best to ensure the accuracy and currency of all the information in **The Rough Guide to Thailand's Beaches & Islands**, however, they can accept no responsibility for any loss, injury, or inconvenience sustained by any traveller as a result of information or advice contained in the guide.

1   3   5   7   9   8   6   4   2

Help us update

We've gone to a lot of effort to ensure that the fourth edition of **The Rough Guide to Thailand's Beaches & Islands** is accurate and up-to-date. However, things change – places get "discovered", opening hours are notoriously fickle, restaurants and rooms raise prices or lower standards. If you feel we've got it wrong or left something out, we'd like to know, and if you can remember the address, the price, the hours, the phone number, so much the better.

Please send your comments with the subject line "**Rough Guide Thailand's Beaches & Islands Update**" to @mail@roughguides.com. We'll credit all contributions and send a copy of the next edition (or any other Rough Guide if you prefer) for the very best emails.

Have your questions answered and tell others about your trip at @wwww.roughguides.com.

Acknowledgements

The **authors** jointly would like to thank: Abigail Silver at London TAT; staff at TAT offices in Surat Thani, Ko Samui, Hat Yai and Nakhon Si Thammarat.

From **Lucy**, thanks to: Serge and Morn in Trat; Bronwen in Chanthaburi; Ian on Ko Chang; Stuart and Ball on Ko Mak; Gai on Ko Kood; Tom and Aroon; Aung on Ko Samet; Paul Embrechts; Heather and Kitty on Ko Yao Noi; Richard on Ko Phayam; Ray and Sao on Ko Jum; Panja in Bangkok; and Mai and Maree in Krabi.

From **Paul**, very special thanks to Gade Taraksa. Thanks also to: Bill Gray; Jack Grassby; Rashi and Bambi on Ko Pha Ngan; Ekkachai Binwaha, Dick te Brake, Anita and all the Siaws in Trang; Bon Satarat and Ratana Kongnual in Satun; Nikki Busuttil, Wannapa Rakkeo, Maria Kuhn and Marion Walsh in Bangkok; on Ko Tao, Matt Bolton, Nathan Cook, Dev and Don; on Ko Lipe, Luca, Boi and Johann; Tom in Phetchaburi; Suda in Chumphon; and Tuppadit Thaiarry at Avis.

Readers' letters

Thanks to all the readers who have taken the time to write in with comments and suggestions (and apologies if we've inadvertently omitted or misspelt anyone's name):

Carla Anderson, Julien Anseau, John Archibald, Luis F Arévalogarcia, Jane Barnett, Alison Batley, Marcel Bokhorst, Paul Bonner, Michelle Brodie, Margo Burgers, Phil Cairns, Adam Cathro, Katie Clare, G Clegg, John & Maggie Coaton, Ryan Collins, Cian Connolly, Diana Coode & Lee J Barnett, Melanie Cook, David Cunningham, Conrad Davies, Kieran Dignam, Chris Eichler, Mike Fletcher, Michael Gardham, Joanne Gardiner, David Gaukrodger, Chris Goward, Kimberley Anne Gray, Bernd Greiner, Pelle Gustafson, John & Shirley Harper, Anna Harrison, Paul Hie, Benjamin L Hilditch, Charlie Hogan, Andrew Hunt, Clare Johnson & Peter Lawrie, Steven Jolly, Grace Kenny, Helen Keynes, Majid Khan, A.G. Klei & Ruth Campbell-Page, Jan Kling, Viviana & Allister Levy, Jason Lewis, Rob van Loo, Bridget MacDonald, Aiden MacFarlane, Monica Mackaness & John Garratt, Anita & Hamish McFarlane, Jim McNalis, Regine De Naegel, James Newton, Matt Nicholls, Jan van Oort, Megan Murphy O'Connell, John, Phil & Sinead O'Reilly, John & Saw Payne, Jan Pennington, Por Fl Pharo, Allan and Margaret Rickmann, Paul Robson, Kimberley Ross, Simon Rowley, Vanessa Ryan & Russ Nash, Riccardo Sai, Beat & Anaida Schmid, Peter Searl, Keith Shaw, Alex Shields, Clayton Smith, Ray Smith, Andrea Spescha, Dave Stark, Jeff Stone, Vicky Stone, Sarah Stuteville, Will Swainson, Neal Teplitz, Robin & Matt Thomsen, Sue Thornton, Nick Trautmann, Wayne Turner, Charlotte Underwood, Gillian Walker, John Weldon, David Whiting, Moritz Winnen, Lisa Wortley

Photo credits

Index

Map entries are in colour.

I

INDEX

INDEX

INDEX

Map symbols

maps are listed in the full index using coloured text

-----	International boundary	⊠	Gate
--- ...	Province boundary	∩	Arch
--- ---	Chapter division boundary	→	One-way street
=====	Pedestrianized road	⊙	Statue
=====	Road	✈	Airport
▥▥▥	Steps	★	Transport stop
------	Unpaved road	✦	Point of interest
------	Path	❢	Museum
━━━	Railway	$	Bank/ATM
— —	Ferry route	@	Internet access
———	River/Canal	ⓘ	Tourist information
———.	Wall	ℂ	Telephone office
•---•	Cable car & station	⊞	Hospital
⤫	Footbridge	⊠	Post office
⤬	Bridge	᠁	Market
▣	Accommodation	❖	Mosque
◉	Restaurants & bars	⩘	Temple
ⵙ	Border crossing	ⴲ	Chinese temple/Pagoda
▲	Peak	⬭	Stadium
⋏	Mountains	⊞	Church
◠	Cave	▬	Building
ⵉ	Waterfall	▱	Swamps/marshes
⁓	Rocks	▦	Park/forest
ⵘ	Lighthouse	▨	Beach
⬇	Viewpoint		